STRUCTURED BASIC

AN INTEGRATED APPROACH

**McGraw-Hill
Book Company**

New York
St. Louis
San Francisco
Auckland
Bogotá
Hamburg
Johannesburg
London
Madrid
Mexico
Montreal
New Delhi
Panama
Paris
São Paulo
Singapore
Sydney
Tokyo
Toronto

Lawrence S. Orilia
Nassau Community College

STRUCTURED BASIC
AN INTEGRATED APPROACH

STRUCTURED BASIC: An Integrated Approach

1234567890VNHVNH8987654

ISBN 0-07-047839-2

This book was set in Century Schoolbook by Progressive Typographers, Inc.
The editors were Eric M. Munson, Christina Mediate, and Frances Koblin;
the designer was Joseph Gillians;
the production supervisor was Joe Campanella.
The cover illustration was done by Greg Couch;
unit and chapter-opening illustrations were done by Joseph Gillians.
Picture research was done by Lorinda Morris/Photoquest, Inc.
The drawings were done by Fred Eckhardt.
Von Hoffmann Press, Inc., was printer and binder.

Library of Congress Cataloging in Publication Data

Orilia, Lawrence.
    Structured BASIC.

    Includes index.
    1. Basic (Computer program language)   2. Structured
programming.   I. Title.   II. Title: Structured B.A.S.I.C.
QA76.73.B3075   1985   001.64'24   84-14334
ISBN 0-07-047839-2

To my sister Joan,

*whose courage will remain
an inspiration to me always.*

CONTENTS

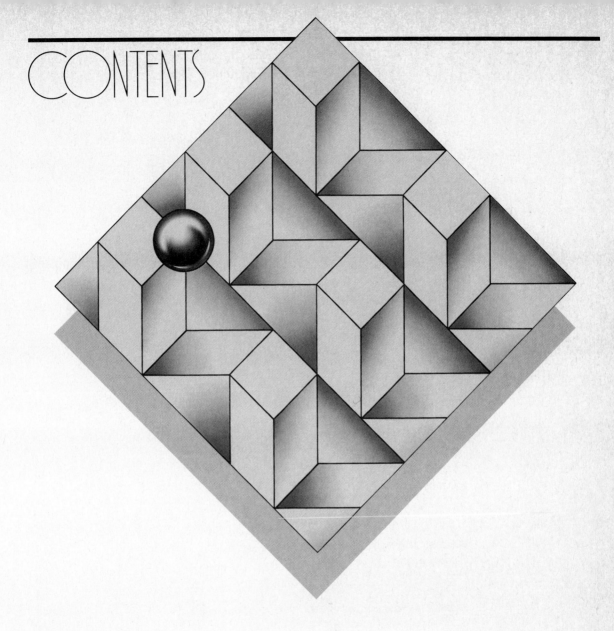

UNIT II
Developing Your
Programming
Skills

UNIT III
Advanced
Programming
Techniques

PREFACE

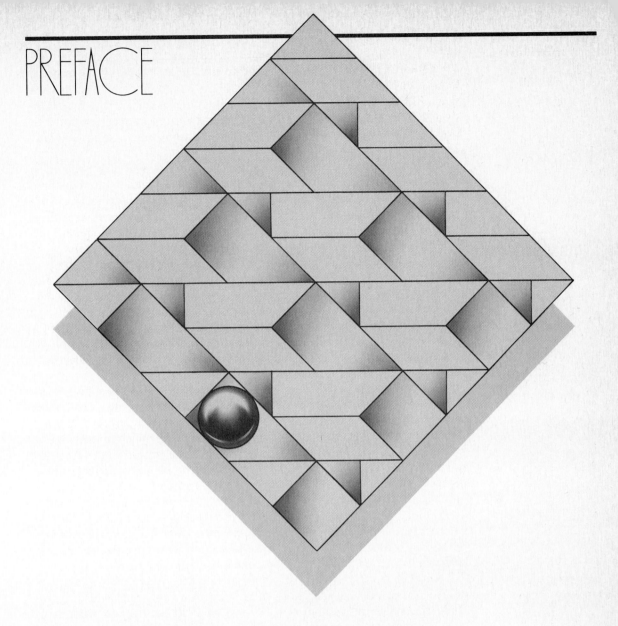

Fifteen years of teaching students about computers have greatly reinforced three of my educational principles. The first is that students learn best by doing, by applying theories taught in the classroom. The second principle is that repetition of illustrative examples reinforces the usefulness of an idea. The third principle is that students should receive instruction about a variety of operational strategies, to broaden their knowledge and create an arsenal of skills applicable to any problem. A careful development of theories enables students to understand the origin of currently popular computer strategies and evaluate their effectiveness.

In writing this text, I attempted to incorporate these ideas into the manuscript. The text offers many illustrative examples to explain the concepts taught, and exercises which require the student to apply them. Carefully worded discussions develop concepts from their origin to their operational formats. A conversational style of writing ties everything together and permits students to learn at their own pace.

This text expresses my strong beliefs about how programming should be introduced to beginning students. It attempts to integrate flowcharting, BASIC, and structured design principles in a unified presentation. Concepts evolve in a continuous flow. This is especially true in the area of structured concepts, where the groundwork is carefully laid for the development and application of principles designed to improve program logic.

Great emphasis has been placed on the use of flowcharts in the text because I believe they are an indispensable tool in problem solving. The pictorial format of the flowchart is also ideally suited for today's media-oriented students. Flowcharts, which adopt both conventional and structured design elements, provide the means of expressing the logic of a program pictorially, avoiding the difficulties associated with psuedo languages or abstract approaches. At the same time, the student is introduced to a documentation tool that is used uniformly throughout the industry.

The conversion of the problem narrative to a flowchart solution has received equal scrutiny. Before you can write a flowchart, you must understand the problem. I have taken great care to guide the student in a step-by-step analysis of the problem narrative. The standard problem narrative format used will also assist student comprehension. The reinforcement provided by the detailed list which follows the illustrative problems highlights critical processing factors drawn from the problem narrative, provides a basis for developing a flowchart, and acts as a checklist when verifying the accuracy of a solution. These lists generate a form of coding sequence which may be used when planning the logic of a flowchart and the resulting program solution. Solutions to illustrative problems are presented with both flowcharts and program listings to stress the effectiveness of their combined use.

Another feature of this text is the diversified nature of the solutions offered. Frequently, two solutions to the same problem are provided to give students an alternative approach for evaluation. This diversity offers students a glimpse of other problem-solving techniques, broadens their base of knowledge, and makes them receptive to new approaches. Insights into the alternate logic employed by other programmers is often invaluable when existing programs must be modified.

The approach of integrating the problem narrative, flowcharting, and program solution has benefits for the instructor too. The comprehensive coverage enables the instructor to focus on specific problems and cover specialized topics. The bulk of the material can be grasped by students working on their own, at their own pace, leaving the teacher free to provide more personalized instruction.

Organization of the Book

This text is organized into three major units; each unit provides the reader with a specific set of information. Unit I, composed of Chapters 1 and 2, provides a brief history of computing and an overview of a computer system. These chapters also introduce the terminology that is a vital part of the programmer's lexicon, and they help explain the computer's functions during the execution of programs.

The second unit, Chapters 3 to 6, covers the development of programming skills. Chapter 3 focuses on the preparation of flowcharts from problem narratives, accentuating the pictorial representation of the flow of data. Chapters 4 and 5 introduce the BASIC language, coordinating the use of flowcharts and the writing of BASIC programs. Major programming concepts are developed in both chapters, and applied within flowcharts and program solutions. Topics relating to structured programming are fully evolved in Chapter 6 with emphasis on modular structure. Great care is exercised to evolve structured design concepts, in the belief that a full understanding of why these principles are employed reinforces their practical use.

Unit III, Chapters 7 to 9, presents advanced topics such as arrays and nested loop sequences. The manipulation of data held in one- and two-dimensional arrays is carefully explained, from their conceptual origins to their use in tables. Multiple sample programs provide readers with examples to learn from and use as prototypes for their program solutions.

Three appendixes are provided to enhance the reader's knowledge. Appendix C discusses the use and manipulation of data held in computer files. Sample programs for the creation and update of sequential and random access files are reviewed on a line-by-line basis in relation to four versions of BASIC. This file software is written for APPLE II, IBM PC, TRS-80, and DEC systems. Appendix B offers a comparison of major statements in the versions of BASIC used by these four types of computers. Appendix A discusses special functions that afford the user specialized processing sequences for handling word strings and user-defined computations. A section of constructing menus explains how to offer users a series of options in a program solution.

Appendixes at the end of each chapter are another feature of this text. They review common student programming errors and show ways to correct these errors. These debugging aids greatly assist students in developing the logic procedures used to correct their programs. The material presented in the chapter appendixes, as well as all the other materials in this text, have been class-tested and refined for over 10 years.

Chapter Outline and Objectives

Each chapter opens with a chapter outline, which gives the student an overview of the material to be covered, and a list of objectives, which act as a guide to the student as to the key concepts to be mastered. Key terms, which represent the operational lexicon of the computer field, are explained fully in the chapter. They are also defined in the glossary at the end of the chapter, giving the student additional reinforcement.

Readability

I have written this text in a conversational style to maintain interest and keep the text from becoming unduly complicated. Readability tests indicate that the reading level is appropriate for college freshmen. The student who does not understand the material at first reading may reread that material, without becoming frustrated.

Flowcharts are carefully explained to ensure student comprehension, as they act as springboards to writing program solutions. To assist students, a point-by-point format follows each problem narrative. This detailed list identifies the major processing factors to be incorporated into both flowchart and program solutions. It aids students by highlighting major points drawn from the original problem narratives. Often, students are stumped not by the programming, but by their inability to convert the problem narrative into a workable solution. The coordinated use of an itemized list of processing objectives and a flowchart is invaluable in mastering problem-solving logic.

Chapter Summary

A summary of the materials covered appears at the end of each chapter. The major concepts presented in the chapter are restated concisely, each point in a few sentences. The summary follows the presentation of material in the chapter, reinforcing the order of topic coverage. Students preparing for examinations will find this summary helpful when reviewing.

Key Symbols and Statements

Chapters 3 to 9 include charts and tables that highlight major flowcharting symbols and BASIC statements. These presentations review the number of ways a statement or symbol can be used and provide further reinforcement.

Glossary

In an introductory text, the mastery of major terms and definitions is of critical importance. To provide immediate reinforcement, each chapter includes a glossary of terms introduced in that chapter. All glossary terms also are listed in **boldface** type in the index of the book, for easy reference.

Exercises

Beginning with Chapter 3, there are three categories of end-of-chapter exercises: in-class exercises, lab exercises, and quiz problems.

In-class exercises are short problems, designed for classroom use. They can be assigned immediately after the class presentation to reinforce a concept. These short exercises are patterned after illustrative examples given in each chapter. They enable the student to apply the concept taught in a shorter problem. Three in-class exercises are provided in each chapter. Instructors can also assign these exercises during lab periods.

Lab exercises are designed as homework assignments. These exercises offer a variety of problems, of varying difficulty. Lab exercises may contain multiple components requiring the student to incorporate several special programming features, or to prepare the solution using two different processing approaches. This last factor is important, as it proves that program solutions may be written using a variety of methods. The lab problems permit the student to incorporate several different programming techniques in the same problem.

These multifaceted lab exercises are designed for flexibility. The student is free to test different programming techniques on the same problem to compare their effectiveness. Instructors may direct students to focus their work on only one part of the problem (which they deem critical to classroom discussions), while permitting the student to research alternative solutions independently.

The Quiz problem tests the student's mastery of material presented within that chapter. The student must proceed from the problem narrative to its program solution.

The solution to the quiz problem is presented right after the problem. Answers to the in-class exercises are at the end of the book. Solutions to the lab exercises are in the Instructor's Manual.

Chapter Appendixes

The chapter appendixes are of particular importance. They enhance student debugging skills, as they advise the student on how to find and correct program errors. Common student programming errors are explained, and students learn how to spot these errors and correct them. Students can also learn how to avoid certain errors and how to improve the logic of their program solutions. Readers should review each chapter appendix before commencing the writing and execution of their program solutions.

Instructor's Manual

This manual is designed to assist in the preparation of classroom support materials, including lecture notes, tests, and illustrations. The Instructor's Manual provides:

1 Lecture notes

2 Answers to lab exercises

3 Extra problems for instructional use

4 A test bank

5 Overhead transparency masters of selected text illustrations

The lecture notes, in outline format, focus on the chapter organization and topical coverage. Lab exercises are answered in outline form, incorporating flowcharts and programs as needed. Extra problems are provided for in-class use. A test bank consisting of short-answer questions and problems is also supplied to test student comprehension and mastery of subject matter.

Acknowledgments

No successful text is written without the contributions of many talented individuals. Many fine people have reviewed and improved this manuscript. I wish to take special note of the contributions of the following reviewers: Donald L. Davis, University of Mississippi; Patrick Graham, Austin Community College; Steve Mansfield, McHenry County College; Jeanne Massingill, Highland Community College; Richard Moller, Fresno City College; William I. Salmon, University of Utah; John Schreiber, Nassau Community College; and Angelo Scordato, Nassau Community College.

I would also like to thank the McGraw-Hill editorial staff for its many creative contributions. My special thanks go to Jim Vastyan for signing the project and Eric Munson and Christina Mediate for seeing it through all phases of preparation. My thanks to Jon Palace, Fran Koblin, and Joe Campanella as well, for keeping the production schedule on track. Joe Gillians' striking design cannot be overlooked.

My last acknowledgments are reserved for my family. My wife and children had to survive my work efforts and the frustrations associated with the text's preparation. Tracy's verbal encouragement, as well as Vanessa's and Adrian's laughter, often gave me the emotional lift necessary to continue this creative effort.

Lawrence S. Orilia

**Getting to Know
the Computer**

ONE

A Historical Perspective of Computing

Chapter Objectives

This chapter will

- Provide an overview of the evolution of computers and the need to automate the handling of data.

- Identify major events in the evolution of computers and researchers contributing to that effort.

- Describe the three generations of computer equipment and the technologies that followed them.

- Discuss technologies of fiber optics, magnetic-bubble memory, low-power lasers, the Josephson switching device, artificial intelligence, and plug compatibility.

- Discuss the use of terminals and interactive languages in teleprocessing activities.

Introduction

With every day that passes, the computer becomes further ingrained into our society. We note its impact on sporting events, business activities, movies, medicine, and manufacturing. Many of us even spend our spare time destroying computerized space invaders to relieve tension after a tough workday.

These modern-day applications of computers are a far cry from the computer's beginning and the rationale for its development. People have always wanted to possess a high-speed computing device with record-keeping capabilities, but only recently has the technology existed.

This chapter focuses on the evolution of computing from the record-keeping efforts of primitive people to the current state of the art. We examine many devices that were stepping stones to today's computers and the rash of technological advances introduced over the past four decades. Many people contributed to the development and success of today's computers.

This historical perspective will provide the reader with an understanding of why computers were developed and a time frame within which these advances were achieved. By highlighting the major achievements, we are able to recognize the series of events which led to our current technology. Readers will realize that even today's achievements are just another plateau in the evolution of computers.

Early human beings used the most obvious method for counting—their fingers. But this limited computations to rather small quantities; in addition, the fingers were not efficient record-keeping devices, particularly when sign language was necessary.

Two early means of record keeping and computation involved the use of diagrams and stones. Charcoal drawings by primitive tribes show the use of tally marks to record quantities of livestock. Marks could be added or deleted as these inventories were consumed or refurbished.

An equally simple approach followed a one-to-one relationship: one stone equalled one unit of inventory or goods. Shepherds utilized this principle to monitor their flocks, associating one stone with a sheep. In today's terminology, we could state that shepherds were keeping an inventory of their sheep. Though the terms may change through time, the principle remains the same. Inventories are monitored on a one-to-one basis.

The difficulty with using stones was their lack of portability. A large flock meant literally hundreds of stones and thus further taxed the physical resources of the shepherd. As such, shepherds resorted to other means of recording flock sizes. Tying knots in thongs made from animal hides provided a solution, with each knot representing 5 or 10 sheep. Carving marks into the shepherd's crook (or staff) offered another vehicle for accounting, with each mark representing a fixed number of animals.

One of the earliest devices to facilitate computation was the **abacus.** This device utilized a numbering scheme based upon the five digits of the hand. It could easily have been an extension of the combined use of leather strips and seeds.

One of the first computational devices to follow the abacus was the **machine arithmétique,** developed in 1642 (Figure 1.1). Its inventor was the 19-year-old French scholar Blaise Pascal, whose ideas for this device evolved while performing tax computations in his father's employ. His device incorporated interlocking gears which functioned to add or subtract quantities. The concepts resulting from Pascal's device would be used in the manufacture of mechanical calculators in the twentieth century.

Pascal to Babbage

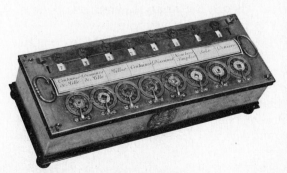

FIGURE 1.1 Pascal's development of the Machine Arithmetique was a milestone in the evolution of mechanical computational devices. Constructed of interlocking gears, this device functioned much the way a car's odometer functions when recording mileage. *(IBM.)*

A fully operational calculator capable of adding, subtracting, multiplying, and dividing was produced in 1671 by the German Gottfried von Leibniz. His invention utilized interlocking gears of different sizes to accomplish all four of the basic arithmetic operations. Though Leibniz's calculator demonstrated its operational principles, it proved unreliable and in need of further refinement.

Other inventors were seeking ways of recording data tangibly so that it could be fed into a machine to control its operation. It is in these activities that we recognize the first seeds of the computer: data recorded on a tangible medium, input to a device which accomplishes some form of processing to produce a desired result.

The first vestiges of these activities are found in France during the 1720s. Perforated paper strips designed by Basile Bouchon were used to control the weaving of cloth. Weaving looms specially constructed to operate under control of these paper strips made this concept a reality.

Many years later, in 1801, the Frenchman Jacquard expanded upon these concepts and invented the **automatic loom.** A series of punched cards controlled the loom and therefore the weaving of fabric. The prosperity that France's textile industry enjoyed in the 1800s was directly related to the use of Jacquard looms.

The importance of this achievement cannot be lost. Inventors realized that it was possible to control machines with data encoded onto tangible mediums. The data provided the means of performing computations and enabling a device to produce a desired product or result. Computational devices that utilized externally oriented data and provided user-related results had become a reality.

It was the Englishman Charles Babbage who synthesized many of the ideas related to computational devices. Drawing on the theories of the German inventor Müller, Babbage attempted to develop a computational device that could handle complex arithmetic operations (up to 20 positions of accuracy) and produce results in a visible printed format. He conceived of his so-called **difference engine** in 1812, though despite 20 years of effort he failed to produce a working model (Figure 1.2).

Though disappointed, in 1833 Babbage conceived of another device which would coordinate the entry, computation, and printing of data in much the same way that current computers operate. Babbage also conceived of using punched cards with this device and of having a memory to store data which resulted from processing. Though the **analytic engine** was never constructed, it pointed the way toward modern computing devices.

Babbage's efforts intrigued a close friend, Augusta Ada Byron, the Countess of Lovelace. Using her background in mathematics, Lady Lovelace was able to analyze many of the algebraic relationships incorporated into Babbage's work and translate them into realistic operational terms. The documentation of these relationships into a cogent series of instructions earned her the title of First Programmer. She is credited with detailing the first sets of programming rules and documenting the essential steps with that process.

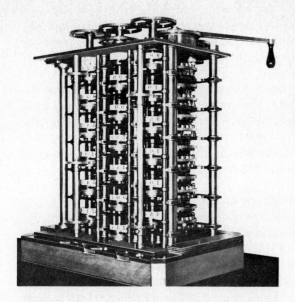

FIGURE 1.2 Much of Babbage's design effort occurred in the early 1800s. Though his designs were well ahead of the times, they were never constructed. Babbage spent over 20 years attempting to build and perfect the difference engine. *(IBM.)*

Other activities in the nineteenth century involved the continued invention of calculating devices for use in business activities. A calculator, commercially introduced by C. X. Thomas in 1820, met with limited success. An adding machine capable of printing its results was invented in 1884 by the American William S. Burroughs. This device, which utilized a keyboard to enter numbers, was capable of adding long columns of figures and printing the resultant totals. A similar device invented in 1885 by a fellow American, Dorr Felt, permitted the performance of multidigit calculations. This device was so successful that it ruled the marketplace until the early 1900s.

A major contribution in the area of automated data processing was made by the American Dr. Herman Hollerith (Figure 1.3). Contacted by the U.S. Census, Hollerith was asked to speed the processing of the upcoming 1890 census. To accomplish this task, Hollerith devised a punched card, a system

Hollerith and the U.S. Census

FIGURE 1.3 Hollerith used computer cards and the tabulating equipment shown to process the 1890 census. *(IBM.)*

to encode data onto the card, and tabulating equipment to manipulate the data. Hollerith was able to perform the demographic analysis of the census data in less than three years, though the U.S. population had risen by over 25 percent.

Some years later, a new punched-card system was introduced to process data relating to the 1910 census. The brainchild of James Powers, this card system was introduced and tested in 1907; Powers was capable of handling the 240 categories of data contained on the census questionnaire. Keys associated with each data category were incorporated into the mechanical processing of the 1910 census, thus increasing both processing speed and accuracy.

1.2 The First Computers

**Getting Started
in the 1930s**

The 1930s saw the emergence of research that was to lead to the first computers. In 1934, under the supervision of Dr. John V. Atanasoff at Iowa State College, a card-processing machine was modified to perform arithmetic computations under mechanically activated controls. Some five years later, Dr. Atanasoff and Clifford Berry constructed the Atanasoff-Berry computer, or **ABC,** which consisted of vacuum tubes and possessed a limited memory in which data undergoing processing could be stored.

Parallel research on electromechanical devices was being conducted elsewhere. At Harvard in 1937, Dr. Howard Aiken and his staff, in conjunction with IBM, conceived the idea of the **Mark I,** which would later be recognized as the first computer. The Mark I weighed over 10,000 pounds, was over 50 feet long and 8 feet high, and contained over 760,000 moving parts. A programlike structure consisting of a series of instructions was employed to direct the Mark I in its calculations.

While the aforementioned activities received public acclaim, British research technicians were secretly conducting work on a computer called **Colussus.** Only recently has information come to light regarding this project and its impact on the British war effort. Colussus was utilized to crack Nazi communication codes and provide insights to German military strategies. This computer could be fed coded data at a rate of 5000 characters per second, analyze its textual contents, and output the converted coded material via an electrified typewriter. The Colussus computer demonstrated that a large quantity of intricate electronic circuitry could reliably handle high-speed computations.

**The Postwar
Effort**

Military theoreticians were quick to recognize the potential that computers could have on modern warfare and urged that funds be made available to continue research on these computational devices. A product of these efforts was the **ENIAC** computer, invented by two researchers at the University of Pennsylvania in 1946 (Figure 1.4). Dr. John W. Mauchly and J. P. Eckert

FIGURE 1.4   One of the primary users of the ENIAC computer was the U.S. Armed Forces. This computer, the first all-electric device built, was the product of the work of Mauchly and Eckert. *(UPI.)*

constructed this computer to prepare ballistic tables for use in artillery operations. ENIAC was a huge device, weighing over 60,000 pounds and using almost 19,000 vacuum tubes. It was assessed as the first all-electric computer.

The importance of the ENIAC device should not be overlooked. Though it possessed a limited storage capacity, it could perform almost 5000 addition operations or 300 multiplications per second. Data could be fed to ENIAC in the form of punched cards. It also possessed the ability to concurrently perform several arithmetic operations, a feat that is only now commonplace in modern computing devices.

Mauchly and Eckert did not stop their research at ENIAC but helped design the **EDVAC** computer. The EDVAC system introduced the internal storage of data in a digital form and demonstrated the successful use of binary numbers with computers. The use of a binary or base 2 system, where data is represented solely in two states as either a 0 or a 1, was a major breakthrough for computing technology and one that would have an impact on the construction of future computers. Research on EDVAC was fully completed in 1952.

The **EDSAC** computer, developed at Cambridge University in England in 1949 by Dr. John von Neumann, incorporated the **stored-program concept,** an idea that revolutionized computing. Most computers prior to EDSAC were directed by control panels wired to perform a specific set of tasks. A change in tasks meant a major rewiring effort, as the program (or set of instructions) controlling the computer would undergo modification. Dr. von Neumann theorized that a computer should not be externally controlled by a set of wires, but directed in its processing by a series of instructions retained within the computer's memory. A program stored within the computer would direct all processing, initiate the entry of data to the computer, direct the computer's printing of the results of processing, and control the performance of arithmetic operations.

A complete set of activities could be controlled by a program stored in the computer and could thus direct the computer's processing of a specific task. The next program to be entered and stored within the computer's memory could undertake a different task without the necessity of rewiring the computer. Essentially, the computer possessed the capacity to perform a variety of different processing operations, any of which could be initiated by the program stored within its memory. EDSAC provided the vehicle to prove the reality of von Neumann's stored-program concept.

One of the first commercially available computers was the **UNIVAC I** introduced in 1951. The computer was designed under the supervision of Mauchly and Eckert for the U.S. Census Bureau. UNIVAC I introduced the prototypes of programming languages and techniques which would be developed for use in future computing devices.

It was about this time that IBM entered the computer industry, introducing its first computer, the IBM 701, in 1953. Within a year IBM introduced its IBM 650 system, which proved to be one of the most popular computers of that era. It could handle operations involving computer cards, with later models of this device supporting more sophisticated devices. Subsequently, IBM promoted its 702 and 704 computers, designed for the areas of business and science, respectively.

The computers discussed in this section, from the Mark I to the IBM 704, were representative of **first-generation computers.** They were extremely large, bulky devices that were difficult to program and limited in their range of activities. The major component in the construction of first-generation computers was the vacuum tube, which generated great quantities of heat and consumed large amounts of electrical power. These computers possessed limited storage capacities and were restricted in the type of data items they could handle. Despite their shortcomings, first-generation computers provided the stepping-stone to future computer systems.

1.3 The Second Generation of Computers

The differences between the first and second generations of computers were their construction and the operational capabilities offered. **Second-generation computers** were constructed with transistors, small electrical components developed at Bell Labs in 1947 and refined over 12 years of work. The transistor was smaller and more reliable than the vacuum tube and offered higher internal processing speeds, measured in microseconds (one-millionth of a second).

One of the technologies refined with second-generation computers was **magnetic-tape storage,** originally introduced with first-generation computers in the mid-1950s. Data was recorded on magnetic tapes in much the same manner as music is recorded on your home tape recorders. Magnetic tape offered users the ability to store vast amounts of data on a medium that was readily accessible.

During the period of second-generation systems, manufacturers placed great emphasis on developing less technical programming languages that were easier for users to employ. Languages introduced during the period of 1958 to 1963 include assembly language, FORTRAN, and COBOL; FORTRAN was applied to scientific problems, and COBOL was specifically designed for use in business.

The concept of separating business and scientific activities was also carried forward to second-generation computers. Two of the major systems in this category were the IBM 1401 and IBM 1600 Series computers. The 1401 Series was designed to handle business data processing operations which involved both numeric and alphabetic data. The 1600 Series was assigned scientific applications, where numeric data was primarily employed. Each type of computer was designed for and restricted to a specific area.

It is appropriate at this time to introduce and define the following terms that relate to the handling of computer data: **Hardware** is the "nuts and bolts" of computers, the machinery that enables the processing of data to occur. **Software** consists of the computer programs that direct the hardware in the performance of its computerized tasks. In order for a computer to undertake any task, a series of instructions in the form of a **program** must be provided. Software is the general term applied to identify the diverse programs which may be used to direct the computerized processing of data.

1.4 The Emergence of the Computer

As with the prior two computer generations, the third generation of computers was marked with a major change in technology. The construction of **third-generation computers** was based upon microminiaturized circuitry, a by-product of the American space effort. This advanced circuitry replaced the conventional wiring associated with prior computer systems and offered higher internal speeds. Third-generation computers were capable of attaining operational speeds in nanoseconds (one-billionth of a second), processing many millions of instructions in a single second.

The Third Generation

It was with the appearance of third-generation systems that the computers began their full emergence into all aspects of American society. Where computers had been little used or secondary processing devices kept in a back office, they now became major tools of organizations handling all types of data. A company's computer system became one of the first things viewed when promoting business, implying the updatedness of the organization and its capacity to service the customer's every need.

One of the major computer systems to emerge during this period was the **IBM System/360** (Figure 1.5). It was the widespread acceptance of the System/360 and its successful usage in all areas of business and science that made it the hallmark of third-generation computers. The System/360 represented such a major departure from second generation hardware that it was classified as a **general-purpose computer.** It was designed to handle both business and scientific processing activities. Its design provided users with the flexibility to carry out the wide range of activities that modern corporations must undertake. It could process a payroll and project economic conditions based upon computer-generated mathematical models.

FIGURE 1.5 *(Above)* The IBM System/360 was a major third-generation computer. *(Right)* Microminiaturized circuits were used in third-generation computers like the IBM 360. *(IBM.)*

FIGURE 1.6   **The advent of magnetic disk marked the emergence of the computer into business and made it a major tool of data processing.** *(Left)* **The disk pack retains data on its many surfaces and is placed in a disk-drive unit** *(right)*, **which accesses data contained on it.** *(Data General.)*

A major hardware unit to complement third-generation computers was the **magnetic disk** (Figure 1.6). The magnetic disk was a significant change from all previous storage devices, as it permitted the random access of data held within computer files. Previously, data could only be stored on a sequential basis, and an individual record could be accessed only after all records before it had been scanned. Using disk storage techniques, programmers found it was possible to access a specific item of data directly, without involving other records in that file. Now computer files could be composed of organized series of records, with any record independently accessible via magnetic disk.

The processing potential offered by magnetic disk was immediately recognized by the business field. Organizations that were previously hindered by the inability to access data directly could now immediately serve their clients; management's desire for more timely data could now be realistically satisfied.

This newly developed capacity was applied to the airline reservation systems. Prior systems required days to confirm customer reservations, much of that data handling performed external to the computer. With disk support, it was possible to respond to ticket reservation requests while customers waited on the phone.

Major breakthroughs were also achieved in the transmission of data between computer systems and users located many miles apart. Computerized data was now transmittable over telephone lines and microwave facilities to remote computer centers, thereby providing high-speed processing support to widely distributed organizations. The term **telecommunications** was introduced to help describe activities related to the transmission of computerized data over communications lines.

Computer manufacturers were quick to recognize that users required computer programming languages more suited to their needs, with operational characteristics not found in second-generation languages. Programming languages had to be more readily learned, understood and supported by adequate documentation to describe their usage. Manufacturers realized that if programming languages were easier to learn and use, more people would be attracted to the computer and potentially adopt its service. The seeds of today's revolution in the use of computers for home and business were sown in this realization.

Two languages that gained major prominence with third-generation hardware were **FORTRAN** and **COBOL.** FORTRAN was the major language of the scientific community, as its algebraic format was readily suited to expressing formulas and scientific problem-solving sequences. COBOL was developed for the specific needs of the business community, readily permitting the manipulation of data held in computer files and the preparation of printed reports. The English-like format of COBOL sharply contrasted with FORTRAN's algebraic format and enabled businesspeople not acquainted with mathematical concepts to understand business-related software. It was a major factor in COBOL's widespread acceptance in the business community.

The surge in computer-related activities resulting from third-generation computers focused on the software needs of individual users. Many people were interested in generating their own software, but had neither the desire nor the inclination to work with the then-existing programming languages. Also, users wanted to interact directly with the computer while developing their software. It was these requirements that led to the development of the **BASIC** programming language.

BASIC is referred to an an **interactive language,** as users can directly interact with the computer on a statement-by-statement basis by means of the computer **terminal.** A user seated at the terminal's keyboard enters the required instructions and immediately observes their effectiveness as the instructions are processed.

Two terms associated with the usage of an interactive language like BASIC are **online** and **teleprocessing.** Online terminal devices are tied directly to the computer, permitting the user to interact directly with the computer; online devices transfer data directly between user and computer. Teleprocessing implies telecommunications data processing activities where terminals possessing TV-like picture tubes are involved. The TV-like screens that display data are called cathode ray tubes **(CRT).**

The Silicon Chip

The advent of the **silicon chip** signaled the next major change in computer construction. However, a lack of consensus on the part of computer experts has left unsettled the issue as to whether the silicon chip constitutes the fourth generation of computer equipment. Despite this controversy, the silicon chip has undergone refinements and has become the major component of current computer construction.

One impact of the silicon chip is the further reduction in size of computer hardware. Currently available silicon chips pack in literally thousands of circuits; one chip can contain program instructions or retain thousands of items of data. Computers once occupying an entire room can now be constructed in the space occupied by an office desk.

The **IBM System/370** is one system that uses silicon chip technology. Figure 1.7 illustrates both the IBM System/370 and the silicon chip used in its construction. The System/370 and its various models are capable of providing data processing support to both large and small organizations alike. Large amounts of disk storage, as well as telecommunications activities, are a keynote of the IBM System/370.

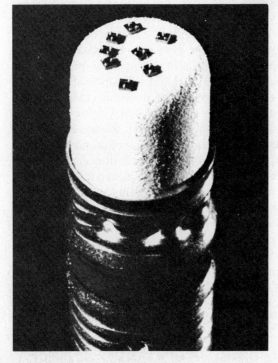

FIGURE 1.7 *(Above)* An IBM System/370, which consists of many devices; *(left)* silicon chips positioned atop a pencil eraser. The silicon chip permitted further reduction in the size of computing devices.

FIGURE 1.8 Minicomputers possess the same operational features as much larger systems. Both magnetic tape and magnetic disk may be used in minicomputer systems to store large quantities of data. *(Sperry Rand.)*

Another type of computer to attain prominence in the 1970s was the **minicomputer.** Minicomputers are smaller than conventional computer systems yet offer parallel processing capabilities at a competitive price. Minicomputers were originally introduced in 1965 by Digital Equipment Corporation but attained their widespread acceptance when data processors discovered their limited but effective processing potential. They offer the same operational capacities of larger systems but to a lesser degree. Figure 1.8 shows the magnetic tape and disk processing capabilities of minicomputers.

The **microcomputer** (or home computer) system is another result of silicon chip technology. The fundamental processing aspects of a computer are duplicated within the intricate circuitry comprising the silicon chip. The microcomputer can be used for both business and home entertainment activities. A principal language used with microcomputers is BASIC.

Microcomputers offer tape and disk storage capacities, also. Small tape cassette devices offer the sequential storage of data on magnetic tape. Small flexible disks, referred to as **floppy disks** or **diskettes** support disk storage operations on microcomputers. These smaller systems also possess CRTs with color display capabilities and many types of printing devices. Many types of business and entertainment software are commercially available for microcomputers.

1.5 Modern Computer Technology

Continuing the pattern developed by earlier generations, modern computers have become faster, smaller, and more reliable. The devices supporting current computers have become equally sophisticated and complex. Technologies developed in other fields have been applied to produce new devices to complement existing computing capabilities. The resultant devices have speeded the flow of computerized data and added new dimensions to the processing of information.

Many new computerized devices have incorporated low-power lasers as part of their operation. Computer printing devices using laser-oriented units have attained speeds as high as 21,000 lines of print per minute. A comparable high-speed printing device capable of preparing multipage reports in minutes utilizes **fiber optics** to transmit and record data. With fiber optics, data is transferred in the form of light impulses through wires made of silicon, thus increasing the operational speed of the device.

The computer industry has also incorporated satellites into its data communications services. Many computerized networks use satellites to rapidly transfer data between continents and widely dispersed corporate headquarters. In some satellite transmissions, low-power lasers are used to temporarily record and transmit data. Currently, national high-speed digital transmission services, reserved solely for computerized data, are in operation with additional satellite centers in the planning. Satellite communications represent some of the most sophisticated telecommunications activities in use today.

Data Communications

The advent of the silicon chip has not stopped research in the area of computer storage. In 1979 a microprocessor chip representing the equivalent of 68,000 transistors was introduced by the Motorola Corporation. Within two years a memory chip approximately $\frac{1}{2}$-inch square and capable of storing 72,000 items of data was introduced by IBM. Research is currently underway to develop a microminiaturized chip which could possess a multimillion-character storage capacity and function in billionths of a second.

Though microchip research is in its developmental stage, other laboratory storage techniques are beginning to demonstrate their practicability. **Magnetic-bubble memory** and the **Josephson switching device** are beginning to show promise. The concept of magnetic-bubble memory relates to the movement of electronic bubbles across a specially magnetized surface. The movement of the bubble creates various impulses which are translated by the computer into coded data formats. Figure 1.9 illustrates a bubble memory surface and a portable printing device in which bubble memory technology is successfully incorporated.

The Josephson switching device is now experimentally used in computer prototypes to perfect its function. This switching device shows great promise

Data Storage

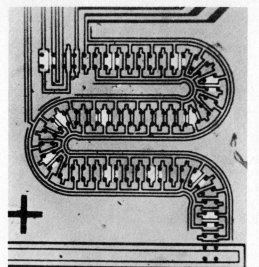

FIGURE 1.9 *(Left)* The bubble memory cell possesses the capacity to retain data used in processing. This one is approximately 1/64 inches (.396 mm) square and can retain millions of data items. *(Right)* This portable printer utilizes magnetic-bubble technology in its construction. *(IBM and Texas Instruments.)*

in terms of its ability to shift data within the computer at extremely high speeds. The Josephson device has attained speeds in the picosecond (one-trillionth of a second) range. Such high speeds, though currently in the experimental stage, would represent another major breakthrough in technology.

The Japanese computer industry, with government assistance, is attempting to forge a technical breakthrough which could define the fifth generation of computers. They are attempting to endow computers with the ability to creatively handle dynamically changing situations via uniquely designed decision-making resources. This technique, referred to as **artificial intelligence (AI),** would provide the computer with a humanoid thought process capable of responding to changing situations for which it has not been programmed. The computer will record facts and use them as a basis for future decision making. Essentially, the Japanese scientists hope to make the computer respond as a human might using a parallel thought process. They anticipate making this technological breakthrough by the 1990s; the prospect of this discovery is certainly intriguing.

Hardware Features

In a more practical vein, current computer systems demonstrate new speed and processing power. New computer systems like the IBM 4300 Series can outperform their previous counterparts by over 600 percent while saving users over half the cost. These systems offer greater reliability and less maintenance. Furthermore, they possess software to diagnose malfunctions, thus greatly assisting technicians by pinpointing the location of any problems.

Key Historical Points

Milestones

date unknown	Abacus
1642	Pascal's *machine arithmétique*
1671	Leibniz's calculator
1720s	Bouchon's perforated paper strips used in weaving
1801	Jacquard's automatic loom
1812	Babbage's difference engine
1820	Thomas's commercially available calculator
1833	Babbage's analytic engine
1830s	Lady Lovelace's analysis of Babbage's ideas
1884	Burrough's adding machine with printing capability
1885	Felt's calculator capable of multidigit calculations
1880s and 1890s	Hollerith's U.S. Census work
1880s–1890s	Hollerith's use of coded punch cards and calculating equipment to analyze census data
1907–1910	Power's new card-processing system for U.S. Census
1930s to 1956	First generation of computers
1934	Atanasoff's work at Iowa State
1937	Aiken's Mark I computer at Harvard
1939	Atanasoff-Berry Computer (ABC)
1941	Britain's Colussus
1946	Mauchly and Eckert invent ENIAC at the University of Pennsylvania
1949	von Neumann's stored-program concept and the invention of EDSAC
1951	Mauchly and Eckert invent EDVAC at the University of Pennsylvania
1951	UNIVAC I
1953	IBM 701
1954	IBM 650
mid-1950s	IBM 702 and 704
mid-1950s	Magnetic tape
1957 to 1963	Second generation of computers
late 1950s to early 1960s	IBM 1401 and 1600 Series
1964 to early 1970s	Third generation of computers
mid-1960s to early 1970s	IBM System/360
mid-1960s	Magnetic disk
1965	Minicomputers
early 1970s	Silicon chip
early 1970s	IBM System/370
late 1970s	Microcomputers
late 1970s	Fiber optics
1979	Microprocessor chip
late 1970s	Magnetic-bubble memory
1980s	Josephson switching device
1980s	Plug-compatible computers
1990s	Artificial intelligence

The IBM 4300 Series also demonstrates another advantage of new computer hardware: it is now possible to link virtually any computer device to any system without encountering the difficulties associated with older hardware. Previously, the interface of different computer hardware represented a major roadblock and expense. For that reason, users tended to stay with one manufacturer. The concept of **plug compatibility** dictates that hardware be designed to facilitate the hookup and interaction of various devices within a computer system; ideally, the attachment of devices should involve no more than plugging in the device.

Glossary

Artificial intelligence (AI) A research technique which attempts to give computers the resources for decision making in response to changes in operational conditions.

BASIC A programming language which permits users to directly interact with a computer.

COBOL The programming language primarily associated with business applications.

CRT The initials of the words *cathode ray tube,* used to describe a terminal which displays data on a TV-like picture tube.

Diskette Small flexible disks used for storage on microcomputer systems.

Fiber optics A technology where data in the form of light impulses are transferred over communications lines made of silicon.

First-generation computers The initial series of computers; they were big, bulky, difficult to program, and constructed of vacuum tubes.

Floppy disk Another term used for diskettes.

FORTRAN A programming language developed in the 1950s that utilizes an algebraic format and is uniquely suited to scientific applications.

General-purpose computer A computer capable of handling both business and scientific problems.

Hardware The term generally applied to all computer devices within which computerized data processing is performed.

Interactive language A computer programming language which permits users to communicate directly with the computer in the processing of data.

Magnetic disk A storage technique where individual data records are randomly accessed from computer files.

Magnetic-tape storage A storage technique where data is sequentially accessed from files recorded on the surface of magnetic tape.

Microcomputer The smallest computer system, constructed of silicon chips and found within business and the home.

Minicomputers Task-oriented computers, originally introduced in 1965, offering processing potential comparable to large systems but at competitive prices.

Online The ability of a user to gain direct access to the computer for data processing purposes.

Plug compatibility The property of most modern computers which enables devices to function properly together by simple, plug-in interconnection.

Program The series of instructions written in a computer language which direct the computer in its processing activities.

Second-generation computers The second major era of computers, where computers were constructed using transistors.

Silicon chip The computer component used to construct post-third-generation computers, in which thousands of integrated circuits exist to retain data or program instructions.

Software The term applied to the programs used to direct and control computer processing.

Stored-program concept The concept originated by von Neumann which dictates that a program and its related data be retained in the computer, thus controlling its operation.

Telecommunications The use of any form of communications line which connects users to their computer systems and permits the online handling of data.

Teleprocessing Telecommunications activities which specifically involve the use of terminals which visually display data.

Terminal The modern computer device which combines a keyboard and the ability to visually display or print data during online processing activities.

Third-generation computers The third era of computers, in which they were constructed with microminiaturized circuitry and became major tools of business.

TWO

An Overview of Computing Concepts

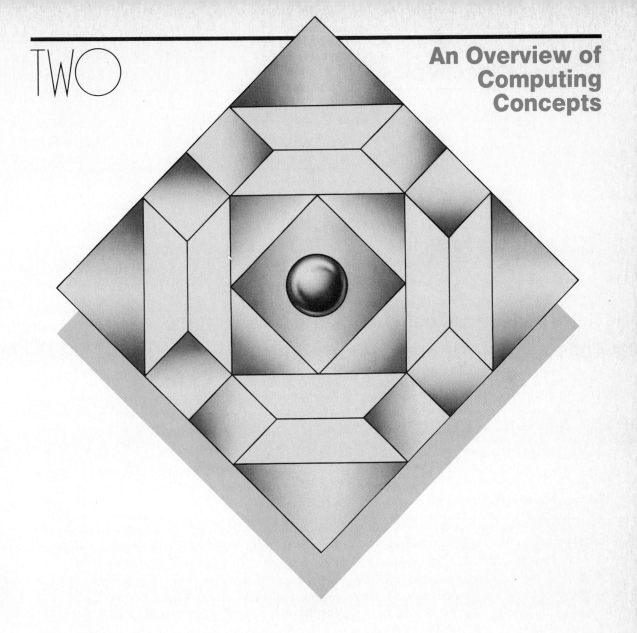

Chapter Objectives

This chapter will

- Discuss the EDP cycle and its components.

- Describe I/O devices and their function.

- Briefly discuss the operational purpose of the CPU and its control, arithmetic logic, and primary storage units.

- Introduce concepts related to secondary storage.

- Describe the operational characteristics and relationship of fields, records, and files.

- Discuss the differences between applications and operational software and the origin of canned software.

- Briefly describe differences between batch and online processing activities.

- Discuss concepts of timeshared processing.

Introduction

As will become apparent from the study of computerized data processing, users may choose from among many methods to process their data. The level of sophistication adopted by users relates directly to their finances and the immediacy of their processing need. Interactive languages such as BASIC can provide a ready and inexpensive means of accommodating users' data processing needs.

In this chapter, we examine a representative computer system in which BASIC is used and discuss the hardware that supports it. Devices that handle data input, processing, and output are discussed. We will also distinguish between software programs that control processing activities and those that relate to specific applications. It is important for readers to understand how these types of software interact, since this defines how programs are actually executed. Lastly, we offer an overview of online processing activities and focus on timeshared processing where BASIC is principally used. Throughout the chapter we will again introduce terminology directly related to computer activities and thus provide an informational base for future discussions.

The analysis of many processing activities often eludes beginning program-mers, as they do not recognize key elements in the overall processing se-quence. In the analysis of programs, many programmers evaluate their solu-tions in terms of the **electronic data processing (EDP)** cycle (Figure 2.1). The EDP cycle describes processing sequences in terms of three key elements: input, processing, and output. Most programming tasks fall within one of these three fundamental tasks.

We shall define the term **input** as the entry of data into the computer system. This definition recognizes the many ways in which computer systems may accept data in preparation for its processing. In Chapter 1 we discussed one input method: the use of a terminal to enter data manually via its key-board and thus input data on an online basis. There are many other methods of input.

Processing is broadly defined as the manipulation of data. This defini-tion accommodates such processing activities as the fundamental arithmetic operations of addition, subtraction, multiplication, and division, as well as the comparison of two data items to determine whether one is equal to, greater than, or less than the other. In addition, processing activities may include the movement of data for its subsequent printing or the ordering of a group of data items in numerical or alphabetic sequence. The processing instructions composing a program solution may be so diverse that only a broad definition of those activities could apply.

It is important for processing instructions to proceed in an orderly and logical sequence of steps in order to produce the correct answer. The logic expressed in a program solution must represent a well-thought-out series of statements, not a haphazardly thrown together group of instructions with no purpose. Programmers must exercise great care in ensuring that program instructions are logically placed and accurately directed toward the develop-ment of the desired result.

Once the input data is processed, it is time to record the results for future processing tasks or present them to the user. This recording or presenting of

FIGURE 2.1   The electronic data processing or EDP cycle is composed of three elements which characterize most programming operations.

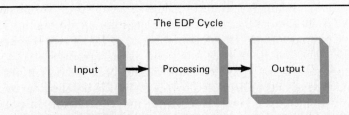

the processing results is called **output,** which we define as the retrieval of information in a predetermined format. This definition is somewhat more specific, as it recognizes distinctions associated with outputs. Not every item involved in processing is automatically output. It is the programmer's responsibility to select and present only those data items that comprise the desired output. The use of the word *information* is deliberate and denotes that input data has undergone processing and is being presented to the user in a more useful format.

The format used to present processed results is also critical. The programmer must specifically instruct the computer in the placement of each item comprising the output, because without these instructions output operations would remain incomplete. The output format must be crisp and legible to permit ready comprehension by its intended users. The visual appearance of printed reports is a major consideration when writing program solutions.

The components of the EDP cycle are useful in both defining the tasks which make up a program solution and determining the actual program instructions which are used. The concept of input, processing, and output can be helpful in the preparation of program solutions.

I/O Devices

Current computer technology permits users to employ a variety of devices for input and output operations. These devices are referred to as **peripheral devices.** Some are restricted solely to input operations; one such is the **card reader.** This input device reads data punched onto a standard 80-column computer card, as shown in Figure 2.2. Input data is recorded onto 80-column cards using the **Hollerith code,** named after its originator. The Hollerith code designates a unique code for each character; one character's code is punched into any of the 80 columns on the card. Once the card is punched, it is read by the card reader, and data on the card is input to the computer. Though BASIC is primarily an interactive language, some users elect to punch their BASIC programs onto cards and process them via cards.

By contrast, the **printer** is solely an output device providing tangible printed reports. These reports provide their users with the data necessary to make decisions, conduct business, or study information. Figure 2.3 shows one type of printer, with a printed output representative of the reports which may be prepared. How many retail statements or invoices have you personally received which were prepared by a similar printing device?

While card readers and printers are respectively limited to input and output operations, terminals may perform both types of tasks. Terminals are used to key in data, as well as to record the results of processing. These terminal devices are referred to as **input-output (I/O) devices** because of their dual capacity to perform both input and output operations.

Terminals are generally divided into two categories, with each category denoting the type of output produced by the device. **Hardcopy terminals** prepare printed outputs on paper and provide users with a tangible permanent document which may be referred to repeatedly. Because of this associa-

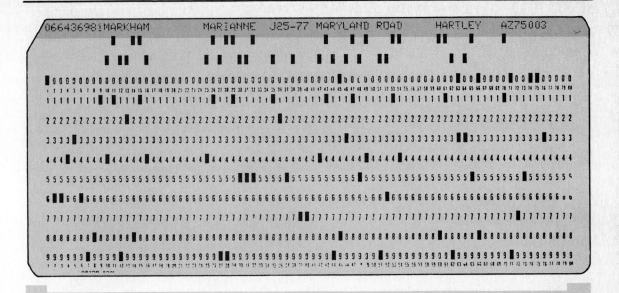

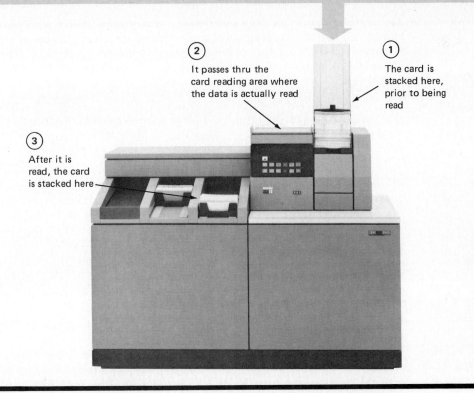

FIGURE 2.2 The card reader is solely an input device that is used to read data punched onto cards, as that card passes through the card reader. Data is punched onto the card using the Hollerith code. In the figure, a card containing student data is read via a card reader. *(IBM.)*

```
  CUSTOMER                    REERENCE   PAYMENT    DISCOUNT
  NO      NAME                NUMBER     DATE       DATE

  ----------------------      ------------------------------

  120017 LAKEVILLE PLBG. CO INC    037924      2-11-82     1-22-82

  CUSTOMER TOTAL

  120079 LICON ASSOCIATES, INC.    037065      2-08-82    12-18-81
  120079 LICON ASSOCIATES, INC.    037452      2-08-82     1-08-82

  CUSTOMER TOTAL

  120097 LIZZA INDUSTRIES

  CUSTOMER TOTAL

  120114 LONG ISLAND LIGHTING CO   035389      2-01-82    10-16-81
  120114 LONG ISLAND LIGHTING CO   008570      2-08-82    12-10-81
  120114 LONG ISLAND LIGHTING CO   008617      2-08-82    12-15-81
  120114 LONG ISLAND LIGHTING CO
```

Printed reports are generated by many types of printers

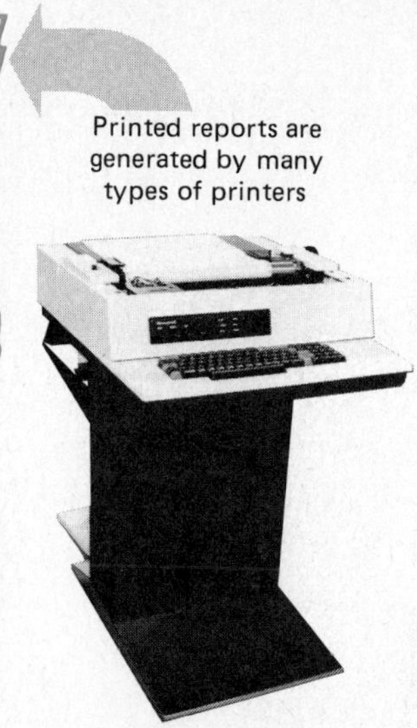

FIGURE 2.3   Printers provide an output capability for the preparation of printed materials. Shown is one type of printing device and a sample report prepared by such a device. *(Data Printer Corporation.)*

tion, printed reports are often called **hardcopy outputs. Softcopy terminals** display a nonpermanent visual output on CRTs, using their TV-like picture screen. These temporary **softcopy outputs** provide a quick and ready reference to program data and are frequently used in software development activities. Examples of softcopy and hardcopy terminals and output are shown in Figure 2.4. Both types of terminals can record the results of processing using their respective formats. Softcopy terminals are generally faster and quieter, but hardcopy terminals provide a permanent record of programming activities.

2.2 The Central Processing Unit (CPU)

The Control Unit and ALU
Whereas peripheral devices are used for input and output operations, they cannot actually process data. All processing activities must occur within the **central processing unit (CPU)** and under its direction. Any programs undergoing processing in a computer must reside in its CPU during their execution.

To accommodate the full and complete processing of all software, the CPU is divided into three functional components:

(a)

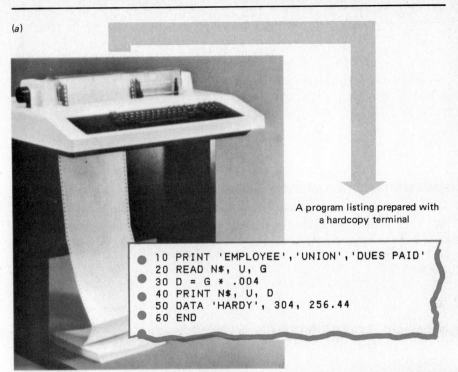

A program listing prepared with a hardcopy terminal

```
10  PRINT 'EMPLOYEE','UNION','DUES PAID'
20  READ N$, U, G
30  D = G * .004
40  PRINT N$, U, D
50  DATA 'HARDY', 304, 256.44
60  END
```

FIGURE 2.4 Hardcopy and softcopy terminals provide radically different types of outputs. In *(a)*, a hardcopy terminal is shown along with an excerpt of a BASIC program which was prepared via that device. In *(b)* a softcopy terminal is shown with a blowup of the visual output possible with these devices. Both types of devices shown are representative of the I/O devices associated with hardcopy and softcopy terminals. *(Digital Equipment and Honeywell.)*

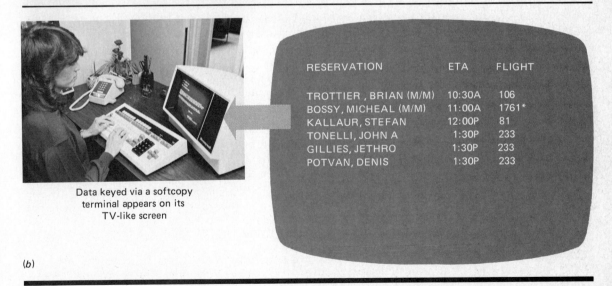

RESERVATION	ETA	FLIGHT
TROTTIER , BRIAN (M/M)	10:30A	106
BOSSY, MICHEAL (M/M)	11:00A	1761*
KALLAUR, STEFAN	12:00P	81
TONELLI, JOHN A	1:30P	233
GILLIES, JETHRO	1:30P	233
POTVAN, DENIS	1:30P	233

Data keyed via a softcopy terminal appears on its TV-like screen

(b)

1 Control unit

2 Arithmetic logic unit (ALU)

3 Primary storage unit

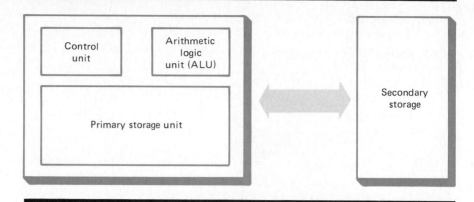

FIGURE 2.5 Data not retainable in primary storage may be placed in secondary storage. Secondary-storage devices must be online to the CPU and retain the data stored in a format that is acceptable to the computer and does not require conversion.

Each CPU component has specific functions which are operationally related, as shown in Figure 2.5.

The **control unit** is designed to oversee the function of all hardware composing the system. It defines the circuitry used in processing and I/O operations, checks circuits employed to verify the accurate transfer of data and its processing, and ensures that all hardware is functioning properly. The control unit directs the system's hardware in processing the operations indicated by the program undergoing execution. It also schedules the execution of all statements slated for processing.

The **arithmetic logic unit (ALU)** is assigned tasks which the control unit cannot perform. Among its principal activities are the performance of arithmetic and logic operations and the handling of the data involved in those activities. Arithmetic operations undertaken by the ALU include the four fundamental arithmetic operations, as well as exponentiation. Logical operations involve the comparison of data items to determine their operational relationships to each other (e.g., greater than, less than, or equal to, etc.). Logical and arithmetic operations are the sole responsibility of the ALU. The ALU performs either task when so directed by the program undergoing execution.

The Storage of Data

The principal storage area of a computer system is the CPU's **primary storage unit.** All programs undergoing processing are retained in primary storage during their execution. You will recall from Chapter 1 that the retention of a program within the computer was a major component of the stored-program concept.

Instructions from a program are individually accessed from the primary storage unit and direct the computer to perform specific processing activities. Program statements might direct the output of a group of data items, the movement of data between two storage locations, or the addition of two numbers. In responding to these program instructions, the computer will involve the control unit, the arithmetic logic unit, and any other hardware required to accomplish that task. Essentially, the control unit supervises the execution of all program statements, the ALU involves itself with arithmetic and logical operations, and primary storage retains the results of processing.

Primary storage is an organized series of storage locations. Each storage location is identified by a specific "address," in much the same manner that numbered addresses designate different homes on the same street. During processing activities, storage locations are operationally linked together and retain both the data used in processing or resultant from processing and the programs being run.

Data is not retained in primary storage in a decimal format but adopts a **base 2,** or binary, format. This format parallels the actual storage mode used by the computer through the usage of 0s and 1s. The 0 and 1 coding of data is referred to as **binary notation** and represents the two types of impulses composing the codes used for the storage of data.

This process takes place as follows. The user inputs data to the computer in a decimal format. The computer must convert this data to the base 2 format to actually process the data in primary storage. The computer performs all processing activities using data coded in base 2, then converts the data back to a decimal format for output. The information output may then be employed by users in decision making.

Though we have simplified this conversionary process, it offers an overview to the computer's storage of data. A similar process is utilized with alphabetic data, with a different coding structure employed that is unique to alphabetic characters. Alphabetic data is inputted, converted to its binary code, and placed in primary storage for processing.

One final point of clarification is necessary. There are no 0s or 1s as such in primary storage. Binary notation is used merely to represent the data in storage; it is designed to assist users in understanding how data is stored. The 0s and 1s represent the electrical impulses generated by the computer to actually store data.

Another important concept associated with the primary storage unit concerns the actual storage of data. During processing operations, the storage locations of data involved in computations are accessed, and exact coded images of that data are removed. It is the duplicate copies of the original data that are used when computations are undertaken. Accessing a storage area to use a data item does not destroy the contents of that storage location.

A representative processing operation is illustrated in Figure 2.6. In this sequence, the contents of storage area A are added to the contents of storage area B. After addition in the ALU, the computed result of 71 is stored in C. The storage of the new result (71) in C destroys the result (39) that was previously contained at the C location. This last transaction denotes how data is altered in primary storage. The only way to destroy the contents of a primary storage location is to move new data into the same location. The movement of 71 into C destroyed its previous contents of 39. The contents of storage areas A and B were not destroyed, as only duplicates of those numbers

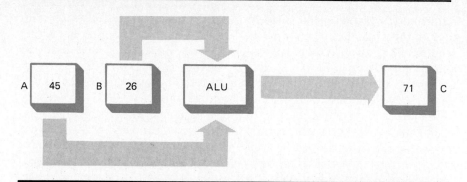

FIGURE 2.6 When performing arithmetic operations, the computer takes copies of the numbers involved and uses them in those activities. In this example, the results of the addition of A and B, 71, is stored in C. The placement of 71 in C destroys its previous contents of C.

were utilized in processing and no new data was moved into those locations. This latter concept is reintroduced when we discuss the handling of data within programs and performance of selected accumulation techniques for developing subtotals.

The capacities of primary storage units are measured in relation to CPU sizes; CPU sizes are denoted multiples of K. The factor **K** is the equivalent of 1024 bytes of storage. A **byte** is generally the equivalent of one character's worth of storage, with that character being alphabetic (A to Z), numeric (0 to 9), or special (e.g., @, :, #, etc.).

A CPU may be said to possess a storage capacity of 64K. The 64K designation implies that the CPU has a storage capacity of *approximately* 64,000 bytes of storage. To compute the *actual* number of storage positions available, the user would multiply 64 by 1024 to find that exactly 65,536 bytes of storage are available within a CPU size of 64K. The next time you read an article on a home computer, observe how the K designation is used in relation to CPU sizes.

2.3 Secondary Storage

The Operational Concept

The concept of **secondary storage** evolved from the limitations of primary storage. Even though CPU sizes may range into millions of bytes of storage, they are limited in their capacity to retain data. Data placed in primary storage cannot be permanently retained in the CPU. A sudden loss of power from the CPU would destroy all data held within primary storage. Also, it would prove impractical for the computer to keep the same data in the CPU permanently, as its limited storage capacity would be quickly filled.

Secondary storage was constructed to overcome these difficulties and provide the computer with the means to permanently retain vast quantities of data that are readily accessible by the computer during processing. The relationship between primary and secondary storage was depicted in Figure 2.5. Secondary storage is tied directly to the CPU, enabling online interaction of both units. With this online link, data is readily accessible from files retained within a secondary storage device.

Data stored on secondary storage devices assumes a permanent form and is not destroyed when power is removed from the device. Data is altered by erasing the entire file or writing new data over the existing data. It is possible to record many billions of characters of data via secondary storage devices and provide access to that information in seconds.

Magnetic Tape and Disk

The two principal means of secondary storage are **magnetic tape** and **magnetic disk.** Both units provide for the permanent storage of data, utilizing different storage techniques.

Magnetic tape storage was introduced in the mid-1950s and represented a major breakthrough in the computerized storage of data. The storage of data on magnetic tape parallels the operation of home tape recorders. As the tape's magnetizable surface passes over the read-write head, data may be written onto the tape or read from its surface (providing that data was previously recorded onto the tape).

This method of accessing data belies the operational concept associated with this secondary storage medium. Magnetic tape is a *sequential-storage medium;* individual items of data are accessed as the tape passes through the device. For the 100th data item to be read, the 99 data items preceding it must be read first.

Though the sequential method of accessing data is suitable for some applications, it does not lend itself to access of individual data items. Magnetic disks have the capacity to directly access individual data items from within a file. Disk is defined as a *direct-access medium,* enabling the computer to individually select specific data records from within a file.

The technology related to magnetic disk is more complex but provides excellent support for secondary storage functions. It was the advent of this technology in the early 1960s that revolutionized the computer field and thrust the computer into the limelight of business. Multiple read-write heads enable disk devices to record data and selectively retrieve single data items from within a large file. The 100th data item may be read *without* the preceding 99 data items being read.

In recent years, emphasis has shifted to magnetic disk from tape because of its direct-access capabilities. Magnetic tape has been relegated to retaining data that rarely changes or serves as a backup medium. The term **backup** defines the set of activities where critical data files are duplicated on tape, thus providing a reserve copy of that file should the original be damaged. Magnetic tape provides an inexpensive and reliable means of backup operations.

The successful use of magnetic disk results from its ability to rapidly retrieve independent items of data from a file. In addition, although magnetic tape once held a significant advantage in storage capacities, this is no longer the case. Current magnetic disks may store as much as 2 billion characters of data and transfer that data at speeds of 3 million characters per second. Both disk operational figures are far in excess of magnetic tape capacities. It is the online support capabilities of magnetic disk that have permitted its widespread acceptance.

File Characteristics

In our discussion of secondary storage we referred to data files, a reference which often confuses some beginning programmers. Let us initially define a **file** as an organized series of records, where each record details data related to a single transaction, event, or person. (That is, files are made up of records, and records are made up of related data items.) The file is sequentially ordered to permit access to any record within its structure and provide a means of logically accessing that data. But to truly understand the structure of a file, we must dig more deeply.

The first concept to be examined is that of a field. A **field** is defined as a series of storage positions set aside to hold a specific data item. Thus, it is possible to have fields representing ZIP codes, social security numbers, states, telephone numbers, last names, departments of work, sex, marital status, and birthdays. Each of these fields, and many others not listed, could easily be associated with a personnel record for a company's file of employees.

The sequential positioning of fields provides the basis of the data record upon which a file is constructed. A **record** may then be defined as a consecutive series of fields defining data items related to a transaction, event, or person. The record becomes the basis of a file. Each record of a file represents data relating to a specific person, event, or transaction and is composed of the same fields. Though the actual data contained in each field can vary, the same fields, in exactly the same order, will constitute each record.

Files must be ordered in some way. A field is selected from each file and becomes the basis for placing all records composing the file in a logical order. This field is referred to as the **key field.** Examples of key fields used to order files of personnel data are social security number or employee number. Both data types provide a ready means of ordering the records which could compose a file of employee data.

An illustration of the hierarchy used in constructing a student file is shown in Figure 2.7. The individual student record noted consists of six fields. The order of these fields is social security number, last name, first name, program of study, semester of study, credits taken. The key field is social security number, as it offers a unique number assigned to all students which is readily used to order a file. Because of its significance, the social security number field is positioned as the first field of the student record.

All records in the student file employ each of the six fields. All six fields are used for student record 1 and are continued for each student record until the last record of the file is defined. The file consists of a logically ordered

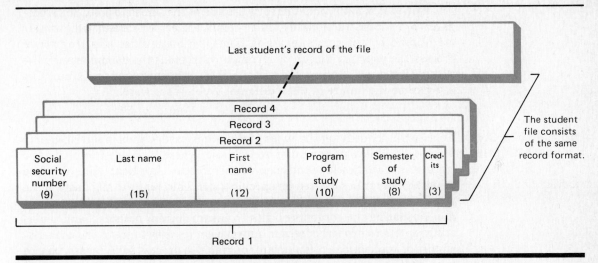

FIGURE 2.7 Files are constructed of a series of records. The student record shown consists of six fields of student data. The social security field is used to order the entire file's data. Each student record contains the same data, from the first to the last record of that file. The numbers placed in parentheses beneath each field name denote the size of each field.

series of student records. Most files generally exhibit the characteristics associated with the student file discussed.

Looking back, we may now summarize the hierarchical structure of a file using the following definitions:

1 A field consists of a series of storage positions reserved for a specific item of data.

2 A record consists of a series of fields identifying data related to a specific transaction, event, or person.

3 A file consists of a logical series of records, ordered on the basis of a key field.

Using these definitions, users can assess the ordered nature of computerized files and note how each factor is employed as a building block when constructing a file.

2.4 Computer Software

By definition, programs are designed to direct the computer in all phases of processing. This rationale evolved from von Neumann's stored-program concept. This concept dictates that programs retained within primary storage control the computerized processing of data.

However, not all computer software serves the same purpose. Some programs provide instructions on how to handle a specific problem, while others are utilized by the computer itself. Thus, we may utilize one program to process the payments made by a company, whereas the computer may use another program to control the processing of a related group of programs. Let us examine the nature of these different types of software.

Applications and Operational Software

To assist in identifying the types of programs used with computerized data processing activities, computer software is generally divided into the two categories of applications and operational software. **Applications software** consists of programs written for specific tasks. They relate to all phases of the processing activity. These programs concern themselves with I/O data handling, updating the contents of files to ensure current accuracy, and generating reports to properly present information for assistance to the user. Examples of applications software are programs to process payroll data, charge sales data for customer credit accounts, advise customers of payments that are due, complete math or science lab assignments, and plot your own biorhythmical chart or horoscope.

Operational software is totally different and helps the computer efficiently supervise processing. Let us define operational software as the set of supervisory programs that control processing and define the processing potential of a computer system. It is the operational software of a computer system which defines what and how things are processed. Thus, in effect, the operational software of a computer system interacts with the applications software for a specific activity, which results in the actual processing of data.

Because the concepts related to operational software are often difficult to digest by the beginning programmer, some further explanation is in order. It is the operational software of a computer (or, as it is sometimes called, the **operating system**) which defines the processing potential of the hardware. Essentially, the operating system defines what processing activities the computer can support. For example, if a computer's operational software is only designed to handle computer cards, it will not support the online use of terminals, teleprocessing activities are out of the question, and all CRTs attached to that computer's CPU will have no effect.

It is possible to obtain computer systems that are identical down to the last nut and bolt and radically alter their processing potential by equipping the systems with different types of operational software. Thus, depending on their operational software, some computers could be limited to a few tasks and others will support an expanded range of data processing activities. The point of this oversimplification is that a computer system will only perform processing tasks which its operational software can support.

Computer manufacturers offer many types of operational software for their computers. Each operating system equips a computer with specific processing capabilities which have been matched against the operational needs of users. Some permit a computer to support the type of interactive processing activities which relate to BASIC. The term **interactive processing** describes the online processing mode where users interact directly with the computer, affecting processing on almost a line-by-line basis. The computer and user interchange program instructions and responses on an online basis. Because of this online interaction, interactive processing is sometimes referred to as **conversational mode.** Most BASIC programs are written and executed within an interactive processing environment. Again, the operational software necessary to support interactive processing must be available within the computer system slated to support such processing activities.

Program Execution

For operational software to be used properly, control languages have been developed. These control languages are often unique to a given system. One of the most frequently encountered is **job control language (JCL),** which is representative of most control languages currently used. JCL is composed of a set of complex operational codes which, when put together in certain combinations, enable users to communicate with the computer's operating system and tell the computer which applications programs are to be executed.

To observe how JCL, operational software, and applications software interact, we should examine how an interactive language like BASIC is used. As we know, BASIC permits users to be online during processing. In order to establish the online communications link between their terminals and the computer, users must follow a special set of JCL procedures which are generally referred to as **LOGON procedures.** The instructions constituting a LOGON procedure are drawn from the JCL used with that system. These control instructions establish that a particular terminal is requesting access to the computer and that the BASIC language will be used on an interactive basis. It directs the computer to ready the operational software needed to support the online use of BASIC. Any special requirements related to the BASIC programs to be processed will come from the JCL composing the LOGON procedure.

The opposite of the LOGON procedure is the **LOGOFF procedure,** which is used when a user wishes to conclude a processing session. The JCL instructions constituting the LOGOFF procedure (1) cancel the existing online status, (2) stop interactive processing activities, (3) permit the operational software to turn toward other programs, and (4) prepare the computer for the next program.

During the interactive processing of BASIC programs, the combined use of JCL commands and operational software is also evident. The successful completion of the LOGON procedure enables the user to start inputting the **source program.** The source program is the term used to describe the program written by the user. Each statement of the source program is entered on an individual basis via the terminal's keyboard. When the entire program has been inputted the user may elect to run the program by keying the appropriate JCL command.

The execution of the source program is accomplished by using a special program within the operating system. This program, referred to as a **compiler,** converts the source program into machine language, the only language the computer can utilize to actually execute a program. BASIC was used to simplify the preparation of software by humans, but it must be converted to machine language to undergo execution. It is the compiler which converts the source program written in BASIC to its equivalent machine language program for actual processing by the computer.

Compilers exist for many currently popular languages, assisting in their conversion and execution. An attractive feature of compilers is their facility to check for errors in statements composing the source program. Compilers scan program statements and ensure that each statement was written according to the rules associated with that language. The failure to observe those rules will cause the processing of that program to stop. The computer's operational software will cancel the program and direct that the source of that error be outputted. These outputs are helpful in correcting program errors. This correction process is sometimes referred to as **debugging,** as the programmer attempts to remove errors, or bugs, from the source program.

A compiler often associated with the conversion of interactive languages such as BASIC is the **interpretive compiler.** The interpretive compiler converts each statement of an interactive program as it enters the computer. With BASIC, each program statement is checked for errors by the interpretive compiler before conversion into machine language. Errors uncovered by an interpretive compiler are immediately outputted, making possible their rapid correction. The interpretive compiler differs from other compilers in that it converts programs on a line-by-line basis, rather than accepting and converting the entire program as one large unit. Both types of compilers are part of a computing system's operational software.

In this brief overview, we have attempted to introduce examples of the operational software commonly encountered during the execution of source programs. This is a complex area and we have barely touched the surface of materials regarding operational software. Your knowledge of operational software will improve with programming experience.

Canned Software

In the past many organizations preferred to have all their applications software written in-house, believing that the final product would be more suited to their needs. Recent increases in software development costs have led many organizations to reevaluate this position. Although hardware costs have gradually declined, the costs associated with programming personnel have risen dramatically. It is the cost of quality programming staff that has increased the expenses related to extensive program development.

As an alternative to writing in-house software, many organizations are now considering the purchase of canned programs. The term **canned program** defines commercially available software that handles one particular type of application. Where once this type of software was scarce or economically prohibitive, canned programs are now readily available for almost every business application and many personal applications as well.

Canned programs may be purchased for the processing of employee payrolls, accounts receivable related to credit cards, inventory control in warehouses, the analysis of economic conditions and budgets, and medical record keeping. On a personal basis, canned software exists to project astrological forecasts, analyze your stock portfolio, prepare personal letters, record social engagements, and teach children how to spell. Most canned programs are prepared by computer manufacturers or private software houses that specialize in commercial applications. A trade-off exists between writing your own software or purchasing the canned software.

2.5 Online Processing Approaches

Batch versus Online Processing

Data may be processed in two different ways: in batches or online. In **batch processing,** groups of data are accumulated over a specific period of time and then processed. This accumulation of data causes delays in processing. By contrast, **online processing** enables the direct handling of data and speeds processing considerably. Online processing activities involve some form of telecommunications. Data entering processing is rapidly inputted to the computer for processing, thus speeding the preparation of results.

Each processing approach has its merits. When a delay in processing will not adversely affect an organization's work, batch processing can prove effective and efficient. Hardware expenses related to batch-processing systems are generally lower than online systems where more sophisticated devices are utilized. Online processing is designed to overcome potential delays. All I/O operations are online, permitting users to interact with their supporting systems. Compare the two processing approaches shown in Figure 2.8.

The weekly processing of a payroll is good example of the batch processing approach. The organization for which the payroll is prepared has seven days to accumulate and prepare the payroll data slated for processing. Once the data is collected, another week is available to process payroll data and print employee paychecks. Compare these time constraints with those of a retail system where credit cards must be checked immediately. To ensure the accuracy of credit sales, clerks must have online access to customer charge card records. Using the online retail system, charged sales are immediately verified and posted against the appropriate customer records. Without online support, this type of direct processing support would not be possible.

Timesharing

An online processing approach which supports the use of an interactive language like BASIC is **timesharing.** Timesharing derives its name from the fact that multiple users can share the resources of a single computer at the same time. The operational software supporting a timesharing system allows each user to work with his or her individual program and to share online I/O

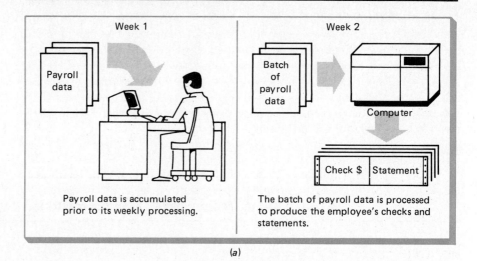

Week 1

Payroll data

Payroll data is accumulated prior to its weekly processing.

Week 2

Batch of payroll data

Computer

Check $ | Statement

The batch of payroll data is processed to produce the employee's checks and statements.

(a)

Sales data is directly input to the computer.

Computer

Secondary storage

Sales data is posted against customer files retained on secondary-storage disk devices.

Sales clerks have online access to customer data.

(b)

FIGURE 2.8 Batch and online processing activities are markedly different in their handling of data. *(a)* In batch processing, data is accumulated over a period of time and then processed. *(b)* Online processing activities permit the immediate entry and processing of data.

operations of the system. Timesharing computers can support multiple users from one organization or users distributed at distant regional offices.

BASIC is ideally suited to a timesharing environment. Many users do not require, or want the expense of, full-scale computer support. Timesharing permits them to plug in to a support system when necessary and receive online data processing services. They pay only for the services they use. Many beginning programming students develop their initial skills at schools that use timesharing. BASIC is effectively used in, but not restricted to, timesharing. Student programmers may also use BASIC as the interactive language for their home computers. BASIC offers advantages to users in either operational environment.

Time-sharing provides a practical example of the concept of **multiprogramming,** a processing environment created by a computer's operational software which permits the concurrent processing of multiple programs. Multiprogramming enables the computer to concurrently retain one or more programs in primary storage and process them as required. This technique takes full advantage of current computer processing speeds. By concurrently storing multiple programs, the computer can rapidly jump from one to another and process instructional sequences from within each program.

The concept of multiprogramming must be compared against **multiprocessing.** Whereas multiprogramming involves a single computer, multiprocessing involves the simultaneous execution of two or more instructions in two or more CPUs. Even with its impressive processing speed, one CPU can execute only one instruction at one given instant. To execute two instructions from two separate programs simultaneously, two CPUs must be involved.

Multiprocessing is normally associated with computer networks, where multiple systems at key locations interact with each other. These networks often support large corporations, sharing the organization's workload and distributing information to all levels of management. Often in a multiprocessing environment, supporting computers will utilize multiprogramming to increase their capacity for data handling and process a larger workload.

Multiprogramming and multiprocessing techniques are often utilized by organizations which rent out computer services. These organizations, referred to as **service bureaus,** rent computer services, including software and hardware support, to users who do not want to own their own computer facilities. Users rent from service bureaus only those facilities they need and only for services used.

Service bureaus offer a wide range of services. Timesharing is available, as is the development of canned software for a user's specific needs. Computer hardware may be leased from service bureaus, including computer systems or specialized I/O units. Service bureaus lease software, run users' software on their own computers and prepare results in a predetermined format, or input users' data, process it with their own software and return these results on a scheduled basis. These results may be printed and returned via messengers, or they may be telecommunicated to your home office and printed in hardcopy form by you for immediate distribution. Online processing activities are offered by many service bureaus and have become increasingly popular over the past few years.

A drawback to the use of service bureaus is the possible loss of security, as your records and files are maintained in their computers and within their offices. It is the responsibility of the user to investigate a service bureau and determine whether it can provide adequate security as well as sufficient processing support.

Chapter Summary

2.1 The EDP Cycle

Programming activities may be represented in terms of the electronic data processing cycle. The EDP cycle is composed of three operational elements: input, processing, and output. Input describes the entry of data into the computer. Processing is broadly described as the manipulation of data. Output describes the retrieval of information in a predetermined format.

Many types of devices are employed to accomplish input and output operations and are generally referred to as peripheral devices. The card reader is an example of a device limited to input tasks. Printers are strictly output devices that are used to prepare the varied printed reports so vital to the management of organizations.

Terminal devices are classified as I/O devices, as they provide for both input and output operations. Terminals may provide either printed or visual-display outputs: hardcopy terminals provide printed, or hardcopy, outputs, and softcopy terminals display their outputs on a TV-like screen. These nonpermanent visual displays of information are called softcopy outputs.

2.2 The Central Processing Unit (CPU)

The focal point of processing activities in a computer system is the central processing unit. The CPU consists of the control unit, arithmetic logic unit (ALU), and primary storage unit. The control oversees the operation of all hardware and the execution of program statements. The ALU assumes control over execution of arithmetic and logical operations. Programs and data undergoing processing are retained within primary storage.

Data retained in primary storage is stored in the form of electrical impulses. As only two types of impulses result, stored data may be represented with a binary notation of 0 and 1 developed from the base 2. Each location in primary storage has its own identifying address. Data within a storage location is altered when new data is moved into that storage area.

CPU sizes are assessed according to a K factor, the equivalent of 1024 bytes of storage. A byte is normally the equivalent of one character's worth of data. To compute the actual capacity of a CPU, multiply the specified K number by 1024. For example, a CPU of 32 K has an actual capacity of 32,768 bytes (32×1024).

2.3 Secondary Storage

The limitations of primary storage led to the development of secondary storage. Data held in secondary storage may be retained for extended periods of time.

The principal methods of secondary storage are magnetic tape and magnetic disk. Magnetic tape is a sequential storage medium whose function parallels the operation of home tape recorders. Magnetic disk is a random-access medium which permits the independent access of individual records.

Data retained on either tape or disk is organized into files. A file is defined as an organized series of records, each record representing one transaction, event, or person. Records are constructed of fields, which are consecutive storage positions set aside to hold specific data items. Key fields provide a basis for ordering files.

2.4 Computer Software

Computer software is generally divided into applications and operational software. Applications software is developed to handle specific user tasks and process data related to those activities. Operational software is a set of supervisory programs which control the processing activities of the computer and define its processing potential. Operating systems equip a computer with specific processing capabilities.

The interactive processing activities associated with BASIC are supported by operational software. With this software, users may interact with the computer on a line-by-line basis; an approach referred to as conversational mode.

Within a computer, applications

software will interact with operational software to complete processing. Users communicate with a computer's operating system using a control language like JCL. JCL consists of a series of complex codes. The LOGON and LOGOFF procedures are defined using JCL, where the online link between user and computer is created and ended. The source program, the user's original program, is converted to machine language by a compiler. Machine language is the only language that the computer uses in its processing. A compiler will search the source program for errors and document their existence for the user to aide the debugging process.

Canned software consists of commercially prepared programs applied to specific tasks. Canned programs may be purchased outright, thus avoiding the need to write that software from scratch. Many organizations find it more economical to buy canned programs than to write their own.

2.5 Online Processing Approaches

Batch and online processing represent two primary data processing modes. With batch processing, data is accumulated over periods of time and processed in batches at regular intervals. Online processing enables the user to interact with the computer and handle data on an immediate basis. Timesharing represents an online processing mode often utilized with BASIC. With timesharing, users concurrently share the resources of the same computer.

Timesharing offers a practical example of the concept of multiprogramming. Multiprogramming is a processing environment created by a computer's operational software in which many programs are held and processed in the CPU concurrently. By contrast, multiprocessing means that two or more computers simultaneously execute statements from separate programs. Both techniques are utilized by service bureaus who rent their computer services to users. These services include hardware and software support, program development, and data handling activities.

Glossary

Applications software Programs that are written for specific problems or tasks (e.g., payroll program, programs for math or business problems).

Arithmetic logic unit (ALU) The CPU component assigned the performance of arithmetic operations and the comparison of data in logical operations.

Backup Processing activities performed to duplicate critical data files to protect their contents, normally associated with magnetic tape.

Base 2 The numbering system which uses 0s and 1s in its representation of computerized data storage.

Batch processing The processing technique where data is accumulated in batches over a period of time and processed at regular intervals.

Binary notation The representation of data in a base 2 format, involving the use of 0s and 1s in its notation.

Byte The storage configuration normally associated with the equivalent of one character's worth of data.

Canned program Prewritten, commercially available software that may be immediately used in a variety of applications.

Card reader The I/O device used in the reading of data coded onto computer cards.

Central processing unit (CPU) The focal point of all processing activities within a computer system; composed of the control, arithmetic logic, and primary storage units.

Compiler A program that is part of a system's operational software and that converts source programs into machine language for execution; during conversion it scans the source program for errors.

Control unit The CPU component assigned to supervise processing activities in a computer, control all hardware interaction, and schedule the execution of all programs and statements.

Conversational mode The interactive processing mode in which an online user communicates with the computer on a line-by-line basis; usually associated with timesharing.

Debugging The scrutiny and correction of programs to remove errors.

Electronic data processing (EDP) cycle The term describing the processing associated with most software; composed of the key elements of input, processing, and output.

Field A series of storage positions set aside for specific items of data.

File An organized series of records where each record relates to a specific transaction, event, or person; ordered on a specific key field.

Hardcopy output Outputs that assume a printed, tangible format (e.g., paychecks, student transcripts).

Hardcopy terminal Terminals which record their outputs in a printed report format.

Hollerith code The code utilized to record data on standard 80-column cards.

Input Data entered into a computer; an element of the EDP cycle.

Input/output (I/O) device A device capable of performing both input and output operations; the general term applied to the devices which may be attached to a computer to perform I/O operations.

Interactive processing The term applied to the process by which online users interact with their supporting computer systems to process their software;

associated with timesharing and conversational mode.

Interpretive compiler A compiler which translates the source program on an individual line basis, as it enters the computer during timesharing.

Job control language (JCL) The special language used to communicate with and direct the activities of a computer's operational software.

K The factor associated with the computerized storage of data representing exactly 1024 bytes of storage; often used to describe the capacity of primary storage units.

Key field The specific field within the record upon which a file is constructed, that is, used to order the entire file.

LOGOFF procedure Those steps used to break the online link between a user and computer; composed of JCL statements.

LOGON procedure Those JCL statements used to construct an online link between a user's terminal and supporting computer system.

Magnetic disk The secondary storage medium which permits the direct access of individual data records from within a computerized file.

Magnetic tape The secondary storage medium which records its data on a sequential basis; often used for the backup storage of file data.

Multiprocessing The simultaneous execution of two or more statements in two or more CPUs in some form of computer network.

Multiprogramming The concurrent handling of two or more programs in a single CPU, where the

computer alternately jumps between programs to process them.

Online processing The processing activities performed via communications lines between a user and distant computer; users directly interact with their supporting computer.

Operational software The set of supervisory programs which oversee all processing activities and define the processing potential of a computer system.

Operating system Another term used for operational software.

Output Information retrieved from the computer in a predetermined format; an element of the EDP cycle.

Peripheral devices The general term applied to all devices which may be attached to a computer to undertake I/O operations; used interchangeably with I/O devices

Primary storage unit The CPU component which retains all programs and data undergoing processing.

Printer The device used to record outputs in a printed (paper) format.

Processing The manipulation of data (to accommodate all types of processing operations); an element within the EDP cycle.

Record The unit upon which a file is constructed; composed of a series of data fields.

Secondary storage Storage media online to the CPU which can permanently record data used in processing, but not retained in primary storage.

Service bureau A computer organization which rents many types of data processing services to users.

Softcopy output An output which

results during processing and assumes a visible, nonpermanent format.

Softcopy terminals A terminal device that display outputs in a visible, nonpermanent format, usually on a TV-like screen.

Source program The original program written by the user.

Timesharing The online processing approach where multiple users share the resources of the same computer at the same time; often used to support the interactive use of BASIC; associated with the terms interactive processing, conversational mode, and multiprogramming.

**Developing Your
Programming Skills**

THREE

Chapter Objectives

- Describe the functional uses of flowcharts and the symbols used in their preparation.

- Introduce flowcharting techniques for processing data in loops.

- Discuss techniques used to control loops to include the LRC, EOF check, and 9s Decision.

- Discuss the impact of literals in creating headings and special labels.

- Briefly discuss the purpose of heading, detail, and summary lines.

- Introduce the concept of a counter and its use with loops.

- Generally describe the use of a checklist when preparing flowcharts and when checking the accuracy of solutions.

- Discuss techniques used in the conversion of problem narratives to flow-chart solutions.

Introduction

For readers that are old movie buffs, the name Charlie Chan has a familiar ring. In pursuit of criminals and their alleged crimes, this learned investigator was known to offer wisdom in the form of Confucious-like parables. One of the statements frequently offered was, "A picture is worth 1000 words," a remark noting the simplicity with which a diagram can explain a complex idea. We have all experienced an incident where a simple diagram was more effective than the barrage of words associated with it.

A **flowchart** is a picture which depicts the logic or series of steps representing a processing activity. Using flowcharts, it is possible to represent the complex series of steps which compose a program solution.

The flowchart serves the user as a roadmap guides the motorist. It offers a link between the start and stop points of processing sequences, defining the path taken in terms of processing activities. The flowchart permits users to lay out all options open to them and detail alternatives which must be considered. The flowchart is a planning vehicle used to describe both the logic and steps critical to a successful processing activity.

This chapter focuses on the development and interpretation of flow-charts in preparation for future programming activities. We examine the derivation of a flowchart from its problem narrative to the symbols used to construct its pictorial solution. The major emphasis applies to the pictorial representation of the flow of processing and the logic employed in those steps. Illustrative problems will reinforce major flowcharting concepts offered throughout the chapter.

For the beginning programming student, the flowchart is a vital learning tool. Most advanced language courses use flowcharts to explain operational concepts and the logic employed in sample solutions. Many instructors rely heavily on the flowchart's pictorial format to introduce difficult topics and the steps related to their software equivalents. Once the steps and logic used are expressed in pictorial form, most students find it a simple task to write the required program statements.

Flowcharts are used in the *development of software:* they are prepared *before* the source program is written to detail the logic of solutions and simplify the task of writing that software. Program flowcharts are diagrams which depict the logic used in relation to program solutions. Employed in this manner, flowcharts are used as

1   A means of documentation

2   An analytic tool

3   A means of communication

Because of their pictorial format, flowcharts serve as an excellent means of *documentation.* They enable programmers to document every step of their program solutions, down to the smallest details. The program flowchart acts as a record of each solution as it is modified. Thus, the programmer can look back and review the evolution of a solution, record the reasons for each modification, and assess their impact.

The importance of adequate program documentation cannot be overestimated. In some data processing organizations programmers are not permitted to advance to the next stage of a project unless the documentation related to the last phase of their work is properly prepared.

Having proper program documentation available has many benefits. For one thing, this documentation helps supervisory personnel manage software development projects. By monitoring the documentation prepared, these supervisors may assess how rapidly a programmer is progressing, what difficulties the individual programmer is encountering, and whether the project is on schedule.

Proper documentation is also extremely helpful in educating programming personnel newly entering a project. By examining flowcharts and other supporting documentation, these employees can quickly acquaint themselves with many aspects of a project and become potentially productive in a shorter time. Also consider the benefits offered by this paperwork when a programmer must take over a partially completed project. Without the assistance offered by adequate documentation, that programmer would have to backtrack and duplicate the work previously performed during the initial stages of program development. If software has been properly documented, the transition between programmers is accomplished smoothly.

The flowchart's capacity to record the logic of a progam solution enables it to be used as an *analytic tool.* Essentially, the flowchart becomes a problem-solving tool. Consider the case of a programmer who is uncertain as to which program approach is best suited for a particular application. Using several flowcharts to detail each alternative, the programmer can depict the logic related to each approach. Each approach may be evaluated as to its merits and compared to the other alternatives.

The advantages of using flowcharts in this fashion are many. It is far easier to draw a flowchart than write an entire program, especially when one is uncertain as to the effectiveness of the proposed logic. The pictorial approach permits fellow programmers to act as critics of your solution and offer comments as to the potential success of each approach. Unsound solutions are readily uncovered, without the programmer's expending the effort associated with writing a complete program. Flowcharts provide a readily available and inexpensive method of assessing the effectiveness of program solutions.

A flowchart diagram can be used to express a host of ideas related to a specific processing activity without the support of a lengthy written narrative. Each step is assigned a symbol which depicts its processing activity and fixes its logical position in the flow of processing. Flowcharts are particularly useful when two or more programmers on a project work in separate offices. Using flowcharts, they may *communicate ideas* regarding an approach toward processing. The analysis of these flowcharts will reveal the thrust of their approaches and serve as a basis of future discussions. Should one programmer wish to modify another's design, the flowchart becomes the vehicle for expressing the recommended changes.

One final advisory note: some critics of flowcharting tend to discount its importance in relation to current EDP operations. These critics are very far from reality. Many data processing (DP) organizations rely heavily on flowcharts as a major analytic and documentation tool. Some programmers elect to forgo preliminary flowcharting activities in critical situations, choosing to concentrate on the problem at hand and the preparation of flowcharts for the final documentation package. Organizations that do not use flowcharts or similar documentation often find themselves spending inordinate amounts of time retracing their steps and duplicating prior programming efforts.

Flowcharts continue to be important beyond the preliminary planning stages. Once the source program is properly tested and certified as operationally sound, a final version of the supporting flowchart is drawn. The flowchart will detail the logic and symbolic equivalents of all instructions composing the final source program. This flowchart is then retained within the project's file (with other flowcharts), serving as the basis for future work on that specific program. All changes made to the original program are documented within subsequent flowcharts, which are appended to the previously prepared final documentation. Make an effort to learn how to use flowcharts, as they offer the user a powerful operational tool.

3.2 Program Flowcharts

Flowcharts, or **flow diagrams** as they are sometimes called, are symbolic diagrams by nature. That is, they are diagrams composed of symbols which specify certain processing or data handling operations. Each symbol is unique in shape and represents a particular processing operation. Within the flowchart, each symbol is logically positioned and connected to the symbol before it. This series of symbols creates the chain of steps which define the processing operations to be performed.

Some programmers consider flowchart symbols the building blocks out of which program solutions are constructed. Each block or symbol describes a specific task and provides the base for the processing operation which follows it. The flowchart is built by positioning each block in its logical place. For this reason flowcharts are sometimes considered **block diagrams.**

For operational purposes, flowcharts are generally divided into two categories: systems flowcharts and program flowcharts. **Systems flowcharts** are broad, all-encompassing diagrams which describe the flow of information through an organization. These flowcharts are used to describe any of the computerized and manual processing activities an organization may employ.

The handling of a credit memo within a retail organization when a sales item is returned can be used as an example. This procedure involves both manual and computer-related actions. A sales clerk must handle the return, manually recording all data relating to the transaction. The transaction is verified and cleared for payment by computer. All steps taken within this procedure, both manual and computerized, would be reflected in a systems flowchart.

A **program flowchart** is a much more restrictive document. It limits itself to only those steps which will compose a computer program. The program flowchart acts as a precursor to the source program written by the programmer. The program logic developed is reflected in the order of symbols used and precedes their conversion to equivalent program statements.

Program flowcharts are used to detail many types of software, whether the program is designed to support a scientific experiment or to process a monthly car loan payment. All processing steps attributed to the problem are logically laid out and depicted via symbols in the flowchart.

Both a program and a systems flowchart are shown in Figure 3.1. At this point we do not expect the reader to fully understand either flowchart's purpose but to observe the differences between them. The systems flowchart reflects the manual and computerized handling of charge card payment, where the program flowchart depicts the handling of a finance charge. The systems flow diagram uses a wider variety of symbols than its program flowchart counterpart. By examining both types of flow diagrams the reader may gain some initial insights into their differences.

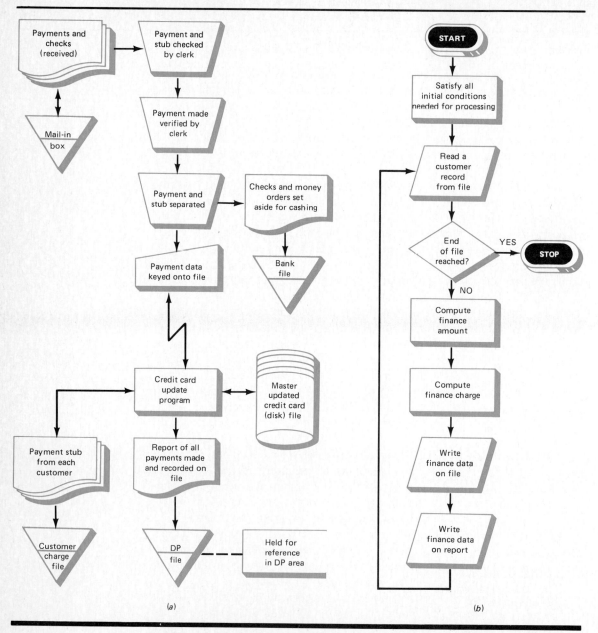

(a)

(b)

FIGURE 3.1 Program and systems flowcharts serve different functions. The systems flowchart can describe the flow of information through an organization and is therefore a broader, more detailed diagram. The program flowchart is more specific, as it is used to detail those steps which compose a software solution and acts as a planning step to the writing of that program. *(a)* The system flowchart depicts the handling of a charge card payment. *(b)* The program flowchart portrays the handling of a finance charge.

The differences between systems and program flowcharts extends not only to their operational use but to the symbols which they use (Figure 3.2). Program flowcharts require fewer symbols than systems flowcharts, as the type of processing activities depicted is more limited. The symbols associated with program flowcharts are primarily concerned with I/O operations and processing activities. Each symbol is assigned a specific operational purpose and must be properly drawn.

The preparation of systems flowcharts is a complex topic, well beyond the scope of this text. It often takes many years to master concepts associated with their preparation. In our discussions, we will focus our attention on program flowchart symbols and their use.

Flowcharts should have start and stop points. The symbol utilized for these purposes is the **terminal symbol** (Figure 3.3). A flowcharting convention dictates that only two terminal symbols be placed in the flowchart, at the beginning and at the end. Convention also directs that the words START and STOP be placed as narratives within the opening and closing terminal symbols, respectively. These terminal symbols are also simply referred to as **START** and **STOP symbols.**

Once the flowchart is started, a variety of processing operations may ensue. The performance of input and output operations is denoted by the use of the parallelogram-shaped **input-output (I/O) symbol.** This symbol serves a dual purpose of identifying both input and output operations. The difference between these I/O operations is indicated by the narrative enclosed within the I/O symbol. The terms READ and INPUT are commonly used to denote input operations, while the words PRINT and WRITE are associated with output operations. Figure 3.4 shows representative uses of these narratives with I/O symbols.

The four sample I/O symbols in Figure 3.4 demonstrate some flowcharting conventions. In Figure 3.4(a), three data items are slated for entry into processing. The word READ indentifies an input operation; it is followed by three other phrases, which define the data to be inputted. The words STUDENT NAME, COURSE NO, and GRADE are referred to as **datanames,** as they stipulate the names assigned by the programmer to the individual data items used in this application. The datanames used in flowcharts (and subsequently in programs) are operationally similar to the variables which are used in algebra. They are names generally applied to data or variables used in solving that problem.

The datanames chosen by user should reflect the data they represent. It is easier to work with datanames that you understand. An important fact to remember is that although the actual data items used will vary continuously during processing, the datanames will not. For example, the dataname STUDENT NAME remains unchanged throughout a program, but data items under that name — Mary Rodrique, John Jackson — will change. Beginning computer students often fail to realize the importance of being consistent in the designation of datanames. For example, within flowcharting and subsequent programming applications, the datanames COURSE NO and

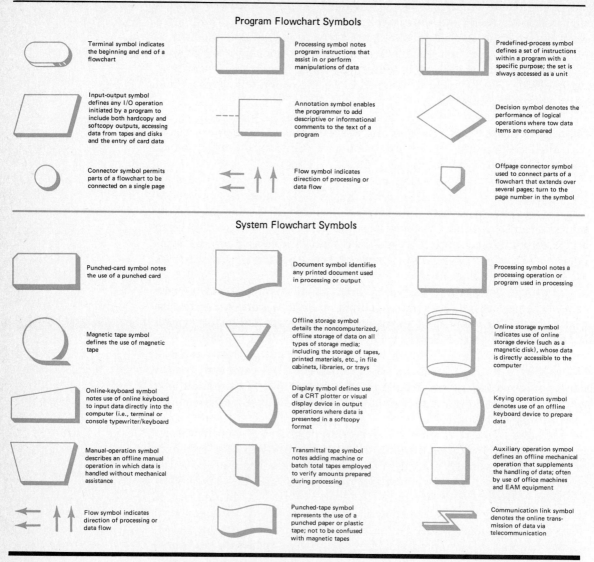

FIGURE 3.2 Specific symbols are used when constructing flowcharts. These symbols are divided into two categories: program and systems flowchart symbols.

COURSE NUMBER refer to two distinctly separate items of data, though they appear to have similar operational purposes.

A more cryptic type of dataname is employed in Figure 3.4(b). In this I/O symbol, two changes are evident. The narrative used is INPUT and the three datanames used are A, B, and C. Concise datanames of this type are normally

FIGURE 3.3   The terminal symbol is used to denote the beginning and end of a program flowchart. The narratives START and STOP are commonly used with terminal symbols; the resulting symbols are referred to as START and STOP symbols, respectively. *(a)* Terminal symbol. *(b)* START symbol. *(c)* STOP symbol.

associated with mathematical or scientific applications, where the notations used are generally abbreviated to accommodate an algebraic formula.

Note the punctuation inserted between the datanames specified. In both I/O symbols, the datanames are separated by commas. However, *no* comma is placed after the last dataname. The placement of a comma there would indicate the existance of additional datanames—which do not exist. This type of error usually adds a measure of confusion to comprehension of the flowchart.

The same punctuation conventions are also evident in Figures 3.4*(c)* and *(d),* where I/O symbols identify output operations. The narratives respectively used are PRINT and WRITE, both denoting the output of data. In

FIGURE 3.4   The input-output (I/O) symbol is used for specifying both input and output operations within flowcharts. The narratives used with I/O symbols are READ, INPUT, PRINT, and WRITE, each denoting its I/O function. Four representative examples of how I/O symbols are written are illustrated.

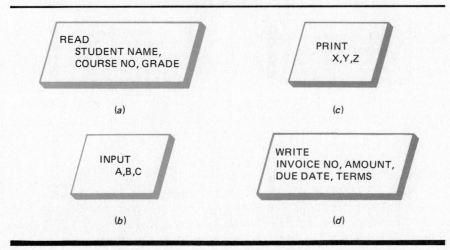

Figure 3.4*(c)*, the output of the three data items of X, Y, and Z is indicated. Figure 3.4*(d)* directs the output of four data items, identified by the datanames INVOICE NO, AMOUNT, DUE DATE, and TERMS.

In an effort to standardize our discussions, we will utilize the narratives READ and PRINT to detail input and output operations, respectively. These notations are closely aligned to BASIC and will ease our conversion of flowchart solutions into BASIC programs. We will also employ a shorthand notation similar to that used with terminal symbols by referring to these I/O symbols as **READ** and **PRINT symbols.**

The **processing symbol** is used to show processing operations involving the arithmetic manipulation of data or the movement of data between storage locations. This rectangular-shaped symbol may represent computations in terms of formulas or sentences which explain the calculations to be performed.

For example, in Figure 3.5*(a)*, the computation of the cost of an inventory item (INV-COST) is expressed as a formula and computed by multiplying its unit cost (UNIT-COST) by the number of those units held in inventory (QUANTITY). Figure 3.5*(b)* shows the same computational format expressed in English terms (MULTIPLY BY, GIVING) instead of symbols (*, =). In both examples the same datanames are employed, as they serve as a reference to the data undergoing processing. Other examples of the processing symbol are shown in Figures 3.5*(c)* and *(d)*. Both illustrations use formulas to represent the processing operations involved. Formulas are often preferred because of their conciseness and simplicity of expression for com-

FIGURE 3.5 Processing symbols are used to depict manipulations of data related to arithmetic operations, as well as the movement or reordering of data. These operations may be represented in the form of formulas or English-like sentences as in Figures 3.5*(a)* and *(b)*. The last two symbols note other uses of the processing symbol.

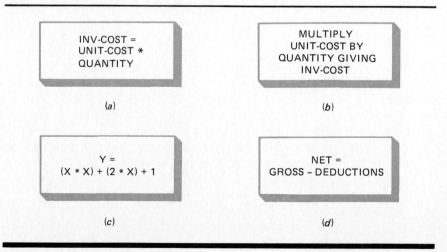

plex processing tasks. In our discussions, we will use formulas because of their operational similarities to BASIC.

Certain conventions are applied when representing computations as formulas. One relates to the placement of only *one variable to the left of the equal sign.* This convention parallels the representation of processing instructions in many currently popular languages, including BASIC. It also reflects the computer's handling of processing tasks and the results produced. The computer undertakes all processing indicated to the right of the equal sign and derives a single result. That result represents the culmination of processing and is retained in the storage location of the variable to the left of the equal sign. By having only one dataname to the left of the equal sign, no confusion arises as to where to store the data. For example, even though $A = B + C$ is *algebraically* equivalent to $B + C = A$, by convention $A = B + C$ must be used.

A second convention relates to the use of symbols to denote arithmetic operations. These symbols are uniformly used in most flowcharting examples and offer a simple and concise method of defining fundamental arithmetic operations. Table 3.1 details the symbols associated with the four fundamental arithmetic tasks. Many of these symbols were exhibited in Figure 3.5.

TABLE 3.1 Arithmetic Symbols for Flowcharts

Operation	Symbol
Addition	+
Subtraction	−
Multiplication	*
Division	/

TABLE 3.2 Logic Symbols Used with Decision Symbols

Definition	Symbol
Equal to	=
Less than	<
Greater than	>
Not equal to	<>
Less than or equal to	<=
Greater than or equal to	>=

Table 3.2 depicts the symbolic operators used in flowcharts to compare data items. These symbols are set inside diamond-shaped **decision symbols,** which indicate that the relationship between two data items is to be tested. The use of these symbolic operators is depicted in Figure 3.6*(a).* This decision attempts to determine whether a data item referred to as HRS (hours) is less than or equal to 40, thus distinguishing between those who have worked overtime and those who have worked a regular work week. The key element in the decision symbol is the question IS HRS $<=$ 40? which is referred to as a **conditional statement.** The conditional statement defines the logical relationship that is to undergo testing. When this statement is eventually converted to a program instruction, the computer will compare the contents of the storage area called HRS against 40 and determine whether it is less than or equal to 40.

Two implications result from this logical operation. The variable HRS is evaluated either as less than or equal to 40 or as greater than 40. This conditional statement was deliberately constructed to elicit this response. A clear

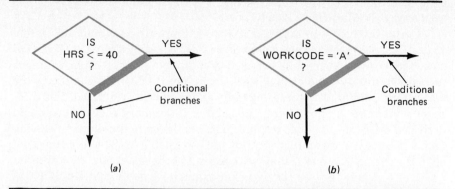

(a)   (b)

FIGURE 3.6 Logical operations in which data items are compared are represented via decision symbols. These operations can determine whether two data items are equal, less than, or greater than each other. Figure 3.6(a) shows a logical operation involving numeric data. Figure 3.6(b) shows a logical operation involving alphabetic data.

distinction must be made between HRS and its relationship to 40. Note that the structure of the conditional statement lends itself to this effort. By deliberately constructing the conditional statement as a question, the possible responses are limited to YES or NO.

These two options define the **conditional branches** which permit the logical flow of processing through the decision symbol. If HRS <= 40, the YES branch is chosen and the flow of processing exits through it. If HRS > 40, the NO branch is opted for and processing continues. One must always remember that in program flowcharts, the decision symbol is the only method available for choosing between two alternatives. The proper use of decision symbols to represent logical operations is critical to most flowchart solutions and the programs which evolve from them.

Conditional operations are not restricted to testing for numeric quantities. Logical operations can determine if the proper alphabetic codes were used in a processing sequence or to identify a specific set of values. In Figure 3.6(b) the conditional statement IS WORKCODE = 'A'? attempts to determine if a work code of A was specified. The input of this code could direct the flow of processing through the YES branch to a set of instructions specifically designed for data related to a code of A. If the work code is not equal to A, the flowchart will exit the NO branch to other processing activities or decisions.

Note the use of single quotation marks around alphabetic data in the conditional statement. These quotes are used to highlight alphabetic data and differentiate it from numeric data items. Thus, any data item specified within quotes in a conditional statement is treated as an alphabetic data item. Even numbers, when positioned within single quotes, are logically tested as alphabetic data items. Many current computer languages, BASIC included, make a distinction between numeric and nonnumeric data items. **Numeric data** consists only of the digits 0 to 9 (and decimal points when used); it may contain no alphabetic or special characters. By contrast, **nonnumeric data** is composed of any combination of numeric, alphabetic, or special characters. Alphabetic characters consist of the characters A to Z and special characters consist of all others ($, @, #, %, etc.). The term *nonnumeric data* identifies all data items not possessing a strictly numeric format. Concepts related to numeric and nonnumeric data items will be reviewed again, when specific data in BASIC is presented.

When flowcharts and program solutions are developed, it is often necessary to group together sets of related instructions. These instructions are handled as a single entity and are accessed as a unit. The flow of processing is transferred to that set or module of instructions which are completely executed. Using this rationale, it is possible to create modules of instructions for specific processing sequences to handle unique or special circumstances. These sets of instructions simplify the handling of unique problems where data is segregated into predefined coded groups. Applying this concept, overtime employees are handled separately from regular workers. Similarly, students possessing different areas of interest are coded into different groupings and handled within their specialized areas.

Within flowcharts, modules of related instructions are identified via the **predefined-process symbol** (Figure 3.7). This one symbol is used to identify a set of instructions which relate to a specific situation. In the predefined-process symbol shown, a set of instructions related to employees with an S pension plan option are specified. This symbol will be discussed later in this book.

The rationale of grouping instructions into a module relates directly to the concept of a **subroutine.** A subroutine is a related group of program instructions which handle a specific processing application. These instructional sets relate directly to programming applications where a specific processing activity must be repeatedly handled. The use of subroutines has become increasingly popular with the current trend toward modularization of program solutions.

Many programmers like to add descriptive comments to flowcharts which serve as advisory notes during their analysis and modification. These comments remind the flowcharter of special conditions which are encountered during processing. The flowchart equivalent of the comment is the **annotation symbol.** (Figure 3.8). This three-sided rectangular symbol utilizes a dashed line to attach itself to the symbol for which the comment is pertinent. The dashed line denotes that the annotation symbol is strictly informative and will not result in any change in the flow of processing.

In Figure 3.8(*b*), an annotation symbol is depicted as it might appear within a flowchart, attached to decision symbol. The annotation symbol shows that the decision is the first of four logical operations. Annotation symbols may be inserted at any point within a flowchart, positioned at the discretion of the programmer. The comments in annotation symbols are of great value when flowcharts are reviewed many months after their prepara-

PENSION 'S'
employees

FIGURE 3.7 Groups of related statements may be referred to through the predefined process symbol. The symbol depicted enables access to the group of statements referring to Pension 'S' employees only.

FIGURE 3.8 The
addition of descriptive
comments to a
flowchart is
accomplished with
annotation symbols.
(a) The annotation
symbol is drawn with a
dashed line to denote
its advisory status. *(b)*
The annotation symbol
is attached to a
decision.

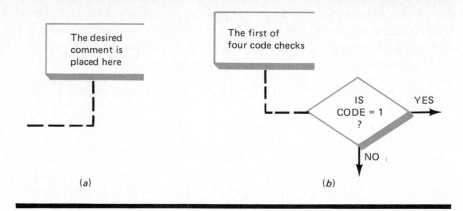

tion. In the intervening period the programmer may have forgotten the particulars of a specific solution. Annotation symbols serve as reminders of these special factors.

A Simple Flowchart

Though the aforementioned symbols have their own uses, they must be integrated into a flowchart to demonstrate their effectiveness. In this section, we will begin our discussion of flowcharts from their problem narratives to the final pictorial formats. The problems will be somewhat simplified at first and gradually increase in difficulty. Also, we will deliberately restrict the problem to manageable proportions so that our discussions can focus on specific points and not range too far afield.

A critical aspect to any flowchart solution is the user's comprehension of the problem narrative. The problem narrative details all aspects of the problem to be worked on and should provide the user with the information necessary to prepare a sound and logical flowchart solution. A careful analysis of the problem is one of the initial keys to a successful flowchart solution. With this fact in mind, let us examine the problem narrative for our first illustrative flowchart.

PROBLEM 3.1 Gross Pay

Input to the problem are the employee's name, hours worked, and hourly rate of pay. The gross pay amount is computed by multiplying the hours worked by the rate of pay. Output only the employee's name and gross pay amount.

The narrative for Problem 3.1 is designed to present all aspects of the problem to be flowcharted. The problem narrative should state the data to be input, the data items slated for output, and the computations required to support processing. It should be as explicit as possible, completely detailing all aspects of the problem. A well-prepared problem narrative is an invaluable ally, as it provides the flowcharter-programmer with the information necessary to prepare a sound flowchart and program solution.

These are the main points in the problem narrative.

1   The flowchart documents the processing of one employee's gross pay.

2   The inputs to the problem are the employee's name, hours worked, and hourly pay rate.

3   The processing of gross pay is represented by the formula

Gross pay = hours worked * rate of pay

4   The outputs of processing are the employee's name and gross pay.

By extracting the above points from the problem narrative, we are beginning the analysis of the problem solution. In effect, we are detailing those factors which when pictorially integrated will form the basis of our flowchart solution.

The flowchart prepared from this analysis is shown in Figure 3.9. It is an uncomplicated solution, exhibiting characteristics generally associated with most flowcharts. The first symbol of the flowchart is the START symbol. It represents the beginning of the flowchart and those instructions necessary for the actual processing of this problem.[1]

The first step involves the input of data. An I/O symbol containing the READ narrative denotes that initial input operation and the entry of the three required data items. The datanames specified within the READ symbol are EMPNAME for the employee's name, HOURS for the hours worked, and RATE for the hourly rate of pay. The datanames used are intended to be representative of the data involved in processing and provide an easy reference to them. Individuals preparing flowcharts are free to choose any datanames they desire, but should avoid those which may tend to confuse subsequent users of those diagrams.

Within the READ symbol, each dataname is clearly specified and separated by commas. This convention helps establish the uniqueness of each dataname. Once specified, datanames must be consistently used throughout the flowchart solution. Even the slightest variation is sufficient to void a solution. The casual reference to a dataname of HOUR, instead of the correct use of HOURS, would result in processing errors. Once specified as HOURS, that dataname must be uniformly used.

In the processing symbol which follows we use a formula to represent the computation of GROSS. Following previously stated conventions, we place only the variable GROSS to the left of the equal sign. The multiplication of

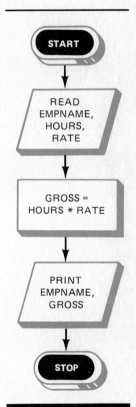

FIGURE 3.9   Flow-chart for Problem 3.1.

---

[1] The term *housekeeping* was introduced many years ago by programmers to identify those instructions executed in preparation for the processing of a program. In recent years, usage of the housekeeping term has decreased, being replaced by phrases related to LOGON procedures.

HOURS and RATE produces a gross pay amount that is stored at a location called GROSS. For processing to occur properly the datanames HOURS and RATE must be correctly specified within the formula shown in the processing symbol. For clarity, only one formula is specified in a processing symbol at any one time.

The computed value of GROSS, along with the employee's name (EMP-NAME), are outputted after processing is completed. The second I/O symbol of this flowchart utilizes a narrative of PRINT to denote this output operation. This PRINT symbol specifies the output of EMPNAME and GROSS, in accordance with the stated problem definition. Following convention, datanames are separated by commas. The selection of only two of the four variables involved in processing reinforces the nature of output operations. The user is free to select and output any of the variables used in processing. The only restriction observed is that all data items slated for output must be defined prior to their actual output. Obviously, it is not possible to print a data item which does not exist.

The flowchart's close is denoted by the STOP symbol, which directs that all processing activities be concluded. No other symbols related to processing are added to the flowchart after the STOP symbol.

One point of clarification must be offered to our readers. For brevity we will sometimes reduce the complexity of a problem in order to simplify the discussion. For example, we may deliberately disregard an operational limit related to social security deductions. Rather than immediately confronting students with illustrations whose size would thwart understanding and create confusion, we will upgrade problems gradually.

Along these lines, let us now expand Problem 3.1 by adding steps related to the computation of a FICA deduction and net pay. These extra steps will enable us to observe how our original flowchart can be expanded.

SIDE BAR 3.1   Tilting the I/O Symbol

The parallelogram-shaped I/O symbol is used to represent the performance of input and output operations. A common error made when drawing this symbol is to tilt the parallelogram the wrong way. The figure below illustrates the correct and incorrect versions of specifying the I/O symbol. This type of error usually occurs from haste and the confusion that arises when a flowcharting solution is unclear. Flowcharters must remember that the input-output (I/O) symbol always leans toward the right.

Correct   Incorrect

PROBLEM 3.2   Net Pay

Input to the problem are the employee's name, hours worked, and hourly rate of pay. Gross pay is computed by multiplying hours worked by rate of pay. The FICA deduction is computed at 6.70 percent of gross pay. Net pay is computed by subtracting the FICA deduction from gross pay. Output the employee's name, gross pay, FICA deduction, and net pay.

These are the main points in the problem narrative.

1   Inputs are the employee's name, hours worked, and rate of pay.

2   The computations of gross pay, the FICA deduction, and net pay utilize the following formulas:

   a   Gross = hours worked * rate of pay
   b   FICA = gross * .0670
   c   Net = gross − FICA

3   Output are the employee's name, gross pay, FICA deduction, and net pay.

4   Only one person's payroll data is handled.

The flowchart prepared from this narrative, encompassing these major points of analysis, is illustrated in Figure 3.10.

     Examining this flowchart will reveal some change from its original configuration. Initially, one can observe that it is a larger flowchart, as more processing steps were incorporated. Also, major changes have been made in the datanames used.

     The flowchart opens with a START symbol, which is followed by an I/O symbol defining the input of the employee's name, hours worked, and pay rate. The datanames used for these data items are NAME, H, and R, respectively. We have chosen to utilize these datanames for brevity and to distinguish between data types. BASIC is a language which tends to use shortened datanames with its processing operations. By using abbreviated datanames, we hope to accustom you to them. The second reason requires a little more explanation.

     As previously mentioned, BASIC differentiates between numeric and nonnumeric data items. We would like to reinforce this concept, as it is a critical operational aspect when programming in BASIC. Thus, we will use shortened datanames like H and R for numeric quantities and slightly longer datanames like NAME for nonnumeric data items. This type of convention parallels BASIC's data-handling rules and also alerts readers to the nature of the data being processed. A one- or two-character dataname will signal nu-

FIGURE 3.10   Flowchart for Problem 3.2. This flow diagram expands our initial solution, as additional processing steps have been added to the problem solution.

meric quantities, whereas longer datanames will highlight nonnumeric (alphabetic) data items. This convention will serve as a quick visual reference to the data undergoing processing.

Examining the three processing symbols that follow the initial READ symbol, we note the computation of gross pay (G), FICA (F), and net pay (N). In all three cases, abbreviated datanames denote the manipulation of numeric data. The three formulas specified are:

1 $G = H * R$ for the computation of the gross pay, G

2 $F = G * .0670$ for the computation of the FICA deduction, F

3 $N = G - F$ for the computation of net pay

Each formula is positioned within its own processing symbol, as per flowcharting convention, and only one dataname is placed to the left of each equal sign. With these formulas, symbols are utilized to indicate multiplication (*) and subtraction (−).

Some students might question the usage of the decimal number .0670 for 6.70 percent in the computation of the FICA deduction. The use of the decimal more closely parallels the actual program instruction which would be written to perform that computation. Generally, percent signs are not commonly represented in formulas. Instead, decimal equivalents are preferred.

The output of the employee's name (NAME), gross pay (G), FICA (F), and net pay (N) is signaled by the PRINT symbol. Logically, this symbol is positioned after the three processing operations, as these required figures must be computed before they can be printed. The same datanames are utilized in the PRINT symbol, as they are uniformly used throughout the flowchart solution. The STOP symbol closes this flowchart.

We may observe by comparing the flowcharts in Figures 3.9 and 3.10 that our initial flowchart solution was expanded by the addition of two processing symbols. These two symbols were logically positioned after the computation of gross pay, to reflect changes in the problem narrative. The important point here is that the original flow diagram was altered with a minimum of effort.

These two flowchart problems were business-oriented, relating to payroll activities. Flowchart exercises are not restricted to business-related problems but may also extend into the areas of science and math. The next illustrative example involves a low-level math problem.

PROBLEM 3.3   An Algebraic Formula

A student is required to substitute an X value into the following equation:

$$Y = 2X^2 + 13X - 27$$

Input to the problem is one value for X. The X value is substituted into the equation and the corresponding Y value computed. Output both the X and Y values.

These are the main points in the problem narrative.

1   One value of X is input.

2   The equation in which the X value is substituted is

$$Y = 2X^2 + 13X - 27$$

3   The computed Y value and initial X value are output.

4   Only one X value is processed.

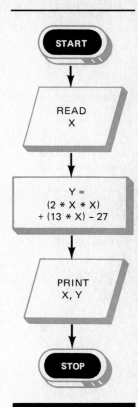

The flowchart prepared for the narrative is shown in Figure 3.11.

A concisely constructed flow diagram is prepared for Problem 3.3. The flowchart opens with a START symbol, which is followed by the input of the X value destined for substitution. The conciseness of the datanames used denotes the numeric orientation of the data undergoing processing.

The representation of the equation in the processing symbol requires some explanation. The result of processing, Y, is positioned to the left of the equal sign, as per convention. On the righthand side of the equal sign, parentheses are used to group components of that equation. The component $2X^2$ is represented as $(2 * X * X)$, where asterisks detail the multiplication of the 2 and X variables. Similarly, the 13X factor is defined as $(13 * X)$, where the asterisk is again positioned between variables. The subtraction of 27 is positioned as the equation's last factor.

The final equation depicted in the processing symbol combines each of these elements and is the flowchart equivalent of the equation originally defined within the problem's narrative. The use of parentheses helps processing activities focus on the accurate handling of each equation's component.

The I/O symbol representing the printing of both the X and Y variables follows the equation's processing. In this illustration, both X and Y are output — one resulting from an input operation, the other from a processing operation. The STOP symbol closes the flowchart.

FIGURE 3.11 Flowchart for Problem 3.3 has a mathematical orientation, as the problem involves an equation.

3.3 Looping Sequences

Flowchart Loops and LRC

Many readers may have recognized that our initial flowcharting examples were capable of processing only one item of data. These examples were not able to represent the repetitive processing of data which is a hallmark of most program solutions. In this section we examine the repetitive processing operations as constructed using a looping sequence and a means of properly ending that sequence without an error condition. These two techniques are referred to as (1) a flowchart loop and (2) a last-record check (LRC).

The incorporation of these two techniques into a flowchart makes possible the repetitive processing of data, permitting variable amounts of data to be processed in any given application. Large or small quantities of data are readily handled, with control over the looping sequence exercised by the

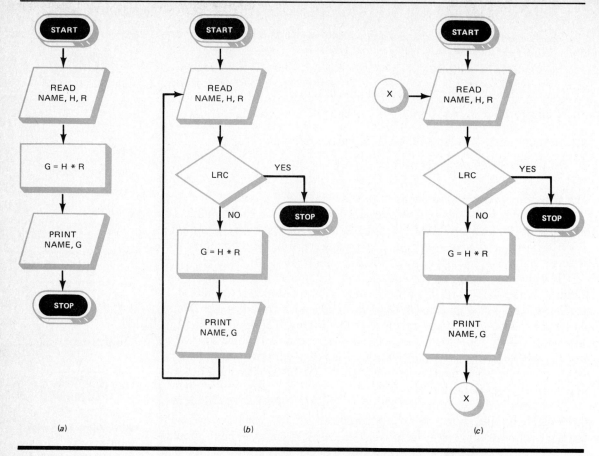

(b)

FIGURE 3.12 *(a)* A simple flowchart for processing one employee's data. *(b)* A looping sequence using a solid flowline. *(c)* The same loop using connector symbols.

flowcharter-programmer. To examine the impact of the flowchart loop and LRC, let us examine the flowcharts presented within Figure 3.12.

As in Problem 3.1, the flowchart in Figure 3.12*(a)* is capable of processing only one employee's data. However, Figure 3.12*(b)* contains a **flowchart loop.** The solid flowline directs processing from the PRINT symbol back to the READ symbol, which inputs the next employee's data. In this fashion, we create a looping sequence where payroll data is repeatedly read and processed.

The unbroken line proceeding from the PRINT symbol back to the READ symbol is referred to as an **unconditional branch.** The unconditional branch is the direct opposite of the conditional branching operation defined via a decision symbol. No deviation is permitted from the path defined by an unconditional branch. Once initiated, the unconditional branch directs the flow of processing to a specific symbol without interruption.

Unconditional branches may also be represented by **connector symbols,** as shown in Figure 3.12*(c)*. Connector symbols are used in pairs — one showing the point of departure and the second noting the point at which the flow of processing continues. Generally, connectors are preferable to solid lines when multiple unconditional branches must be drawn into a flowchart solution. They avoid the confusion that sometimes arises from the crisscrossing of flowlines. Any character or group of characters may be used within a connector symbol as long as pairs are identical.

When a looping sequence is established, an obvious question relates to how the sequence is properly concluded. We cannot permit the flowchart loop to merely run out of data, as that would create an error condition which would cancel all processing operations. It is far better if we construct a means of

SIDE BAR 3.2   The Correct Flow of Processing

The connector symbol is a valuable flowcharting tool, as it enables us to replace the solid flowline. Using two connector symbols, it is possible to represent a branching operation from its start to its end. When using these symbols, we must properly specify the flow of processing. Two examples of the use of connector symbols are illustrated below.

In Figure A, the flowline arrow points toward the bottom connector, having left the I/O symbol at the loop's end. The second matching connector has its flowline leaving its symbol and the flow of processing is toward the READ symbol. This flowcharting sequence is correct, as the processing flow is returning toward the top of the loop.

Compare this initial flow to that of Figure B. The direction of the arrowheads in this case is critical. The flow of processing correctly leaves the I/O symbol and proceeds toward the connector symbol at the loop's end. However, the top connector symbol is not properly drawn. There, the flowline's arrow incorrectly points from the READ symbol to the connector, reversing the processing flow. The reversal of this flow is similar to the merging of two one-way streets at a dead end.

Flowcharters must remember that the arrows delineating the flow of processing should be properly drawn and represent a logical processing flow.

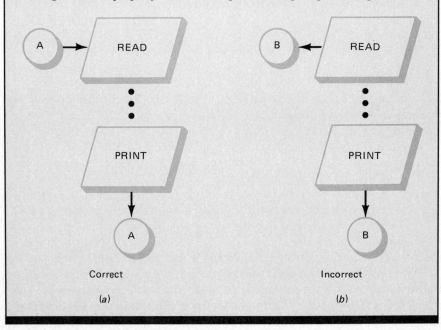

Correct	Incorrect
(a)	(b)

controlling the loop's close and have it occur when we desire. The **last-record check (LRC)** provides a vehicle for controlling the close of a looping sequence.

The decision defined by the last-record check recognizes the fact that a finite amount of data will enter processing, be handled via a looping sequence, and that the flowchart loop should end when the last data item is read and processed. The critical decision established by the LRC is whether to continue processing or exit the looping sequence. In Figure 3.12*(b)* and 3.12*(c),* the LRC chooses between the NO branch and the YES branch. As long as valid payroll data exists, the flow of processing will pass through the NO branch. After the last record has been read and processed and the LRC has determined that no additional data exists, the flow of processing will proceed out of the looping sequence via the YES branch.

The reader may recognize that the bulk of processing activities will proceed down the NO branch of the LRC as long as valid employee data exists. In effect, the LRC's YES branch is used only once, after the last payroll data has been processed. It is the lack of input data which triggers the LRC and causes the flow of processing to exit the flowchart loop via the YES branch.

PROBLEM 3.4   Final Sales Price

Inputs to the problem are the item purchased and its sales price. The sales tax is computed at 4 percent of the original sales price. The final sales price is computed by adding the sales tax to the original sales price. Output the item's name, original sales price, sales tax, and final sales price. A number of sales items will be processed, so create a looping sequence and control its execution with an LRC.

These are the main points in the problem narrative.

1   Inputs are the item's name and the original sales price.

2   Processing includes computation of sales tax and final sales price. The formulas used are as follows:
   a   Sales tax = sales price * .04
   b   Final sales price = sales price + sales tax

3   Output each item's name, original sales price, sales tax, and final sales price.

4   A looping sequence is required, as multiple sales items will be processed.

5   An LRC decision controls the looping sequence.

The flowchart for this problem is depicted in Figure 3.13.

Examining the flowchart for Problem 3.4, we note the creation of the looping sequence and the placement of the LRC. The unconditional branch from the PRINT to READ symbol completes the looping sequence and is represented by two connector symbols. For ease of identification, matching

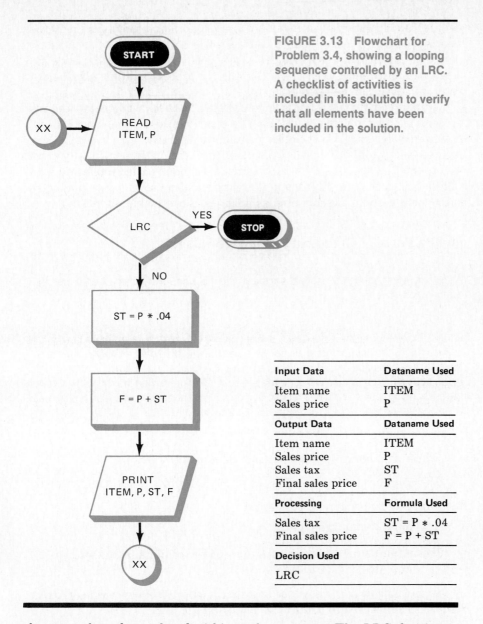

FIGURE 3.13 Flowchart for Problem 3.4, showing a looping sequence controlled by an LRC. A checklist of activities is included in this solution to verify that all elements have been included in the solution.

Input Data	Dataname Used
Item name	ITEM
Sales price	P
Output Data	**Dataname Used**
Item name	ITEM
Sales price	P
Sales tax	ST
Final sales price	F
Processing	**Formula Used**
Sales tax	ST = P $*$ .04
Final sales price	F = P + ST
Decision Used	
LRC	

characters have been placed within each connector. The LRC decision is properly positioned after the READ symbol, acting as a control for the flow of processing. As long as data exists, the NO branch is followed and processing continues. The YES branch of the LRC permits the flow of processing to exit the looping sequence and commence the flowchart's close.

In all other aspects, the flowchart solution follows established norms. A START symbol opens the flow diagram, and a READ symbol acts as the start of the flowchart loop. The LRC follows the READ symbol, with the NO branch leading to the normal flow of processing. The first processing symbol details the calculation of sales tax (ST), and the second computes the item's final sales price (F). Both computations precede the output of each item's name (ITEM), original sales price (P), sales tax (ST), and final sales price (F). The looping sequence creates the capacity to process multiple sales items, with one sales item handled per loop.

Introduced in Figure 3.13 is a **checklist.** The checklist serves to identify all aspects of a problem's solution and act as a reminder when composing a flowchart solution. The checklist contains all datanames, processing formulas, decisions, and I/O tasks composing the solution. By continually referring to the checklist, the user can ensure that a required dataname or operation has not been omitted. Many flowcharters also use this checklist when subsequently preparing software, as it serves as a valuable reference.

PROBLEM 3.5   Computing Production Costs

A formula representing the costs associated with the production of a particular mechanical component is

$$C = 2.50 * U + 8500$$

where C represents the total cost, U the number of units to be manufactured, the constant 2.50 the cost of materials per unit, and 8500 a fixed cost related to the cost of manufacturing equipment. The user is to input the desired number of Units (U) to be manufactured. The formula will compute the cost (C) of producing that quantity. Output the cost and the number of units related to it on each loop. As there are many estimates, a looping sequence should be created and controlled via an LRC.

These are the main points in the problem narrative.

1   The only input, U, represents the number of units to be manufactured.

2   The formula used in processing is

$$C = (2.50 * U) + 8500$$

3   The outputs to the problem are the number of units manufactured (U) and the computed cost (C).

4   As multiple data items will be inputted, a looping sequence is needed. An LRC decision is used to control the exit from the loop.

The flowchart and checklist prepared for Problem 3.5 are provided in Figure 3.14.

The flowchart developed for this problem parallels previous solutions. The flowchart opens with a START symbol, which is followed by a READ symbol where only one variable, U, is input. In the processing symbol, the constant 2.50 is multiplied against U and added to 8500 to generate C. Both U and C are outputted via the I/O symbol at the flowchart loop's end. Two connectors containing the symbol 4 denote the unconditional branch which completes the loop.

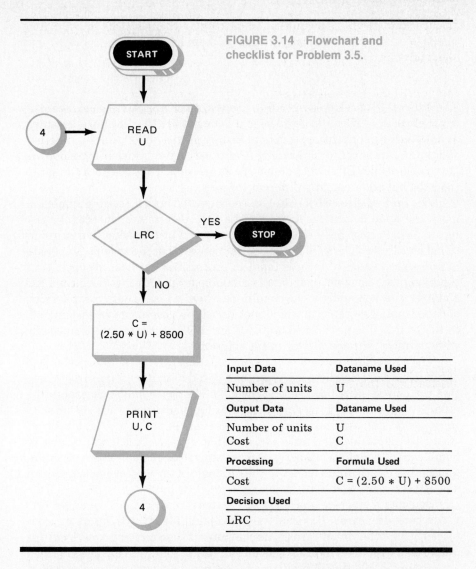

FIGURE 3.14   Flowchart and checklist for Problem 3.5.

Input Data	Dataname Used
Number of units	U
Output Data	**Dataname Used**
Number of units Cost	U C
Processing	**Formula Used**
Cost	C = (2.50 ∗ U) + 8500
Decision Used	
LRC	

The exit from the looping sequence is accomplished through the last-record-check decision, which is logically positioned after the READ symbol. As long as U is input, the looping sequence will continue down the NO branch of the LRC. When all data has been processed, the flow of logic will exit the LRC's YES branch and processing activities will cease at the STOP symbol. By inputting a variety of U values, the user can obtain a series of estimates as to the costs associated with those production levels.

Factors related to all phases of Problem 3.5 are detailed within the checklist developed for this problem. Though the problem has a limited number of I/O variables, they are specified in the checklist, as are all formulas and decisions. The checklist is drafted as the user reads the problem narrative and then rechecked when the final flowchart solution is reached. In this manner the checklist serves as a guide when developing the flowchart and a double check to ensure that all aspects of the problem have been incorporated into the final solution.

EOF and 9s Decision

The last-record check is essentially a check against whether the last record or data item of a group has been processed. Though the LRC decision is accepted as flowcharting convention, it is not the only means of determining whether additional data exists for processing. Two other methods for exiting a loop are (1) an end-of-file (EOF) check and (2) a 9s decision. They are both similar to the LRC but adopt slightly different formats.

The **end-of-file (EOF) check** is constructed with a decision symbol in much the same manner as an LRC. The LRC determines whether the last record or data item has been read and processed by assessing that no additional data exists. The EOF check determines whether the end of a file of data (an organized series of records input to processing) has been reached, thus signifying that no additional data is available for processing. Both the LRC and EOF checks highlight the conditions where no more data records exist, and the looping sequence in which such data is processed may be terminated. In flowcharts, it is possible to use LRC and EOF decisions interchangeably without affecting the accuracy of the solution.

The **9s decision** is somewhat more complex. It represents a special type of last-record check where the input of a coded data item serves to indicate that the end of a file has been reached. The 9s decision also attests to the different ways in which modern computer languages deal with the close of input operations. An important point to remember is that not all languages treat LRC operations the same way and that a programmer must be able to handle each technique properly and recognize parallels between each approach. Let us orient the reader to the rationale of the 9s decision through an analogy.

Consider a program where the data slated for processing is punched into yellow computer cards. To signal the close of that file of cards, a purple card is placed behind the yellow cards. The computer is then directed to seek out the purple card which will indicate that an end-of-file condition has been reached and looping should stop. A problem arises, since the computer is colorblind. It can, however, read the holes on the purple card. So, instead of the color purple, a special code is substituted, and the computer is directed to check for that coded data item. The coded data triggers the EOF condition and the looping sequence is closed.

The coded data item chosen must relate to one of the data items being input. The use of a string of 9s in that data field makes that data item really stand out and minimizes the mix-up which might occur if the coded item is accidentally sensed prior to the actual EOF condition. For example, if a 9s decision were constructed against an hours field in a payroll problem, we would want to test against $H = -99.99$, not $H = 40$. Figure 3.15 illustrates this 9s decision. If $H = 40$ was used as the 9s decision, a good chance would exist that the EOF or LRC condition would be triggered prematurely. How-

(a)   (b)

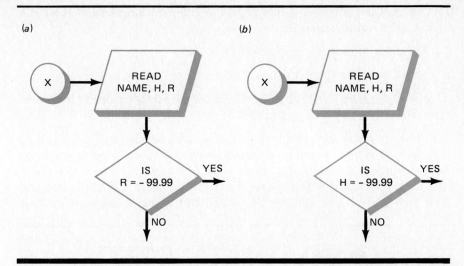

FIGURE 3.15 The 9s decision symbol is placed after the READ symbol in the flowchart loop. It can replace the LRC and EOF check in flowchart solutions. Any input variable may be used when constructing the 9s decision.

ever, the use of the conditional statement IS H = −99.99? ensures that the EOF condition will be activated only by the 9s data. The special 9s data is always placed behind all other data items; the only way to access that data is to read all of the cards before it.

A question that often arises relates to the data items upon which the 9s decision is constructed. It is possible to use *any* of the input datanames in a 9s decision. In Figure 3.15*(b)*, for example, rate of pay (R) is used instead of the hours (H). The use of either type of 9s decision will effectively support processing.

The reader may be wondering about the use of the 9s decision instead of the LRC or EOF. Whereas other languages have EOF checking features built into their input instructions, BASIC does not. Thus, it is the responsibility of the programmer to construct a means of identifying the LRC or EOF decision when program processing is actually undertaken. The EOF or LRC decisions are adequate for flowcharting, but the 9s decision will probably be written into the program.

PROBLEM 3.6 Student Averages

Inputs are the students' names and three test grades. Each student's average is computed by adding the three grades and dividing that total by 3. Output each student's name and average. As an unspecified number of students are to be processed, use a 9s decision to control processing.

These are the main points in the problem narrative.

1 Four data items are input: each student's name and three test grades. Each test grade is assigned its own dataname.

2 The required processing relates to the computation of each student's average. The formula used is:

Average = (grade 1 + grade 2 + grade 3)/3

3 Output only the student's name and computed average.

4 The looping sequence should be controlled by a 9s decision. Test against any of the three grades that are input.

The flowchart and checklist for this problem are provided in Figure 3.16.

The flowchart prepared for Problem 3.6 incorporates a looping sequence that is effectively controlled by a 9s decision. The flowchart loop commences with a READ symbol which inputs the student's name (SNAME) and the three test grades (G1, G2, and G3). Each test grade is assigned its own

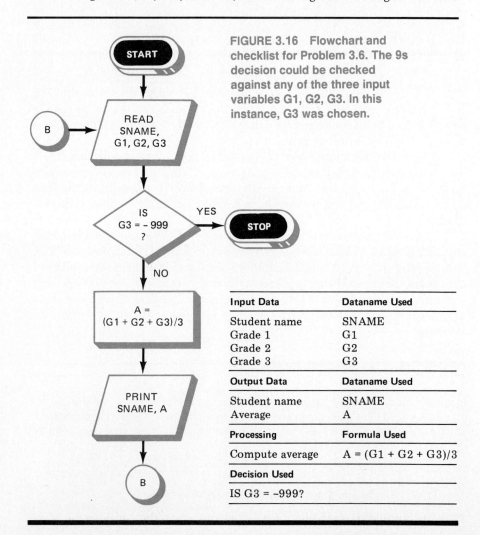

FIGURE 3.16   Flowchart and checklist for Problem 3.6. The 9s decision could be checked against any of the three input variables G1, G2, G3. In this instance, G3 was chosen.

Input Data	Dataname Used
Student name	SNAME
Grade 1	G1
Grade 2	G2
Grade 3	G3
Output Data	**Dataname Used**
Student name	SNAME
Average	A
Processing	**Formula Used**
Compute average	A = (G1 + G2 + G3)/3
Decision Used	
IS G3 = –999?	

dataname, enabling individual access to each grade and the specific use of each grade in the computation of each student's average.

Individual access to each grade is essential to properly define the flowchart's 9s decision. We have elected to use G3 in that decision, but either G1 or G2 could have been used. The 9s decision, IS G3 = −999? will check against each G3 value that is input. On all loops, processing will proceed down the NO branch. The YES branch of the 9s decision is executed only once, when the −999 data for G3 is input as the last data item.

The computation of each student's average is accomplished in one step. The addition of the three grades is performed within the parentheses, with that sum divided by 3. The PRINT symbol following that computation outputs both the student's name and his or her average.

When drafting this flowchart, some students ask if it is possible to perform the computation of the student average in two steps, that is, to add the three grade values in one processing symbol and in a second symbol divide that total by 3 resulting in the desired average. The two-step processing sequence is valid, requiring one additional processing symbol to the solution.

A far more intriguing question relates to the proper use of parentheses in the processing symbol of Figure 3.16. This symbol contains the formula

$$A = (G1 + G2 + G3)/3$$

Some students ask whether the formula which follows would prove equally effective.

$$A = G1 + G2 + G3/3$$

The answer is no. The formula without parentheses will result in the addition of grades 1 and 2 to one-third of grade 3; this approach will not result in the desired answer and will incorrectly compute the average. The proper placement of parentheses within the formula will result in the initial addition of the three grades and the division of that sum by 3. As a general rule of thumb, use parentheses to define the arithmetic operation in question.

3.4 More Flowcharting Tools

Prior discussions have concentrated on the processing of data within loops and the proper ways of terminating those loops. As yet, we have not focused on the descriptive types of outputs which support the visual or printed display of information. For example, Problem 3.6 provided for the output of student's name and average. The flowchart did not contain any means of printing column headings or other special labels, features which normally complement printed or visual outputs.

Headings and Labels

To observe the impact that these specially generated outputs can have, examine the accounts receivable listing in Figure 3.17. In Figure 3.17*(a)*, only

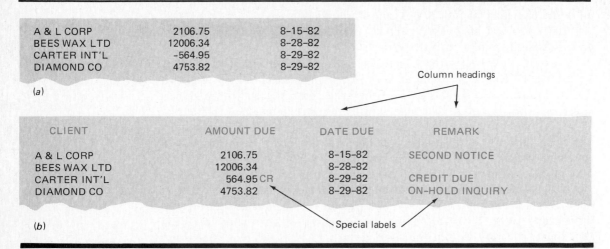

A & L CORP	2106.75	8-15-82
BEES WAX LTD	12006.34	8-28-82
CARTER INT'L	-564.95	8-29-82
DIAMOND CO	4753.82	8-29-82

(a)

Column headings

CLIENT	AMOUNT DUE	DATE DUE	REMARK
A & L CORP	2106.75	8-15-82	SECOND NOTICE
BEES WAX LTD	12006.34	8-28-82	
CARTER INT'L	564.95 CR	8-29-82	CREDIT DUE
DIAMOND CO	4753.82	8-29-82	ON-HOLD INQUIRY

(b)

Special labels

FIGURE 3.17 Output for a report of accounts receivable. (a) No advisory outputs are evident. (b) Column headings and special labels make the report comprehensible.

the original output is provided. Without additional prompting of some type, the user may be confused as to the nature of the information provided. After all, what useful information does an organization's name, an amount of money, and a date impart?

Compare this format to the report depicted in Figure 3.17(b). Here, the inclusion of column headings and special labels gives the report added meaning, as well as making it more useful. The **column headings** positioned atop each column of data identify the items appearing beneath them. The **special labels** appended to the end of each line of output offer additional information regarding each account's status.

The flowchart technique used to generate column headings and special labels is the **literal.** A literal is a desired group of characters contained within a pair of single quotation marks. In flowcharts, the output of literals is defined in PRINT symbols, as shown in Figure 3.18. Figure 3.18(a) denotes the four literals which were used as column headings in Figure 3.17(b). Each literal in the PRINT symbol is framed by single quotation marks and separated from the other literals by commas. The four literals will generate the four column headings appearing atop the accounts receivable report.

The special-label literal depicted in Figure 3.18(b) serves a different purpose. Special labels highlight special conditions that result from processing and should be brought to the attention of the user. The PRINT symbol shown is associated with the first line of the report of Figure 3.17(b). It directs the output of the organization's name (COMPANY), the amount of money due (AMT), the due date of the payment (DD), and the special label ('SECOND NOTICE'). Note that though the quotes appear in the PRINT symbol, they do not appear when the special label is actually printed. The special label in Figure 3.18(b) is designed to alert the user to the fact that a second notice regarding payment was mailed to that client. The literal defining that label makes possible that specialized output.

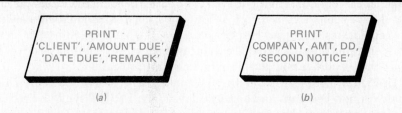

FIGURE 3.18 Literals are framed by single quotation marks and separated from other literals by commas. They are defined in PRINT symbols.

This second illustration also points to the combined use of special labels and datanames in a single output operation. Literals may be employed separately or in conjunction with datanames. This latter use permits the flowcharter-programmer to highlight conditions to which the user's attention must be drawn. In reports where that type of output is essential, the combined output of individual data items and special labels is especially beneficial.

A good rule of thumb to remember with regard to literals is that the characters placed within the quotation marks are exactly — *literally* — what you get on output. A second point to remember is that column headings and

---

SIDE BAR 3.3 Literally Anything Goes, Except . . .

The use of literals to create column headings and labels is a great boon to flowcharters, as these output features greatly assist in the preparation of legible and informative user-oriented outputs. However, care must be exercised when defining literals to accurately convey the desired output activity.

Examining the I/O symbols below, we see two common mistakes. In Figure A, though the literal appears correct, the column heading is improperly written. The comma used to separate the literals 'NAME' and 'AVERAGE' is misplaced. It should appear outside the end quote of the literal 'NAME'. If it were translated into the source program as is, a syntax error would ensue.

The second error also involves punctuation but relates to the single quotation marks used to define literals. In this case, the quotes at the end of NAME and before GROSS were omitted. A literal will result, but it will not represent the desired column headings. Instead of outputting two column headings, a lone heading of 'NAME,GROSS' will result. The lack of the two required quotes caused that literal to be treated as one column heading consisting of 10 characters, the comma included.

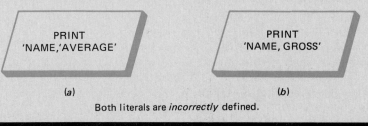

Both literals are *incorrectly* defined.

special labels serve different purposes. A column heading identifies the column of data composing a report, whereas a special label highlights exceptional conditions with that report's data. Each is an integral part of computer-generated outputs and can enhance their usability. Let us observe the impact that headings and labels could have on Problem 3.6.

In Figure 3.19, the flowchart solution for Problem 3.6 is redrawn to include column headings and a special label. The PRINT symbol directing the output of column headings is logically placed after the START symbol and before the READ symbol which identifies the start of the flowchart loop. This positioning ensures that the column headings are printed atop the report and that all other outputs generated by processing appear beneath those headings. In this flowchart, the two column headings output are 'STUDENT NAME' and 'AVG GRADE'.

It should be pointed out that the column headings specified must properly coincide with the data to be printed beneath them. Only two column headings were detailed, as only two data items are printed within the looping sequence. The output of each student's name (SNAME) and average (A) will probably appear beneath their respective assigned column headings of STUDENT NAME and AVG GRADE. Many student flowcharts initially overlook this relationship and must therefore be reworked.

The remainder of this new solution parallels the original one. The YES branch of the 9s decision in this solution does not proceed directly to the STOP symbol. A special label, PROCESSING OVER, was inserted to highlight the close of processing activities. The characters composing that message were positioned with the required pair of quotes. The printing of this label indicates the feasibility of performing many types of processing operations on the YES branch of the LRC, EOF, or 9s decision. This availability was omitted from previous illustrative examples to simplify their structure and enable us to focus on other critical concepts. The branch from a looping sequence may lead to other required processing sequences.

The discussion of headings and labels leads us to introduce terms related to printed outputs. Through the years, terms have been associated with outputs that appear atop reports, within their context on a line-by-line basis, and at the close of reports. These types of printed lines may be respectively referred to as heading, detail, or summary lines.

A **heading line** represents those lines which appear at the top of reports or outputs. It indicates the report's name or function and identifies the columns of data composing the report. The headings STUDENT NAME and AVG GRADE in Figure 3.19 are representative of heading lines.

The output of data relating to specific people, transactions, or events on individual loops is representative of detail lines. A **detail line** is an individual line of output which details information specifically related to one person, event, or transaction. In most applications, the outputs that result from processing data within a loop are examples of detail lines. The output of each student's name and average is representative of a detail line.

Summary lines normally appear at the end of reports or at the bottom of specific report pages and summarize a group of actions. Thus, a total of dollars paid to all employees, when printed as the last line of a payroll report, would represent a summary line. A line of output indicating the number of people processed during a particular pay period would also serve as a sum-

FIGURE 3.19   The flow diagram for Problem 3.6 is modified to include the output of column headings and a closing label.

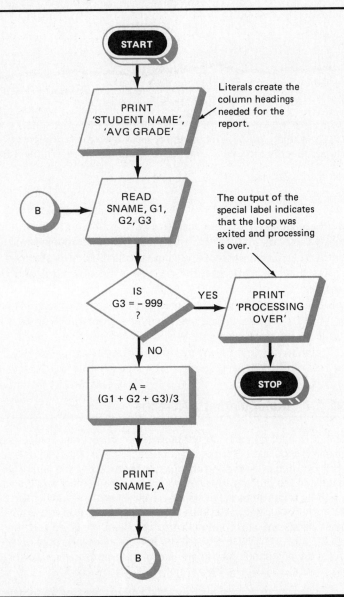

Column headings define the data items listed with
each column of the report.

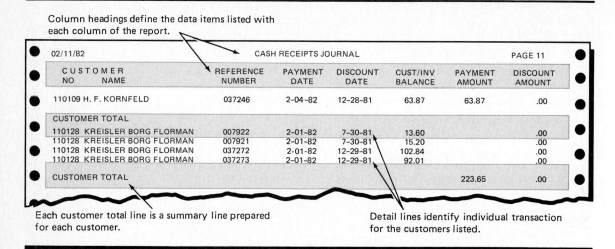

Each customer total line is a summary line prepared
for each customer.

Detail lines identify individual transaction
for the customers listed.

FIGURE 3.20 **Heading, detail, and summary lines are an integral part of most report formats. Observe the use of each type of output line within this report excerpt.**

mary line. These lines report the results of a combined group of activities. Summary lines are an integral part of most business reports and are extremely useful when an analysis of aggregate totals must be performed. Figure 3.20 illustrates how each of these three types of lines is employed within a printed report.

Literals are not restricted to business applications but may also be used to enhance outputs related to math and science problems. Our next sample flowchart will illustrate this point.

PROBLEM 3.7   Manipulating a Number

A single number is input on each loop of processing. In separate computations, the number is squared and cubed. The results of processing are outputted on three separate lines. The first output is the original number preceded by the label, 'ORIGINAL NO ='. The second line outputs the squared value of the number and the label, 'NO SQUARED ='. The third output line prints the cubed value of the number and the label, 'NO CUBED ='. A looping sequence is established and controlled by a 9s decision.

Two other literals are incorporated into this problem. A heading advising that '3 LINES OF OUTPUT PER NUMBER' should be printed prior to the start of the looping sequence. A special label should be printed when the looping sequence is exited, prior to the flowchart's close. This label should state 'PROCESSING OVER'.

These are the main points in the problem narrative.

1   A heading of '3 LINES OF OUTPUT PER NUMBER' must be printed before the looping sequence is started.

2   Only one numeric variable is inputted to the problem.

3   Two processing operations are required and defined by the formulas:
  a   X1 = number * number
  b   X2 = number * number * number

4   Three outputs are required to include:
  a   The output of the original number preceded by the label 'ORIGINAL NO ='.
  b   The output of the squared number preceded by the label 'NO SQUARED ='.
  c   The output of the cubed number preceded by the label 'NO CUBED ='.

5   A 9s decision controls the exit from the looping sequence.

6   On the YES branch of the 9s decision, the output of the special label 'PROCESSING OVER' is required.

The flowchart and checklist associated with Problem 3.7 are presented in Figure 3.21.

Examining this solution, we note a variety of outputs and the creation of a looping sequence. After its opening, the flowchart directs that a heading of '3 LINES OF OUTPUT PER NUMBER' be printed before the start of the loop. The first task of the loop is represented in a READ symbol, which inputs the number to undergo processing. This I/O symbol is logically followed by a 9s decision, which depicts the conditional statement, IS N = −999?. The NO branch of the 9s decision leads to the required processing activities.

The first processing symbol identifies the computation of X1, the dataname associated with the squaring of N. The second processing task defines X2, the cubed valued of N. The values of N, X1, and X2 are thus available for the output operations which follow.

The flowchart utilizes three PRINT symbols to denote the three output operations required by the problem narrative. Each I/O symbol results in a line of output. The use of separate I/O symbols avoids the confusion that sometimes arises when an attempt is made to represent multiple line formats in one PRINT symbol.

Each of these outputs consists of a special label and a dataname. This type of output format is often used when critical items must be highlighted. Though we have chosen to accent mathematical results, similar labels relating to business data may be outputted in other applications. Note that the processing of X1 and X2, the squared and cubed values of N, were completed before output operations commenced.

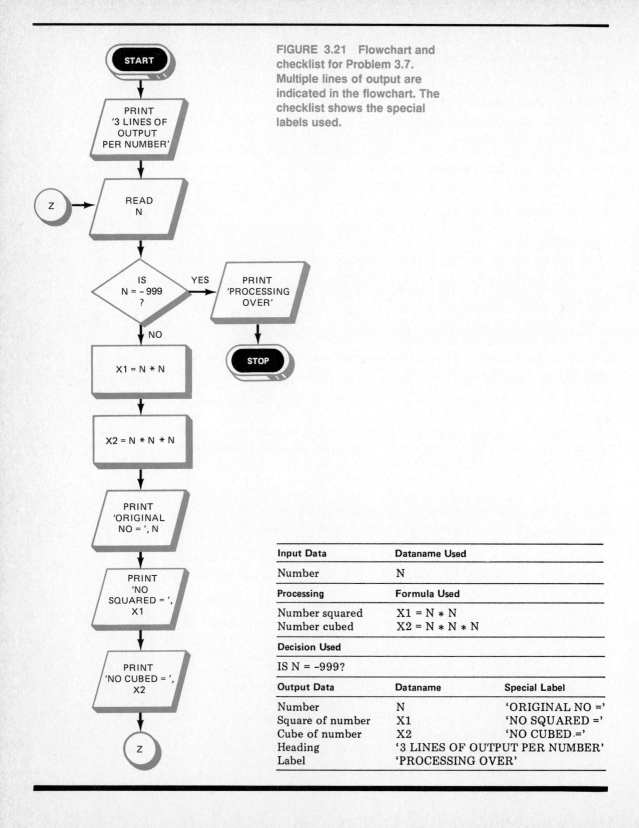

FIGURE 3.21 Flowchart and checklist for Problem 3.7. Multiple lines of output are indicated in the flowchart. The checklist shows the special labels used.

Input Data	Dataname Used	
Number	N	
Processing	**Formula Used**	
Number squared	X1 = N * N	
Number cubed	X2 = N * N * N	
Decision Used		
IS N = –999?		
Output Data	**Dataname**	**Special Label**
Number	N	'ORIGINAL NO ='
Square of number	X1	'NO SQUARED ='
Cube of number	X2	'NO CUBED.='
Heading		'3 LINES OF OUTPUT PER NUMBER'
Label		'PROCESSING OVER'

Looping activities continue until a value of -999 is input for N, thus activating the 9s decision and causing the processing flow to exit the loop via the YES branch. The output of a special label, 'PROCESSING OVER', is indicated and precedes the flowchart's close.

The varied activities of this flowchart are reflected in its checklist. We may also note the general use of heading, detail, and summary lines. The output of a heading line was evident at the flowchart's opening, advising that three lines were to be printed. Detail lines were employed to output the values of N, X1, and X2, along with their special labels. The closing special label on the YES branch of the 9s decision is representative of a summary line.

Multiple Decisions

Until this point, the decisions incorporated into our flowcharts have related to the control of looping sequences. Other decisions are required to support the varied processing activities which constitute more complex problems. Flowcharts can detail decision symbols to distinguish between two commissions, FICA rates, the formulas used to describe the trajectory of a rocket, and so forth. Essentially, the more complex a problem, the greater the need for decisions to select the paths processing can follow. Decisions provide the means of choosing between alternative processing steps. Consider how two commission rates could be handled.

PROBLEM 3.8 Sales Commissions Using Two Rates

Input on every loop are a salesperson's name, the name of the item sold, and its sales price. The salesperson's commission is computed by multiplying the sales price by the commission rate. If the sales price exceeds $100, a commission rate of 8 percent is used. If the sales price is less than or equal to $100, the commission rate is 5 percent. Output on each loop the salesperson's name, the item's name, the sales price, and the commission amount. Print the following headings atop the report: 'SALESPERSON', 'ITEM', 'PRICE', and 'COMMISSION'. Use an LRC to control looping. Output the label 'COMMISSIONS DONE' after the last data item is processed and before the flowchart's close.

These are the main points in the problem narrative.

1   A heading consisting of four literals is required atop the output.

2   Inputs are the salesperson's name, item name, and sales price.

3   Two commission rates are available: if the sales price is greater than 100, the 8 percent rate is used; if not, the 5 percent rate is used.

4   The formula required for processing is

Commission = sales price * commission rate

5   Outputs are the salesperson's name, item name, sales price, and commission.

6   An LRC is used to control looping.

7   The literal 'COMMISSIONS DONE' is output on the LRC's YES branch.

The flowchart and checklist for Problem 3.8 are presented within Figure 3.22.

The flowchart solution developed incorporates two decision symbols. Both decisions are logically positioned within the flowchart loop. The flowchart opens with the output of the required four column headings. The placement of the I/O symbols ensures that the literals SALESPERSON, ITEM, PRICE, and COMMISSION will appear atop the respective columns of data. The READ symbol initiates the input of the salesperson's name (SNAME), item name (ITEM), and sales price (P).

The READ symbol immediately precedes the LRC, the first of the solution's two decisions. This decision is properly positioned to ensure the rapid detection of the LRC condition. The decision regarding sales price, IS P > 100?, directly follows the LRC. This decision determines which rate to use to calculate commission amounts. Thus, it must follow the LRC decision and precede the computation of the sales commission.

Note that processing symbols appear on either branch of the commission decision. This configuration exists because one of the two percentage rates must be used. If it is not the 5 percent figure, the 8 percent rate is employed. Whichever rate is used, the flow of processing returns to the PRINT symbol. Output on each loop are the salesperson's name (SNAME), item name (ITEM), sales price (P), and commission (C).

An unconditional branch to the READ symbol completes the loop, which continues until the last sales record is fully processed. The YES branch of the LRC leads to the output of the label 'COMMISSIONS DONE', noting the close of processing.

One note must be made regarding the sales price decision. The conditional statement IS P > 100? does not contain a dollar sign, a special character some people might want to incorporate into that decision. The inclusion of the $ would render the decision invalid, as the variable P is numeric but $100 is nonnumeric (contains both numbers and symbols). The integrity of the conditional statements composing decision symbols must be maintained. You cannot utilize nonnumeric data to test against numeric variables.

Some students also wonder why a second decision, IS P <= 100? is not used. The reason is simple: it is not required. The original decision was sufficient to distinguish between sales prices that are greater than $100 and those that are less than or equal to that amount. That decision directs the flow of processing to the appropriate sales commission formula. Decisions should not be specified unless they are truly needed. Another illustrative problem will demonstrate the use of multiple decisions.

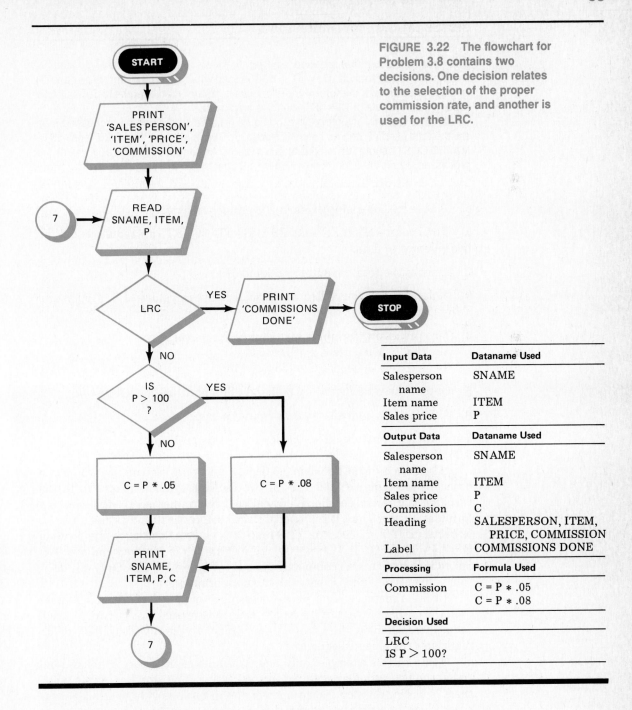

FIGURE 3.22 The flowchart for Problem 3.8 contains two decisions. One decision relates to the selection of the proper commission rate, and another is used for the LRC.

Input Data	Dataname Used
Salesperson name	SNAME
Item name	ITEM
Sales price	P

Output Data	Dataname Used
Salesperson name	SNAME
Item name	ITEM
Sales price	P
Commission	C
Heading	SALESPERSON, ITEM, PRICE, COMMISSION
Label	COMMISSIONS DONE

Processing	Formula Used
Commission	$C = P * .05$
	$C = P * .08$

Decision Used	
LRC	
IS $P > 100$?	

PROBLEM 3.9   Inventory Costs

Two straight-line formulas are used to project the costs related to maintaining a monthly inventory. The first formula, $C = .5T + 500$, is used when the total inventory on hand (T) is under 5000 units. If the total number of units is greater than or equal to 5000, then a second cost formula of $C = .35T + 750$ is employed.

Input is the total-inventory-on-hand figure (T). The outputs of the processing loop are the total used (T) and its estimated cost (C). Two headings, 'INV SIZE' and 'ESTIMATED COST', should be printed atop the report. An unspecified number of values are processed, so create a loop controlled by a 9s decision.

These are the main points in the problem narrative.

1   Two heads, 'INV SIZE' and 'ESTIMATED COST', are required atop the two columns of data.

2   Input is the total inventory on hand (T).

3   A decision is required to distinguish between values of $T < 5000$ and $T >= 5000$.

4   Two processing formulas are required for processing:
   a   If $T < 5000$, use $C = .5T + 500$
   b   If $T >= 5000$, use $C = .35T + 750$

5   Output the total inventory on hand (T) and its associated cost (C).

6   A 9s decision controls the exit from the loop.

The flowchart and checklist developed for this problem is shown in Figure 3.23.

The flowchart for Problem 3.9 depicts a looping sequence in which two decisions are required. The first of two decision symbols relates to the 9s decision. The second decision is critical, as it determines which of the two cost formulas is used. Thus, it is properly placed before the formulas and after the 9s decision. If $T < 5000$, the YES branch is chosen, leading to the formula $C = (.5 * T) + 500$. If $T >= 5000$, the NO branch is followed and the estimated inventory cost is computed using $C = (.35 * T) + 750$. Only one decision is required to choose between the two formulas.

In either instance, the flow of processing returns to the I/O symbol where both the on-hand inventory total (T) and its estimated cost (C) are printed. Connectors complete the unconditional branch to the READ symbol, which reinitiates the looping sequence.

Again in this example, only one decision was necessary to choose between the two formulas required for processing. The situation exists when there is a clear division indicating when each formula is to be used. Essentially, if one formula is not used, the other must be employed. The exactness of the decision specified makes the choice easy. If more than one alternative exists, then possibly a series of decisions might be required to unravel the

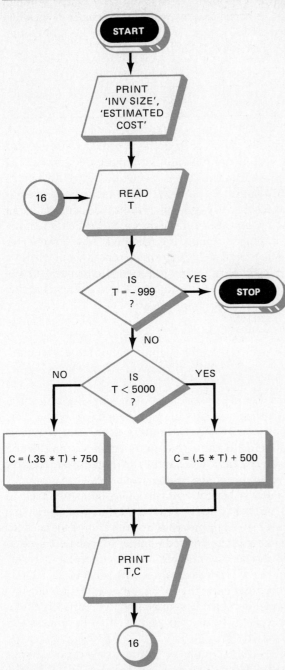

FIGURE 3.23 Flowchart and checklist for Problem 3.9, using multiple decisions.

Input Data	Dataname Used
Total inventory on hand	T

Output Data	Dataname Used
Total inventory on hand	T
Estimated inventory cost	C
Heading	INV SIZE, ESTIMATED COST

Processing	Formula Used
Inventory cost	C = .5 * T + 500
	C = .35 * T + 750

Decision Used
IS T = -999?
IS T < 5000?

logic as to when specific formulas might be invoked. Not every problem possesses two exactly opposite processing sequences. Logically positioned decision symbols make it possible to control processing and dictate when specific processing operations are undertaken.

3.5 Counting Loops

There are occasions when an LRC, EOF, or 9s decision prove inadequate for our processing needs. Those techniques are valid for unspecified amounts of data because they loop until the end of the data is reached. They could loop 21 times in one example and 614 times in the next. These techniques are not constructed to handle the execution of a specific number of loops. Such an operation requires a counter. A **counter** establishes a controllable looping sequence where a specific number of loops are executed. The flowcharter defines the series of tasks to be repetitively performed, places them within a loop controlled via a counter, initiates the looping sequence, and monitors the results produced by executing the desired number of loops. Flowcharting characteristics normally associated with counters are:

1   The initialization of the counter at 1

2   The use of a counter decision to monitor the number of loops executed

3   The increment of the counter by a factor of 1

As with any variable used within processing, counters must be initialized at a specific value to establish a point at which processing activities may begin. We choose to start counters at 1, thus beginning the looping sequence with that value. The concept being to have the counter equal to 1 on the first loop, 2 on the second loop, 3 on the third loop, and so on. Setting our counter at 1 initializes this looping sequence at the proper value.

Once the looping sequence is begun, a check must be established to ensure that only the desired number of loops is executed. The vehicle for this check is the counter decision, which examines the current value of the counter and compares it against the value of the desired number of loops. As long as the counter has not reached the desired number of loops, looping will continue. When the desired number of loops is attained, the counter decision is triggered and the flow of processing exits the loop via the YES branch.

Figure 3.24 shows the same flowchart that appeared in Figure 3.10, but a counter is used. For this example, assume that we are going to process 100 people and need to perform exactly 100 loops.

The flowchart's opening START symbol is immediately followed by a processing statement which sets $K = 1$. The $K = 1$ instruction initializes the counter (K) at 1 and establishes the counter for subsequent loops. The initialization of K is performed before the looping sequence commences. Operations of this type are generally referred to as **initial conditions,** as they are conditions which must be established before processing begins.

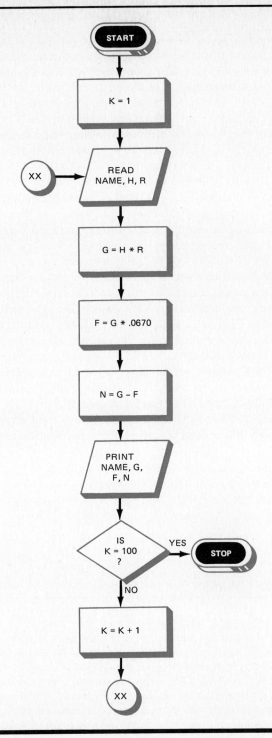

FIGURE 3.24 Flowchart showing use of a counter. The counter is initialized at 1, a counter decision checks that exactly 100 loops are executed, and the counter increment of 1 is positioned on the NO branch of the counter decision.

With K initialized at 1, the loop begins at the READ symbol. As an LRC is not used, a processing symbol representing the computation of gross pay (G) follows the READ symbol. The processing of FICA (F) and net pay (N) follow, with the required output of G, F, and N defined by a PRINT symbol.

The output of the employee's payroll data signals the end of processing within that loop. This is where the counter decision, IS K = 100? is positioned. The counter decision determines whether the hundredth loop has been completed. On the first loop, when K = 1, the counter decision compares 1 (the current value of K) to 100 (the number of loops to be executed). As long as the number of loops executed remains under 100, the NO branch of the counter decision is followed. On this branch is located the counter increment K = K + 1. This computation increases the counter by 1 on each loop. Its positioning, prior to the unconditional branch to the READ symbol, ensures that the counter is increased before the next loop is begun. As such, K becomes 2 before the second loop, 3 before loop 3, and so on.

The counter K is incremented to 100 before loop 100 begins. After the hundredth employee is processed, the counter decision is encountered. At this point K = 100, and the YES branch is followed, exiting the looping sequence. In this problem, the YES branch leads to a STOP symbol and the flowchart's close. The counter has served its purpose, controlling the looping sequence and completing exactly 100 loops.

Reviewing the flowchart, we can observe the three operations associated with use of a counter. The operation K = 1 initializes the counter prior to the start of the flowchart loop. The counter decision IS K = 100? determines whether the hundredth loop was executed. The computation K = K + 1, positioned on the NO branch of the counter decision, increments the counter by 1.

In this problem, we chose to use the dataname K for the counter, but flowcharters can use any dataname to represent a counter. Also, the problem utilized 100 loops, but that value will vary with each application. Another problem demonstrates the use of a counter to control looping.

PROBLEM 3.10   Student Grades Report

Headings consisting of 'STUDENT', 'AVERAGE', and 'COMMENT' should appear above all outputs. Input to the problem are student's name and three grades. The average of the three grades is computed by adding the grades and dividing that sum by 3. A decision is required to distinguish between two different outputs. If the computed average is greater than or equal to 90, output the student's name, grade, and the label 'WITH HONORS'. If the average is less than 90, output only the student's name and average. As exactly 76 students will be processed, a counter is used to control looping. After processing the last student, output the label 'ALL DONE' before ending the flowchart.

These are the main points in the problem narrative.

1   Column headings consisting of three literals, 'STUDENT', 'AVERAGE', and 'COMMENT', are required atop the report.

2   Inputs are the student's name and three grades, each using separate datanames.

3   The student's average is calculated using the formula

Average = (Grade 1 + Grade 2 + Grade 3)/3

4   A decision is required to determine which type of output is used. If the average is greater than or equal to 90, output the student's name, average, and the label 'WITH HONORS'. If the average is less than 90, output only the student's name and average.

5   A counter is used to control the looping sequence. Exactly 76 students are to be processed. Ensure that the counter is properly initialized and incremented by 1.

6   After the 76 students have been processed output the literal 'ALL DONE' before closing processing.

The flowchart and checklist prepared for Problem 3.10 are detailed in Figure 3.25.

Two tasks occur at the flowchart's opening. The first task is the initialization of K, which is accomplished within the processing symbol via the formula $K = 1$. Immediately following that operation is the output of the required column headings. A PRINT symbol directs the output of the three literals which will compose the headings. These two initial conditions are performed prior to the start of the loop sequence.

The READ symbol inputting student data opens the loop and precedes the computation of the student's average. This processing symbol is logically placed after the READ symbol because an LRC (or similar decision) was not used.

The computation of the student's average must precede the decision symbol, which dictates which of two outputs are executed. If $A >= 90$, the student's data is printed with a special label of 'WITH HONORS'. If $A < 90$, then only the student's name and average is outputted. Either output is the last task required for any student's data and provides the basis for placement of the counter decision.

The counter decision IS $K = 76$? continually checks for the execution of the seventy-sixth loop. It is positioned at the end of the flowchart loop, acting as a control to whether another loop is started. If the seventy-sixth loop has not been performed, processing proceeds down the NO branch to the counter increment. The formula $K = K + 1$ increases K by 1, in preparation for the next loop's processing. The unconditional branch to the READ symbol starts the next loop.

The looping and increment of the counter will continue until the

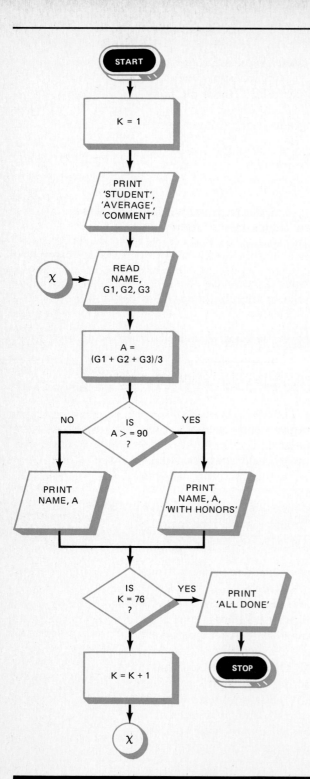

FIGURE 3.25 Flowchart and checklist for Problem 3.10. A counter (K) is used.

Input Data	Dataname Used
Student name	NAME
Grade 1	G1
Grade 2	G2
Grade 3	G3

Output Data	Dataname Used
Student name	NAME
Average	A
Label	WITH HONORS, ALL DONE
Heading	STUDENT, AVERAGE, COMMENT

Processing	Formula Used
Average	A = (G1 + G2 + G3)/3
Counter initialization	K = 1
Counter increment	K = K + 1

Decision Used
IS K = 76?
IS A >= 90?

seventy-sixth loop is completed. When $K = 76$, the counter decision will assess this fact and cause the flow of processing to exit via the YES branch. The output of the 'ALL DONE' literal is then performed before the flowchart's close.

Chapter Summary

3.1 Why Use a Flowchart?

Flowcharts provide an excellent means of depicting the logic of solutions related to computer programs. Their pictorial format enables users to detail the logic of every step in a solution. Specifically, flowcharts are used as

1　A means of documentation

2　Analytic tools

3　A means of communication

Flowcharts provide a means of documenting all solutions developed for a particular application down to the smallest detail. They record all modifications made to specific solutions and act as a historical record of the evolution of a project's final solution.

Flowcharts are used to develop alternative solutions to the same problem, without having to write the software necessary to test each alternative. This latter approach reveals another purpose of flowcharts as analytic tools. Using flowcharts it is possible to detail potential design approaches and test their possible effectiveness.

Flowcharts serve as an excellent means of communicating new ideas. Flowcharts enable programmers to express complex ideas and have them evaluated without recourse to elaborate narratives. Symbols within the flowchart define specific processing activities and their logic. They are an integral and vital component of any project's final documentation.

3.2 Program Flowcharts

Flowcharts are sometimes referred to as flow or block diagrams. Two types of flowcharts encountered are systems and program flowcharts. Systems flowcharts are generally much larger than program flowcharts and describe the flow of information through an organization. Program flowcharts focus on those steps that constitute a computer program. They are smaller and more concise and detail the logic of program solutions.

Flowcharts employ a set of symbols to which predefined operations are associated. The entire group of symbols is respectively divided into those which are used with program or systems flowcharts. Each symbol has a specific purpose and is generally restricted to either type of flowchart.

The terminal symbol is used to denote the opening and close of flowcharts. Input-output (I/O) symbols depict I/O operations. Terms written into I/O symbols include READ and INPUT for input operations and PRINT and WRITE for output tasks. Through convention, I/O symbols may be referred to as READ or PRINT symbols. The narratives associated with variables used in I/O operations and processing are referred to as datanames. Whenever possible we will assign shortened datanames to variables associated with numeric data and longer datanames to nonnumeric variables.

Computations of any type are defined within processing symbols via formulas or English-like sentences. When a formula is used, convention dictates that only one dataname be placed to the left of the equal sign. A specific set of symbols are used to represent arithmetic operations.

The performance of logical operations is accomplished within decision symbols. The use of decision symbols enables the comparison of two data items. Symbols can identify the operators used in decision symbols.

In a decision symbol, logical operations are defined as questions and referred to as conditional statements. Conditional statements are constructed to elicit a YES or NO response. These responses direct the flow of processing from the decision symbol via the appropriate conditional branch. The decision symbol is the only means of choosing between alternative paths.

In logical operations, the distinction between numeric and nonnumeric data items is again emphasized. Numeric data consists solely of numeric characters and should contain no alphabetic or special characters (with the exception of decimal points). Nonnumeric data may consist of any combination of alphabetic, numeric, or special characters. In conditional statements, nonnumeric data items are highlighted by the use of quotation marks.

Groups of related statements— define modules of activity—are represented via the predefined-process symbol. This symbol permits flowcharters to identify a group of processing tasks as a single entity with one symbol. The concept of grouping statements provides a ready means of identifying subroutines. A subroutine is a concept common to languages where sets of instructions must be accessed as a single unit.

Descriptive comments are appended to flowcharts using annotation symbols. This symbol is attached to any other symbol using a dashed line to show its informational function. The desired comment is placed within this three-sided figure to advise the reader of a specific fact.

3.3 Looping Sequences

Looping sequences enable the repetitive processing of data and the handling of more than one data item. Two techniques utilized in this repetitive process are the flowchart loop and last-record check (LRC). The flowchart loop creates the sequence by which the same tasks are repeated. An unconditional branch provides a means of reinitiating the loop. Connector symbols may be used to denote unconditional branches.

The last-record check (LRC) provides a means of continuing the looping sequence or exiting from it. The LRC decision determines whether the last record has been read and processed. If it has, no additional data exists, the YES branch of the LRC is followed, and the loop is exited. If additional data is sensed, processing is continued via the LRC's NO branch.

A checklist is often associated with flowchart solutions. It acts as a list of all factors which constitute the flowchart and may be used to check the correctness of the flowchart drawn. All input, output, processing statements, decisions, and related factors are listed within the checklist.

Two equivalents of the LRC are the end-of-file (EOF) check and the 9s decision. They may each be used interchangeably with the LRC. The EOF check is similar to the LRC in that it checks to see that no additional data exists and that the end of the file of data has been reached. The 9s decision is similarly positioned, but checks against the input of a coded data item which notes that the last data item was read. The 9s decision must involve one of the variables inputted on each loop. Sensing of the 9s data means that the last item has been read, no more data exists, and looping must cease.

3.4 More Flowcharting Tools

Computer outputs are embellished to make them as useful as possible. This includes the use of column headings placed atop reports and special labels which highlight critical data items. Both column headings and special labels are created through literals — character groupings framed within single quotation marks. Literals are defined in PRINT symbols and may be exhibited anywhere within a flowchart. Literals and datanames may be mixed within a PRINT symbol.

Column headings are generally created prior to the start of a looping sequence, with special labels sprinkled through a flowchart as needed. Special labels are often viewed on the YES branch of an LRC, signaling the close of processing.

The outputs associated with literals help define the use of heading, detail, and summary lines. These designations provide a uniform reference to the types of outputs presented. A heading line appears atop reports, defining the data items that are printed beneath it. Detail lines constitute the bulk of a report, listing data regarding individual transactions, events, or persons involved in processing. Summary lines appear at a flowchart's close, listing information which reflects results drawn from a group's data.

The more complex the flowchart, the greater the need for decisions. Multiple decisions are commonly employed to distinguish between data-handling activities, to code data into groups, and to control the looping sequence. Decisions may be positioned throughout a flowchart, in response to processing needs.

3.5 Counting Loops

When the need arises to perform a specific number of loops, a counter may be used. The counter provides a means of executing an exact number of loops and processing a specific amount of data. The counter controls the looping sequence, completing only the desired number of loops. Using a counter, the flowcharter performs three tasks:

1 Initializes the counter at 1

2 Creates a counter decision to check whether the proper number of loops has been executed

3 Increments the counter by 1

The initialization of the counter variable prior to the looping sequence (e.g., K = 1) is referred to as an initial condition. The counter decision is positioned at the close of the flowchart loop. It determines whether the exact number of loops has been performed. The counter decision compares the current value of the counter variable against the numeric equivalent of the desired number of loops to be executed.

The counter increment (e.g., K = K + 1) is positioned on the NO branch of the counter decision. This formula increases K by 1 on each loop until a desired number of loops are completed. The increment occurs before the start of the next loop. An unconditional branch normally follows the counter increment, providing the link to the start of the next loop. The counter offers an alternative to controlling a looping sequence.

Key Flowcharting Symbols

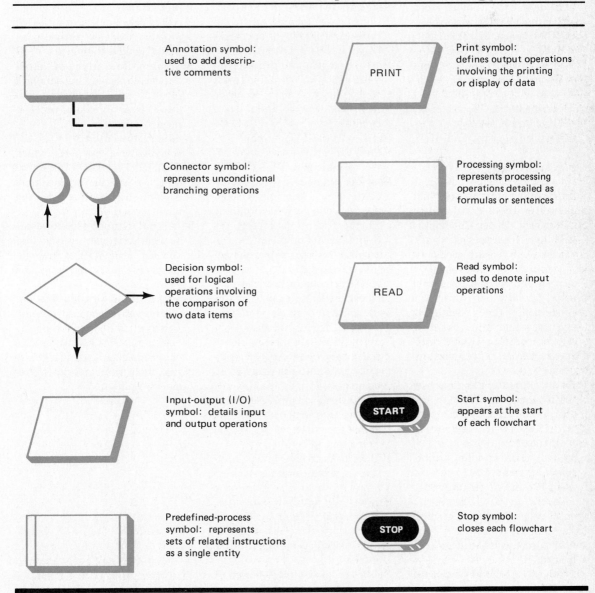

Annotation symbol: used to add descriptive comments

Print symbol: defines output operations involving the printing or display of data

Connector symbol: represents unconditional branching operations

Processing symbol: represents processing operations detailed as formulas or sentences

Decision symbol: used for logical operations involving the comparison of two data items

Read symbol: used to denote input operations

Input-output (I/O) symbol: details input and output operations

Start symbol: appears at the start of each flowchart

Predefined-process symbol: represents sets of related instructions as a single entity

Stop symbol: closes each flowchart

Glossary

Annotation symbol The symbol employed to record descriptive comments within a flowchart, attached by a dashed line.

Block diagram A term applied to flowcharts which recognizes that each symbol of a flowchart solution represents a block upon which that solution was built.

Checklist A list of components derived from the problem narrative, upon which the flowchart solution is based; can act to verify the accuracy of a solution.

Column heading Characters positioned atop reports, represented as literals within PRINT symbols.

Conditional branches The exits from decision symbols.

Conditional statements The question within a decision symbol which defines the logical operation being tested for.

Counter A flowchart technique used to create and control the execution of a specific number of loops.

Datanames The identifying names assigned variables within flowcharts which permit reference to the data undergoing processing.

Decision symbol The flowchart symbol used to represent logical operations where the comparison of two data items is possible.

Detail line A type of output line related to a specific person, event, or transaction.

End-of-file (EOF) check A decision similar to a last-record check which determines whether the end of a file has been reached; controls the looping sequence.

Flowchart A pictorial description of the logic used to process data for a specific application.

Flowchart loop A series of steps composing the repetitive processing of data in a flowchart.

Flow diagram Another term for a flowchart.

Heading line An output line positioned atop reports which describes the data items appearing below; a column heading.

Initial condition A processing requirement which is fulfilled prior to the start of a looping sequence (e.g., the initialization of a counter.)

Input-output (I/O) symbol The flowchart symbol used to detail I/O operations in a flowchart.

Last-record check (LRC) A decision which controls a looping sequence by determining whether the last data record has been read and processed.

Literal A desired group of characters framed within quotes, used to define column headings and labels in PRINT symbols.

9s decision A decision paralleling the LRC which controls a looping sequence by testing for a coded data item (usually a string of 9s) placed after the last item to be processed.

Nonnumeric data Data items composed of any combination of alphabetic, numeric, or special characters.

Numeric data Data items consisting of only numeric characters.

Processing symbol The flowchart symbol used to describe processing operations; may contain formulas or English-like sentences.

Program flowchart A flowchart depicting the logical steps from which a computer program will be written.

Special label A literal used to highlight critical data items or bring attention to special situations.

Subroutine A programming concept which emphasizes the use of program modules consisting of sets of related statements.

Summary line A type of output line which usually appears at a report's end, summarizing data drawn from a group of processing activities.

Systems flowchart A broad, encompassing flowchart which documents the flow of information through an organization, depicting both computerized and manual operations.

Terminal symbol The flowchart symbol positioned as the first and last symbol of a flow diagram, noting its opening and close.

Unconditional branch The uninterrupted branch to another flowchart symbol where no deviation is possible; often used to close a looping sequence by branching to a previously executed operation.

Exercises

1   For the flowchart excerpts of Figure 3.26, insert the narratives necessary to initial-   **In-Class Exercises**
ize and use a counter called K for the indicated number of loops.
   a   Figure 3.26*(a):* 62 loops
   b   Figure 3.26*(b):* 107 loops
   c   Figure 3.26*(c):* 19 loops

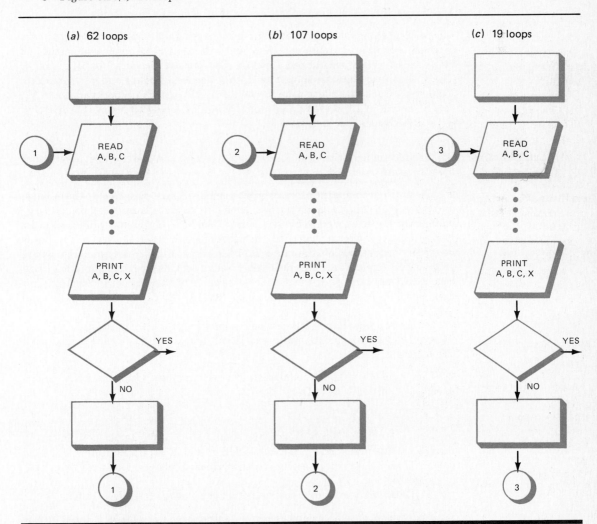

FIGURE 3.26   Complete the counters for the indicated number of loops. Use K as the counter variable.

2   For the problem narrative that follows, prepare a flowchart, with a checklist, that represents the processing described.

The problem entails the computation of pension benefits. Input to the problem are an employee's name, identification code, and gross pay amount. If the identification code is M (for management), the pension rate is 1.2 percent of the gross pay amount. If the code is S (for salaried employees), the rate used is .8 percent of gross pay. The pension amount is computed by multiplying the gross pay amount by the pension rate. Output the employee's name, identification code, gross pay, and computed pension amount. Column headings of 'EMPLOYEE', 'CODE', 'GROSS', and 'PENSION AMT' should be printed. Use a 9s decision to control looping.

3   For the problem narrative that follows, draw a flowchart solution.

The problem entails solving a math formula. The general formula for a straight line is $Y = MX + B$, where M represents the slope of a line and B the point at which the line crosses the Y axis when graphed. Input on each loop are the values for M, X, and B. These three data items are substituted into the general formula and Y is computed. Output after each computation are the values of M, X, B, and Y. Four headings of 'M', 'X', 'B', and 'Y VALUE' are printed atop that output. As exactly six sets of values will be processed, a counter is used.

Lab Exercises   For the problem narratives that follow, prepare a flowchart and checklist to represent the processing described.

1   The problem entails the processing of an employee's net pay. Input to the problem are the employee's name, hours worked, and hourly pay rate. Gross pay is computed by multiplying the hours worked by the pay rate. The FICA deduction utilizes two rates. If the gross pay is greater than $750, the FICA rate is 6.70 percent. If the gross pay is less than or equal to $750, the rate is 5.75 percent. Multiply the specific rate by the gross pay to compute the FICA deduction. Net pay equals gross pay minus the FICA deduction. Output the employee's name, gross pay, FICA deduction, and net pay. This data should appear beneath the headings 'EMPLOYEE', 'GROSS', 'FICA', and 'NETPAY'.
   a   Draw a flowchart solution where looping is controlled by an LRC.
   b   Draw a flowchart to process exactly 162 employees. Use a counter to control the looping sequence.

2   The problem entails the completion of a math exercise. Using the following formula, solve for the value of D

$$D = 3B^2 - 6B - 17$$

Input a value of B which is used in the computation of D. Output both B and D, preceded by the labels 'FOR THE B VALUE =' and 'D =', respectively.
   a   Draw a flowchart to process an unspecified number of B values. Use an LRC to control looping.
   b   Draw a flowchart to process exactly five values of B. Use a counter.

3   The problem entails the processing of a salesperson's commission. Input are the salesperson's name and four sales amounts (which must have four distinct data-names). The total sales amount is calculated by adding the four sales amounts. The commission amount is computed by multiplying the total sales amount by a commission rate of 8 percent. Print the salesperson's name, total sales amount, and commission amount. Column headings of 'SALESPERSON', 'TOT SALES' and 'COMM' should be printed atop all outputs. An unspecified number of salespeople are pro-

cessed, so use an LRC to control looping. On the YES branch of the LRC, print the label 'COMMISSIONS DONE' before the flowchart's close.

4   Redo problem 3, but substitute the following requirements:
    a   Replace the LRC with a 9s decision, testing for a sales amount of -9999.99 against sales amount 2.
    b   Instead of one commission rate, two rates now exist. If the total sales amount is greater than $300, a rate of 11 percent is used. If not, the commission rate is 8 percent.

Draw new flow diagrams with these features.

5   This problem entails the computation of a pressure factor. The headings 'POUNDS', 'AREA-SQ. FT.' and 'LBS/SQ. FT.' appear atop the report. Input are three data items: weight of the object (in pounds) and the length and width (in feet) of the floor space it will occupy. Multiply the length and width values to compute the area of the floor space (in square feet). The pressure factor is calculated by dividing the weight by the floor space area. Output the weight, computed floor space area, and pressure factor. Use an LRC to control looping.

6   The problem entails calculating winning percentages for a baseball league. Inputs to the problem are the team's name, the number of games won, and the number of games lost. The winning percentage is computed by dividing the number of games won by the total number of games played by a team. The total number of games played is computed by adding a team's games won and lost. Output the team's name, games won, games lost, and winning percentage. Use the headings 'TEAM', 'WON', 'LOST', and 'PCT' atop the report. Exactly eight teams compose the league and are processed. Use a counter to control looping. A closing label of 'PROCESSING DONE' is printed.

7   The problem entails the printing of data related to two formulas. A teacher defines a line via the following functions:
    a   If $X < 0$, $Y = 3X + 6$
    b   If $X >= 0$, $Y = X^2 + 6$

Input on each loop is the X value. The solution must decide which formula to use by testing against the X value, comparing it to zero. When the proper formula is accessed, a value of Y is computed. Output the X and Y values, placing the labels 'X =' and 'Y =' before their respective values. Use an LRC to control the loop.

8   The problem entails the computation of simple interest. Interest is paid quarterly on the lowest balance of a savings account. Two rates are used in this special account. If the balance is greater than or equal to $100, a rate of 1.5 percent is used. If the balance is less than $100, the interest rate is zero and no interest is paid. Input to the problem are the account number and its balance of funds. The interest amount is computed by multiplying the balance by the interest rate. The computed interest is added to the existing balance to create each account's new balance. Output the account's number, opening balance, computed interest, and new balance. Column headings include 'ACCOUNT', 'OPEN BAL', 'INTEREST', and 'NEW BAL'. A counter is used to control the looping required to process 850 accounts.

9   The problem entails the computation of mileage expenses. Two formulas are used to compute mileage expenses, depending upon the type of car. If a small car is used, the expense formula used is $E = .15M + 160$ where E equals the expense and M the miles traveled. If a large car is operated, the expense formula is $E = .18M + 225$. Input are

the car's identification number, the car's code, and the miles traveled. A car code of 1 denotes a small car, and a code of 2 denotes a large car. Substitution of the mileage figure is necessary to compute the mileage expense. Output the car's number, mileage, and computed expense. Three literals, 'CAR', 'MILES', and 'EXPENSE', create the required column headings. Use a 9s decision to control the looping sequence.

Quiz Problem   Draw a flowchart for the problem narrative that follows.

The problem entails the computation of weekly bowling averages. Input are the player's name and the individual scores of the three games for that week. These three scores are added and the sum is divided by 3, to produce the weekly average for that bowler. If that average is greater than 200, output the bowler's name, weekly average, and the label 'PLUS 200'. If not, output only the player's name and weekly average. These outputs should appear under the headings 'BOWLER', 'WEEKLY AVG', and 'SPECIAL'. Use a loop control sequence of your choice to process the 60 bowlers in the league.

Quiz Solution   The flowcharts for the quiz narrative are shown in Figure 3.27. An LRC is used in Figure 3.27(a) and a counter is used in Figure 3.27(b).

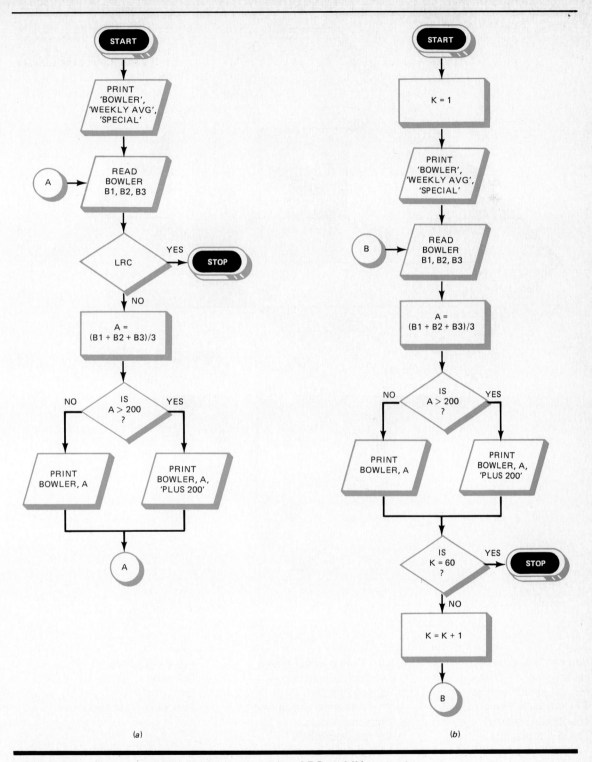

FIGURE 3.27 Solution to quiz problem, using (a) an LRC and (b) a counter.

FOUR

A BASIC Introduction

Chapter Objectives

- Describe the general line format for BASIC instructions.

- Discuss the conversion of problem narratives to flowcharts and program solutions.

- Discuss the use of literals in PRINT statements.

- Describe the use of IF/THEN and GO TO statements in looping sequences.

- Discuss the relationship between READ and DATA statements and the alternate use of INPUT statements.

- Describe the use of LET statements in arithmetic operations.

- Describe BASIC's handling of counters and looping sequences.

- Discuss the use of the IF/THEN/ELSE statement to distinguish between alternative computations or branching operations.

Introduction

In the early 1980's there has been an explosion of computer products. Computerized games, video cartridges, home computers, small computers in the kitchen, and computer-filmed movies are just a few examples of the computer mania sweeping the country. BASIC is one of the principal languages associated with these smaller computer systems. It is a good learning language because of its relative simplicity; beginners can quickly master preliminary programming skills. Many users find that they are able to write and execute programs within hours of their initial instructional periods.

BASIC was introduced in the mid-1960s as the brainchild of Dr. John Kemeny of Dartmouth College. Kemeny was a proponent of computer literacy for all college graduates. The then-existing languages were overly technical, with formats that did not lend themselves to rapid student learning; these drawbacks led to Kemeny's development of BASIC. Since its initial use, BASIC has been expanded to permit its handling of industrial, business, and scientific applications.

Originally, only one version of BASIC existed, but now various forms of BASIC are available from computer manufacturers. These newer versions are fairly similar, with each manufacturer incorporating selected special instructions to highlight the effectiveness of their BASIC. Throughout these discussions, we will advise the reader of potential differences between the various versions of BASIC.

In this chapter we will follow the practice of presenting a problem, developing a flowchart, and writing a BASIC program related to it. We will introduce BASIC instructions that will enable us to perform arithmetic and I/O operations, as well as looping sequences. Statements related to the performance of logical operations via decisions, the creation and output of literals and the use of counters will also be presented.

4.1 A BASIC Overview

The word BASIC is an acronym of *B*eginner's *A*ll-purpose *S*ymbolic *I*nstructional *C*ode. BASIC is referred to as a free-form language because of its simple structure and minimal number of rules. The rules of a programming language are called its *syntax,* which defines the conventions associated with its usage. BASIC possesses its own syntax, but one with far fewer rules than most. Whatever rules do exist must be followed strictly, however.

While executing programs the BASIC compiler will enforce the syntax rules and highlight errors. The manner in which these errors are displayed relates to the hardware being used and the processing mode. Generally, since BASIC is principally used in a timesharing, interactive environment, program errors will be revealed as they occur.

Statements written in BASIC programs normally follow the general line format defined for that language, with few exceptions. This general line format consists of three elements: (1) line number, (2) command, and (3) variable(s). Each component in this format serves a different operational function.

The **line numbers** assigned to BASIC instructions serve as a means of identification and define the order in which a series of instructions are executed. The line number is positioned at the start of each instruction and assumes a numeric, integer format. The spread of acceptable line numbers generally ranges from 1 to 99999, with the upper limit varying between systems in which BASIC is executed. Generally, the line number 99999 is the last statement number possible, though it is very rarely used.

In BASIC, program statements are executed by their line number in ascending numeric order. Thus, line 10 is executed before line 20, line 20 before line 30, 30 before 40, and so on. A sequence of instructions may be repeated many times to process data, as might occur within a looping sequence.

When writing BASIC programs, the reader may observe that gaps exist in the sequencing of instructions. That is, a program may be written using the line numbers 10, 20, 30, 40, 50, and so on. Though this may seem wasteful, it serves a valuable purpose and represents much foresight. Consider what might happen if a program was written using line numbers 1 through 10. If after entering these 10 statements a programmer notes the omission of a statement that should have been placed between lines 2 and 3, the lines numbered 3 to 10 must all be renumbered to make room for the omitted statement. Contrast this with a program that has employed the line numbers 10, 20, 30, 40, 50, 60, 70, 80, 90, and 100. An omitted statement can be placed between lines 20 and 30 and assigned any line number between 21 to 29. None of the existing statements have to be renumbered. The operational software supporting BASIC will accept this newly inputted statement and logically position it between lines 20 and 30, the new order of statements becoming, for example, lines 10, 20, 25, 30, 40, 50, 60, 70, 80, 90, and 100.

This facility gives BASIC a true advantage. Users are free to enter BASIC instructions in any order, with the knowledge that they will be properly reordered prior to their execution. Users can easily make program corrections with no fear of lengthy corrective sessions, thus simplifying the debugging process. Statements may be inserted as the programmer requires and immediately phased into processing.

The function of a specific BASIC instruction is defined by its **command.** The command is the equivalent of an operational code, defining the processing task assigned to that statement. For example, if the BASIC command READ was incorporated into a line, an input operation would be indicated. Similarly, the command PRINT would invoke an output operation. Essentially, without a command the instruction would have no purpose.

If a statement defines an operation, it must also dictate the data to be worked on. The **variable** (or variables) within this line format defines the data to be processed. Thus, if an input operation of READ is directed, the instruction must specify the variables to be read.

Most of BASIC's instructions are constructed using a combination of these three elements. The actual format of each specific instruction will vary in relation to its operational usage.

In introducing BASIC programming concepts, we have chosen to reuse problems previously discussed in the flowcharting chapter. This approach enables students to focus on the BASIC instructions introduced, as they are familiar with the logic of prior solutions.

4.2 An Initial Program

As with any other language, BASIC employs a syntax which is unique. It does not employ the wealth of statements available with other more complex languages but instead relies heavily on a fundamental group of instructions to handle the bulk of processing activities. The instructions relate to the input, processing, and output operations and define the data used in a problem and general comments added to the program solution to aid understanding. A sample program will help introduce these BASIC instructions.

PROBLEM 4.1   Individual Gross Pay

Input to the problem are the employee's name, hours worked, and hourly pay rate. Gross pay is computed by multiplying the hours worked by the pay rate. Output the employee's name and gross pay amount. Only one person is processed in this example. For test purposes, use the following data:

Employee Name	Hours Worked	Pay Rate
John Smith	35	$3.25

These are the main points in the problem narrative.

1   No headings are required for the problem.

2   Only one person's data will be handled.

3   Input are the employee's name, hours worked, and pay rate.

4   Processing consists of the formula:

Gross = hours worked * rate of pay

5   Output only the employee's name and computed gross pay.

The flowchart and BASIC program prepared from this narrative are shown in Figure 4.1.

Let us first turn our attention to the flowchart, which serves as a layout for the logic of our solution. The flowchart opens with a START symbol, inputs the three data items involved in processing, and proceeds to the computation of the employee's gross pay. A single I/O symbol defines the output of the employee's name and gross pay. A STOP symbol closes the flow diagram.

The flowchart provides the stepping stone to the BASIC program for Problem 4.1. Most of the five statements composing that BASIC program are expressed in its flow diagram. The preparatory statements used to LOGON are the equivalent of the START symbol. No statements are written into the program for these purposes. Our BASIC program begins with the entry of data for processing, that is, the equivalent of the READ symbol.

The READ Statement   Line 10 of this BASIC program is defined as a **READ statement** and adheres to the general line format of all BASIC instructions. The line number is 10, the command READ denotes an input activity, and the three variables following READ define the data to be worked on.

The different spelling of the three datanames in the flowchart and the program is significant. From the flowchart, we know that the input data consists of the employee's name, the hours worked, and rate of pay. The name

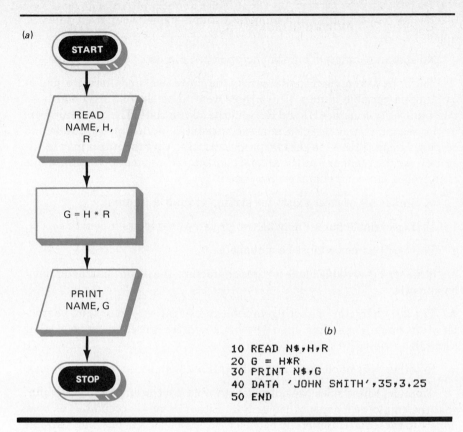

FIGURE 4.1 The flowchart solution depicts the processing of exactly one person's data and is the basis of the BASIC program shown. Note the relationship between (a) the symbols composing the flowchart and (b) the statements of the BASIC program.

```
10 READ N$,H,R
20 G = H*R
30 PRINT N$,G
40 DATA 'JOHN SMITH',35,3.25
50 END
```

is represented as nonnumeric data, whereas the hours worked and pay rate items are numeric data. This distinction between numeric and nonnumeric data items is carried forward to BASIC. The nonnumeric dataname N$ is called a string-variable name, and the numeric H and R are called numeric-variable names. Both numeric- and string-variable names are formed according to specific rules.

The following rules are associated with **numeric-variable names:**

1   Numeric-variable names are one or two characters long.[1]

2   The first or only character of a numeric-variable name must be alphabetic.

---

[1] For consistency and to avoid confusion we have chosen to apply these rules throughout the text. However, many versions of BASIC provide users with special statements that permit the creation of datanames that are longer than two or three elements. These commands vary extensively between manufacturers. Users are free to experiment on their own computers and use datanames of their choice.

3 The second character of a numeric-variable name, when used, must be numeric.

4 No special characters may be incorporated in numeric-variable names.

Both the datanames H and R satisfy the above rules and therefore qualify as numeric-variable names. If two rates were to be used in processing, the numeric-variable names R1 and R2 would be appropriate. The use of numbers as the second characters of a numeric variable is perfectly acceptable and helps distinguish between the two proposed rates. Note that users may legitimately use the number 0 as the second character of a numeric-variable name if and when a second character is desired.

A similar set of rules exists for **string-variable names.**

1 String-variable names may be two or three characters in length.[2]

2 The first character must be alphabetic.

3 If the string-variable name is three characters, the second character must be numeric.

4 The last character of a string-variable name (the second or third character of the name, depending upon whether a number is used) must be a dollar sign ($).

5 No other special characters may be utilized with string-variable names.

Applying these rules, we note that it would have been possible to represent the employee's name as N$ or N4$. Either name is acceptable, as both adhere to these rules. Generally, most users restrict the size of string-variable names to two characters, thus simplifying references to them. We will adhere to this practice in our examples, unless otherwise indicated. Table 4.1 illustrates both valid and invalid forms of both numeric- and string-variable names.

TABLE 4.1   Numeric- and String-Variable Names

Numeric-Variable Names						String-Variable Names					
Valid			**Invalid**			**Valid**			**Invalid**		
B4	G0	X	B@	9Z	3X	A$	B8$	R$	GR$	D?$	BR
Y9	D7	P3	XX	3D	PR	C1$	W$	N$	7C$	ON$	P-$
C	A1	H0	9	15	K—	Z$	M$	L4$	B	$F	CH$

---

[2] See footnote 1.

One rule of thumb is generally applied to the use of *both* types of variable names: never position two alphabetic characters together. Specification of variable names in that way is a definite mistake, resulting in a syntax error. The appearance of datanames such as GR$, BR, NR, or BB$ should alert the student programmer to potential error conditions.

The punctuation used with a READ statement is also quite specific. A comma is the only punctuation employed with READ statements. Note that in line 10, commas are used to separate the variable names. No commas are placed between the READ command and the first variable name following it. The comma following a variable name essentially implies the existence of another variable for which data must be read. Commas follow N$ and H, but not R. The comma following N$ directs the computer to look for H, and the comma following H directs the search for R. A comma is not placed after the numeric variable R, as no additional datanames follow it. To do so would induce a syntax error, and the program would not be processed.

SIDE BAR 4.1   READing Dilemma

The READ statement is one of the principal data-handling statements of BASIC. Because of its operational use and normal placement at the start of a program, its proper specification is critical. If the READ statement is not written properly, the program's processing will quickly end.

To help overcome these types of difficulties, we will point out errors commonly associated with the incorrect READ statements. The following sample statements illustrate four common errors.

```
Error 1: 20    READ N$ H R          ⎫
Error 2: 20    READ N$; H; R        ⎪ These statements
Error 3: 20    READ N$, H, R,       ⎬ are WRONG!
Error 4: 20    READ 'JONES', 40, 2.50 ⎭
```

In error 1, the programmer has omitted the placement of the correct punctuation between variables. Commas should have been positioned after N$ and H. A parallel exists in error 2. Here, incorrect punctuation was used, as semicolons were incorrectly substituted for the required commas.

In error 3, too many commas were used. It is incorrect to place a comma after the last variable of a READ statement, as the computer views that comma as a pointer to another variable, which, in this case, is nonexistent.

The last mistake, error 4, results from carelessness. It is not possible to specify actual data items in a READ statement. READ statements utilize variable names to refer to the actual data items which are specified in DATA statements.

The LET Statement

With the input of data accomplished at line 10, processing operations are undertaken at line 20. Processing activities involving the use of formulas are completed using the **LET statement**.[3] At one time it was necessary to write the command LET into the statement, but recent versions of BASIC have relaxed that requirement. The user is free to insert the word "LET" in the command or omit its usage when writing processing statements. As noted from line 20, we have chosen to omit the word "LET" and will follow this practice throughout the remainder of the text.

Examining line 20, we observe that only one variable is placed to the left of the equal sign. This convention must be followed in BASIC, as any other positioning would result in an error.

Symbolic operators are used in BASIC to denote the fundamental arithmetic operations. Table 4.2 identifies the appropriate BASIC symbols and the arithmetic operations they represent. Exponentiation, raising a number to a power, is represented via the up arrow ($\uparrow$). Accordingly, A^3 (A cubed) is represented by $A \uparrow 3$ (pronounced "A up 3"). The use of these symbols is consistent with our flowcharting discussions where they were incorporated into our formulas.

TABLE 4.2   Arithmetic Symbols Used in BASIC

Operation	Symbol
Exponentiation	$\uparrow$
Multiplication	*
Division	/
Addition	+
Subtraction	−

As only the two numeric variables of H and R were specified in line 20, on the rightside of the equal sign, we did not employ parentheses in the equation. Paralleling our flowcharting discussions, we advise the use of parentheses whenever any doubt exists as to how the formula will be handled. Table 4.3 illustrates some sample formulas and their equivalent in BASIC using parentheses. Future problems will reinforce concepts related to the use of parentheses in computations.

Whenever processing operations are undertaken, the programmer should ensure that datanames are consistently employed. That is, the variable names used to input data should be the same as those used within subsequent processing statements. Thus, if the numeric-variable name R1 is used to input data, the same name must be used within processing statements where needed.

---

[3] LET statements are sometimes referred to as assignment statements, as they use formulas to define relationships between variables. We will use the LET statement reference in our discussions.

TABLE 4.3 Sample Formulas Represented in BASIC

Formula		BASIC Statement
$G = .4 \cdot P + 1.6 \cdot Q$	30	$G = (.4 * P) + (1.6 * Q)$
$A = 3 \cdot C^2 + 12 \cdot C - 4^*$	150	$A = (3 * C * C) + (12 * C) - 4$
	150	$A = (3 * (C \uparrow 2)) + (12 * C) - 4$
$P = 2(1.5 \cdot B + 12.9 \cdot C - 15)/5$	120	$P = 2 * ((1.5 * B) + (12.9 * C) - 15)/5$

* This formula has two correct BASIC statements: one uses asterisks, the other the up arrow for exponentiation.

The computation of G, the gross pay amount, provides the last data item required for output. As shown in the **PRINT statement,** line 30, only two data items are output. The string variable N$ and the numeric variable G follow the PRINT command and direct the output of the employee's name and gross pay. Note the consistent use of these datanames.

Output operations in BASIC are somewhat simplified by its print syntax. BASIC establishes a print area of a specific number of characters and divides that area into a set of major print zones. The size of the print area will vary between the various versions of BASIC that are available today. Print areas generally range between 60 to 80 characters wide and may be divided into four or five zones. For our discussions we will use a print area of 70 characters that is broken into five zones of 14 characters each. The size of other zones and print areas may vary, but the concepts associated with their usage are fairly standard.

The structure of this print area is depicted in Figure 4.2. Each print zone identifies a specific set of print positions into which data is positioned for output. Print positions 1 through 14 are assigned to print zone 1, positions 15 to 28 are assigned to print zone 2, and so on. Each zone is composed of exactly 14 characters; each print position is numbered from 1 through 70.

Access to each zone relates to the punctuation specified in the program's PRINT statement. Let us examine the impact of using commas and semicolons. When used in a PRINT statement, the comma directs that the output proceed to the *first position of the next available print zone.* By contrast, the semicolon directs that the output of data commence with the *next available*

The PRINT Statement

FIGURE 4.2 A BASIC print area composed of five major print zones of 14 characters each. A total of 70 characters, representing 70 print positions, may be printed on a line.

Print Zone 1	Print Zone 2	Print Zone 3	Print Zone 4	Print Zone 5
1 14	15 28	29 42	43 56	57 70

70 Characters wide

print position. With the semicolon, the computer does not advance to the next print zone.

Figure 4.3 shows how different punctuation can affect the output of essentially the same data. For this illustration, assume the N$ represents the name Hardy and G, the amount $125.48. In Figure 4.3*(a)*, the PRINT statement incorporates a comma between the output of N$ and G. As N$ is the first variable to follow the PRINT command, its output is automatically assigned to print zone 1, starting with print position 1. The comma following N$ directs the output of G to the first position of the next zone, print zone 2. Thus, data relating to G will commence output with print position 15, the first position of zone 2.

In Figure 4.3*(a)* HARDY properly occupies the first five print positions of zone 1 and 125.48 correctly occurs in print zone 2. Note, however, that the amount 125.48 is preceded by a blank space and apparently commences with print position 16, not 15 as implied by the use of the comma. This blank is unique to BASIC and requires some explanation.

In actuality, the output of G commences with position 15 — even though it is not filled. In output operations related to numeric variables, BASIC sets aside the first position immediately in front of the number being output. This position is reserved for a minus sign if the number is negative or remains blank if the quantity is positive. In the output shown, print position 15 remains blank as the quantity 125.48 is positive. Had 125.48 been negative, that print position would have been occupied by a minus sign.

In Figure 4.3*(b)* a semicolon was inserted in line 30. Again, data related to N$ is printed in zone 1, as it is the first variable to follow the command PRINT. However, the semicolon following N$ directs the output of G to the next available *print* position, which is position 6. The output of G occupies print positions 6 through 12, with position 6 left blank to accommodate the positive number 125.48.

FIGURE 4.3   The use of the semicolon and the comma in a PRINT statement alter the output it produces. Figure 4.3(*a*) uses a comma, resulting in the output of N$ data into zone 1 and G data in zone 2. Figure 4.3(*b*) uses a semicolon, resulting in the output of both N$ and G data in zone 1. The blank space preceding 125.48 indicates that the number is positive.

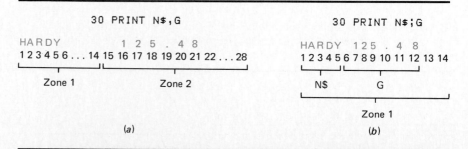

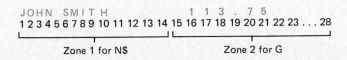

FIGURE 4.4   The output resulting from processing of Problem 4.1. JOHN SMITH occupies the first 10 positions of zone 1, with the gross pay amount of 113.75 positioned in zone 2.

Punctuation enables users to tailor outputs to their needs. The semicolon positions the entire output of N$ and G in print zone 1; these two variables are butted together, one behind the other with no gaps in between. If the user wants to position only one variable in each print zone, the comma is specified. Commas and semicolons may be interspersed within a single PRINT statement to produce stylized outputs. They represent one of the many output techniques available with BASIC that we will review.

Figure 4.4 shows the output from Problem 4.1. The employee's name JOHN SMITH, represented by the string-variable name N$, is outputted in print zone 1. As the entire name is treated as a single item consisting of 10 characters, it will occupy the first 10 positions of print zone 1. The comma preceding G directs its output to zone 2. The gross pay amount of 113.75 commences with print position 15 and extends to position 21; print position 15 is left blank for the possible insertion of a minus sign. The print positions not used within print zones 1 and 2 — that is, 11 to 14 in zone 1 and 22 to 28 in zone 2 — remain blank.

The operational use of commas and semicolons is fairly uniform between most versions of BASIC. In many applications, the use of commas to assign and align data in print zones will suffice. Future discussions will present other output techniques which enable users to embellish their outputs.

Handling Program Data

Referring back to the program in Figure 4.1 we see that the PRINT statement in line 30 is followed by the DATA statement in line 40.

The **DATA statement** follows the general line format adopted for all BASIC statements: the specification of a line number, the command of DATA, and a group of actual data items which correspond to the variables listed in the READ statement. The association of these two statements is not accidental. Whenever a READ statement is used in a program, one or more DATA statements will be required to provide the supporting data. The READ statement cannot be used without its supporting DATA statement.

The operational link of the READ and DATA statements is evident from

---

SIDE BAR 4.2   Moving Data in Print Zones

The PRINT statement uses commas and semicolons to shift output data through the print zones that compose BASIC's print area. Most PRINT statements are uniformly written as follows:

    70   PRINT N$, G, F, N

where the first variable following the command PRINT is assigned to print zone 1. This assignment occurs because no punctuation is placed between the PRINT command and the first variable to be output.

    The question arises as to the validity of the following statement and the output that might result.

    70   PRINT, A, B, C

This instruction is perfectly valid, as BASIC permits punctuation to be positioned after the PRINT command. The placement of this comma would result in the printing of A in zone 2, not in zone 1.

    As no variable follows the command PRINT, the computer reads through the statement and encounters the first comma. It concludes that nothing is to be printed in zone 1 and adheres to the dictates of commas by moving to print zone 2. It outputs A there, printing B and C respectively in zones 3 and 4, as commas were specified. Similarly, examine the impact of the PRINT statement below.

    60   PRINT N$,,G

In this case, N$ is output in zone 1 and G is shifted to zone 3. Commas are an efficient way of moving outputs between zones and may be advantageously used when aligning totals beneath the proper columns of data.

---

the manner in which each specifies its variables or data items. In line 10, we note that the READ statement has specified a string-variable name (N$) followed by two numeric-variable names (H and R). This statement requests the input of an employee's name (nonnumeric data) and the number of hours worked and pay rate of that employee (numeric data). By specifying this sequence of variables, the READ statement dictates the order in which the DATA statement must present those data items. This order of presentation is adhered to in line 40. Three items of data are specified following the required command of DATA, namely, JOHN SMITH, 35, and 3.25. The data item JOHN SMITH is associated with N$, the number 35 with H, and the rate of 3.25 with R.

    The supporting terminology is just as important. Whereas N$ is referred to as a string-variable name, the item 'JOHN SMITH' is defined as a **string-variable data item.** To distinguish it from numeric data, string-variable data is specified within single quotes. These quotes are not printed on output but serve to denote the exact number of characters composing that string-variable data item. From line 40, we determine that 'JOHN SMITH' is a string-variable data item consisting of 10 characters. The blank space between JOHN and SMITH is included in that total of 10 characters, but the quotation marks are not counted.

The maximum size of a string-variable data item is defined by the size of the print zone. The string-variable data item must fit exactly within the print zone and cannot exceed its maximum size. Thus, in our discussion, a string-variable data item may be 14 characters or less, exclusive of its required quotes.[4]

A common error made by beginning BASIC programmers is to confuse the rules associated with string-variable names and data items. Each serves a different purpose and possesses its own syntax. String-variable names are two or three characters in length, require a $ as their last character, and provide a reference to the data undergoing processing. String-variable data items are a maximum of 14 characters (or the equivalent size of a print zone), defined within quotes, and provide a means of designating the actual nonnumeric data items used in processing.

Numeric data items employ a similar logic but possess their own rules of syntax. In a manner similar to handling string variables, numeric-variable names must be matched against numeric data items. Numeric data items are composed of the numbers 0 to 9, decimal points when necessary, and minus signs. They normally range in size from 1 to 7 digits. They are *not* specified in quotes, as that would convert them to nonnumeric, or string-variable data items.

Figure 4.5 depicts the relationship between READ and DATA statements and between string-variable and numeric-variable names and data items. Note that the order of presentation of data items must correspond to that of the datanames in the READ statement.

An important fact to gain from the coordinated usage of lines 10 and 40, the READ and DATA statements of our program solution, is the ordered

```
10 READ N$,H,R

40 DATA 'JOHN SMITH',35,3.25
```

String-Variable Dataname	String-Variable Data Item	Numeric-Variable Dataname	Numeric-Variable Data Item
N$	'JOHN SMITH'	H R	35 3.25

FIGURE 4.5 The order of variables presented in the READ statement defines the sequence of data items specified in the DATA statements.

---

[4] In other versions of BASIC, the size of a string-variable data item can vary, with a potential maximum of 18 characters.

sequence of both variables and data. The order specified with the READ statement line 10, was a string variable name, followed by two numeric variable names. The specification of data within the DATA statement of line 40 was matched against those requirements. The string variable data item of 'JOHN SMITH' had to precede the amounts of 35 and 3.25 representing the numeric data items for H and R. The use of any other order would produce a data error and prevent the processing of the program to completion.

Note also that each data item is separated from the one preceding by a comma. No commas are placed after the last data item of a DATA statement, however. The comma is the only punctuation permitted in a DATA statement.

SIDE BAR 4.3   Data, Data Everywhere . . .

DATA statements suffer from afflictions similar to those encountered with READ statements. Beginning programmers often do not change incorrectly specified DATA statements, believing that the computer will intervene and correct all errors. Nothing could be further from the truth.

The following statements detail errors commonly found in DATA statements.

```
Error 1: 100    DATA 60 81 94    ⎫
Error 2: 100    'SMITH', 40, 2.50  ⎬  These statements are WRONG!
Error 3: 100    DATA 'XXX', 0,    ⎭
```

The initial error statement lacks the correct punctuation. No commas were utilized to separate data items, as required by the syntax for the DATA statement. Commas are the only punctuation used to separate data items.

In error 2, the command DATA is omitted from the statement and invalidates its use, causing an error condition to occur. In error 3, the placement of an additional comma triggers an error state. The computer scans the rest of line 100 for the data item promised by the comma following the numeric data item 0.

The close of a BASIC program is denoted by the **END statement,** as in line 50 of our sample program. No numbers can follow the END statement number. Users who accidentally use line numbers higher than the END statement's line number will find those statements ignored during processing. This restriction does not preclude users from entering new statements after inputting the END statements. It just prevents them from using line numbers that are higher than the END statement's line number. Thus in this case, any statements with line numbers greater than 50 are ignored as they are beyond the END statement's line number. Another unusual feature of the END statement is its lack of a variable. The END statement is one of the few BASIC instructions that does not use a variable.

PROBLEM 4.2   Student Average

Input to the problem are the student's name and three test grades. The student average is computed by adding the three grades and dividing that sum by 3. Output the student's name, the three test grades, and the computed average. Add a descriptive note to the flowchart and program solution to identify the problem. The data used in the problem follows:

Student	Grade 1	Grade 2	Grade 3
G. HOPE	79	72	68

These are the main points in the problem narrative.

1   A descriptive comment placed in the program and flowchart solution will identify the problem.

2   No headings are required.

3   Input includes the student's name and three test grades, which should carry their own unique data names.

4   The computation of the student average will use the formula:

Average = (grade 1 + grade 2 + grade 3)/3

5   Output the student's name, the three grades, and the computed average.

6   Only one student's data is processed.

The flowchart and BASIC program for Problem 4.2 are presented in Figure 4.6.

Analyzing the flowchart solution, we note that an annotation symbol is attached to the opening READ symbol. The annotation symbol is used to add descriptive commentary to the flowchart to help subsequent users. Comments of this type are frequently added to both flowcharts and program solutions to help comprehension or advise of special conditions.

The remainder of the flowchart is similar to other problems we have reviewed. The opening READ symbol details the input of a student's name and three grades, each possessing its own dataname. The computation of the average precedes the output of all five data items.

The translation of the flowchart solution into a BASIC program is also shown in Figure 4.6. The first line of this program corresponds to the advisory comment in the flowchart's annotation symbol. This instruction, referred to as a **REMARK statement,** identifies the fact that this solution relates to a student average program. When writing this instruction, the letters REM are sufficient to identify the REMARK statement.

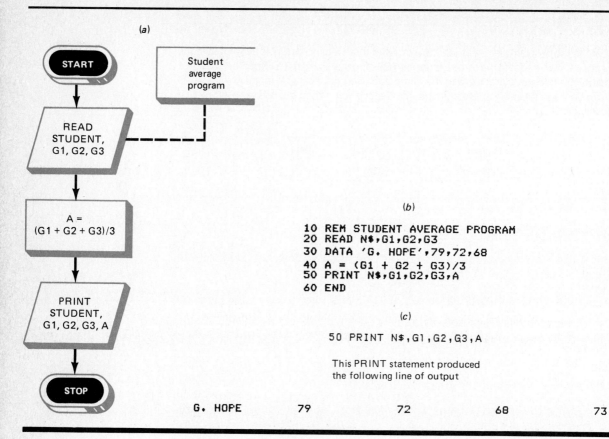

(a)

(b)

```
10 REM STUDENT AVERAGE PROGRAM
20 READ N$,G1,G2,G3
30 DATA 'G. HOPE',79,72,68
40 A = (G1 + G2 + G3)/3
50 PRINT N$,G1,G2,G3,A
60 END
```

(c)

```
50 PRINT N$,G1,G2,G3,A
```

This PRINT statement produced
the following line of output

```
G. HOPE        79            72            68            73
```

FIGURE 4.6   *(a)* Flowchart and *(b)* BASIC program for Problem 4.2. Note the use of the annotation symbol in the flowchart and the placement of the DATA statement in the program solution. *(c)* The output resulting from Problem 4.2. Each output item is assigned to its respective print zone through the use of commas in the PRINT statement of the program.

With the REM statement, a line number must be specified. The user is free to write any desired comment following the REM command, consisting of any combination of characters. Any advisory comment added via the REM instruction will have no effect on the program in which it is written other than to advise users of a special fact or condition.

One point should be noted regarding the REMARK statement. Some versions of BASIC require that users use only the characters REM when specifying the REMARK statement. The use of the full REMARK command will result in errors in those cases and prevent the program from running. We will use the universally accepted REM command in our discussions.

Following the REM statement at line 10, the actual processing of data commences. The READ statement at line 20 directs the input of the student's name via the string-variable name N$ and the entry of the three grades represented by the numeric-variable names G1, G2, and G3. The three numeric-variable names are necessary to refer to the three individual data items which are utilized in processing. In line 20, commas are properly utilized to separate the variables undergoing input.

The actual data items used in processing are specified in the DATA statement, line 30. The student name of 'G. HOPE' is correctly specified as a string-variable data item and followed by the grades of 79, 72, and 68. The order used in line 30 parallels the sequence of variables used in line 20, the READ statement. This statement specifies a string-variable name followed by three numeric-variable names and thus dictates the order in which the actual data items are written. Within line 30, commas were used to separate the four data items specified.

An additional fact to be drawn from line 30 is the positioning of the DATA statement. In this program, the placement of the lone DATA statement was advanced and placed after the READ statement. This relocation emphasizes the fact that DATA statements may be positioned anywhere in a program, prior to the END statement.

With the data input via lines 20 and 30, processing may commence. The actual computation of the average, A, is accomplished via line 40. In this statement, the three grades are added and that sum divided by 3. The use of parentheses ensures that G1, G2, and G3 are totalled before that sum is divided by 3. Again, only one variable, A, is positioned to the left of the equal sign.

The output of all data items is revealed in the PRINT statement, line 50. Here, all five variables are outputted at one time on one line. Because the comma is used this PRINT statement will assign one variable to each of the five major print zones. Each variable will commence its output at the first position of each major print zone. The resultant output from this program is also illustrated in Figure 4.6.

The output of the PRINT statement precedes the close of the program. The END statement, line 60, indicates that no further processing will be accomplished.

4.3 The Looping Process

As we discussed in flowcharting concepts, the ability to repeatedly perform processing operations via a flowchart loop is critical to computerized activities. The conversion of the flowchart loop to software results in the creation of the **program loop,** which permits a series of instructions to be repeatedly executed.

When there is a looping sequence in a program the user must be able to control it. The two principal means of controlling the flowchart loop are the last-record check (LRC) and the 9s decision. Both permit the looping sequence to continue until the last record is processed and the loop ended. The 9s decision, a special case of the LRC, responds to the existence of a specially coded data item which indicates that the last data record has been processed.

To use these two flowchart techniques, the programmer must convert them to their program equivalents. This is not as easy as it sounds, as each language handles these decisions differently. For example, the 9s decision is readily converted to a program instruction, since it is represented as a logical operation. However, the LRC is not so easily converted. Though other languages possess a built-in last-record-check sensing feature when reading data within a program, BASIC does not. However, as the 9s decision is as easily used, our writing of program solutions is not hindered.

Conditional Branching

The vehicle for writing conditional statements in BASIC is the **IF/THEN statement:** "IF this condition occurs, THEN go to that line number." For example: the format of the IF/THEN statement used in conditional testing is as follows:

XXX   IF _____ THEN _____

line   conditional   line
number   statement   number

Within this format, the first line number is used to identify the logical position of the IF/THEN statement within the entire program. The terms IF and THEN are required phrases within the structure of the IF/THEN statement. The logical operation being tested against is written as the conditional statement and represents the focal point of the instruction.

The line number at the end of the IF/THEN format identifies the line that the program will branch to — the line that is the equivalent of the conditional statement's YES branch — if the indicated condition is met.

Incorporating the components of the 9s decision into an IF/THEN format produces the following sample instruction:

40   IF H $= -99.99$ THEN 300

This IF/THEN statement is identified as line 40. The conditional statement H $= -99.99$ is the 9s decision used to test for that specially coded data. When H $= -99.99$, the program will branch to line 300 (the equivalent of the YES branch). If H is *not* equal to -99.99, the program will *not* branch to 300 but advance to the statement immediately following line 40. The branch to the statement following line 40 is the equivalent of the NO branch and usually leads to the normal flow of processing inside the loop.

Accompanying the IF/THEN statement representing the 9s decision is a DATA statement which contains the 9s data for that test. The 9s DATA statement is positioned behind all other DATA statements, so that it is read as the last data record. The program must read through all DATA statements ahead of the 9s data to reach it. Thus, when the 9s data is read, all prior data items have been processed and the program loop may be brought to a close.

Conditional testing is accomplished via the IF/THEN statement. Unconditional branching operations are handled in BASIC via the **GO TO statement.** The general format of the GO TO instruction is:

XXX   GO TO   XXX

line   line

number   number

The opening line number of the GO TO statement notes its position in the source program. The terms GO TO act as the instruction's command, defining its operational purpose. The line number after the GO TO notes the statement to unconditionally branch to when that instruction is executed.

To focus on the impact of these conditional branching instructions, one must see them used in a programming exercise. Let us incorporate a 9s decision and program-looping sequence into the solution developed for Problem 4.2. Additional data items are added for the program loop, as is a 9s DATA statement. The flowchart and BASIC program for this updated solution are illustrated in Figure 4.7.

Reviewing the flowchart, we note the insertion of the 9s decision after the opening READ symbol and the unconditional branch back to the I/O symbol to complete the flowchart loop. The NO branch of the 9s decision leads to the normal flow of processing inside the loop. The YES branch exits the looping sequence and closes the flowchart. When writing the source program, the 9s decision and unconditional branch are converted to their BASIC equivalents via the IF/THEN and GO TO statements.

How these statements are incorporated into our previous solution for Problem 4.2 is evident in Figure 4.7. The program opens with a REM instruction, line 10, which advises that the program solution now incorporates a 9s decision. This advisory comment is followed by line 20, a READ statement, which enters the student's name (N$) and the three test grades used to compute an average (G1, G2, and G3).

Paralleling our flowchart solution, the instruction following the READ statement relates to the 9s decision. Using the format of the IF/THEN statement, line 30 of the program tests the numeric variable G3 against a value of -999. If G3 equals -999, the program will branch to line 200, execute the END statement, and close processing. If G3 is not equal to -999, the program does not exit the loop but continues on to line 40 — the statement immediately after line 30.

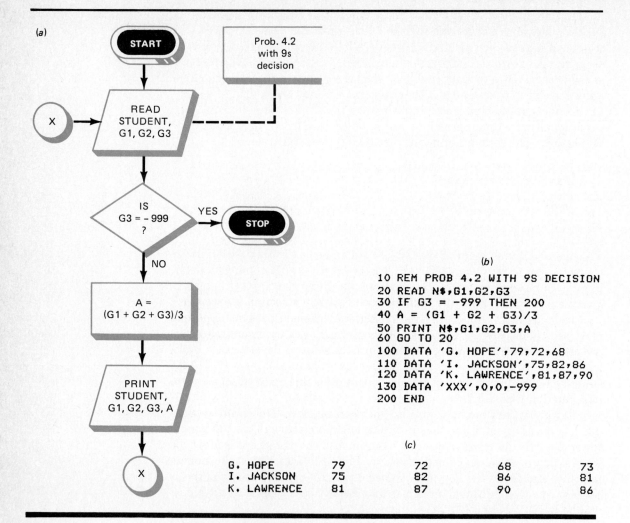

FIGURE 4.7 *(a)* Flowchart and *(b)* program for Problem 4.2. A looping sequence makes possible the repeated processing of data. A loop under control of a 9s decision is incorporated into a revised version of the program written for Problem 4.2. *(c)* The output for Problem 4.2 consists of three lines spanning five print zones. The 9s data is not outputted.

At line 30, we choose to use the numeric variable G3 as the basis for our 9s decision. Though G3 was used, any of the other two numeric variables could have been as easily used to test for the −999 data. When writing the 9s decision IF/THEN statement, unless otherwise stipulated, the programmer is free to use any variable appearing within the preceding READ statement. If either G1 or G2 were incorporated into line 40, those statements would have assumed the following formats.

```
30     IF G1 = −999 THEN 200
30     IF G2 = −999 THEN 200
```

Either of these two statements could have been satisfactorily substituted for the current line 30 of the existing program solution.

The computation of the student's average grade at line 40 follows the IF/THEN statement. We should carefully examine the proper use of parentheses in this LET statement. Their positioning around the addition of the three grades ensures that they are added before that sum is divided by 3. The resulting average, identified by the numeric variable A, is positioned to the left of the formula's equal sign.

The output of this program results from the PRINT statement at line 50. Exactly five variables are outputted. The use of commas ensures that one variable will be assigned to each of the major print zones. The string variable N$ is assigned to zone 1, with the numeric variables G1, G2, and G3 printed in zones 2, 3 and 4, respectively. The computed average A is printed in zone 5, the last print zone on that line of output.

The output of the five variables represents the last processing operation of that program loop and precedes the unconditional branch to the top of the loop. The GO TO statement at line 60 results in the unconditional branch to the READ statement at line 20. The execution of line 20 inputs the next set of student data and continues the looping sequence. The loop is designed to continue until the 9s data, G3 = −999, is encountered, thus triggering the exit from the loop.

The DATA statements used in this program appear at lines 100 to 130. Statements 100 to 120 represent the type of student data that would be processed in a normal looping sequence. Though only three sets of data are employed, they are sufficient to illustrate the impact of a looping sequence. Essentially, if the loop works with two or more sets of values, it will adequately serve any amount of data.

The presentation of the individual data items within the program's DATA statements parallels the datanames in the READ statement, line 20. The string-variable and numeric-variable names of line 20 properly align with their respective data items in lines 100 to 130. This alignment ensures that G. HOPE is inputted for N$ and 79, 72, and 68 are respectively assigned to G1, G2, and G3. The data contained within line 100 is correctly associated with its intended variables. The DATA statements of lines 110 and 120 are similarly processed, thus inputting grades data related to 'I. JACKSON' and 'K. LAWRENCE'.

The order of data items must be also adhered to in line 130, the DATA statement containing the 9s data. Line 130's purpose is to provide the 9s data for the 9s decision at line 30 and permit the program to properly end the looping sequence without error. For the string-variable name N$, a string-variable data item of 'XXX' is specified. The use of a data item of 'XXX' is deliberate, as it serves to note the fictitious nature of that data entry. Data items of this nature are referred to as **dummy data items,** as they fill required data fields in a way that will not adversely affect processing. The same logic is used when filling the data slots for G1 and G2. The dummy data used for both numeric variables is 0. Dummy data must be provided for N$, G1 and G2 in order that the computer properly access the −999 data for G3. Without the specification of 'XXX', 0, 0, in line 130, the 9s data would not be properly read.

Many beginning programmers believe that the program will account for any potential data error, seek out the 9s data, and properly end the program without error. This is a common misconception. The 9s data of −999 must be aligned with input of data for the G3 variable; otherwise the 9s decision will be incorrectly performed. Samples of four incorrectly written DATA statements follow, each resulting in an error and the aborting the 9s decision.

```
130    DATA −999
130    DATA 'XXX', −999        These statements are incorrectly
130    DATA 'XXX', 0, −999     written for this program.
130    DATA 'XXX', 0, 0
```

In each case, an insufficient amount of data is provided. A total of four data items are required to satisfy the READ statement (line 20) and provide G3 with its value of −999.

The result of properly implementing the 9s decision via the IF/THEN statement and program loop is evident in the output produced (see Figure 4.7). Exactly three lines of output are printed, one line for each of the three student DATA statements specified. The 9s data is not outputted because of the positioning of the IF/THEN statement representing the 9s decision at line 30. The 9s data input at the READ statement (line 20) is immediately checked by the IF/THEN statement (line 30). If it is the 9s data, the loop is exited and the program branches to line 200. No other data items preceding the 9s data activate that decision. The 9s data was not designed to enter processing.

Some readers may also question the sequence of line numbers employed in our program. An attempt was made to distinguish between the various components of our solution by using different sets of line numbers. The main portion of our program used line numbers 10 through 60. To help distinguish them, the DATA statements were grouped as statements 100 to 130. The END statement, which closes this revised version of Problem 4.2, was assigned line number 200. This placement of the END statement ensures that all other program statements appear well before its line number.

Printing Literals　　Notice the absence of column headings in Figure 4.7. In our discussion of flowcharts we observed that column headings and labels are vital output features, as they provide a means of identifying the information generated by program outputs. As with flowcharts, BASIC can generate these outputs via literals defined within quotation marks in PRINT statements.

SIDE BAR 4.4   Spelling Counts

The IF/THEN statement is a principal instruction of BASIC programs, as it supports the testing of variables in conditional operations. Common errors related to IF/THEN statements occur in the spelling and punctuation used when it is specified.

Many students initially write the IF/THEN as follows:

    30   IF X = −999 THAN 600   (Wrong!)

and wonder why the BASIC compiler rejects it as incorrect. The misspelling of THEN is the reason. The correct term is THEN, *not THAN*. It is essential that statements be properly written if you want the programs to run.

A second error commonly related to the IF/THEN statement is

    30   IF R = −99.99, THEN 600   (Wrong!)

This line includes punctuation that is not part of the statement's syntax. The insertion of a comma is a common error and relates to the preparation of conditional statements when writing conventional English grammar. The insertion of a comma might satisfy a grammatical need but is definitely incorrect for BASIC.

We could embellish the output of Problem 4.2 by adding column headings. This additional output could be created by adding the following PRINT statement to the solution appearing in Figure 4.7.

    15   PRINT 'STUDENT', 'GRADE1', 'GRADE2', 'GRADE3', 'AVG'

This statement would be inserted between lines 10 and 20, resulting in the output of a string of five literals to compose five column headings. The seven-character literal 'STUDENT' will occupy the first seven positions of zone 1. The use of commas will subsequently assign each of the following literals to print zones 2 to 5. The literals 'GRADE1', 'GRADE2', 'GRADE3', and 'AVG' are output, commencing with the first print positions of zones 2, 3, 4, and 5, and appear as headings atop each column of data.

Special labels are as easily created. The PRINT statement which follows could have appeared at the end of Problem 4.2.

    200   PRINT 'PROCESSING IS COMPLETE'

This statement would displace the END statement from line 200 and reposition it at line 210. This 22-character literal would appear beneath the last student's data item and denote the end of processing.

The reconstruction of the revised solution for Problem 4.2 is shown in Figure 4.8; depicted are the flowchart, BASIC program, and output. The flowchart notes the inclusion of the PRINT symbols creating the column headings and closing label. The PRINT symbol for the column heading is properly placed before the start of the looping sequence. The closing literal is

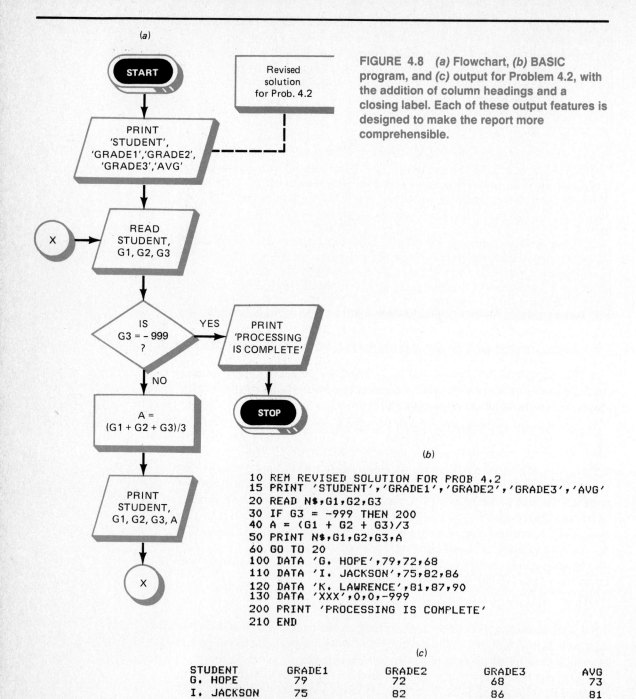

(a)

START

Revised
solution
for Prob. 4.2

PRINT
'STUDENT',
'GRADE1','GRADE2',
'GRADE3','AVG'

X → READ
STUDENT,
G1, G2, G3

IS
G3 = – 999
?   —YES→   PRINT
'PROCESSING
IS COMPLETE'

NO

A =
(G1 + G2 + G3)/3

STOP

PRINT
STUDENT,
G1, G2, G3, A

X

FIGURE 4.8 *(a)* Flowchart, *(b)* BASIC program, and *(c)* output for Problem 4.2, with the addition of column headings and a closing label. Each of these output features is designed to make the report more comprehensible.

(b)

```
10 REM REVISED SOLUTION FOR PROB 4.2
15 PRINT 'STUDENT','GRADE1','GRADE2','GRADE3','AVG'
20 READ N$,G1,G2,G3
30 IF G3 = -999 THEN 200
40 A = (G1 + G2 + G3)/3
50 PRINT N$,G1,G2,G3,A
60 GO TO 20
100 DATA 'G. HOPE',79,72,68
110 DATA 'I. JACKSON',75,82,86
120 DATA 'K. LAWRENCE',81,87,90
130 DATA 'XXX',0,0,-999
200 PRINT 'PROCESSING IS COMPLETE'
210 END
```

(c)

STUDENT	GRADE1	GRADE2	GRADE3	AVG
G. HOPE	79	72	68	73
I. JACKSON	75	82	86	81
K. LAWRENCE	81	87	90	86
PROCESSING IS COMPLETE				

positioned on the YES branch of the 9s decision, after the flowchart loop and before the flowchart's close.

These output operations are incorporated in the BASIC program at lines 15 and 200. The PRINT statement at line 15 produces the five column headings. The closing literal results from the execution of line 200. This closing label 'PROCESSING IS COMPLETE' will occupy all of zone 1 and part of zone 2 when output. Literals may exceed the size of print zones without requiring special punctuation.

Figure 4.8 depicts the output resulting from processing this program. Each student's data is properly positioned beneath the appropriate column headings. A total of five lines of output are printed. The top line represents the column headings, the next three lines relate to student data, and the last line of output display the closing literal. The 9s data is not outputted because of the logic used in this program's solution. Additional problems will reinforce the use of looping sequences and the output of literals.

PROBLEM 4.3   Baseball League Stats

The final report requires column headings of 'TEAM', 'WON', 'LOST', and 'PCT'. Input are each team's name and the number of games won and lost. A team's winning percentage is calculated by dividing the number of games won by the total number of games played by that team. The total games played is determined by adding a team's games won and lost. Output each team's name, games won, games lost, and winning percentage on each loop beneath their proper column headings. After printing the last team's statistics, print out a label which states 'LEAGUE DATA ENDS'. Use a 9s decision to control processing. The data used in this problem is as follows:

Team	Games Won	Games Lost
Astros	20	6
Bullets	17	9
Cayotes	15	11
Devils	8	18
Eagles	0	26

These are the main points in the problem narrative.

1 A descriptive comment is required to identify the program.

2 A heading consisting of four literals is required to create column headings.

3 Input are each team's name, games won, and games lost.

4 A 9s decision is required to control the looping sequence.

5   The formulas necessary to support processing are

a   Total games = games won + games lost
b   Winning percentage = games won/total games

6   Output on each loop the team's name, games won, games lost, and the computed winning percentage.

7   After processing the last data item, output the label 'LEAGUE DATA ENDS'.

8   Data for five teams is involved.

The flowchart and BASIC program prepared for Problem 4.3 are shown in Figure 4.9.

The flowchart for Problem 4.3 is designed to handle the data related to five teams. After the opening START symbol, a PRINT symbol details the output of the four literals which create the required column headings. An annotation symbol advises of the handling of baseball standings. The READ symbol opens the flowchart loop, immediately followed by a 9s decision, which controls the looping sequence.

The NO branch of the 9s decision leads to the computation of a team's winning percentage. Two processing operations are indicated: the first computes the total number of games played by a team, and the second computes its winning percentage. The output of the team's name, games won, games lost, and winning percentage is noted by the PRINT symbol at the loop's bottom. Two connectors identify the unconditional branch to the READ symbol, thus restarting the loop and processing the next team's data.

The YES branch of the 9s decision causes processing to exit the loop and output the closing special label. Then the flowchart ends at its STOP symbol.

The BASIC program naturally follows the logic developed in this flowchart. A REMARK statement opens the program at line 10. The PRINT statement, line 20, will generate the four column headings required by the problem. The use of commas successively assigns each literal to the first four print zones. Each literal is defined by single quotation marks.

The input of a team's data is accomplished via line 30, the READ statement. The sequence of variables is string variable (T$), numeric variable (W), and numeric variable (L). This sequence defines the format of the DATA statements described in lines 100 to 150. Each of the five teams has its own DATA statement which specifies its name, games won, and games lost.

The last DATA statement, line 160, is reserved solely for the 9s decision. It is read after all other data items are processed and enables the program to exit the loop. The IF/THEN statement at line 40 directs that when W equals −99, the program should branch to line 200 and print the closing literal, 'LEAGUE DATA ENDS'. For the first five loops, however, the program proceeds to line 50 to accomplish its processing.

We have chosen to use two statements to compute a team's winning percentage. At line 50, the total number of games played by a team (T) is

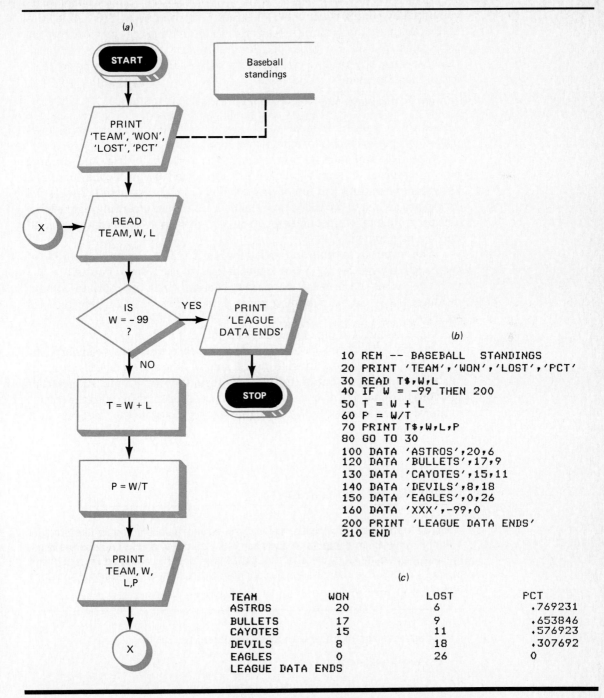

(a)

```
10 REM -- BASEBALL  STANDINGS
20 PRINT 'TEAM','WON','LOST','PCT'
30 READ T$,W,L
40 IF W = -99 THEN 200
50 T = W + L
60 P = W/T
70 PRINT T$,W,L,P
80 GO TO 30
100 DATA 'ASTROS',20,6
120 DATA 'BULLETS',17,9
130 DATA 'CAYOTES',15,11
140 DATA 'DEVILS',8,18
150 DATA 'EAGLES',0,26
160 DATA 'XXX',-99,0
200 PRINT 'LEAGUE DATA ENDS'
210 END
```

(b)

(c)

TEAM	WON	LOST	PCT
ASTROS	20	6	.769231
BULLETS	17	9	.653846
CAYOTES	15	11	.576923
DEVILS	8	18	.307692
EAGLES	0	26	0
LEAGUE DATA ENDS			

FIGURE 4.9 (a) Flowchart, (b) program, and (c) output for Problem 4.3. The output prepared from this program uses headings and a special label.

computed by adding the number of games won (W) and lost (L). Line 60 is used to compute the winning percentage (P) by dividing the games won by the total games played. For those people that prefer a more compact computational scheme, the formula which follows will calculate the winning percentage in one statement.

    50   P = W/(W + L)

This latter formula replaces the need to compute T, the total number of games played by a team. Either computational approach is valid.

The output of each team's name, games won, games lost, and winning percentage occurs at line 70. Each output is assigned to a print zone, matching the column headings printed at line 20. The GO TO instruction directs the flow of processing to the READ statement at line 30, thus continuing the loop. The program loop of lines 30 through 80 continues until the 9s data is sensed and the loop exited.

The output from this program is shown in Figure 4.9. Note the position of each heading and the way print zones help align each item of output.

The teams' data items are output beneath their appropriate column headings, each output spanning zones 1 to 4. The close of processing is signaled by the printing of the special label 'LEAGUE DATA ENDS'. A total of six lines of printed data composes the output for Problem 4.3.

In addition to their successful use in report formats, literals can highlight individual items of data. In these cases, special labels precede the output of variables, drawing attention to the data items following them. As noted in previous flowcharting discussions, it is acceptable to combine both the output of literals and variables on the same line. Let us illustrate the prior point via an example.

PROBLEM 4.4   Solving for Y

Input on each loop is a value of X. This value is substituted in the formula $Y = X^2 - 8X + 12$ to compute Y. On each loop, output X and Y on separate lines. Precede the output of X by the label 'VALUE OF X =' and the computed value of Y with the label 'Y VALUE ='. Use a looping sequence controlled by a 9s decision. The values of X are 0, 2, 4, 6, and 8.

These are the main points in the problem narrative.

1   No headings are required.

2   A single value of X is inputted on each loop.

3   The formula used in processing is:

$$Y = (X * X) - (8 * X) + 12$$

4   Output X and Y on separate lines in each loop, using the labels 'VALUE OF X =' for X and 'Y VALUE =' for Y.

5   A 9s decision is used to control looping.

The flowchart and program solution prepared for Problem 4.4 are detailed in Figure 4.10.

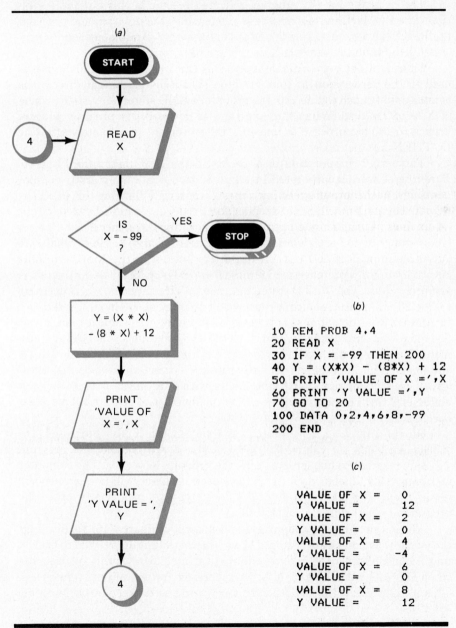

(a)

(b)

```
10 REM PROB 4.4
20 READ X
30 IF X = -99 THEN 200
40 Y = (X*X) - (8*X) + 12
50 PRINT 'VALUE OF X =',X
60 PRINT 'Y VALUE =',Y
70 GO TO 20
100 DATA 0,2,4,6,8,-99
200 END
```

(c)

```
VALUE OF X =      0
Y VALUE =         12
VALUE OF X =      2
Y VALUE =         0
VALUE OF X =      4
Y VALUE =        -4
VALUE OF X =      6
Y VALUE =         0
VALUE OF X =      8
Y VALUE =         12
```

FIGURE 4.10
(a) Flowchart and *(b)* program for Problem 4.4. In this solution, only one variable is input and used with the 9s decision. Separate lines of output are employed with each variable. *(c)* The output from Problem 4.4 consists of five sets of data. Each output grouping possesses two lines — one for the X value and one for each Y value. The −99 value, inserted for use with the 9s decision, is not printed.

The flowchart demonstrates a looping sequence controlled via a 9s decision involving the numeric variable X. The NO branch of the 9s decision leads to the computation of Y, and the YES branch indicates the flowchart's close. After computing the Y value, the output of both X and Y is directed. Each variable is output on a separate line, preceded by its own special label.

The resulting BASIC program reflects the logic of this flowchart solution. The REMark statement at line 10 identifies the program and precedes the READ statement at line 20. Note that the only variable needed for processing, the numeric variable X, is read on each loop.

Since X is the only variable input, it is the only variable which may be used in the 9s decision at line 30. This IF/THEN statement directs the computer to branch to line 200, the program's END statement, when a value of X = −99 is read. When the −99 value is not read, the program will not branch to 200 but proceed to line 40 — the statement immediately after the IF/THEN instruction.

The actual computation of Y occurs in the LET instruction, line 40. Parentheses were incorporated into line 40 to operationally group components within the formula used and ensure accuracy. Following this logic, the (X * X) component will have (8 * X) subtracted from it and 12 added to that result. Both X and Y are outputted at lines 50 and 60, respectively. Special labels designed for each variable precede both X and Y. Both labels are outputted in print zone 1 of their respective lines, with the X or Y variable output in zone 2. Commas used in lines 50 and 60 help align the output of the X and Y values. The GO TO statement, line 70, directs the flow of processing to line 20, where the loop continues with the entry of the next X value.

Exactly five data items are processed before the −99 value is read. These five data items are defined within line 100, the program's sole DATA statement. For expediency we have placed all of the data items into one DATA statement. This approach is perfectly safe and correct and avoids the necessity to use six separate DATA statements, with only one data item listed per statement. Such an approach would be inefficient and require the needless specification of extra DATA statements.

On the first loop, a value of 0 is inputted for X and processed. On subsequent loops, the values of 2, 4, 6, 8, and −99 are handled. The program will only read one value per loop until the program loop ends. The computer will keep track of what data items have been used and will not erroneously reread them. The specification of DATA statements is normally left to the programmer, who will efficiently utilize them.

The output from Problem 4.4 is also shown in Figure 4.10. No headings are evident, as none were required. Two lines of output are related to each X and Y value. A total of 10 lines of output are printed. As the program branches when the −99 value is read, it is not processed and no outputs relate to it. This is exactly how the 9s decision should work, as directed by our program solution.

4.4 Additional Statements

In our previous illustrations we utilized the combined resources of the READ and DATA statements to provide the data items involved in processing. These statements enabled us to recognize the coordinated nature of variable names and the actual data items they represent. We learned that string-variable names must be aligned with string-variable data items and numeric-variable data items are specified with numeric-variable names.

Interactive Inputs

Though READ and DATA statements are satisfactory for some applications, they are not suited to every problem. On occasion users want to interact with the computer and input data that varies for each application. Data input for one problem may not be usable for the next processing of the same program. Also, users may want to key in their data from the keyboard of an online terminal and obtain an immediate response to their processing needs. The combined use of the READ and DATA statements is often too cumbersome for this purpose.

The BASIC statement introduced to satisfy the need for an online entry is the **INPUT statement.** This instruction enables users to enter one or more data items via an online keyboard and effectively replaces the teamed use of the READ and DATA statements. The INPUT statement is not used with either READ or DATA statements. The structure of the INPUT statement follows BASIC's general line format and may appear as follows:

```
20      INPUT N$, G1, G2, G3
```

This sample instruction is representative of the INPUT statement's format. A line number of 20 is indicated and followed by the command INPUT. This command is followed by the variables to be input — in this case, one string variable and three numeric variables. Commas are used to distinguish between variables in the INPUT statement.

The major operational difference in using the INPUT statement occurs when that instruction is executed. The program literally requests the entry of data from the user, while the program is undergoing processing. To observe how the INPUT statement is used, let us examine Figure 4.11.

Figure 4.11(a) shows a program excerpt of three statements: the INPUT statement and the processing of data entered with that statement. After inputting data at line 30, the data items are added (line 40) and outputted (line 50). In Figure 4.11(b), the output of executing lines 30, 40, and 50 is depicted and illustrates those differences related to INPUT statements.

The INPUT statement is an interactive statement, requesting data from the user. As such, it must prompt the user to key in data. BASIC uses the question mark for this purpose, printing a ? when the INPUT statement is actually processed and data should be keyed in. The ? is output and then the computer waits for the required data items to be entered.

FIGURE 4.11 INPUT
statements handle
data in a markedly
different fashion from
READ statements. The
statements composing
(a) the program
excerpt will produce
(b) the output.

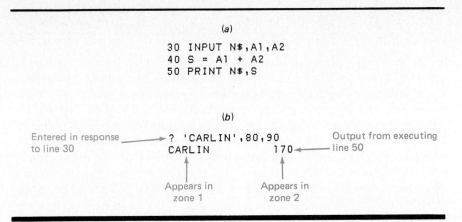

(a)

```
30 INPUT N$,A1,A2
40 S = A1 + A2
50 PRINT N$,S
```

(b)

Entered in response → ? 'CARLIN',80,90   Output from executing
to line 30   CARLIN   170 ← line 50

Appears in   Appears in
zone 1   zone 2

In this latter sense, the INPUT statement is similar to the READ and DATA statements. The data keyed in must match the order of the requesting INPUT statement. In line 30, the INPUT statement specifies a string variable (N$), followed by two numeric variables (A1 and A2). That is the exact order in which the data items must be entered.

Reexamining Figure 4.11*(b)*, we may observe the adherence to that sequence. The ? was used to alert the user to the need to key in data. The data item 'CARLIN' was entered for N$, with 80 and 90 keyed for A1 and A2. The sequence defined by line 30 dictates the order of the data input.

Users initially using the INPUT statement make a common error when they want to enter the word DATA following the prompting question mark. This should not be done, as it would result in an error serious enough to stop the program's processing. The command DATA is not keyed in when the INPUT statement is used.

The second line of Figure 4.11*(b)* illustrates the output that would follow the data keyed in response to the INPUT statement. Line 50 of our program excerpt directs that we output N$ and S, where S represents the sum of A1 and A2. This PRINT statement directs the N$ data, 'CARLIN', to print zone 1 and the value of S, 170, to zone 2. The data keyed in and the resulting output would appear on consecutive lines, as the program does not separate the entry of data and the outputs which follow it.

To further examine the impact of the INPUT statement, let us apply it to our program solution for Problem 4.4. Figure 4.12*(a)* shows the original program and output for this problem using READ and DATA statements. In Figure 4.12*(b)* a new solution is presented — one in which an INPUT statement is used. The program appears substantially the same as the original, except for the absence of line 100. The DATA statement is not needed, as the required data will be supplied when the INPUT statement is executed. This mode of data entry is observed in the output. Here, three lines of output result for each value processed. The computer uses ? to request data for the value of X; the next two lines reflect the execution of lines 50 and 60 of the program using the same output format as the original program. The major difference between the two outputs is the extra line used to record the entry of data for the INPUT statement, line 20 of the solution in Figure 4.12(b).

In substituting an INPUT statement for the READ and DATA statements, we note that this modification has no effect on the looping sequence or the execution of the 9s decision. When the −99 value is input, the program completes processing and ends, as per the instructions in line 30 of both programs. The entry of the −99 data item was recorded as part of the program's output, since it was keyed in. This output will always result, as the 9s data is entered in response to the INPUT statement and characteristic of the INPUT statement.

In examining Figure 4.12(b), we note a potential drawback of the INPUT statement. Some users believe that the prompting ? is not sufficient advisory

FIGURE 4.12 Two solutions to Problem 4.4. (a) Program and output using READ and DATA statements. (b) Program and output using an INPUT statement. Note the absence of line 100 and the extra line of output in version (b).

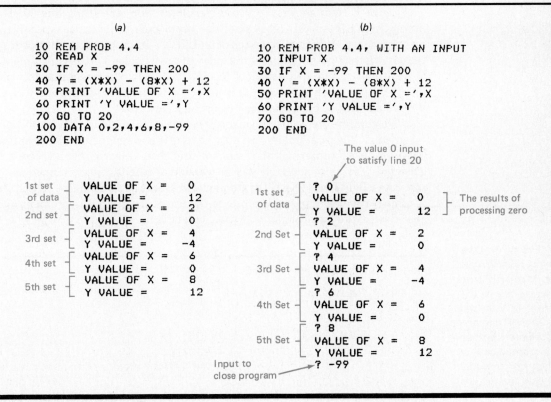

guidance to the user in that it does not remind the user of what data to key in. They believe that the user should be continually reminded of what data to enter and that the reminder should take the form of a message. This can be accomplished through the combined use of a PRINT and INPUT statement. The PRINT statement will generate the prompting literal, with the INPUT statement handling the actual entry of data.

Figure 4.13 illustrates the integrated use of these two statements and the output resulting from their execution. Statements 30 and 40 define back-to-back PRINT and INPUT statements. Line 30 generates a prompting literal of 'ENTER A VALUE FOR X' which is output on a line above ? where the value of 0 is input. Note that the literal and ? appear on two different lines, as they are generated by separate statements. These two lines would be printed each time a loop is executed.

Some versions of BASIC offer a slightly different approach to the same situation, where the prompting literal is incorporated directly into the INPUT statement. Instead of requiring two distinct statements, only one instruction is necessary. A sample of this alternative type of INPUT statement is shown in Figure 4.14(a). The literal becomes part of the instruction. It is created by a pair of quotes in the instruction and precedes the variable (or variables) to be input. Here, the required punctuation is a semicolon. The literal serves to advise the user of what data to enter.

Figure 4.14(b) shows the output resultant from executing line 30. The literal 'ENTER A VALUE FOR X' is output before the appearance of the question mark, denoting the usage of an INPUT instruction. Both appear on the same line of output, as does the entry of the 0 value to processing. Instead of printing two lines, this form of the INPUT instruction requires only one line of output when executed. This may be a valuable consideration when a limited amount of data must be output on a terminal.

We caution the reader regarding the use of this version of the INPUT instruction. This statement may only be used if it is supported. The user may test for its use by entering this statement and observing whether it is properly executed. If it is not available in your version of BASIC, the combined use of separate PRINT and INPUT statements will serve as an adequate substitute. An illustrative example will reinforce the use of the INPUT statement and, specifically, the latter version of that instruction.

FIGURE 4.13 One way of prompting a user to enter the right data, via the INPUT statement, is by placing a PRINT statement immediately before it. This instructional sequence is noted in *(a)*, with the resulting output in *(b)*.

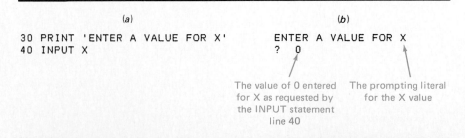

```
              (a)                              (b)
30 PRINT 'ENTER A VALUE FOR X'        ENTER A VALUE FOR X
40 INPUT X                            ?  0
```

The value of 0 entered for X as requested by the INPUT statement line 40

The prompting literal for the X value

(a)

```
30 INPUT 'ENTER A VALUE FOR X'; X
```

(b)

ENTER A VALUE FOR X ?   0

The question mark associated with the INPUT statement

The value of 0 for X, entered by the user

The prompting literal

FIGURE 4.14 One version of the INPUT statement permits the user to include the prompting literal within its structure. *(a)* The prompt precedes the variable name within the INPUT statement. *(b)* When the line 30 is executed, the prompting literal, the required ?, and the input data all appear on the same line.

PROBLEM 4.5   Cost Estimates

The following formula estimates the costs associated with a specific product:

$$C = .4 * U + 650$$

In this formula, C represents the costs associated with the number of units (U) manufactured. Using a prompting literal with an INPUT statement, key in each U value on a separate loop. The prompting literal should read 'ENTER NUMBER OF UNITS'. After computation of the cost C, output that amount preceded by the label 'COSTS = $'. Separate each data grouping by a blank line. Use a 9s decision to control the processing loop. Compute costs for the following units: 500, 2500, 5000, 10000. Use a closing literal, 'PROCESSING OVER', to note the program's end.

These are the main points in the problem narrative.

1   No headings are required.

2   An INPUT statement is used with a prompting literal of 'ENTER NUMBER OF UNITS'.

3   The formula used to compute production costs (C) is

$$C = (.4 * U) + 650$$

4   A label of 'COSTS = $' precedes the output of C.

5   Each output grouping is separated by a blank line.

6   A 9s decision is used to control looping.

7   A closing literal of 'PROCESSING OVER' is positioned on the YES branch of the 9s decision.

The flowchart and program developed for Problem 4.5 are shown in Figure 4.15.

The flowchart solution shows no initial conditions and moves directly to the input of the number of units to be processed. An I/O symbol with an INPUT statement notes the entry of U and the use of the prompting literal 'ENTER NUMBER OF UNITS'. A 9s decision follows that input and enables a choice between continuing the loop via the NO branch and exiting via the YES branch.

The computation of the cost (C) using the U value occurs on the NO branch and precedes its output. A label of 'COSTS = $' is placed before the printing of C. No output is provided for U, as none was defined in the problem narrative. The PRINT symbol possessing no variables denotes the blank line that is to separate data groups. The unconditional branch to the opening I/O symbol completes the loop.

The flowchart is converted directly into the BASIC solution, also shown in Figure 4.15. A REMARK statement at line 10 opens the program and is placed ahead of the INPUT statement at line 20. This instruction includes a prompting literal, which identifies the entry of U, the number of units for which a cost estimate must be prepared. At line 30, an IF/THEN statement representing the 9s decision tests to see if a value of −999 was input for U. That specific value will cause the program to branch to line 200, print a closing literal of 'PROCESSING OVER', and end the program.

If the −999 value is not inputted, processing moves to line 40, where the cost estimate is computed. Here, the U value input is substituted into that equation and C is calculated. This cost is outputted at line 50, with the cost appearing immediately after the label 'COSTS = $'. The use of a semicolon directs that the C value appear immediately after that literal. The blank PRINT statement, line 60, is BASIC's way of skipping a line and puts a blank line between each output grouping. The GO TO statement at line 70 moves the flow of processing to line 20, where the input of the next U value restarts the looping sequence.

The output from this program is also shown in Figure 4.15(c). Four groups of output data related to the values of 500, 2500, 5000, and 10000 are separated by blank lines and denote the cost associated with each unit value. The last data grouping has the −999 value and the closing literal resulting from its entry. This last output notes that processing has been concluded.

Multiple Decisions

Our discussion of flowcharts demonstrated that many problem solutions incorporate more than one decision to facilitate processing. IF/THEN statements may be used to support processing, in addition to branching activities. In previous programs, we have utilized the IF/THEN format of

```
200      IF H = −99.99 THEN 200
```

which permitted the branching to line 200 when H was equal to −99.99.

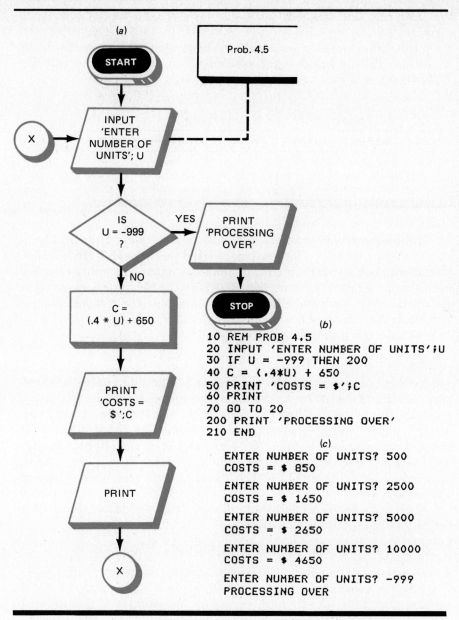

FIGURE 4.15 The flowchart *(a)* and BASIC program *(b)* for Problem 4.5. This problem is constructed around the use of the INPUT statement and its interactive capabilities. *(c)* The output of Problem 4.5 reflects the use of the interactive form of the INPUT statement. The program handles the values of 500, 2500, 5000, and 10000 units and places them in separate groups. The entry of the −999 value is essential for the execution of the 9s decision. Each output group is separated by a blank line, the result of a blank PRINT statement.

```
                                        (b)
10 REM PROB 4.5
20 INPUT 'ENTER NUMBER OF UNITS';U
30 IF U = -999 THEN 200
40 C = (.4*U) + 650
50 PRINT 'COSTS = $';C
60 PRINT
70 GO TO 20
200 PRINT 'PROCESSING OVER'
210 END
                            (c)
ENTER NUMBER OF UNITS? 500
COSTS = $ 850

ENTER NUMBER OF UNITS? 2500
COSTS = $ 1650

ENTER NUMBER OF UNITS? 5000
COSTS = $ 2650

ENTER NUMBER OF UNITS? 10000
COSTS = $ 4650

ENTER NUMBER OF UNITS? -999
PROCESSING OVER
```

When processing demands, the format of the IF/THEN statement may be altered to include a processing statement. For example, we could test against a value and if that condition is met, perform another computation. The statement that follows demonstrates this approach.

400   IF G > 250 THEN F = G * .067

In this statement, if G is greater than 250, the computer is directed to compute F via the formula provided after the word THEN. This is a perfectly valid statement and an alternative to branching to another statement via the IF/THEN. Table 4.4 details the symbols which may be used within IF/THEN statements and the logical conditions they represent.

TABLE 4.4   Symbols For Logical Operations

Symbol	Condition Represented	Symbol	Condition Represented
=	is equal to	<>	is not equal to
<	is less than	<=	is less than or equal to
>	is greater than	>=	is greater than or equal to

In problems where two alternatives exist, another form of the IF/THEN statement may be used. This version, referred to as the **IF/THEN/ELSE statement,** permits the user to incorporate alternative computations or line numbers in a single statement. The IF/THEN/ELSE can represent those actions taken on both the YES and NO branches of a decision. Sample statements will illustrate how the IF/THEN/ELSE is used.

Consider the IF/THEN/ELSE that follows:

200   IF C = 1 THEN 500 ELSE 600

defines branching operations for the YES and NO conditional exits. Statement 200 directs that if C = 1, the program should branch to line 500. This is the equivalent of the YES branch. However, if C is not equal to 1, the ELSE option is chosen and the program branches to line 600. The ELSE instructional component reflects the NO branching condition. When the IF/THEN/ELSE is so defined, the program must branch to the line number following either THEN or ELSE. The logical operation chooses one alternative or the other.

Another format specified within the IF/THEN/ELSE statement may include two alternative computations:

70   IF P < 500 THEN C = 200 + (.5 * P) ELSE C = 300 + (.2 * P)

In this statement, the YES and NO conditionals define two computations. IF P < 500, the equation C = 200 + (.5 * P) is processed. If P >= 500, the equation C = 300 + (.2 * P), representing the NO alternative, is performed.

A major difference evident with this statement is what happens after either computation is performed. In this latter format, the instruction does not direct the program to a line number. Thus, after processing either equation, the program proceeds to the statement following line 70. This format permits a series of alternative computations to be performed, the program selecting the required processing via IF/THEN/ELSE statements. To observe how this latter version of the IF/THEN/ELSE may be advantageously used, let us examine another sample solution.

PROBLEM 4.6   Sales Report

A heading atop the report consists of the literals 'SALES NO', 'SALES TOT', and 'COMMISSION'. Input are a salesperson's number and three sales amounts. These three amounts are added to create the sales total. If that sales total is greater than $300, a commission rate of 20 percent is used. If not, a rate of 10 percent is employed. The commission amount is calculated by multiplying the rate by the sales total. For each sales number on each loop, output the sales number, sales total, and computed commission. Use a 9s decision to control the program loop. Use READ and DATA statements to handle the below data.

Sales No	Amt 1	Amt 2	Amt 3
1106	126.35	52.45	113.55
3128	206.12	83.27	485.16
4067	83.47	19.67	75.11
8010	175.38	60.42	84.45

These are the main points in the problem narrative.

1   A three-part heading of 'SALES NO', 'SALES TOT', and 'COMMISSION' should appear at the top of the report.

2   Input are a salesperson's number and three sales amounts, each requiring its own dataname.

3   A 9s decision controls looping.

4   The formulas needed to support processing are:

   a   Sales total = Amt 1 + Amt 2 + Amt 3
   b   Commission = sales total * commission rate (where the rate is either 10 or 20 percent).

5   A decision which tests against the sales total to determine whether it is greater than $300 is needed to determine which commission rate to use. IF sales total > 300, THEN use the 20 percent rate, ELSE use the 10 percent rate.

6   Output the salesperson's number, sales total, and commission.

7   Four data items and an additional 9s data item are processed.

8   No closing literal is required.

The flowchart and program prepared from this problem narrative are shown in Figure 4.16.

The flowchart prepared for Problem 4.6 reflects the use of two decisions. One decision entails determining the correct commission rate to use, and the second details the 9s decision used for loop control.

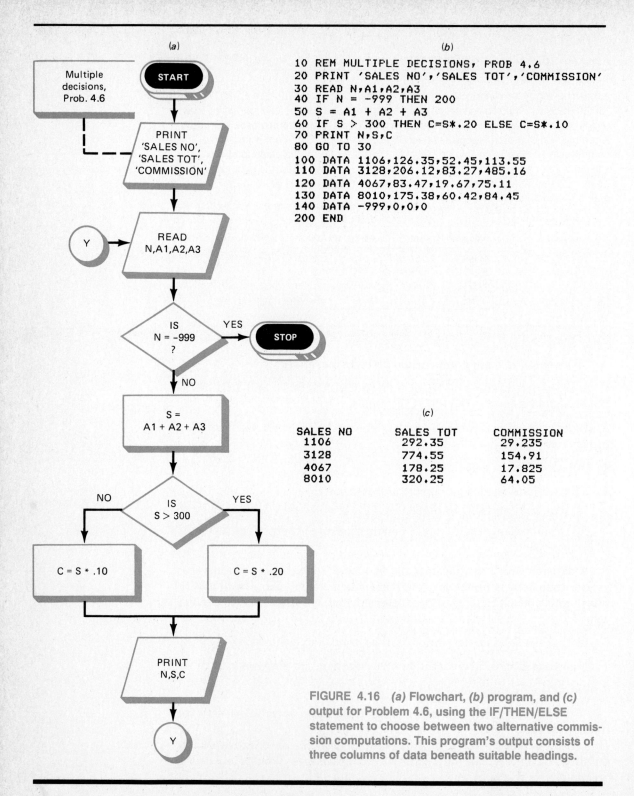

(a)

(b)

```
10 REM MULTIPLE DECISIONS, PROB 4.6
20 PRINT 'SALES NO','SALES TOT','COMMISSION'
30 READ N,A1,A2,A3
40 IF N = -999 THEN 200
50 S = A1 + A2 + A3
60 IF S > 300 THEN C=S*.20 ELSE C=S*.10
70 PRINT N,S,C
80 GO TO 30
100 DATA 1106,126.35,52.45,113.55
110 DATA 3128,206.12,83.27,485.16
120 DATA 4067,83.47,19.67,75.11
130 DATA 8010,175.38,60.42,84.45
140 DATA -999,0,0,0
200 END
```

(c)

SALES NO	SALES TOT	COMMISSION
1106	292.35	29.235
3128	774.55	154.91
4067	178.25	17.825
8010	320.25	64.05

FIGURE 4.16 (a) Flowchart, (b) program, and (c) output for Problem 4.6, using the IF/THEN/ELSE statement to choose between two alternative commission computations. This program's output consists of three columns of data beneath suitable headings.

Note that the second decision symbol has processing symbols on both the YES and NO branches, each representing the computation of a commission amount. This is valid, as either one or the other computation must be used. If the 20 percent rate is used, then the 10 percent rate is not, or vice versa. Both computations lead to a PRINT symbol which outputs the salesperson's number, sales total, and computed commission amount.

The looping sequence will execute four complete loops before encountering the 9s data and exiting via the YES branch of the 9s decision. In this case, we have chosen to test against the salesperson's number to complete the 9s decision. In the flowchart, the conditional statement IS $N = -999$? represents the 9s decision, where N defines the variable for salesperson number. Any one of the three variables representing sales amounts could have been used, but we elected to use N. Remember, the choice of the variable used, unless stipulated by the problem narrative, is left to the programmer.

The program prepared from the flowchart solution of Figure 4.16 reflects the logic discussed. An opening comment via the REMARK statement, line 10, indicates the program's purpose. The PRINT statement that follows generates the required three-part column heading, positioning each literal within one of the first three print zones. Each literal is defined by its own set of quotes, and commas are used to position this output.

The READ instruction, line 30, commences the looping sequence. It is used to enter the four numeric variables undergoing processing. The numeric-variable names A1, A2, and A3 define the three sales amounts used in processing. Line 40 defines a 9s decision. A branch to line 200 will only occur when $N = -999$; otherwise the program continues on to line 50. The sales total amount, the variable S, is computed at line 50 by adding the three sales amounts.

The test to determine which commission rate to employ occurs with the IF/THEN/ELSE statement at line 60. If the sales total > 300, the equation $C = S * .20$ is used; otherwise $C = S * .10$ is processed. Using either formula will result in a commission amount, which is output at line 70. The unconditional branch to line 30 continues the loop, processing all four data items until the 9s data is read.

All data items are configured within lines 100 to 140. Each DATA statement specifies data related to a salesperson's number and three sales amounts. No string-variable data items are used in this program. The last DATA statement, line 140, contains the -999 required for the 9s decision. Note that the -999 data is positioned in the DATA statement in relation to the numeric variable N, so that it is properly entered for use in statement 40. The three 0s following -999 are necessary to complete the 9s DATA statement.

The output from Problem 4.6 is also shown in Figure 4.16. Note the positioning of the column headings in print zones 1, 2, and 3 and the printing of the appropriate sales data beneath them. Four lines of sales data are outputted, with each line single-spaced. No closing literal is printed.

Additional problems will reinforce the use of the IF/THEN/ELSE statement, with recommendations as to where it is best used. One advisory note must be made with regard to the IF/THEN/ELSE: some versions of BASIC may not allow use of this instruction. If the IF/THEN/ELSE statement cannot be used, it may be replaced by two sequential IF/THEN statements. For example, the statement

```
60      IF S > 300 THEN C = S * .20 ELSE C = S * .10
```

could be effectively replaced by

```
60      IF S > 300 THEN C = S * .20
65      IF S<= 300 THEN C = S * .10
```

4.5 Using a Counter

The use of a looping technique controlled by a 9s decision is adequate for many types of computer applications. As we recognized in our flowcharting discussions, counters provide a means of executing a specific number of loops when an exact number of repetitions are required in a program. The components composing a counter are easily converted to their BASIC equivalents via LET and IF/THEN statements.

Table 4.5 shows the three components that are required to construct a counter: (1) a counter must be initialized at 1; (2) a counter decision must determine whether the desired number of loops has been executed; and (3) a counter increment must exist. Assuming for discussion purposes that 25 loops should be executed, observe how the three counter components are converted to their equivalents in BASIC.

TABLE 4.5   Three Operational Elements of a Counter

Counter Components	Sample BASIC Statements	
Initialization of counter	20	K = 1
Counter decision and the YES branch out of the loop	100	IF K = 25 THEN 200
Counter increment	110	K = K + 1

The counter is initialized on line 20. That instruction, $K = 1$, establishes the counter variable K equal to a value of 1 and initializes the counter for use. The counter decision that checks for the completion of 25 loops is written using an IF/THEN statement: IF K = 25 THEN 200. This instruction compares the value of K against 25 and branches out of the loop to line 200 when K = 25. When K < 25, the program branches to the statement following line 100, representing the counter increment. The counter increment is always positioned on the equivalent of the NO branch of the counter decision. The LET statement, line 110, represents the counter increment.

Some students question whether the equation of K = K + 1 is correct. Though algebraically questionable, that computation is valid for processing in BASIC. Its validity results from the manner in which K = K + 1 is actually executed.

The computer processes the right side of the equation, K + 1, first. It takes the current value of K and adds 1 to it, thus increasing that value by 1 for the next loop's use. This result is stored back in K, the lone variable on the left side of the equal sign. The instruction K = K + 1 is valid for use as a counter increment and representative of statements used in counter-oriented applications. For illustrative purposes, let us observe how a counter could be applied to create a looping sequence for Problem 4.2.

The counter-oriented version of Problem 4.2 is depicted in Figure 4.17. As we note from the flowchart solution, the three counter components are evident within the solution. The counter initialization of K = 1 is placed as an initial condition prior to the looping sequence. The counter decision is logically positioned at the loop's end, checking on the performance of three loops. One loop is needed to process each of the three data items involved in processing. The counter increment of K = K + 1 is properly positioned on the NO branch of the counter decision and precedes the branch to the loop's start.

The BASIC program written from this flowchart parallels its logic. A REMARK statement opens the program at line 10 and indicates the use of a counter. Line 20 serves to initialize the counter by specifying K = 1. The PRINT statement, line 30, defines the five column headings of the printed output. Line 40, the READ statement, inputs the student's data and defines the first instruction of the program loop. A 9s decision **is not used** when a counter is incorporated into a program solution. The 9s DATA statement is also omitted from this program, as it is also not needed. Examining the program solution, note that only three DATA statements exist matching the number of students undergoing processing.

The entry of data via line 40 begins the processing loop. The LET statement, line 50, computes the student's average (A) and precedes the output of all data at line 60 via that PRINT statement. A variable is assigned into each of the five print zones beneath its respective heading. As all processing related to a student is concluded, we can turn our attention to the counter decision at the loop's close.

The counter decision is stipulated at line 70 via an IF/THEN statement. It checks for the execution of exactly three loops, by comparing K against a value of 3. If K = 3, the program is directed to branch to line 200 where a closing literal of 'PROCESSING IS OVER' is printed. This label notes the close of processing and precedes the program's end. If K < 3, the branch from the loop is not made and the program proceeds to line 80.

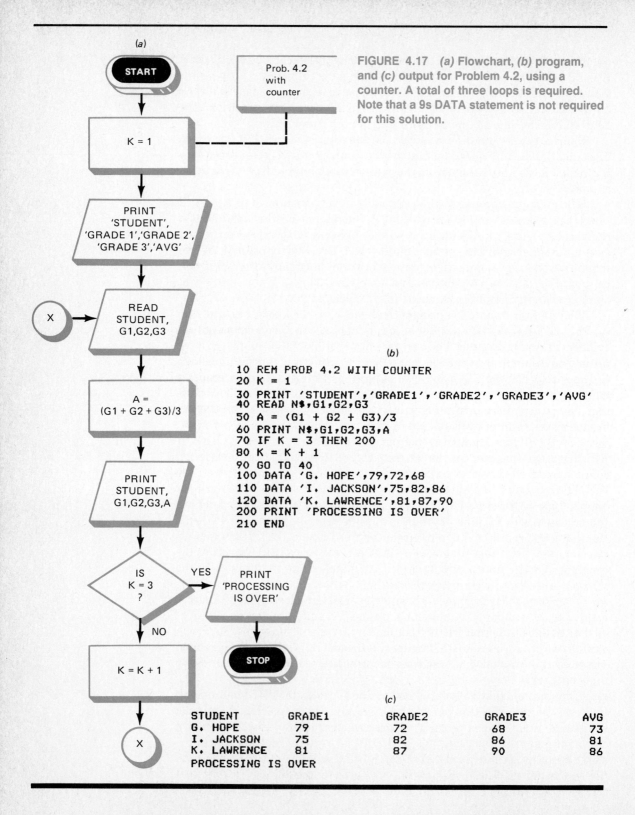

(a)

START

K = 1

PRINT
'STUDENT',
'GRADE 1','GRADE 2',
'GRADE 3','AVG'

X → READ
STUDENT,
G1,G2,G3

A =
(G1 + G2 + G3)/3

PRINT
STUDENT,
G1,G2,G3,A

IS
K = 3
?   —YES→ PRINT
'PROCESSING
IS OVER'

NO

K = K + 1

X

STOP

Prob. 4.2
with
counter

FIGURE 4.17 (a) Flowchart, (b) program, and (c) output for Problem 4.2, using a counter. A total of three loops is required. Note that a 9s DATA statement is not required for this solution.

(b)

```
10 REM PROB 4.2 WITH COUNTER
20 K = 1
30 PRINT 'STUDENT','GRADE1','GRADE2','GRADE3','AVG'
40 READ N$,G1,G2,G3
50 A = (G1 + G2 + G3)/3
60 PRINT N$,G1,G2,G3,A
70 IF K = 3 THEN 200
80 K = K + 1
90 GO TO 40
100 DATA 'G. HOPE',79,72,68
110 DATA 'I. JACKSON',75,82,86
120 DATA 'K. LAWRENCE',81,87,90
200 PRINT 'PROCESSING IS OVER'
210 END
```

(c)

STUDENT	GRADE1	GRADE2	GRADE3	AVG
G. HOPE	79	72	68	73
I. JACKSON	75	82	86	81
K. LAWRENCE	81	87	90	86
PROCESSING IS OVER				

At line 80 the counter is increased by an increment of 1 and prepares itself for the next loop's processing. The GO TO at line 90 sends the program flow to line 40, the READ statement which inputs the next student's data. Exactly three loops are executed in this fashion to process the three students' data.

Students may want to compare this solution with the program written in Figure 4.8. That program focused on use of a 9s decision and processed exactly the same data. Comparison of the outputs from both programs reveals that both listings provide the same results. The programmer is usually free to choose a processing approach suited to his or her needs.

Let us redraft the program written for Problem 4.6, originally presented in Figure 4.16. However, instead of controlling the looping sequence with a 9s decision, we incorporate a counter to execute exactly four loops. All other aspects of the problem are maintained. The flowchart and program for this new counter-oriented solution are shown in Figure 4.18.

This revised flowchart notes three activities that occur prior to the start of the loop: an annotation symbol offers an introductory comment, the K counter is initialized at 1, and the output of column headings are noted prior to the main loop's opening READ symbol.

Processing within the loop parallels the prior solution of Figure 4.16. The READ symbol enters the four required items of data. The 9s decision is omitted; it is not required, since a counter is being used. The three sales amounts are added and that sales total (S) compared against the $300 limit in a decision symbol. This comparison enables the selection of the proper commission rate, which precedes the output of sales data.

The counter decision is positioned after the required PRINT symbol. The counter decision will verify whether four loops have been completed. If $K < 4$, the counter increment of $K = K + 1$ is executed and the flowchart unconditionally branches to the READ symbol. At the fourth loop's close, the loop is exited and the flowchart closes via its STOP symbol.

The statements composing the revised solution for Problem 4.6 parallel the logic of the flowchart. The REMARK statement, line 10, advises of the change to a counter in our solution. Line 20 initializes the counter with $K = 1$ and precedes the output of column headings at line 30. Again, each literal is assigned to one of the first three print zones through the use of commas in that PRINT statement.

The READ statement starts the program loop and enables the entry of the four required data items. The three sales amounts are added at line 50 to produce the sales total (S). It is this sales total that is compared against 300 to determine whether a rate of 10 or 20 percent should be used. An IF/THEN/ELSE statement (line 60) is used to determine whether $S > 300$ and to compute the proper commission amount. The PRINT statement, line 70, outputs the sales number (N), sales total (S), and commission amount (C) on each of the four loops performed.

Line 80 signals the position of the IF/THEN statement representing the counter decision. On the fourth loop, $K = 4$, the program is directed to exit the loop and branch to the END statement at line 200. On the three preceding

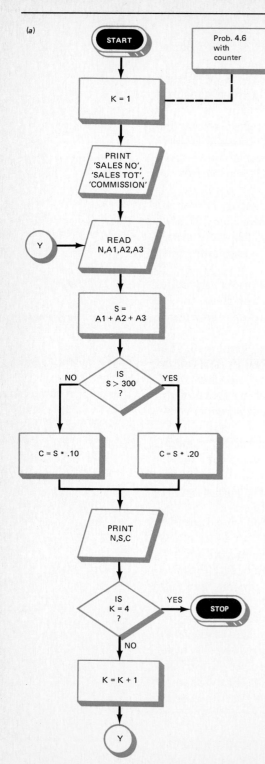

(a)

FIGURE 4.18   (a) Flowchart, (b) program, and (c) output for Problem 4.6, using a counter. A total of four loops is undertaken by the counter in this solution.

(b)

```
10 REM PROB 4.6 WITH COUNTER
20 K = 1
30 PRINT 'SALES NO','SALES TOT','COMMISSION'
40 READ N,A1,A2,A3
50 S = A1 + A2 + A3
60 IF S > 300 THEN C=S*.20 ELSE C=S*.10
70 PRINT N,S,C
80 IF K = 4 THEN 200
90 K = K + 1
100 GO TO 40
110 DATA 1106,126.35,52.45,113.55
120 DATA 3128,206.12,83.27,485.16
130 DATA 4067,83.47,19.67,75.11
140 DATA 8010,175.38,60.42,84.45
200 END
```

(c)

SALES NO	SALES TOT	COMMISSION
1106	292.35	29.235
3128	774.55	154.91
4067	178.25	17.825
8010	320.25	64.05

loops, the program branches to line 90 and increments K by 1. The unconditional branch at line 100 continues the loop.

The four DATA statements required for this program are listed at lines 110 to 140. Note that an additional DATA statement for the 9s data is not required. The hierarchy of variables in each DATA statement parallels the order of the READ statement. The order dictated by statement 40 is four numeric variables, led by the sales number and followed by three sales amounts.

The output, as shown in Figure 4.18(c), once again reveals that when a counter is properly used, it can produce exactly the same report data as any other looping sequence. This fact will become even more evident as additional looping control techniques are introduced. Each looping technique has its own merits which programmers must learn to take advantage of. A final problem will reinforce the use of a counter.

PROBLEM 4.7   Ticket Lists

Headings are 'ORDER', 'TICKET HOLDER', 'QUANTITY', 'PRICE', and 'TICKET COST'. Input are the ticket holder's name, number of tickets purchased, and the individual cost per ticket. The ticket cost is prepared by multiplying the cost per ticket by the number of tickets purchased. Output are the sequence number of the transaction, ticket holder's name, number of tickets bought, and the individual and total cost of these tickets. The sequence number of each transaction is obtained by printing the current value of the counter controlling the looping sequence. The flowchart should close by outputting the label 'TICKET SALES CLOSE'. The data used in this problem is listed below.

Ticket Holder Name	Number of Tickets	Price of Ticket
Abacrombie	5	8.25
Beckett	8	9.24
Carolyn	7	6.55
Darwink	3	10.75
Enriquez	4	12.66
Faintly	6	7.32

These are the main points in the problem narrative.

1   A counter is used to control the looping sequence of exactly six loops.

2   Five column headings are to be outputted.

3   Input are the ticket holder's name, quantity of tickets bought, and their individual price.

4   The cost for each batch of tickets is computed by

Cost = quantity * price

5   Output the current value of the counter, ticket holder's name, quantity of tickets purchased, ticket price, and the total cost of those tickets.

6   A closing literal of 18 characters is outputted.

7   Exactly six sets of data are involved.

The flowchart and program prepared for this problem are shown in Figure 4.19.

The flowchart opens with the initialization of the counter at 1 and the printing of the five required column headings. The flowchart loop commences with a READ symbol where three data items are input. The two numeric data items (Q and P) are immediately used to compute the cost of tickets (C). All data items are output, including the current value of K. The K value will generate an itemized list, ranging from 1 to 6, identifying in sequence each order handled.

The counter decision signals the test for the sixth loop. If K < 6, the counter is incremented and the flowchart branches back to the opening READ symbol, where the next ticket holder is handled. The completion of the sixth loop results in the output of a closing literal, which advises that ticket sales have ended.

The program is fairly straightforward. Line 10 identifies the program's purpose, with the counter K initialized at 1 by line 20. The following PRINT statement positions each literal into one of the five print zones, no literal exceeding the size of any zone. Statement 40 enters the ticket holder's name (N$), number of tickets bought (Q), and their individual purchase price (P) on each loop. Line 50 computes the total cost for each set of tickets (C).

The output of these variables occurs at line 60. The output of K in zone 1 provides the numbered itemized listing which identifies each transaction in order. The initialization of K at 1 ensures that the correct sequence number is recorded for each loop's processing. All other variables occupy print zones 2 through 5, beneath their proper headings.

The counter decision and increment follow on lines 70 and 80, with the unconditional branch to line 40 noted at statement 90. When K = 6, the program will cease looping and execute the output of the closing 18-character literal 'TICKET SALES CLOSE'. This label appears beneath the last item of output.

An interesting aspect to this problem relates to how the DATA statements are specified. Instead of assigning each data item to a single DATA statement, we doubled up the data listed per statement. This enabled us to use fewer DATA statements. On each loop, three data items are drawn from each DATA statement, using the order of a string variable and two numeric variables. This order was dictated by the READ statement, line 40. Thus, 'ABACROMBIE', 5, and 8.25 are used in loop 1, 'BECKETT', 8, and 9.24 on loop 2,

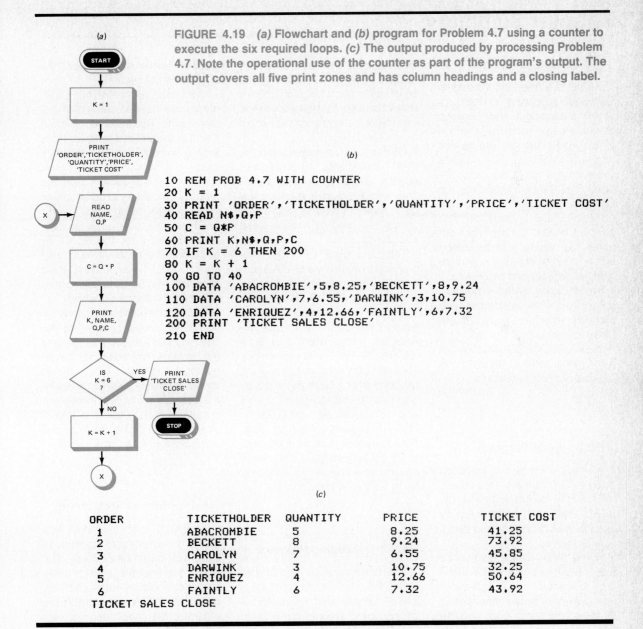

(a)

FIGURE 4.19 *(a)* Flowchart and *(b)* program for Problem 4.7 using a counter to execute the six required loops. *(c)* The output produced by processing Problem 4.7. Note the operational use of the counter as part of the program's output. The output covers all five print zones and has column headings and a closing label.

(b)

```
10 REM PROB 4.7 WITH COUNTER
20 K = 1
30 PRINT 'ORDER','TICKETHOLDER','QUANTITY','PRICE','TICKET COST'
40 READ N$,Q,P
50 C = Q*P
60 PRINT K,N$,Q,P,C
70 IF K = 6 THEN 200
80 K = K + 1
90 GO TO 40
100 DATA 'ABACROMBIE',5,8.25,'BECKETT',8,9.24
110 DATA 'CAROLYN',7,6.55,'DARWINK',3,10.75
120 DATA 'ENRIQUEZ',4,12.66,'FAINTLY',6,7.32
200 PRINT 'TICKET SALES CLOSE'
210 END
```

(c)

ORDER	TICKETHOLDER	QUANTITY	PRICE	TICKET COST
1	ABACROMBIE	5	8.25	41.25
2	BECKETT	8	9.24	73.92
3	CAROLYN	7	6.55	45.85
4	DARWINK	3	10.75	32.25
5	ENRIQUEZ	4	12.66	50.64
6	FAINTLY	6	7.32	43.92
TICKET SALES CLOSE				

and so on until 'FAINTLY', 6, and 7.52 are inputted on the sixth and last loop.

The output related to this program is shown in Figure 4.19*(c)*. Note the itemized listing of K from 1 to 6 in the lefthand column of data. Each detail line of ticket sets is so identified, until the final literal is printed.

Chapter Summary

4.1 A BASIC Overview

BASIC is a free-form interactive language supporting online program development and provides students with a computer language that is readily learned. The general format of BASIC instructions uses line numbers, commands, and variables. The line number defines the order of execution for program statements and uniquely identifies each statement. The command denotes the operation to be undertaken, with the variables noting the items of data used in processing.

When writing BASIC programs, programmers are urged to use line numbers separated by units of 10. This separation of statement numbers simplifies the entry of program instructions without having to renumber existing statements.

4.2 An Initial Program

A simple program can introduce many BASIC formats. One vehicle for entering program data is the READ statement, which may be used to specify numeric and string-variable names.

Numeric-variable names may be one or two characters long, with the first character being alphabetic. String-variable names may be two or three characters long, with the last character specified as a $. No other special characters should be utilized with either variable, and at no time should two alphabetic characters be used for variable names.

Processing activities involving arithmetic manipulations are handled in LET statements. Only one variable is placed to the left of the equal sign in formulas. Parentheses should be used to group arithmetic expressions and ensure their accuracy.

Outputs are prepared using the PRINT statements. To align these outputs, BASIC establishes a print area and subdivides it into major print zones. Commas and semicolons are used to access these print zones.

The data used in BASIC programs is specified via DATA statements, which must be used in conjunction with READ statements. The order of variables specified within the READ statements defines the order in which data items are specified in DATA statements. The use of any other order results in program errors. Data items are divided into the categories of numeric and string-variable data items. DATA statements may be positioned anywhere in a program, prior to its END statement. Descriptive comments are added to programs using REMARK statements.

4.3 The Looping Process

The repetitive processing of data is defined within a program loop. BASIC incorporates 9s decisions into programs to control looping sequences and exit from them. Conditional operations are processed using IF/THEN statements, where the equivalent of the YES branch causes the program to branch out of the program loop. If the loop is not exited, the flow of processing leads to the instruction following the IF/THEN statement.

Unconditional branching statements are defined using GO TO statements. This statement is often found at the end of a program loop, leading to the start of a program loop.

When the 9s decision is used, the programmer is free to utilize any of the data items being input. The IF/THEN representing the 9s decision is positioned after the READ instruction. The program must also contain a DATA statement which specifies the 9s data associated with that conditional statement.

BASIC possesses a means of outputting literals. Literals are defined in PRINT statements, placing the desired characters in single quotes. Using literals, we can define column headings and special labels. It is possible to mix both literals and conventional data items in PRINT statements, with both commas and semicolons used as punctuation.

4.4 Additional Statements

As BASIC is an interactive language, it must possess the ability to input data on an online basis. The INPUT statement is used for these purposes and does not require support of the DATA statement. Rules regarding the specification of variable names and data are still consistently used. When the INPUT statement is written into a program, users key data from their terminals. Data is keyed in in the order requested by the statement. To alert the user to the execution of an

INPUT statement, a ? is output.

Some versions of BASIC support the use of an INPUT statement that incorporates a literal to prompt users. The prompting INPUT statement offers users additional guidance when keying data into a program. It too places a ? on the screen to alert users, but the ? appears after the prompting literal.

BASIC programs must accommodate multiple decisions. BASIC utilizes the IF/THEN statement and its longer version, the IF/THEN/ELSE statement. The IF/THEN/ELSE is ideal for conditions where two alternatives are involved in processing. If the IF/THEN/ELSE statement is not available in your version of BASIC, it can be replaced using two IF/THEN statements.

4.5 Using a Counter

Counters are constructed in BASIC programs using LET and IF/THEN statements. The initialization of the counter occurs prior to the start of the program loop. The counter decision is positioned at the loop's close, determining whether the desired number of loops has been performed. If that is the case, the IF/THEN statement representing the counter decision will direct the flow of processing out of the program loop. If not, processing passes to the counter increment, the statement after that decision.

When a counter is used, the 9s decision is not. As such, a DATA statement possessing the 9s data is not specified. A counter also permits users to output information in an itemized format, where the counter value is the first value printed.

Key BASIC Statements

Statement	Examples	
DATA statement	100	DATA 36, 70, 82
	100	DATA 'SMITH', 40, 2.50
END statement	200	END
GO TO statement	90	GO TO 30
IF/THEN statement	40	IF H = −99.99 THEN 200
	80	IF S > 250 THEN C = S * .12
	100	IF K = 7 THEN 200
IF/THEN/ELSE statement	50	IF S > 300 THEN C = S * .20 ELSE C = S * .10
	80	IF B = THEN 100 ELSE 30
INPUT statement	20	INPUT N$, H, R
	40	INPUT X
	30	INPUT 'ENTER C VALUE'; C
LET statement	50	LET I = P * R
	50	I = P * R
	80	Y = (3 * A * A) + (6 * B) + 13
PRINT statement	20	PRINT 'SALESPERSON', 'SALES', 'COMMISSION'
	60	PRINT N$, G, F, N
	70	PRINT 'THE CURRENT X VALUE ='; X
	80	PRINT 'THE PROGRAM IS CLOSED'
READ statement	30	READ X
	40	READ B$, C, R1, R2
REMARK statement	10	REM PROBLEM 6 WITH COUNTER
	60	REM CHECKS COMMISSION AMOUNT

Glossary

Command The general line component which dictates the processing activity to be undertaken by that instruction.

DATA statement The instruction, used with READ statements, which provides the data used in processing.

Dummy data items DATA items used in a 9s DATA statement to complete the statement and satisfy the request for data.

END statement The closing statement of any BASIC program; no statements may possess line numbers in excess of this instruction.

GO TO statement The unconditional branching statement in BASIC.

IF/THEN statement A conditional instruction which can direct the flow of processing to another line or execute a processing operation if that condition is met.

IF/THEN/ELSE statement The conditional statement which specifies both alternatives of a decision within the same statement; the YES alternative is placed after the THEN command and the NO alternative after the ELSE command.

INPUT statement The interactive statement where users enter data on an online basis; some versions of BASIC permit a prompting literal to be part of its format; does not require use of a DATA statement.

LET statement The statement supporting processing specified in terms of an equation, where one variable is placed to the left of the equal sign.

Line number The general line component which uniquely identifies an instruction and defines its position in the order of execution.

Numeric data items Data items possessing a solely numeric format.

Numeric-variable name Data-name utilized to refer to numeric data items.

PRINT statement The statement used for outputting literals and other data items.

Program loop The looping sequence created for the repeated processing of data.

READ statement A statement used to enter the data for processing; must be used with DATA statements.

REMARK statement The instruction used for advisory comments within a program; cannot initiate any processing activities.

String-variable data item Data item consisting of nonnumeric characters; cannot exceed the size of a print zone.

String-variable name Data-name assigned to a string-variable data item, with the last character a dollar sign ($).

Variable The general line component which identifies the variables used in processing.

Exercises

In-Class Exercises

1 To acquaint yourself with the entry of programs into your computer, try keying the following short program and noting the results.

```
10    REM SAMPLE PROGRAM
20    PRINT 'HELLO--MY NAME IS HAROLD'
30    PRINT 'WHAT IS YOUR NAME'
40    INPUT N$
50    PRINT 'HI', N$, 'GLAD TO MEET YOU'
60    END
```

2 For the following program excerpts enter the statements necessary to complete the 9s decision or counter indicated.

a A 9s decision via an IF/THEN statement at line 30

```
20      READ N$, P, R
30      — — — — — — — — — — — — —
```

b A counter (K) to execute 15 loops with line 20 the counter initialization, line 60 the counter decision, and line 70 its increment.

```
10      REM SAMPLE COUNTER
20      — — — — — — — — — — — — —
30      READ X
40      Y = 3X + 17
50      PRINT X, Y
60      — — — — — — — — — — — — —
70      — — — — — — — — — — — — —
80      GO TO 30
        .
        .
        .
400     END
```

3 Write a flowchart and BASIC program for the following narrative:

This problem entails the computation of union pension benefits. A heading of the following literals is required: 'EMPLOYEE', 'UNION', and 'PENSION AMT'. Input are the employee's name, union code, and base amount on which the pension amount is based. If that base amount is greater than $3000, the pension rate used is 2.2 percent. If the base amount is less than or equal to $3000, the pension rate is 1.6 percent. The pension amount is computed by multiplying the base amount by the proper pension rate. Output the employee's name, the union code, and the computed pension amount. Use any looping sequence. Data items appear below.

Employee Name	Union Code	Base Amount
Arnoudt	303	4620
Barends	46	2830
Carlton	303	7780
Dooley	303	8940
Paterno	46	1460
Reilly	46	2560

Lab Exercises

1 Examine the statements that follow, and determine whether they are properly written. Correct only those statements deemed to have syntax errors.

a 20 READ N$, B; Z; R3
b PRINT' PROGRAM ENDS'
c 60 IF K = 6, THEN 705
d 100 DATA 44; 6; −14.2
e LET 16 + (3 * X) = Y
f 210 G = (B1 + B2 + B3)/3
g INPUT 'ENTER THE VALUE R1', R1
h 10 PRINT 'NAME' 'COL1' 'COL2'
i 75 IF J = 1 THEN 200 ELSE C = 6
j 40 READ 'NAME', 'RATE1', 'RATE2'

2 Represent the following formulas in terms of their LET statement equivalents.

a $Y = 6 \cdot A^2 + 7 \cdot B \cdot A - 5B^2$
b $C = 4 \cdot H^3 / 3 \cdot R$
c $V = (1/3) \cdot B \cdot H^2$
d $P = ((X^2 - 16) \cdot (3X + 7))^2$

For the problem narratives that follow, prepare flowcharts and BASIC programs representing the processing described.

3   The problem relates to the computation of sales commissions. Input to the problem are the salesperson's name and four sales amounts. The sales amounts are added to create a total sales amount. If the total sales amount is less than or equal to $200, then the commission rate used is 5 percent. If not, a commission rate of 10 percent is used. The commission amount is computed by multiplying the commission rate by the total sales amount. Output the salesperson's name, total sales amount, and commission amount. Use the column headings 'SALESPERSON', 'TOTAL SALES', and 'COMMISSION'.

   a   Prepare the flowchart and program to process the five data items listed below. Use a 9s decision to control looping.

Salesperson	Amt 1	Amt 2	Amt 3	Amt 4
Marshall	59.46	48.25	19.39	70.30
Nussbaum	49.38	10.29	89.70	54.43
Oversony	168.75	106.25	75.33	62.27
Pietzrak	19.83	60.73	32.92	45.72
Queen	83.06	42.14	15.20	58.30

   b   Prepare the flowchart and program for a counter of exactly five loops. Use the data items listed in 3(a).

4   The problem entails substituting values in the algebraic formula

$$F = 28 + 3X - X^2$$

Input on each loop is a value for X. This X value is substituted into the above equation to compute the F value. On each loop, output the values of X and F on separate lines. Precede the X value with the literal, 'FOR A VALUE', with the F value preceded by the literal, 'THE RESULT ='. Before ending the solution, print the closing literal 'WORK CLOSES'.

   a   Using READ and DATA statements and a counter, prepare the flowchart and program to process the seven values of X, as follows: $-6, -4, -2, 0, 3, 8$, and 10.
   b   Using an INPUT statement to enter the values of X and a 9s decision to control looping, enter the five values of X as follows: $-5, -1, 2, 4$, and 7.

5   The problem entails preparing and printing the results of a soccer league. The problem requires column headings of 'TEAM', 'WON', 'LOST', 'TIED', and 'POINTS'. Input on each loop are a team's name and the number of games won, lost, and tied. The latter three numeric data items are used to compute points gained by each team. A game won is worth two points, a tied game worth one point, and a loss receives no points. By multiplying the games won, lost, or tied by their respective point equivalent and then adding them up, you obtain the total points assigned to that team. Output on each loop each team's name, games won, games lost, games tied, and the points earned by that team. A total of six teams are to be handled in this application, with their data listed below. Use READ and DATA statements to handle these data.

Team Name	Won	Lost	Tied
Oilers	19	7	4
Roughriders	15	6	9
Whitecaps	15	10	5
Minutemen	10	10	10
Carltons	8	16	6
Strokers	5	23	2

a Prepare the flowchart and program using a counter to process each team on one of six loops.

b Prepare a flowchart and program which utilizes a 9s decision, being sure to add a 9s data statement.

c In both instances, use a REMARK statement to identify each program.

6 The problem entails the estimation of production costs. Input on each loop are the number of units to be produced. Depending on that number, one of two formulas is used to compute costs. If the number of units exceeds 4000, the formula used is C = 5000 + (.0426 * U), where U equals the number of units produced and C the cost. If the number of units is less than or equal to 4000, the formula used is C = 3500 + (.0573 * U). On each loop, output the units produced and the estimated cost of producing them. Print them on separate lines, using the labels 'UNITS PRO-DUCED =' and 'ESTIMATED COSTS ='. Print a blank line between each set of outputs. The units data for this problem include 1800, 4600, 3200, 8700, 2900, 5400, and 6100. Prepare your flowchart and program using a 9s decision to control looping and READ and DATA statements to enter data. Output a label of 'COSTS END' to denote the program's close.

7 The problem relates to the estimation of the price of Treasury bills. The equation used in this estimation process is:

$$P = F * \left(1 - \frac{D * T}{360}\right)$$

where P = the price paid for the bill, D = the rate of discount given in a percent, T = the days to maturity of that bill, and F = the face value of the bill being purchased. On each loop, the variables related to F, D, and T are entered via INPUT statements. These variables are entered into the above formula and used to compute the price of the Treasury bill. Output on four separate lines the discount rate (D), the face value of the bill (F), the days to maturity (T), and the computed price (P) of the bill, preceded by the respective labels of 'DISCOUNT RATE =', 'FACE VALUE OF BILL =', 'DAYS INVESTED =', and 'ACTUAL PRICE OF BILL ='. Separate each output group by a blank line. Use a 9s decision to control the looping sequence and print the label 'PROCESSING BILLS OVER' when that loop is exited. The data for the problem are listed below.

Face Value	Discount Rate (%)	Days to Maturity
100,000	6.0	364
100,000	8.5	350
50,000	9.2	364
75,000	9.875	180
40,000	10.29	364

8   The problem entails the computation of an employee's payroll deductions. Input for each employee are name and gross pay amount. The gross pay provides the basis of computing the employee's union dues, medical insurance premium, and pension benefits per pay period. If the gross pay amount > $500, the union dues deduction is 2.5 percent of the gross amount; otherwise a 2 percent figure is used. The medical deduction uses a flat fee schedule. If gross pay > $400, the medical fee is $5.78, otherwise a fee of $4.93 is charged. Pension benefits are also tied to the gross amount. If gross pay is less than $1000, pension benefits are calculated at 1 percent of the gross amount; otherwise a 1.5 percent figure is employed in that computation. All three deductions are added to produce the total deductions for that employee. Output each employee's name, union deduction, medical insurance deduction, pension deduction, and the total of all three deduction amounts. These five outputs should be printed beneath the respective headings of 'EMPLOYEE', 'UNION', 'MEDICAL', 'PENSION', and 'TOTAL DED'. Print a blank line between the headings and the first line of output. Use READ and DATA statements to handle the data items which follow:

Employee	Gross Pay	Employee	Gross Pay
Sterling	526	Waterford	1258
Thomas	317	Xenoas	463
Unterberg	834	Younghans	287
Villiams	393	Zerkins	752

Quiz Problem   For the quiz narrative that follows, prepare a flowchart and BASIC program to describe the processing outlined.

The problem entails computing an employee's net pay. A report heading consisting of the literals 'EMPLOYEE', 'GROSS', 'FICA', and 'NETPAY' is required. Input to the problem are an employee's name, hours worked, and hourly rate of pay. The employee's gross pay is computed by multiplying the hours worked by the rate of pay. If gross > $500, the FICA rate is 2.2 percent; otherwise a rate of 1.6 percent is used. The FICA deduction is computed by multiplying the appropriate FICA rate by gross pay. Net pay is calculated by subtracting the FICA deduction from gross pay. Output each employee's name, gross pay, FICA deduction, and net pay amount. When the loop is exited, output the label 'PAYROLL OVER' and close the program. The data items used in processing are listed below.

Employee Name	Hours Worked	Pay Rate
Harrison	36	4.00
Jacquline	40	12.10
Lampiere	30	18.20
Norton	42	22.00

Quiz Solution   The flowcharts and programs for this quiz problem are shown in Figures 4.20 and 4.21.

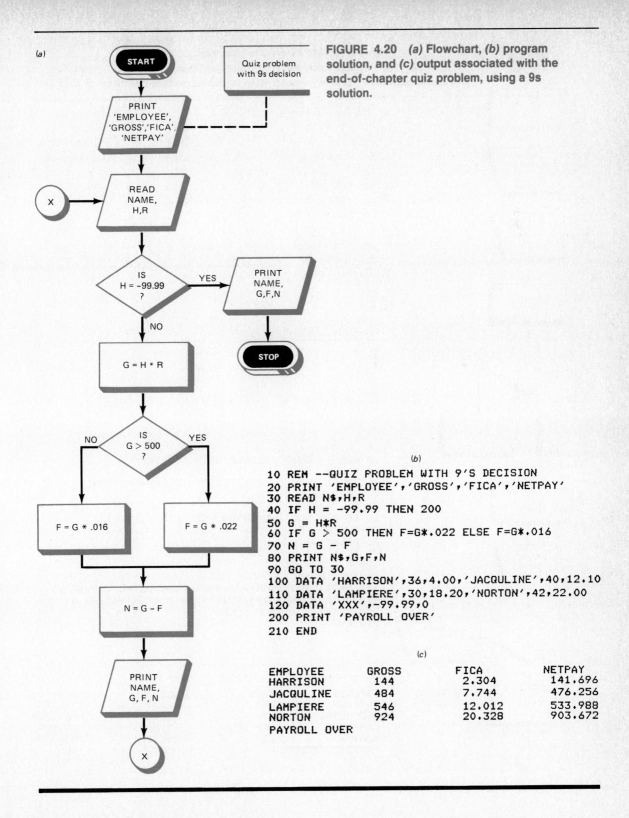

(a)

Quiz problem with 9s decision

FIGURE 4.20 *(a)* Flowchart, *(b)* program solution, and *(c)* output associated with the end-of-chapter quiz problem, using a 9s solution.

(b)
```
10 REM --QUIZ PROBLEM WITH 9'S DECISION
20 PRINT 'EMPLOYEE','GROSS','FICA','NETPAY'
30 READ N$,H,R
40 IF H = -99.99 THEN 200
50 G = H*R
60 IF G > 500 THEN F=G*.022 ELSE F=G*.016
70 N = G - F
80 PRINT N$,G,F,N
90 GO TO 30
100 DATA 'HARRISON',36,4.00,'JACQULINE',40,12.10
110 DATA 'LAMPIERE',30,18.20,'NORTON',42,22.00
120 DATA 'XXX',-99.99,0
200 PRINT 'PAYROLL OVER'
210 END
```

(c)

EMPLOYEE	GROSS	FICA	NETPAY
HARRISON	144	2.304	141.696
JACQULINE	484	7.744	476.256
LAMPIERE	546	12.012	533.988
NORTON	924	20.328	903.672
PAYROLL OVER			

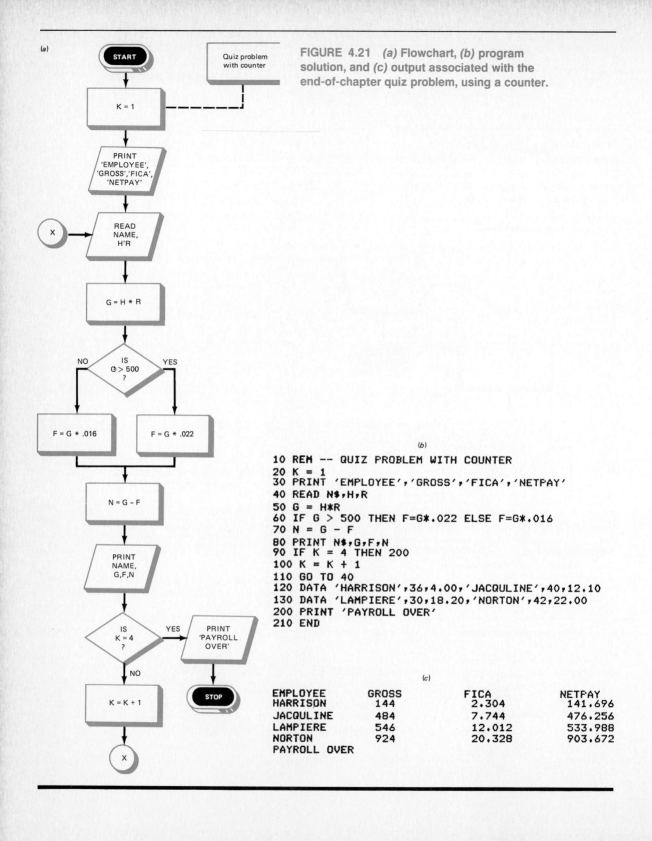

(a)

FIGURE 4.21 (a) Flowchart, (b) program solution, and (c) output associated with the end-of-chapter quiz problem, using a counter.

(b)
```
10 REM -- QUIZ PROBLEM WITH COUNTER
20 K = 1
30 PRINT 'EMPLOYEE','GROSS','FICA','NETPAY'
40 READ N$,H,R
50 G = H*R
60 IF G > 500 THEN F=G*.022 ELSE F=G*.016
70 N = G - F
80 PRINT N$,G,F,N
90 IF K = 4 THEN 200
100 K = K + 1
110 GO TO 40
120 DATA 'HARRISON',36,4.00,'JACQULINE',40,12.10
130 DATA 'LAMPIERE',30,18.20,'NORTON',42,22.00
200 PRINT 'PAYROLL OVER'
210 END
```

(c)

EMPLOYEE	GROSS	FICA	NETPAY
HARRISON	144	2.304	141.696
JACQULINE	484	7.744	476.256
LAMPIERE	546	12.012	533.988
NORTON	924	20.328	903.672
PAYROLL OVER			

Appendix: Debugging Hints

Many students express great anxiety about the debugging (or correcting) of their programs. This uncertainty results from inexperience, as beginning programming students do not know what errors to anticipate or how the computer identifies selected error conditions. Through practical experience, the programmer develops a sense of what program states trigger certain types of errors and where to look for error-generating statements.

This appendix, as well as other appendixes to follow, will act as a guide to debugging techniques by pointing out the steps used to locate errors and make corrections. The debugging of a program is *not magic!* It is a carefully planned elimination process, where facts lead to certain conclusions and the discovery of errors. Each potential error state is scrutinized and eliminated or leads to further analysis until the problem is found. Once a potential source of an error is located, corrections are initiated and evaluated as to their effectiveness and the program is rerun. The debugging process is repeated as long as errors exist.

This appendix will discuss errors which relate to the handling of program loops, DATA statements, and counters. Our discussions will illustrate the program, the error message or condition which results, the likely source of the error, and the way to correct it.

Proper Program Loops

As we have noted, the looping sequence is the basis of most processing sequences where a group of data items is handled. It is important that the loop be properly created and that a conditional branch be established to properly exit the loop. It is generally not acceptable practice to end a program via an error state.

An example of this type of programming error is depicted in Figure 4.22, where two programs are listed. In Figure 4.22(a) the program does not possess an IF/THEN statement and therefore does not possess a conditional statement with which to control and exit the looping sequence. Thus, when the program is run after the third loop, the following error message appears:

? Out of data at line 20

The significance of this error statement is twofold. It denotes that the program has failed to run to completion without incurring an error and that the error occurred at line 20. If the program was properly written, the program would have been processed and *no error message would have resulted.*

The specification of line 20 often puzzles some readers. This line was specified because it was the line at which the program error occurred. The out-of-data message denotes that the computer, under command of the READ statement at line 20, went to read data that was nonexistent. In three previous loops, a total of nine data items was read, three variables per loop. The out-of-data condition occurred when the program looped and tried to read data at the start of the fourth loop.

The out-of-data error state occurred because a conditional statement permitting an exit from the loop did not exist. Compare the solution offered in Figure 4.22(b), where a 9s decision via an IF/THEN statement was written into that solution. Here the programmer foresaw the need to properly exit the loop, after handling the third set

FIGURE 4.22 Programs and outputs for two programs. *(a)* Program 1 shows an error condition because there is no way to properly exit the loop. *(b)* Program 2 shows that error condition corrected, with the addition of a 9s decision.

(a) Program 1

```
10 REM -- ERROR PROGRAM 1
20 READ A,B,C
30 X = A*B + C
40 PRINT A,B,C,X
50 GO TO 20
60 DATA 4,6,9,-3,4,-5,12,1,7
100 END
```

```
    4              6              9              33
   -3              4             -5             -17
   12              1              7              19
?Out of data at line 20
```

(b) Program 2

```
10 REM -- NEW LOOP SEQUENCE
20 READ A,B,C
30 IF A = -999 THEN 100
40 X = A*B + C
50 PRINT A,B,C,X
60 GO TO 20
70 DATA 4,6,9,-3,4,-5,12,1,7
80 DATA -999,0,0
100 END
```

```
    4              6              9              33
   -3              4             -5             -17
   12              1              7              19
```

of data items. When the 9s data is input on the start of the fourth loop, it is properly read and tested, with the program exiting to line 100.

In examining the output from this program, note that *no error* message was printed as *no error existed*. The program was not permitted to run into an error condition but was properly designed to exit on loop 4 when the -999 data was input for A.

READ statements are often the point at which error conditions are noted, as a program may run out of data or input invalid data items. Programmers must provide for looping sequences that are properly executed. Looping sequences should not be closed because of error conditions.

An Errant 9s DATA Statement

Even when looping sequences are properly created, the potential for errors still exists. A common source for errors is the DATA statement provided for the 9s data item. One type of mistake is to completely omit the 9s DATA statement; the program

```
10 REM -- ERROR PROGRAM 2        NAME          GROSS
20 PRINT 'NAME','GROSS'          SMITH         100.75
30 READ N$,H,R                   BROWN         195.65
40 IF H = -99.99 THEN 200        GREENE        131.75
50 G = H*R                       XXX           0
60 PRINT N$,G                    ?Out of data at line 30
70 GO TO 30
100 DATA 'SMITH',31,3.25
110 DATA 'BROWN',43,4.55
120 DATA 'GREENE',25,5.27
130 DATA 'XXX',0,-99.99
200 END
```

FIGURE 4.23 A program and its output, indicating an error condition at line 30. Often the incorrect positioning of the 9s data used by a program is responsible for an error, which closes that program's processing.

will then generate an out-of-data message. This error message recognizes that the 9s data was not incorporated into the solution and that the program literally ran out of data. This type of error parallels the error condition discussed in the previous section of this appendix.

A far more subtle error is evident when the 9s DATA is specified but incorrectly written. Figure 4.23 illustrates a program in which such a condition occurs. At an initial inspection the gross pay program appears to have all of the required components. The program possesses column headings and a looping sequence controlled by a 9s decision; the DATA statements use the proper format and data sequence; and a 9s DATA statement exists. However, when the program's output is examined, it is apparent that an error condition was encountered.

The initial three lines of output related to SMITH, BROWN, and GREENE are expected and valid. However, the output of the dummy data items of XXX for N$ and 0 for G, as well as the out-of-data error message, confirm the error state. The output of XXX tells the programmer that data from line 130, the 9s DATA statement, was incorrectly outputted. This error tells us to focus our attention at line 130.

The out-of-data message indicates that the program kept on looping until it ran out of data and that the 9s decision was not invoked. This condition usually results from an improperly written 9s decision (IF/THEN) statement or improperly specified 9s data.

At line 40, the IF/THEN statement representing the 9s decision reveals no errors. The same is true for line 130, as the statement correctly follows the BASIC syntax. The error at line 130 does not result from a lapse in coding; it results from the incorrect positioning of the 9s data. Line 40 tests against the H variable, the second variable input on line 30. However, when line 130 is examined, we note that the −99.99 data item is aligned for input against the R variable and 0 will be input for H. When line 130 was accessed, the data input caused the computer to invalidate the 9s decision and continue looping.

Generally, since data drawn from a 9s DATA statement is not normal, we must look for an error. To correct this type of error, we must rewrite line 130, so that the

−99.99 item is positioned as the second data item input. The new statement shown below

    130   DATA 'XXX', −99.99, 0

will cause the 9s decision to be properly executed. The looping sequence will properly end after the third loop, and only the three required lines of output will result.

Finding the DATA Error

When many data items are listed in one DATA statement, the potential for error increases greatly. Through fatigue or carelessness, data items can be improperly specified—often by the insertion of unwanted characters. Common mistakes are the substitution of commas for decimal points, the placement of two decimals in a number, or the omission of required commas between data items. The sample program listing of Figure 4.24 presents this type of error condition.

An initial reading of the program would probably not reveal a DATA error. The resultant output serves as a far better guide to errors. The output of column headings reveals that the program was free from errors, compiled, and entered processing. One of the secondary purposes of outputting column headings is to provide those indications. The appearance of column headings, whose PRINT statements are executed at the program's start, denote the satisfactory acceptance and execution of the program before an error was encountered.

FIGURE 4.24   A program and its output, indicating a data format error. The incorrect specification of data within DATA statements is the source of many program errors. Programmers must exercise great care when inputting their program data.

```
10 REM -- ERROR PROGRAM 3
20 PRINT 'SALESPERSON','TOTAL SALES','COMMISSION'
30 READ N$,A1,A2,A3,A4
40 IF A1 = -999.99 THEN 200
50 S = A1 + A2 + A3
60 C = S*.10
70 PRINT N$,S,C
80 GO TO 30
100 DATA 'HECKER',19.45,26.31,56.98,87.36
110 DATA 'GERMAN',15.20,93.57,70.68,43.15
120 DATA 'FRANCOIS',49.26,62.36,18,75,30.83
130 DATA 'ERIGONT',16.38,19.72,66.24,73.16
140 DATA 'XXX',-999.99,0,0,0
200 END
```

```
SALESPERSON    TOTAL SALES    COMMISSION
HECKER           102.74         10.274
GERMAN           179.45         17.945
FRANCOIS         129.62         12.962
%Data format error at line 30
```

The output of data related to the first three salespeople points our attention to a potential error in the fourth DATA statement. Evaluation of line 130, the fourth data statement, reveals that it is correctly written and follows the form specified in the READ statement of line 30.

A second indicator is the error message of %DATA format error at line 30, which normally indicates an attempt to mix string-variable data with numeric variables and vice versa. As the READ statement (line 30) is correctly written, we must turn our attention back to the program's DATA statements. Each DATA statement must be reread and its accuracy assessed. By this method, we can verify the accuracy of statements 100 and 110; the same cannot be said for line 120.

The DATA statement at line 120 is incorrectly written, resulting from improper punctuation. The error occurs at the third data item. Instead of being 18.75, the data item was written as 18,75. A comma was incorrectly keyed in place of a decimal point. This type of error occurs from haste or fatigue and is encountered by programmers with a variety of experience.

The error message resulted from the fact that the data was not properly specified. In executing the program, it assigned 'FRANCOIS' to N$, 49.26 to A1, 62.36 to A2, 18 to A3 and 75 to A4. The comma broke what was to be 18.75, into 18 and 75. This completed the input operation of line 30, but left 30.83 unhandled.

On the fourth loop, the program attempted to assign 30.83 to N$, as it was the next data item available. This mismatch created the error condition, aborted the program's processing, and produced the DATA format error message.

The correction to this program is easily accomplished by retyping line 120. The correction of 18,75 to 18.75, with no additional errors, will produce the desired outputs and complete processing of the program.

FIVE

- Introduce the concept of an accumulator and its application to program solutions involving totals.

- Describe the use of program modules and the use of the GOSUB statement to create them.

- Describe the use of the TAB function when aligning output data.

- Describe the use of the PRINT USING statement in the formatting of outputs.

- Discuss the operational relationship between a counter and looping sequences defined by FOR/NEXT statements.

- Illustrate the use of the STEP option with a FOR/NEXT statement.

Introduction

In Chapter 3 we discussed the general types of lines which are employed when printing reports. One of these types was the summary line, a line of output representing a form of total computed by adding values from a group of people or transactions. The summary line contains the many grand totals or subtotals used when preparing business reports. A representative sample of these totals is illustrated in Figure 5.1, where individual-customer totals and a grand total of all accounts is printed.

Chapter 5 discusses a critical component in the computation of any total, the **accumulator.** The accumulator provides a means of adding values to create running totals. Accumulators are selectively applied to add values undergoing processing or values identified with a specific group or code. Programmers can use as many accumulators as the problem requires.

The accumulation of data is often one computation within a group of related tasks. A group of related statements is often combined into a modular unit to control execution and simplify access to that module when debugging. This chapter reviews the composition of such modules using BASIC's GOSUB instruction and its application to program development.

Another topic presented in Chapter 5 is the creation of automated looping sequences via the FOR/NEXT instruction. This instruction offers a concise replacement for the counter, as well as adding many user-oriented features to improve its processing potential. The FOR/NEXT is applied to a variety of problems to highlight its universality. The STEP option permits the user to vary the increment employed with the FOR/NEXT.

CUST NO	CUSTOMER NAME	ORIGINAL INVOICE		
		NUMBER	DATE	AMOUNT
050055	EMPIRE CITY SUBWAY CO	008702	01/08/82	75.00
		037570	01/15/82	64.95
		008687	01/06/82	75.00
		037780	01/20/82	64.95
		037612	01/18/82	64.95
		037635	01/18/82	70.36
CUSTOMER TOTAL				415.21
050161	ENERGY ADMINISTRATION	037303	01/06/82	140.73
CUSTOMER TOTAL				140.73
050077	EXXON CO., USA	032780	07/06/81	100.00
		037339	01/07/82	346.40
CUSTOMER TOTAL				446.40
050099	J. F. EVANS, INC.	007238		
		007983	08/10/81	75.00
CUSTOMER TOTAL				−9.00
050162	L M ERICSSON TELE-	037811	01/21/82	96.53
CUSTOMER TOTAL				96.53
GRAND TOTALS				71144.94

CUSTOMER totals provide individual totals for each company's transactions.

GRAND totals represent the activities of the entire group of transactions.

FIGURE 5.1   Accumulated totals provide users with information related to the addition of data for a group. In the report shown, customers are provided with their own totals and a grand total is provided for the entire group of activities.

In addition to these topics, other BASIC instructions and techniques are presented. These concepts supplement previously introduced statements and assist in the preparation of outputs or help refine processing techniques.

5.1 Accumulated Totals

Accumulators provide the vehicle for developing totals that reflect data drawn from a group of transactions. The computerized preparation of an accumulated total is entirely different from the manual computation of that same sum. During the computerized processing of an accumulator, it is not possible to run down a column of figures and add them. Instead, a quantity must be added to the accumulator during the program loop in which it is computed. In this fashion, the accumulator serves as a form of running total, always providing the most current total. A simple analogy illustrates this point.

The Concept of an Accumulator

Assume that you are working in a small retail outlet as a sales clerk. When a sale is made, you must compute the sales tax and record it within a separate journal. Each time you enter an amount, you must add it to the previous total and compute the new subtotal. The first sales tax amount becomes the basis for the first subtotal. The second amount is added to the first, and the second subtotal is computed. The third amount is added to the sum of the first two amounts, producing the next subtotal.

This sequence of additions continues until the last sales record is processed. The handling of that last data item signals the close of processing. It denotes that the last tax item was added to the previous accumulated total and that the subtotal is now a final total, as no new data items are forthcoming.

Within this operational sequence, each new tax amount is added to the prior total, producing a new accumulated total. The sequence of accumulations continues as long as data is being generated. When the last sales amount is handled the accumulated total becomes final.

Converting this sequence into computer terms, we code the sales tax routine as a looping sequence. Each sale is an input to the computation of a sales tax, which is added to the accumulator on each loop. When an LRC condition is satisfied, the loop is exited and the finalized total is outputted.

The translation of this concept into flowcharting and programming terms requires the execution of two statements. One statement defines the accumulator and initializes it at a value of zero. This statement acts as an initial condition to use an accumulator and must precede its use within a looping sequence. The second statement accomplishes the actual addition of the amount to the accumulator and appears inside the looping sequence. On each loop the computed amount is added to the previous total, producing the new total which is retained in the accumulator.

Two statements used to represent the initialization of an accumulator and its subsequent update may appear as follows:

1   $T = 0$

2   $T = T + A$

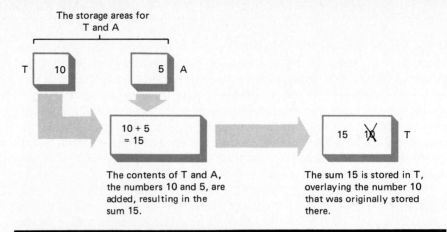

The storage areas for T and A

The contents of T and A, the numbers 10 and 5, are added, resulting in the sum 15.

The sum 15 is stored in T, overlaying the number 10 that was originally stored there.

FIGURE 5.2 The execution of the instruction $T = T + A$ causes the amounts of T and A to be added and the result to be stored back in T.

T is the variable representing the accumulator, and A is the variable to be accumulated. Though we have chosen the variable A in this case, any other variable could have been used in an actual application.

The statement $T = 0$ serves two purposes: it defines the accumulator as the variable T and initializes T at zero. This step is critical, as it ensures that the accumulator begins adding from a zero base and does not incorrectly include a carryover amount from another problem. It is positioned prior to the start of the loop sequence in which the accumulator is used, acting as an initial condition to its processing.

The statement $T = T + A$ is the instruction which actually updates the accumulated total on each loop. The value to be accumulated, A, is added to the current value of T, and the result is stored back in T. The addition of T and A occurs first, as their addition is on the righthand side of the equal sign. Their sum is then stored in T, the sole variable to the equal sign's left. This operational sequence is illustrated in Figure 5.2.

In the indicated operation, an A value of 5 is added to an existing T total of 10. The result of 15 is then stored in T, which overlays and eliminates the old value of 10. The old accumulated total is updated on each loop and stored away for update on the next loop. The process continues until the last record is processed, the loop exited, and that total outputted.

Critical to the computation of $T = T + A$ is the initialization of T prior to the first loop. On that first loop, an A value is computed and an attempt is made to add it to T. Without an initial value for T, the $T = T + A$ computation cannot be executed. By using an initial value of zero, T has a valid number which can be added to A and not throw off our final total. Any value other than zero will result in an error. The flowchart and BASIC program shown in Figure 5.3 illustrate this point.

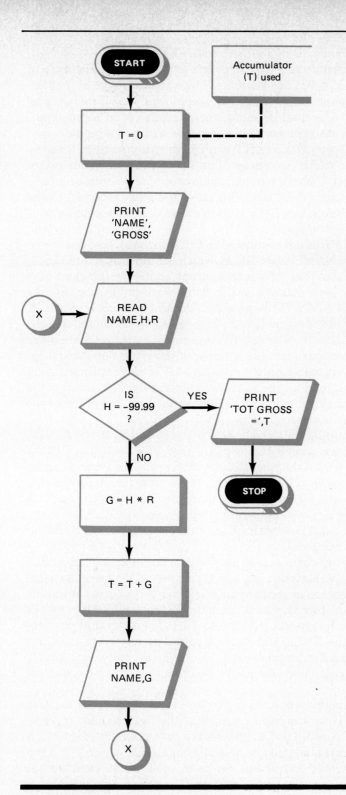

FIGURE 5.3 The flowchart and BASIC program shown incorporate an accumulator, which totals the gross pay amounts for three employees. The resulting output appears below.

```
10 REM -- ACCUMULATOR(T) USED
20 T = 0
30 PRINT 'NAME','GROSS'
40 READ N$,H,R
50 IF H = -99.99 THEN 200
60 G = H*R
70 T = T + G
80 PRINT N$,G
90 GO TO 40
100 DATA 'SMITH',31,3.26
110 DATA 'BERGEN',41,5.25
120 DATA 'CHEERIOS',36,4.11
130 DATA 'XXX',-99.99,0
200 PRINT 'TOT GROSS =',T
210 END
```

```
NAME          GROSS
SMITH          101.06
BERGEN         215.25
CHEERIOS       147.96
TOT GROSS =    464.27
```

The overall problem entails the computation of a gross pay amount and the accumulation of all gross pay amounts. This particular type of problem has been already discussed a few times; its overall logic should therefore be familiar. Here we have inserted those statements related to an accumulator, thus illustrating how easily an accumulator can be added to a problem.

Our flowchart opens with a START symbol, which is directly followed by the first accumulator-related statement. The $T = 0$ initial condition establishes the accumulator T at the required value of zero and is properly positioned prior to the start of the loop. An annotation was attached to the processing symbol containing $T = 0$ to remind us that an accumulator is being used.

Following the $T = 0$ initial condition is a PRINT symbol that directs the output of two literals, NAME and GROSS, which will serve as column headings. The READ symbol that follows this output begins the flowchart loop and inputs the employee's name (NAME), hours worked (H), and pay rate (R). The H variable is used in the 9s decision to control the looping sequence. Its NO branch leads to the computation of the gross pay amount G and the update of the accumulator T. Note that the accumulator update equation was altered to properly accommodate the addition of the gross amount and appears as $T = T + G$. On each loop, the gross amount is added to the accumulator and updates that total for the next loop's processing. The output of the employee's name and computed gross pay closes the loop and precedes the unconditional branch to the loop's top.

The looping continues until the 9s data is recognized by the 9s decision and causes the program to exit the loop. On that YES branch, a PRINT symbol is directed to output the label TOT GROSS = and the actual accumulated total represented by T. This output is vital to accumulators, as the computer must possess a way of providing the results of its processing. After all, of what value are processed results if they are not accessible to their users. The specification of a special label, prior to outputting T, merely aids in identifying the total printed.

A similar series of steps is used in the program prepared from that flowchart. The REMARK statement, line 10, advises of the use of an accumulator. The initialization of the accumulator T via $T = 0$ occurs at line 20. The PRINT statement, line 30, directs the output of the two literals in zones 1 and 2 that compose the report's column heading. The program loop commences at line 40, the READ statement, where data related to the three variables of N\$, H, and R enter processing. The IF/THEN statement, line 50, represents the 9s decision and enables the program to choose between lines 200 and 60.

The NO branch equivalent leads to line 60, where the gross pay amount, G, is computed. This statement precedes the accumulator update, $T = T + G$, where G is added to T to produce the new accumulated total. It is at this instruction that many people note the importance of the $T = 0$ initialization. Without that instruction, no value of T would exist for the $T = T + G$ computation to be processed. With $T = 0$, the G value is added to

0, the result stored back in T, such that processing can continue into the loops that follow.

The output N$ and G occurs via line 80, the PRINT instruction, placing both variables beneath their respective headings. The GO TO, line 90, returns the flow of processing to the READ statement at line 40 and continues the looping sequence.

The 9s data, specified at the DATA statement of line 130, activates the IF/THEN statement. When H = −99.99, the program exits the loop and branches to line 200. Unlike previous solutions, line 200 is not an END statement. Instead, it is a PRINT statement which will output the accumulated total T, preceded by the literal TOT GROSS =. This output is executed before the END statement closes the program.

The output from this sample program is also shown in Figure 5.3. Note that headings appear atop each column of output. Three detail lines are printed, matching the number of employees processed. A summary line representing the output of the accumulated total T is the last line printed; T appears in zone 2, beneath all other values, as planned.

The important thing to draw from this example are the three program components associated with processing an accumulated total of data. In order, they are:

1   The initialization of the accumulator at zero (T = 0)

2   The update of the accumulator (T = T + G)

3   The output of the accumulated total

These three elements ensure the accurate processing of the accumulator and its output once that final total is attained.

In our first illustration the accumulator was used in a processing sequence to total a data item after its computation. The program in Figure 5.3 accumulated gross pay amounts subsequent to their computation on each loop. Some applications require that an accumulator add a specific input amount, prior to the use of that total in a computation. A sales commission problem provides an opportunity to examine such a sequence.

Applying the Accumulator

PROBLEM 5.1   Sales Commissions

Input on each loop includes a sales item and its sales price. The individual sales price is accumulated on each loop prior to printing each sales item and its price. The headings SALES ITEM and PRICE appear at the top of the output of all items. When all the data is processed, the actual sales commission is computed after the loop is exited. The commission is computed by multiplying the accumulated total by the appropriate rate. If the accumulated total is greater than $250, a rate of 10 percent is used; otherwise a 5 percent rate is employed. Output the resultant commission, preceded by the label

COMMISSION =. The commission amount should appear beneath the column of data related to sales prices. The data for this problem appears below.

Sales Item	Sales Price
Armchair	289.63
Coffee table	157.37
Desk lamp	169.25
Light fixture	124.45

Use a 9s decision to control the looping sequence needed to process this data.

These are the main points in the problem narrative.

1   The headings SALES ITEM and PRICE appear atop the final output.

2   Input on each loop are a sales item and its sales price.

3   A 9s decision is used to control the looping sequence.

4   An accumulator is needed to total the individual sales prices. The accumulator must be initialized at zero prior to looping and updated on each loop.

5   The formulas required for processing are

a   Total = total + price
b   Commission = total * commission rate

6   Two commission rates are available for use. If the accumulated total is greater than $250, the rate used is 10 percent. If not, a 5 percent rate is used to compute the commission.

7   Within the loop's processing, output only the sales item and its price.

8   After looping ceases, the commission is computed and outputted, preceded by the label COMMISSION =.

The flowchart and BASIC program for this problem are shown in Figure 5.4.

In the flowchart for Problem 5.1, we observe that this solution is divided into two major groups. The first group relates to the looping sequence, in which each price (P) is added to the accumulator (T) on each loop. The loop is preceded by the initialization of T at zero and the output of the two column headings. The loop is framed by the READ symbol, which enters the sales item (ITEM) and price (P), and the PRINT symbol, which outputs the same two variables.

It is the exit of the flowchart loop via the 9s decision that leads to the second major component of this solution. The decision symbol that tests whether T is greater than 250 is essential to determining which commission rate to use. The computation of the actual commission amount is positioned ahead of its output, which incorporates the label COMMISSION =. As you may conclude, the sequence of tasks on the YES branch of the 9s decision is external to the looping sequence and executed just once.

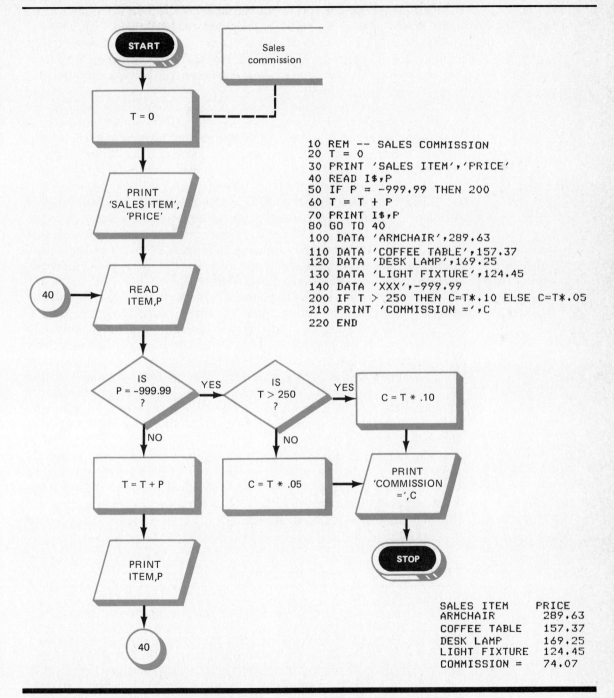

```
10 REM -- SALES COMMISSION
20 T = 0
30 PRINT 'SALES ITEM','PRICE'
40 READ I$,P
50 IF P = -999.99 THEN 200
60 T = T + P
70 PRINT I$,P
80 GO TO 40
100 DATA 'ARMCHAIR',289.63
110 DATA 'COFFEE TABLE',157.37
120 DATA 'DESK LAMP',169.25
130 DATA 'LIGHT FIXTURE',124.45
140 DATA 'XXX',-999.99
200 IF T > 250 THEN C=T*.10 ELSE C=T*.05
210 PRINT 'COMMISSION =',C
220 END
```

```
SALES ITEM      PRICE
ARMCHAIR        289.63
COFFEE TABLE    157.37
DESK LAMP       169.25
LIGHT FIXTURE   124.45
COMMISSION =     74.07
```

FIGURE 5.4   The flowchart and program written for Problem 5.1, which entails the computation and accumulation of sales commission amounts. The output reveals the results of processing.

The looping sequence is used to accumulate the total price of all items sold, with no commission amounts computed within the loop. Only when no further data exists and the 9s data is read can the accumulated total be tested against $250. The problem narrative dictated that only the accumulated total be compared to 250, prohibiting the computation of individual commission amounts within the loop.

The logic depicted in the flowchart of Figure 5.4 provides the basis for writing the program solution. After the opening REM instruction, the accumulator is initialized at line 20 and the column headings printed via line 30. Line 40 identifies a READ statement, which opens the program's looping sequence. In that READ instruction, the variables I$ and P relate to the sales item and sales price, respectively.

The P variable is used in the IF/THEN statement, line 50, which is a 9s decision. The update of the accumulator occurs at line 60, where the computation $T = T + P$ adds the new price to the current accumulated total. The PRINT statement that follows on line 70 outputs I$ and P beneath their respective column headings in zones 1 and 2. The GO TO statement, line 80, completes the loop and restarts the looping sequence.

Exactly four loops are completed before the 9s data is read and the program exits the loop. At line 200 an IF/THEN/ELSE statement tests T against 250, causing the program to choose between the commission rates of 5 and 10 percent. If T is greater than $250, the 10 percent rate is used; otherwise the 5 percent rate is employed. The two required commission computations are positioned within either leg of the IF/THEN/ELSE statement. This line is followed by the output of the commission (C) and its label before the program ends. The punctuation used in line 210 results in the label appearing in zone 1 and the commission in zone 2. The output from this program is shown in Figure 5.4.

The number of accumulators incorporated into a program relates directly to the number required by the problem. Regardless of the number employed, each accumulator is handled similarly and must satisfy the three constraints associated with all accumulators. Consider the following problem where multiple accumulators are required.

PROBLEM 5.2   Payroll Deductions

Input to the problem are an employee's name and gross pay amount. The gross pay amount is involved in the computation of the pension and unemployment deductions. The pension deduction is computed at 5 percent of the gross pay amount. The unemployment deduction is calculated at 1 percent of gross pay. The problem requires two separate accumulators, one for the pension deductions and one for the unemployment deductions. Output each employee's name, gross pay, pension deduction, and unemployment deductions. These outputs should be printed beneath the headings EMPLOYEE, GROSS PAY, PENSION, and UNEMPL. After processing the last employee, as noted via a 9s decision, output the two accumulated totals on separate lines. Use the labels TOT PENSION = and TOT UNEMPL = before their respective outputs and position them beneath their columns.

The data for the problem is as follows:

Employee	Gross	Employee	Gross
Cartright	479	Ninski	523
Eagleton	345	Porterhouse	377
Markham	287	Tarshisian	601

These are the main points in the problem narrative.

1 Two accumulators are required to separately total amounts related to pension and unemployment deductions. Each must be individually initialized at zero.

2 A heading consisting of four literals is required.

3 Input are an employee's name and gross pay amount. A total of six sets of employee data are involved.

4 A 9s decision is used to control the loop's processing.

5 The formulas used to support processing include

a Pension deduction = gross pay * .05
b Unemployment deduction = gross pay * .01
c Tot pension = tot pension + pension deduction
d Tot unemployment = tot unemployment + unemployment deduction

6 The output within each loop are the employee's name, gross pay, pension deduction, and unemployment deduction.

7 When the loop is exited, output both accumulated totals on separate lines. Precede each total's output with its respective label, either TOT PENSION = or TOT UNEMPL =. Ensure that the amount printed appears beneath its respective column of output (e.g., the pension total is printed beneath the column of pension data).

The flowchart and program for Problem 5.2 is presented in Figure 5.5.

The flowchart in Figure 5.5 details the planned logic of our solution. Three initial conditions are indicated before the start of the looping sequence. Two accumulators are initialized, as the problem calls for two separate totals. The T1 accumulator is assigned to total pension deductions, with the T2 accumulator serving the same function for unemployment deductions. The output of the four literals composing the column headings completes those tasks which must be accomplished before the start of the looping sequence. Two annotation symbols, which accompany these initial symbols, advise of the flowchart's purpose and each accumulator's assignment.

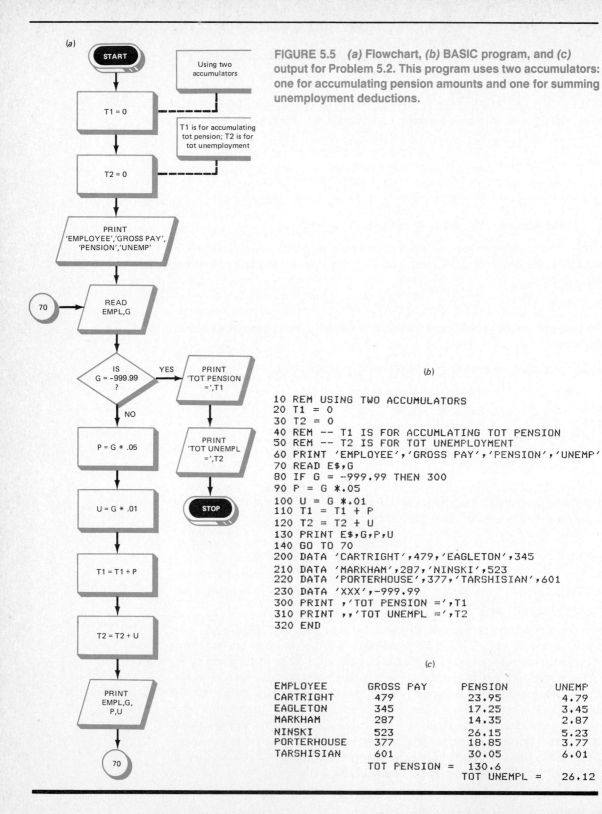

FIGURE 5.5 (a) Flowchart, (b) BASIC program, and (c) output for Problem 5.2. This program uses two accumulators: one for accumulating pension amounts and one for summing unemployment deductions.

(a)

Using two accumulators

T1 is for accumulating tot pension; T2 is for tot unemployment

(b)

```
10 REM USING TWO ACCUMULATORS
20 T1 = 0
30 T2 = 0
40 REM -- T1 IS FOR ACCUMLATING TOT PENSION
50 REM -- T2 IS FOR TOT UNEMPLOYMENT
60 PRINT 'EMPLOYEE','GROSS PAY','PENSION','UNEMP'
70 READ E$,G
80 IF G = -999.99 THEN 300
90 P = G *.05
100 U = G *.01
110 T1 = T1 + P
120 T2 = T2 + U
130 PRINT E$,G,P,U
140 GO TO 70
200 DATA 'CARTRIGHT',479,'EAGLETON',345
210 DATA 'MARKHAM',287,'NINSKI',523
220 DATA 'PORTERHOUSE',377,'TARSHISIAN',601
230 DATA 'XXX',-999.99
300 PRINT ,'TOT PENSION =',T1
310 PRINT ,,'TOT UNEMPL =',T2
320 END
```

(c)

EMPLOYEE	GROSS PAY	PENSION	UNEMP
CARTRIGHT	479	23.95	4.79
EAGLETON	345	17.25	3.45
MARKHAM	287	14.35	2.87
NINSKI	523	26.15	5.23
PORTERHOUSE	377	18.85	3.77
TARSHISIAN	601	30.05	6.01
	TOT PENSION =	130.6	
		TOT UNEMPL =	26.12

The flowchart loop opens and follows previously discussed norms. The READ symbol allows for the input of the employee's name (EMPL) and gross pay (G) and is placed prior to the 9s decision. The NO branch leads to processing within the loop and a string of four processing symbols. The first processing symbol details the computation of the pension deduction (P), and the second the computation of the unemployment deduction (U). Both involve the use of the gross pay amount (G) and a decimal which is the equivalent of the specified percent figure.

The next two processing steps relate to the update of the two accumulators. The $T1 = T1 + P$ formula updates the accumulator assigned to pension amounts (T1), whereas the $T2 = T2 + U$ equation adds unemployment deductions to the T2 accumulator. We have placed the two update computations together as a means of grouping like computations.

After the update of both accumulators, we print each employee's data. This output occurs at the end of each loop and precedes the continuation of the loop via an unconditional branch. Once looping stops, the output of the accumulated totals is possible. Each accumulated total is printed on a separate line, with T1 appearing before T2. Two distinct special labels, TOT PENSION = and TOT UNEMPL =, are printed before the accumulated totals of T1 and T2, respectively. These two outputs mark the close of processing.

As you might surmise, the BASIC program illustrated within Figure 5.5 adheres to the logic developed within our flowchart. In the program, statements 10 to 60 precede loop activities. Lines 10, 40, and 50 are REM statements, serving as advisory notes. Statements 20 and 30 initialize the T1 and T2 accumulators at zero. The PRINT statement, line 60, outputs each literal into one of the first four print zones.

The program loop is defined by lines 70 to 140. The READ statement, line 70, precedes the IF/THEN statement representing the 9s decision. The two variables input are the employee's name (E$) and the gross pay amount (G). The gross pay variable is used in lines 90 and 100 to sequentially compute the pension deduction (P) and the unemployment deduction (U). Both deductions are updated into their accumulators via lines 110 and 120. The output of the variables E$, G, P, and U occurs at line 130.

The required DATA statements are grouped in statements 200 to 230. We have placed two sets of employee data within each DATA statement. Line 230, the 9s DATA statement, is excepted from this format and presents data relating solely to the 9s decision. Note that it is positioned in relation to the G variable on input, as G is tested against in the IF/THEN statement of line 80. When $G = -999.99$, the flow of processing transfers to line 300. This is the first of two PRINT statements, outputting the accumulated totals of T1 and T2 on separate lines.

Of interest is the punctuation used within lines 300 and 310. Note that one comma is placed after the PRINT command of line 300 and two commas are similarly positioned in line 310. The commas will shift the output of variables by one or two print zones. As shown in Figure 5.5(c), the output from line 300 appears in print zones 2 and 3; zone 1 is deliberately blank. The single comma placed after the PRINT command shifts the output one print zone to the right. Thus, the label TOT PENSION = is printed in zone 2, and the quantity for T1 in zone 3. The output of T1 in zone 3 places it beneath the column of pension deductions, as requested in the problem narrative.

The same logic is applied to the output directed by the PRINT statement at line 310. In this case, however, the outputs of the literal TOT UNEMPL = and T2 are offset by two print zones, as two commas are positioned after the PRINT command. This offset leaves print zones 1 and 2 blank and places the outputs related to T2 in zones 3 and 4. Again, the accumulated total for T2 is printed beneath unemployment deductions.

SIDE BAR 5.1   Don't Lose T = 0

For any accumulator to be effectively used, it is essential that it be properly initialized and updated. A common error found in many programs is the failure to establish the initial condition of T = 0. This instruction is omitted from the preloop activities and renders the subsequent update of the accumulator ineffective.

The programmer must remember to initialize any accumulator before it is used. If more than one accumulator is used, each accumulator must be initialized at 0.

5.2 Program Modules and the GOSUB

FIGURE 5.6   The predefined-process symbol is used in flowcharts to identify program modules. The narrative in the symbol identifies the program module's name.

Often, in addition to updating an accumulator, the problem requires that a program undertake other processing activities directly associated with that update. This may be the case when two or more categories of data are handled by the same program and the processing related to each category is separated into its own group of statements. The programming module contains only those statements which relate directly to that category.

The concept of organizing modules of program instructions is currently popular and has many advantages. It enables the programmer to group related statements into one unit. When errors are encountered in relation to a specific category or coded entry, the programmer does not have to search the entire program but can turn directly to the module which contains only those instructions. The use of program modules also helps programmers organize their thoughts, as they have to deal with only one component at a time.

The **predefined-process symbol** is used to define program modules in flowcharts (Figure 5.6). This rectangular symbol, which was previously introduced in Chapter 3, identifies the point at which that module of instructions is referenced. The actual set of instructions composing that module are then outlined in a second flow diagram, which accompanies the main flowchart and details only those steps relating to that specific category.

BASIC's operational equivalent of the program module is defined by the GOSUB and RETURN statements. The **GOSUB statement** is the operational reference to a specific module of instructions and enables the program to branch to that module and commence processing. The **RETURN statement** is the operational counterpart of the GOSUB and directs that the flow of processing return to the main program from the module. Whereas the GOSUB statement is positioned within the main part of the program, the RETURN statement is positioned at the end of the program module and is invoked when the module's end is encountered.

The structure of the GOSUB statement adheres to BASIC's general line format. A sample GOSUB statement is

    60   GOSUB 2000

where 60 is the line number of the statement, GOSUB its command, and 2000 the line that identifies the first statement of a module to which the program will branch.

Assuming that the module employs lines 2000 to 2100, the RETURN statement is positioned as the last statement of that module. Hypothetically, that RETURN statement could be written as

    2100   RETURN

where 2100 is the line number and RETURN the command. Nothing follows RETURN, as the statement's sole purpose is to direct the flow of processing back to the statement which precipitated the branch to the module. To further illustrate the use of both statements, consider the example which follows.

PROBLEM 5.3   Union Deductions

Input to the problem are an employee's name, union code, and gross pay. If the union code is 1, that union deduction is computed to 1 percent of the gross pay amount. If the union code is 2, the union deduction is computed at 2 percent of gross pay. Each type of union deduction should be accumulated separately. Output on each loop is the employee's name, gross pay, union deduction, and a literal specifying the union's name. A union code of 1 identifies a CLERICAL union worker, whereas a code of 2 notes a TWU union person. All computations and outputs related to either union should be performed within their separate modules. A heading of EMPLOYEE, GROSS PAY, UNION DED, and UNION NAME appears atop the report. Output both accumulated totals when the loop is closed, using the labels TOTAL CLERICAL DUES = $ and TOTAL TWU DUES = $, respectively. Each of these outputs should appear on a separate line, the actual totals appearing beneath the union deductions column. Use a counter to control looping.

The data for the problem is as follows:

Employee Name	Gross	Code	Employee Name	Gross	Code
Adams	463	1	Graddock	371	1
Barnowski	577	2	Hartman	576	2
Charleston	363	2	Inderoff	675	1
Dalton	258	1	Jackson	309	2

These are the main points in the problem narrative.

1   Two types of union deductions are handled, each within its own module.

2   Two accumulators are required to total the dues related to union 1 and union 2 separately.

3   A report heading consisting of four literals is printed atop the final output. The last column of data notes the union's name in which that employee is enrolled.

4   Input are each employee's name, union code, and gross pay.

5   Two union codes exist: codes 1 and 2.

6   A union code of 1 notes:

  a   A union deduction of 1 percent of gross, computed as

  Union1 = gross pay ∗ .01

  b   This amount is accumulated separately using the formula

  Tot1 = tot1 + union1

  c   The output related to union 1 consists of the employee's name, gross pay, computed union deduction, and the label CLERICAL.

7   A union code of 2 notes:

  a   A union deduction of 2 percent of gross, computed as

  Union2 = gross pay ∗ .02

  b   This amount is accumulated separately using the formula

  Tot2 = tot2 + union 2

  c   The output related to union 2 consists of the employee's name, gross pay, computed union deduction, and the label TWU.

8   A counter will control the eight loops needed to process data. It must be initialized, incremented, and checked to ensure that only eight loops are executed.

9   After the eighth loop is completed, output the accumulated totals computed for both unions on separate lines. Use the labels TOT CLERICAL

DUES = \$ and TOT TWU DUES = \$ prior to their respective union totals. Both totals are printed in column 3 of the output format.

The flowchart written for Problem 5.3 is shown in Figure 5.7.

This flowchart solution consists of three flow diagrams — one main flowchart for the overall problem and two smaller diagrams related to each GOSUB module. We have deliberately used the term GOSUB to highlight each module. Both modules are referenced in the main flowchart via predefined-process symbols.

The main flowchart contains the following major components. There are symbols defining initial conditions, a looping sequence controlled by a counter in which the program modules are accessed, and the output of the two accumulated totals. The first initial condition, K = 1, establishes the counter K at a starting value of 1. An annotation symbol advises of the problem's intention. The next two processing symbols initialize the two accumulators required to sum union deductions. A second annotation symbol advises that the T1 accumulator is used for union 1, while its T2 counterpart is assigned to union 2. The PRINT symbol directs the output of the four literals composing the requested column headings. The reader should note that the order of these four symbols has no effect on processing, as they are not logically dependent upon each other. All four actions must be undertaken before the looping sequence is initiated.

The READ symbol denotes the start of the flowchart loop, inputting the employee's name (EMPL), union code (C), and gross pay (G). As a counter is used in place of a 9s decision, we may proceed directly to processing. Our first processing activity is to determine which of the two union codes was input, thus leading to the proper module to handle that deduction's processing. A decision symbol accomplishes this test, specifying the conditional statement IS C = 1?. If C is 1, the flow of processing will pass to the GOSUB 500 module; otherwise the GOSUB 600 module is selected. The logic depicted will force the processing flow to either one module or the other.

The two GOSUB modules are markedly similar, as they must perform essentially the same processing tasks. They differ only in the specifics of processing. For example, different percentages are used to compute each deduction, different accumulators are needed to total the two deductions, and the resulting outputs vary because of different union names.

In the GOSUB 500 module, the variable U1 denotes the union deduction for clerical workers. The T1 accumulator adds each of the U1 amounts and precedes the output of that employee's deductions data. The GOSUB 600 is similar but varies in the datanames used. Its union deductions are referenced by the U2 dataname, the accumulator carries a T2 notation, and the TWU literal is incorporated into its output.

Both modules close with a processing symbol using a RETURN narrative. This reminds us that the flow of processing returns to the main flowchart at the point at which the individual module was referenced. Thus, if the GOSUB 500 module was chosen, the processing would return to its predefined-process symbol and proceed to the next symbol following it.

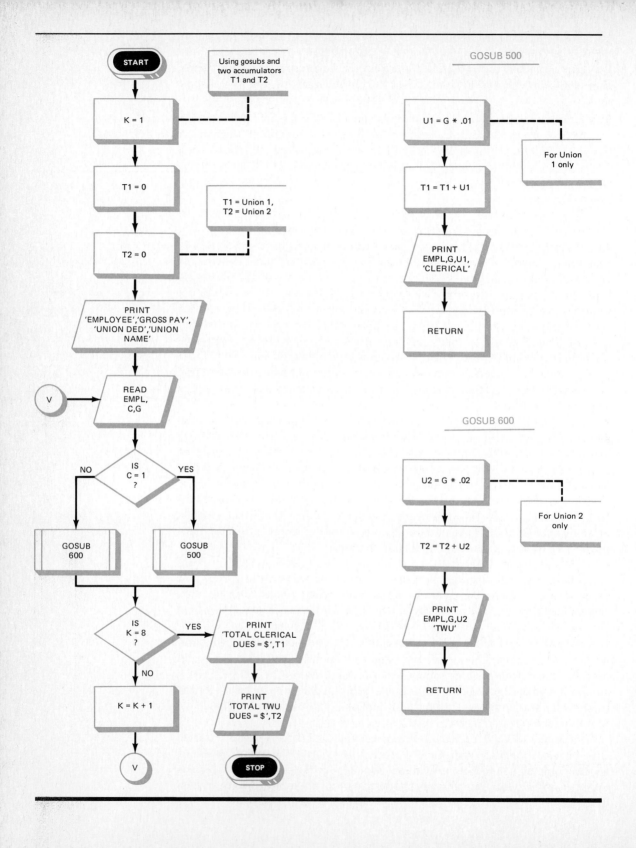

In both instances, the symbol following each module is the counter decision. This decision symbol identifies a check to determine whether exactly eight loops have been executed. If $K < 8$, the counter increment of $K = K + 1$ is invoked and looping continues. The completion of the eighth loop leads to the output of the accumulated totals on two separate lines. Separate labels indicated within each PRINT symbol precede the output of T1 and T2, respectively. Note that the $, a special character which is part of the literal, should not be considered as part of the numeric data that has undergone processing.

The conversion of the entire flowchart to a BASIC program follows from the logic depicted. The resulting program shown in Figure 5.8 reflects the modular structure of Problem 5.3. This structure is reflected in the use of GOSUB modules and in the line numbers used for program statements.

The BASIC program opens with a REMARK statement, which notes that GOSUBs and two accumulators are involved in this solution. In addition to line 10, a second REMARK statement at line 50 advises of the specific assignments made to the T1 and T2 accumulators. These two accumulators were initialized in lines 30 and 40, after the initialization of the counter K. The PRINT statement, line 60, directs the output of the literals EMPLOYEE, GROSS PAY, UNION DED, and UNION NAME into print zones 1, 2, 3, and 4, respectively.

The program loop effectively starts at line 70 with a READ statement, which enters data relating to the employee's name (E$), union code (C), and gross pay amount (G). An IF/THEN/ELSE statement, line 80, enables the program to choose between the two GOSUB modules.

The GOSUB 500 module utilizes statements 500 to 540. The REM statement opening that module serves an identification function. The LET statements in lines 510 and 520 compute the U1 deduction and update the T1 accumulator. The CLERICAL literal, incorporated into the PRINT statement, line 530, specifies that union and appears in zone 4 when output. The differences in each union's PRINT statement required their output in their respective modules.

The GOSUB 600 module is similarly detailed, except for the different datanames and the TWU literal. Line 600 offers an opening REM comment, followed by the computation of the U2 union deduction and the update of the T2 accumulator in lines 610 and 620. The PRINT statement, line 630, outputs the employee's name, union code, and gross pay prior to the TWU union identification. Accordingly, the first four print zones are filled, paralleling the output produced by line 530 of the GOSUB 500 module.

The RETURN statement closes both modules and returns the flow of processing back to the main program. The program advances to line 90 — the next statement in the program. The RETURN statement must appear at the

FIGURE 5.7   The flowchart for Problem 5.3 consists of three flow diagrams: one defines the main flowchart, and two represent the modules incorporated within the solution.

FIGURE 5.8 The program for Problem 5.3. Note the outputs of the two totals at the report's end.

```
10 REM --USING GOSUBS & 2 ACCUMULATORS T1 & T1
20 K = 1
30 T1 = 0
40 T2 = 0
50 REM T1 = UNION 1, T2 = UNION 2
60 PRINT 'EMPLOYEE','GROSS PAY','UNION DED','UNION NAME'
70 READ E$,C,G
80 IF C = 1 THEN GOSUB 500 ELSE GOSUB 600
90 IF K = 8 THEN 700 ELSE K = K + 1
100 GO TO 70
200 DATA 'ADAMS',1,463,'BARNOWSKI',2,577
210 DATA 'CHARLESTON',2,363,'DALTON',1,258
220 DATA 'GRADDOCK',1,371,'HARTMAN',2,576
230 DATA 'INDEROFF',1,675,'JACKSON',2,309
500 REM -- FOR UNION 1 ONLY
510 U1 = G *.01
520 T1 = T1 + U1
530 PRINT E$,G,U1,'CLERICAL'
540 RETURN
600 REM -- FOR UNION 2 ONLY
610 U2 = G *.02
620 T2 = T2 + U2
630 PRINT E$,G,U2,'TWU'
640 RETURN
700 PRINT 'TOTAL CLERICAL DUES =$',T1
710 PRINT 'TOTAL TWU DUES =$',T2
720 END
```

EMPLOYEE	GROSS PAY	UNION DED	UNION NAME
ADAMS	463	4.63	CLERICAL
BARNOWSKI	577	11.54	TWU
CHARLESTON	363	7.26	TWU
DALTON	258	2.58	CLERICAL
GRADDOCK	371	3.71	CLERICAL
HARTMAN	576	11.52	TWU
INDEROFF	675	6.75	CLERICAL
JACKSON	309	6.18	TWU
TOTAL CLERICAL DUES =$		17.67	
TOTAL TWU DUES =$		36.5	

end of each module in order that the processing flow return to the main part of the program. Every time a GOSUB statement is invoked, a RETURN statement must conclude that module's activity. The two statements must be used together.

The counter decision statement, line 90, also adopts the IF/THEN/ ELSE format. However, the choice here is not between alternative GOSUB modules but between branching out of the loop created by the counter or incrementing the counter by 1. As long as K is less than 8, the increment of K = K + 1 is selected for processing. Only when K = 8 and the eighth loop has been completed, will the program choose to branch to line 700 and exit the loop. By writing this statement in the form of an IF/THEN/ELSE, we save one statement in our program. We avoid having to write a separate IF/THEN statement for the counter decision and the LET statement to increment the counter which immediately follows it. The GO TO statement at line 100 directs the program to the loop's start and commences the processing of the next employee's data.

All of the DATA statements used in this program are grouped in lines 200 to 230. To conserve program statements, we have elected to double up on the number of data items appearing in each DATA statement. This alignment matches the needs of the READ statement, defined at line 70. As a counter is used to execute the required eight loops, a 9s DATA statement is not necessary.

The completion of the eighth program loop leads to line 700. Lines 700 and 710 are PRINT statements related to outputting the two accumulated totals, T1 and T2. Both numeric quantities will appear in zone 3, as the labels preceeding either total will occupy zone 1 and part of zone 2. The overlays occur because of the size of each label, as both exceed the print zone size of 14 characters: the CLERICAL accumulator's label is 22 characters long, and the TWU label totals 17 characters. The output of these two lines completes this program's processing.

The output for Problem 5.3 is shown in Figure 5.8. Note that all employee data is positioned beneath the column headings. The two accumulated totals are printed on separate lines in the union deduction's column (print zone 3). The placement of a $ before the accumulated totals reminds users of the dollar figures involved. The dollar sign was created as part of the special label to precede the totals and is not part of either T1 or T2. Each total reflects the four individuals found in each union grouping.

The next illustrative problem involves a program which uses one GOSUB for processing and one for I/O activities and requires two accumulators. One accumulator adds individual values to compute an average, and the second counts the number of people falling into that special category.

PROBLEM 5.4   Student Grades

A heading atop this report consists of the literals STUDENT, MARK1, MARK2, MARK3, and AVG. Input to the problem are a student's name and three test grades. The average of these test grades is computed by adding the grades and dividing that sum by 3. Of interest are those students whose averages are greater than 80. Within a separate module, only the plus 80 averages should be accumulated, as well as the number of students falling into that category. For all students processed, print their name, three test grades, and computed average.

A 9s decision should be used to control the looping sequence. When the 9s data is encountered, the loop should be exited and a series of final processing steps undertaken. These tasks are handled in a module, accessed at the solution's close. The average for these students falling into the plus 80 category is computed by dividing the accumulated total of those averages by the accumulated total of students possessing plus 80 averages. Print that average with the label AVG FOR PLUS 80 STUDENTS =. On a second line, place the label NO OF STUDENTS IN PLUS 80 CATEGORY = before that accumulated total.

The data for this problem is as follows:

Student	Mark1	Mark2	Mark3
Mary	70	65	83
Nancy	67	89	86
Olivia	75	89	73
Pat	98	87	86
Quinn	72	75	63
Roseann	86	74	83
Susie	68	92	81

These are the main points in the problem narrative.

1   The problem requires the use of two accumulators and two modules. One accumulator is used to total all averages greater than 80, and the second is used to add (by 1) the number of students with plus 80 averages. One module groups statements related to the processing of students with averages greater than 80 and is accessed inside the loop. The second module appears at the program's close and relates to the computation and output of information for plus 80 students.

2   The report heading consists of five literals: STUDENT, MARK1, MARK2, MARK3, and AVG.

3   Input are the student's name and three test grades.

4   Each student average is computed using the formula

Avg = (mark1 + mark2 + mark3)/3.

5   The handling of student averages greater than 80 is accomplished in a separate module. One accumulator totals each student average, whereas the second accumulator is incremented by 1 (representing each student in the plus 80 category).

6   Printout each student's name, three test grades, and computed average.

7   A 9s decision controls the looping sequence

8   The closing module contains the computation of the average for plus 80 students, and the output of that average and number of students with plus 80 averages. The formula used for computing the average for plus 80 students is

Plus 80 avg = total of plus 80 averages/no of plus 80 students

The output of this average uses the label AVG FOR PLUS 80 STUDENTS =.

The total of students in the plus 80 group is outputted on a separate line, preceded by the label NO STUDENTS IN PLUS 80 CATEGORY =.

The flowchart prepared for Problem 5.4 is shown in Figure 5.9.

The overall solution consists of three flow diagrams. One flowchart details the logic of the main program solution, with the two smaller diagrams depicting each module's processing. The main flowchart opens with the initialization of the two accumulators used in handling plus 80 student data. The second of two annotation symbols advises that the T1 accumulator is used to total plus 80 averages, while the T2 accumulator totals the number of students possessing averages in excess of 80. The output of the five literals comprising the report's column headings completes all processing operations prior to the looping sequence.

The loop opens with a READ symbol, which precedes the 9s decision symbol that tests against M1. The normal flow of processing leads to the computation of each student's average. The decision symbol which tests to determine whether the average is greater than 80 is designed to separate student data into two categories. Data related to students with averages greater than 80 is handled within the GOSUB 300 module. Students with averages that are less than or equal to 80 are not handled in that module, with the processing flow leading to the PRINT symbol at the loop's bottom.

The update of the two accumulators occurs within the GOSUB module. The equation $T1 = T1 + A$ updates the T1 accumulator by adding only those averages that are greater than 80. The second accumulator's update is written to increase T2 by 1. It is this accumulator that counts the number of students which fall into the plus 80 category. The rationale for the update by 1 is that we are counting students, who are handled one at a time.

When using an update of 1, some readers ask why the accumulator is not initialized at 1 also. They theorize that since we count individual quantities, we should start at 1 in preparation for the first student processed. This approach would result in error and throw off the final total. To understand this error, consider what would occur if the accumulator was initialized at 1 but no students were found to have averages greater than 80. The actual total is zero, but the accumulator would contain the incorrect value of 1. To avoid the potential for this type of error, accumulators are initialized at 0.

It is the YES branch of the 9s decision which leads to the GOSUB 400 module and performs the last phase of processing. The computation of P, the average of only those students with averages greater than 80, is the first task undertaken. The P computation involves both accumulators, T1 and T2, as the total of plus 80 averages (T1) is divided by the number of plus 80 students (T2) to produce P. Though T1 and T2 were computed in another module, these variables are accessible in the GOSUB 400 module.

The computation of P immediately precedes both its output and the printing of T2. Each variable is output on its own line, preceded by its own special label. The two literals used are important in the identification of these two outputs.

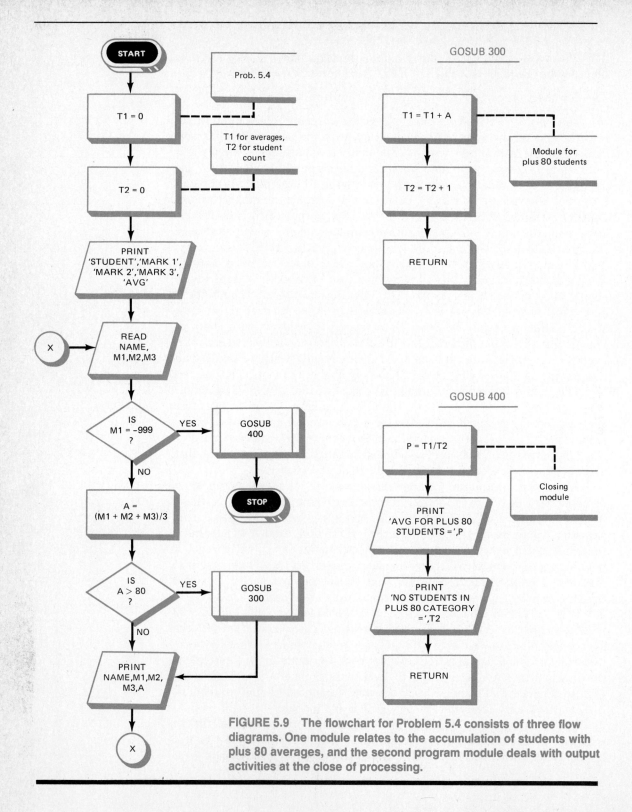

FIGURE 5.9 The flowchart for Problem 5.4 consists of three flow diagrams. One module relates to the accumulation of students with plus 80 averages, and the second program module deals with output activities at the close of processing.

The use of the GOSUB 400 highlights the use of modules anywhere in a flowchart or program solution. Modular units are not restricted to looping sequences and may be used to consolidate related statements into one group. The GOSUB 400 module made it possible to group statements related to the computation of P and output both P and T2. As all three activities are performed prior to the end of processing, they could be combined into one processing module.

If desired, a module could have been created for the initial conditions performed prior to the loop's start. We elected not to do that, however, choosing instead to handle those tasks individually. Let us now turn our attention to how both modules and other tasks were handled in the BASIC program written from this flowchart solution.

The resulting BASIC program opens with two REMARK statements (Figure 5.10). Line 10 advises that the program relates to Problem 5.4, and

```
10 REM PROB 5.4
20 REM -- T1 FOR AVERAGES, T2 FOR STUDENT COUNT
22 T1 = 0
24 T2 = 0
30 PRINT 'STUDENT','MARK1','MARK2','MARK3','AVG'
40 READ N$,M1,M2,M3
50 IF M1 = -999 THEN 600
60 A = (M1 + M2 + M3)/3
70 IF A > 80 THEN GOSUB 300
80 PRINT N$,M1,M2,M3,A
90 GO TO 40
200 DATA 'MARY',70,65,83,'NANCY',67,89,86
210 DATA 'OLIVIA',75,89,73,'PAT',98,87,86
220 DATA 'QUINN',72,75,63,'ROSEANN',86,74,83
230 DATA 'SUSIE',68,92,81,'XXX',-999,0,0
300 REM -- MODULE FOR PLUS 80 STUDENTS
310 T1 = T1 + A
320 T2 = T2 + 1
330 RETURN
400 REM -- CLOSING MODULE
410 P = T1/T2
420 PRINT 'AVG FOR PLUS 80 STUDENTS =',P
430 PRINT 'NO STUDENTS IN PLUS 80 CATEGORY =',T2
440 RETURN
600 GOSUB 400
610 END
```

FIGURE 5.10   The program prepared from the flowchart solution for Problem 5.4. GOSUB statements were employed to define two program modules.

STUDENT	MARK1	MARK2	MARK3	AVG
MARY	70	65	83	72.6667
NANCY	67	89	86	80.6667
OLIVIA	75	89	73	79
PAT	98	87	86	90.3333
QUINN	72	75	63	70
ROSEANN	86	74	83	81
SUSIE	68	92	81	80.3333

```
AVG FOR PLUS 80 STUDENTS =    83.0833
NO STUDENTS IN PLUS 80 CATEGORY =        4
```

line 20 details the responsibilities assigned to the accumulators T1 and T2. Lines 22 and 24 are utilized to initialize both accumulators at 0. The PRINT statement which follows generates the five literals needed for the column headings. Each literal is individually assigned to one of the five print zones, responding to the use of commas in the PRINT statement of line 30.

The program loop is opened via line 40, the READ statement. The string variable name N$ is assigned as the student's name, where M1, M2, and M3 individually identify the three test grades input. The IF/THEN statement, line 50, defines a 9s decision, making possible the conditional branch to line 600 when the 9s data is read. The normal flow of processing leads to line 60, where the average A is computed.

The test to see if A is greater than 80 occurs at statement 70. If A > 80, the program accesses the GOSUB 300 module where the two accumulators are updated. Line 310 adds A to the T1 accumulator, updating it whenever a plus 80 average is computed. Line 320 updates T2 by 1 each time a student is found to have a plus 80 average. It is T2 which monitors the number of students with averages greater than 80. The RETURN statement, line 330, closes that module and returns the processing flow to the requesting GOSUB instruction.

Despite the computed average, all student data are output via line 80. The branch to GOSUB 300 related to handling plus 80 average data and affected no other processing. The PRINT instruction at line 80 was intended for use with all student data and was placed in the main program loop, not in the GOSUB 300 module. The positioning of that PRINT statement within that module would have restricted its use to students with averages greater than 80. The five data items output via line 80 appear beneath their respective headings, printed within the five print zones.

The loop continues until the 9s data is encountered, with the program branching to line 600. The access to GOSUB 400 occurs from this line and leads to the final group of processing tasks. We choose to use line 400 for this module, as the use of any line numbers greater than 600 would have incorrectly exceeded the END statement at line 610.

A REM statement at line 400 offers an opening identification for the closing module. The numeric variable P represents the average of students possessing plus 80 averages and is computed at line 410. The computation of P is accomplished by dividing the accumulated total T1 by T2. The PRINT statements of lines 420 and 430 respectively output data relating to P and T2 on separate lines. The RETURN statement closes the module and permits the program to return to line 600. The program's close at line 610 immediately follows the return from the GOSUB 400 module.

In examining this program's close, the reader may question why the following statement was not used:

```
50      IF M1 = −999 THEN GOSUB 400
```

Though this instruction appears correct, *it is not*. This new line 50 does not properly replace the statement originally used in our solution. If this statement was used, the program would access the GOSUB 400 module and perform its processing and outputs. The error would occur when the GOSUB module was over and the program returned to line 50. Instead of proceeding to the END statement at line 610, the program would proceed from line 50 to line 60. The loop would therefore continue and an out-of-data error would occur the next time the READ statement was executed.

The purpose behind branching to line 600, in our successful program solution, was to avoid this type of error. The original statement

50   IF M1 $= -999$ THEN 600

ensures that the program branches out of the loop and accesses the GOSUB 400 module, where it is executed once. The module performs its processing before the program's close.

The output from this program is shown in Figure 5.10. As desired, the five headings appear atop each column of data. A total of seven students' data is outputted, with four of those students attaining averages in excess of 80. This fact is confirmed by the second summary line, NO OF STUDENTS IN PLUS 80 CATEGORY $= 4$. The average grade for these plus 80 students is printed above it. The length of both literals has caused the data printed on both summary lines to appear in print zones 3 and 4.

Modules enable programs to group related processing activities into readily accessible groupings. We will attempt to use them whenever they favor the handling of a group of related tasks.

5.3 Aligning Printed Outputs

The output from Problem 5.4 exhibited two characteristics. Examining Figure 5.15, we may observe that this output spans the five print zones which compose the printing area related to our version of BASIC. This printout is spread across the entire page. Also, evident was the variety of output formats used to print data related to the variable A, the average computed for each student.

Two questions are often raised at this point.

1   Does BASIC provide a means of outputting data in a more compact format?

2   Is there a means of formatting output data, such that each item printed adheres to a predetermined format?

BASIC does provide a means of satisfying both output requirements, thus improving the readability of its printed results. Let us initially examine one way of aligning printed outputs and use it as a stepping stone to future discussions.

The TAB Function

BASIC provides several means of refining the outputs prepared through its application. One of the methods available for the alignment of output data is the **TAB function.** This option is incorporated into the syntax of the PRINT statement and keys itself to aligning output data by specific print positions rather than print zones.

Essentially, the TAB function is designed to override the print zone structure and permit users to position output data anywhere along the line of output. Evaluation of a sample PRINT statement utilizing the TAB function will illustrate its use.

```
40      PRINT TAB(8);A;TAB(26);D$
```

The TAB function is appended to variables undergoing output, positioned prior to every variable's dataname. Examining line 40, we note the output of two variables — A and D$. Without the use of the TAB function, these variables might be printed in print zones 1 and 2. With it, we can output these variables in any other available print position.

The print positions you want to use are specified in the parentheses which follow the term TAB. Our sample statement directs that A be output starting with print position 8 and D$ be printed commencing with print position 26. The TAB function alerted the computer to override the use of print zones and employ the print positions detailed within the parentheses associated with each TAB variable. Note also the specific use of semicolons as the punctuation with the TAB function and its variables. The semicolon defers control to the TAB function, enabling each variable to be properly positioned for output.

The TAB function may also be used to prepare headings and summary lines. The following two statements illustrate these uses:

```
20      PRINT TAB(5);'EMPLOYEE';TAB(20);'GROSS';TAB(28);'UNION DUES'
600     PRINT TAB(11);'TOTAL DUES PAID =';TAB(28);T
```

Statement 20 is used to create a report's heading, with line 600 preparing the output of an accumulated total of union dues.

The heading created via line 20 consists of three literals. Each literal is respectively printed commencing with print positions 5, 20, and 28. The heading resulting from line 20 would be more tightly configured than if each literal were printed within one of the first three zones.

The summary statement, line 600, possesses a special label and variable. The label TOTAL DUES PAID = starts at print position 11 and precedes the output of T at position 28. The TAB function makes it an easy task to align outputs, as the desired print positions are readily specified within the indicated parentheses. Let us apply the TAB function to a problem where columns of data are involved.

PROBLEM 5.5   Tabulating Data

A counter is utilized to control a looping sequence of five repetitions. On each loop, variables A, B, and C are input. The three variables are added to find their sum and that sum is accumulated to produce the grand total of all 15 values that will undergo processing. The three variables and their sum are outputted on the same line. Column headings COL1, COL2, COL3, and TOTAL are to appear atop the report. The grand total of all 15 numbers is outputted when the five loops are completed, preceded by the label GRAND TOTAL =. This total should be printed in the last column of the output format. Also, compute the average of these numbers by dividing the accumulated total by 15. Print that average in the fourth column with the label AVG =. As a concise output format is desired, override the print zone structure and place five spaces between each column of output. Also, double-space the lines for legibility and indent the first column by five print positions.

The data used for this problem is as follows:

X: 16, 87, 273, 39, 40, 6, 19, 85, 71, 130, 57, 43, 94, 48, 29

These are the main points in the problem narrative.

1   An accumulator is needed to total the sum of the 15 numbers inputted. A counter controls the required five loops. Both are initialized before the looping sequence starts.

2   A heading for four columns of output is created and must adhere to a predetermined format. It is indented by five spaces, with an equal number of spaces between each column. A blank line follows the column heading to create a double-spaced format.

3   Input are three data items referred to by the variables A, B, and C.

4   The three variables are added to create the sum of that row's data, with that sum accumulated on each loop. The required formulas are

a $Row = A + B + C$
b $Total = total + row$

5   Output the variables A, B, and C on each loop, in addition to the row total, on the same line. Each should appear within its own column of data. A blank line of print creates the double-spacing format required.

6   The counter decision checks for the processing of the fifth loop.

7   The output of the accumulated total, in the fourth column of output, initiates the last phase of work. The computation of the average of the 15 numbers processed occurs next, using the formula

Average = total/15

This average is also printed in the fourth output column, using the label AVG =.

8   To accommodate the alignment of all outputs, the TAB function will be incorporated into the program solution.

The flowchart and program solution for Problem 5.5 are shown in Figure 5.11.

The flowchart solution possesses three major components: a series of initializations, the main loop, and closing activities. The initial conditions include setting T at 0 and K at 1, each step respectively establishing the accumulator T and counter K. The output of the four column headings is defined in the PRINT symbol, which precedes a blank PRINT symbol. This latter symbol reflects the need to double-space all outputs.

The main loop of the solution is controlled by the counter. The READ symbol inputs the three variables involved in processing. The row total R adds A, B, and C and is subsequently accumulated in the next processing symbol. The variables A, B, C, and R are outputted in four separate double-spaced columns before encountering the counter decision. Its NO branch leads to the K = K + 1 update, while the YES branch is accessed when K is 5.

The last phase of processing is accessed after the fifth loop is concluded. Initially, the accumulated total T is printed with its label GRAND TOTAL =. This leads to the computation of the average of the 15 numbers processed, represented by the variable F. This average is then printed, along with its label AVG =. Both of the numeric quantities represented by T and F should appear in the fourth and last column of output, with their respective labels positioned before them on the same line.

Of major interest in our BASIC program is how the TAB functions are written. After an opening REM statement (line 10) and the initialization of the accumulator and counter (lines 20 and 30), we encounter the first PRINT statement with a TAB function. Each TAB function carries parentheses, defining the number of print positions in which that data will start to be printed. Line 40 relates specifically to the output of the four column headings.

The first literal COL1, representing column 1, is designated to start in print position 6. This four-character literal will occupy print positions 6, 7, 8, and 9 and leave the first five print positions blank. This offset of five positions satisfies the narrative's request that the report be indented by five spaces.

The output of the second literal COL2 commences at position 15, which leaves print positions 10 to 14 blank. This gap of five print positions was designed into the output to separate each column of figures by five spaces, as required. A similar technique is applied to the COL3 literal, whose output begins in position 24 and runs to 27. The gap of five spaces occupies positions 19 to 23. The last literal TOTAL starts at print position 33 and is preceded by

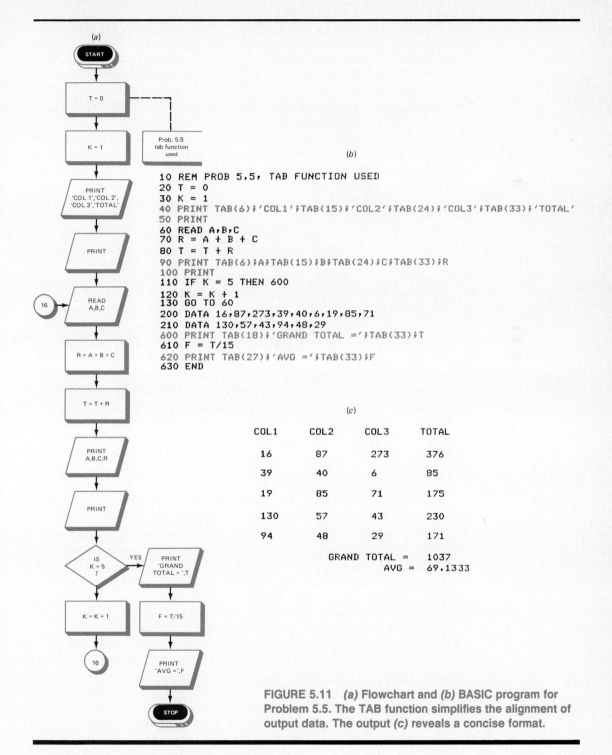

```
(a)

START

T = 0  -----  Prob. 5.5
                tab function
K = 1           used

PRINT
'COL 1','COL 2',
'COL 3','TOTAL'

PRINT

16 → READ
      A,B,C

R = A + B + C

T = T + R

PRINT
A,B,C,R

PRINT

IS
K = 5
?  → YES → PRINT
            'GRAND
            TOTAL = ',T

K = K + 1       F = T/15

16              PRINT
                'AVG = ',F

                STOP
```

(b)

```
10 REM PROB 5.5, TAB FUNCTION USED
20 T = 0
30 K = 1
40 PRINT TAB(6);'COL1';TAB(15);'COL2';TAB(24);'COL3';TAB(33);'TOTAL'
50 PRINT
60 READ A,B,C
70 R = A + B + C
80 T = T + R
90 PRINT TAB(6);A;TAB(15);B;TAB(24);C;TAB(33);R
100 PRINT
110 IF K = 5 THEN 600
120 K = K + 1
130 GO TO 60
200 DATA 16,87,273,39,40,6,19,85,71
210 DATA 130,57,43,94,48,29
600 PRINT TAB(18);'GRAND TOTAL =';TAB(33);T
610 F = T/15
620 PRINT TAB(27);'AVG =';TAB(33);F
630 END
```

(c)

COL1	COL2	COL3	TOTAL
16	87	273	376
39	40	6	85
19	85	71	175
130	57	43	230
94	48	29	171

```
            GRAND TOTAL =   1037
                    AVG =   69.1333
```

FIGURE 5.11 (a) Flowchart and (b) BASIC program for Problem 5.5. The TAB function simplifies the alignment of output data. The output (c) reveals a concise format.

blanks in positions 28 to 32. The TAB function made it possible to align each column heading and provide the required spacing between columns.

A similar alignment is configured for the variables output within the main loop. The READ statement (line 60) opens the loop's processing, inputting the three numbers for A, B, and C. Their sum R is produced via line 70, and its addition in the accumulator update occurs in line 80. The TAB function makes its reappearance at line 90's PRINT statement.

In this case, each TAB notation is positioned ahead of a numeric variable name. The variables A, B, C, and R respectively commence their output at print positions 6, 15, 24, and 33. This output aligns each of the four variables with their respective column headings, as the same TAB positions were defined. As no data item exceeds three digits, each number output will fall well beneath the size of its heading.

The blank output of line 100's PRINT statement creates the double-spacing required to provide legibility. The counter decision (line 110) completes the loop and enables the choice between its continuance or exit. Lines 200 and 210 provide the two DATA statements containing the 15 numeric items of data. Exactly three data items are inputted on each of the five loops. No 9s data is required, as the 9s decision technique is not written into this program.

The closing phase of this solution begins at line 600. As noted in the initial narrative, the last two outputs must coincide with the last column of output. This column commences at print position 33, the position noted by the TAB functions of lines 600 and 620. The printing of T (line 600) commences at position 33 and carries a special label with it. The TAB notation dictates that the label GRAND TOTAL = be printed at position 18 and thus allow sufficient space for its length. A similar logic is used with the AVG = label of line 620. As it is smaller, this label commences at print position 27 and provides for the output of F at position 33. Again, the alignment of outputs was somewhat simplified through the use of the TAB function.

The output from Problem 5.5 reflects the impact of using the TAB function (see Figure 5.11(c)). Instead of an output that stretches over four print zones, a more concise output is evident using approximately 40 characters. The TAB function enabled a tighter, more cohesive report format and simplified the alignment of data in each column. The summary lines were as easily handled, as each of those two outputs were readily positioned in the last column of output via the TAB setting.

The TAB function is ideally suited to applications where columns of output data require alignment, with little emphasis placed upon specific stylized output formats. The outputs resulting from Problem 5.5 were well handled via the TAB function and aligned each column of data. However, it merely positioned the computed average result and did not affect its output. That is, the TAB function could not alter the digits printed or restrict the number of digits printed. If we only wanted two decimal positions, the TAB function would not support that format. A different BASIC instruction can accommodate that request.

In the output of Problem 5.5, Figure 5.11, the computed average of the 15 data items was printed as 69.1333. The computer printed as many digits as it could, since no restriction was placed upon the output of F — the variable representing that final average. What would we need if we chose to utilize a format of XXXX.XX, with four positions before the decimal point and two places after it?

The term **editing** is often associated with programming techniques which stylize or affect outputs and cause them to conform to predetermined formats. The **PRINT USING statement** affords one way of accomplishing that editing feature. When combined with the TAB function, the PRINT USING statement permits the user to edit and align output data. As an example, consider outputting the final average of Problem 5.5 through the combined use of these instructions.

```
610     F = T/15
620     L$ = '####.##'
630     PRINT TAB(27);'AVG =';TAB(33);
640     PRINT USING L$,F
650     END
```

This program excerpt incorporates the TAB and PRINT USING options and may be substituted for statements 610 to 650 in Figure 5.11*(b)*. These instructions will align the output of F within the original output format and apply an edited format to the number printed for F.

An examination of these new statements reveals some changes within instructional formats previously discussed. Line 610 is the LET statement used to compute the average (F) of the 15 numbers that underwent processing. This average was computed by dividing the accumulated total (T) by 15.

The next instruction, line 620, is also a LET statement, but it serves a function other than an arithmetic manipulation. Line 620 is used to define the format which we wish to apply when printing F. The LET statement was used, as it enables the user to specifically dictate a desired output format. The use of a string-variable name to define the format is deliberate, as it establishes a nonnumeric format applicable only to output tasks and not usable in arithmetic operations.

The desired format is defined within quotes, in much the same manner as a literal. The pound sign (#) is the special character required by the BASIC syntax that defines the size and nature of the output format. In line 620 we have chosen to place four digits before the decimal and two after it. Essentially, we have defined a seven-position output field consisting of six digits and a decimal point. Line 620 enables the user to access this output format through the string-variable name L$.

The output of data relating to the computed average F commences with line 630. In this statement, the initial TAB function establishes the output of the literal AVG = at print position 27 and prepares for the output of F at position 33. The actual output of F must be initiated at line 640.

The need to continue the actual output of F (at line 640) relates to the

The PRINT USING Statement

nature of the PRINT USING statement. This statement may not be incorporated into any other PRINT statement and must appear separately within its own instruction. It may be used, however, in conjunction with TAB settings to align data.

To accomplish this coordinated use, a simple output convention is employed. A semicolon is positioned at the end of the PRINT statement preceding the PRINT USING to establish the link between both statements. When so positioned, the semicolon directs the computer to hold the printer on that same line and operationally ties the output of the PRINT USING statement to the end of the prior statement.

In effect, we must consider the output of F resulting from two program statements. Line 630 aligned the literal AVG = at position 27 and readied the output of F for position 33. The PRINT USING instruction applied the L\$ format to the output of F, completing that line's output. The link between both statements is accomplished by means of the semicolon. The resultant output is shown in Figure 5.12. Except for the computed average, it is similar to the output in the original solution to Problem 5.5. The original output was 69.1333 and no format was applied. The new output, 69.13, adheres to the ####.## format. The L\$ format was made available via the PRINT USING statement, the alignment defined with the TAB function. The coordination of the two statements was handled by the semicolon placed at the end of line 620. No semicolon is placed at the end of line 622, as none is required and no other PRINT statements are needed.

A semicolon may be used to advantage to link together multiple PRINT statements in other situations. Consider the preparation of the heading for Problem 5.4, as shown in Figure 5.10. This program required column headings consisting of five literals, namely, STUDENT, MARK1, MARK2, MARK3, and AVG. PRINT statements within the original program assigned each literal to one of the five available print zones. The resultant output was printed across the width of the entire page.

If we wanted a more compact output, we could use the TAB function. Its incorporation into the PRINT statement required for Problem 5.4 would result in an instruction which might possess over 80 characters — an instruction that could conceivably exceed the capacity of some terminals. To overcome any potential problem, this lengthy instruction could be written in two PRINT statements. Both statements would be operationally linked via the semicolon, as listed below.

```
30     PRINT TAB(1);'STUDENT';TAB(20);'MARK1';TAB(26);'MARK2';
35     PRINT TAB(32);'MARK3';TAB(40);'AVG'
```

The column headings produced by these two PRINT statements would be more compact than the original output, consisting of 42 characters. The entire heading appears on one line, as lines 30 and 35 are tied together by the semicolon at the end of line 30.

As the report heading is altered, the PRINT statement outputting student data would have to be changed accordingly. Combining the TAB function and PRINT USING statement would enable us to align the student data

(a)

```
10 REM PROB 5.5, TAB FUNCTION USED
20 T = 0
30 K = 1
40 PRINT TAB(6);'COL1';TAB(15);'COL2';TAB(24);'COL3';TAB(33);'TOTAL'
50 PRINT
60 READ A,B,C
70 R = A + B + C
80 T = T + R
90 PRINT TAB(6);A;TAB(15);B;TAB(24);C;TAB(33);R
100 PRINT
110 IF K = 5 THEN 600
120 K = K + 1
130 GO TO 60
200 DATA 16,87,273,39,40,6,19,85,71
210 DATA 130,57,43,94,48,29
600 PRINT TAB(18);'GRAND TOTAL =';TAB(33);T
610 F = T/15
616 L$ ='####.##'
620 PRINT TAB(27);'AVG =';
622 PRINT USING L$,F
630 END
```

(b)

COL1	COL2	COL3	TOTAL
16	87	273	376
39	40	6	85
19	85	71	175
130	57	43	230
94	48	29	171
	GRAND TOTAL =		1037
	AVG =		69.13

FIGURE 5.12 (a) BASIC program and (b) output for Problem 5.5 employing the PRINT USING statement. The result, 69.13, adheres to the format defined by the PRINT USING instruction and L$. Lines 600 to 622 highlight the statements responsible for generating this stylized output.

with its column headings and apply a format of ###.##. The three statements that follow would replace line 80 in the original solution for Problem 5.4 and result in this stylized output.

```
80    D$ = '###.##'
82    PRINT TAB(1);N$;TAB(20);M1;TAB(26);M2;TAB(32);M3;TAB(40);
84    PRINT USING D$,A
```

The LET statement, line 80, defines the output format which will be applied to the printing of the average. The initial PRINT statement, line 82, outputs the student's name and three grades, aligning each variable within its appropriate column. The semicolon at the end of line 82 joins that PRINT statement with the PRINT USING statement that follows it. Line 84 applies the decimal format, defined at line 80, to the output of A. The revised program and output appear in Figure 5.13. It shows the tighter design overall and the two-place decimal format applied to the printing of the average A.

The revised output is more compact and illustrates the usefulness of the

FIGURE 5.13 *(a)* BASIC program and *(b)* output for Problem 5.4 using the TAB function and PRINT USING statements to produce a more stylized and compact output.

(a)

```
10 REM PROB 5.4 REVISED
20 REM -- T1 FOR AVERAGES, T2 FOR STUDENT COUNT
22 T1 = 0
24 T2 = 0
30 PRINT TAB(1);'STUDENT';TAB(20);'MARK1';TAB(26);'MARK2';
35 PRINT TAB(32);'MARK3';TAB(40);'AVG'
40 READ N$,M1,M2,M3
50 IF M1 = -999 THEN 600
60 A = (M1 + M2 + M3)/3
70 IF A > 80 THEN GOSUB 300
80 D$ = '###.##'
82 PRINT TAB(1);N$;TAB(20);M1;TAB(26);M2;TAB(32);M3;TAB(40);
84 PRINT USING D$,A
90 GO TO 40
200 DATA 'MARY',70,65,83,'NANCY',67,89,86
210 DATA 'OLIVIA',75,89,73,'PAT',98,87,86
220 DATA 'QUINN',72,75,63,'ROSEANN',86,74,83
230 DATA 'SUSIE',68,92,81,'XXX',-999,0,0
300 REM -- MODULE FOR PLUS 80 STUDENTS
310 T1 = T1 + A
320 T2 = T2 + 1
330 RETURN
400 REM -- CLOSING MODULE
410 P = T1/T2
420 PRINT 'AVG FOR PLUS 80 STUDENTS =',P
430 PRINT 'NO STUDENTS IN PLUS 80 CATEGORY =',T2
440 RETURN
600 GOSUB 400
610 END
```

(b)

STUDENT	MARK1	MARK2	MARK3	AVG
MARY	70	65	83	72.67
NANCY	67	89	86	80.67
OLIVIA	75	89	73	79.00
PAT	98	87	86	90.33
QUINN	72	75	63	70.00
ROSEANN	86	74	83	81.00
SUSIE	68	92	81	80.33

```
AVG FOR PLUS 80 STUDENTS =    83.0833
NO STUDENTS IN PLUS 80 CATEGORY =            4
```

TAB function and PRINT USING statements. Each student's name appears in the left-hand column and proceeds to three columns of test marks. Using the TAB function, we are able to closely align these three columns of data, along with their headings. The effect of the PRINT USING is readily observed in the AVG column; where the ###.## format is applied to the output of the student averages, which are rounded off to two decimal places instead of four. The computed averages which previously possessed no decimals now have two zeros in their decimal positions. The application of ###.## to A requires that the zeros be printed in those unoccupied positions. The standardization of printed outputs is applied to all items printed.

SIDE BAR 5.2   Drafting Column Headings

Many students have difficulty visualizing the outputs they are required to prepare for their program solutions. This difficulty relates to laying out the position of each heading and the number of spaces between columns, as well as the placement of both summary and detail lines beneath these headings. Often, it is the data printed within the column that dictates the spacing required.

A convenient way of preparing program output is to draft the proposed format onto graph paper, as shown below. The individual boxes of the graph paper provide a ready format in which to describe on a character-by-character basis each line composing that output. One can readily observe how that output will appear. This approach is very helpful when anticipating the use of the PRINT USING statement.

One final advisory note is necessary. Do not expect to lay out and finalize your output format in a single try. Normally, it takes anywhere from one to three attempts to properly draft an output so that it is properly aligned and can be used as a basis for writing your output instructions. This is especially true if a complex edited format is involved. Take the time necessary to draw your format properly, and this effort will simplify your programming task.

Most programmers find it very helpful to lay out their program outputs before writing the actual program. This detailing will include all headings, detail lines, and any summary lines that are required. Any type of graph or lined paper may be used to assist these design activities.

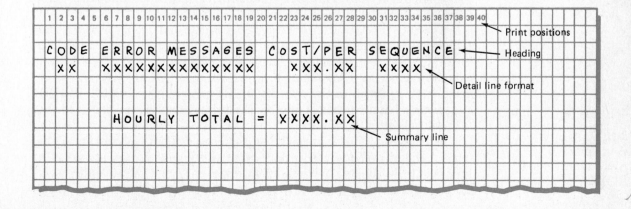

Another Output Version

With some modification, the PRINT USING statement can be used to position, as well as to format, output data. When used in this fashion, it eliminates the need to invoke the TAB function. To illustrate this point, let us replace lines 80, 82, and 84 of Figure 5.13 with two new statements, lines 80 and 82, as shown in Figure 5.14. These statements relate directly to the printing of student grade data. As their format is somewhat complex in appearance, they require some explanation.

The LET statement at line 80 is essentially a detailed format for the output of student data. This format is matched against the literals which compose the column headings, so that each output is properly positioned. The string-variable name, F$, provides a reference to the entire format when output operations are undertaken.

Each component of the F$ format serves a specific purpose. The opening and closing quotes define the format in its entirety. The two backslash symbols (\) are separated by 14 positions and relate to the output of each student's name via N$. The 14 positions defined between both backslashes (inclusive) parallel the maximum number of characters needed to compose a string-variable data item. To align this with print position 1 and the output of N$, the opening backslash is placed immediately after the opening quote.

The three ##### formats are positioned at the equivalent of print positions 20, 26, and 32, thus aligning them with the outputs slated for the MARK1, MARK2, and MARK3 columns and relating them to the printing of data for the M1, M2, and M3 variables, respectively. The blank spaces between the last backslash of the N$ format and the first # of the M1 format serve to separate both columns of data and will result in the printing of blank spaces in those positions.

The last edited format, ###.##, is different from the three prior formats because it relates to the variable A. Through the PRINT USING we are directing the computer to apply that format when printing A. Thus, all data printed for A is limited to three digits before the decimal point and two decimals after it.

The well-trained eye may note subtle differences between the outputs in Figures 5.13 and 5.14. In Figure 5.13, grades in the MARK1, MARK2, and MARK3 columns are moved left, whereas these same grades appear more to the right in Figure 5.14. This slight difference relates to the nature of the TAB function and PRINT USING statement.

The TAB function attempts to left-justify data undergoing printing. The term **left-justify** describes the computer's attempt to move the printed data to the farthest left position in which it can be printed. This is a logical extension from the TAB function, which requires that the lefthand print position be specified in the instruction. By contrast, the PRINT-USING statement attempts to **right-justify** the printed data by moving it to the farthest right print position.

Either output format is valid, but users may prefer the visual impact of one statement over the other. Both types of statements may appear in a program, with the user applying them where they best serve. Many users

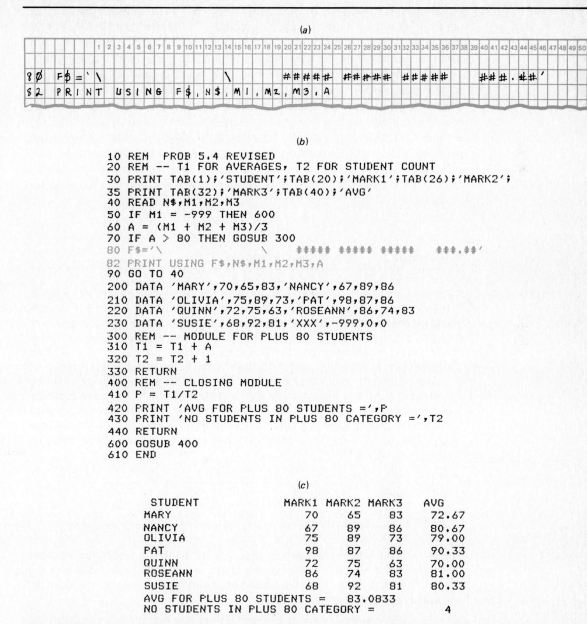

(a)

```
80  F$='\                    \         #####  #####  #####      ###.##'
82  PRINT USING F$,N$,M1,M2,M3,A
```

(b)

```
10 REM  PROB 5.4 REVISED
20 REM -- T1 FOR AVERAGES, T2 FOR STUDENT COUNT
30 PRINT TAB(1);'STUDENT';TAB(20);'MARK1';TAB(26);'MARK2';
35 PRINT TAB(32);'MARK3';TAB(40);'AVG'
40 READ N$,M1,M2,M3
50 IF M1 = -999 THEN 600
60 A = (M1 + M2 + M3)/3
70 IF A > 80 THEN GOSUB 300
80 F$='\                    \         #####  #####  #####      ###.##'
82 PRINT USING F$,N$,M1,M2,M3,A
90 GO TO 40
200 DATA 'MARY',70,65,83,'NANCY',67,89,86
210 DATA 'OLIVIA',75,89,73,'PAT',98,87,86
220 DATA 'QUINN',72,75,63,'ROSEANN',86,74,83
230 DATA 'SUSIE',68,92,81,'XXX',-999,0,0
300 REM -- MODULE FOR PLUS 80 STUDENTS
310 T1 = T1 + A
320 T2 = T2 + 1
330 RETURN
400 REM -- CLOSING MODULE
410 P = T1/T2
420 PRINT 'AVG FOR PLUS 80 STUDENTS =',P
430 PRINT 'NO STUDENTS IN PLUS 80 CATEGORY =',T2
440 RETURN
600 GOSUB 400
610 END
```

(c)

```
STUDENT         MARK1 MARK2 MARK3    AVG
MARY               70    65    83   72.67
NANCY              67    89    86   80.67
OLIVIA             75    89    73   79.00
PAT                98    87    86   90.33
QUINN              72    75    63   70.00
ROSEANN            86    74    83   81.00
SUSIE              68    92    81   80.33
AVG FOR PLUS 80 STUDENTS =     83.0833
NO STUDENTS IN PLUS 80 CATEGORY =           4
```

FIGURE 5.14 *(a)* The PRINT USING statement detailed on a character-by-character basis. This detailing ensures proper spacing and permits us to lay out the instruction accurately. *(b)* The revised program and *(c)* output for Problem 5.4. This newer version of the PRINT USING statement allows the programmer to align and edit a line of output.

prefer to right-justify with the PRINT USING statement when outputting detail lines, as it is more compact. Similarly, a preference for the TAB function when laying out headings is often expressed. Through experience, each programmer develops a sense of what statement to apply in which situations.

In versions of BASIC where the TAB function and PRINT USING statements are not available, the user may duplicate the spacing between fields using commas and semicolons. This is a much more elaborate process, requiring infinite patience to concurrently detail each heading and data item appearing in that column. The formatting or editing of output data is not possible using that punctuation, however, and sufficient space must be allocated to accommodate the printing of numeric data. To reinforce the usefulness of the TAB and PRINT USING options, let us develop another program solution.

PROBLEM 5.6　Estimating Project Costs

A company wants to project the costs related to a work project for exactly six months. Expenses are estimated using the formula $E = 400 + (8.34 * H)$, where E is the estimated expense and H the number of hours for that month. In two separate accumulators, total the number of hours worked that month and the estimated expense for that month's work. For each month's data, output the number of that month, hours worked, and the estimated expense, using the printed format accompanying this narrative.

Use a counter to control the looping process. When the looping ends, print the two accumulated totals. Use the format depicted and the label TOTAL. For better organization, group into separate modules the output of headings, the initialization of accumulates, and the closing output activities. Use a TAB function when printing the headings and the PRINT USING when outputting the edited formats. The hourly data used in the problem is as follows:

Month	1	2	3	4	5	6
Hours	10.3	15.6	8.6	21.7	12.5	18.1

The desired output format is depicted in Figure 5.15. It was prepared by the programmer and details the position of the heading, detail, and summary lines needed for this solution. The reader should note the spacing and types of output formats applied to the variables used in the problem.

These are the main points in the problem narrative.

1　A counter is used to execute exactly six loops, with each loop representing one month's processing.

2　Two accumulators are necessary to total the number of hours worked each month and the estimated expense for each month's work on the project.

PRINT			POSITIONS						
1 2 3 4 5 6 7 8 9 10 11 12 13 14 15 16 17 18 19 20 21 22 23 24 25 26									
MON		HOURS		EXPENSE			Heading line		
###		###.#		####.##			Format for detail lines		
TOTAL	###.#			####.##			Summary line format		

FIGURE 5.15 The programmer should detail every aspect of the program output to be used before writing any statement. A character-by-character layout removes much of the guesswork and simplifies the specification of the actual program instructions. The detailed format shown describes the heading, detail, and summary lines associated with Problem 5.6. With this format, the writing of TAB function and PRINT USING statements is greatly simplified.

3 A heading consisting of the literals MON, HOURS, and EXPENSE appear at the top of this compact (edited) format.

4 Both the initialization of the accumulators and output of the heading line should occur within one module.

5 Input to the problem on each loop is the number of hours per month for the specific project.

6 The estimated project expense for that month is based on the formula

Expense = 400 + (8.34 * hours)

7 The accumulation of the two separate totals uses the equations

a Total1 = total1 + hours
b Total2 = total2 + expense

8 On each loop output the month's number, hours, and expenses, using the indicated edited format.

9 After the sixth loop, branch to the module containing closing output tasks. In that module, define the edited format applied to the required summary line. Print the label TOTAL prior to the edited output of the two accumulated totals.

The flowchart for Problem 5.6 is shown in Figure 5.16.

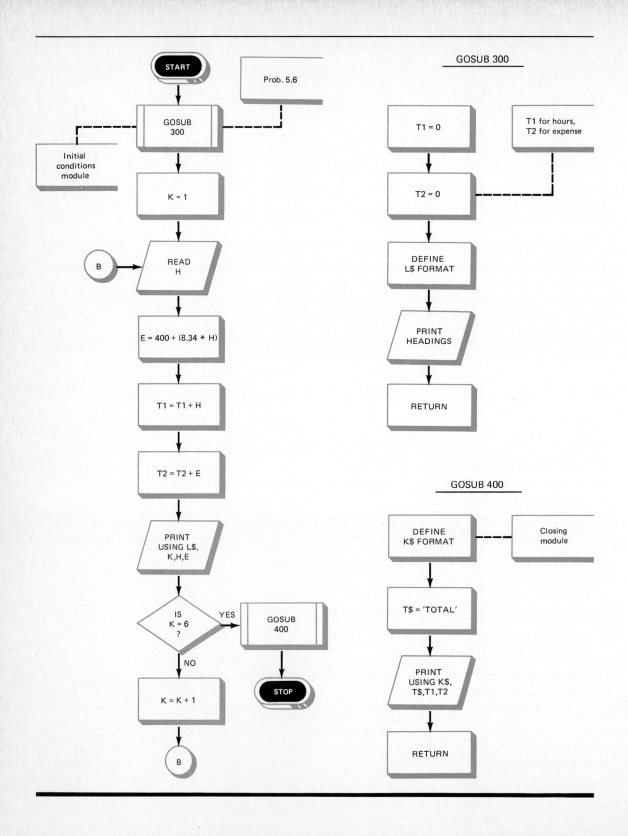

The flowchart solution for Problem 5.6 consists of three flow diagrams. The main flowchart describes the flow of processing through the counter-oriented loop and references both program modules. The first of these modules, GOSUB 300, opens the flowchart and serves to initialize both accumulators, T1 and T2, and define printed formats. The processing symbol with the narrative DEFINE L\$ FORMAT is used to detail the format applied to each month's output. This format is eventually employed with the PRINT USING statement later in the solution's loop. Because of the complexity of the actual BASIC statement, we have simply identified the L\$ instruction and left the actual specification of that format for the program.

The same rationale is applied with the PRINT symbol of the opening module. The symbol's narrative of PRINT HEADINGS identifies its function and fixes the point at which that output should occur. Again, the length and complexity of the instruction (which will incorporate the TAB function) prohibits its specification within a single PRINT symbol. Actual program statements will subsequently detail every character of those output instructions, with each respective symbol noting the position of each task. A RETURN symbol indicates the opening module's close and return to the main flowchart.

The initialization of the counter, K = 1, readies the loop for processing and the input of H. A series of processing activities follow the READ symbol, incorporating the hourly value into processing. The first task involves the computation of E, using the formula E = 400 + (8.34 * H). The next two symbols depict the update of the accumulators. The first update accumulates the number of hours (H) in the T1 accumulator, with the second accumulator (T2) adding that month's expense.

The PRINT symbol following these updates outputs that month's data and applies the L\$ format defined in the opening module. As this notation is somewhat more compact, we have chosen to specify the PRINT USING reference. The counter decision for the execution of six loops follows, as does the counter increment on its NO branch. An unconditional branch to the READ symbol continues the looping sequence.

The YES branch of the counter decision leads to the closing module. Before outputting the required summary line, it is necessary to define two factors. The K\$ instruction establishes the output format applied to the summary line. The second processing task defines T\$ = 'TOTAL' to permit the output of the label within the summary line. It is the subsequent PRINT symbol which applies the K\$ format through the PRINT USING option. The RETURN symbol concludes that closing module and facilitates the flowchart's close.

The resulting BASIC program and output is shown in Figure 5.17. The program reflects the use of two GOSUB modules and the specialized output

---

FIGURE 5.16   The flowchart developed for Problem 5.6. Observe the use of modules for handling a set of initial conditions and closing output activities.

FIGURE 5.17 *(a)*
BASIC program and
(b) output for Problem
5.6. This output shows
the successful
integration of the TAB
function and PRINT
USING statements to
produce a stylized
output.

(a)

```
10 REM PROB 5.6
20 GOSUB 300
30 K = 1
40 READ H
50 E = 400 + ( 8.34 * H )
60 T1 = T1 + H
70 T2 = T2 + E
80 PRINT USING L$,K,H,E
90 IF K = 6 THEN 600
100 K = K + 1
110 GO TO 40
200 DATA 10.3,15.6,8.6,21.7,12.5,18.1
300 REM -- INITIAL CONDITIONS MODULE
310 T1 = 0
320 T2 = 0
330 REM --T1 FOR HOURS, T2 FOR EXPENSES
340 L$ ='###    ###.#    ####.##'
350 PRINT 'MON';TAB(7);'HOURS';TAB(15);'EXPENSE'
360 RETURN
400 REM -- CLOSING MODULE
410 K$ ='\      \###.#    ####.##'
420 T$ ='TOTAL'
430 PRINT USING K$,T$,T1,T2
440 RETURN
600 GOSUB 400
610 END
```

(b)

```
MON     HOURS    EXPENSE
  1      10.3    485.90
  2      15.6    530.10
  3       8.6    471.72
  4      21.7    580.98
  5      12.5    504.25
  6      18.1    550.95
TOTAL    86.8   3123.91
```

formats. The program begins with an opening REM statement which precedes its access of the GOSUB 300 module. It is this introductory module which initializes the accumulators and output formats.

Within the GOSUB 300 module, lines 310 and 320 initialize T1 and T2 at zero and precede a REM statement at line 330 commenting on their use. The LET statement, line 340, serves to define L$ and the output format applied to each item of data printed within the looping sequence. Where a general reference was permitted in the flowchart, the LET statement defines this format on an individual-character basis. Within line 340's quotes, the ### format is applied to the number of the month (K), the ###.# format to the hours worked that month (H), and the ####.## format to the related expense (E). Blanks inserted between these edited formats ensure that they are properly positioned in their respective columns.

The headings defining these columns of data are supplied by line 350. The PRINT statement, with the assistance of TAB functions, creates the column headings MON, HOURS, and EXPENSE. As the literal MON is the first item to follow the command PRINT, it is printed starting at position 1 and does not really require a TAB setting of its own. To ensure the proper positioning of the two literals that follow, TAB functions are applied to HOURS and EXPENSE, respectively, at print positions 7 to 11 and 15 to 21.

To avoid any potential confusion, we should advise the reader that no direct operational relationship exists between lines 340 and 350, where one statement is required to precede the other. They carry companion output formats, as the headings define the columns in which the loop's data is output, but they may be executed separately. We have chosen to position these statements sequentially in our opening module because of their parallel relationship.

The completion of the GOSUB 300 module enables a return to the main program and the initialization of K = 1. The start of the six looping sequences begins at line 40, where a READ statement enters data related to H — the number of hours applied to the project. The computation of E occurs at line 50, with the updates of the T1 and T2 accumulator completed via lines 60 and 70.

The PRINT USING statement at line 80 invokes the L$ format and prints project data. Though L$ was defined in the opening module, it is directly usable for printing throughout the program's processing. Formats may be defined in a fashion similar to an initial condition and used throughout a program. The use of the PRINT USING coordinates the output of K, H, and E through the L$ format and aligns their printing with the column headings originally defined from line 350's execution.

The next three statements, lines 90 to 110, oversee the counter's processing and complete the looping sequence. The counter is incremented until the sixth loop is executed and the closing output module is accessed. Line 200 dictates the hourly data used in processing. Exactly six data items are needed to support this program's processing.

Access to the closing GOSUB 400 module is facilitated through line 600. Again, we chose to group our closing output-related statements in a single module. The format prepared for the final summary line is defined as K$ in line 410. Within the quotes of this statement, the opening two backslashes define the position for a label, with the ###.# and ####.## formats reserved for T1 and T2. Line 420 defines T$ = 'TOTAL', thus creating the label that will be inserted into the K$ format. We chose to define the TOTAL label in this manner and enable its use in the PRINT USING statement, line 430. Using conventional methods to define this literal would have resulted in another series of output instructions. The statements which follow offer an alternative to lines 410 to 430 and produce the same output.

```
410     K$ = '###.# ####.##'
420     PRINT 'TOTAL';TAB(7);
430     PRINT USING K$,T1,T2
```

The compact output, noted in Figure 5.17, parallels the desired format specified in Figure 5.15. Edited formats were applied to K, H, and E, as well as to the accumulated totals, T1 and T2.

5.4 Automated Looping Sequences

The concept of a counter was introduced to permit the processing of an exact number of loops. Through the years, the importance of this concept was recognized and an attempt to provide a simplified means of representing a counter-oriented looping sequence was initiated. This work was designed not to eliminate the counter, but to offer users an easy way of invoking a loop.

FOR/NEXT Statement

By integrating the **FOR/NEXT statement** into a program it is possible to create a looping sequence both to parallel a counter and to offer the user other processing features. In actuality there are two statements — the **FOR statement** and the **NEXT statement.** The FOR instruction initializes the looping sequence, whereas the NEXT is positioned at its close.

The general format of the FOR statement is outlined below.

```
40    FOR I = 1 TO 8
```

The commands of FOR and TO are required parts of this statement's syntax, as is the equal sign before the first number. The variable I is referred to as the counter variable, as it is the numeric-variable name used to monitor the loop sequence throughout processing. A numeric-variable name must be used with the FOR instruction to enable the computer to determine whether the desired number of loops has been executed. The numeric-variable name is generally restricted to one alphabetic character for easy handling within the FOR statement's syntax.

The numbers 1 and 8 relate directly to the number of loops to be executed. The number 1 represents the starting point of the looping sequence, where the number 8 represents the closing point of the looping sequence. Effectively, this FOR instruction will start looping at a value of I = 1 and continue until I = 8. As the implied increment of this instruction is 1, a total of exactly eight loops is indicated.

Where the FOR instruction opens the automated looping sequence, the NEXT instruction denotes its close. The abbreviated syntax of the NEXT statement belies its importance to the looping operation. The companion instruction to the previous FOR instruction is shown below.

```
40     FOR I = 1 to 8
 .
 .                    } Statements within the loop
 .
100    NEXT I
```

Within this format, the line number 100 identifies the logical position of the NEXT statement in the program and precedes the NEXT command. The variable I is needed to complete the I-oriented loops, initiated by line 40. The same variable name must be jointly used in both parts of the FOR/NEXT sequence, otherwise a program error results and all processing ceases.

The NEXT instruction defines the loop's close and serves to identify the point at which the program will branch to the loop's top and continue processing. This FOR/NEXT sequence provides eight loops of processing, as defined by those instructions. On the initial seven loops, the program will execute line 100, increment I, return to line 40, and continue the loop. On the last loop, when I = 8, the program will pass through the NEXT statement (line 100), continue on to the statement immediately following line 100, and permit processing of another series of tasks.

The use of the FOR/NEXT instruction enables the programmer to create a looping module in which a series of tasks is repeatedly performed. It is an effective substitute for the counter and, as subsequent discussions will show, offers its users some other advantages.

In our two sample statements we indicated the execution of exactly eight loops and use of the variable I. As you may have concluded, the FOR/NEXT may be used to execute any number of loops and use almost any numeric-variable name. To reinforce its varied use, let us consider applying the FOR/NEXT statement to a counter-based solution previously covered in Chapter 4. Figure 5.18 offers a side-by-side comparison of the FOR/NEXT solution and its counter-oriented counterpart. For the sake of brevity, we have not incorporated many of the special features previously reviewed; this enables us to focus readily on the application of the FOR/NEXT instruction.

This side-by-side comparison of both program solutions permits us to observe how easily a FOR/NEXT looping sequence is substituted for a counter, when desired. Essentially, the program solutions are identical.

In the counter-based program, Figure 5.18(a), line numbers 30, 70, 80, and 90 are of particular interest. These statements relate directly to the counter K, which controls the execution of four loops in this solution. Other than these statements, both solutions are identical and produce the same results.

These four statements are effectively replaced by two statements in the FOR/NEXT solution of Figure 5.18(b). Here, lines 30 and 70 are sufficient to replace the counter and yet create a looping sequence where exactly four loops are executed. Line 30, the FOR statement, establishes a looping sequence of four loops and a loop variable of K which will range from 1 to 4. The NEXT instruction, line 70, closes the loop and serves to replace lines 70, 80, and 90 of the original solution.

The net effect of applying the FOR/NEXT statement is to create a more compact program solution. A secondary effect of the FOR/NEXT statement is to eliminate the use of the GO TO statement, which many currently popular programming techniques de-emphasize. Though this unconditional branching activity is actually performed by the program's looping sequence, it is

(a)   (b)

```
10 REM -- GROSS PAY WITH COUNTER        10 REM -- GROSS PAY WITH FOR/NEXT
20 PRINT 'NAME','GROSS'                 20 PRINT 'NAME','GROSS'
30 K = 1                                30 FOR K = 1 TO 4
40 READ N$,H,R                          40 READ N$,H,R
50 G = H * R                            50 G = H * R
60 PRINT N$,G                           60 PRINT N$,G
70 IF K = 4 THEN 200                    70 NEXT K
80 K = K + 1                            100 DATA 'HARRISON',36,4.00
90 GO TO 40                             110 DATA 'JACQULINE',40,12.10
100 DATA 'HARRISON',36,4.00             120 DATA 'LAMPIERE',30,18.20
110 DATA 'JACQULINE',40,12.10           130 DATA 'NORTON',42,22.00
120 DATA 'LAMPIERE',30,18.20            200 PRINT 'PROCESSING OVER'
130 DATA 'NORTON',42,22.00              210 END
200 PRINT 'PROCESSING OVER'
210 END
```

and its output   and its output

```
NAME            GROSS                   NAME            GROSS
HARRISON         144                    HARRISON         144
JACQULINE        484                    JACQULINE        484
LAMPIERE         546                    LAMPIERE         546
NORTON           924                    NORTON           924
PROCESSING OVER                         PROCESSING OVER
```

FIGURE 5.18   One of the best ways to observe the effectiveness and operational similarities of the FOR/NEXT instruction to a counter is to compare parallel solutions where both are applied. Here a gross pay problem is programmed using a counter (a) and a FOR/NEXT sequence (b) to control the looping sequence of four repetitions. Note that the outputs resultant from either solution are identical.

masked within the FOR/NEXT instructional format. Additional discussions related to these concepts are introduced in Chapter 6.

An additional point relating to Figure 5.18(b) must be made. Some students question the progression of processing, after the four loops are completed and the program continues from the NEXT instruction. From line 70, the program will continue through the DATA statements, lines 100 to 130, onto the PRINT statement at line 200. The DATA statements are essentially bypassed, as they have already been used. The next instruction to be processed is line 200, where a closing literal of PROCESSING OVER is output. The program closes after executing that PRINT instruction. The printouts resulting from both programs are also shown in Figure 5.18 and permit readers to observe the similarity of those results.

The FOR/NEXT statement is applicable to more complex problems such as the solution developed for Problem 5.6. This program involved six loops, specialty output statements, and two GOSUB modules. Let us examine Figure 5.19 and observe the impact of a FOR/NEXT statement.

Again, we have chosen to employ a side-by-side comparison of both BASIC solutions for Problem 5.6. An initial analysis of both solutions reveals the effect of the FOR/NEXT. In the original solution, lines 30, 90, 100, and 110 were directly related to a counter-oriented sequence of six loops. In the FOR/NEXT solution, Figure 5.19(b), these instructions were replaced by lines 30 and 90. Statement 30 was the FOR instruction which initiated the necessary six-loop sequence and defined K as the loop variable. The NEXT statement, line 90, defines the loop's close and the point which the program will pass through when the sixth loop is processed.

FIGURE 5.19   Similar solutions for Problem 5.6 are compared. (a) The original solution used a counter to control the execution of the required six loops. (b) A FOR/NEXT is substituted for the counter, resulting in a more compact and simplified program.

```
                    (a)                                          (b)

10 REM PROB 5.6 WITH COUNTER              10 REM PROB 5.6 WITH FOR/NEXT
20 GOSUB 300                              20 GOSUB 300
30 K = 1                                  30 FOR K = 1 TO 6
40 READ H                                 40 READ H
50 E = 400 + ( 8.34 * H )                 50 E = 400 + ( 8.34 * H )
60 T1 = T1 + H                            60 T1 = T1 + H
70 T2 = T2 + E                            70 T2 = T2 + E
80 PRINT USING L$,K,H,E                   80 PRINT USING L$,K,H,E
90 IF K = 6 THEN 600                      90 NEXT K
100 K = K + 1                             100 GOSUB 400
110 GO TO 40                              110 STOP
200 DATA 10.3,15.6,8.6,21.7,12.5,18.1     200 DATA 10.3,15.6,8.6,21.7,12.5,18.1
300 REM -- INITIAL CONDITIONS MODULE      300 REM -- INITIAL CONDITIONS MODULE
310 T1 = 0                                310 T1 = 0
320 T2 = 0                                320 T2 = 0
330 REM --T1 FOR HOURS, T2 FOR EXPENSES   330 REM -- T1 = HOURS, T2 = EXPENSE
340 L$ ='###    ###.#    ####.##'         340 L$ ='###    ###.#    ####.##'
350 PRINT 'MON';TAB(7);'HOURS';TAB(15);'EXPENSE'  350 PRINT 'MON';TAB(7);'HOURS';TAB(15);'EXPENSE'
360 RETURN                                360 RETURN
400 REM -- CLOSING MODULE                 400 REM -- CLOSING MODULE
410 K$ ='\      \###.#    ####.##'        410 K$ ='\      \###.#    ####.##'
420 T$ ='TOTAL'                           420 T$ ='TOTAL'
430 PRINT USING K$,T$,T1,T2               430 PRINT USING K$,T$,T1,T2
440 RETURN                                440 RETURN
600 GOSUB 400                             600 END
610 END
```

```
MON   HOURS   EXPENSE              MON   HOURS   EXPENSE
 1    10.3    485.90                1    10.3    485.90
 2    15.6    530.10                2    15.6    530.10
 3     8.6    471.72                3     8.6    471.72
 4    21.7    580.98                4    21.7    580.98
 5    12.5    504.25                5    12.5    504.25
 6    18.1    550.95                6    18.1    550.95
TOTAL 86.8   3123.91              TOTAL 86.8   3123.91
                                  Stop at line 110
```

The statement which follows the NEXT instruction is another change in our revised solution. The placement of line 100 relates directly to the pass-through quality of the NEXT instruction. In the original solution, the counter decision branched to line 600 when K = 6, in order to execute the GOSUB 400 closing module. By placing the GOSUB 400 statement at line 100 in our revised solution, we ensure that the closing module is executed after the sixth loop sequence has ended.

Without positioning this new line 100, the program will have continued from line 90, the NEXT statement, to line 200 and then on to both modules. This would have resulted in the reexecution of the GOSUB 300 and 400 modules, which was not intended. By positioning the GOSUB 400 instruction at line 100, we ensure that the closing module is executed immediately after the last loop's processing. The **STOP statement** at line 110 acts as a substitute END statement, which permits the user to close a main program and cause it to immediately suspend processing. As we noted, we did not want to reexecute the GOSUB modules out of their intended order. Placement of the STOP statement at line 110 ensures that this situation does not occur.

The operational sequence implied by statements 90, 100, and 110 of Figure 5.19*(b)* is as follows:

1   The NEXT statement closes the loop and the program continues through line 90 when the last or sixth loop is over.

2   The GOSUB 400 instruction prints the required summary line only once.

3   The STOP statement, line 110, causes the program to conclude processing.

The specific importance of the STOP statement is to prohibit the reexecution of the GOSUB modules which follow it in the program. If one decided not to use the STOP statement to bypass the GOSUB 300 and 400 modules, a GO TO statement could have been used. The statement 110 GO TO 600 could have been substituted for 110 STOP, causing the program to unconditionally branch around those two modules and access the END statement at line 600. We elected not to use a GO TO but to illustrate the operational use of the STOP statement instead.

The STEP Option Loop

In the FOR/NEXT statements of the prior two sample problems, the implied increment was 1. When the need arises to utilize an increment other than 1, the **STEP option** is invoked. The STEP option is appended to the end of the FOR statement and alters the increment used during the looping sequence. To illustrate this fact, consider the following FOR/NEXT statement:

```
40      FOR I = 1 TO 15 STEP 2
.
.
.
100     NEXT I
```

SIDE BAR 5.3   The FOR/NEXT Variable

The programmer must ensure that the correct loop variable is used within a FOR/NEXT instructional sequence. A common error, normally made through confusion, is to specify one variable in the FOR instruction and a different one in the NEXT instruction. This incorrect program sequence is illustrated below.

```
20      FOR K = 1 TO 25
.
.                          This sequence is
.                          incorrect.
100     NEXT I
```

Here, the variable K was initialized as the loop counter and should run from 1 to 25. However, the companion NEXT statement specifies a variable of I, disagreeing with line 20.

This FOR/NEXT sequence will not work and results in a program error serious enough to prevent the looping sequence. The variables specified in both the FOR and NEXT statements must be the same. In this case, changing line 100 to

```
100     NEXT K
```

would correct the error and enable the FOR/NEXT to be properly executed.

In this FOR/NEXT sequence, the loop appears to run from I = 1 TO 15, resulting in 15 loops. However, the STEP option alters this sequence, increasing the loop counter I by 2, not 1. The new increment will force I to assume the values of 1, 3, 5, 7, 9, 11, 13, and 15 — for a total of 8 loops. By altering the increment, it is possible to affect the number of loops executed by a FOR/NEXT sequence. To illustrate this use of the STEP option, examine the sample flowchart and program solution of Figure 5.20.

The STEP option defines an increment of 3, within a looping sequence that will range from K = 1 to 49. The program is designed to accumulate every value of K as it is incremented and accumulate the number of loops executed to reach the final loop value of 49.

Note that no READ or INPUT instructions are used in this example. The data involved in processing is generated by the FOR statement. It is perfectly acceptable to use the loop variable (K) in processing, as long as those subsequent processing steps do not adversely effect the FOR/NEXT looping sequence. In Figure 5.20 one accumulator (T1) adds each K value on every loop, while the second accumulator (T2) adds the loops executed until the K = 49. Since a STEP option of 3 is involved, the number of loops actually executed will be much less than 49.

Once K = 49, the FOR/NEXT sequence will close and the program will proceed to statements 90 and 100, where the output of both accumulated

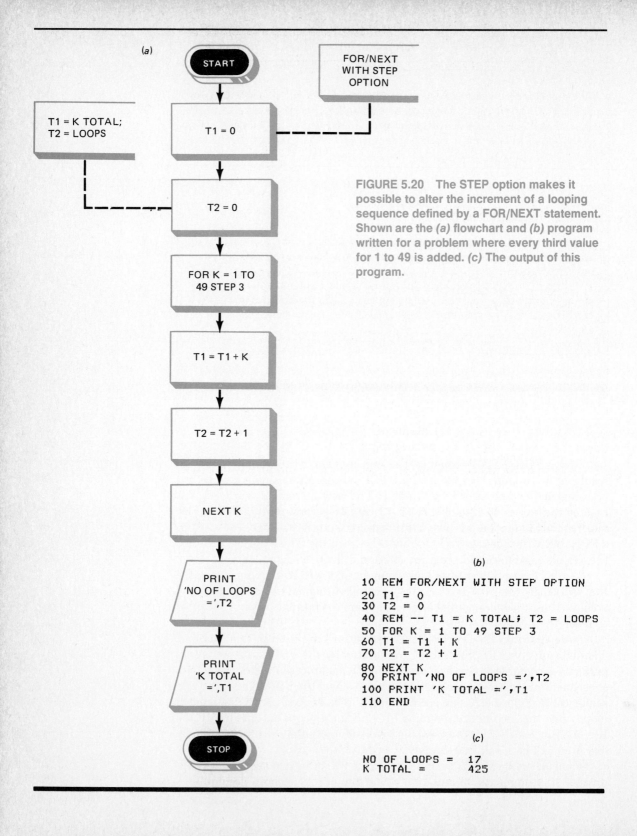

FIGURE 5.20 The STEP option makes it possible to alter the increment of a looping sequence defined by a FOR/NEXT statement. Shown are the *(a)* flowchart and *(b)* program written for a problem where every third value for 1 to 49 is added. *(c)* The output of this program.

(a)

START

FOR/NEXT WITH STEP OPTION

T1 = K TOTAL; T2 = LOOPS

T1 = 0

T2 = 0

FOR K = 1 TO 49 STEP 3

T1 = T1 + K

T2 = T2 + 1

NEXT K

PRINT 'NO OF LOOPS =',T2

PRINT 'K TOTAL =',T1

STOP

(b)

```
10 REM FOR/NEXT WITH STEP OPTION
20 T1 = 0
30 T2 = 0
40 REM -- T1 = K TOTAL; T2 = LOOPS
50 FOR K = 1 TO 49 STEP 3
60 T1 = T1 + K
70 T2 = T2 + 1
80 NEXT K
90 PRINT 'NO OF LOOPS =',T2
100 PRINT 'K TOTAL =',T1
110 END
```

(c)

```
NO OF LOOPS =   17
K TOTAL =      425
```

totals occurs. The results reveal that exactly 17 loops were executed and the total of K values is 425.

The coordinated use of the STEP option and loop variable can be a valuable tool. Often by analyzing the results of such processing activities, users may derive answers to specific questions. Consider the following illustrative problem.

PROBLEM 5.7   Analyzing a Curve

A math student wishes to analyze the path of the curve $Y = X^2 + .5X - 3$, from a value of $X = 3$ to $X = -3$. The student wants to decrement each X value on each loop by steps of .5. On each loop, output the X and Y values beneath the headings of X VAL and Y VAL. Apply the edited format of ##.# to the X values and the format ##.## to all Y values, when outputting both. Use a FOR/NEXT statement and STEP option to control looping.

These are the main points in the problem narrative.

1   No inputs are utilized in this problem.

2   A heading consisting of the literals X VAL and Y VAL is required. The spacing of these literals is left to the programmer.

3   The edited formats of ##.# and ##.## are applied to the X and Y outputs, respectively.

4   A FOR/NEXT looping sequence is employed. The X value acts as the loop variable and input to the equation. The X value will vary from 3.0 to -3.0, by increments of $-.5$.

5   Output X and Y values on each loop, using their intended formats.

The flowchart, program, and results associated with Problem 5.7 are displayed in Figure 5.21.

The flowchart prepared for Problem 5.7 is compact and focuses on the looping sequence. A PRINT symbol noting the output of both headings and a TAB function opens the flowchart. The definition of the L$ format establishes the editing associated with the printing of X and Y. The FOR statement identifies the start of the looping sequence, with X ranging from 3.0 to -3.0. A negative increment of $-.5$ is noted to facilitate use of the declining values of X.

Within the loop, each X value is properly utilized in the equation to compute Y. A PRINT USING I/O operation details the application of the L$ format to the output of X and Y. The NEXT instruction notes the loop's close, positioning itself before the STOP symbol.

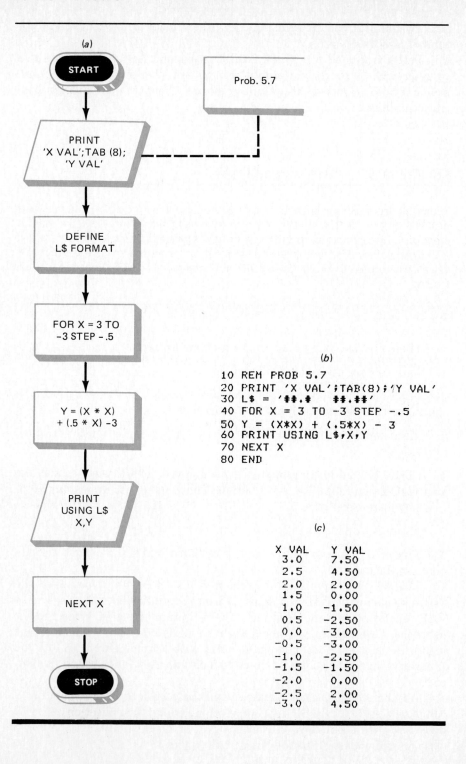

(a)

START

PRINT
'X VAL';TAB (8);
'Y VAL'

Prob. 5.7

DEFINE
L$ FORMAT

FOR X = 3 TO
−3 STEP − .5

Y = (X * X)
+ (.5 * X) −3

PRINT
USING L$
X,Y

NEXT X

STOP

(b)

```
10 REM PROB 5.7
20 PRINT 'X VAL';TAB(8);'Y VAL'
30 L$ = '##.#   ##.##'
40 FOR X = 3 TO −3 STEP −.5
50 Y = (X*X) + (.5*X) − 3
60 PRINT USING L$,X,Y
70 NEXT X
80 END
```

(c)

```
X VAL    Y VAL
 3.0      7.50
 2.5      4.50
 2.0      2.00
 1.5      0.00
 1.0     −1.50
 0.5     −2.50
 0.0     −3.00
−0.5     −3.00
−1.0     −2.50
−1.5     −1.50
−2.0      0.00
−2.5      2.00
−3.0      4.50
```

The resultant program follows the logic of this flowchart, incorporating many of the previously discussed techniques. The REM statement, line 10, advises of Problem 5.7's solution. The PRINT statement at line 20 directs the output of the literals X VAL and Y VAL at print positions 1 and 8, respectively. The TAB function is used within line 20 to properly position the second column heading. The edited format applied to X and Y within the loop is specified at line 30. The L$ format assigns the ##.# format to X values and the ##.## format to Y values. The spaces in L$ separate both edited formats and ensure the proper positioning of the second format.

The structure of line 40, the FOR instruction, requires some explanation. In this case, a negative increment is specified, as the looping sequence will proceed from 3.0 to -3.0. This situation represents an advantage associated with using the FOR/NEXT structure. It is perfectly acceptable to specify a negative increment as the STEP option and a higher and lower value as the starting and ending values of the FOR/NEXT sequence. In this case, we will start looping at a value of X $= .0$ and proceed at increments of $-.5$ to X $= -3.0$. The FOR/NEXT sequence permits users to proceed from low to high loop values, as well as vice versa. STEP option values may be positive or negative and may assume a decimal form, too.

A total of 13 loops will be executed, in which 13 sets of X and Y values will be printed. The X and Y values will adopt the L$ format created for them and are applied via the PRINT USING statement, line 60. The NEXT statement will permit the flow of processing to pass to the END statement, only after the thirteenth loop is processed (when X $= -3.0$).

The series of X and Y outputs reveals that at values of X $= 1.5$ and X $= -2.0$, the corresponding values of Y $= 0$. This identifies those X values as roots of the equation and assists the math student in analyzing the problem. The student is able to use a BASIC program as a problem-solving tool.

It should be pointed out that it was possible to have written this solution where the FOR/NEXT sequence ran from -3.0 to 3.0 and the increment was .5. However, we elected to show that negative increments and decreasing loop variables may be satisfactorily used in FOR/NEXT statements.

FOR/NEXT looping sequences may be applied to a wide range of business, math, and science problems, as they facilitate the repetitive processing of data. The critical factor in all cases is to recognize the range of the looping sequence and its related increment. The variable representing the loop variable may be incorporated into processing if the problem requires it. The FOR/NEXT loop may contain a complete set of processing activities or involve itself directly into processing.

FIGURE 5.21   The flowchart, program, and output related to Problem 5.7. Carefully note the use of a decreasing STEP option tacked onto the program's FOR/NEXT instruction.

Chapter Summary

5.1 Accumulated Totals

The accumulator provides the means of creating totals which reflect data drawn from groups of people or transactions. Accumulators are operationally similar to running totals, which provide users with the most current total.

Two initial conditions of using accumulators are: $T = 0$, for the initialization, and $T = T + A$, for the update, where T is the dataname for the accumulator and A represents the amount being accumulated. The initial condition of $T = 0$ is positioned prior to the loop and the update placed within the loop to sum up data.

Accumulators are used in any application where a total must be computed. The number of accumulators used relates directly to the number of totals required. Labels are usually applied to the output of accumulated totals, helping to distinguish between them when multiple totals are printed.

5.2 Program Modules and the GOSUB

Because of certain operational requirements, a set of related statements must often be grouped together and handled as a single entity, or program module. In flowcharts, program modules are depicted with the predefined process symbol. In BASIC, the GOSUB instruction enables the program to branch to a specified module, perform the required series of tasks, return to the main program, and proceed to the statement immediately following the GOSUB. A vital component of the GOSUB structure is the RETURN statement, which closes each module and signals the return to the main program. Each module may support all types of processing activities, including arithmetic and I/O operations.

Modules provide a means of distinguishing between operational groups supporting separate processing activities. It is possible to assign to separate modules processing activities relating to different codes and have them handled solely within one module. GOSUB modules also permit the grouping of related tasks, such as a series of initial conditions or closing output activities. Program modules are referenced in the main flowchart and detailed in separate flow diagrams.

5.3 Aligning Printed Outputs

In addition to the alignment of data within print zones, BASIC provides a means of editing output data. The term *editing* describes the tailoring of outputs to suit a particular user's needs. This may include the introduction of special characters to embellish a report's appearance or the laying out of a report in a compact format.

One technique of aligning outputs involves the use of the TAB function. With the TAB function the user can specify the exact print positions at which the output of variables should commence. This control of outputs may be extended to literals as well as to numeric and string variables. Data output via the TAB function is left-justified; that is, output starts at the farthest left print position available.

The editing of data items, especially those with numeric formats, involves the PRINT USING statement. This statement allows the user to control the number of digits or decimal positions printed in the output. Edited formats are defined as nonnumeric or string variables and executed via the PRINT USING statement. Within certain types of outputs, features of the TAB function and PRINT USING statements are combined to produce edited and aligned formats.

5.4 Automated Looping Sequences

An alternative to the counter to control a looping sequence is BASIC's FOR/NEXT statement. The FOR/NEXT is composed of two instructions—the FOR statement, which initializes the loop, and the NEXT statement, which fixes the loop's end. The FOR statement requires the specification of a line number, a loop counter via a numeric variable, and the starting and ending points of the looping sequence. The NEXT statement closes the indicated loop and contains the matching numeric variable used as the loop counter.

The implied increment of the FOR/NEXT statement is 1, closely paralleling the counter-based sequence. When a different increment is desired, the STEP option is invoked. The increment specified may be positive or negative but must match the sequence of the opening and closing values of the FOR statement.

The FOR/NEXT instructional sequence brackets those statements which are executed within the loop. It is valid for the numeric variable representing the loop counter to be involved in processing activities, as long as that variable is not improperly altered. The use of the loop variable in processing lends itself to math and science problems.

The combined use of the FOR/

NEXT and GOSUB statements can present some operational problems. The NEXT instruction is designed to let the program pass through it when the loop has ended. If the FOR/NEXT loop has GOSUB modules following it and before the END statement, the program flow may incorrectly reexecute those

modules. To prevent this type of program error, the STOP statement is used. The STOP statement is placed at the program's logical conclusion and ahead of any subsequent modules. Use of the STOP instruction causes the program to close processing and denies access to those modules.

Key BASIC Statements

		Examples
FOR statement	40	FOR K = 1 TO 16
	80	FOR J = −7 TO 11
	70	FOR I = 212 TO 32 STEP −2
	20	FOR N = 2.5 TO 6.0 STEP .25
GOSUB statement	100	GOSUB 600
NEXT statement	120	NEXT K
PRINT USING statement	80	PRINT USING L$,A$,B,C
	30	PRINT USING D$,H
RETURN statement	450	RETURN
STEP option (with FOR statement)	60	FOR I = 6.1 TO 3.2 STEP −.1
	80	FOR J = 2 TO 30 STEP 2
	50	FOR K = −300 TO 400 STEP 50
STOP statement	120	STOP
TAB function (with PRINT statement)	100	PRINT N$;TAB(20);A;TAB(30);B
	110	PRINT TAB(5);'COL1';TAB(15);'COL2'
	40	PRINT TAB(6);'TOTAL';TAB(20);
	45	PRINT USING D$,T

Glossary

Accumulator The technique which enables the computation of totals.

Editing The formatting of data undergoing output.

FOR statement The opening instruction of a FOR/NEXT sequence; defines the loop variable and opening and closing values and may include a STEP option.

FOR/NEXT statement The

combination of FOR and NEXT statements to create an automated looping sequence.

GOSUB statement The instruction used to access a module of instructions; must be used in conjunction with a RETURN statement.

Left-justify The leftmost positioning of data within an I/O field.

NEXT statement The companion to the FOR statement in a FOR/NEXT sequence; positioned at the logical close of the loop.

Predefined process symbol The flowcharting symbol used to represent modules of related instructions.

PRINT USING statement An I/O statement which enables the formatting and editing of output data.

RETURN statement The last statement of a program module which directs the flow of processing back to the main program.

Right-justify The rightmost positioning of data within an I/O field.

STEP option The clause appended to a FOR statement to specify an increment other than 1.

STOP statement The instruction placed at the end of the main program which prohibits the processing flow from reentering and executing GOSUB modules,

thus resulting in the program's close.

TAB function An output clause which when incorporated into a PRINT statement enables the alignment of literals and variables to specific print positions.

Exercises

In-Class Exercises

1 For the program excerpts shown, enter the FOR/NEXT statements for the indicated number of loops.

a A looping sequence of 24 loops, commencing at 1.

```
10      REM--24 LOOPS ARE EXECUTED
20      _ _ _ _ _ _ _ _ _ _ _ _ _
30      READ N$,H,R
40      G = H * R
50      PRINT N$,H,R,G
60      _ _ _ _ _ _ _ _ _ _ _ _ _
 .
 .
 .
```

b A looping sequence in which the loop variable X varies from -1.8 to 2.4 in increments of .2.

```
10      REM--A FOR/NEXT AND STEP OPTION
20      _ _ _ _ _ _ _ _ _ _ _ _ _ _ _
30      Y = (.5 * X) + .3
40      PRINT 'X =';X,'Y =';Y
50      _ _ _ _ _ _ _ _ _ _ _ _ _ _ _
 .
 .
 .
```

c A loop in which the loop variable C varies from 100 to 0 in increments of -5.

```
10      REM-A FOR/NEXT WITH A NEGATIVE STEP
20      _ _ _ _ _ _ _ _ _ _ _ _ _
30      F = 32 + (9 * C)/5
40      PRINT 'A TEMPERATURE OF';C,'EQUAL F DEGREES OF';F
50      _ _ _ _ _ _ _ _ _ _ _ _ _
 .
 .
 .
```

2   Prepare a flowchart and program to accumulate all of the even numbers from 2 to 100. Utilize a FOR/NEXT to define the looping sequence and the loop variable which is involved in the accumulation of the even numbers. A STEP option is used to properly increment each loop. When the looping is complete, print out the total of even numbers with the label, EVEN NOS =.

3   Write a flowchart and BASIC program for the following problem.

A manufacturing agent wants to estimate the cost of producing a particular line of goods. The formula used to estimate these costs is:

$$C = (.0012 * U^2) + (.08 * U)$$

where U is the number of units to be manufactured. The agent wants to track these costs for a series of units ranging from 500 to 800 units, in increments of 50. Use a FOR/NEXT to create the looping sequence and a STEP option to generate the increment.

Use a TAB function to position the headings NO OF UNITS and MFG COST at print positions 10 and 25, respectively. The units used in processing and their related costs should be printed in their columns, commencing at print positions 14 and 25, respectively. The edited formats of ### and ###.## should be respectively assigned to the units and cost amounts, when output using a PRINT USING instruction. The program should end after the last cost's data is printed.

1   Examine the following statements and determine whether each is properly writ- **Lab Exercises**
ten. Correct only those statements you believe are incorrect.

    a   40   FOR I = 1 TO 17, STEP 2
    b   100 PRINT N$;TAB(20);A;TAB(30);B
    c   280 FOR J = −5 TO 8 STEP .5
    d   30   LET D$ = '#### ####'
        40   PRINT USING F$,A,B
    e   60   FOR K = 39 TO 1 STEP 2
    f   140 PRINT TAB(5) 'EMPLOYEE', TAB(20) 'GROSSPAY'
    g   80   L$ = '###.##'
        85   PRINT USING L$,T

For the problem narratives that follow, prepare a flowchart and BASIC program for the processing described.

2   The problem entails the accumulation of FICA deductions. Input to the problem are the employee's name, hours worked, and rate of pay. Gross pay is computed by multiplying the hours worked by rate of pay. The FICA rate is computed in relation to the amount of gross pay. If the gross pay amount > $300, the FICA rate is 7.5 percent of gross pay. If gross pay <= $300, the FICA rate is 6.7 percent of gross. The FICA deduction is computed by multiplying the FICA rate by the gross amount. Net pay is computed by subtracting the FICA deduction from gross pay. Accumulate the FICA deduction computed for each employee in a separate accumulator on each loop. For each employee, print name, gross pay, FICA deduction, and net pay. These data items should be outputted beneath the headings EMPLOYEE, GROSS PAY, FICA DED, and NET PAY. When the looping sequence ends, output the accumulated total of

FICA deductions preceded by the label TOT FICA = $. The data used for this problem is as follows:

Employee	Hours	Rate	Employee	Hours	Rate
Collins	40	4.31	Henrick	56	10.92
Davidoff	35	15.25	Isuzi	38	7.64
Eazory	32	9.74	Jackson	36	4.65

a   Prepare a flowchart and program solution in which the loop is controlled via a 9s decision.

b   Prepare a flowchart and program solution in which the looping is controlled by a FOR/NEXT statement, with an increment of 1. Incorporate a TAB function and PRINT USING statement to control outputs. Print the employee name in position 4 and the gross, FICA, and net pay amounts in positions 20, 30, and 40. Edit each dollar amount to include the accumulated FICA deduction total, using the edited format of ####.##.

3   The problem entails the computation of a probability. A pair of dice is rolled 40 times, with possible outcomes ranging from 2 to 12. The problem requires that you accumulate the number of times a 6 is rolled. Using a FOR/NEXT to create the looping sequence, two data items (D1 and D2) representing each die are read per loop. Each time the sum of both dice equals 6, update the accumulator by 1. After the fortieth loop, compute the probability of rolling a 6 by dividing the accumulated total of 6s rolled by 40. Output this result with the label, PROB OF A 6 =. No other outputs are used in this problem. The data for this problem is as follows:

Roll	Die 1	Die 2	Roll	Die 1	Die 2
1	6	3	21	2	1
2	3	3	22	4	4
3	4	6	23	2	2
4	1	6	24	1	2
5	2	5	25	3	4
6	3	3	26	1	5
7	6	3	27	3	4
8	1	4	28	3	3
9	6	1	29	1	3
10	5	6	30	2	2
11	6	5	31	6	4
12	2	3	32	4	3
13	6	6	33	5	2
14	4	5	34	5	5
15	3	6	35	4	1
16	3	4	36	1	5
17	1	5	37	4	4
18	2	4	38	6	1
19	4	4	39	3	1
20	5	6	40	2	6

Because of the nature and quantity of data in this problem, the user may elect to use an INPUT statement rather than READ and DATA statements.

4 The overall problem entails the computation and output of sales data. It requires the use of TAB functions and PRINT USING statements. The heading used for the output of data is SALESPERSON, SALE1, SALE2, SALE3, TOT SALES, and COMMISSION. The opening print positions associated with each of these six column headings are positions 1, 20, 28, 36, 44, and 54. Each sales amount is formatted as ###.##, with total sales and commission amounts formatted as ####.##. Two accumulators are used to compute the total sales made by all salespeople and the commissions paid to all salespeople. Each will use the ####.## format when output.

Input to the problem are each salesperson's name and three separate sales amounts. The three sales amounts are added to produce the total sales amount for that salesperson. This sales total is accumulated on each loop into the first of two accumulators. If the sales total > $200, a commission of 8 percent is used; otherwise a 5 percent rate is used. The commission amount is computed by multiplying the total sales amount by the correct rate. Accumulate each commission into the second accumulator. Print each salesperson's name, three sales amounts, total sales amount and commission.

After processing the last salesperson, output the data held within each accumulator. Use the label TOTAL OF ALL SALES = for the accumulated total of all sales and the label TOTAL COMM PAID = for the sum of commissions paid to all salespeople. The data for the problem follows:

Salesperson	Sale 1	Sale 2	Sale 3
Camille	56.95	89.63	41.20
Rosebud	295.08	96.91	128.75
Willard	68.40	70.65	63.95
Lucretia	189.76	206.93	488.35

Prepare a flowchart and program using a 9s decision to execute the four loops required. Utilize GOSUB modules to group related statements.

5 The problem entails estimating advertising costs. An advertising agency uses the following formula to estimate the sales revenues derived from dollars spent on advertising.

$$R = (.025 * C^2) + (.16 * C)$$

R represents the revenue estimate, and C the advertising cost (in dollars) per product. The agency wishes to estimate the revenue gained by spending from $500 to $1000 in increments of $100.

Use a FOR/NEXT to create the looping sequence and a STEP option to handle the increment. On each loop, output the cost used and the estimated revenue. Use an edited format of #####. when outputting both amounts. A heading of COSTS and EST REVENUE is required at the top of the report. No inputs or accumulators are utilized in this problem.

6　The problem entails accumulating a table of values. On each of eight loops, two data items are input. These two data items are added to compute the sum of that row. In addition, that sum is accumulated in an effort to prepare a total of all 16 data items. On each loop, output both data items and the row total beneath the column headings of ROW1, ROW2, and ROW TOTAL. After the last loop is completed output the accumulated total of all 16 values using the label TOTAL =. This total should appear in the third column of output, acting as a sum of all row totals. The data for the problem is as follows:

Loop	1	2	3	4	5	6	7	8
Item 1	33	68	17	39	106	179	65	83
Item 2	72	24	15	143	117	57	5	49

Use a FOR/NEXT statement to establish the required loop.

7　The problem entails the computation of a payroll. This program is designed to segregate the computation of the regular weekly payroll and overtime pay (including regular pay) into two separate processing modules. Despite this separation, only one report format is to be prepared. This format consists of headings EMPL NO, REG PAY, O/T PAY, GROSS PAY, FICA DED, and NET PAY, each literal positioned at print positions 5, 15, 25, 35, 45, and 55, respectively. The edited format for employee number is #####, where all dollar amounts will utilize ####.##.

Input on each loop is the employee's payroll number, the hours worked that week, and the hourly pay rate. The key to determining whether overtime pay should be computed is whether the number of hours worked is greater than 35. If the employee has worked > 35 hours, both regular and overtime pay are computed in one module. If the hours <= 35, regular pay is computed in the second module.

In the regular pay module, gross pay is computed by multiplying hours worked by pay rate. The FICA deduction is 6.7 percent of gross pay. Net pay is the gross pay minus the FICA deduction. Print out the employee's number, regular pay, gross pay (which is the same as regular pay as no overtime was worked), FICA deduction and net pay amounts in their respective columns. The O/T pay column is left blank.

In the overtime pay module, two payroll figures are computed. Regular pay is computed by multiplying 35 by the hourly pay rate. Overtime pay is computed by multiplying the number of hours worked over 35, by twice the hourly rate. The regular and overtime pay rates are added to compute the gross pay. The FICA deduction is computed 7.2 percent of the gross pay amount. Net pay is calculated by subtracting the FICA deduction from gross pay. Use two accumulators to separately accumulate the number of people paid overtime and the total amount of overtime paid. Print the employee's payroll number, regular pay, overtime pay, gross pay, FICA deduction, and net pay amounts in this module.

After handling the last employee, print the two accumulated totals in separate lines. Precede the overtime paid total with the label TOT O/T PAID = $ and the people paid O/T total with, OT PEOPLE =. The data for the problem follows:

Employee no	Hours	Rate
01263	35	14.26
08096	42	15.60
12534	36	12.73
15667	56	6.45
21345	32	17.67
24609	45	13.69

Prepare the flowchart and program using a FOR/NEXT statement to control looping. Use GOSUB to create the payroll modules and other desired program modules.

Quiz Problem

For the narrative that follows, prepare a flowchart and BASIC program to describe the processing outlined.

The problem entails projecting costs on a straight-line basis. A company desires to project the costs associated with product A over a six-month period using the formula:

$$Cost = (.067 * units) + 175$$

C and U will represent the monthly cost generated and units manufactured. Each monthly cost is accumulated after its computation to produce a total cost estimate for that six-month period. The number of units for that month and the related costs are output on each loop, which is controlled via a FOR/NEXT instruction. A heading consisting of MONTH, UNITS, and COST should appear at the top of the report, with each output commencing at print position 5, 15, and 25, respectively. The month column will range from 1 to 6, for each of the six months involved. Each line will represent that month's activity. After the sixth month is processed, output the accumulated total of costs with the label, COSTS FOR PROJ A =. Output this total cost in the COSTS column of the report. All dollar figures should use the edited format of ####.##. The data for this problem is as follows:

Month	1	2	3	4	5	6
Units	160	425	1000	872	667	315

The flowchart and program written for this quiz problem are shown in Figure 5.22.

Quiz Solution

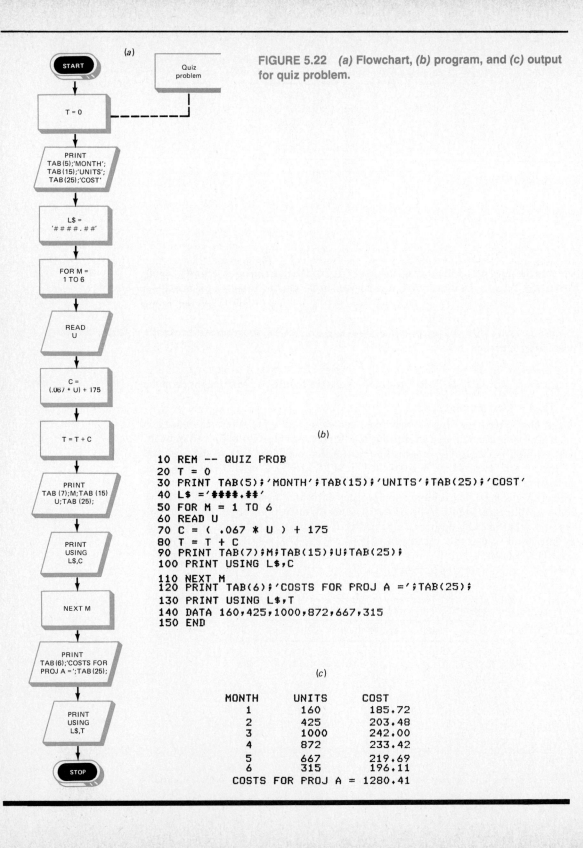

FIGURE 5.22 *(a)* Flowchart, *(b)* program, and *(c)* output for quiz problem.

(a)

START

Quiz problem

T = 0

PRINT
TAB(5);'MONTH';
TAB(15);'UNITS';
TAB(25);'COST'

L$ =
'####.##'

FOR M =
1 TO 6

READ
U

C =
(.067 * U) + 175

T = T + C

PRINT
TAB(7);M;TAB(15)
U;TAB(25);

PRINT
USING
L$,C

NEXT M

PRINT
TAB(6);'COSTS FOR
PROJ A =';TAB(25);

PRINT
USING
L$,T

STOP

(b)

```
10 REM -- QUIZ PROB
20 T = 0
30 PRINT TAB(5);'MONTH';TAB(15);'UNITS';TAB(25);'COST'
40 L$ ='####.##'
50 FOR M = 1 TO 6
60 READ U
70 C = ( .067 * U ) + 175
80 T = T + C
90 PRINT TAB(7);M;TAB(15);U;TAB(25);
100 PRINT USING L$,C
110 NEXT M
120 PRINT TAB(6);'COSTS FOR PROJ A =';TAB(25);
130 PRINT USING L$,T
140 DATA 160,425,1000,872,667,315
150 END
```

(c)

MONTH	UNITS	COST
1	160	185.72
2	425	203.48
3	1000	242.00
4	872	233.42
5	667	219.69
6	315	196.11
COSTS FOR PROJ A =		1280.41

Appendix: Debugging Hints

This appendix continues our discussions about debugging BASIC programs. It focuses on the reinitialization of accumulators, the failure to output accumulated totals, and the incorrect specification of the FOR/NEXT instruction.

The Initialization of T

It is vital that an accumulator be initialized prior to the start of the looping sequence. This initialization should occur once, thus ensuring that all subsequent accumulations properly commence at 0. However, through programmer error the accumulator may be reinitialized on each loop, thus defeating its operational purpose. An example of this type of program error is illustrated in Figure 5.23.

A preliminary analysis of this program fails to disclose an error, but it is readily evident from the output. The columns of data printed correctly itemize each data item, with the exception of the accumulated total of T. There a total of 0 is printed, noting that an error exists in the accumulation process.

Initially, one could conclude that the error exists with lines 20, 60, and 200 — statements relating directly to the accumulator. Each of these statements is correctly written and positioned. Thus, the error must lie elsewhere.

Since T = 0 is output, the potential for an error in relation to line 20 seems possible. That is the only point in the program at which T is set equal to 0. Examining the entire program on a line-by-line basis, we note no unusual problems until the end of the program loop, line 80.

This GO TO instruction reveals the source of our error. Instead of completing the loop by branching to the READ statement at line 30, this instruction unconditionally branches to line 20 where T is initialized at zero. The net effect of this sequence is to repeatedly initialize T at zero, at the start of each loop. As a result, one accumulation is performed on each loop and then that total is erased as T is set back to zero.

FIGURE 5.23 *(a)* Program showing an error state in the initialization of the accumulator. *(b)* An accumulated total of zero in the output signals an error.

```
        (a)                              (b)

10 REM -- ACCUMULATOR ERROR      24        57        88
20 T = 0                         39        92        77
30 READ A,B,C                     8        46        61
40 IF A = -999 THEN 200          59        13        28
50 G = A + B + C              TOTAL =       0
60 T = T + G
70 PRINT A,B,C
80 GO TO 20
100 DATA 24,57,88,39,92,77
110 DATA 8,46,61,59,13,28
120 DATA -999,0,0
200 PRINT 'TOTAL =',T
210 END
```

Prior to reading the 9s data, T was set equal to zero. Thus, when -999 was input for A, the 9s decision was triggered and the program branched to line 200. As the value in T was zero, that was the number output by the PRINT statement at line 200.

The correction of this problem is readily done. The programmer must alter line 80 from GO TO 20 to a statement which branches to the READ statement — GO TO 30. By branching to line 30, the looping sequence will continue properly, as will the update of the accumulator T on each loop.

Where Did T GO?

The output of the accumulated total T is often an indicator of whether the programming sequence is being properly executed. The absence of an accumulated total on output or an incorrect output is a signal that something is amiss in that solution. The prior discussion noted the source of an incorrect accumulated total. What happens when no total is output?

To observe this type of error, we can examine Figure 5.24. The printout from this program properly lists the three required outputs. However, the required output of an accumulated total was missing. An examination of the program reveals that a PRINT statement related to outputting T exists at line 190. Why, then, was T not output?

Scanning the program, we note that all aspects of the solution are properly included in the program. The accumulator is initialized and updated and a statement defining is output exists. Our next step is to determine whether the accumulator output is accessed.

As that PRINT statement is noted on line 190, we must search our program for the means of accessing that statement. Access to that PRINT statement is accomplished via the IF/THEN statement at line 40. Examining this statement, we note the source of this program error. Instead of branching to line 190, that IF/THEN statement directs that the program branch to line 200 — the program's END statement. In performing that branching activity, the program branches around line 190 and does

FIGURE 5.24   *(a)* Program with a printing error. *(b)* The absence of an output for the total T alerts the programmer to a potential error in the source program.

```
           (a)                           (b)
10 REM -- PRINTING ERROR        SMITH        100.75
20 T = 0                        STOVE        312.48
30 READ N$,H,R                  FRANKLIN     286.96
40 IF H = -99.99 THEN 200
50 G = H * R
60 T = T + G
70 PRINT N$,G
80 GO TO 30
100 DATA 'SMITH',31,3.25
110 DATA 'STOVE',42,7.44
120 DATA 'FRANKLIN',34,8.44
130 DATA 'XXX',-99.99,0
190 PRINT 'TOT GROSS =',T
200 END
```

not output the required accumulated total T. That total was not printed, as the program statement defining such an activity was bypassed and not executed.

The correction of this error is easily accomplished. The existing IF/THEN statement at line 40 must be changed to

40   IF H = −99.99 THEN 190

This statement will cause the program to properly branch to line 190 and output the accumulated total T. Completing that output, the program will branch from line 190 to line 200 and execute the END statement.

It should be noted that these two error conditions did not result in the output of an error message, as the errors resulted not from program syntax but from faulty programmer logic. The BASIC compiler can uncover syntax errors, but it is the responsibility of the programmer to figure out errors in program logic.

A Fitting End to a FOR/NEXT

One kind of program error results from the incorrect specification of the FOR/NEXT sequence. Consider the output shown in Figure 5.25.

In this program listing the use of a FOR/NEXT is indicated at lines 30 and 80. However, a careful examination of both lines reveals a program error. In line 30 the loop variable is defined as I, ranging from 1 to 5. At line 80 the indicated loop variable is K. Obviously, an error was made, as it is not possible to use two different loop variables in one FOR/NEXT sequence.

This error was discovered by the compiler, as it generated the error message of:

? NEXT without FOR at line 80
? FOR without NEXT at line 30

These messages reflect the use of the loop variables I and K. The computer is essen-

FIGURE 5.25   (a) A program with an incorrect FOR/NEXT sequence. (b) The failure to properly specify a FOR/NEXT statement results in its nonexecution.

```
               (a)                          (b)

10 REM -- FOR/NEXT PROB           ?NEXT without FOR at line 80
20 T = 0                          ?FOR without NEXT at line 30
30 FOR I = 1 TO 5
40 READ N$,G
50 M = G *.065
60 T = T + M
70 PRINT N$,G,M
80 NEXT K
90 PRINT 'TOT MED $=',T
100 DATA 'BROWN',450,'EMILE',540
110 DATA 'FRANCIS',480,'CARROLL',660
120 DATA 'HANDRAIL',810
200 END
```

tially asking if the program lacks a NEXT I statement or a FOR K = 1 TO 5 instruction. Both errors cancel the program's processing.

The rewriting of line 80 will correct both errors and enable the program's processing. The new line 80 NEXT I properly completes the FOR/NEXT instruction and correctly matches the FOR statement initially written at line 30. Programmers must exercise great care when defining FOR/NEXT loop variables, as they have a considerable impact on processing.

SIX

Chapter Objectives

- Discuss the three control block structures principally used in the formulation of structured-programming solutions.

- Describe the operational concept of the priming read and its use in looping sequences.

- Explain and illustrate the concept of a break-even point.

- Briefly describe the hierarchical structure of top-down solutions and the use of GOSUB statements to create program modules.

- Discuss sample programs that use structured principles, with emphasis on top-down designs.

- Introduce the FOR/UNTIL and FOR/WHILE instructions and the STEP option.

Introduction

Software specialists are always seeking ways to improve their ability to prepare and document programs. In the past few years, structured programming has been introduced and successfully applied to program development. Originally perceived as the panacea for virtually all software-related difficulties, it has proven to be extremely beneficial to software development when properly applied. Proponents of structured-design concepts believe that the application of those concepts will result in logically sound, well-thought-out program solutions.

The structured approach lends itself to the development of programs in which a hierarchy of program modules provides the basis of the solution. Essentially, a structure similar to an organization chart is constructed, with modules at each level that define specific processing activities. This approach is very helpful when it is applied to the design of large program solutions, where many complex components must be integrated throughout all levels of that design.

Though BASIC is not a fully structured language, it lends itself to the application of many structured concepts. It is important that beginning programmers master these concepts, as they are incorporated into many currently popular languages. Structured concepts also provide a means of self-discipline and greatly assist in the preparation of programs that are logical and easy to debug.

6.1 The Structured-Design Approach

Though many people believe that the concepts associated with structured designs are very new, this is not the case. The first technical papers related to structured designs appeared in 1965 and marked the emergence of this programming concept.

From those initial ideas, **structured,** or **top-down, designs** have been refined and improved. The basic steps in top-down design are:

The Top-Down Concept

1 Break down the problem into a modular structure, such that each major module of activity is individually attacked.

2 Minimize the use of unconditional-branching (GO TO) statements.

3 Establish a hierarchical structure for program modules.

Structured design eliminates solutions that are a hodgepodge of elements; that is, it eliminates unintegrated, illogical *bottom-up solutions.* By examining a problem from the top down and dividing it into modules, the programmer is forced to integrate each module logically into the overall design. Thus, a logical flow of information will result.

The application of structured-design principles to software development is called **structured programming.** Statements are logically placed within the resulting solution and compose a workable program. This does not mean that other programming techniques are unsound. Rather, when structured-programming principles are properly applied, well-conceived software results. Three advantages associated with structured programming are:

1 Sound solutions whose logic is readily followed

2 Reduced testing and debugging time

3 Improved programmer output

The impact of structured-programming efforts is best measured in larger, more complex programs, where logical relationships must be clearly defined. Large programs adopting these principles are more readily maintained and easier to modify when upgrading is necessary.

One concept of structured programming is that any program may be represented by three control block sequences: the processing sequence, the IF/THEN/ELSE conditional sequence, and the looping sequence. Figure 6.1 illustrates these control block sequences. In the **processing sequence,** a

Control Block Structures

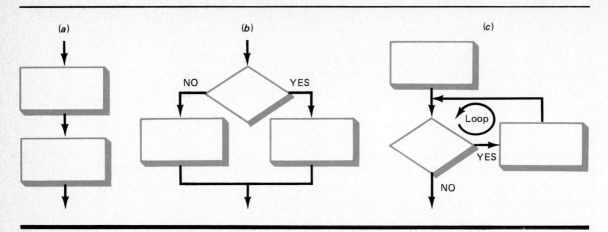

FIGURE 6.1   The three fundamental control block sequences used in top-down designs: *(a)* the processing sequence, *(b)* the IF/THEN/ELSE sequence, and *(c)* the looping sequence.

series of processing activities is sequentially accomplished, where one task logically precedes the next. The **IF/THEN/ELSE sequence** identifies a conditional operation where the program must select between two alternative processing paths. These paths may include a single statement or a module of instructions. The last control block is the looping sequence. It is the cornerstone of many processing activities and must be properly documented.

Minimizing the Use of GO TOs

If a program solution is not properly developed, its components will be attached by a series of GO TO instructions. In many instances, instead of properly analyzing a solution and its modules, the programmer makes a patchwork of statements — each unit linked by GO TOs. Though the original idea of structured programming was to eliminate *all* GO TOs, most programmers now merely deemphasize their use. The GO TO instruction may be used in certain applications. Often it is the most expedient way of accomplishing a transfer of program control. However, its excessive use often reflects insufficient planning and foresight by the programmer.

The elimination of the GO TO instruction will not resolve the problem of poor logic and ill-conceived program solutions. It is still the responsibility of the programmer to carefully develop and document a logically correct program solution.

Similarly, the blind application of structured principles does not ensure a logical or sound solution. These concepts are only valid when applied with sufficient time and effort. Logical, well-conceived solutions result from the application of sound analytical techniques.

6.2 The Priming Read

One of the special techniques to evolve from structured programming is the **priming read.** This technique is incorporated into looping sequences to handle the input of data. It helps construct and control loops and minimizes the use of GO TOs.

The priming read is incorporated into a looping sequence as any other reading operation might be, except that the READ symbol is placed both inside and outside of the loop. Previous READ symbols were positioned at the top of the loop only, but the priming read places one READ symbol before the loop and a second one in the loop at its close.

Figure 6.2 illustrates the conventional looping sequence and its priming read counterpart. In Figure 6.2*(a),* the processing flow places the READ symbol at the loop's top and follows it with a 9s decision. The NO branch leads to the looping sequence. Of importance are the connectors which represent the unconditional branch to the READ symbol. In many languages, unconditional branches are converted to GO TO instructions, which are shunned by most structured programmers.

Figure 6.2*(b)* depicts the use of the priming read, where the READ symbol and 9s decision are positioned at the loop's close. If data exists, the NO branch leads to the loop's top and undertakes its processing. If all records have been processed, the processing proceeds out of the loop. This exit is preferable, as no processing activities are bypassed and the YES branch logically leads to the next series of tasks.

Some critics question the NO branch's unconditional branch back to the loop's top, stating that it is in effect a form of GO TO instruction. The 9s decision placed at the loop's close adopts the form of an IF/THEN/ELSE sequence and is therefore more than a logical operation and branching operation. In effect, the IF/THEN/ELSE enables the solution to choose between continuing or exiting the loop in one logical operation. The unconditional branch is thus suppressed within the IF/THEN/ELSE structure. This point will become apparent when the IF/THEN/ELSE sequence is converted to its program equivalent.

A second question relates to the use of two READ symbols in the flow-chart of Figure 6.2*(b).* The second of the two READ symbols is the loop's primary input activity, handling all data processed within the normal processing loop. If that is the case, what is the purpose of the first READ symbol?

It should be evident from Figure 6.2*(b)* that the first READ symbol is external to the main loop and executed only once. The branch back to the loop is placed beneath that initial READ symbol, so the first READ symbol is encountered only once before the looping sequence starts. It provides the first set of data items to be processed within the loop. The initial READ acts in a manner similar to an initial condition, making data available so that processing may proceed properly.

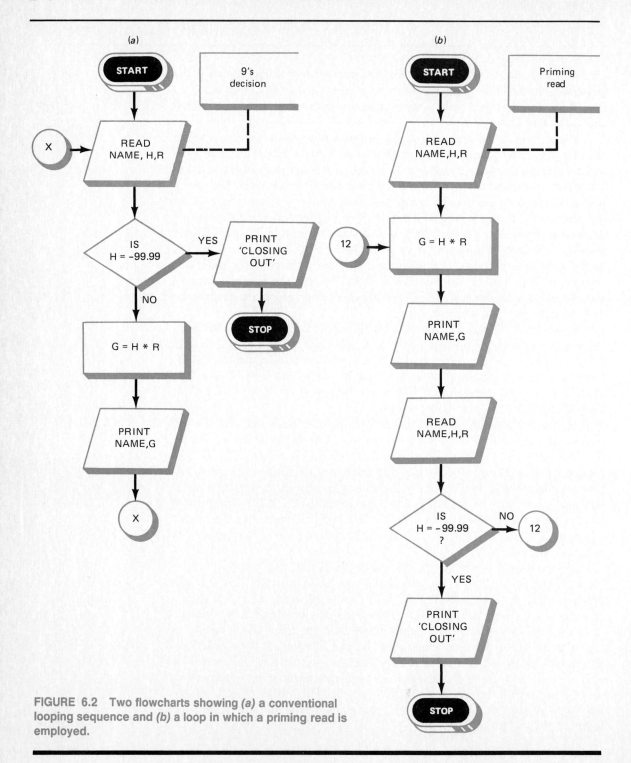

FIGURE 6.2 Two flowcharts showing (a) a conventional looping sequence and (b) a loop in which a priming read is employed.

To verify the importance of this initial READ operation, let us imagine that it is removed from the flowchart of Figure 6.2*(b)*. Without that input, no H and R values exist and the computation of G is not possible. The initial READ represents only half of the priming-read technique but is critical to the processing performed inside a loop.

The effectiveness of the priming read can be seen when it is translated into an actual program solution. Figure 6.3 details the programs written for the two flowcharts of Figure 6.2. Though the results are the same, the program solutions are markedly different. The solution in Figure 6.3*(a)* uses a GO TO statement; in Figure 6.3*(b)* an IF/THEN/ELSE statement is used as part of the priming-read technique. The statement at line 60 represents a 9s decision and enables the program to choose between lines 200 and 30. When H = −99.99, the program will exit the loop and proceed to the output of a literal at line 200. If the 9s data is not encountered, the IF/THEN/ELSE causes the program to branch to line 30 and the computation of G. The unconditional branch still occurs, but it is now part of the IF/THEN/ELSE statement. The elimination of the GO TO instruction was a desired result of structured programming.

Note the application of the priming read in Figure 6.3*(b)*. The first half of the priming read occurs at line 20, where the first set of employee values is

FIGURE 6.3 The programs and outputs written from the flowcharts in Figure 6.2. In *(a)* a conventional looping sequence is employed, whereas in *(b)* a loop with priming read is used.

(a)	(b)

```
10 REM -- 9S DECISION          10 REM -- PRIMING READ
20 READ N$,H,R                 20 READ N$,H,R
30 IF H = -99.99 THEN 200      30 G = H * R
40 G = H * R                   40 PRINT N$,G
50 PRINT N$,G                  50 READ N$,H,R
60 GO TO 20                    60 IF H = -99.99 THEN 200 ELSE 30
100 DATA 'SMITH',42,2.51       100 DATA 'SMITH',42,2.51
110 DATA 'BROWN',31,3.66       110 DATA 'BROWN',31,3.66
120 DATA 'DANTE',35,4.67       120 DATA 'DANTE',35,4.67
130 DATA 'XXX',-99.99,0        130 DATA 'XXX',-99.99,0
200 PRINT 'CLOSING OUT'        200 PRINT 'CLOSING OUT'
210 END                        210 END
```

    and the resultant   and the results of processing
        output

```
SMITH         105.42          SMITH         105.42
BROWN         113.46          BROWN         113.46
DANTE         163.45          DANTE         163.45
CLOSING OUT                   CLOSING OUT
```

inputted before the looping sequence. The second READ instruction, line 50, handles *the remainder of all inputs in the loop.* Essentially, the loop structure exists from lines 30 to 60. The successful use of the priming read is shown in Problem 6.1.

SIDE BAR 6.1   The Loop Back Up

Programmers must ensure that the looping sequence created when using a priming read and 9s decision is correctly designed. A common error involves the branch to the top of the loop, after the second half of the priming read is executed. The program excerpt that follows illustrates this type of error.

```
20      PRINT 'NAME','AVERAGE'
30      READ N$,M1,M2,M3
40      A = (M1 + M2 + M3)/3
 .
 .
 .                                          This sequence
90      READ N$,M1,M2,M3                     is incorrect.
100     IF M3 = −999 THEN 600 ELSE 30
 .
 .
600     END
```

The looping sequence is designed to process student averages, commencing at line 40. But, if we examine the IF/THEN statement at line 100, we observe that this is not the case. Line 100 chooses between a branch to the END statement, line 600, or a branch to the READ statement, line 30. This latter option is incorrect.

The program should correctly branch to line 40, the true top of the loop. The opening half of the priming read, line 30, should be executed only once. The correct 9s decision should be written as follows.

```
100     IF M3 = −999 THEN 600 ELSE 40
```

This statement will ensure that the loop is properly executed and that the priming-read technique correctly inputs data for processing.

PROBLEM 6.1   Student Grades

The overall problem entails the processing of student grades. Inputs are students' names, a grade code, and two scores corresponding to their midterm and final exam grades. If the grade code is A, the student's grade is computed where the midterm and final exam grades represent 30 and 70 percent of the final average. Output that student's name, midterm grade, final grade, final average, and the label PLAN A.

If the grade code is B, a different calculating scheme is used. The midterm and final exam grades are valued at 45 and 55 percent of the final average, respectively. This plan's output uses the student's name, midterm grade, final grade, final average, and the label PLAN B. The headings for all outputs are STUDENT NAME, MIDTERM, FINAL,

FIGURE 6.4 The edited output format applied to Problem 6.1.

AVERAGE, and PLAN CODE. These literals, respectively, commence at print positions 1, 16, 24, 30, and 38. The coordination of this heading and the output formats needed for the student line are shown in Figure 6.4.

The problem requires that the number of students with final averages greater than 85, within either category, be accumulated. This total should be output after the 9s data is handled. Use the label NO OF PLUS 85 GRADES = when outputting this accumulated total. A priming read should be used to input the problem's data which is listed below.

Student	Midterm	Final	Code	Student	Midterm	Final	Code
Abigail	90	84	A	Betty	72	90	A
Carolyn	90	80	B	Diane	76	88	A
Ellen	77	89	B	Frances	96	76	A
Georgia	93	81	B	Harriet	68	95	A

These are the main points in the problem narrative.

1   The headings consist of five literals: STUDENT NAME, MIDTERM, FINAL, AVERAGE, and PLAN CODE. The starting print positions associated with these five literals are 1, 16, 24, 30, and 38, respectively.

2   A specialized format is needed to output variables in each column of data, so that a PRINT USING statement can be employed. The starting print positions for the columns of data are 1, 18, 25, 31, and 39. The numeric formats applied are ### for the two grades and ##.## for the final average.

3   An accumulator totals the number of students in either category who have attained final averages greater than 85.

4   Inputs are the student's name, grade code, midterm, and final exam grades. The priming read in conjunction with a 9s decision controls looping.

5   a   If the grade code is A, the midterm is 30 percent of the final average and the final exam is 70 percent. For code A students, print their names, midterm grades, final exam grades, computed final averages, and the literal PLAN A in the preplanned format.

    b If the student grade code is B, the midterm is 45 percent of the final grade and the final exam is 55 percent. Output the same five data items, except that the last literal should be PLAN B.

    c Each coding plan is handled within its own separate module.

6 In both modules, search out students whose final computed average is greater than 85. For every student found, increment the accumulator by 1.

7 When the 9s decision is activated, exit the looping sequence and output the accumulated total of plus 85 students using the label NO OF PLUS 85 GRADES =.

    The flowcharts prepared for Problem 6.1 are given in Figure 6.5. Note that the modules applied to each grading scheme are separately defined within two smaller flow diagrams.

    This flowchart parallels our previous solutions, incorporating the priming read as desired. The flowchart opens with the output of column headings, the definition of the L\$ format which will be used to print each student's grade data, and the initialization of the accumulator T at 0. The last symbol before the start of the looping sequence is the READ symbol representing the first half of the priming read. This READ symbol is positioned outside the loop and used to prime the loop for processing the first set of student data items.

    A conditional statement acts as the loop's first symbol. With this decision, we test for the student's code. A code of A results in a branch to the GOSUB 400 module. The NO branch leads to the GOSUB 500 module, where all code B students are processed. This decision exhibits the format of an IF/THEN/ELSE sequence.

    Each module contains the computational formula associated with that category. After computing the student's average, each module tests to determine whether the average is 85. If so, the T accumulator is incremented by 1. This test and update are incorporated in both modules. This ensures that each average is tested immediately after its computation. The outputs related to each category are also placed within their modules, as each format possesses a PLAN A or PLAN B literal. The use of a PRINT USING statement is anticipated with the L\$ format and is so indicated.

    In the main flowchart, the return from either module leads to the second half of the priming read. The READ symbol is operationally linked with a 9s decision. This sequence directs that the flowchart choose between continuing the loop or exiting from it. The YES branch, if followed, leads to the output of the accumulated total of plus 85 students and the close of processing.

    The BASIC program prepared from this flow diagram is detailed in Figure 6.6. An opening REM statement precedes the PRINT statements of lines 20 and 25, which detail the printing of the column headings via TAB functions. Line 30 defines the L\$ format which is used with the PRINT USING instructions of each module. The initialization of T occurs at line 40.

    The READ statement at line 50 notes the opening half of the priming read, with the second READ statement placed at line 70. The IF/THEN/

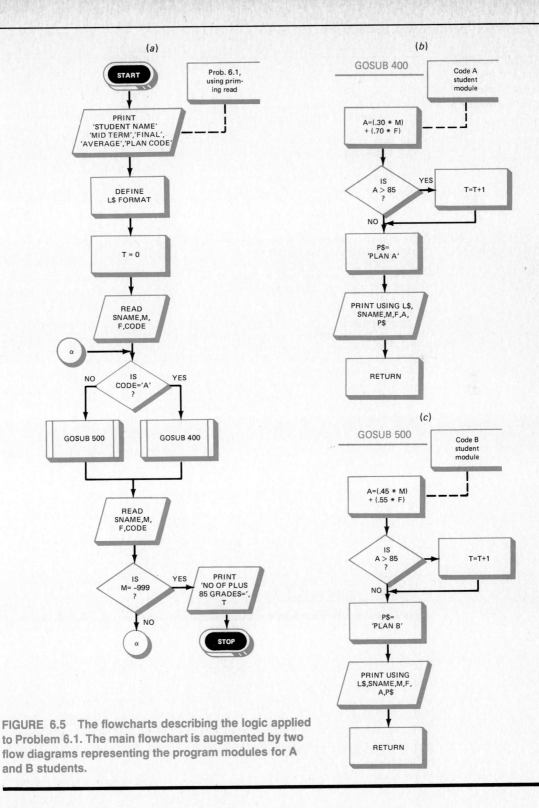

FIGURE 6.5 The flowcharts describing the logic applied to Problem 6.1. The main flowchart is augmented by two flow diagrams representing the program modules for A and B students.

FIGURE 6.6 *(a)* The
program and *(b)* the
output for Problem 6.1,
using the priming read
to input data.

(a)

```
10 REM PROB 6.1, USING PRIMING READ
20 PRINT 'STUDENT NAME';TAB(16);'MIDTERM';TAB(24);'FINAL';
25 PRINT TAB(30);'AVERAGE';TAB(38);'PLAN CODE'
30 L$ ='\              \   ###   ###   ##.##   \      \'
40 T = 0
50 READ N$,M,F,C$
60 IF C$ = 'A' THEN GOSUB 400 ELSE GOSUB 500
70 READ N$,M,F,C$
80 IF M = -999 THEN 600 ELSE 60
100 DATA 'ABAGAIL',90,84,'A','BETTY',72,90,'A'
110 DATA 'CAROLYN',90,80,'B','DIANE',76,88,'A'
120 DATA 'ELLEN',77,89,'B','FRANCES',96,76,'A'
130 DATA 'GEORGIA',93,81,'B','HARRIET',68,95,'A'
140 DATA 'XXX',-999,0,'XX'
400 REM -- CODE A STUDENT MODULE
410 A = (.30 * M) + (.70 * F)
420 IF A > 85 THEN T = T + 1
430 P$ = 'PLAN A'
440 PRINT USING L$,N$,M,F,A,P$
450 RETURN
500 REM -- CODE B STUDENT MODULE
510 A = (.45 * M) + (.55 * F)
520 IF A > 85 THEN T = T + 1
530 P$ = 'PLAN B'
540 PRINT USING L$,N$,M,F,A,P$
550 RETURN
600 PRINT 'NO OF PLUS 85 GRADES =',T
610 END
```

(b)

```
RUN

STUDENT NAME    MIDTERM FINAL AVERAGE PLAN CODE
ABAGAIL             90    84   85.80  PLAN A
BETTY               72    90   84.60  PLAN A
CAROLYN             90    80   84.50  PLAN B
DIANE               76    98   84.40  PLAN A
ELLEN               77    89   83.60  PLAN B
FRANCES             96    76   82.00  PLAN A
GEORGIA             93    81   86.40  PLAN B
HARRIET             68    95   86.90  PLAN A
NO OF PLUS 85 GRADES =      3
```

ELSE instruction separates these statements and enables the program to
choose between both categories. Note that this decision involves C$, the
dataname assigned to the group code for each student. As such, the IF/THEN
statement must test C$ against a nonnumeric data item framed in quotes.
This principle is also carried to the program's DATA statements, lines 100 to
140, where the data items associated with C$ are treated as string-variable
data items.

The main looping sequence of this program essentially involves lines 60, 70, and 80. Access to either program module is controlled via the IF/THEN/ELSE statement, line 60. The next loop's data is input via line 70 and tested against the 9s decision at line 80. This IF/THEN/ELSE statement continues the loop via line 60 or causes the program to branch to line 600.

Both GOSUB modules are similarly constructed. They open with identifying REM instructions and the computation of A, using the assigned percentages. A test of A against 85 determines whether the accumulator is incremented by 1. The next statement in either module defines P$ as the proper plan code, in preparation for its output. The PRINT USING statements invoke the L$ format (defined earlier in the program) and use the literals defined via P$. RETURN statements close both modules and pass control back to the main loop.

The reading of the 9s data causes the program to exit the loop to line 600. The output of the accumulated total of plus 85 students completes all output activities and precedes the END statement.

Students should become acquainted with use of the priming read, since it is commonly used in most currently popular languages. It is easily combined with a 9s decision to control and exit from a loop and minimize the use of GO TO statements.

6.3 A Program Hierarchy

A major principle of structured solutions is the use of program modules. Each module is logically positioned within a series of modules which define processing. As each module is executed, the program handles data and accomplishes its intended function.

The Top-Down Structure

Though BASIC is not a fully structured language, it does enable the user to define a modular program structure. The GOSUB statement is the principal instruction upon which this modular sequence is based. The logic used in sequencing modules is defined in a hierarchical structure which parallels the format of an organization chart. Each module is defined in relation to all other modules in that hierarchical structure.

One type of fundamental program structure is shown in Figure 6.7(a). This organization divides the program solution into three major modules consisting of:

1 An initial-conditions module

2 A main-loop module

3 A closing module

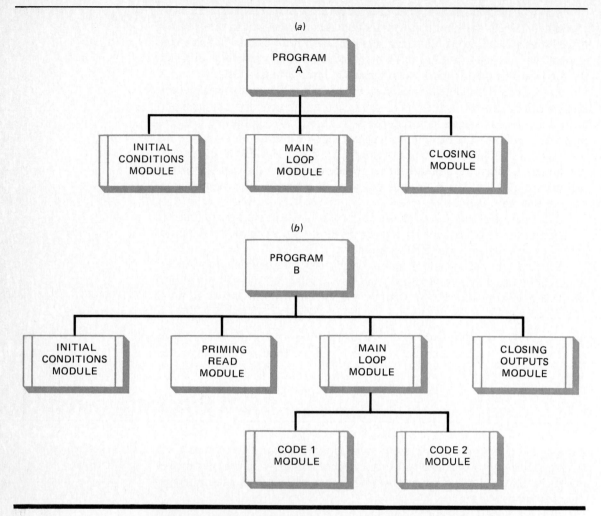

FIGURE 6.7 Two different hierarchical structures are depicted. *(a)* A program solution is divided into three modules of activity. *(b)* The hierarchy of program B shows an initial level of four modules, with the main module further subdivided into two modules.

These modules represent the principle activities composing a program. The first module defines the initial conditions performed in preparation for processing. These activities may include the initialization of accumulators, the output of headings, or the definition of the edited output formats.

The main-loop module defines activities related to the processing effort performed within the main loop. This loop would most likely use an automated looping sequence (for example, FOR/NEXT). All I/O activities, equations, and decisions used in this main loop are defined.

The closing module contains statements which conclude all phases of processing. These activities may include the output of accumulated totals, closing labels, summary data, or any processing activities required to close the program.

In defining each module, we establish its existence and its relationship to the other modules. Each module is depicted in a smaller flow diagram, each activity composing the module defined by its own symbol. When the program is eventually written, each symbol is converted to its equivalent program statement and grouped within its own module.

A slightly different modular structure is described in Figure 6.7(b). This hierarchical structure has added an additional level, as another set of modules is indicated. The first level consists of four modules which represent:

1 An initial-conditions module

2 A priming-read module

3 A main module in which the bulk of processing is accomplished

4 A closing module to conclude processing

The second level of modules is a subdivision of the main module. The two modules define processing for two codes which distinguish between two processing modes. The hierarchy diagram dictates that access to the two code modules is only possible from the main-loop module. Thus, when writing the program, the programmer must be aware that access to those modules is controlled from the main loop.

The vehicle for constructing program modules of Figure 6.7 is the GOSUB statement. GOSUB statements provide access to modules as processing requires. To illustrate the use of GOSUBs, let us examine a flowchart and BASIC program which uses a modular logic.

Applying the GOSUB Module

PROBLEM 6.2   Break-Even Analysis

The problem entails the computation of a break-even point between costs and sales revenue. One equation is used to predict product costs, while a second formula estimates revenue produced by sales of that product. The point at which both lines intersect defines the break-even point — the point at which revenues equal costs.

From estimates already developed, we know that the break-even point lies somewhere between 4900 and 5100 units. The revenue and costs formulas are, respectively, $R = 1.12 * X$ and $C = (.67 * X) + 2250$. R represents the revenue amount, C the cost of production, and X the number of units upon which that cost or revenue amount was based. Figure 6.8 illustrates the relationship of those equations.

Use a FOR/NEXT to control looping; the loop variable of X ranges from 4900 to 5100, with an increment of 10. On each loop, print the units used, their cost, and

FIGURE 6.8 The intersection of the cost and revenue lines defines the break-even point of the two lines. It is the point at which costs equal revenues.

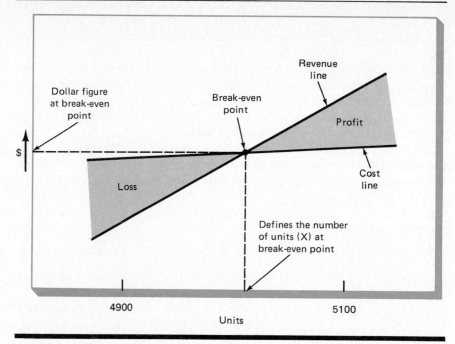

the revenue for that level of sales. When costs equal revenue, cease looping and print the label BREAK-EVEN POINT ATTAINED. The column headings UNITS, PROD $, and REVENUE are needed, with literals commencing at print positions 5, 13, and 21, respectively. The units amount is edited as #####, with all dollar amounts edited as ###.##. These edited formats start at the same print positions as the column headings.

These are the main points in the problem narrative.

1   Two formulas are used. One is used to compute production costs, whereas the other computes revenues possible at that same level of production.

2   The headings UNITS, PROD $, and REVENUE are used, with literals commencing at print positions 5, 13, and 21, respectively.

3   Edited outputs use a ##### format for units and a ###.## format for dollar amounts.

4   A priming-read technique is not required, as the values used are generated by the FOR/NEXT.

5   The required looping sequence is generated by a FOR/NEXT, using a STEP option with an increment of 10. When R = C, the lines intersect and the break-even point is reached.

6   Output the units, costs, and revenue figures in each loop.

7   When R = C and the loop is exited, print out the label BREAK-EVEN POINT ATTAINED.

8   Use GOSUB statements to create a modular structure.

The hierarchical structure in Problem 6.2 is shown in Figure 6.9. Figure 6.9(a) shows the three main modules which compose this solution and define the modular components of the main program. In Figure 6.9(b), the flow-charts defining the processing performed in those modules are detailed.

The main program indicates access to the three modules via GOSUB modules. Each module is annotated with a descriptive comment to identify its function. Symbols within each module define the specific processing steps undertaken and the logical positioning of each task. The program derived from this flow diagram is described in Figure 6.10.

The program is divided into the modules, as represented within the flow diagrams accompanying the solution. The main program is defined by the statements 10 to 60, with the three modules defined at lines 100, 200, and 300, respectively. The modular structure makes possible the grouping of related statements into a single entity and makes debugging easier.

The important factor in this solution is the conversion of the modular structure to a program format. Every module was set off by itself; access to each module is controlled via GOSUB statements. The main looping sequence was defined in the GOSUB 200 module. The FOR/NEXT loop was not affected by its placement in that module. When the third module is completed, the program ends at line 60 via a STOP statement.

The STOP statement is used instead of a GO TO to deny access to the modules commencing at line 100. The GOSUB 100 module defines the column headings and edited formats applied to the break-even report prepared by this program.

The second main-loop module, lines 200 to 270, performs the break-even analysis within a FOR/NEXT loop. The FOR statement, line 210, defines the range of X values from 4900 to 5100, with a STEP of 10. After C and R are computed, both values are printed via line 240. The test for the equality of C and R, the break-even point, occurs at line 250. If C = R, the break-even point is found and the program should branch out of the FOR/NEXT loop to line 270. This IF/THEN statement illustrates that it is possible to branch out of a FOR/NEXT controlled loop before reaching its closing value.

The RETURN statement, line 270, causes the processing flow to return to the main program and commence execution of the GOSUB 300 module. A label advising of the attainment of the break-even point is printed beneath those values. The output tells us that the break-even point is achieved at 5000 units.

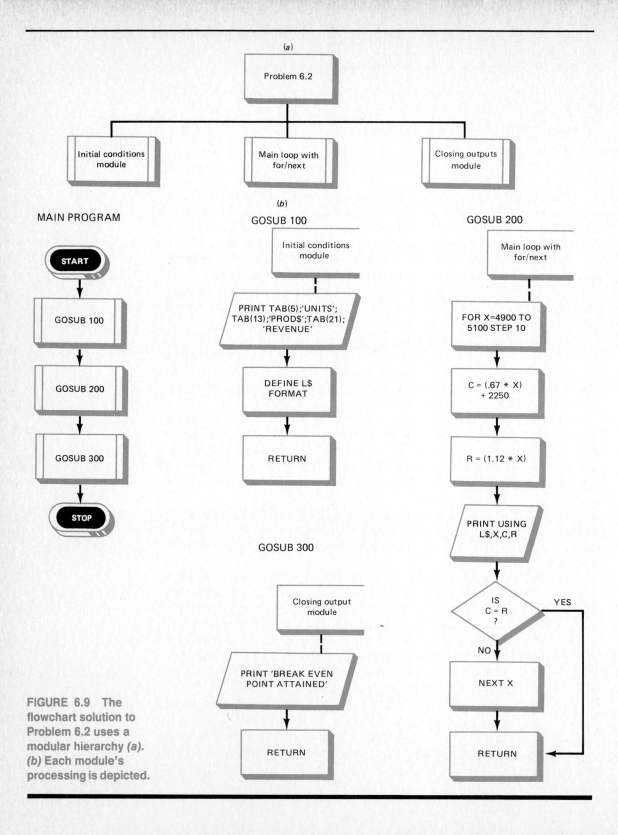

FIGURE 6.9 The flowchart solution to Problem 6.2 uses a modular hierarchy *(a)*. *(b)* Each module's processing is depicted.

(a)

```
              ┌10 REM PROB 6.2
              │20 REM -- MAIN PROGRAM
MAIN          │30 GOSUB 100
PROGRAM       │40 GOSUB 200
              │50 GOSUB 300
              └60 STOP
              ┌100 REM INITIAL CONDITIONS MODULE
MODULE        │110 PRINT TAB(5);'UNITS';TAB(13);'PROD $';TAB(21);'REVENUE'
1             │120 L$ = '    #####   #####.   #####.'
              └130 RETURN
              ┌200 REM -- MAIN LOOP WITH FOR/NEXT
              │210 FOR X = 4900 TO 5100 STEP 10
              │220 C = (.67 * X) + 2250
MODULE        │230 R = (1.12 * X)
2             │240 PRINT USING L$,X,C,R
              │250 IF C = R THEN 270
              │260 NEXT X
              └270 RETURN
              ┌300 REM -- CLOSING OUTPUT MODULE
MODULE        │310 PRINT 'BREAK EVEN POINT ATTAINED'
3             │320 RETURN
              └400 END
```

(b)

```
          UNITS   PROD $  REVENUE
          4900    5533.   5488.
          4910    5540.   5499.
          4920    5546.   5510.
          4930    5553.   5522.
          4940    5560.   5533.
          4950    5567.   5544.
          4960    5573.   5555.
          4970    5580.   5566.
          4980    5587.   5578.
          4990    5593.   5589.
          5000    5600.   5600.
      BREAK EVEN POINT ATTAINED
      Stop at line 60
```

FIGURE 6.10   (a) The program and (b) the output for Problem 6.2. Note the three modules which compose this solution.

PROBLEM 6.3   Utility Billings

The problem entails the computation of utility bills. Three rates are used when computing customer bills. A modular structure is required. In the initial-conditions module, three accumulators are initialized. An accumulator is used to total the billings in each of the three categories. A four-literals ACCT, RATE, KW USED, and AMT, are printed in positions 5, 14, 20, and 29, respectively. A TAB function is used for alignment. An edited format of ###### is applied to account number, ### to the rate code, ####.# to kilowatts used, and ####.## to the amount billed.

A priming read with 9s decision is used with the main loop. Three decisions open processing and provide access to the three modules in which processing is performed. Within each loop, the amount billed is computed, that amount added to the accumulator for that code rate, and the account number, rate code, kilowatts used, and billed amount are outputted. Access to each rate module occurs from the main loop. The formulas for each rate group follow:

1   For the 180 rate code, $B = 36.50 + .0056 * K$

2   For the 280 rate code, $B = 39.25 + .0048 * K$

3   For the 480 rate code, $B = 40.75 + .0042 * K$

B is the billed amount, and K the kilowatts used.

The closing module provides a summary of processing. Each accumulated total is outputted with its own literal (for example, TOT 180 ACCTS =). All three accumulators are added to compute the grand total of accounts billed, which is output with the label TOTAL BILLINGS =.

The data utilized in this problem are as follows:

Acct No	Code	KW Used	Acct No	Code	KW Used
010638	180	1316.4	010773	280	2605.7
010907	480	4166.2	011038	280	1917.4
012655	180	2937.8	012984	480	5603.5
014483	280	1006.7	015056	480	3962.9

These are the main points in the problem narrative.

1   A modular structure is used, with GOSUB modules creating the required program modules. The main module is divided into three submodules, each module handling a specific rate code.

2   The first module initializes the three accumulators used for each rate code. This module directs output of the heading and defines the edited format used when outputting each account's billing information.

3   A priming read is used to input data. The first half of the priming read follows the initial-conditions module, with the second read placed within the main loop. Input includes the account number, rate code, and the kilowatts used by that customer.

4   The main module contains three decisions, which lead to three submodules. The rate codes of 180, 280, and 480 are used. The amount billed is computed by its specific formula, with that amount added to its respective accumulator. The output of the account number, code, kilowatts used, and amount billed is accomplished in each module. The rate formulas are:

    a   For the 180 rate, $B = 36.50 + .0056 * K$
    b   For the 280 rate, $B = 39.25 + .0048 * K$
    c   For the 480 rate, $B = 40.75 + .0042 * K$

5   The input of an Acct No $= -9999$ triggers the close of the main loop. The closing module is accessed to print summary data. Each accumulated total is

printed with its own label. The sum of the three totals is computed and output with the label TOTAL BILLINGS =.

The hierarchical and flow diagrams prepared for Problem 6.3 are displayed in Figure 6.11. The hierarchical chart shown in Figure 6.11(a) reveals a main level of four tasks and a subdivision of the main module into three modules. Each module's components are defined on the flowcharts of Figure 6.11(b).

The main program diagram defines the three major modules of the solution and the first half of the priming read. The GOSUB 100 module identifies the initial-conditions module. Three accumulators—T1, T2, and T3—are initialized for the three rate codes. The output of column headings via a TAB function precedes definition of the L$ edited format.

The main module, GOSUB 200, reflects the main processing loop. A main loop is defined and continues until the A = −9999 data is sensed. Three decisions control access to the three rate modules. The GOSUB 400, 500, and 600 modules handle the 180, 280, and 480 rates, respectively. The second half of the priming read and 9s decision close the main module.

Within each rate module, the assigned formula computes the amount billed to each account. This amount is posted against the proper accumulator, which precedes the output of that accounts data. The accumulators T1, T2, and T3 are applied to the 180, 280, and 480 rates, respectively.

FIGURE 6.11 *(a)* The hierarchical structure and *(b)* flow diagrams prepared for Problem 6.3. In this solution, the main looping module is broken into three submodules.

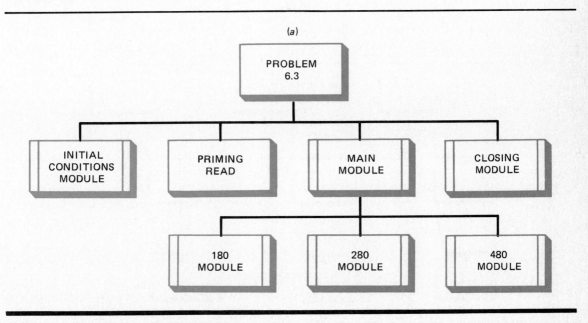

(a)

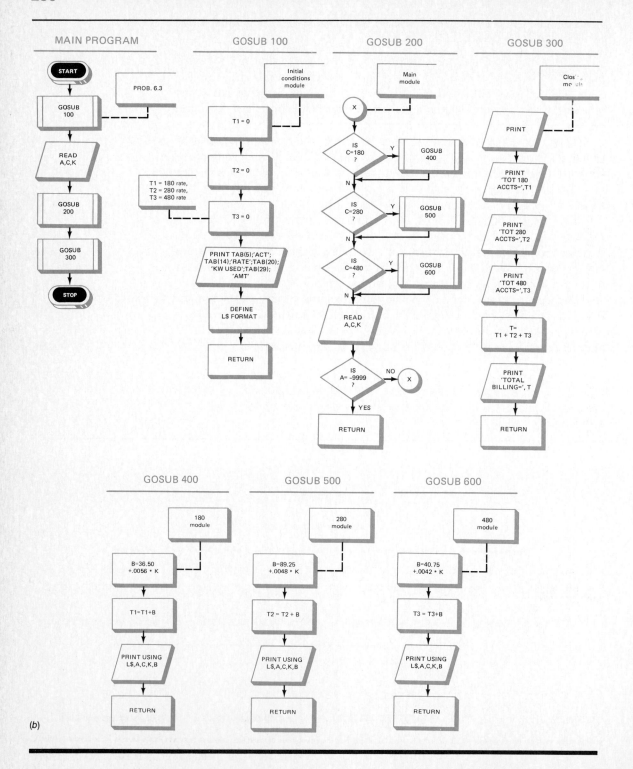

(b)

The closing module possesses four output tasks. Each accumulated total is outputted with its own label. The three accumulators are added to create the grand total of all accounts billed, which is then output. Figure 6.12 details the program written for these diagrams.

(a)

```
10 REM PROB 6.3
20 GOSUB 100
30 READ A,C,K
40 GOSUB 200
50 GOSUB 300
60 GO TO 800
100 REM -- INITIAL CONDITIONS MODULE
110 T1 = 0
120 T2 = 0
130 T3 = 0
140 REM -- T1=180 RATE, T2=280 RATE, T3=480 RATE
150 PRINT TAB(5);'ACCT';TAB(14);'RATE';TAB(20);'KW USED';TAB(29);'AMT'
160 L$ = '   ######   ###   ####.#   ####.##'
170 RETURN
200 REM -- MAIN MODULE
210 IF C = 180 THEN GOSUB 400
220 IF C = 280 THEN GOSUB 500
230 IF C = 480 THEN GOSUB 600
240 READ A,C,K
250 IF A = -99.99 THEN 260 ELSE 210
260 RETURN
300 REM -- CLOSING MODULE
310 PRINT
320 PRINT 'TOT 180 ACCTS =',T1
330 PRINT 'TOT 280 ACCTS =',T2
340 PRINT 'TOT 480 ACCTS =',T3
350 T = T1+T2+T3
360 PRINT 'TOTAL BILLING =',T
370 RETURN
400 REM -- 180 MODULE
410 B = 36.50 + (.0056 * K)
420 T1 = T1 + B
430 PRINT USING L$,A,C,K,B
440 RETURN
500 REM -- 280 MODULE
510 B = 39.25 + (.0048 * K)
520 T2 = T2 + B
530 PRINT USING L$,A,C,K,B
540 RETURN
600 REM -- 480 MODULE
610 B = 40.75 + (.0042 * K)
620 T3 = T3 + B
630 PRINT USING L$,A,C,K,B
640 RETURN
700 DATA 010638,180,1316.4,010773,280,2605.7
710 DATA 010907,480,4166.2,011038,280,1917.4
720 DATA 012655,180,2937.8,012984,480,5603.5
730 DATA 014483,280,1006.7,015056,480,3962.9
740 DATA -99.99,0,0
800 END
```

FIGURE 6.12 *(a)* The program and *(b)* the output of Problem 6.3. Program modules were constructed using GOSUB statements.

(b)

ACCT	RATE	KW USED	AMT
10638	180	1316.4	43.87
10773	280	2605.7	51.76
10907	480	4166.2	58.25
11038	280	1917.4	48.45
12655	180	2937.8	52.95
12984	480	5603.5	64.28
14483	280	1006.7	44.08
15056	480	3962.9	57.39

```
TOT 180 ACCTS =          96.8235
TOT 280 ACCTS =          144.293
TOT 480 ACCTS =          179.927
TOTAL BILLING =          421.043
```

The main program is defined via lines 10 through 60. Three GOSUBs are utilized to access the initial-conditions module (GOSUB 100), the main module (GOSUB 200), and the closing module (GOSUB 300). Line 20 defines a READ statement, which represents the opening half of the priming read.

The GOSUB 100 module consists of the statements 100 to 170; of interest are lines 150 and 160. The PRINT statement positions the required headings via a TAB function. Line 160 defines the edited format used with the PRINT USING statements of each rate module.

The main module, GOSUB 200, utilizes statements 200 to 260. Three IF/THEN statements, line 210, 220, and 230, provide access to the rate modules. A priming read and 9s decision, lines 240 and 250, close the main loop and precede that module's RETURN statement.

The 180 rate module begins at line 400. After inputting K and computing the billing amount (line 410), the B amount is added to T1 (line 420). The PRINT-USING statement, line 430, outputs that account's billing data. The other two modules are similarly constructed. The 280 rate module consists of lines 500 to 540, with lines 600 to 640 noting the 480 rate GOSUB module. The T2 and T3 accumulators are used to total the billing amount associated with the 280 and 480 rates.

The closing module, lines 300 to 370, handles the output of data summarizing each rate grouping. The three accumulators are outputted separately via lines 320, 330, and 340. The grand total is computed at line 350; its output at line 360 ends processing.

Some readers may question the use of the GO TO statement, line 60. This statement causes the program to branch to line 800, the END statement, and close the program. Because we used the GO TO statement, we did not use a STOP statement and suppressed the printing of an advisory note in our output. It offers another alternative to the programmer.

The outputs for Program 6.3 are shown in Figure 6.12. They reflect the data defined by lines 700 to 740 of the program. Note that the 9s data is appended to the required eight sets of data, at line 740.

Some additional effort is required for users to master concepts related to structured designs. Though these structured solutions may appear confusing when applied to smaller problems, they provide a valuable means of defining program solutions to larger, more complex problems.

Future program solutions will alternate between conventional and structured formats. We will use the format that best explains the solution, so as not to detract from its major points. Our emphasis is on explaining the solution's logic and how each BASIC instruction contributes to a successful program. It is important that future programmers understand both analytic approaches, possess the capacity to handle either a conventional or a structured technique, and be capable of properly expressing the logic used in any solution.

Chapter Summary

6.1 The Structured-Design Approach

Three key elements of top-down designs are

1 The subdivision of a solution into modular components.

2 Minimal use of GO TO statements

3 Use of a hierarchical structure where a solution is analyzed from the top elements down

Proper application of these principles will avoid the preparation of fragmented, illogically prepared, and incomplete solutions. The top-down approach is designed to avoid bottom-up solutions.

The application of top-down designs to software development is called structured programming. The advantages associated with structured principles are

1 Sound solutions with readily followed logic

2 Reduced amounts of time for testing and debugging

3 Higher productivity by programming personnel

The impact of structured programming is most readily seen in complex solutions. Large problems need a clear definition of operational relationships.

Three control structures have been developed for structured programming solutions.

1 Processing sequence

2 IF/THEN/ELSE sequence

3 Looping sequence

The processing sequence identifies two or more consecutive processing activities. The IF/THEN/ELSE sequence is a conditional statement where alternative operations are placed within either branch of the decision. The looping sequence permits the creation and control of a loop where data is repeatedly processed.

6.2 The Priming Read

A programming technique which evolved from structured solutions is the priming read. It utilizes two read instructions—one prior to the loop's start and a second within the loop at its close. The initial read is executed once and inputs the first set of values to undergo processing. The second read is in the loop and is repeatedly executed to input data for each loop's processing.

The positioning of the second read is designed to assist in controlling the looping sequence. If valid data is read, the loop continues. If the last, or 9s, data record is read, the logical flow continues through the closing decision and the loop is exited. The priming read may be used with a 9s decision to control looping.

The priming read affects only the input of data and does not change other programming techniques. Structured concepts are designed not to alter the instructional formats but to encourage the preparation of logical, well-conceived programs.

6.3 A Program Hierarchy

The creation of program modules is a major aspect of structured solutions. Each module's activities are clearly defined, and the module is logically positioned within the overall solution. The GOSUB statement provides the means of constructing these modules in BASIC.

Using GOSUB modules, it is possible to create a main program from which all processing is controlled. The program is constructed using a hierarchical structure similar to an organization chart. This structure enables the programmer to establish modules of only initial conditions, main processing loops, or closing output statements.

Any program module may be subdivided into smaller module components. Each lower-level module directs processing related to the higher module's activities. Hierarchical structures establish relationships between modules at any level of a solution.

Key BASIC Statements

	Examples	
IF/THEN/ELSE Statement	60	IF C = 1 THEN GOSUB 200 ELSE GOSUB 400
	100	IF H = −99.99 THEN 400 ELSE 30
Priming read sequence with 9s decision	40	READ A,B,C
	50	G = A + B + C
	.	
	.	
	.	
	80	READ A,B,C
	90	IF A = −99.99 THEN 600 ELSE 50

Glossary

Break-even point A business term describing the point at which costs and revenues are equal and the lines representing these estimates intersect.

IF/THEN/ELSE sequence One of the three control block sequences associated with structured designs, making choice between two alternatives possible via one decision.

Looping sequence A control block sequence which defines a loop in which a group of tasks are repeatedly performed.

Priming read An input technique consisting of two read instructions—one prior to the loop's start and one at its close; simplifies exit from a loop within a structured solution.

Processing sequence A control block sequence using structured-design solutions to define a series of two or more processing activities.

Structured design The application of top-down concepts to create program solutions which are modular and logically correct, minimize the use of GO TOs, and utilize a hierarchical structure.

Top-down design A term interchangeable with structured design.

Exercises

1 The problem entails the computation of sales tax on retail purchases. Use a priming read within a looping sequence controlled via a 9s decision. Input is the sales price. The program computes the sales tax using the formula

Sales tax = (sales price) ∗ .0425

The sales tax is added to the sales price to produce the final sales price. Each sales tax amount is accumulated, outputting that sum when processing ends. Output on each program loop, the original sales amount, the computed sales tax, and the final sales price. The headings SALES PRICE, SALES TAX, and FINAL PRICE are used, with

positions 1, 12, and 24. Output the accumulated sales tax total using the label TOT
SALES TAX =. All dollar amounts outputted use the edited format of ####.##. The
data is as follows:

Sales No	1	2	3	4	5	6
Sales Price	1.89	26.78	79.85	209.63	760.04	1489.36

Write a flowchart and BASIC program for the problem narrative.

2   The problem entails computing the break-even point of two cost estimates. A
manufacturing concern uses two lines to estimate production costs. Line A is estimated by the formula $C1 = 525 + (.38 * U)$, and line B is estimated by the formula
$C2 = 625 + (.33 * U)$. The variables C1, C2, and U represent the two production costs
and units involved. It is estimated that the break-even point lies between 1500 and
2500 units. Using a FOR/NEXT to establish a looping sequence, test to determine
where the break-even point lies. Use an increment of 50 units on each loop. When the
break-even point is reached, exit the loop and print the label, BREAK-EVEN POINT
FOUND. On each loop, print the units used and their estimated cost. The headings
UNITS, COST A, and COST B, at print positions 1, 7, and 15 respectively, are needed.
Edit each cost with the format ####.## and units as ####.
Write a flowchart and BASIC program for the problem narrative.

3   The problem involves the accumulation of taxes until a limit of $1000 is exceeded.
A priming read is incorporated with an initial-conditions module, main-loop module,
and closing-output module. Use GOSUBs to create those modules. The initial module
initializes the accumulator at zero and outputs the heading ACCT, INCOME, and
EST EXPENSE. The main loop computes estimated tax expense using the formula
Estimated tax expense = 100 + (.16 * income). The tax expense is accumulated before outputting the account number, income amount, and estimated tax. The second
half of the priming read follows, inputting the account number used and an income
amount. This looping sequence should be exited when the accumulated total of tax
expense exceeds $1000. The closing module prints the total of tax expense, using the
label EST EXP TOT =. The data items are as follows:

Acct No	Income	Acct No	Income
10635	879	30075	3474
42738	1497	93137	2106
24663	2983	55024	4678

1   Write a flowchart and BASIC program for the problem narrative.

Lab Exercises

The problem entails computing the royalties owed to commission accounts. Input
includes the account number, book title, copies sold, and retail price of a text. The
commission computation involves three steps. First, the discount book price is com-

puted by multiplying the retail price by .75. Second, the commission amount per book is computed by multiplying the discount price by 10 percent. Last, the commission is calculated by multiplying the commission amount per book by the number of copies sold. For each book, output the account number, book title, copies sold, the commission amount per book, and the total commission amount due. Use the headings ACCT NO, TITLE, COPIES SOLD, COMM AMT, and COMM AMT DUE. The data is as follows:

Acct No	Book Title	Copies Sold	Retail Price
40467	Home Repair	479	9.25
13389	Kids Today	2006	14.95
06755	World History	1086	20.58
63971	Midwifery	168	39.95
21743	Mom and Pop	4502	6.95
33802	Bonds and Stocks	7663	12.56

Write a flowchart and BASIC problem for this problem narrative. Use a priming read and a 9s decision to control the loop. Accumulate the total of all commission amounts due and output this sum with the label TOTAL ROYALTIES DUE =.

2   The problem entails plotting the path of a curve between two points. The curve in question is:

$$Y = 8X - X^2$$

Find the X and Y values between $X = -1$ and $X = 9$, at intervals of .5. Print both values on each loop beneath the headings X VALUE and Y VALUE.

Write the flowchart and program to satisfy the student's problem. Use a FOR/NEXT statement to control the loop, with a STEP of .5. No inputs are required, as the loop variable will serve to define the values of X. Create opening output and main-loop modules, using GOSUBs, to construct your program.

3   The problem entails describing the trajectory of a cannon shell. A cannon is fired from the top of a hill, with the arc of the shell following a trajectory defined by the curve

$$H = 200 + 70T - 9T^2$$

T represents the time in seconds, and H the height. Compute the height of the shell as it flies through the air from a time of 0 until it strikes the ground. Print the H and T values employed in each loop under the headings TIME and HEIGHT.

   a   Prepare a flowchart and program for this narrative. Use a FOR/NEXT to control the loop, testing for the shell's impact on the ground.
   b   From the data output, answer the following questions:
      (1)   What was the shell's highest altitude?
      (2)   How many seconds elapsed after firing before the shell struck the ground?

4 The problem entails a break-even analysis and profit estimation. A retail sales organization uses two formulas to estimate their sales revenues and product costs:

Revenue = .49 * units
Costs = 675 + (.24 * units)

The estimate of revenues and costs are based upon the units sold and manufactured. When estimates are made, the program must print the units used, the costs incurred, the revenue produced, and the potential profit or loss. Profit (or loss) is computed by subtracting the costs from the revenues. The headings UNITS, COSTS, REVENUE, and PROFIT/LOSS are placed at the top of the report, with the editing of #### applied to units and ####.## applied to dollar amounts. No inputs are used.

a Write the flow diagram and program to determine the break-even point. Use a FOR/NEXT statement to create the looping sequence, with the number of units (U) ranging from 2000 to 3000 in increments of 50. When the break-even point is reached, close the loop and print the label B/E POINT ATTAINED.

b Write a flowchart and program to determine the point at which a profit of $500 is attained. Use a FOR/NEXT statement for the loop, starting at a value of U = 2000, in increments of 100. When the $500 profit is attained or exceeded, exit the loop and end the program.

5 The problem entails the computation and highlighting of bowling scores. Input to the problem are a bowler's name and the score of three games bowled. These scores are averaged by adding the three scores and dividing that sum by three. Each individual average is accumulated to eventually produce the average of all bowling scores processed. On each loop, each bowler's name and average are outputted. The average should be edited as ###.##. The headings BOWLER NAME and AVERAGE are printed at the top of the report.

The league also wants to highlight bowlers that have average scores of 200 or more. Outputs should contain their name, average and a literal 200 PLUS. The 200 plus averages and the number of people in that category are accumulated separately. The 200 plus bowlers should be handled in their own module.

After the last bowler's data is processed the main loop is closed and processing of the averages commences. The average of all bowling scores is computed by dividing the accumulated total of all averages by the number of bowlers processed. The average of plus 200 bowlers is computed by dividing their accumulated total by the number of plus 200 bowlers. Output both averages on separate lines, using the labels LEAGUE AVG = and AVG FOR PLUS 200 BOWLERS =. Also, print the number of plus 200 bowlers found, preceded by the label NO OF PLUS 200 BOWLERS =. The data for this problem is as follows:

Bowler	Game 1	Game 2	Game 3
Kucharski	167	206	210
Romanski	246	278	263
Polanski	187	243	174
Wotecha	217	206	168
Pakus	154	186	225
Kilakowski	278	290	266
Jastrow	194	216	190
Anastaskis	278	280	292

Write a flowchart and program for this problem. Use a priming read to input data. Use GOSUB statements to construct an initial-conditions module, a main-loop module, and a closing-outputs module. Processing related to plus 200 bowlers should be handled in a separate module. Follow the narrative carefully when detailing the logic of your solution.

6 The problem entails the computation of a payroll. Three modules are used to process regular, overtime, and part-time payroll amounts. A priming read is used to input each employee's number, name, hours worked, and pay rate. The headings EMP NO, EMPLOYEE NAME, REG PAY, OT PAY, GROSS PAY, FICA, and NET PAY are required, with each literal respectively commencing at the print positions 1, 8, 22, 30, 38, 46, and 54. The employee number is edited as #####, with all dollar amounts edited as ####.##.

Each payroll type is processed within its own module. The normal work week consists of 35 hours. If more than 35 hours are worked, the overtime pay module is accessed. If exactly 35 hours are worked, the regular pay module is used. Employees working less than 35 hours are treated in the part-time module.

Overtime pay amount is computed at twice the pay rate for the number of hours worked in excess of 35 hours. This amount is added to the regular pay to produce gross pay. The FICA deduction is computed at 9.2 percent of gross pay. Net pay equals the gross amount minus the FICA deduction. Print the number, name, overtime pay, regular pay, gross pay, FICA deduction and net pay amounts of each overtime worker.

Regular pay is 35 hours times the hourly pay rate and equals the gross pay for that employee. The FICA deduction is computed at 6.2 percent of gross pay. Net pay equals the gross amount minus the FICA deduction. Output each employee's number, name, regular pay, gross pay, FICA deduction, and net pay in their respective columns.

Part-time pay is the number hours worked times the hourly rate. The FICA deduction is 5.6 percent of the gross amount and subtracted from it to produce net pay. Output the part-time employee's number, name, gross pay, FICA deduction, and net pay amounts in their respective columns.

While processing all employees, accumulate the totals of all overtime paid, the accumulated total of all gross pay paid, the total of all FICA deducted, and the total net pay paid. These four accumulated totals should be outputted using appropriate labels and handled in a separate closing module.

The data for this problem is as follows:

Number	Name	Hours	Rate	Number	Name	Hours	Rate
00162	Alberto	35	6.20	01632	Bacchus	25	3.90
04625	Cicero	42	8.63	05163	Dante	37	10.62
09308	Euripides	40	9.23	10065	Ficus	28	14.68
20657	Grimaldi	40	12.27	22028	Hannibal	30	8.67
25998	Izvestia	60	3.10	28090	Jupiter	35	25.49

Write the flowchart and program to satisfy this narrative. Use GOSUBs to create your modules. Employ a looping sequence using a priming read. Ensure that each output line is executed within its module, as they vary with the type of payment.

The problem entails the monthly estimation and accumulation of manufacturing costs. The formula $C = 180 + (16 * U) - (.24 * U^2)$ is used to estimate the monthly costs (C) based on the units (U) produced. Input on each loop representing each month is the number of units to be manufactured. A priming read is needed to input these items within a loop sequence. The cost computed for each month is accumulated after its computation, as the company wants to determine when the $2000 limit is exceeded. On each loop, output the units used and their resultant costs beneath the headings UNITS and MFG COSTS. When looping ends, output the accumulated total which exceeded the $2000 limit with the label TOT COSTS =. The data for the problem follows.

Quiz Problem

Month	1	2	3	4	5	6	7
Units	40	28	12	18	31	26	11

The solution to the quiz problem is shown in Figure 6.13. The solution uses an accumulator and priming read with 9s decision.

Quiz Solution

Appendix: FOR/UNTIL and FOR/WHILE Statements

The priming-read technique and 9s decision were integrated to provide a means of controlling loops. The same level of success was not achieved when an attempt was made to combine the use of the priming read and the FOR/NEXT statement. The difficulty arises in trying to coordinate the double reading operations of the priming read and the automated loop of the FOR/NEXT. There is always one more read than the number of FOR/NEXT loops, or the program is short one item of data. The conventional loop structure, where a single READ statement is at the loop's top, is better suited for use with the FOR/NEXT.

To accommodate use of the priming read and structured concepts, an automated loop technique was developed to complement those ideas. The results were two other versions of the FOR instruction which created a loop and incorporated a conditional statement to control execution of those loops: (1) the FOR/UNTIL statement and (2) the FOR/WHILE statement.

Not all versions of BASIC support the FOR/UNTIL and FOR/WHILE statements. Readers are advised to check their technical manual to see whether their computer supports these instructions. If they are not available, programmers may still use the priming read technique, since it is not dependent upon them. Concepts presented here should be applicable to similar FOR/UNTIL-like statements in other current languages.

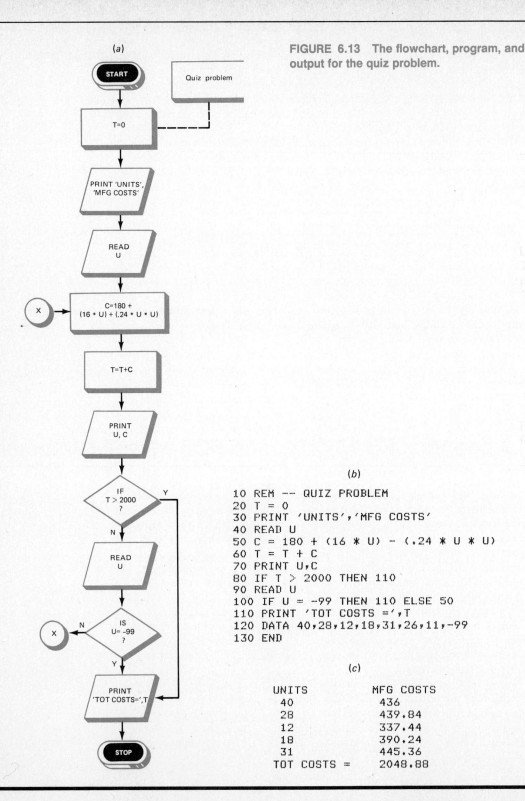

Quiz problem

START

T=0

PRINT 'UNITS',
'MFG COSTS'

READ
U

X

C=180 +
(16 * U) + (.24 * U * U)

T=T+C

PRINT
U, C

IF
T > 2000
?   Y

N

READ
U

IS
U= -99
?   N   X

Y

PRINT
'TOT COSTS=',T

STOP

FIGURE 6.13 The flowchart, program, and output for the quiz problem.

(b)

```
10 REM -- QUIZ PROBLEM
20 T = 0
30 PRINT 'UNITS','MFG COSTS'
40 READ U
50 C = 180 + (16 * U) - (.24 * U * U)
60 T = T + C
70 PRINT U,C
80 IF T > 2000 THEN 110
90 READ U
100 IF U = -99 THEN 110 ELSE 50
110 PRINT 'TOT COSTS =',T
120 DATA 40,28,12,18,31,26,11,-99
130 END
```

(c)

UNITS	MFG COSTS
40	436
28	439.84
12	337.44
18	390.24
31	445.36
TOT COSTS =	2048.88

The FOR/UNTIL Statement

The **FOR/UNTIL statement** is an automated looping statement, with a conditional statement built into its format. Essentially, it dictates that the looping continues *until* a specific condition is met. For this reason, the FOR/UNTIL is often referred to as a posttest loop statement, verifying the test value at the loop's end. The FOR portion of the statement creates the loop, whereas the UNTIL establishes the condition which, when encountered, will close the looping sequence. For example:

```
40       FOR I = 1 UNTIL H = −99.99
  .
  .        }  Statements in loop.
  .
100      NEXT I
```

The FOR/UNTIL statement on line 40 defines the start of the loop, with the NEXT statement closing it. The concurrent use of the FOR/UNTIL and NEXT statements frames the looping sequence undertaken. In this manner, the FOR/UNTIL statement parallels its FOR/NEXT counterpart.

The command FOR precedes the loop variable I. An equal sign is required and placed prior to the loop's opening value. Unlike the FOR/NEXT instruction, no closing value is specified.

The UNTIL command follows the opening value (here, I = 1) and defines the conditional statement which controls looping. The H = −99.99 represents the conditional statement appended to our FOR/UNTIL statement. Virtually any condition may be used with the FOR/UNTIL syntax, but we have chosen to illustrate a 9s decision.

The NEXT instruction is positioned at the end of the desired loop, line 100. The variable used with the NEXT command must match the variable name of the opening FOR/UNTIL statement. When the last loop occurs, the program passes through the NEXT statement onto the statement following it.

In Figure 6.A.1, we reworked our gross pay problem to illustrate the ease with which the FOR/UNTIL instruction is integrated into a program. We use an accumulator to total the gross pay amounts. Headings highlight the employee's name and gross pay columns. The priming-read technique inputs the required data, coordinating its use with the FOR/UNTIL.

The flowchart opens with the initialization of T and the output of column headings. The first half of the priming read is properly positioned prior to the FOR/UNTIL. These three activities act as initial conditions.

The looping sequence begins and ends with FOR/UNTIL and NEXT instructions. The FOR/UNTIL establishes a loop with I at 1, which continues until H = −99.99. This symbol identifies the true nature of the FOR/UNTIL, where the conditional statement is part of the FOR statement.

After the computation of G, the update of T, and the output of employee data, the second part of the priming read is placed. This placement is critical to the coordinated use of the priming read and FOR/UNTIL. It is the input of the 9s data (H = −99.99) at the second READ symbol which triggers the UNTIL portion of the FOR/UNTIL. As the NEXT command follows the READ symbol, the looping sequence is closed. By positioning the second half of the priming read before the NEXT instruction, the loop is quickly closed without processing any extra data. As long as the last, or 9s, data record is not sensed, the loop continues.

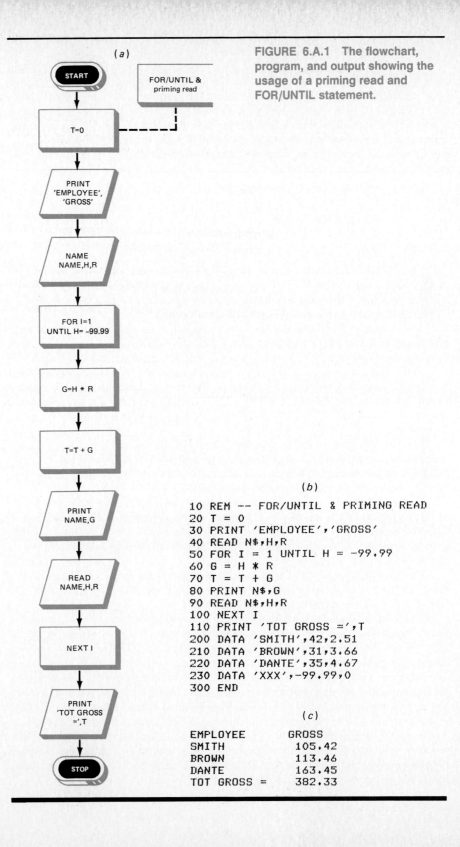

FIGURE 6.A.1 The flowchart, program, and output showing the usage of a priming read and FOR/UNTIL statement.

(a)

START

FOR/UNTIL & priming read

T=0

PRINT 'EMPLOYEE', 'GROSS'

NAME NAME,H,R

FOR I=1 UNTIL H= -99.99

G=H * R

T=T + G

PRINT NAME,G

READ NAME,H,R

NEXT I

PRINT 'TOT GROSS =',T

STOP

(b)

```
10 REM --- FOR/UNTIL & PRIMING READ
20 T = 0
30 PRINT 'EMPLOYEE','GROSS'
40 READ N$,H,R
50 FOR I = 1 UNTIL H = -99.99
60 G = H * R
70 T = T + G
80 PRINT N$,G
90 READ N$,H,R
100 NEXT I
110 PRINT 'TOT GROSS =',T
200 DATA 'SMITH',42,2.51
210 DATA 'BROWN',31,3.66
220 DATA 'DANTE',35,4.67
230 DATA 'XXX',-99.99,0
300 END
```

(c)

EMPLOYEE	GROSS
SMITH	105.42
BROWN	113.46
DANTE	163.45
TOT GROSS =	382.33

The exit from the loop causes the processing to pass on to the PRINT symbol following the NEXT command. The accumulated gross total is output with its label of TOT GROSS =. The flowchart ends at the STOP symbol.

The BASIC program prepared from this flowchart also is depicted in Figure 6.A.1. The logic expressed provides the basis of the program. A REM statement mentions the combined use of the FOR/UNTIL and priming read. At line 20, the T accumulator is initialized at zero. Line 30 reflects the placement of the literals EMPLOYEE and GROSS in print zones 1 and 2. The READ instruction, line 40, establishes the first half of the priming read.

At line 50, the FOR/UNTIL instruction establishes a looping sequence. The required loop variable I is initialized at 1 with the loop continuing until a value of H is read which equals -99.99. Processing returns to line 50 when each subsequent loop is executed. On each loop, I is incremented by 1 and maintained at that value.

The computation of G and update of T occur successively at lines 60 and 70. The output of N$ and G beneath their respective headings is accomplished at line 80. The READ statement, line 90, completes the priming read and becomes the main input vehicle for data within the loop. The NEXT I instruction denotes the loop's close. Remember, the loop variables used with the FOR/UNTIL and NEXT statements must match and, as such, the variable I was specified at line 100.

Some students comment at the absence of an IF/THEN statement, representing the 9s decision, following the priming-read instruction. The reasoning is simple: none is required. The equivalent of the 9s decision was incorporated into the FOR/UNTIL and is represented by the $H = -99.99$ conditional statement. Reexamine line 50 to ensure that this point is not overlooked.

With the exit from the looping sequence, the program proceeds from line 100 to line 110 and the output of the accumulated total of gross, T. The program then passes through the DATA statements, line 200 to 230, to the END statement at line 300. Carefully observe that the 9s DATA statement is not overlooked and is positioned at line 230.

PROBLEM 6.4   Customer Credit Statement

The problem entails preparing a customer credit statement. The statement uses the literals ITEM NO, TRANSACTION, CHARGE, and CREDIT beginning in print positions 1, 9, 24, and 31, respectively. Inputs are the item number of the transaction, the type of transaction, the transaction code (1 or 2), and the amount. A priming read handles the input of data, with a FOR/UNTIL controlling looping.

After the loop is opened, check to determine whether the transaction code is a 1. If it is, branch to a module where the amount is added to an accumulator, as that amount is a charge. Output the item number, the transaction type, and the amount, each output commencing with print positions 1, 9 and 24, respectively. Use a TAB function.

If the code is 2, then branch to the other module. Subtract this amount from the accumulated total. Output the item number, transaction type, and credit amount in print positions 1, 9, and 31. Note that this amount is printed in the credits column, whereas code 1 items are printed in the charge column.

An IF/THEN/ELSE controls access to either module and precedes the second half of the priming read. When the 9s data is sensed the looping sequence ends. If the accumulated total is less than zero, output the total using the label TOT CREDIT =. If the total is the same as or greater than zero, output the total and the label TOT DUE =.

The data used in the problem follows:

Item No	Transaction	Code	Amount
10063	Coats	1	139.65
10125	Return	2	206.72
10213	Candy	1	29.89
10226	Cassettes	1	49.68
10367	Payment	2	24.55
10473	Cabinets	1	67.83
10539	Coveralls	1	26.01

These are the main points in the problem narrative.

1 An accumulator is needed to compute the total of credits and charges. If the transaction code is 1, the amount is added; otherwise, the amount is subtracted from the accumulator.

2 Headings ITEM NO, TRANSACTION, CHARGE, and CREDIT appear in print positions 1, 9, 24, and 31, respectively.

3 Inputs include the item number, transaction type, transaction code, and amount of the transaction. A priming read is used.

4 A FOR/UNTIL instruction with a 9s decision controls looping.

5 Each of the codes' activities is handled in its own module. If the code is 1, add the amount to the accumulator. Output item number, transaction description, and amount using positions 1, 9, and 24. If code is 2, subtract the amount from the accumulator. Print out the same three items starting with positions 1, 9, and 31. This places the amount in the credits column.

6 Once looping ends, print the accumulated total with the proper label.

The flowchart for Problem 6.4 is shown in Figure 6.A.2. The initial conditions are the initialization of the accumulator T and the output of four column headings. The READ symbol for the priming read precedes the FOR/UNTIL looping sequence. As noted, the loop will continue until A equals -99.99.

Within the loop is the check of the transaction code. If $C = 1$, branch to the GOSUB 400 module to handle all charge transactions. All code 2 activities are handled within the GOSUB 500 module. Code 1 amounts are added to the accumulator, whereas code 2 amounts are subtracted from T. The update of T is handled via $T = T + A$, with subtractions accomplished using $T = T - A$. This latter formula is the exact opposite of the preceding one, as it subtracts an amount from a total. After updating the accumulator in either module, output the item number, transaction and amount. A TAB function places the transaction amount in either the charge or credit column.

The exit from either module leads to the latter half of the priming read and the NEXT portion of the FOR/UNTIL. When looping ends, the processing flow leads to two consecutive decisions which test T against 0. If $T < 0$, a credit is indicated, as more money has been paid than charged. The opposite condition is apparent if $T >= 0$, as charges have exceeded credits. The decisions control which literal and total is printed, before closing the flowchart.

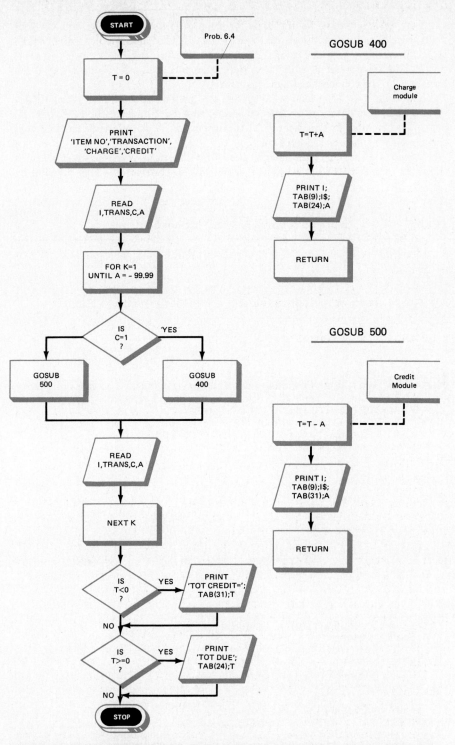

FIGURE 6.A.2 The flowchart prepared for Problem 6.4. Note the use of two program modules.

This flowchart provides the basis for the solution shown in Figure 6.A.3. The main program focuses on the priming read, FOR/UNTIL loop, modules which handle each transaction code and closing outputs. Line 10 opens the program with an advisory REMARK statement, with the initialization of T at line 20. Using a TAB function, line 30, the column headings are printed.

The priming-read technique is applied via lines 40 and 70. The initial READ statement primes data for the loop's opening, which occurs from the FOR/UNTIL instruction at line 50. The second READ instruction is placed inside the loop and executed prior to the next loop's start.

The looping sequence initiated by the FOR/UNTIL instruction continues until the value of A = −99.99 is read. The FOR/UNTIL incorporates a 9s decision by

FIGURE 6.A.3   The program and output for Problem 6.4.

(a)

```
10 REM PROB 6.4
20 T = 0
30 PRINT 'ITEM NO';TAB(9);'TRANSACTION';TAB(24);'CHARGE';TAB(31);'CREDIT'
40 READ I,I$,C,A
50 FOR K = 1 UNTIL A = -99.99
60 IF C = 1 THEN GOSUB 400 ELSE GOSUB 500
70 READ I,I$,C,A
80 NEXT K
90 IF T < 0 THEN PRINT 'TOT CREDIT =';TAB(31);T
100 IF T >= 0 THEN PRINT 'TOT DUE';TAB(24);T
110 GO TO 600
200 DATA 10063,'COATS',1,139.65,10125,'RETURN',2,206.72
210 DATA 10213,'CANDY',1,29.89,10226,'CASSETTES',1,49.68
220 DATA 10367,'PAYMENT',2,24.55,10473,'CABINETS',1,67.83
230 DATA 10539,'COVERALLS',1,26.01,0,'XXX',0,-99.99
400 REM -- CHARGE MODULE
410 T = T + A
420 PRINT I;TAB(9);I$;TAB(24);A
430 RETURN
500 REM -- CREDIT MODULE
510 T = T - A
520 PRINT I;TAB(9);I$;TAB(31);A
530 RETURN
600 END

Ready
```

(b)

ITEM NO	TRANSACTION	CHARGE	CREDIT
10063	COATS	139.65	
10125	RETURN		206.72
10213	CANDY	29.89	
10226	CASSETTES	49.68	
10367	PAYMENT		24.55
10473	CABINETS	67.83	
10539	COVERALLS	26.01	
TOT DUE		81.79	

adding that conditional after the word UNTIL. The loop counter K was initialized at 1 to permit the program to monitor each loop. Though K is not an integral part of this solution, it must be specified. The use of a value of K = 1 was deliberate, as it parallels the concept of a counter and enables the user to monitor each loop's execution.

Only two statements comprise the FOR/UNTIL loop. Line 70 is the latter half of the priming read, and line 60 establishes a conditional which controls access to the GOSUB modules. In the IF/THEN/ELSE statement, a code of C = 1 directs the program to the GOSUB 400 module, with the C = 2 code handled at GOSUB 500. In the GOSUB 400 module, the amount A is accumulated in T (line 410). As it represents a charge, it is output in the CHARGE column, starting at print position 24, via line 420.

A similar set of tasks compose the GOSUB 500 module for credits. At line 510, the amount is subtracted from T, reducing it by that amount. The amount is printed in the CREDIT column, line 520, commencing in print position 31. It follows the output of the item number I and transaction I$ at positions 1 and 9, respectively. A RETURN statement closes each GOSUB module processing and returns the program flow to the main loop.

The DATA statements are grouped at lines 200 to 230, with two sets of data written into each statement. The second set of data, line 230, contains the A = −99.99 data which is used to terminate the FOR/UNTIL loop. Let us again note this loop-closing sequence. The A = −99.99 is read at line 70 and thus signals the loop's close, once the NEXT statement is executed. This action is immediately undertaken, as the program moves from statements 70 to 80. The successive positioning of these statements was deliberate and permits the looping sequence to close once the 9s data is read.

Exiting the loop, two consecutive IF/THEN statements control access to two PRINT statements. If T < 0, a negative total identifies a credit due and line 90 is output. If T >= 0, an amount due is indicated and line 100 is printed. It is acceptable to initiate an output operation via a PRINT statement on the YES branch of an IF/THEN statement. The statements at lines 90 and 100 illustrate this new wrinkle.

The output for Problem 6.4 utilizes the desired compact format. In effect, the use of two columns for charges and credits helps to highlight each type of transaction. This technique of visually highlighting specific outputs by their positioning is important when designing printed outputs. It permits the user to easily distinguish between two or more types of data items.

The STEP Option

As noted with the FOR/NEXT instruction, the STEP option is used to specify an increment other than 1. The STEP option is similarly used with the FOR/UNTIL (or the FOR/WHILE) to alter the increment of the loop counter. The STEP option precedes the UNTIL command in the statement's syntax, as in the following examples:

```
60      FOR K = 1 STEP 2 UNTIL A = −99.99
100     FOR X = 50 STEP 10 UNTIL X = 120
50      FOR I = 5 STEP .5 UNTIL I > 30
180     FOR J = 12.5 STEP − .1 UNTIL P <= 10.8
```

SIDE BAR 6.2   A READ Statement at the Loop's Top?

Some readers pose a question regarding the input of data and the execution of the FOR/UNTIL and FOR/WHILE instructions. Why must the READ statement be positioned at the loop's close via the priming read? Why is it not logically correct for the READ statement to be placed at the loop's top? The following program excerpt illustrates their quandary:

```
100     FOR K = 1 UNTIL H = −99.99
110     READ N$,H,R
.
.
140     PRINT N$,G,F,N
150     NEXT K
.
.
```

The READ statement positioned at line 110 appears to be correct but will produce an undesirable side effect. It will cause the 9s data to be read and outputted before the looping sequence is closed. If you recall from previous problems, the output of the 9s data was not a desired byproduct of the 9s decision.

The placement of the READ statement at the loop's top, after the FOR statement, forces the program to use the 9s data in processing. This may result in the 9s data adversely affecting previously processed answers, causing the invalidation of previously correct results and their output.

It was for this reason that the priming read placed the READ statement at the loop's end. Once the 9s data was read, the loop's closing mechanism was triggered and the loop was exited. With the FOR/UNTIL and FOR/WHILE instructions, the priming read properly positions its two READ statements before and within the looping sequence.

The four examples noted offer different glimpses of how the STEP option is applied. In the first example, an increment of 2 is specified, causing the odd values of K to be generated. The looping sequence will continue until a value of A = −99.99 is sensed. In the second sample instruction, line 100, the increment noted was 10 and was applied to an intial value of X = 50. In this instance, the looping will continue until X is equal to 120. Generally, when the FOR/UNTIL is so specified, the loop variable is used in processing and substituted into a formula.

The next two FOR/UNTIL instructions note different aspects of their format. In statement 50, I is initialized at 5 and an increment of .5 is indicated. The conditional statement uses a logical operator other than an equal sign; thus, the loop will continue until I is greater than 30. Specifying the instruction in this fashion enables the program to execute a loop with I = 30 before activating the UNTIL conditional. This condition is not triggered until I actually becomes greater than 30.

The fourth example demonstrates the use of a negative increment. In line 180, the statement initializes J at 12.5 and directs that a STEP of − .1 be applied to J on each loop. The loop continues until P is less than or equal to 10.8. Again, this statement incorporates a looping sequence which is terminated when a specific value is attained.

The FOR/WHILE Statement

The **FOR/WHILE statement** is similar to the FOR/UNTIL, establishing a looping sequence controlled by a conditional statement. The operational difference between both instructions lies in their use of the conditional. The FOR/UNTIL continues to loop *until* a specific condition occurs, whereas the FOR/WHILE continues to loop *while* a condition exists. The FOR/WHILE is a pretest looping statement, evaluating its conditions at the loop's start. While the defined condition exists, the looping sequence continues.

The general format of the FOR/WHILE statement is as follows:

```
60      FOR K = 1 WHILE H <> −99.99
 .
 .      }  Statements in loop.
 .
200     NEXT K
```

The FOR/WHILE statement defines its loops within the required FOR and NEXT statements. The looping sequence commences at a value of K = 1 and continues *while* H is not equal to −99.99. The logical operators <> represent the "not equal to" conditional statement.

When used in this fashion, the FOR/WHILE statement can be successfully combined with a priming read, as in the example shown in Figure 6.A.4. At line 50 the FOR/WHILE invokes a loop, which continues while H is not equal to −99.99. When the 9s data is read, the FOR/WHILE prepares to close the loop at the NEXT statement. This occurs at line 100, when the program passes from the READ statement to the loop's NEXT instruction. The loop's close leads to line 110, where a PRINT statement outputs the accumulated total of T with its label of TOT GROSS =. The program's output is also viewed in Figure 6.A.4 with no visible difference. The loop control instructions should have no impact on the processed results.

A revised version of Problem 6.2 offers another glimpse of the FOR/WHILE instruction. In our earlier solution, we attempted to determine the break-even point between two lines representing costs and revenues. How could we use the FOR/WHILE instruction to assist in finding the point at which profits initially exceed $500?

Profits result when the revenue line is above the cost line. The break-even point was shown to be at 5000 units. From that point on, profits accrue and may be measured by subtracting the costs from revenues as the following formula directs:

Profits = revenues − costs

Using the structure of Problem 6.2 and making slight variations in that solution, we can derive a program which identifies profits in excess of $500. The new program will commence processing at the break-even point and move forward at an increment of 100 units until that specific profit point is found. The new program incorporates a FOR/WHILE and STEP option (Figure 6.A.5). As the logic is already familiar to the reader, we will suspend use of the flowchart. The real impact of the solution is evident in its program instructions.

A modular structure is employed with the three GOSUBs accessed from the main program. GOSUB 100 handles initial conditions; printing column headings and defining an edited output. TAB functions, line 110, align their headings with the L$ format of line 120.

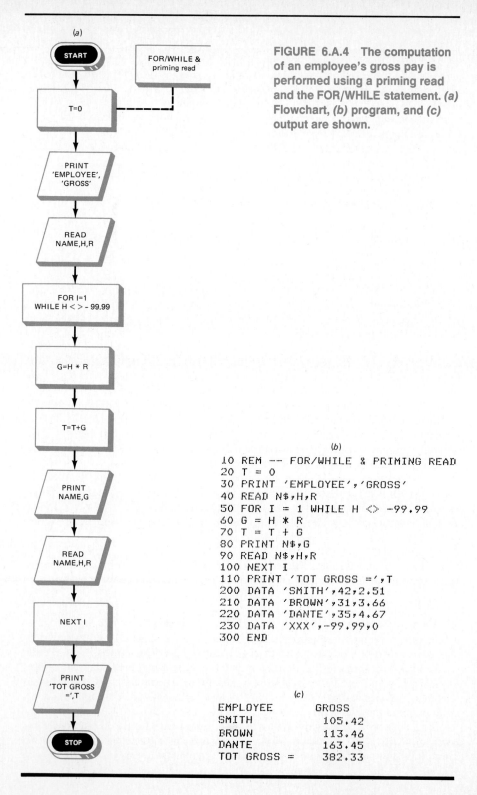

FIGURE 6.A.4 The computation of an employee's gross pay is performed using a priming read and the FOR/WHILE statement. (a) Flowchart, (b) program, and (c) output are shown.

(a)

START

FOR/WHILE & priming read

T=0

PRINT 'EMPLOYEE', 'GROSS'

READ NAME,H,R

FOR I=1 WHILE H < > - 99.99

G=H * R

T=T+G

PRINT NAME,G

READ NAME,H,R

NEXT I

PRINT 'TOT GROSS =',T

STOP

(b)

```
10 REM --- FOR/WHILE & PRIMING READ
20 T = 0
30 PRINT 'EMPLOYEE','GROSS'
40 READ N$,H,R
50 FOR I = 1 WHILE H <> -99.99
60 G = H * R
70 T = T + G
80 PRINT N$,G
90 READ N$,H,R
100 NEXT I
110 PRINT 'TOT GROSS =',T
200 DATA 'SMITH',42,2.51
210 DATA 'BROWN',31,3.66
220 DATA 'DANTE',35,4.67
230 DATA 'XXX',-99.99,0
300 END
```

(c)

```
EMPLOYEE        GROSS
SMITH            105.42
BROWN            113.46
DANTE            163.45
TOT GROSS =      382.33
```

(a)

```
10 REM REVISED SOLUTION PROB 6.2
20 REM -- MAIN PROGRAM
30 GOSUB 100
40 GOSUB 200
50 GOSUB 300
60 GO TO 400
100 REM INITIAL CONDITIONS MODULE
110 PRINT TAB(5);'UNITS';TAB(13);'PROD $';TAB(21);'REVENUE';TAB(29);'PROFIT'
120 L$ = '   #####   #####.   #####.   #####.'
130 RETURN
200 REM -- MAIN LOOP WITH FOR/WHILE MODULE
210 FOR X = 5000 STEP 100 WHILE P < 500
220 C = (.67 * X) + 2250
230 R = (1.12 * X)
240 P = R - C
250 PRINT USING L$,X,C,R,P
260 NEXT X
270 RETURN
300 REM -- CLOSING OUTPUT MODULE
310 PRINT 'THE $500 PROFIT LIMIT WAS REACHED'
320 RETURN
400 END
```

(b)

UNITS	PROD $	REVENUE	PROFIT
5000	5600.	5600.	0.
5100	5667.	5712.	45.
5200	5734.	5824.	90.
5300	5801.	5936.	135.
5400	5868.	6048.	180.
5500	5935.	6160.	225.
5600	6002.	6272.	270.
5700	6069.	6384.	315.
5800	6136.	6496.	360.
5900	6203.	6608.	405.
6000	6270.	6720.	450.
6100	6337.	6832.	495.
6200	6404.	6944.	540.

THE $500 PROFIT LIMIT WAS REACHED

FIGURE 6.A.5 The revised modular solution for Problem 6.2. (a) Program and (b) output.

The FOR/WHILE with STEP option is placed in the second GOSUB at line 210. The FOR opens X at 5000, the break-even point from which looping begins. A STEP of 100 precedes the WHILE condition, P < 500. While the profit P is less than 500, looping will continue. When P exceeds 500, the program exits the FOR/WHILE loop.

The program records the units, production costs, revenue, and profit computed on each loop. The last item listed notes the value which caused the profit to exceed $500. This output is followed by a closing literal, the main feature of the GOSUB 300 module. This program's output verifies the results of processing and the logic used.

Some students ask why the conditional WHILE P = 500 was not used, as that was the critical profit level under investigation. The reason lies in the nature of the computation of P and the high probability that the profit will never be exactly equal to 500. The FOR/WHILE loop will continue as long as P < 500 and cease only when P has exceeded that point. With the P = 500 conditional, the potential exists that the loop could continue indefinitely, as P may never be exactly equal to 500. A profit of 499.99 or 500.01 is not sufficient to suspend a processing loop initiated under a WHILE P = 500 conditional.

PROBLEM 6.5   A Rocket's Path

The problem entails estimating the trajectory of a rocket, as described by the formula

$$H = 825 + (20T) - 16T^2$$

where H is the height (in feet) at a given moment and T the time (in seconds) from its release at T = 0. A science student wishes to track the flight of the rocket, and determine the time necessary for the rocket to strike the ground. Use a FOR/WHILE to create a loop in which this formula is processed. Begin at an initial value of T = 0 and increment it by 1 second. Under the headings TIME and HEIGHT output T and H, commencing with print positions 5 and 10. The formats of ##.# and ####.# are applied to T and H, respectively. Looping ceases when the rocket strikes the ground. Figure 6.A.6 illustrates the projected trajectory.

FIGURE 6.A.6   The projected trajectory of a rocket described by the formula used in Problem 6.5.

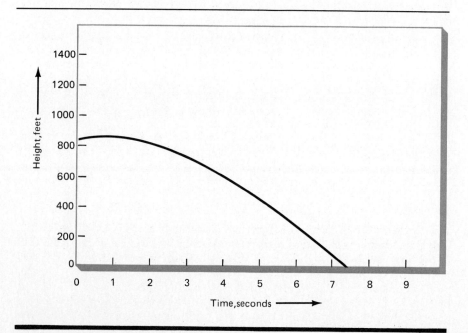

These are the main points in the problem narrative.

1   No inputs are required and a priming read is not needed.

2   A heading TIME and HEIGHT are outputted, starting at print positions 5 and 10, respectively. The edited formats of ##.# and ####.# are applied to time and height variables.

3   The FOR/WHILE is initialized at T = 0, with looping continuing while H > 0. An increment of 1 is used.

4   The required processing is described by the formula

$$H = 825 + (20 * T) - (16 * T * T)$$

where H is the rocket height (in feet) above the ground and T the time (in seconds) since firing.

5   Output T and H on each loop, using their respective edited formats.

The flowchart, Figure 6.A.7, opens with the output of the column headings and the definition of the L$ format applied to T and H. TAB functions are used to align the two headings with the edited L$ format. The initialization of H at 1 precedes the FOR/WHILE statement and permits the loop to start. Without this initialization, the FOR/WHILE does not have any value to test against H and looping could not start. Though we used a value of H = 1, any H value greater than zero is acceptable.

The FOR/WHILE loop is initiated by a processing symbol. The WHILE condition of H > 0 denotes that looping should continue while H is greater than zero. While H > 0, the rocket is above the ground and therefore airborne. When H <= 0, the rocket has struck the ground and the loop should end. The use of H > 0 in line 40 was deliberate, as it covers all heights above the ground.

The computation of H precedes the output of T and H on each loop. The use of a PRINT USING instruction is indicated, enabling the specification of the desired edited formats. The NEXT statement identifies the loop's end and precedes the flowchart's close.

The BASIC program closely parallels the flowchart from which it was prepared. Lines 20 and 30 specify this program's headings and output formats. Lines 40 to 70 define the FOR/WHILE looping sequence.

The FOR/WHILE statement, line 40, initializes T at zero and dictates that the loop continue while the value of H is greater than zero. The absence of a STEP option denotes an increment of 1 on each loop. The T value is substituted into the formula at line 50. The resultant H value is checked on each loop. A value of H <= 0 will cause the loop to cease.

The output of T and H on each loop is accomplished by line 60. This PRINT USING statement applies the L$ format to T and H, printing each in their respective columns. The NEXT T statement, line 70, acts as a loop control point. While H > 0, the loop continues and T and H values are computed. When H <= 0, processing ends and the program exits the loop through line 70.

The output for Problem 6.5 shows that at a starting value of T = 0, H was equal to 825. These results also reveal that it took almost eight seconds for the rocket to strike the ground. At T = 7, the height (H) value is positive, meaning that the rocket was still above ground. At T = 8, H adopts a negative value, meaning that it has hit the ground. The user is free to use a host of other looping techniques to determine the exact time at which the rocket struck the ground.

FIGURE 6.A.7 (a)
Flowchart, (b)
program, and (c)
output for Problem 6.5.

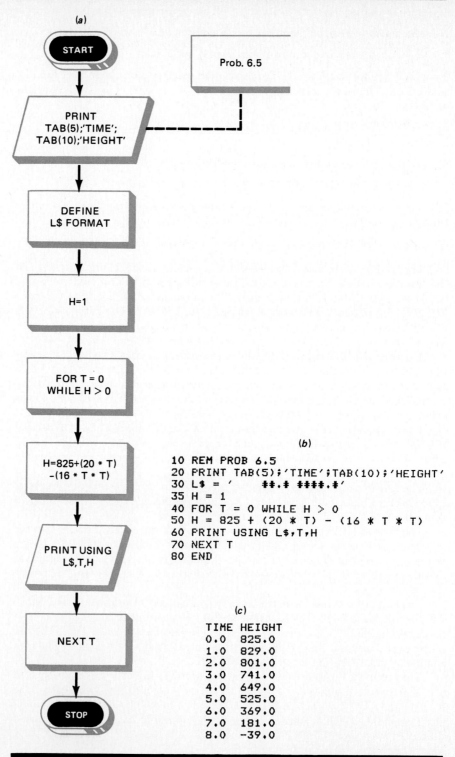

(a)

START

Prob. 6.5

PRINT
TAB(5);'TIME';
TAB(10);'HEIGHT'

DEFINE
L$ FORMAT

H=1

FOR T = 0
WHILE H > 0

H=825+(20 * T)
-(16 * T * T)

PRINT USING
L$,T,H

NEXT T

STOP

(b)

```
10 REM PROB 6.5
20 PRINT TAB(5);'TIME';TAB(10);'HEIGHT'
30 L$ = '     ##.# ####.#'
35 H = 1
40 FOR T = 0 WHILE H > 0
50 H = 825 + (20 * T) - (16 * T * T)
60 PRINT USING L$,T,H
70 NEXT T
80 END
```

(c)

```
TIME HEIGHT
0.0   825.0
1.0   829.0
2.0   801.0
3.0   741.0
4.0   649.0
5.0   525.0
6.0   369.0
7.0   181.0
8.0   -39.0
```

Advisory Note:

Any of the problems listed within the lab exercises of Chapter 6 can be solved using the FOR/UNTIL or FOR/WHILE instructions. The reader can substitute these statements into those solutions and observe their impact.

**Advanced
Programming
Techniques**

SEVEN

One-Dimensional Arrays

Chapter Objectives

Introduction

One of the difficulties associated with loops is that data items are only used once. Each time a new data item is inputted, the data previously stored at that location is destroyed permanently. Thus, looping sequences which might follow the initial or main loop are denied access to the destroyed data. Also it is now impossible to reuse the original data in a different sequence of tasks.

The ideal solution to this dilemma is to create special data storage locations. Once a data item is placed in this storage position, it may be accessed any number of times without being destroyed.

The realization of this concept is the array. An **array** is generally defined as a series of special storage locations identified as a single entity. This definition recognizes the protected status of each storage cell and the grouping of those cells under a common name. Referencing the array as a single entity provides a ready means of accessing data in it.

The **one-dimensional (1-D) array** is the most fundamental type of array. It is essentially a list of values identified by a common dataname in which each data item is assigned a position in the sequence of storage cells. To fully comprehend this structure, we must review the origin and evolution of the one-dimensional array.

A programmer wishes to use a set of six data items repeatedly within a series of loops. The programmer assigns the numeric-variable names of X1, X2, X3, X4, X5, and X6 to these six data items. Because each variable has a unique dataname, the computer treats them as independent items, not as a group. However, using a one-dimensional array, the programmer can assign each variable a unique dataname, place each variable in its own storage position, and access to all six items as a single unit.

The Conceptual Structure

In this case, the entire unit is referred to as the X array and consists of six cells: $X(1)$, $X(2)$, $X(3)$, $X(4)$, $X(5)$, and $X(6)$.[1] These six cells are referred to as **subscripted variables** and carry the pronunciation "X-sub-1" for $X(1)$, "X-sub-2" for $X(2)$, and so on. The **subscript** is the number placed in parentheses and defines the logical position of the item in the array. Thus, $X(1)$ is the first item of the X array and identifies its first cell. Similarly, $X(2)$ is the second item of the X array and identifies the second storage cell. This naming sequence continues until the last storage cell, $X(6)$, is identified. Each storage cell in the X array must possess a subscript which renders it independent of all other cells.

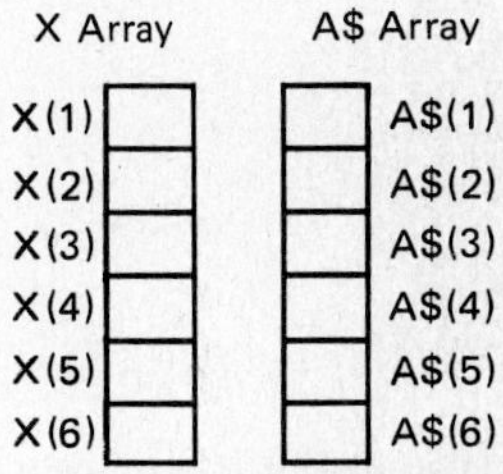

In BASIC, the variable name placed in front of the parentheses is important because it defines the type of data stored in the array. An X array is capable of storing only numeric data items, as X is a numeric-variable name. If a string-variable name such as A$ is used, the array can retain nonnumeric data. The relationship of these two arrays is illustrated in Figure 7.1.

FIGURE 7.1 Two six-cell arrays are depicted. The X array holds numeric data, whereas the A$ array holds nonnumeric data items.

The DIM Statement

Before an array can be used in a program, its type and size must be defined via the **DIMension statement.** The DIM statement will generally appear as the first executable statement of a program. It uses the following format:

```
10    DIM X(6),A$(6)
```

The line number 10 identifies the logical position of the DIM statement as the first instruction. The letters DIM represent the operational command

---

[1] A seventh cell, X(0), is also created in the X array. All one-dimensional arrays possess the X(0) cell when created. As it is rarely used, most people place a minimal amount of importance on its existence. We will not consider it in future discussions.

which directs the computer to establish the arrays listed. The subscripted variables X(6) and A$(6) identify the two arrays the programmer wishes to use by type and size. The subscripts specified refer not to a single array cell but to the total number of positions needed by that array. Hence, both are defined as six-cell arrays.

The array names also indicate that the X array will handle numeric data and the A$ array will handle nonnumeric data. Remember, that the same size rules apply to each type of data when stored in an array. Many students incorrectly believe that a new set of rules applies when data is stored in an array. This is not the case.

The order in which the arrays are specified is not critical, nor does it define the order in which they may be accessed. Thus, the DIM statement could have been written as follows:

```
10    DIM A$(6),X(6)
```

The net effect is the same; two six-cell arrays result.

The DIM statement should only appear once in a program, as its initial statement.[2] This requires that all arrays slated for use be defined at the start of a program. Even though an array may only be used at a program's end, it *must* be defined at its start. It is totally wrong to define arrays throughout the program. The incorrect positioning of DIM statements will result in a program error sufficient to end processing.

7.2 Loading the Array

The primary function of the DIM statement is to define the array by name, type, and size. However, the DIM statement does not place any data in the array.[3] For this, a separate series of inputs is used, normally in a looping sequence. Data that will be used during processing is usually loaded during the initial stages of a program. Data that results from programming can also be loaded into array cells and retained for subsequent analysis. Both loading techniques may be combined in one program.

---

[2] For most programs, the DIM statement will be the first instruction. Some versions of BASIC offer selected statements for specialized processing tasks which must precede the DIM statement. As these situations are reserved for highly complex tasks, we will assign them minimal importance and continue to stress the placement of the DIM statement as the first executable program statement.

---

[3] Some versions of BASIC are designed to load array cells with either the null set (blanks) or zeros upon its definition. This feature varies between computer systems. Most programmers consider it poor procedure to rely on these features, preferring to specifically load each array cell with data of their design. This procedure ensures that the array is properly loaded, with the programmer controlling that input and dictating the data actually entered into the cells. In later examples we will follow the practice of actually loading each array, avoiding any potential difficulty.

SIDE BAR 7.1   A DIM View of Things

A common error associated with the use of DIMension statements relates to its spelling. Many users want to spell out the entire command, thus producing a statement such as this:

    10   DIMENSION X(10),N$(10)   *(Wrong)*

This format is incorrect, as the BASIC compiler is seeking not the full command but only DIM. A DIM statement is properly specified like this:

    10   DIM X(10),N$(10)

This format ensures the accurate processing of this statement and the definition of the arrays specified.

One critical point must be made with regard to the life of an array. An array is not a file. It is created and used by the program and lasts only for the life of that program. Once the program ends, data loaded into the array is destroyed.

There are two basic approaches to loading data into an array. If the contents of an array will remain stable for the duration of the program—for example, when an array is used as a table or an index—the array may be loaded by means of READ and DATA statements. If the contents of an array will constantly change between program applications—for example, when statistics are being accumulated—READ and DATA statements may prove to be too cumbersome. Interactive arrays of this type are best loaded by means of INPUT statements.

Loading Stable Arrays

One of the methods used to load data into arrays involves the combined use of READ and DATA statements. This loading technique is best used when the contents of the array will remain unchanged. Figure 7.2 illustrates a program in which an array is loaded using READ and DATA statements.

The DIM statement, line 10, defines a Y array consisting of eight cells. The variable name Y denotes that only numeric data is stored in this array. The first FOR/NEXT module, lines 20 to 50, loads the array. The FOR instruction, line 20, opens an eight-loop sequence in which each array cell is loaded. The loop variable I will range from 1 to 8 and use an increment of 1. The variable I will also serve as the subscript for the array variables.

This selection of the FOR/NEXT and its variable was deliberate. It easily creates a looping sequence to control the loading of each array cell and provides a loop variable readily used as a subscript. As I varies from 1 to 8, the FOR/NEXT will cause the program to methodically move through each Y(I) array cell and load one number.

The actual loading of each array cell occurs at the READ statement, line 30. The focal point of this statement is the subscripted variable Y(I). The Y(I) identifies the array on a general basis, with the computer substituting the

FIGURE 7.2   READ
and DATA statements
are used to load
stable arrays. Here, an
eight-loop sequence
frames statements
used to load the Y
array.

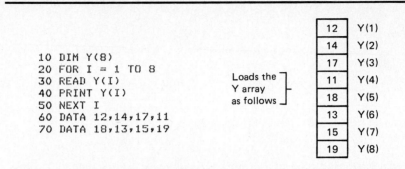

```
10 DIM Y(8)
20 FOR I = 1 TO 8
30 READ Y(I)
40 PRINT Y(I)
50 NEXT I
60 DATA 12,14,17,11
70 DATA 18,13,15,19
```

current value of I to identify the specific cell into which the data item will be stored. The association of the FOR/NEXT variable I and its use as the subscript is not accidental. The FOR/NEXT provides a means of helping the program carefully pass through each array cell, using the loop variable as the subscript.

Thus, on the first loop, I = 1; the Y(1) cell is accessed and a value of 12 is stored in that cell. On the second loop, I = 2 and the Y(2) cell is filled with a value of 14. When I = 3, the program loads the number 17 in the Y(3) cell. This process continues until the eighth and last value, 19, is loaded into Y(8). With that final input, the FOR/NEXT looping sequence ends and the program exits the loop. The data used in loading the Y array is specified in two DATA statements, lines 60 and 70.

The important point to focus on is the combined use of the FOR/NEXT and READ statements, which enabled the program to systematically access and load each array cell. The procedure is a principal means of working with arrays when I/O activities must be undertaken.

This latter point is evident in discussing the purpose of the PRINT statement, line 40. This instruction is specifically used to verify the contents of the array cell into which data was just loaded. We are checking to see if the data inputted into each cell was properly stored. Line 40 causes the computer to go to each Y(I) cell, obtain an image of the data stored in that cell, and print it for the user's information. In this fashion, the user has a record of data stored in each cell and can verify the accuracy of the data intially used in processing.

This printout of the array's data may seem trivial, but it is the kind of small point that good programmers incorporate into their solutions. It provides the programmer with a valid point from which to start analysis of the program should errors result from processing. Without this output, the user may be uncertain as to the data initially used to commence processing. The documentation of data stored in an array is especially critical when data is loaded on an interactive basis.

The program presented in Figure 7.3 consists of two major modules and shows how the data stored in the Y(I) array is used. The first FOR/NEXT

FIGURE 7.3 Data retained in the Y array is used to compute an average. The program (a) and its output (b) are listed.

```
              (a)                                    (b)

10 DIM Y(8)                              12
20 FOR I = 1 TO 8                        14
30 READ Y(I)                             17
40 PRINT Y(I)                            11
50 NEXT I                                18
60 DATA 12,14,17,11                      13
70 DATA 18,13,15,19                      15
100 T = 0                                19
110 FOR I = 1 TO 8            AVG AGE =          14.875
120 T = T + Y(I)
130 NEXT I
140 A = T/8
150 PRINT 'AVG AGE =',A
160 END
```

module, lines 20 to 50, loads the $Y(I)$ array — a processing sequence we have already reviewed. The second looping module, also controlled via a FOR/NEXT sequence in lines 110 to 130, demonstrates how array data is used in processing. This second module accumulates each array value in preparation for computing the average of all eight values.

Once data is stored in an array, it is available for processing. The second program module, lines 100 to 150, is designed to accumulate the sum of the eight ages stored in the Y array.

The LET statement, line 100, initializes the accumulator T at zero. T is used to add up each $Y(I)$ value. Access to the array cells is again controlled via the FOR/NEXT statements, lines 110 and 130. The accumulation of data commences with $Y(1)$ and sequentially proceeds through each array cell until $Y(8)$ is accessed. The accumulation of each cell is dictated by line 120, where the computation $T = T + Y(I)$ is specified.

Some users question whether the $T = T + Y(I)$ equation is affected by the use of the subscripted variable. This is not the case. The type of variable name used does not affect the update of an accumulator.

Some users believe that a READ statement must be specified to access data stored in an array. The use of a READ statement to access array data is *incorrect*. Once an array is loaded, the programmer need only specify the subscripted variable of the array cell in question to access its contents.

Hence, a READ statement at line 120 is *not* necessary to read the contents of the Y array. The specification of the subscripted variable $Y(I)$ is sufficient. This is why most programmers choose to isolate the loading of an array in a separate module. Essentially, one program module loads the array(s), and each subsequent module has access to that data.

The second FOR/NEXT sequence executes exactly eight loops, with the contents of cells 1 to 8 respectively added to the accumulator. On the last loop, the program passes through the NEXT statement and computes the average of the eight ages at line 140. This average is output at line 150, preceded by the label AVG AGE =. This output concludes processing and precedes the program's END statement, line 160.

The first eight lines of output relate directly to the input of data to the array. Each data item is printed immediately after its storage in one of the eight array cells. The last line printed reveals the average age computed within the second module's processing. This last output was the only line resultant from the second module's execution and reveals the successful use of data retained in arrays.

Loading Interactive Arrays

It is also possible to use INPUT statements when loading array data. This statement is advantageously used when new data is processed each time a program is rerun. It avoids having to rewrite numerous READ and DATA statements and enables the user to readily input data as the program is executed. The interactive capacity of the INPUT statement lends itself to the online entry of data. Let us consider a revised version of the previous program, where an INPUT statement is used to load the array.

The revised solution, Figure 7.4, again consists of two modules. The biggest change in this revised solution is the use of the INPUT statement, line 30. As array data is input on an online basis, the need to utilize DATA statements is eliminated. The INPUT statement is positioned within the eight-loop FOR/NEXT sequence, lines 20 to 50. On each loop one value is inputted to its respective array position. The cell used is defined by the value of the loop variable I. When I = 1, the first cell is accessed and the value input stored therein. The sequential loading of each cell continues until the eighth

FIGURE 7.4   Arrays may be loaded on an interactive basis using INPUT statements. Our initial solution is modified to incorporate the use of INPUT statements and enable the online entry of data. The appearance of questions marks (?), in the program's output, reflects these online data entries.

```
10 DIM Y(8)                              ? 12
20 FOR I = 1 TO 8                          12
30 INPUT Y(I)                            ? 14
40 PRINT Y(I)                              14
50 NEXT I                                ? 17
100 T = 0                                  17
110 FOR K = 1 TO 8                       ? 11
120 T = T + Y(K)          The revised      11
130 NEXT K                program and —  ? 18
140 A = T/8                its output      18
150 PRINT 'AVG AGE =',A                  ? 13
160 END                                    13
                                         ? 15
                                           15
                                         ? 19
                                           19
                                         AVG AGE =      14.875
```

cell is filled. Whether INPUT or READ and DATA statements are used, the FOR/NEXT statement controls access to the Y array.

The effect of using the INPUT statement is evident in this program's output. The entry of each item is preceded by a ? which prompts the user. A series of eight question marks note the entry of the eight ages used in processing and stored in the Y array. Each ? is then followed by the printing of that data item, resultant from line 40. Again, the PRINT statement is used to verify the proper storage of that cell's data. The NEXT statement closes the looping sequence.

The second module of processing is identical to that of the first solution discussed. The T accumulator is initialized at line 100, with the FOR/NEXT loop evident from lines 110 to 130. The accumulator is updated at line 120 and the average age computed at line 140. The average printed uses the label AVG AGE =.

A slight variation was incorporated into the second module. Instead of reusing I for the loop variable of the second FOR/NEXT statement, we chose to use K. The decision to use K was deliberate and demonstrates that the same variable does not have to be continuously reused in a series of FOR/NEXT loops. The programmer must ensure that the correct subscripts are employed when referencing array positions.

For example, in the initial FOR/NEXT loop, lines 20 to 50, the loop variable I was used. As a result, a subscript of I was required to access each array cell. In the second looping sequence, a loop variable of K was specified. The FOR instruction, line 110, defined K as ranging from 1 to 8 in the same fashion as the previously used I variable. As such, the subscripted variables were defined as Y(K), *not Y(I)*. The K subscript had to be used in the second module, as it provided access to the array. It is perfectly acceptable to switch FOR/NEXT variables in successive loops, providing that the programmer uses the appropriate subscripts.

The solutions presented in Figure 7.3 and 7.4 were substantially similar, with the exception of how each program handled its array data. In both instances, the initial loading of the arrays was performed in a module separated from processing. This isolated the array handling, ensuring the integrity of that module. It is generally a good idea to separate the loading of arrays from the modules in which their data are actually processed.

Error Checking

One of the difficulties associated with the interactive data entry is the potential for inputting incorrect data. Another factor is the need to prompt users as to what data items should be keyed in. The INPUT statement used in Figure 7.4 did not incorporate a prompting literal and only specified the subscripted variable Y(I). Generally, when using online inputs, it is good practice to prompt the user.

Figure 7.5 shows how this program may be modified to satisfy the requirements of error handling and user prompting. The revised program uses prompting literals in the opening loop's INPUT statements, as well as an

FIGURE 7.5 The interactive program is revised to include an error-checking sequence. Note the occurrence of an error when the data 33 was input and the way the program handled the reentry of the correct data item, 11.

```
10 DIM Y(8)
20 FOR I = 1 TO 8
30 INPUT 'ENTER ONE AGE VALUE';Y(I)
40 INPUT 'IS AGE CORRECT---ENTER Y OR N';R$
50 IF R$ = 'N' THEN 30
60 PRINT Y(I)
70 NEXT I
80 PRINT 'THE ARRAY IS LOADED'
100 T = 0
110 FOR K = 1 TO 8
120 T = T + Y(K)
130 NEXT K
140 A = T/8
150 PRINT 'AVG AGE =',A
160 END
```

```
ENTER ONE AGE VALUE? 12
IS AGE CORRECT---ENTER Y OR N? Y
 12
ENTER ONE AGE VALUE? 14
IS AGE CORRECT---ENTER Y OR N? Y
 14
ENTER ONE AGE VALUE? 17
IS AGE CORRECT---ENTER Y OR N? Y
 17
ENTER ONE AGE VALUE? 33
IS AGE CORRECT---ENTER Y OR N? N
ENTER ONE AGE VALUE? 11
IS AGE CORRECT---ENTER Y OR N? Y
 11
ENTER ONE AGE VALUE? 18
IS AGE CORRECT---ENTER Y OR N? Y
 18
ENTER ONE AGE VALUE? 13
IS AGE CORRECT---ENTER Y OR N? Y
 13
ENTER ONE AGE VALUE? 15
IS AGE CORRECT---ENTER Y OR N? Y
 15
ENTER ONE AGE VALUE? 19
IS AGE CORRECT---ENTER Y OR N? Y
 19
THE ARRAY IS LOADED
AVG AGE =        14.875
```

An error is caught and the correct data rekeyed.

IF/THEN statement for error detection. It also maintains the two-module structure of prior solutions. The first module monitors the loading of the Y array, while the second module directs the computation of the average age.

The program opens with a DIM statement defining the eight-cell Y array. The FOR instruction, line 20, initiates a looping sequence of eight repetitions and defines I as the loop control variable. The first of two INPUT statements with prompting literals is encountered at line 30. This statement advises the user to ENTER ONE AGE VALUE and accepts that numeric value using the subscripted variable Y(I).

This new statement 30 serves essentially the same purpose as its previous counterpart. It accepts each age value and stores that number in one of the eight array cells. The subscripted variable Y(I) is employed in exactly the same fashion, substituting the existing I value for the subscript. The prompting literal is incorporated to advise the user when to key in the next age.

The error-checking capacity of this revised solution is evident in the next two instructions, lines 40 and 50. These statements ask the user to verify the accuracy of the data just entered and enable the user to rekey that data if an error is made. The prompting literal of line 40 asks whether the age keyed in is correct and requires that the user actively accept or reject that data. The entry of the letter Y indicates that the age entered was correct and processing may continue. The N response will trigger the error-checking mechanism within line 50.

The IF/THEN statement is constructed to catch the N response in which the user believes an error has occurred. The string-variable name R$ was used in line 40 to accept the input of Y or N. If R$ is equal to N, the program branches to line 30 and gives the user an opportunity to rekey the data into the same array cell. A response of Y will cause the program to branch to line 60, output the Y(I) value, and continue the loop.

The importance of lines 40 and 50 lies in their error-checking capacity and the ability to re-input data into the same array cell. This latter point is critical, as these instructions hold I at that value and permit the same cell to be loaded. The user is capable of entering a corrected value and storing that value in the same array cell. The new value totally replaces the old (incorrect) value and ensures that the array holds only the correct data. The correction process may be repeatedly executed, without advancing the loop counter I. It is only when R$ = 'Y' that the program will pass through to line 60 and permit processing to continue.

The literal output via line 80 is another embellishment designed to assist the user. The output of THE ARRAY IS LOADED advises that the first phase of processing, the loading of the array, is complete. This type of advisory literal is often used in programs where READ and DATA statements are employed to load arrays. In those instances, users cannot readily track the loading process. The advisory literal alerts the user to completion of one module and the start of the next phase of processing.

The output from our revised solution is shown in Figure 7.5. This output records the entry of each data item and the program's request to verify each value input. One error is noted on the fourth try, where an age of 33 was erroneously entered for a value of 11. The error was handled and the correct value substituted in cell Y(4). The complete loading of the Y array is highlighted by THE ARRAY IS LOADED label, which precedes the output of the computed average age. This last output signals the close of the second phase of processing and the entire program.

We have just touched the surface with regard to error checking and the use of advisory literals. These statements reflect a brief introduction to a phase of programming that can become as elaborate or as intricate as the programmer desires. The important point is that the user possesses a way of changing an incorrectly inputted data item without affecting the loop sequence. Also, the user is alerted when the program passes from one phase of processing to another, via advisory literals.

SIDE BAR 7.2   The Proper Subscript

Most of the errors initially made when specifying subscripted variables relate to the uncertainty of using them. Many programmers simply forget to use the same subscript consistently or fail to specify the proper subscripted-variable name. For example, a variable may be input using the variable S(I), but when a statement is written it may appear as:

    60   C(I) = S * .06

Instead of correctly specifying the subscripted variable S(I), the programmer erroneously wrote the nonsubscripted variable S. This type of error usually occurs from haste and is readily corrected by rewriting the statement.

Programmers should expend some time and effort rereading their programs before actually running them. Frequently, this form of error checking can uncover carelessness and save needless repeated processing of a program.

7.3 Array Applications

Program Organization with FOR/NEXT Statements

The primary purpose of arrays is to provide the program with repeated access to the same data. It is often advantageous when working with arrays to establish program modules. Positioned in logical order, they compose the program and direct its processing. Each module can be worked on in isolation without affecting another module, greatly simplifying debugging. Also, the use of modules is closely aligned to the structured-programming concepts discussed in Chapter 6.

Along these lines, let us undertake a sample program consisting of three separate modules. One module will assume the responsibility of loading the array, and the remaining two modules will perform separate processing tasks. To simplify these discussions, we will limit this problem to numeric arrays.

PROBLEM 7.1   Above-Average Values

The problem entails the computation of an average and the number of values that exceed that average. A modular structure is used, with each module performing specific tasks. A total of 12 numbers are involved.

The first program module loads the array, which is called the X(12) array. This loading sequence should input and output all array values. Use READ and DATA statements to define the 12 values.

The second module accumulates each value and computes the average of the 12 numbers. This average is output using the label COMPUTED AVG =.

The third module searches the entire array for all values which exceed the computed average. For each such value, the accumulator (which is counting the number of above-average values) increases by 1. When all array cells have been searched, output the total using the label NUMBER OF ABOVE AVG VALUES =. This output concludes processing. The data used in processing is as follows:

54.81	87.68	56.58	51.04	50.03	39.81	49.65
49.98	14.57	47.93	43.65	61.73		

These are the main points in the problem narrative.

1   The problem solution uses three modules: Module 1 handles the loading of the array, module 2 computes the average, and module 3 determines the number of above-average values.

2   No headings are required.

3   An array consisting of 12 cells is needed. It will use the dataname X.

4   In module 1, one value is read per loop. This value is loaded into the X array and output. After the last value is loaded, output the literal THE 12 CELLS ARE LOADED.

5   Two accumulators are needed. One accumulator will total the sum of 12 values and the second accumulator is incremented each time an above-average value is found. The first accumulator is used in module 2, and the second is used in module 3.

6   Module 2 focuses on the computation of the average. A loop controls the accumulation of the 12 cells, which precedes the computation of the average. The formula used is:

Average = total/12

The average is outputted using the label COMPUTED AVG =.

7   Module 3 uses a loop to compare each array cell to the computed average of all 12 values. If the cell is greater than the average, the second accumulator

is increased by 1. After scanning all 12 cells, the second total is outputted with its own label.

The flowchart and program for Problem 7.1 are illustrated in Figure 7.6.

In the flowchart, the array is loaded in module 1 by means of a FOR/NEXT sequence. It is preceded by a DIMension statement, which defines a 12-cell array called X. One number is input per loop until the last loop is executed. The closing 12-cell literal denotes the end of the first program module and the first phase of processing.

Module 2 opens with the initialization of the accumulator T1, which is used to compute the sum of all 12 values retained in the array. In the second FOR/NEXT loop, the X(I) cell values are accumulated into T1. After the completion of the twelfth loop, the average A is computed by dividing T1 by 12. This average is outputted with its own label, denoting the close of the second phase of processing.

Some readers question why T1 was not initialized at the start of the entire program. This initialization could have been accomplished then; however, we chose to initialize T1 prior to the module in which it is used. This approach tends to reinforce the modularity of processing activities. If we had initialized T1 at the program's start, we might have omitted it from the solution. By defining T1 at the start of module 2, we ensure that it is specifically associated with that module's activities.

This rationale is repeated at the third module's opening, where the T2 accumulator is initialized at zero. T2 is used to total the number of values that are greater than the computed average. Each time that an array cell is found to be greater than A, T2 is incremented by 1. The comparison of X(I) against A is identified by a decision symbol and performed in the third FOR/NEXT loop. The accumulated T2 total is outputted after every cell in the X array has been tested against A. The output of T2 closes the third module's processing and notes the end of this solution.

The program written from this flow diagram parallels its logic. It opens with a DIM statement defining an array called X of 12 cells. The REM which follows identifies the first phase of processing, the loading of 12 data items into the X array.

The vehicle for controlling the loading operation is the FOR/NEXT statement, lines 30 to 60. The FOR instruction defines a 12-loop sequence, with I serving its dual role as loop control variable and subscript. The READ statement, line 40, individually loads each data item into its respective array cell. The PRINT statement, line 50, records the data entered into each cell and precedes the loop's required NEXT instruction. The DATA statements specifying the 12 data items are provided at lines 80 and 90, with each statement defining 6 items apiece.

The 12 CELLS literal outputted via the PRINT statement at line 70 has many uses. It signifies that the array was loaded without incident and the accumulation of data has begun. It serves as a debugging aid. If an error occurs at this point, the error must exist in the second module, as the first module was executed without error. Similarly, the output of the

(a)

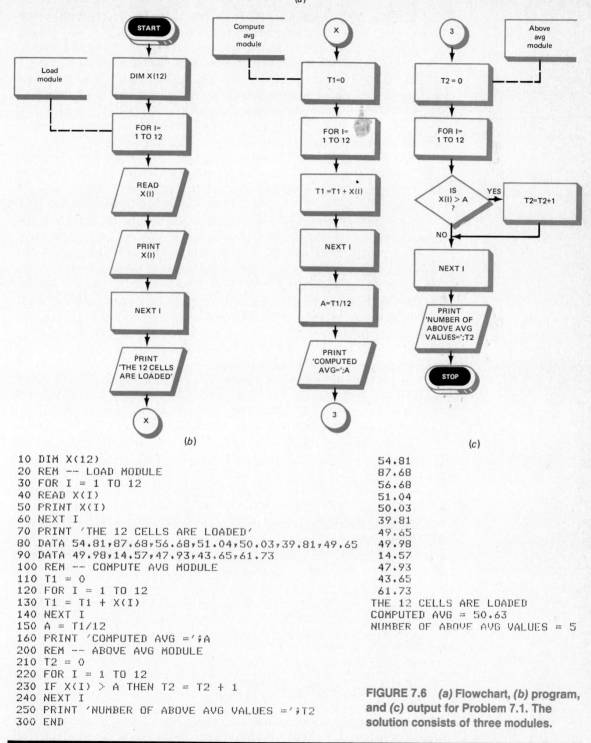

(b)

```
10 DIM X(12)
20 REM --- LOAD MODULE
30 FOR I = 1 TO 12
40 READ X(I)
50 PRINT X(I)
60 NEXT I
70 PRINT 'THE 12 CELLS ARE LOADED'
80 DATA 54.81,87.68,56.68,51.04,50.03,39.81,49.65
90 DATA 49.98,14.57,47.93,43.65,61.73
100 REM --- COMPUTE AVG MODULE
110 T1 = 0
120 FOR I = 1 TO 12
130 T1 = T1 + X(I)
140 NEXT I
150 A = T1/12
160 PRINT 'COMPUTED AVG =';A
200 REM --- ABOVE AVG MODULE
210 T2 = 0
220 FOR I = 1 TO 12
230 IF X(I) > A THEN T2 = T2 + 1
240 NEXT I
250 PRINT 'NUMBER OF ABOVE AVG VALUES =';T2
300 END
```

(c)

```
54.81
87.68
56.68
51.04
50.03
39.81
49.65
49.98
14.57
47.93
43.65
61.73
THE 12 CELLS ARE LOADED
COMPUTED AVG = 50.63
NUMBER OF ABOVE AVG VALUES = 5
```

FIGURE 7.6 (a) Flowchart, (b) program, and (c) output for Problem 7.1. The solution consists of three modules.

COMPUTED AVG = label, line 160, means that the second module was completed and the third module started. Many programmers deliberately place literals at the end of each program module to aid the debugging process and record the passage of program control from one module to another.

The second module consists of lines 100 to 160. A REM statement, line 100, identifies this module and precedes the initialization of the T1 accumulator. The accumulator update is executed in the FOR/NEXT loop, lines 120 to 140. Again, the I variable is used as subscript and loop variable. Access to each cell is available via the subscripted-variable name X(I).

The accumulated total T1 is employed in the computation of the average A, line 150. This computed average is outputted via line 160, along with its identifying label. This output serves to note the close of the second phase of processing.

The third and last processing module begins at line 200, a REM statement advising of the attempt to find all above-average values. The T2 accumulator, initialized at line 210, is used to total the number of array values that exceed the computed average. Testing against that average occurs in the FOR/NEXT loop, lines 220 to 240.

The IF/THEN statement, line 230, compares each value held within the X array against the average A. Each cell is accessed via the subscripted variable X(I). If X(I) > A, the T2 accumulator is updated by 1. If the cell value defined by X(I) is not greater than the average A, the accumulator is not affected and the loop tests the next value.

When a total of 12 comparisons have been made, the looping sequence ends. The PRINT statement at line 250 outputs the label NUMBER OF ABOVE AVG VALUES = and the value of T2. The program then proceeds to the END statement at line 300.

The output from Problem 7.1 is shown in Figure 7.6(c). This printout consists of the outputs of the 12 array values, the computed average, and the number of above-average values. The user should examine the printout and ensure that the results of processing are valid. Is the number of above-average values correct?

The secret to the success of this solution lies in the program's ability to access data held in the array. Once the array was loaded, that data was available for repeated use. As long as new data was not input to the X array, data within its cells was unchanged and available for reuse.

Problem 7.1 demonstrated a numeric array that was created and loaded at the program's inception. Programs may also involve alphameric arrays and arrays that are created and filled *during* processing. Such arrays are useful in the preparation of printed reports, as in the next example.

PROBLEM 7.2   Employee Benefits

The problem entails the computation and reporting of employee benefits. A total of four arrays are required. In the original loading of data, only two arrays are accessed. Input on each loop are the employee's name and gross pay, which are loaded to their separate arrays. The two remaining arrays, one each for pension benefits and union dues, are filled with the results of processing.

Module 1 loads the name and gross pay arrays. The computation of the pension and union data is handled in module 2. These two amounts are computed separately and stored in their respective array positions. The union dues are a flat percentage, computed at 3.2 percent of the gross pay amount. The pension benefits are 8.9 percent if gross pay is greater than or equal to $275; otherwise pension benefits are 6.7 percent. It is necessary to accumulate all union dues and pension benefits separately, so initialize two accumulators at the beginning of the second module. No outputs result from this module.

The third and fourth modules serve output functions. Module 3 will output a report on union dues deductions, and module 4 will output pension benefits. The column headings for the union report are EMPLOYEE, GROSS PAY, and UNION DUES, each output respectively commencing at print positions 5, 20, and 30. All dollar amounts are edited with ####.##. Exactly the same report format is used with the pension report, except that the headings are EMPLOYEE, GROSS PAY, and PENSION AMT. At the end of each report, output the respective accumulated total with an appropriate label beneath its column. The data is as follows:

Name	Gross	Name	Gross
Dunphy	489.60	Granito	673.89
Clark	163.27	Chomiscz	273.65
Donofrio	760.04	Tessar	327.82
Conlon	224.36	Rector	517.44

These are the main points in the problem narrative.

1   Four arrays are required to support processing — one array each for the employee's name, gross pay, union dues, and pension benefits. Each array consists of eight cells.

2   Four modules compose this problem solution: module 1 is used for loading the name and gross arrays; module 2 involves processing operations; modules 3 and 4 prepare reports.

3   Input to the arrays are the employees' names and gross pay amounts. The pension and dues arrays are filled with data that results from processing.

4   Processing consists of the computation of union dues, pension benefits, and totals for each amount. Dues are 3.2 percent of gross pay, with two rates used for pension deductions. If gross pay is less than $275, a rate of 6.7 percent is used; otherwise, a rate of 8.9 percent is used.

5   Two report formats are executed by modules 3 and 4: one outputs union dues, and the other outputs pension benefits. Totals for these amounts are outputted at the end of the reports. An edited format of ####.## is applied to dollar amounts.

6   Looping sequences are controlled via FOR/NEXT statements.

The flowchart written for Problem 7.2 is shown in Figure 7.7.

The flowchart for this narrative is lengthy, as the problem consists of many parts. Module 1 of our flowchart details the creation of the four required arrays and the loading of the two input arrays. Within an eight-loop FOR/NEXT sequence, the name and gross pay arrays are loaded and their contents printed. A closing literal, specially placed at the end of this opening module, signals its completion.

In module 2, data in the N$ and G arrays are used to process employee dues and benefits. Two accumulators are initialized at the start of this module. The T1 accumulator is used to total the dues paid, whereas T2 will accumulate individual pension benefits. In a second eight-loop sequence, the variables U(I) and P(I) represent the union dues and pension benefits computed for each individual on each loop. A decision helps select the proper pension rate to use when computing each pension amount. No outputs are accomplished in module 2, as it serves solely a computative role.

Module 3 opens the report-making sequence by focusing on the printing of union dues data. Two formats are defined, one each for a detail and summary line. The L$ format is used with the detail lines when outputting both the union dues and pension amounts. The T$ format is constructed to align summary lines when outputting the two accumulated totals.

The heading output in module 3 appears at the top of the union dues report. It precedes the looping sequence in which that employee's data is output. The printing of the T1 accumulator, with its label TOT UNION DUES = immediately follows the last employee's line. A blank line is output to separate the union dues report from the pension report that follows in module 4.

The fourth module opens with the printing of its heading. It uses a format which parallels the previous report but replaces the last literal with one that reads PENSION AMT. It is not necessary to redefine the L$ and T$ formats, as those formats will remain intact unless they are specifically altered. The last FOR/NEXT loop enables the output of pension data held in the N$, G, and P arrays. After printing the last employee's data, the accumulated total held in T2 is outputted with a label TOT PENSION AMT =.

The actual program written from this expanded flowchart is shown in Figure 7.8(a). The DIM statement defines each of the four arrays by type and size. Though the N$ and G arrays are accessed immediately and the P and U arrays are not used until later, all four arrays *must* be defined in the opening DIM statement. Otherwise, a program error will result.

The initial program module consists of lines 20 to 80. After an identifying REM statement, the FOR statement initializes an eight-loop sequence where N$(I) and G(I) arrays are loaded. The READ and PRINT statements, lines 40 and 50, serve to load and output the contents of those two arrays. The NEXT statement closes the looping sequence and marks the point at which the program continues when the loop is exited. A literal, line 70, and a blank line of output, line 80, mark the completion of the opening module.

The DATA statements for the eight sets of employee data are grouped at

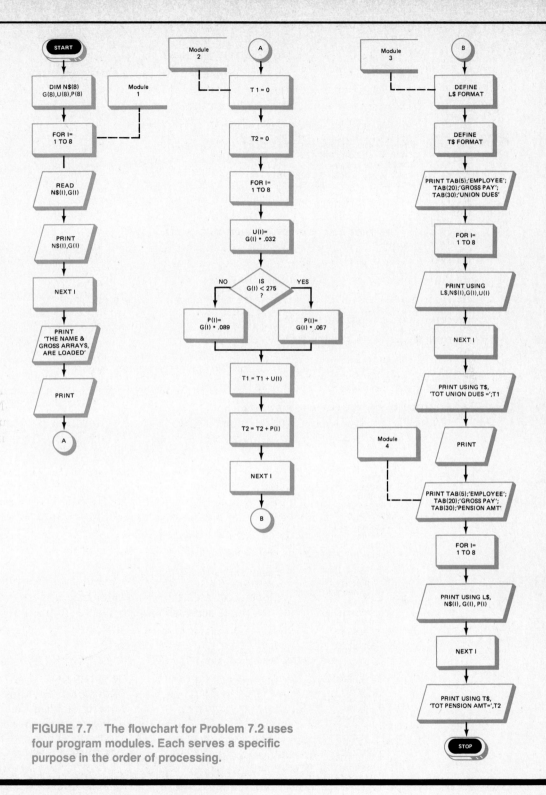

FIGURE 7.7   The flowchart for Problem 7.2 uses four program modules. Each serves a specific purpose in the order of processing.

```
10 DIM N$(8),G(8),U(8),P(8)
20 REM -- MODULE 1
30 FOR I = 1 TO 8
40 READ N$(I),G(I)
50 PRINT N$(I),G(I)
60 NEXT I
70 PRINT 'THE NAME & GROSS ARRAYS ARE LOADED'
80 PRINT
200 DATA 'DUNPHY',489.60,'GRANITO',673.89
210 DATA 'CLARK',163.27,'CHOMISCZ',273.65
220 DATA 'DONOFRIO',760.04,'TESSAR',327.82
230 DATA 'CONLON',224.36,'RECTOR',517.44
300 REM -- MODULE 2
310 T1 = 0
320 T2 = 0
330 FOR I = 1 TO 8
340 U(I) = G(I) * .032
350 IF G(I) < 275 THEN P(I) = G(I)*.067 ELSE P(I) = G(I)*.089
360 T1 = T1 + U(I)
370 T2 = T2 + P(I)
380 NEXT I
400 REM -- MODULE 3
410 L$ = '      \            \    ####.##  ####.##'
420 T$ = '      \            \             \  ####.##'
430 PRINT TAB(5);'EMPLOYEE';TAB(20);'GROSS PAY';TAB(30);'UNION DUES'
440 FOR I = 1 TO 8
450 PRINT USING L$,N$(I),G(I),U(I)
460 NEXT I
470 PRINT USING T$,'TOT UNION DUES =',T1
480 PRINT
500 REM -- MODULE 4
510 PRINT TAB(5);'EMPLOYEE';TAB(20);'GROSS PAY';TAB(30);'PENSION AMT'
520 FOR I = 1 TO 8
530 PRINT USING L$,N$(I),G(I),P(I)
540 NEXT I
550 PRINT USING T$,'TOT PENSION AMT =',T2
600 END
```

```
DUNPHY         489.6
GRANITO        673.89
CLARK          163.27
CHOMISCZ       273.65
DONOFRIO       760.04
TESSAR         327.82
CONLON         224.36
RECTOR         517.44
THE NAME & GROSS ARRAYS ARE LOADED

        EMPLOYEE       GROSS PAY UNION DUES
        DUNPHY           489.60    15.67
        GRANITO          673.89    21.56
        CLARK            163.27     5.22
        CHOMISCZ         273.65     8.76
        DONOFRIO         760.04    24.32
        TESSAR           327.82    10.49
        CONLON           224.36     7.18
        RECTOR           517.44    16.56
              TOT UNION DUES =    109.76

        EMPLOYEE       GROSS PAY PENSION AMT
        DUNPHY           489.60    43.57
        GRANITO          673.89    59.98
        CLARK            163.27    10.94
        CHOMISCZ         273.65    18.33
        DONOFRIO         760.04    67.64
        TESSAR           327.82    29.18
        CONLON           224.36    15.03
        RECTOR           517.44    46.05
            TOT PENSION AMT =    290.73
```

FIGURE 7.8 *(a)* Program and *(b)* output for Problem 7.2. The program adheres to the logic depicted in its flowchart, Figure 7.7.

lines 200 to 230. By doubling up each statement, it was possible to use only four DATA statements. Essentially, we have a data module in which all data items are found.

Module 2 commences at line 300 with its identifying REM statement. The initialization of the accumulators T1 and T2 occurs at lines 310 and 320, which precede the FOR statement of this module's looping sequence. Within these eight loops, the union dues and pension benefits are computed at lines 340 and 350. Note that in both computations, the subscripted variable G(I) provides access to the individual gross amounts. Subscripted variables are used like any other variables in computations.

The same is true for IF/THEN/ELSE statements where they are employed in conditional testing. At line 350, G(I) is tested against 275 and then involved in the computation of P(I), the individual pension benefits. The use of subscripted variables continues at lines 360 and 370, where U(I) and P(I) are posted against their respective accumulators to update T1 and T2. The looping sequence is framed at line 380, a NEXT statement.

One of the initial activities performed in module 3 is to establish the line formats used in both output modules. The L$ line format parallels the column headings, specifying the edited formats and spacing necessary to output both pension and union dues amounts. By planning the L$ format, we were able to use it in both output modules. The T$ format was constructed according to a similar rationale. It allocates space for the special labels preceding both accumulated totals and the editing of both quantities.

The actual output of the union dues report begins with line 430. A PRINT statement using TAB functions aligns each column heading and defines three columns of output. The only statement in the FOR/NEXT loop is the PRINT USING instruction, line 450. Note that subscripted variables provide access to data stored in each array cell and enable their output. The FOR/NEXT statement, lines 440 to 460, also illustrates that a series of outputs may be controlled via a looping sequence.

The output of the eighth cell's union dues marks the loop's close. Line 470 outputs the accumulated total T1, using the label TOT UNION DUES =. The T$ format was designed to position the T1 amount beneath the union dues column. A blank line separates the close of the union dues report and the pension report.

Once defined, the L$ and T$ formats are available to all output statements that wish to use them and fit their format. As such, it is not necessary to redefine them in the fourth module. The second report's heading is provided via line 510; note that the last column is entitled PENSION AMT. The alignment of variables is similar to that of the previous report.

Again, an eight-loop FOR/NEXT sequence is invoked to control the printing of pension data. The PRINT USING instruction employs the L$ format to output the contents of N$(I), G(I), and P(I). Each employee's pension data is printed out via line 530. The accumulated total T2 is printed beneath these eight lines and aligned with the pension column's output. The T$ format of line 550 provides for the positioning of the special label and T2 total. The output for Problem 7.2 is shown in Figure 7.8(b).

**Program
Organization
with GOSUBs**

In the two previous programs we organized our solutions into modules constructed around FOR/NEXT looping sequences. GOSUB statements provide another vehicle for organizing modules. Using GOSUB statements, we can divide a solution into a main program and its supporting submodules, each module supporting a specific operational task.

These principles were applied to Problem 7.2; the revised program is detailed in Figure 7.9. The major difference in the revised solution is the specification of a main program and the shifting of the first module. Other than these changes and the insertion of RETURN statements in each GOSUB module, the solution is identical and produces the same results.

The use of GOSUB statements made it simpler to construct program modules. Four GOSUB modules were used. The GOSUB 100 loads the arrays. The GOSUB 300 computes pension benefits and union dues. GOSUBs 400 and 500 report dues and pension information.

To reinforce the use of GOSUB modules when working with arrays, we will present another sample problem. For variety, we will use an INPUT statement and demonstrate the extraction of data from a larger array into a smaller one.

PROBLEM 7.3   Finding Average and Above-Average Values

The problem entails the computation of an average value and the identification and output of each above-average value. An INPUT statement is used, as the quantity and type of data varies. The maximum number of values used in any example cannot exceed 50, so all arrays must accommodate that quantity of data. Data is loaded within an opening GOSUB module. All modules are created via GOSUBs to form a structured solution. An error-checking feature should be used.

Module 2 involves the computation of the average of all values held within the array. This average should carry the label AVG VALUE = when output.

Module 3 involves two processing activities. The first task is to identify all array values that are greater than the average computed in module 2. Each time an above-average value is found an accumulator is increased by 1. In addition, a copy of each above-average value is stored in a second array for subsequent output.

Module 4 serves an output function. Initially, it will output the number of above-average values with an appropriate label. Beneath that line, the program will list each above-average value. These values are drawn from the second array that was specifically established for that purpose. The data is as follows:

46.89	37.12	73.62	93.57	89.02	49.55
14.06	43.10	28.04	59.98	62.77	56.31

As the nature of this problem is very similar to Problem 7.1, we will refrain from detailing all aspects of the solution. Instead we will focus on the

```
10 DIM N$(8),G(8),D(8),P(8)
20 REM MAIN PROGRAM, REVISED PROB 7.2
30 GOSUB 100
40 GOSUB 300
50 GOSUB 400
60 GOSUB 500
70 GO TO 600
100 REM --- MODULE 1
110 FOR I = 1 TO 8
120 READ N$(I),G(I)
130 PRINT N$(I),G(I)
140 NEXT I
150 PRINT 'THE NAME & GROSS ARRAYS ARE LOADED'
160 PRINT
170 RETURN
200 DATA 'DUNPHY',489.60,'GRANITO',673.89
210 DATA 'CLARK',163.27,'CHOMISCZ',273.65
220 DATA 'DONOFRIO',760.04,'TESSAR',327.82
230 DATA 'CONLON',224.36,'RECTOR',517.44
300 REM --- MODULE 2
310 T1 = 0
320 T2 = 0
330 FOR I = 1 TO 8
340 U(I) = G(I) * .032
350 IF G(I) < 275 THEN P(I) = G(I)*.067 ELSE P(I) = G(I)*.089
360 T1 = T1 + U(I)
370 T2 = T2 + P(I)
380 NEXT I
390 RETURN
400 REM --- MODULE 3
410 L$ = '        \              \  ####.##   ####.##'
420 T$ = '        \              \              ####.##'
430 PRINT TAB(5);'EMPLOYEE';TAB(20);'GROSS PAY';TAB(30);'UNION DUES'
440 FOR I = 1 TO 8
450 PRINT USING L$,N$(I),G(I),U(I)
460 NEXT I
470 PRINT USING T$,'TOT UNION DUES =',T1
480 PRINT
490 RETURN
500 REM --- MODULE 4
510 PRINT TAB(5);'EMPLOYEE';TAB(20);'GROSS PAY';TAB(30);'PENSION AMT'
520 FOR I = 1 TO 8
530 PRINT USING L$,N$(I),G(I),P(I)
540 NEXT I
550 PRINT USING T$,'TOT PENSION AMT =',T2
560 RETURN
600 END
```

FIGURE 7.9 The revised solution for Problem 7.2 using four GOSUB statements.

structural aspect of the problem and special features built into its solution. Figure 7.10 illustrates the flow diagrams and logical structure of this solution.

The difficulty in this problem relates to the unknown quantity of data to be input. It is not possible to fix the array size or the number of loops in each FOR/NEXT statement. Each time this program is run, a different quantity of data is involved, so we must devise a way to handle both the variable nature of

FIGURE 7.10   The hierarchical flowcharts prepared for Problem 7.3. The *(a)* diagram defines the relationship between all modules, with the respective flow diagrams appearing in *(b)*.

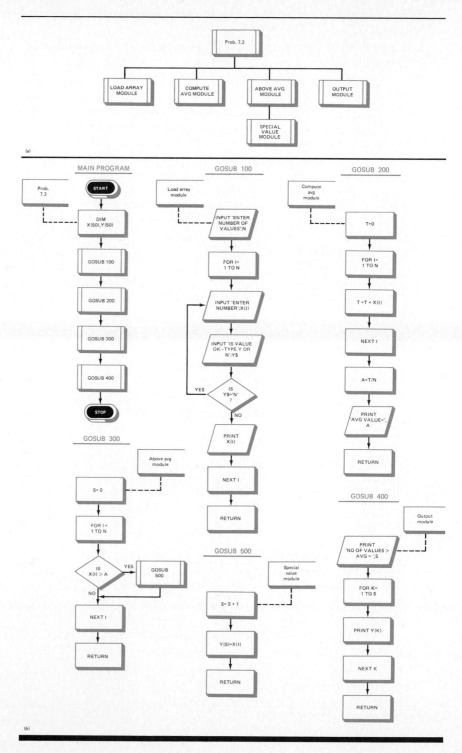

our data requirements and the required loop sequences in which array data is manipulated.

The overall structure of the main program indicates a series of five GOSUB modules, following the definition of two arrays. The X array is the array in which input data is originally retained. The Y array will hold all values deemed to be above average. Both arrays consist of 50 cells, the maximum number of items which can be involved in processing. Establishing each array at that size ensures their correct use throughout processing. Though not every cell may be used in processing, all 50 are available if they be desired.

The technique used to accommodate varying amounts of data is demonstrated via GOSUB 100, the initial program module. The first operation of that module is the input of N, the variable representing the number of data items to be processed. Before undertaking any processing, the user must collect the data to be used and count the number of values. That sum is referenced via N and defines the number of data items to undergo processing.

The N variable may range from 1 to 50, in line with the program's original design. A sufficient number of array cells exists to handle up to 50 data items. The vehicle for loading arrays is the FOR/NEXT sequence that follows the opening INPUT statement.

To understand the impact (and usefulness) of inputting N, we must carefully examine the opening FOR statement. It is designed to commence looping at a value of I = 1 and proceed to a closing value of N. In defining the FOR/NEXT structure, we substituted the variable N for a closing value. Thus, the number of loops executed relates directly to the value of N input. That, in turn, defines the number of values undergoing processing. If the N value is correct, the program will loop N times and enable the input of exactly N data items.

Once the looping commences, each X(I) value is inputted and stored in its respective cell. A second, prompting INPUT statement is used to verify the accuracy of each item input. The recognition of an invalid data item enables the user to rekey that data item without advancing the loop counter. If the data input is correct, the X(I) data is printed and the loop continues. The completion of the N loop completes the FOR/NEXT sequence and closes module 1.

The compute-average module, GOSUB 200, parallels the logic of previous solutions. An accumulator T is used to total X(I), with that total used to compute the average of all values entered. Again, the FOR/NEXT sequence loops N times and N is divided into T to produce the computed average A.

The GOSUB 300 module, module 3, encompasses a looping sequence of N times and offers access to the GOSUB 500 module. Module 3 opens with the initialization of S, which is used to sum up the number of values which are determined to be greater than the average. The looping sequence repeats the required N loops, permitting every item in the X(I) array to be compared against A. If the X(I) value is less than or equal to A, no processing is undertaken and the loop continues. If, however, X(I) is greater than A, then the GOSUB 500 module is accessed.

This module consists of only three tasks. Upon recognition of an above-average X(I) value, the S accumulator is increased by 1. This update precedes the storage of the X(I) value into the Y(S) array.

The use of the S and I subscripts is required, as each array possesses a different sequencing mechanism. If, for example, the first above-average value is found at X(4), we want to store that value at S(1), *not* at S(4). In the GOSUB 500 module, S is updated from 0 to 1, and the X(4) value stored at S(1). When the second above-average value is found, S is updated to 2, and that value is stored at S(2). The N loop permits the program to access every X array value, with S monitoring the storage of values in the Y array.

When the GOSUB 300 module has looped N times, each array cell will have been tested, and those selected stored in the Y array. The exact number of above-average values is recorded by S, whose value is used in the GOSUB 400 module.

The first action in this last module is the output of S with the label NO OF VALUES > AVG =. A FOR/NEXT sequence is then initiated, with the number of loops defined by S. Since only S values were stored in the Y array, only S loops are needed to output them. The loop variable K ranges from 1 to S, and serves as the subscript to access each Y(K) value. Exactly S loops are executed, with exactly S array values printed. The completion of this module closes the program.

One of the questions often asked about this type of problem is, What happens to the unused array cells? The answer is nothing; they remain unused. It is perfectly acceptable to define an array which is larger than necessary and leave some cells unused. However, an error will result if the number of data items exceeds the number of array cells. When INPUT statements are incorporated into a solution, the program will often specify arrays larger than desired to avoid any potential errors.

The program for Problem 7.3 is shown in Figure 7.11(a). The program's structure closely follows its flowchart logic, in that each module is carefully constructed to handle a specific activity. The DIM statement, line 10, opens the program and defines two numeric arrays of 50 cells each. The X array holds input data, whereas the Y array will retain all values greater than the computed average. GOSUB statements define access to the four modules which compose the main program. An unconditional branch to line 600 results in the program's close.

The program's capacity to handle a varying amount of data, up to a maximum of 50 data items, is evident at the start of the GOSUB 100 module. This module opens with an INPUT statement that requests the entry of the number of data items slated to undergo processing. The input of N is critical, as many loops are geared to that value. This is immediately apparent at line 120, where a FOR statement is defined to run from 1 to N.

The entry of each data item into X(I) is accomplished via the statements 130 to 150. The prompting INPUT statement at line 130 accepts and loads the value into X(I). Statements 140 and 150 permit the user to catch a miskeyed value and input a corrected one. The loop counter is not incre-

(a)

```
10 DIM X(50),Y(50)
20 REM PROB 7.3
30 GOSUB 100
40 GOSUB 200
50 GOSUB 300
60 GOSUB 400
70 GO TO 600
100 REM --- LOAD ARRAY MODULE
110 INPUT 'ENTER NUMBER OF VALUES';N
120 FOR I = 1 TO N
130 INPUT 'ENTER NUMBER';X(I)
140 INPUT 'IS VALUE OK - TYPE Y OR N';Y$
150 IF Y$ = 'N' THEN 130
160 PRINT X(I)
170 NEXT I
180 RETURN
200 REM -- COMPUTE AVG MODULE
210 T = 0
220 FOR I = 1 TO N
230 T = T + X(I)
240 NEXT I
250 A = T/N
260 PRINT 'AVG VALUE =',A
270 RETURN
300 REM -- ABOVE AVG MODULE
310 S = 0
320 FOR I = 1 TO N
330 IF X(I) > A THEN GOSUB 500
340 NEXT I
350 RETURN
400 REM -- OUTPUT MODULE
410 PRINT 'NO OF VALUES > AVG =',S
420 FOR K = 1 TO S
430 PRINT Y(K)
440 NEXT K
450 RETURN
500 REM --- SPECIAL VALUE MODULE
510 S = S + 1
520 Y(S) = X(I)
530 RETURN
600 END
```

(b)

```
ENTER NUMBER OF VALUES? 12
ENTER NUMBER? 46.89
IS VALUE OK - TYPE Y OR N? Y
 46.89
ENTER NUMBER? 93.57
IS VALUE OK - TYPE Y OR N? Y
 93.57
ENTER NUMBER? 14.06
IS VALUE OK - TYPE Y OR N? Y
 14.06
ENTER NUMBER? 59.98
IS VALUE OK - TYPE Y OR N? Y
 59.98
ENTER NUMBER? 37.12
IS VALUE OK - TYPE Y OR N? Y
 37.12
ENTER NUMBER? 89.02
IS VALUE OK - TYPE Y OR N? Y
 89.02
ENTER NUMBER? 43.10
IS VALUE OK - TYPE Y OR N? Y
 43.1
ENTER NUMBER? 62.77
IS VALUE OK - TYPE Y OR N? Y
 62.77
ENTER NUMBER? 73.62
IS VALUE OK - TYPE Y OR N? Y
 73.62
ENTER NUMBER? 49.55
IS VALUE OK - TYPE Y OR N? Y
 49.55
ENTER NUMBER? 28.04
IS VALUE OK - TYPE Y OR N? Y
 28.04
ENTER NUMBER? 56.31
IS VALUE OK - TYPE Y OR N? Y
 56.31
AVG VALUE =      54.5025
NO OF VALUES > AVG =           6
 93.57
 59.98
 89.02
 62.77
 73.62
 56.31
```

FIGURE 7.11 *(a)* Program and *(b)* output for Problem 7.3, demonstrating the modularity of its solution. During its execution the program passes from one module to another.

mented, as the IF/THEN statement causes the program to flow back to line 130 where the data is entered into the same cell. This corrective procedure may be repeated for a single cell until the correct data item is input.

The correctly entered value is output via line 160, providing the user with an opportunity to verify its storage within the X array. The NEXT I statement, line 170, frames this initial loop and marks the point at which the looping sequence is exited when N loops are completed. The RETURN statement forces the program flow back to the main program and anticipates access to the second GOSUB module.

The specific purpose of the second module, statements 200 to 270, is the computation of an average. An accumulator T is needed to total each X(I) value, line 230. The variable N is also an integral part of the average formula, line 250. By using N and not a constant (for example, 27 or 6), the program offers flexibility to its users. The value input for N provides a basis for all computations. Before the close of the GOSUB 200 module, the average A is printed with a supporting label at line 260.

The computed average is critical to the third module. It is within this GOSUB module that the number of X(I) values exceeding the average is determined and moved to the Y array. A second accumulator, a program module, and looping sequence are integral components of the GOSUB 300 module.

The second accumulator, S, serves to add up the number of above-average values and acts as the subscript for the Y(S) array. To observe its function, we must examine the GOSUB 500 module accessed by line 330. If the value stored in X(I) is greater than A, the GOSUB 500 is accessed. In successive operations, the S value is updated by 1, line 510, and the X(I) value is stored in Y(S), line 520. When the first above-average X(I) value is found, the S value goes from 0 to 1 and the value is stored within Y(1). When the second value is uncovered, S becomes 2 and that value is stored in Y(2). The process continues as each X(I) value is determined to be greater than A.

The subtlety of using S is often lost on some readers. The S variable enables the program to sequentially access each cell in the Y array without leaving any gaps. When S is 1, the first Y cell is used. When S becomes 2, the Y(2) cell is accessed. S is incremented before the Y(S) cell is loaded. When the N looping sequence is completed, S will define the number of above-average values uncovered by the third module. The S value defines the number of Y(S) cells loaded and must be output in module 4.

The GOSUB 400 module outputs the number of above-average values, line 410, and the contents of the Y(S) array, line 430. The FOR/NEXT statement loops exactly S times, as that is how many values are held in the Y array. The structure of line 420 parallels our use of the N variable in previous FOR/NEXT statements. It should be obvious that we cannot loop through the Y array N times. Not every value can be above average and be stored in the Y array. As S has counted every value entering the Y array, that number of loops is sufficient to properly access each above-average value. The listing of those values identifies each number determined to be above average and permits the user to check the results of processing.

The output for Problem 7.3 is shown in Figure 7.11(b). A total of 12 values were employed in processing. An average of 54.5025 was computed, and 6 values were determined to be above average. The highest number of values input, 12, represents the user's response to the number of values to undergo processing. The lines that follow denote each of the 12 input values and user verification. By expanding the array size, users may utilize the program for larger quantities of data.

7.4 Subscript Manipulations

In our previous examples the I/O activities were handled in FOR/NEXT controlled loops, one variable at a time. For example, 16 values were input on an individual basis in 16 loops, or 8 values were printed on individual lines in 8 loops.

Though these techniques are effective, often the need arises to input or print multiple values concurrently. Our dependence on the FOR/NEXT loop is contingent on the orderly use of its loop variable as a subscript. The conventional use of the FOR/NEXT statement presents some difficulties when dealing with I/O activities involving multiple variables. A method must be found to access two or more subscripted variables sequentially without confusing the looping sequences or the subscripts.

The key to successfully handling multiple subscripted variables lies in the manipulation of the subscripts. To date, we have expressed our subscripts without alteration. It is possible, however, to manipulate subscripts and benefit from these actions.

Subscript handling may involve arithmetic manipulations. The majority of subscript manipulations involve the addition or subtraction of subscripts to access specific array cells. Subscript manipulations involve FOR/NEXT statements with STEP options.

Inputting Multiple Variables

Figure 7.12 shows the impact of array manipulations on multiple data entries. In Figure 7.12(a) an array of 12 cells is loaded, one value at a time. A FOR/NEXT loop performs 12 loops, and one value is loaded into the X(K) cell on each loop. The K subscript reflects the use of K as the loop variable, as defined in line 20.

By comparison, examine the program excerpt of Figure 7.12(b). A FOR/NEXT sequence using the K variable is again defined, but a STEP 2 option is added. Instead of executing 12 loops, this revised FOR/NEXT statement results in 6 loops, where K assumes the values of 1, 3, 5, 7, 9, and 11. A second change is evident: two subscripted variables are used, X(K) and X(K + 1). Where one variable was previously used, now two exist. Instead of handling one variable per loop, the program can now handle two.

The relationship between the FOR/NEXT sequence and the subscripted variables is vital and must be properly understood. On each loop, two array cells are accessed until all 12 cells are loaded. When K equals 1, cells X(1) and

(a)	(b)

```
10 DIM X(12)              10 DIM X(12)
20 FOR K = 1 TO 12        20 FOR K = 1 TO 12 STEP 2
30 READ X(K)              30 READ X(K),X(K+1)
40 PRINT X(K)             40 PRINT X(K),X(K+1)
50 NEXT K                 50 NEXT K
60 DATA -7,9,31,4,6,17    60 DATA -7,9,31,4,6,17
70 DATA 8,-5,-12,13,26,5  70 DATA 8,-5,-12,13,26,5
```

FIGURE 7.12 It is possible to enter more than one data item into an array by manipulating the subscripts of the variables involved. Figure *(a)* notes the input of single data items. Figure *(b)* provides instructions for the entry of two data items per loop.

$X(2)$ are filled with the data items -7 and 9. The subscripted variable $X(K)$ used the current value of K without modification. The $X(K + 1)$ cell manipulated its subscript by adding 1 to the current value of K resulting in $X(2)$. The output of both $X(1)$ and $X(2)$ resulted from line 40 before the next loop began.

On the next loop, because of the STEP 2 option, K assumes a value of 3. The data items of 31 and 4 are read into cells $X(3)$ and $X(4)$ as the subscripts of K and $K + 1$ are invoked. Similarly, on the next loop when K equals 5, the cells of $X(5)$ and $X(6)$ are accessed and their contents filled with 6 and 17. A total of 6 loops are completed, with K assuming a value of 11 on the last loop and the cells $X(11)$ and $X(12)$ respectively loaded with 26 and 5. Instead of loading 1 cell in 12 loops, we loaded 2 cells in 6 loops, the net effect being the accurate entry of 12 cells worth of data.

In both cases the $X(12)$ array is properly loaded with data, but the second method speeds the process by handling two values at a time. The key element is the manipulation of the subscripts specified with each input variable.

The manipulation of subscripts is also permissible with INPUT statements, when the online entry of data is desirable. The program excerpt in Figure 7.13 illustrates the entry of data into the same 12-cell array. Two changes are evident: the use of an INPUT statement and the entry of three items at a time.

FIGURE 7.13 The interactive entry of array data may also implement subscript manipulations to handle multiple data items. Here, three subscripted variables are input per loop.

```
10 DIM X(12)
20 FOR K = 1 TO 12 STEP 3
30 INPUT X(K),X(K+1),X(K+2)
40 PRINT X(K),X(K+1),X(K+2)
50 NEXT K
```

The same X(12) array is defined by the DIM statement, line 10. However, changes result from the desire to concurrently input three variables. The FOR/NEXT statement carries a STEP 3 option, and three subscripted variables are specified in both the INPUT and PRINT statements. The loop variable K assumes the values of 1, 4, 7, and 10 when executing exactly four loops.

On the first loop, when K equals 1, the cells X(1), X(2), and X(3) are loaded with three data items. These cells are defined by the variables X(K), X(K + 1), and X(K + 2). The current value of K is substituted in each subscript, resulting in the use of the first three array cells. On the second loop, when K equals 4, the next three cells are loaded. In this case, the cells X(4), X(5), and X(6) were defined from the use of X(K), X(K + 1), and X(K + 2).

The remaining two loops generate K values of 7 and 10 and result in the loading of data into cells X(7) to X(12). This processing sequence results in the loading of 12 cells, with 3 cells being loaded on 4 loops. Users are free to use any processing approach they desire or require.

SIDE BAR 7.3   Correct Array Multiples

The ability to enter multiple data items into arrays in a FOR/NEXT sequence is extremely helpful. The STEP option ensures that the subscripts are correctly spaced and that all array cells are accessed the proper number of times.

Frequently, when planning I/O operations using arrays, a mistake is made. The size of the array is not coordinated with the STEP option of the FOR statement. Thus, some array cells are accessed twice, while some remain unaffected.

Consider the loading of data into an array defined as X(20). It is possible to load data into this array two, four, or five items at a time, since each amount can divide into 20 without leaving a remainder. Any of the following FOR statements could be successfully used.

```
20      FOR I = 1 TO 20 STEP 2
20      FOR I = 1 TO 20 STEP 4
20      FOR I = 1 TO 20 STEP 5
```

However, the following FOR statement would be inappropriate.

```
20      FOR I = 1 TO 20 STEP 3          (Wrong)
```

As 20 is not divisible by 3, an exact number of loops cannot be coordinated with the number of array cells and subscripted variables.

Tabular Outputs

The output of data from a one-dimensional array is often lengthy when single data items are printed on a line-by-line basis. By applying techniques similar to those used when inputting multiple subscripted variables, we are able to print data in a tabular format. That data appears within a table composed of columns and rows.

```
100 FOR I = 1 TO 15 STEP 3
110 PRINT X(I),X(I+1),X(I+2)
120 NEXT I
```

FIGURE 7.14   Subscript manipulations make possible the tabular output of data held in arrays. The excerpt shown produces a table of five lines, with three values per line.

To accomplish this feat, it is only necessary to reuse a FOR/NEXT statement with STEP option and variables whose subscripts have been properly altered. For example, consider the output of data from a 15-cell array where the user wants to have 5 rows of output with 3 data items per row. Statements capable of generating this type of 5-line output are provided in Figure 7.14.

The program excerpt shown consists of three statements, lines 100 to 120. The FOR/NEXT sequence shows that I ranges from 1 to 15 with an increment of 3. The PRINT statement, line 110, incorporates three subscripted variables to output three numbers per line. In evaluating the looping sequence, we note that when I equals 1, the data drawn from the cells $X(1)$, $X(2)$, and $X(3)$ are printed. These data items were defined by the variables $X(I), X(I + 1)$, and $X(I + 2)$. The subscripts were manipulated through addition to produce the desired output and access the correct array cells.

A total of five loops will result from the indicated FOR/NEXT statement. On loop 1, as we have discussed, cells 1, 2, and 3 are output. On loop 2, the 4, 5, and 6 cell values are printed. In the third loop, when I equals 7, the cells 7, 8, and 9 are displayed. The last two loops will respectively output cells 10, 11, and 12 and 13, 14, and 15 before exiting that five-loop sequence. Another sample program will reinforce concepts related to subscript manipulations.

PROBLEM 7.4   Analysis of Target Scores

The problem entails the analysis of target scores. The 20 values should be entered into an array of 20 cells, 2 at a time. An initial module should be used to load and print these values.

A second module serves to accumulate the number of scores falling above or below a target score of 170. Two accumulators are needed to add scores less than 170 and scores greater than or equal to 170.

The third phase of processing involves outputting the results of processing and the original 20 scores in a tabular format. Print the headings COL1, COL2, COL3, and COL4. Each column is separated by two spaces. Beneath the headings is a blank line followed by the output of five lines, with four scores printed per line. A second blank line precedes the output of the two accumulated totals and the labels ABOVE 170 SCORES = and BELOW 170 SCORES =. The data is as follows:

No	Score	No	Score	No	Score	No	Score
1	170	6	171	11	163	16	161
2	189	7	167	12	156	17	177
3	162	8	178	13	140	18	157
4	144	9	169	14	183	19	182
5	193	10	201	15	185	20	190

These are the main points in the problem narrative.

1   The problem is divided into three processing modules. Module 1 loads the data, module 2 performs processing, and module 3 serves output activities.

2   A total of 20 data items are input to the array, two at a time. These values are loaded and outputted. A numeric array of 20 cells is defined.

3   Each value is tested against a score of 170. Two accumulators will separately total the number of values less than 170 and those values greater than or equal to 170. All 20 values must be tested.

4   When outputting data in module 3, employ a tabular format. A four-part column heading is placed at the top of the report, using the indicated literals. Five lines of output consist of four data items each. Two summary totals note the number of values in either category, using the indicated labels.

The flowchart prepared for Problem 7.4 is shown in Figure 7.15. The modular structure of our flowchart solution groups related activities and helps focus the processing performed within each module. The first task performed is the definition of the N array consisting of 20 cells. A FOR/NEXT controlled loop monitors the loading of the N array, which consists of the input and output of the array data. This opening looping sequence executes 10 loops, with 2 values read per loop. Two subscripted variables handle the I/O activities required by that opening loop.

The second phase of processing opens with the initialization of two accumulators, T1 and T2. The T1 accumulator will total all N(I) values that are less than the 170 test score, with T2 counting all other scores. The actual comparison of N(I) against 170 occurs within a 20-loop cycle. The 20 loops are necessary to permit the individual testing of each value. The result of each logical test will update either the T1 or T2 accumulator by 1.

The third and last module outputs the results of processing using a tabular format. The required four-column heading is defined as one large literal, as it is easily accomplished in one PRINT statement. The L$ format was created to match that heading. The blank line separates headings from the first line of data.

The output of four array values per line is accomplished with a FOR/NEXT loop, in increments of 4. Exactly five loops are executed with four subscripted variables output per line. The manipulation of subscripts permits the output of each array value in coordination with the looping sequence. A

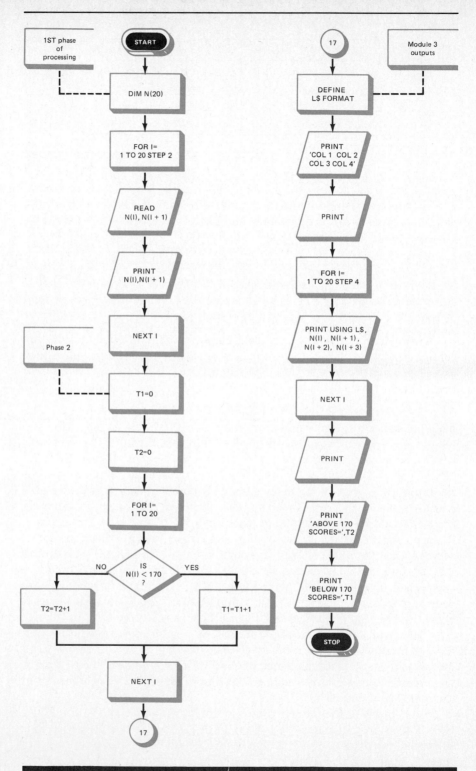

FIGURE 7.15 The
flowchart for Problem
7.4.

second blank line separates the output of the two accumulated totals from the tabular listing of the 20-N array values.

The program written from this flowchart, Figure 7.16*(b)*, is a direct development of its logic. We have chosen to present the solution in a modular fashion, without use of GOSUB modules. As each module flows into the next, the logical flow is fairly self-evident. The program opens with a DIM statement which defines the N(20) array before the first module's activities.

The FOR statement, line 30, establishes a loop, with I going from 1 to 20 at increments of 2. This statement reflects the input of two data items per loop, accessed by the subscripted variables of N(I) and N(I + 1). A similar format is applied to the PRINT statement, line 50, where the contents of each cell are outputted. The loop closes at line 60, a NEXT I statement. The DATA statements, lines 70 and 80, reflect the 20 scores involved in processing.

The second module of processing begins at line 100. The initialization of T1 and T2 occurs before the second loop begins at line 130. The FOR instruction specifies a 20-loop sequence, with each value tested against 170. The actual comparison of N(I) < 170 occurs at line 140. If N(I) < 170, the T1 accumulator is updated; otherwise, T2 is increased by 1. No outputs are undertaken in this loop, as those tasks are assigned to module 3.

The output module consists of lines 200 to 290 and supplies a heading line, a tabular format for the 20 data items, and two summary lines. The

FIGURE 7.16   *(a)* Program and *(b)* output generated by Problem 7.4.

(a)

```
10 DIM N(20)
20 REM -- 1ST PHASE OF PROCESSING
30 FOR I = 1 TO 20 STEP 2
40 READ N(I),N(I+1)
50 PRINT N(I),N(I+1)
60 NEXT I
70 DATA 170,189,162,144,193,171,167,178,169,201
80 DATA 163,156,190,183,185,161,177,157,182,190
100 REM -- PHASE 2
110 T1 = 0
120 T2 = 0
130 FOR I = 1 TO 20
140 IF N(I) < 170 THEN T1 = T1 + 1 ELSE T2 = T2 + 1
150 NEXT I
200 REM -- MODULE 3 OUTPUTS
210 L$ = '###    ###    ###    ###'
220 PRINT 'COL1   COL2   COL3   COL4'
230 PRINT
240 FOR I = 1 TO 20 STEP 4
250 PRINT USING L$, N(I), N(I+1), N(I+2), N(I+3)
260 NEXT I
270 PRINT
280 PRINT 'ABOVE 170 SCORES =',T2
290 PRINT 'BELOW 170 SCORES =',T1
300 END
```

(b)

170		189	
162		144	
193		171	
167		178	
169		201	
163		156	
190		183	
185		161	
177		157	
182		190	

COL1	COL2	COL3	COL4
170	189	162	144
193	171	167	178
169	201	163	156
190	183	185	161
177	157	182	190

ABOVE 170 SCORES =	12
BELOW 170 SCORES =	8

definition of the L$ format, line 210, is aligned with the column headings in line 220. A long literal was used in the PRINT statement, as it was simpler to format than TAB functions. The blank PRINT statements at lines 230 and 270 serves to bracket the table of 20 values.

The tabular output of five lines, four data items per line, is controlled by the FOR/NEXT statements of lines 240 to 260. The FOR instruction denotes that I will assume values of 1 to 20, but in *steps* of 4. The desired output of four variables per line is accomplished at line 250, where a PRINT USING statement applies the L$ format to four subscripted variables. The output will have four data items per line on five separate lines.

The last two lines of output, the accumulated totals of T1 and T2, are initiated via lines 280 and 290. Each total is printed on a separate line, preceded by its label. Users may verify the accuracy of processing by scanning the output of Figure 7.16(b).

7.5 Specialized Statements

With arrays we can undertake more difficult problems, as we can retain and access array data for repeated processing. Users undertaking complex solutions may find it necessary to perform special tasks to fully process their data. These tasks may include taking a square root or determining the absolute value of an expression. As these tasks are fairly common, many computer manufacturers have incorporated these features into their versions of BASIC. The user need only specify a code and that special feature is made available.

Predefined Functions

Predefined functions are manufacturer-supplied programs that generally fill a common processing need. Two common predefined functions are:

1 Square root, or SQR, function

2 Absolute value, or ABS, function

The **SQR function** enables the user to take the square root of a value that results from processing. The function makes it possible to obtain a square root without lengthy computation. Specification of the SQR code directs the computer to access the prewritten program necessary to take the square root of a number. Thus, using the SQR function, we may determine that the square root of 9 is 3.

The SQR function is generally written as follows:

```
60      Y = SQR(X)
```

In this example, 60 is the line number, Y the resulting variable, SQR the BASIC code name assigned to the square root function, and X the variable for which the square root is taken. Note that X is in parentheses. For subscripted variables, double parentheses are employed and the SQR function is written as follows:

    60   Y = SQR(A(I))

This computation will derive the square root of the number stored in A(I) and store the result in Y.

The predefined function often associated with the SQR function is the **ABS function.** The absolute value function derives the largest value of a number, in positive terms. Thus, −576 possesses an absolute value of 576, when that function is applied. The structure of the ABS instruction is written

    100   B = ABS(X)

In this example, 100 represents the line number, B the resulting variable, ABS the function code, and X the value for which the absolute value is taken. Again, note that X is in parentheses.

When used together, the ABS and SQR functions are generally written as follows:

    100   V = ABS(X)
    110   Z = SQR(V)

Line 100 derives the absolute value of X, ensuring that a negative value does not exist (as it is not possible to take a square root for a negative amount). Line 110 computes the square root of V and stores the result in Z. A sample program will illustrate the use of these functions with arrays.

PROBLEM 7.5 Pythagorean Theorem

The problem entails the computation of values using the Pythagorean theorem, of

$$C^2 = A^2 + B^2$$

In this formula, the variables A and B represent two sides of a right-angle triangle and C the hypotenuse (Figure 7.17).

In the first phase of processing, six sets of data are loaded into the A and B arrays. In the second program module, the C values related to each set of data are computed and stored within the C array.

The third module is solely for output. A heading of SIDE A, SIDE B, and SIDE C is required, commencing at print positions 1, 9, and 17. The editing applied to each result is ###.##. The data for this problem is as follows:

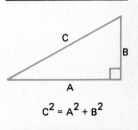

$$c^2 = A^2 + B^2$$

FIGURE 7.17 The Pythagorean theorem defines the relationship between the sum of the squares of the sides (A and B) of a right-angle triangle and its hypotenuse (C).

Triangle	Side A	Side B	Triangle	Side A	Side B
1	5.0	12.0	4	2.6	3.9
2	13.6	27.3	5	8.7	13.2
3	83.5	60.9	6	27.6	55.7

These are the main points in the problem narrative.

1 Three arrays are defined and used to hold the A, B, and C values. A total of six data items are used.

2 The first module loads the A and B arrays. Output all data items that are input.

3 In module 2, each C value is computed and stored within its array. These computations require the use of the ABS and SQR functions. No outputs are generated.

4 In the last module, a report format is established for the output of A, B, and C. Three column headings are outputted, with each A, B, and C printed beneath them. Each array value carries an edited format of ###.##.

The flowchart for Problem 7.5 (Figure 7.18) assumes a structured format divided into three modules. The three arrays related to processing are defined at the start of the main program. The first module loads only the A and B arrays with data, as the computation of C is performed in module 2.

Both of the first two modules are framed in FOR/NEXT sequences, each looping six times. Of interest in module 2 is the use of the ABS and SQR functions. The squaring and addition of A and B is temporarily assigned to the variable V1, whose absolute value is derived in the next processing step. This ensures that no negative number may be accessed by the SQR function that follows. The square root of V2 — a second dummy variable — is obtained, and the result is stored in C(K) array cell. All six values of C are computed in exactly this manner.

The third module prepares a report format in which all three variables are outputted. A three-column heading precedes the definition of the L$ format used by a PRINT USING statement. All three array values are outputted with a loop, causing each A(K), B(K), and C(K) value to appear on one line.

The program and output of Problem 7.5 are detailed in Figure 7.19. The main program consists of lines 20 to 60, with the DIM statement fixed at line 10. The DIM instruction creates A, B, and C arrays, consisting of six cells each. The succeeding three GOSUB statements direct the flow of processing to each of the program's three modules.

The initial module, GOSUB 100, frames the loading of the A and B arrays in a FOR/NEXT statement of six loops. The array variables A(K) and B(K) are operationally used to input and output data at lines 120 and 130.

A six-loop sequence is also used in the GOSUB 200 module, where each C(K) value is calculated. Here, dummy variables are used to simplify processing and enable the user to track the flow of events. Initially, at line 220 the variable V1 is used to record the sum and squaring of A(K) and B(K). For simplicity, we compute V1 first and then substitute it in line 230, where its absolute value was derived.

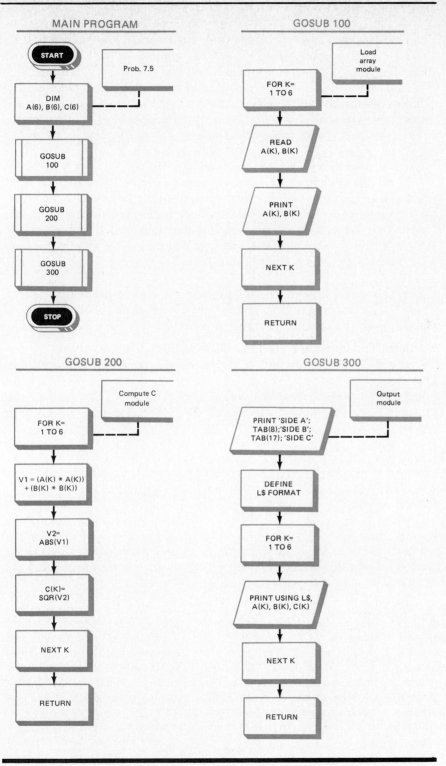

FIGURE 7.18 The modular flowchart for Problem 7.5.

The absolute value was recorded in V2 using exactly the same rationale. The SQR function was isolated in its own statement, line 240, where the V2 value substituted. The square root of V2 represents the triangle's third side and is stored at C(K). The process is repeated six times to facilitate the handling of each triangle's data.

Dummy variables are used by many programmers to simplify program instructions and syntax. Intermediate dummy variables also help monitor processing, as the variables may be outputted to determine whether the intermediate computations are being properly performed.

The third module again assumes an output role. After the output of column headings by means of TAB functions, each array value is outputted via a six-loop FOR/NEXT sequence. The definition of the L$ format, line 320, is sandwiched between these instructions and awaits its use with the PRINT USING statement, line 340. The resulting six lines of output are positioned beneath the column headings which are aligned at positions 1, 9, and 17.

In this solution, we choose to group our data near the program's end. These DATA statements, lines 400 to 420, hold all six sets of data. Line 60 of the main program causes it to branch around all following statements to line 500, the END statement, closing the program.

Chapter Summary

7.1 One-Dimensional Arrays

One-dimensional arrays retain data within a program and enable the repeated use of that data. An array consists of a series of storage cells, with each array cell identified by its own position.

Access to array cells requires the use of a subscripted-variable name. In the subscripted name X(5), the array name is X and the subscript is 5. The X(5) specifically designates the fifth cell in the X array. Array types are defined by the variable name specified. A numeric-variable name identifies a numeric array, whereas a string-variable name de-

notes an array retaining nonnumeric data.

Within BASIC programs, arrays are defined via DIM statements. The DIM statement defines each array by size and type. The following DIM statement defines a numeric array of 15 cells and a string-variable array of 20 cells, respectively.

    10   DIM H(15), M$(20)

The order in which the arrays are specified is not critical, as BASIC handles each separately. DIM statements *must* be written at a program's start.

7.2 Loading the Array

A separate series of instructions must be written to load data into an array. A common method of loading arrays involves FOR/NEXT statements.

The FOR/NEXT loop creates the framework within which an array is systematically loaded, from the first to the last cell. The input or computative statements are positioned within the FOR/NEXT loop, with the loop variable used as the subscript. As the loop variable ranges upward from 1 on each loop, each array cell is loaded with a data item. This technique is effectively used with READ

(a)

```
10 DIM A(6), B(6), C(6)
20 REM PROB 7.5
30 GOSUB 100
40 GOSUB 200
50 GOSUB 300
60 GO TO 500
100 REM -- LOAD ARRAY MODULE
110 FOR K = 1 TO 6
120 READ A(K), B(K)
130 PRINT A(K), B(K)
140 NEXT K
150 RETURN
200 REM -- COMPUTE C MODULE
210 FOR K = 1 TO 6
220 V1 = ( A(K) * A(K) ) + ( B(K) * B(K) )
230 V2 = ABS(V1)
240 C(K) = SQR(V2)
250 NEXT K
260 RETURN
300 REM -- OUTPUT MODULE
310 PRINT 'SIDE A';TAB(9);'SIDE B';TAB(17);'SIDE C'
320 L$ = '###.##  ###.##  ###.##'
330 FOR K = 1 TO 6
340 PRINT USING L$, A(K), B(K), C(K)
350 NEXT K
360 RETURN
400 DATA 5.0,12.0,13.6,27.3
410 DATA 83.5,60.9,2.6,3.9
420 DATA 8.7,13.2,27.6,55.7
500 END
```

produces the following output

(b)

```
5               12
13.6            27.3
83.5            60.9
2.6             3.9
8.7             13.2
27.6            55.7
SIDE A   SIDE B   SIDE C
  5.00    12.00    13.00
 13.60    27.30    30.50
 83.50    60.90   103.35
  2.60     3.90     4.69
  8.70    13.20    15.81
 27.60    55.70    62.16
```

FIGURE 7.19   Using GOSUB statements, we are able to convert the modular solution of Figure 7.18 to an actual program *(a).* **The resulting output is also shown** *(b).*

and INPUT statements or LET statements when the array data is derived from computations. When loading array cells it is common to output the contents of each cell. This output serves as a check on whether the array cell was correctly loaded.

Data in any array cell is available for use. Programs do not have to use READ statements to access array data. The respecification of a READ statement is a common error.

The method used to load an array depends on the programmer's design. The use of READ and DATA statements is well suited to applications where the data remains constant. INPUT statements make it possible to enter new array data each time a program is run.

The interactive approach to loading arrays requires the user to provide a means of checking the accuracy of the data input. Users should follow INPUT statements with an error-checking sequence, whereby

the program requests verification of the data input. This is readily accomplished using a prompting INPUT statement and an IF/THEN statement. If the data is correctly input, processing continues; otherwise, the data is rekeyed into the same array cell.

7.3 Array Applications

When manipulating data held in arrays, the use of program modules is advantageous. It permits the user to group related activities and restrict processing to specific modules. For example, one module can load the arrays, a second can do computations using array data, and another can output array data. Each module satisfies a particular processing need.

A handy vehicle for creating program modules is the GOSUB statement. It permits the formulation of modules which are referenced by a main program, an approach introduced with top-down designs. Each GOSUB module handles a specific task and is accessed from the main program.

It is possible to define an array that is larger than required. This is often done when a program is used on an interactive basis. A second array may also be used to hold data that is extracted from another array. When this approach is adopted, the user must ensure that two looping sequences are invoked. One loop counter supports the sequential access from data on the first array, while a second variable monitors the placement of data in the second array.

The FOR/NEXT statements used with array data may use INPUT statements, tying the closing loop variable to that instruction. By inputting an N variable and having the FOR/NEXT loop run from 1 to N, users can build into their program a flexibility to apply a program to a wide range of input values.

7.4 Subscript Manipulations

It is possible to increase the operational use of arrays by the manipulation of their subscripts. Subscript manipulations are employed to input multiple data items or print array values on a single line.

An important feature in subscript manipulations is the coordinated use of FOR/NEXT statements. The loops used must declare an increment paralleling the number of cells accessed. The STEP option is incorporated into FOR/NEXT statements to modify increments. Users must carefully monitor each loop's increment to ensure its accuracy.

The creation of reports which assume a tabular format is readily accomplished via subscript manipulations. Data drawn from a one-dimensional array is printed across a line in a tabular form. These outputs may appear beneath headings and be handled within output modules.

7.5 Special Statements

Processing often requires the use of specialized functions to include the computation of square roots or absolute values. The features are made available through predefined functions, which are manufacturer-supplied software invoked by predefined codes. The specification of the ABS or SQR codes within BASIC statements alerts the computer to compute an absolute value or square root.

Key BASIC Statements

	Examples	
ABS function for absolute value	100	B = ABS(X)
	150	N(I) = ABS(P(K))
	200	J = ABS(Y(I))
DIM statement	10	DIM X(15)
	10	DIM N$(30), H(30), R(30)
	10	DIM B(50), C(50), D(10)
SQR function for square root	100	R = SQR(X)
	180	T = SQR(A(I))
	200	C(I) = SQR(P)

Glossary

Array A series of storage cells referenced by a common name, in which data is retained during a program's processing.

ABS function A predefined function used to derive the absolute value of a number.

DIMension statement The statement used to define the arrays used within a program; specifies arrays by type and size.

One-dimensional array An array consisting of a consecutive series of storage areas; access to each cell is provided through a subscripted variable.

Predefined function A manufacturer-supplied program assigned to a specific application, referenced through a predefined coded statement.

SQR function A predefined function used to derive the square root of a number.

Subscript The means of accessing each array cell; the number in the parentheses of the subscripted-variable name; often the loop variable of the FOR/NEXT statement.

Subscripted-variable name The variable name used to access individual array cells; consists of the array name and subscript (for example, H$(I), B(J)).

Exercises

In-Class Exercises

1 For the conditions indicated, write the program excerpt necessary to input or output from the array. Remember to define the looping sequence and subscripted variables.

    a A numeric array of 20 cells is defined as D(20). The user desires to enter D values, two at a time, using a READ statement to enter data and a PRINT statement to record it.

    b The contents of the X(28) array must be output in a tabular format, four data items per line. Use a PRINT statement, placing each item into one of four print zones.

    c Input data into the N$(45) array, three data items at a time. Use an INPUT statement to accomplish that input. Insert an error-checking measure in that input sequence.

2 As a practical exercise, key in the program listed in Figure 7.20. This program derives the standard deviation of data in an array that you will fill. This program will illustrate the speed with which the computer can access and use array data. It will probably take you longer to key the data than to process it. The data is as follows:

33.6	46.8	30.2	40.3	36.4	11.7
17.9	7.8	28.7	12.3	31.9	23.6
24.5	13.9	21.5	9.8	27.1	35.4
22.2	19.2	16.7	15.1	19.5	21.6

3 The problem entails the computation of the average of 10 numbers and the number of below-average values that result. The first module requires the loading of the X

```
10 DIM X(24)
20 REM -- STANDARD DEVIATION PROGRAM
30 FOR K = 1 TO 24
40 INPUT 'ENTER ONE DATA ITEM';X(K)
50 INPUT 'IS THE ITEM CORRECT -- Y OR N';Y$
60 IF Y$ = 'N' THEN 40
70 PRINT X(K)
80 NEXT K
100 REM -- COMPUTE STD DEV
110 T1 = 0
120 T2 = 0
130 FOR I = 1 TO 24
140 T1 = T1 + X(I)
150 T2 = T2 + ( X(I)*X(I) )
160 NEXT I
170 V1 = T2 - ((T1*T1)/K)
180 V2 = V1/K
190 V3 = ABS(V2)
200 S = SQR(V3)
210 PRINT 'STANDARD DEV = ',S
220 END
```

FIGURE 7.20   In-class exercise problem 2. The program depicted handles the processing of a statistic referred to as the standard deviation.

array with 10 values. Module 2 computes the average of the 10 array values, which is outputted at the end of module 2 with a label AVG =. The third module reads through the X array and determines the number of below-average values. An accumulator is needed for this task, as well as when computing the computed average in module 2. Print out the total number of below-average values using the label NO OF BELOW AVG VALUES =. The data is as follows:

23.6	21.5	22.8	21.8	23.2
22.4	20.9	23.9	22.3	22.9

Prepare a flowchart and program for the above narrative.

Lab Exercises   1   The problem entails loading an array with data, computing another value, and outputting all data items in a report format. A three-module program is anticipated.

In module 1, two arrays are loaded with data. The N$ array is loaded with employee names, while the G array is filled with gross pay amounts. Each item read is printed after its entry. A looping sequence of seven times is performed.

In module 2, insurance deductions are computed and stored in the I array. The insurance deduction for each employee is computed as 1.8 percent of the gross amount and stored. No outputs result.

In module 3, the contents of the N$, G, and I arrays are printed beneath the headings EMPLOYEE, GROSS, and INS DED. Processing closes after printing all seven employees' data. The data for the problem follows.

Name	Gross	Name	Gross
Albert	510	Bernie	240
Carlo	320	David	430
Ernie	640	Frank	770
George	890		

Prepare a flowchart and program to satisfy this narrative.

2   The problem entails the estimation of future royalties to be paid to employees. The solution requires the use of three arrays — one for the employee's name, a second for the current royalty paid, and the third for the estimate of next year's royalty amount. A total of three program modules are anticipated.

In the first module, the name and royalty arrays are loaded with data. Output every item input. The second module computes the next year's estimate, based upon this year's royalty. A projected increase of 8 percent is anticipated in next year's royalty. After computation, the new estimate is stored in its own array. Accumulate the total of these new estimates.

The third module is output-oriented. A heading placed at the top of the report consists of AUTHOR NAME, CURR RLTY, and EST RLTY. These headings start at positions 1, 20, and 30. The editing applied to all royalty amounts is ######. Output the accumulated total of the estimated royalties in the third column. Insert blank lines at your discretion to improve the report's appearance. The data for this report follows:

Author	Royalty	Author	Royalty
Clarke	9,006	Barber	20,963
Sittler	12,155	Holmgren	13,825
Froese	1,739	Sinisalo	4,967
Howe	6,440	Linkdren	16,010

a   Prepare a flowchart and program to satisfy this narrative.

b   Write a flowchart and program to accommodate the following modification. Assume that the user wants to project for two years, not one. Assume a first-year increase of 8 percent and a second-year increase of 7 percent. Use a fourth array to hold the second-year estimate. Output all four arrays in a report adding a fourth heading at position 40 of 2ND EST RLTY. Also accumulate the second year's royalty estimates and output that total beneath the last output column.

3   The problem involves the analysis of a group of numbers. Two arrays are required: one array holds the original set of data, and the second holds specially selected data items. A total of 12 data items are involved. The data is initially loaded into the first array, two data items at a time. Output each data item upon input.

In module 2, read through the array and compute the average of all values. Output the computed average using the label COMPUTED AVG =. In the third module determine the number of array values that are less than or equal to the average. When such a value is found, place it in the second array. Ensure that you place all such values, commencing with the first cell of the second array. Count the number of values entered in the second array.

The last two modules are output-oriented. The fourth module outputs the contents of the original 12-cell array, using a format that prints four data items per line. The last module outputs data from the second array. Output the number of values held in that array, using the label NO OF VALUES <= AVG =. Print the values stored in the second array, one line at a time, beneath the literal A LIST OF THESE VALUES FOLLOWS. Output the closing literal PROCESSING CLOSED.

The 12 data items for this problem are as follows:

128.6	98.7	86.3	92.9	101.3	96.7
114.2	100.3	92.5	106.4	119.5	95.1

Prepare a flowchart and program to satisfy the above narrative.

4 The problem requires the computation and output of payroll data. A total of five arrays are required to hold the employee's number, hours worked, rate of pay, gross pay, and overtime pay. The initial three arrays are loaded with input data, while the latter two arrays receive data resulting from processing. The opening module loads each employee's number, hours worked, and pay, using INPUT statements. Within that looping sequence, design an error-checking procedure.

Module 2 results in the computation of the gross pay amount and an overtime amount, if warranted. To receive overtime, an employee must work over 35 hours. Overtime is computed at 2.5 times the normal pay rate for only those hours in excess of 35. For employees who work a normal week, the gross is equal to hours times rate, and that amount is stored in the gross array. An amount of zero is stored in the overtime array. If hours are greater than 35, compute the overtime amount and add it to the normal pay (computed at 35 hours) to create the gross amount. Store the gross and overtime amounts in their respective arrays.

Module 3 produces a gross pay report. A heading of EMP NO, HOURS, RATE, and GROSS PAY is required. Position each heading at positions 1, 8, 14, and 20 respectively. Edit employee number as #####, hours as ##.#, rate as ##.##, and gross as ####.## when outputting each amount.

Module 4 outputs data relating solely to overtime. The heading EMP NO and OVERTIME $ starts at positions 1 and 10. Edit each amount as ##### and ####.##, respectively. The data for this problem is as follows:

Emp. No	Hours	Rate	Emp. No	Hours	Rate
1076	35.0	12.60	14339	40.0	20.87
14263	33.5	17.82	26026	34.5	9.68
8307	41.6	15.60	5118	39.2	16.55
19552	37.5	14.85	10665	38.7	18.26

a Prepare the flowchart and program for the above narrative.

b Revise the flowchart and program solutions to accommodate the use of two accumulators: one to total all gross pay totals, and a second to total only overtime pay. Print the gross pay total at the end of the gross pay report, beneath its column. Use the label GROSS TOT =. Output the accumulated overtime total in its report, preceded by the label OT PAY =. Position it beneath the column of overtime data.

5 The problem entails computing sales commissions. A total of five arrays are required to include an array for salesperson's name, total sales amount, earned com-

mission, and two for selected names and commissions. At the program's start, the salesperson's name and total sales arrays are loaded. Module 2 computes commissions. The commission rate is 12 percent. Each computed commission is stored in its own array cell.

The third module identifies those individuals attaining commissions greater than $500. The program should read through the commission's array and identify those people, moving both their name and commission to the second name and commission arrays.

The fourth module produces the first of two reports. It uses the heading SALESPERSON, SALES TOTAL, and EARNED COMM. The data drawn from each array is positioned beneath these headings. The fifth module will highlight only those salespeople with commissions above $500. This second report draws its data from the second name and commission arrays. It carries the title SPECIAL COMMISSIONS LEVEL and will have the name and commission of each person found in those two arrays. The data for this problem is as follows:

Salesperson	Sales Total	Salesperson	Sales Total
Brooks	4962	Pavelitch	4163
Mio	7629	Fotiv	3856
Hedberg	5206	Andersson	2971
Grescaner	3637	Hanlon	4018

Prepare a flowchart and program to satisfy this narrative.

This problem entails the computation of water taxes. A total of three arrays are required for processing. On input, data is loaded into an account number array and a gallons array. The output of each cell's contents follows its input, in module 1.   **Quiz Problem**

The second module controls the computation of water taxes. The formula called for is

$$W = 12.25 + (.057 * G)$$

where W is the water tax and G is the number of gallons used. The computed water tax is stored in its array.

The third module focuses on computation of the average water tax. The water tax array is accessed, with each cell added to an accumulator. Divide that total by 8 to compute the average.

The fourth module acts to output array data. Print water taxes in a report using the headings ACCT NO, GALLONS, and WATER TAX. Output data from each array beneath its appropriate heading. Print out the average water tax in the tax column, preceded by the label AVG WATER TAX =. The data for the problem is as follows:

Acct No	Gallons Used	Acct No	Gallons Used
10634	1260	11063	1140
10395	1740	12845	1320
14608	1660	13903	1830
15006	1490	15887	1570

The flowchart, program, and output for the quiz problem are shown in Figure 7.21.   **Quiz Solution**

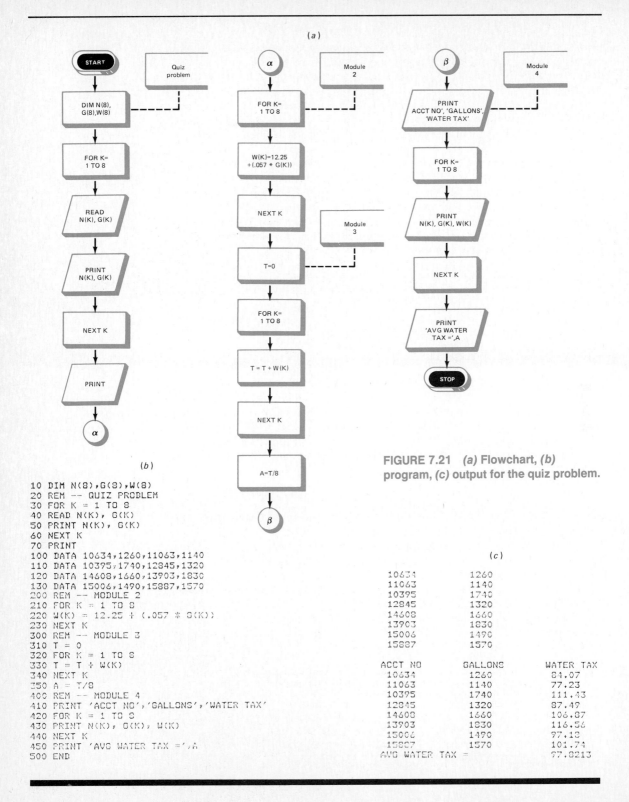

(a)

(b)

```
10 DIM N(8),G(8),W(8)
20 REM -- QUIZ PROBLEM
30 FOR K = 1 TO 8
40 READ N(K), G(K)
50 PRINT N(K), G(K)
60 NEXT K
70 PRINT
100 DATA 10634,1260,11063,1140
110 DATA 10395,1740,12845,1320
120 DATA 14608,1660,13903,1830
130 DATA 15006,1490,15887,1570
200 REM -- MODULE 2
210 FOR K = 1 TO 8
220 W(K) = 12.25 + (.057 * G(K))
230 NEXT K
300 REM -- MODULE 3
310 T = 0
320 FOR K = 1 TO 8
330 T = T + W(K)
340 NEXT K
350 A = T/8
400 REM -- MODULE 4
410 PRINT 'ACCT NO','GALLONS','WATER TAX'
420 FOR K = 1 TO 8
430 PRINT N(K), G(K), W(K)
440 NEXT K
450 PRINT 'AVG WATER TAX =',A
500 END
```

FIGURE 7.21 *(a)* Flowchart, *(b)* program, *(c)* output for the quiz problem.

(c)

ACCT NO	GALLONS	WATER TAX
10634	1260	
11063	1140	
10395	1740	
12845	1320	
14608	1660	
13903	1830	
15006	1490	
15887	1570	

ACCT NO	GALLONS	WATER TAX
10634	1260	84.07
11063	1140	77.23
10395	1740	111.43
12845	1320	87.49
14608	1660	106.87
13903	1830	116.56
15006	1490	97.18
15887	1570	101.74
AVG WATER TAX =		97.8213

Appendix: Debugging Hints

Most mistakes involving arrays occur when users try to access data from individual array cells or when subscripts are specified incorrectly.

The Incorrect Rereading of Data

As stated in the chapter, once data is stored in an array, it is ready for use in processing. In the program of Figure 7.A.1, data is loaded into the array in the first module, lines 20 to 60. Once the 10 values are stored in the array the program can proceed to compute their average.

In examining the second phase of processing, we note the specification of a READ statement at line 110. The attempt to reread the data via a READ statement is totally incorrect. The program need only specify the subscripted-variable name of the desired cell to access its data. The READ statement on line 110 will only succeed in generating a program error sufficient to cancel processing. The attempt to execute line 110 will create an out-of-data condition, as no data other than the 10 array values is defined. This error is identified in the program listing. It notes the error as occurring at line 110, as that is where the execution of the READ statement resulted in the error.

The correction of the program is quite simple. The removal of line 110 will eliminate the incorrect rereading operation and permit processing to continue. The only time additional READ statements are required is when there is additional data. In that case, the DATA statements supporting such a task must be used.

Inconsistent Subscripts

The programmer must always use subscripts consistently in a program. That is, the variable used as a subscript must be properly defined. To observe this type of error, examine the program excerpt of Figure 7.A.2.

In Figure 7.A.2(a) the error results from the specification of the subscript I where the variable K should have been used. The I subscript is incorrect because the loop

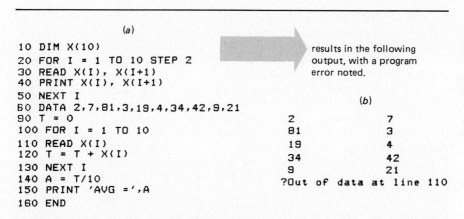

(a)

```
10 DIM X(10)
20 FOR I = 1 TO 10 STEP 2
30 READ X(I), X(I+1)
40 PRINT X(I), X(I+1)
50 NEXT I
60 DATA 2,7,81,3,19,4,34,42,9,21
90 T = 0
100 FOR I = 1 TO 10
110 READ X(I)
120 T = T + X(I)
130 NEXT I
140 A = T/10
150 PRINT 'AVG =',A
160 END
```

results in the following output, with a program error noted.

(b)

2	7
81	3
19	4
34	42
9	21

?Out of data at line 110

FIGURE 7.A.1 The attempt to re-READ data from its array positions results in a program error. (a) Incorrect use of READ statement in program. (b) Output notes error at line 110.

FIGURE 7.A.2 Great care must be exercised when working with subscripts, as their mis-specification will result in program errors. Two examples of this type of error are illustrated in the program excerpts shown.

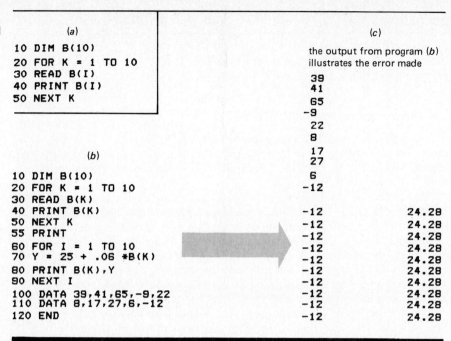

variable specified by the controlling FOR/NEXT statement is K. The I variable is not defined and will result in a program error, prohibiting processing to continue. To correct the problem, the programmer need only specify K as the subscript in lines 30 and 40.

A more subtle error is evident in Figure 7.A.2(b). Here, the array is properly loaded in the first FOR/NEXT loop, where K was correctly used as the subscript. However, the K subscript is improperly used in module 2, lines 60 to 90.

In these statements, the I variable is used in the FOR/NEXT loop and the program improperly specifies a K subscript in lines 70 and 80. A syntax error will not be outputted, as one does not exist. The error is in the program's logic. All statements adhere to accepted syntax, but the wrong subscript has been used.

A tip-off to this error state is evident from the program's output. If you will note, the same results are printed 10 times. When executing lines 70 and 80, the program used the B(10) cell, as 10 was the value substituted for K in lines 70 and 80. The repeated results mean that the same data was repeatedly employed.

To correct the error, the programmer can change the K subscript to I or substitute K as the loop variable for the FOR/NEXT statements in lines 60 and 90. Either substitution will correct the error condition.

A simple way of avoiding this error is to read your program carefully before actually keying it into the computer. Often this step is sufficient to catch many errors.

EIGHT

Selecting and Sorting

Chapter Objectives

This chapter will

- Describe the selection of specific items from an array.

- Discuss how lists and tables are constructed and data is accessed from one-dimensional arrays.

- Discuss the structure and use of compound conditionals.

- Discuss the concept of nested loops using FOR/NEXT statements.

- Describe how negative accumulators reduce amounts on a regular basis.

- Discuss the concept of sorting data held in arrays and the sorting of numeric and nonnumeric array data.

- Demonstrate the integration of sorting, compound conditionals, tables, and nested loops.

Introduction

In this chapter, we build upon the concepts mastered in Chapter 7. We demonstrate how to select and retain specific data items from an array. The construction and handling of data held within tables are principal features in most advanced languages. A sound understanding of how arrays are used to create tables and how data is extracted from them is important.

Data sorting is carefully explained and then illustrated in a program format. We review the concurrent use of two looping sequences, one nested inside the other. Nested loops are critical components of data sorting. Their importance will be even more evident in future discussions of more complex array configurations.

In a previous illustrative problem we were able to pass through an array and identify data items which exceeded a particular limit. Using a second array, we were able to retain data items which fell into a desired category.

Often the need arises to read through an array and select a specific data item which satisfies a predetermined set of characteristics. For example, we might desire the largest (or smallest) value in a series of data items loaded into an array. The key element in this sequence is the process by which that special data item is identified and retained. Essentially, we want to read sequentially through each array cell, examine its contents, and test for the desired data item. Processing will most likely occur within a looping sequence, each loop-handling activity related to one array cell. It is also conceivable that many data items may be initially chosen and replaced before the exact or final data item is selected.

PROBLEM 8.1   Finding the Largest Value

The problem entails identifying the largest value held in an array consisting of 12 cells. The array is loaded, two data items at a time, in the opening module. In program module 2, the data held within the array is examined, and the largest value sought. This task is performed within a loop, with the largest value retained under its own variable name. After testing all cells, the largest value found is output with the label BIG VALUE =. The 12 data items are as follows:

| 46.9 | 62.7 | 50.2 | 88.3 | 59.3 | 93.4 |
| 38.1 | 86.4 | 93.6 | 64.7 | 42.9 | 78.6 |

These are the main points in the problem narrative.

1   The problem consists of two program modules. Module 1 loads the 12-cell array, and module 2 tests all cells for the largest value.

2   Data is loaded two items at a time and outputted to verify each cell's contents. A second output occurs at the end of module 2, where the largest value found is printed with a label.

3   Processing involves the testing of each cell and the retention of the largest value found. The program must replace that value when a larger value is found.

4   No accumulators, headings, or other special features are noted. Ensure that the array is properly defined.

The flowchart and program for Problem 8.1 are shown in Figure 8.1. Processing occurs in a two-module sequence. The flowchart shows the loading of the 12-cell X array in module 1 after its definition by DIM X(12). The loop in which the array data is read and printed uses a loop variable I running from 1 to 12, with an increment of 2. This sequence enables the solution to handle two data items per loop.

In the second module, I loops from 2 to 12. This change results from our desire to select the largest array value. The logic of our solution requires that we identify one data item as the largest value and then compare each array item against it. Each time a larger value is found, we replace the existing value with the larger number. Module 2 reflects this processing approach, as follows.

The value stored in the X(1) cell is taken, initially identified as the largest number, and stored in B. We choose the variable B to represent the BIG value. Loading it with the data stored in X(1) provides a value with which to commence processing.

Having used X(1) to define B, it is illogical to start testing with X(1). Our comparison of array values against B should begin with X(2), the second array cell. The second looping sequence is so constructed that I ranges from 2 to 12. This permits all remaining array values, beginning with X(2), to be tested against B.

The actual comparison is dictated by the conditional statement IS X(I) > B? If the array value X(I) is greater than B, the X(I) value becomes the new B, this processing occurring on the YES branch of the decision. If X(I) is less than or equal to B, no swap is performed (as the existing B value is larger than the data item in the X(I) cell). After the testing of X(12) is completed, the loop closes, enabling the output of B.

Our BASIC solution opens with a DIM statement, line 10, defining the X(12) array. At line 20, a REM statement advises that the solution to Problem 8.1 follows. The FOR statement, line 30, defines a six-loop sequence in which array cells are loaded two at a time. The STEP option causes I to assume values from 1 to 12 in increments of 2. The required NEXT statement appears at line 60.

In this looping sequence we observe that the statements at lines 40 and 50 are indented. This technique is favored by some programmers to focus attention on each loop's processing and to highlight the modular structure of program solutions. Though indentation is not part of BASIC's syntax, we will use this visual effect in future solutions.

Within lines 40 and 50, the array cells are handled two at a time. The subscripts X(I) and X(I + 1) are defined in both the READ and PRINT statements, as they are coordinated with the STEP 2 increment. The tabular output of the 12 array values, in 6 rows of 2 data items each, is also viewed in Figure 8.1. The manipulation of subscripts can assist in simplifying I/O operations related to arrays.

The series of steps used to isolate the largest array value begins at line 100. Here, the value stored in the first array cell, X(1), is assigned to B and

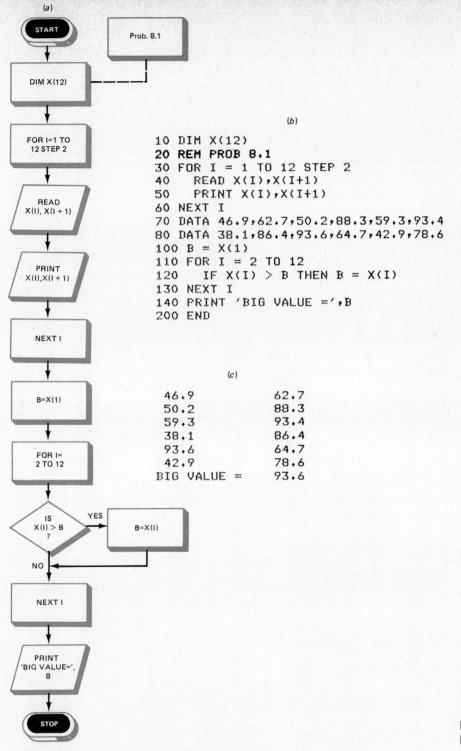

(a)

(b)

```
10  DIM X(12)
20  REM PROB 8.1
30  FOR I = 1 TO 12 STEP 2
40     READ X(I),X(I+1)
50     PRINT X(I),X(I+1)
60  NEXT I
70  DATA 46.9,62.7,50.2,88.3,59.3,93.4
80  DATA 38.1,86.4,93.6,64.7,42.9,78.6
100 B = X(1)
110 FOR I = 2 TO 12
120    IF X(I) > B THEN B = X(I)
130 NEXT I
140 PRINT 'BIG VALUE =',B
200 END
```

(c)

```
46.9            62.7
50.2            88.3
59.3            93.4
38.1            86.4
93.6            64.7
42.9            78.6
BIG VALUE =     93.6
```

FIGURE 8.1 (a) Flowchart, (b) program, and (c) output for Problem 8.1.

thus provides a basis for comparison with the other array values. The purpose of line 100 is to establish an initial value for B.

Beginning with X(2), data is compared to B. Therefore the second FOR/NEXT statement is designed to execute 11 loops. The looping sequence is controlled via line 110, the FOR statement, which directs that I assume the values of 2 to 12. Using I, each array cell from X(2) to X(12) will be compared against B.

The actual test of whether X(I) is greater than B is performed at line 120. This IF/THEN statement is indented to note its positioning within that FOR/NEXT loop. Line 120 indicates that if X(I) is greater than B, then that cell's data becomes the new B value. Only when the X(I) value is greater than B, will B be replaced. This processing sequence ensures that only the largest array value is stored in B.

The NEXT I instruction, line 130, concludes the second loop and precedes the output of B and its label BIG VALUE =. This output indicates that the largest value of 93.6 was retained in B, as a result of processing. To verify this fact, we may scan the 12 data items in lines 70 and 80.

The retention of a single data item is somewhat simplified, as only one special storage area is necessary. Let us observe how we can select the largest value resulting from processing, along with the data associated with that item.

PROBLEM 8.2   Selecting Cost Data

The problem entails the estimation of costs and the selection of the largest of them. Within the first module, two of the three arrays are loaded with data. A total of six data items each are loaded into the project number and units arrays.

The costs array is filled in module 2. Two computations are employed, depending upon their project number. If the project number is 2000 or less, the equation is $C = 245 + .65U$, where U and C represent the units and costs, respectively. For project numbers of the 9000 plus range, the formula used is $C = 376 + .59U$. The cost amount is stored in its own array cell as a result of this computation. No other processing or outputs are anticipated.

Module 3 serves to search through the costs array and identify the largest cost amount. This amount, as well as the related project number and units used, should be retained for subsequent output when looping stops. Output each with appropriate labels and close processing. The output of all other array data is not required. The data for this problem is as follows:

Proj No	Units	Proj No	Units
1106	1820	9006	1970
1554	1790	1806	1940
9217	1860	9665	1930

These are the main points in the problem narrative.

1 The problem involves the use of three arrays consisting of six cells each. The project and units arrays are loaded in module 1, and the costs array is filled in module 2.

2 The computation of costs uses two formulas. If the project number is less than or equal to 2000, the formula is $C(I) = 245 + (.65 * U(I))$. Project numbers greater than 9000 must use the formula $C(I) = 376 + (.59 * U(I))$. The subscripted variable $C(I)$ enables the costs figure to be stored in the costs array.

3 The third phase of processing selects the largest cost. The project number and units related to that cost are also retained.

4 After completion of the loop in which the testing for the largest value is performed, that data is output. On three separate lines, the project number, units, and largest cost data are printed with labels.

The flowchart, program, and output for Problem 8.2 are depicted in Figure 8.2. After defining the three arrays involved in processing, the flowchart's opening loop depicts the loading of the project number and units arrays. The subscripted variables $P(I)$ and $U(I)$ are used in the I/O symbols of that loop.

The flowchart's second six-loop sequence tests for the correct formula to use in computing the projected cost and loading the costs array. We have used two consecutive decisions to choose between the two rate formulas; this ensures that each project is properly associated with its formula. We did not specify an IF/THEN/ELSE sequence, as it is not a clear-cut case of one formula or the other: project numbers between 2000 and 9000 could enter processing and cause errors.

The $C(I)$ array must be loaded before the costs array can be searched for the largest value. Prior to the search of C cells 2 through 6, we establish $C(1)$ as the largest cost. To record the unit and project numbers associated with the largest cost, we have also retained the values in $P(1)$ and $U(1)$. Whenever we record a new largest value, we must also retain the project number and units associated with that larger value.

Within module 3, where I ranges from 2 to 6, each cost array cell is compared against the larger value. If the largest value, B3, is greater than the value of the cell being accessed, $C(I)$, the flow branches to loop's end to continue processing. If B3 is less than or equal to $C(I)$, then a new larger value is found and we must swap values. The three processing steps following the $B3 > C(I)$ decision accomplish that swap. The current $P(I)$, $U(I)$, and $C(I)$ values replace the existing B1, B2, and B3 values, respectively.

The search for the largest cost figure ends after the sixth cost cell is examined. The output of this largest cost, with related units and project data, follows in three separate outputs. The first variable output is B1, which represents the project number and carries the label PROJ ID =. The units

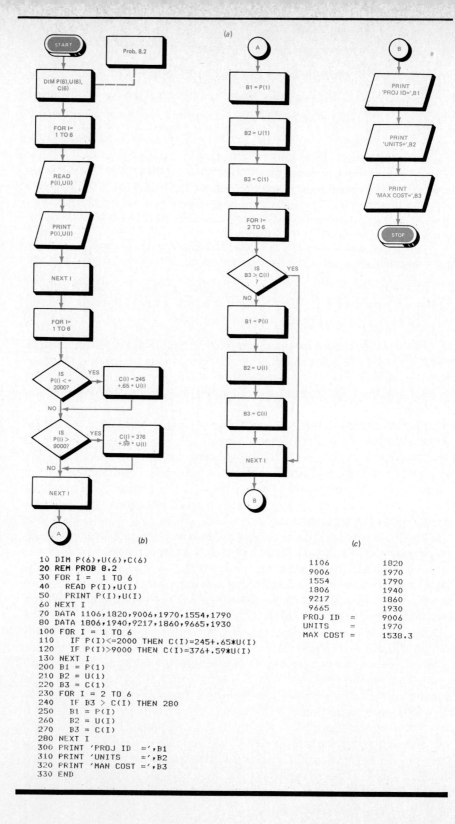

```
10 DIM P(6),U(6),C(6)
20 REM PROB 8.2
30 FOR I =  1 TO 6
40    READ P(I),U(I)
50    PRINT P(I),U(I)
60 NEXT I
70 DATA 1106,1820,9006,1970,1554,1790
80 DATA 1806,1940,9217,1860,9665,1930
100 FOR I = 1 TO 6
110    IF P(I)<=2000 THEN C(I)=245+.65*U(I)
120    IF P(I)>9000 THEN C(I)=376+.59*U(I)
130 NEXT I
200 B1 = P(1)
210 B2 = U(1)
220 B3 = C(1)
230 FOR I = 2 TO 6
240    IF B3 > C(I) THEN 280
250    B1 = P(I)
260    B2 = U(I)
270    B3 = C(I)
280 NEXT I
300 PRINT 'PROJ ID =',B1
310 PRINT 'UNITS    =',B2
320 PRINT 'MAN COST =',B3
330 END
```

```
1106            1820
9006            1970
1554            1790
1806            1940
9217            1860
9665            1930
PROJ ID  =      9006
UNITS    =      1970
MAX COST =      1538.3
```

FIGURE 8.2 (a) Flowchart, (b) program, and (c) output for Problem 8.2.

variable, B2, is outputted, using the label UNITS =. The printing of the largest cost, B3, is preceded by the literal MAX COST = and concludes processing.

The program developed from this flowchart adheres to its logic. To accent their modular nature, we have indented statements within each FOR/ NEXT loop.

The DIM statement at line 10 establishes each of the three six-cell arrays for their eventual use. A REM statement precedes the FOR/NEXT loop sequence created by lines 30 to 60. The project and unit arrays are loaded, respectively using the variables P(I) and U(I). The data related to processing is defined at lines 70 and 80.

In the loop defined via lines 100 to 130, we compute each cost value and load it into the C(I) array. Two IF/THEN statements control access to each equation and ensure that only the proper formula is used for the correct project number. Each cost cell must be filled prior to assessing the largest cost estimate.

The three statements in lines 200, 210, and 220 initially define the values stored in P(1), U(1), and C(1) as the project number and units related to the largest cost. This initialization is needed to start the comparison of values and thus find the largest value in the cost's array. Our third loop is set to run from 2 to 6 and defined by the FOR/NEXT statement, lines 230 to 280.

Each time a C(I) value is larger than the existing B3, the swap of data relating to the new value is performed. The swap is controlled via the statements at lines 250 to 270. As noted at line 240, if B3 is greater than C(I), the program branches to line 280 and the loop continues. The loop closes after the sixth cell's data is evaluated.

Three PRINT statements close the program's activities and represent the only output of data other than the initial loading sequence. Lines 300, 310, and 320 respectively print the project number, units used, and costs related to the largest estimated cost found. Each uses a special label to uniquely identify that output. Figure 8.2(c) shows that the outputs are aligned.

The output of these three values is an option open to programmers. Rather than print an entire list of data, we often want to focus on a set of critical values. By outputting only vital statistics, we enable users to focus on data of immediate concern. It is not always essential that every data item be output.

8.2 One-Dimensional Tables

Though one-dimensional arrays are used to hold processed results, they may effectively be employed as tables or lists to retain data that is repeatedly used in processing.[1] Using the structure of an array, it is possible to establish

The Structure of an Array Table

---

[1] The terms *table* and *list* may be used interchangeably when discussing one-dimensional arrays that hold reference data.

categories into which data items may fall. Each cell holds data relating to a specific category and provides that data each time that cell is accessed.

Figure 8.3*(a)* shows a list of royalty rates for each of four products produced by a particular company. Every product manufactured by this company must use one of these four rates. If retained in an array, they are more readily available for processing. The program need only specify the product code to get the proper rate.

The key to translating the product code to its rate equivalent is the one-dimensional array, shown in Figure 8.3*(b)*. The existing product codes serve as keys to array subscripts. Product 1 becomes $X(1)$, where the $X(1)$ cell holds the rate of .052. Similarly, products 2, 3, and 4 become $X(2)$, $X(3)$, and $X(4)$, with rates of .059, .068, and .073, respectively.

In a program, the specification of a product code as the subscript serves to access data in the rate array. If the product code P is inputted, access to the X array is provided by the variable $X(P)$. Figure 8.3*(c)* shows the sequence of program statements needed for this input of data.

Reviewing lines 100 to 120, we may observe the access of data from the rate array and its use in processing. In line 100, we input the data items P and A, the product code and the amount for which a royalty is computed. The rate to be used in processing is obtained at line 110, where P becomes the subscript for the variable $X(P)$. As P must equal 1, 2, 3, or 4, it provides access to the four cells of the X array. Thus, R is set equal to one of the four rates at line 120. The commission due (C) for the amount (A) is computed by multiplying A by R.

The advantage of this tabular structure is that only one royalty formula is specified. The input of the product code provides the key to accessing the rate array and obtaining the correct royalty rate. The program provides for the conversion of a product code into a rate and its use in a subsequent processing step. We define the series of steps by which an array is so accessed as a **table look-up.** To reinforce the use of this procedure, let us review the program shown in Figure 8.4.

FIGURE 8.3   *(a)* A list of royalty rates for four company products. *(b)* A one-dimensional rate array with each cell containing the royalty rate for one product code. *(c)* Statements used to access data in the rate array.

(a)	*(b)*	*(c)*
A list of royalty rates.	Royalties are loaded into the rate (X) array.	The X array is accessed by using the statements below.

Product Code	Royalty Rate		X array				
1	.052		X(1)	.052		100	INPUT P,A
2	.059		X(2)	.059		110	R=X(P)
3	.068		X(3)	.068		120	C=A * R
4	.073		X(4)	.073			

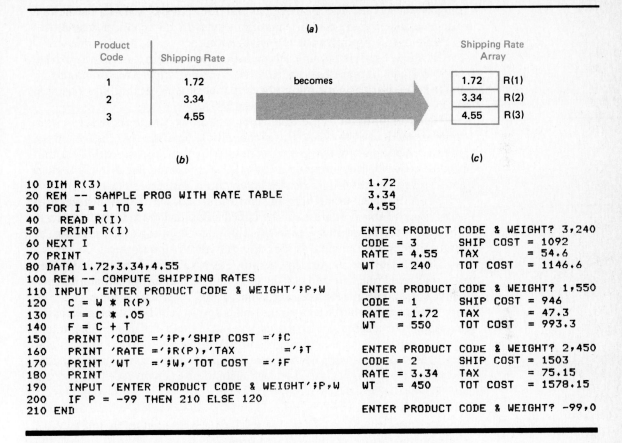

FIGURE 8.4   (a) The rate array is defined from the table of shipping rates. (b) Program and (c) output using the rate array.

The problem entails the computation of shipping costs. The freight clerk keys in the product code and its weight, and the computer provides the cost of shipping that item. The program supporting the clerk uses an array to hold shipping rates, which are keyed to product codes. The shipping rates list and array are illustrated in Figure 8.4(a).

Three shipping rates are defined for product codes 1, 2, and 3. These codes determine the three rates in array cells R(1), R(2), and R(3). The program in Figure 8.4(b) shows that the R array is loaded in a three-loop sequence in lines 30 to 60.

The choice of using READ and DATA statements to load the array is deliberate. Data in the rate array will remain constant for each application. The READ and DATA statements provide a sure means of handling stable data and properly assigning each data item to a desired array cell.

By contrast, an INPUT statement is used in the program's second module. Once the rate array is defined, access to its data may commence immediately. By using the INPUT statement and priming read, the user can enter a variety of data items in response to various weights. The looping sequence will continue until a product code of -99 is keyed.

The REM statement, line 100, defines the opening to the second program module. Line 110 represents the first half of the priming-read technique and enables the user to input the first product code and weight. The loop that commences at line 120 continues to line 200.

The computation of the total shipping cost occurs in three steps. Two tasks are evident at line 120, where the initial shipping cost C is computed. The statement multiplies the weight input W by the rate associated with that product code. The subscripted variable R(P) represents the rate and provides access to the correct cell in the rate array. Since P assumes the values of 1, 2, or 3, the R(P) variable will draw the correct rate data from one of those three cells. The variable C represents the initial shipping cost amount.

A sales tax figure must be added to the initial shipping cost to produce the total shipping cost amount. In line 130, the initial shipping cost C is multiplied by .05, the 5 percent sales tax rate. The addition of the initial shipping cost and sales tax, line 140, produces F, the final total cost of shipping. A blank line of output separates each computational group.

The second half of the priming read is specified at line 190. The looping sequence will continue until the user keys in a value of $P = -99$. At that point, the program passes through line 200 and closes.

The output is presented in Figure 8.4(c). The array contents are outputted before the shipping data. Each set of shipping costs precedes the entry of the 9s data.

Alphabetic Codes

Some readers wonder if a FOR/NEXT loop can be used in module 2. With slight modifications of the existing program, it is possible to redraft the solution. Users may elect to substitute a FOR/NEXT statement, supported by an IF/THEN statement (for a 9s decision), to control looping.

The use of alphabetic product codes poses a somewhat more difficult problem, as a link must be created between these codes and array cells. We must remember that access to array cells occurs via a numeric subscript. For example, a product code of A is of no value unless it can be converted to a numeric subscript. Thus, if A is established as the equivalent of 1, we may use 1 as a subscript and access the first cell of the rate array, R(1). Similarly, numeric equivalents must be established for codes of B, C, etc. so that the codes can be assigned numeric subscripts.

With the program itself, an IF/THEN statement controls access to each array and the computation of shipping costs. The statement may appear as

```
130     IF P$ = 'A' THEN C = W * R(1)
```

where P$ is the string-variable name used for alphabetic codes, C is the initial shipping cost, W is the weight, and R(1) is the first array cell. The specification of R(1) ensures that only the first array cell is used with a product code of A.

(a)

```
10 DIM R(3)
20 REM - REVISED PROGRAM
30 FOR I = 1 TO 3
40    READ R(I)
50    PRINT R(I)
60 NEXT I
70 PRINT
80 DATA 1.72,3.34,4.55
100 REM -- COMPUTE SHIPPING RATES
110 INPUT 'ENTER PRODUCT CODE & WEIGHT';P$,W
120 IF P$ = 'A' THEN I=1
130 IF P$ = 'B' THEN I=2
140 IF P$ = 'C' THEN I=3
150 C = W * R(I)
160 T = C *.05
170 F = C + T
180 PRINT 'CODE = ';P$,'SHIP COST =';C
190 PRINT 'RATE =';R(I),'TAX        =';T
200 PRINT 'WT   =';W,'TOT COST  =';F
210 PRINT
220 INPUT 'ENTER PRODUCT CODE & WEIGHT';P$,W
230 IF W = -999 THEN 300 ELSE 120
300 END
```

```
    1.72
    3.34
    4.55

ENTER PRODUCT CODE & WEIGHT? C,240
CODE = C       SHIP COST = 1092
RATE = 4.55    TAX       = 54.6
WT   = 240     TOT COST  = 1146.6

ENTER PRODUCT CODE & WEIGHT? A,550
CODE = A       SHIP COST = 946
RATE = 1.72    TAX       = 47.3
WT   = 550     TOT COST  = 993.3

ENTER PRODUCT CODE & WEIGHT? B,450
CODE = B       SHIP COST = 1503
RATE = 3.34    TAX       = 75.15
WT   = 450     TOT COST  = 1578.15

ENTER PRODUCT CODE & WEIGHT? XXX,-999
```

(b)

```
10 DIM R(3)
20 REM -- REVISED PROGRAM
30 GOSUB 100
40 GOSUB 200
50 GO TO 400
100 REM -- LOAD ARRAY MODULE
110 FOR I = 1 TO 3
120    READ R(I)
130    PRINT R(I)
140 NEXT I
150 PRINT
160 DATA 1.72,3.34,4.55
170 RETURN
200 REM -- COMPUTE RATES MODULE
210 FOR K = 1 TO 3
220    INPUT 'ENTER PROD CODE & WEIGHT';P$,W
230    IF P$ = 'A' THEN I=1
240    IF P$ = 'B' THEN I=2
250    IF P$ = 'C' THEN I=3
260    C = W * R(I)
270    T = C*.05
280    F = C + T
290    PRINT 'CODE = ';P$,'SHIP COST =';C
300    PRINT 'RATE =';R(I),'TAX        =';T
310    PRINT 'WT   =';W,'TOT COST  =';F
320    PRINT
330 NEXT K
340 RETURN
400 END
```

```
    1.72
    3.34
    4.55

ENTER PROD CODE & WEIGHT? C,240
CODE = C       SHIP COST = 1092
RATE = 4.55    TAX       = 54.6
WT   = 240     TOT COST  = 1146.6

ENTER PROD CODE & WEIGHT? A,550
CODE = A       SHIP COST = 946
RATE = 1.72    TAX       = 47.3
WT   = 550     TOT COST  = 993.3

ENTER PROD CODE & WEIGHT? B,450
CODE = B       SHIP COST = 1503
RATE = 3.34    TAX       = 75.15
WT   = 450     TOT COST  = 1578.15
```

FIGURE 8.5 Revised solutions to the shipping-rates program, linking the alphabetic codes. Program *(a)* uses a priming read with 9s decision, whereas program *(b)* uses GOSUBs and a FOR/NEXT.

Figure 8.5 shows the impact of alphabetic product codes and their linkage to array values, and two solutions to the shipping-rates problem. In Figure 8.5*(a)*, we use alphabetic codes and a looping sequence for module 2 that is controlled via a priming read and 9s decision. In Figure 8.5*(b)*, a FOR/NEXT statement controls both required loops, alphabetic product codes are used, and each program module is defined via GOSUB statements. The outputs for each revised program are printed beneath their listings. The two revised programs shown in Figure 8.5 illustrate that any number of programming techniques can be successfully integrated into a single solution.

Searching between Categories

Though it is desirable to create codes that readily translate into subscripts, it is not always possible. Often a program defines a table in which an array cell is associated with a range of values. Instead of having a code of 1 which relates to array cell 1, the program stipulates that array cell 1 is used for any code with a value from 1 to 1000. Similarly, cell 2 is applied to codes from 1001 to 2000, and so on. This new structure requires a program that converts a range of values to its equivalent array cell. Consider the table shown in Figure 8.6 and the instructions used to access data from its equivalent array.

The indicated range of units consists of three categories, each with a specific cost per unit: $1.25 for 0 to 999 units, $1.12 for 1000 to 4999 units, and $0.83 for 5000 or more units. These three rates occupy cells 1, 2, and 3 of the rates array. During processing, one of the three rates is accessed, depending on the number of units shipped.

Figure 8.6(a) shows how the number of units shipped is converted to the correct array equivalent. After inputting the units shipped, U, the program tests for the category in which that quantity falls and the array cell in which the appropriate rate is stored. Each IF/THEN statement provides the subscript for the desired rate.

Note that a slightly different format is used in the IF/THEN statements. The alteration is designed to accommodate the test for a range of values and is

FIGURE 8.6   The contents of array cells are often used to represent categories within tables. Two program excerpts denote how to access array data and define those categories for testing. (a) The conditional statements define the subscript before accessing the array. (b) The computational use of the array data is built into the IF/THEN statement.

Range of Units	Shipping Cost per Unit		Rate Array	
0 to 999	$ 1.25	becomes	R(1)	1.25
1000 to 4999	$ 1.12		R(2)	1.12
5000 to more	$ 0.83		R(3)	0.83

(a)

(b)

```
100 INPUT U
110 IF U>=0 AND U<=999 THEN I=1
120 IF U>=1000 AND U<=4999 THEN I=2
130 IF U>=5000 THEN I=3
140 C=U*R(I)
```

```
100 INPUT U
110 IF U>=0 AND U<=999      THEN C=U*R(1)
120 IF U>=1000 AND U<=4999  THEN C=U*R(2)
130 IF U>=5000              THEN C=U*R(3)
```

referred to as a **compound conditional.** A compound conditional joins two or more conditionals in a single IF/THEN statement. In essence, two questions are asked at line 110: Is U >= 0? and Is U <= 999? This set of values defines the first category of rates relating to the first cell of the rate array. If the units value falls within that range, the I subscript equals 1. The same logic is applied to the compound conditional in line 120. If U falls within 1000 to 4999, I is equal to 2 and the second cell of the rate array is accessed.

The last IF/THEN statement, line 130, does not use a compound conditional, as it is not required. All units greater than or equal to 5000 set I at 3, thus accessing the shipping rate stored in R(3). As only three rates exist, the rate array consists of only three cells.

Each of the three IF/THEN statements defines a subscript of I from 1 to 3. The definition of the I subscript enables the correct rate to be accessed when computing costs, C, at line 140. The C value is computed by multiplying the number of units, U, by the proper rate drawn from the rate array, R(I). The I subscript defines the correct cell from which that rate is drawn.

An alternative approach to computing shipping costs is occasionally used. Instead of defining the subscript for subsequent use, the cost computation is positioned after the compound conditional. This new series of statements is shown in Figure 8.6*(b)*.

Each IF/THEN statement tests for a desired category and then dictates the correct cost formula. Each formula stipulates a specific rate cell, in accordance with the category defined. As such, the first category uses R(1) to compute costs, with categories 2 and 3 respectively using the R(2) and R(3) rates.

In creating the compound conditional, we used the **AND operator** to connect two decisions. Another option is the **OR operator,** as shown in these two examples.

```
40      IF A > 60 OR B <= 100 THEN I = 4
140     IF P >= 5000 OR P < 2000 THEN C = P * R(5)
```

The OR operator connects two decisions where one or the other argument has validity. So if one or both of the conditions exist, that is the equivalent of a YES answer, and the operation on that branch is performed.

In the first example, if A is greater than 60 *or* B is less than or equal to 100, the variable I is equal to 4. In the second example, if P is equal to or greater than 5000 *or* less than 2000, the formula C = P * R(5) is applied. The OR operator provides another means of constructing compound conditionals.

If the need arises, the AND and OR operators may be combined into a single IF/THEN or IF/THEN/ELSE statement. This situation might arise when a test involves two categories. Here is a sample instruction.

```
20      IF (A < 5 AND A > 0) OR (B > 10 AND B < 20) THEN C = 2
```

Here, two sets of A and B values are tested, with either category sufficient to set C at 2.

This sample illustrates just one of the many ways compound conditions are used. Problem 8.3, which follows, uses compound conditionals to control access to an array.

PROBLEM 8.3   Utility Billing

The problem entails computing monthly utility statements. A four-cell array holds rates used to compute each customer's bill. The first program module loads the rate's array.

The second module focuses on computing each customer's utility bill. Inputted on each loop are the customer's account number and the past and current (kilowatts) meter readings. The rate formula used is

Amount billed $= 5.22 +$ (kw used $*$ rate)

The number of kilowatts used is computed by subtracting the past reading from the current reading. The result is then used to search the rate table for the proper billing rate. Output each customer's account number, kilowatts used, and monthly bill beneath the headings ACCT NO, KW USED, and AMT DUE. Align these outputs starting with print positions 3, 12, and 20, using the ##### format for account number and kilowatts used and ####.## for the billed amount. Customer data and rate values are as follows:

Rates Data			Customer Meter Data		
Kw Used	Rate ($/kw)		Acct No	Current	Old
0–999	.028		4,062	28,762	26,943
1,000–3,000	.023		13,775	14,776	13,908
3,001–10,000	.019		9,801	7,630	1,442
10,000 and over	.016		83,009	56,334	53,018
			10,801	21,055	8,669

These are the main points in the problem narrative.

1   A four-cell array will hold rate data in four categories of kilowatt usage. These rates are used in computing each customer's bill.

2   Module 1 will load the array, and module 2 will compute each utility bill.

3   On each loop, each customer's bill is computed using the following steps:
    a   Subtract the old reading from the current reading to determine the amount of kilowatts used.
    b   Use the number of kilowatts used to determine the proper billing rate from the rate array.
    c   Substitute the rate and kilowatts used into the billing formula to compute the customer's bill.

4   For each customer, output the account number, kilowatts used, and amount due beneath the defined headings. Apply the desired edited formats.

The flowchart for Problem 8.3 appears in Figure 8.7.

The flowchart reveals two major program modules. After defining the R(4) array, the initial FOR/NEXT loop loads the array with the four billing rates for kilowatts used. Prior to the start of the second loop, the report heading is printed and the desired line format (L$) defined.

The second FOR/NEXT sequence consists of five loops, processing one customer per loop. The customer's account number A, old meter reading M1, and current meter reading M2 are inputted ahead of the computation of the kilowatts used W. The W variable is critical in determining which rate to use.

Four decisions are at the heart of module 2. Each decision uses a compound conditional to test against one of the four categories. Each YES branch leads to defining the variable C which serves as a subscript when accessing data from the rate array. With that subscript selected, the computation of the customer's billing amount B is possible. The customer's billing data is outputted before the loop's end.

The program solution and output are shown in Figure 8.8. The first FOR/NEXT statement utilizes four loops to load the R array, one cell per loop. The data for this array is defined at line 70. The second set of DATA statements in lines 300 and 320 holds customer data slated for processing in the second module.

The output of the three column headings occurs at line 100; TAB functions are used to position each literal. The L$ format, line 110, creates the edited formats applied to account numbers and kilowatts used (####) and the amount billed (####.##). A five-loop FOR/NEXT sequence, lines 120 to 210, is required to handle customer data.

Of interest in this five-loop sequence are the compound-conditional statements used to determine which rate cell should be accessed. Each compound conditional parallels the category for which it is testing. The result of a successful test defines the subscript C of the array cell holding the correct rate. Lines 150 to 170 use compound conditional formats. Line 180 adopts a conventional IF/THEN structure, as the last category does not possess an upper and lower limit.

The computation of the customer's bill B occurs at line 190 via the selected rate R(C). The C subscript derived from the IF/THEN statements ensures that the proper rate is employed. The PRINT USING statement, line 200, outputs A, W, and B in accordance with their edited formats.

This program effectively uses the compound conditional to control access to the rate array. If desired, each conditional could have specified a separate billing computation. A sample instruction for category 1 would have been written as follows:

```
150     IF W > 0 AND W <= 999 THEN B = 5.22 + W * R(1)
```

This instruction specifies the exact array cell to use and substitutes that value for processing. The use of similar statements would have been equally successful.

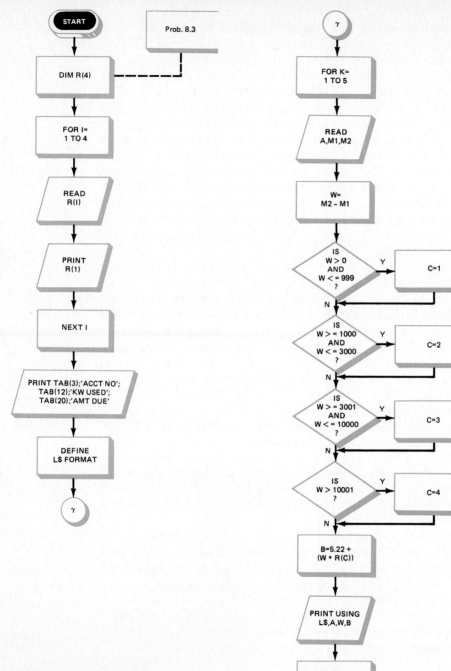

FIGURE 8.7   The flowchart for Problem
8.3 consists of two major modules. The
opening module defines and loads the rate
array. Module 2 depicts the processing
used in relation to its contents.

FIGURE 8.8 *(a)* Program and *(b)* output for Problem 8.3.

(a)

```
10 DIM R(4)
20 REM PROB 8.3
30 FOR I = 1 TO 4
40   READ R(I)
50   PRINT R(I)
60 NEXT I
70 DATA .028,.023,.019,.016
100 PRINT TAB(3);'ACCT NO';TAB(12);'KW USED';TAB(20);'AMT DUE'
110 L$ ='    #####      #####  ####.##'
120 FOR K = 1 TO 5
130    READ A, M2,M1
140    W = M2 - M1
150    IF W > 0 AND W <= 999 THEN C=1
160    IF W >= 1000 AND W <= 3000 THEN C=2
170    IF W >= 3001 AND W <= 10000 THEN C=3
180    IF W >= 10001 THEN C=4
190    B = 5.22 + (W * R(C))
200    PRINT USING L$,A,W,B
210 NEXT K
300 DATA 4062,28762,26943,13775,14776,13908
310 DATA 9081,7630,1442,83009,56334,53018
320 DATA 10801,21055,8669
400 END
```

(b)

```
.028
.023
.019
.016
  ACCT NO   KW USED  AMT DUE
    4062      1819     47.06
   13775       868     29.52
    9081      6188    122.79
   83009      3316     68.22
   10801     12386    203.40
```

SIDE BAR 8.1 Illogical Logic

A common error occurs when programmers use consecutive conditional statements, where an IF/THEN/ELSE sequence is involved. It is a subtle error. The statements used appear correct but create a gap within the testing of values.

Consider an application where four codes of 1, 2, 3, and 4 are used to designate four product lines. The program written must test for and identify each code and assign it to a specific module. The statements specified are written below.

```
160   IF C = 1 THEN GOSUB 500                    }
170   IF C = 2 THEN GOSUB 700                    } (Wrong)
180   IF C = 3 THEN GOSUB 900 ELSE GOSUB 1100    }
```

Though the statements appear to handle all four code structures, they do not. The IF/THEN statements at lines 160 and 170 are properly written to control access for codes of 1 and 2. The error lies in the logic of line 180. In that statement, if C = 3, the program branches to the module at GOSUB 900, which is correct. The error in logic occurs in the ELSE portion of the statement.

The programmer's intent was to check for the codes in sequential statements. Thus, if a code equal to 4 was not handled at line 160 and 170, it would be selected in the ELSE part of line 180. The format of line 180 will accomplish that, as well as assign codes of 1 and 2 to the GOSUB 1100 module.

If you examine line 160, you will note that if C equals 1, the program branches to the GOSUB 500 module and returns to line 160 when that module's work is performed. The program will then proceed onto lines 170, 180, and so on. The C = 1 code is ignored at line 170, but is again handled at line 180.

The reason for the error lies in the nature of the IF/THEN/ELSE statement. Line 180 tests for a code of 3. A 3 code is assigned to the 900 module, where all non-3 codes (of which 1, 2, and 4 are possible) are assigned to the 1110 module. The implied logic — if 1 and 2 are processed, the remaining codes of 3 and 4 may be separately handled — is not correct.

A correct alternative to the above sequence of statements is listed below. Every statement is assigned to a specific code, thereby controlling access to each module — only if the correct code is found.

```
160     IF C = 1 THEN GOSUB 500
170     IF C = 2 THEN GOSUB 700    } (Correct)
180     IF C = 3 THEN GOSUB 900
190     IF C = 4 THEN GOSUB 1100
```

Though there is one additional statement, it removes the potential for error. Only the correct code is used in relation to its module.

8.3 Nested Loops

In many applications, the necessity arises to use **nested loops,** that is, loops positioned one inside the other. Within the nested-loop structure, the inner loop is repeatedly performed under control of the outer loop. Each loop is separately defined with its own loop variable and set of tasks.

The concept of nested loops has many parallels in everyday life. The odometer in your car functions as a series of loops, where tenths of a mile turn into miles after 10 loops and miles turns into tens of miles in 10 loops and so on. Most clocks operate in series of nested loops of 60, 60, 12, and 2 — 60 seconds, 60 minutes, 12 hours, twice a day. A loop within a loop permits programmers to create solutions where one loop's activity is performed within a sequence defined by the other loop.

Nested FOR/ NEXTs

Multiple FOR/NEXT statements are a key to the construction of nested loops. Figure 8.9(a) shows one FOR/NEXT nested within the other. The nested FOR/NEXT statements define an outer, I, loop of four repetitions and an inner, J, loop of three loops. The FOR instruction, line 100, initializes I at 1 and defines an ending value of 4. This instruction is situated ahead of line 110, where J is initialized at 1 and the J loop commences. Effectively, while I equals 1, the second loop continues as J assumes the values of 1, 2, and 3. When J equals 3, the third loop ends, the program continues through the NEXT J statement at line 190 and executes line 200. That NEXT I statement recognizes that I is only equal to 1, increments I to 2, and continues the loop at line 100.

When I equals 2, program flow again accesses the FOR J instruction at line 110. The J loop is reinitialized and again directed to execute three loops.

FIGURE 8.9 *(a)* Using two FOR/NEXT statements, it is possible to nest the J loop inside the I loop. A total of 12 loops results. *(b)* Values of the I and J loop variables are shown.

(a)

```
100 FOR I = 1 TO 4
110    FOR J = 1 TO 3
           •
           •
           •
190    NEXT J
200 NEXT I
```

(b)

When I is equal to . . .	J is equal to . . .
1	1, 2, 3
2	1, 2, 3
3	1, 2, 3
4	1, 2, 3

A total of 12 (4 × 3) loops are performed.

The loop variable J will again be set equal to 1, 2, and 3, but in this case I is equal to 2. Since the J loop is nested within the I loop, it will undergo repeated loops while the I variable remains fixed. Upon completion of the second set of J loops, the entire sequence is repeated with I equal to 3 and 4. On the last loop, when I equals 4 and J equals 3, program control passes from lines 190 to 200 and out of the nested-loop sequence. The instruction following the outer NEXT statement, line 200, is then accessed to continue processing.

An important thing to understand are the values assumed by both the loop variables I and J, as shown in Figure 8.9*(b).* They illustrate the repetitive and nested nature of these looping sequences. Essentially, while I equals 1, J has values of 1, 2, and 3. The J loop of 1, 2, and 3 is repeated for the I values of 2, 3, and 4. A total of 12 loops results from the nested execution of these 2 loops.

To illustrate the practical nature of this nested sequence, consider the use of I and J as month counters in a banking sequence. The J loop could represent the three months in a quarter, whereas the I loop could define the four quarters constituting a calendar year. When I equals 1 in the first quarter of the year, three J months pass. Another three months, when J equals 1 to 3, will pass when I equals 2. In the final two quarters, when I equals 3 and 4, J will again run from 1 to 3 each time to indicate the three-month duration.

Negative Accumulators

The term **negative accumulator** is assigned to accumulators whose function is to reduce a total on a regular basis. Instead of using an equation $T = T + A$, the negative accumulator is defined by $T = T - A$, where A represents the amount by which the total T is reduced. Negative accumulators provide a means of systematically reducing a total.

A major difference with the negative accumulator is the value at which it is initialized. Where the conventional accumulator is initialized at zero, the negative accumulator is established at a value from which data may be subtracted. It is not uncommon for a negative accumulator to be initialized at a large value (for example, 1000 or 10000) and have the program monitor the reduction of that value. A sample program illustrates the combined use of a negative accumulator and nested FOR/NEXT sequence.

PROBLEM 8.4   Analysis of a Declining Inheritance

The problem entails estimating the balance of a declining inheritance. A family is left $26,700 in an account and wants to withdraw exactly 3.56 percent of that amount monthly for one year. Interest is added to the account at the end of each three-month period, at a rate of 2.14 percent of the lowest balance of the account that quarter. The family wants an itemized printout of the account's activity for that year. Identify the principal at the start of each quarter, the balance at the end of each month, the interest added each month, and the final balance. Accumulate the total amount of all monthly deductions and the total interest earned. Use headings whenever desired. Apply the ####.## format to the principal.

These are the main points in the problem narrative:

1   The problem requires a nested-looping sequence to accommodate quarterly withdrawals and interest computations. A three-loop sequence for the months is positioned inside a four-loop sequence for the four quarters in a year.

2   One negative accumulator and two accumulators are needed. The negative accumulator will reduce the account principal by each month's withdrawal. The two accumulators will separately total the withdrawals made and interest paid.

3   Each withdrawal is subtracted from the principal. All interest is added to the account at the end of each quarter. The withdrawal amount is computed at 3.56 percent of the principal, and interest is computed at 2.14 percent of principal at the quarter's end. The opening principal is $26,700.

4   Edited formats are applied to all outputs, each line format prepared by the programmer.

The flowchart for Problem 8.4 is shown in Figure 8.10.

Essentially, the flowchart is divided into three major components. The opening phase of processing serves to initialize the two required accumulators, establish the initial principal amount, define two edited formats and print the report's heading. The second phase depicts the nested loops in which the account's processing is accomplished. The closing module outputs data relating to the account's financial condition.

Focusing on module 2, we note that a loop of three cycles is placed within a loop of four repetitions. The interior loop represents the monthly processing within each quarter, while the outer loop defines the four quarters which constitute the processing performed within one year. After opening the outer loop Q, we identify the quarter to undergo processing and its opening principal. These outputs occur at the start of each quarter's data and prior to the processing of the three monthly withdrawals.

The monthly looping sequence M consists of three loops. Processing involves computation of the withdrawal amount W, the negative accumula-

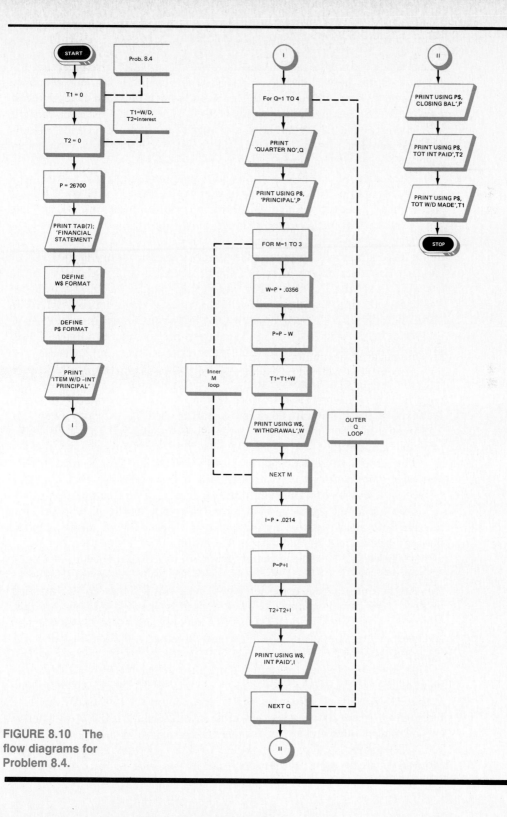

FIGURE 8.10 The flow diagrams for Problem 8.4.

tion of P to produce the current balance, and the update of the T1 accumulator to sum up the withdrawals made. The end of the three-loop sequence closes the quarter's processing and precedes the computation of the interest earned. All interest amounts are posted to the account for the next quarter. The update of the T2 accumulator monitors the interest earned for the current quarter. The interest earned for that quarter is output before commencing the Q loop and the next cycle of withdrawals.

The combined processing of the quarterly Q and monthly M nested loops produces a total of 12 loops, the equivalent of one year's activity. The last three lines of output are printed to summarize the account's status. The output of the account's closing balance, total interest paid, and total withdrawals made close this solution.

The program and output for Problem 8.4 are shown in Figure 8.11. An opening REM statement identifies the program's origin and precedes the initialization of the T1 and T2 accumulators at lines 20 and 30. The principal P is defined at line 50 and precedes the centering of the report title FINANCIAL STATEMENT. Two edited formats, W\$ and P\$, are defined at lines 70 and 80 for later use in PRINT USING statements. Column headings, line 90, are outputted before the nested loops are processed.

The nested-loop sequence extends from lines 100 to 240. An interior M loop of three cycles is nested within an outer Q loop of four cycles. The opening FOR statement is positioned at line 100, with the nested FOR statement appearing at line 140. Prior to the start of each M loop, outputs at lines 110 and 120 define the quarter to undergo processing (Q) and the opening principal amount (P).

The interior M loop consists of lines 140 to 190. The indentation of these and other statements visually highlights each loop's activities. Within three consecutive statements, the computation, posting, and accumulation of the withdrawal amount are performed. Line 150 computes the withdrawal (W); line 160 directs the negative accumulation of the withdrawal, resulting in the update of the current principal P; and the accumulator T1 updates the total of all withdrawals made. The output of the withdrawal amount occurs before the M loop is closed.

At the end of each three-loop sequence, the interest on the existing balance is computed via line 200. That amount is then added to the principal at line 210, with line 220 updating the T2 accumulator (where all interest paid is added). The output of the interest earned is completed, line 230, before the next quarter starts.

After the fourth quarter, the program passes through the NEXT Q statement at line 240 to the closing output statements. PRINT USING statements at lines 300 to 320 provide a summary of the account's activities. On separate lines the program outputs the account's closing balance, the total interest earned in each quarter, and the total of all 12 withdrawals made within that year. The report displayed in Figure 8.11(b) offers a detailed list of all transactions and can be used to advise the family on their planned withdrawal scheme.

(a)

```
10 REM PROB 8.4
20 T1 = 0
30 T2 = 0
40 REM -- T1 = W/D, T2 = INTEREST
50 P = 26700
60 PRINT TAB(7);'FINANCIAL STATEMENT'
70 W$ = '\                \ ####.##'
80 P$ = '\                \          #####.##'
90 PRINT 'ITEM          W/D - INT  PRINCIPAL'
100 FOR Q = 1 TO 4
110    PRINT 'QUARTER NO',Q
120    PRINT USING P$,'PRINCIPAL',P
130       REM -- INNER LOOP
140       FOR M = 1 TO 3
150          W = P * .0356
160          P = P - W
170          T1 = T1 + W
180          PRINT USING W$,'WITHDRAWAL',W
190       NEXT M
200    I = P * .0214
210    P = P + I
220    T2 = T2 + I
230    PRINT USING W$,'INT PAID',I
240 NEXT Q
300 PRINT USING P$,'CLOSING BAL',P
310 PRINT USING P$,'TOT INT PAID',T2
320 PRINT USING P$,'TOT W/D MADE',T1
330 END
```

(b)

FINANCIAL STATEMENT

ITEM	W/D - INT	PRINCIPAL
QUARTER NO	1	
PRINCIPAL		26700.00
WITHDRAWAL	950.52	
WITHDRAWAL	916.68	
WITHDRAWAL	884.05	
INT PAID	512.50	
QUARTER NO	2	
PRINCIPAL		24461.25
WITHDRAWAL	870.82	
WITHDRAWAL	839.82	
WITHDRAWAL	809.92	
INT PAID	469.53	
QUARTER NO	3	
PRINCIPAL		22410.22
WITHDRAWAL	797.80	
WITHDRAWAL	769.40	
WITHDRAWAL	742.01	
INT PAID	430.16	
QUARTER NO	4	
PRINCIPAL		20531.17
WITHDRAWAL	730.91	
WITHDRAWAL	704.89	
WITHDRAWAL	679.80	
INT PAID	394.09	
CLOSING BAL		18809.67
TOT INT PAID		1806.29
TOT W/D MADE		9696.62

FIGURE 8.11   (a) Program and (b) output for Problem 8.4.

8.4 The Program Sort

Sorting, that is, the orderly sequencing of data, is essential to many programming problems. Sorting allows us to alphabetize names or sequence a list of account numbers. Frequently, data must be sorted before many processing activities can be undertaken.

Though other sorting theories exist, the most common approach to sorting data involves the concept of the **bubble sort.** It parallels the concept of selecting, which was previously discussed, as the program continually seeks a key value within a looping sequence, retaining that data in a specific cell.

The purpose of sorting is to isolate a desired value and retain that data in a specific array cell. If, for example, we are sorting array data in ascending numerical order, we seek the lowest value and store it in cell 1. The process continues, with the second lowest value stored in cell 2, the third lowest in cell

The Concept of Sorting Data

3, and so on until the highest value is stored in the last cell. When the sort is over, data retained in the array is ordered from the lowest to the highest value.

The key to sorting is the logical comparison of two data items in an array. In the case of ascending values, each array cell is compared first with cell 1. If the contents of cell 1 are smaller than those of the comparison cell, no change takes place. However, if the contents of the comparison cell are smaller, then they are switched with the contents of cell 1. The process is performed for cell 2, cell 3, and so on, until the last data items are found. A nested-loop sequence is used to create the repetitive sequence in which these cells are compared.

To illustrate the actual operation of the sort, let us examine a five-cell array containing five numbers to be sorted in ascending order (Figure 8.12). The X(5) array holds these data items in their unsorted sequence, with the values 48, 63, 32, 52, and 19 in cells X(1) to X(5), respectively.

Figure 8.12(a) shows the looping sequence of the first sorting pass. In the first loop, X(2) is compared to X(1). Since 48 is less than 63, the value stored in X(1) is smaller, and the cell contents are not swapped. In the second comparison, cells X(1) and X(3) are tested. Since 32 is less than 48, the cell contents are swapped. In the revised array, 32 is now stored in the X(1) and 48 in X(3). It is important to recognize that only the contents of the X(1) and X(3) cells are affected. This swap does *not* push down or reorder any other array cells — contrary to the assumptions of many beginning students. The X(1) and X(4) cells are compared in the third loop. Again, as the value in X(1) is less than the value in X(4), no swap is performed and the array remains unchanged. This is not the case for the comparison of X(1) and X(5), the last test of this initial sort sequence. As the contents of X(5) are less than X(1), these cells are swapped, placing 19 in X(1) and 32 in X(5). The final array configuration is noted in the last diagram in Figure 8.12(a), where the X(1) contains the lowest value of all five cells.

Figure 8.12(b) show the steps involved in the second sort sequence. The contents of the X(1) cell remain unchanged. X(2) is compared with all other array cells in a series of loops, beginning with X(3). The swap of the X(2) and X(3) cells occurs, as 48 is less than 63. No swap occurs when X(2) is tested against X(4), as 48 is less than 52. The contents of X(2) and X(5) are swapped because 32 is less than 48. This second pass of this sort fixes 19 and 32 in X(1) and X(2), respectively, and leaves the contents of the last three cells unsettled.

The third series of tests commences with the X(3) and X(4) cells. The contents of these cells are reversed, as 52 is less than 63. The comparison of X(3) and X(5) also results in a swap, as 48 is less than the 52. The swap of these cells leaves 48 in X(3) and 52 in X(5). The array configuration after three sorting passes is noted in Figure 8.12(c).

In the last sequence the contents of X(4) and X(5) are compared. Since 52 is less than 63, these two cells are swapped. This completes the sort and finds all data in ascending order, as desired. Figure 8.12(d) depicts the final array configuration.

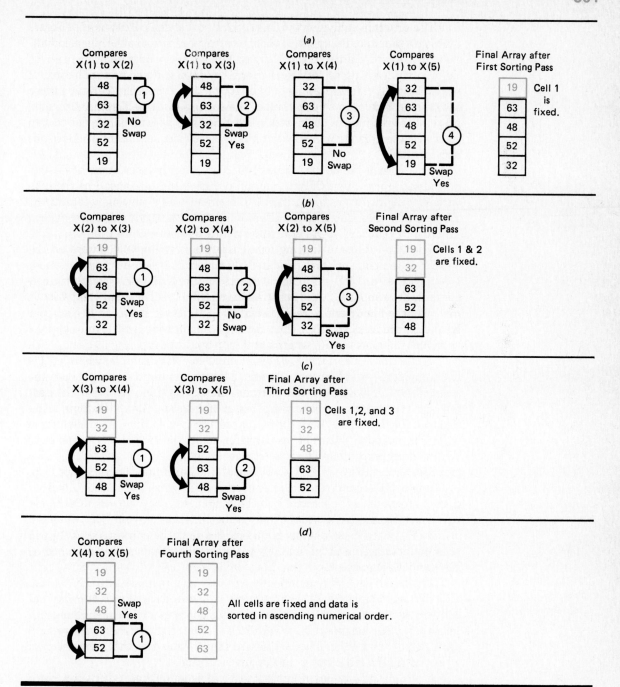

FIGURE 8.12 The four phases of sorting the five cells of the X array are illustrated.

The program equivalent of this sorting sequence is illustrated in Figure 8.13. This sequence assumes (1) that the array was previously loaded, and (2) that the data contained in the X array is ready for sorting.

Examining this set of instructions, we immediately notice the use of nested loops. A careful reading of lines 100 to 120 notes the integrated nature of these nested loops to accomplish the sorting of data. These statements possess a slight modification within their nesting, which enables the sort to start with the next higher array cell when each subsequent set of comparisons is performed.

This linkage is evident in lines 100 to 120, the critical statements in this nested sequence. The FOR instruction of line 100 establishes I as the loop variable ranging from 1 to 4. Line 110 increments the I value by 1, defining K. The nested J loop, line 120, links its starting value to K and ensures that each nested J loop always starts at a value that is one more than I.

The importance of linking I to J is evident at line 130, where an IF/THEN statement compares the data held in two array cells in preparation for a potential swap. If $I = 1$, then J starts at 2 and the first comparison is between $X(1)$ and $X(2)$. As J is incremented from 2, subsequent comparisons occur between $X(1)$ and $X(3)$, $X(1)$ and $X(4)$, and $X(1)$ and $X(5)$. In each case when the value in $X(1)$ is less than the $X(J)$ cell, no swap is performed and the program branches to 170, where the J loop continues.

When the value in the $X(J)$ cell is smaller — for example, when $X(2)$ is less than $X(1)$ — a cell swap is directed. Though apparently a simple task, the swap of data in two cells requires three statements. Line 140 takes the contents of $X(I)$ and stores it in a temporary storage area called S. Without using S, one of the data items would be overlayed and lost. At line 150, the contents of $X(J)$ is moved to $X(I)$. The last transfer causes the data in S to be moved to $X(J)$ and properly completes the transfer sequence. From line 160, the program continues to the NEXT J statement and continues the interior J loop.

When the second set of comparisons is performed, the nested loop sequence starts with $I = 2$ and $J = 3$. This indicates that all comparisons are performed against $X(2)$, and the first test of this set is between $X(2)$ and $X(3)$. By starting with $X(2)$, the program ensures that the contents of $X(1)$ will remain unchanged and the smallest value stored in that cell is untouched by subsequent comparisons.

The second set of comparisons will test $X(2)$ against $X(3)$, $X(4)$, and $X(5)$. When completed, $X(2)$ will contain the second smallest value and that cell will remain fixed when the next set of comparisons begins. The third phase of sorting begins with $I = 3$ and $J = 4$. The resulting tests involve $X(3)$ against $X(4)$ and $X(5)$. The last nested sequence causes the comparison of $X(4)$ and $X(5)$, thus closing the sorting sequence.

It is the I and J values of this last test which define the closing values used within the FOR statements at lines 100 to 120. The closing value of the outer loop must be one less than the closing value of the inner loop, for the proper completion of the nesting sequence and sort. If they were the same, the comparison of $X(5)$ and $X(5)$ in our example would have no significance.

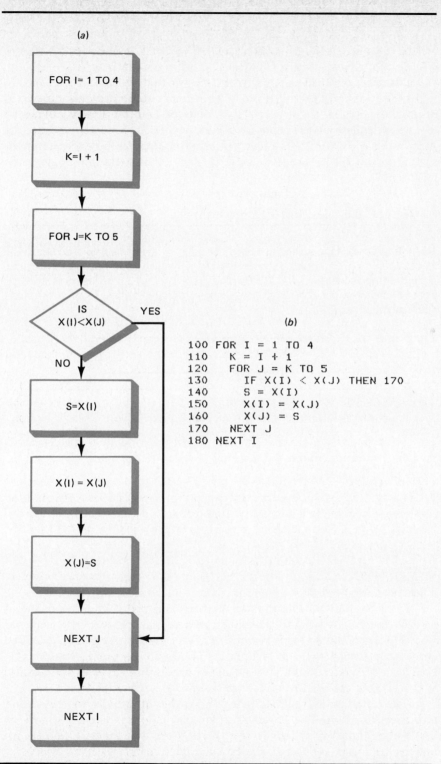

(a)

FOR I= 1 TO 4

K=I + 1

FOR J=K TO 5

IS
X(I)<X(J)

YES

NO

S=X(I)

X(I) = X(J)

X(J)=S

NEXT J

NEXT I

(b)

```
100 FOR I = 1 TO 4
110    K = I + 1
120    FOR J = K TO 5
130       IF X(I) < X(J) THEN 170
140          S = X(I)
150          X(I) = X(J)
160          X(J) = S
170    NEXT J
180 NEXT I
```

FIGURE 8.13 (a)
Flowchart and (b) pro-
gram providing the
instructional sequence
to accomplish the
numerical sort of the X
array's cells.

With I = 4 and J = 5, the comparison of X(I) and X(J) has meaning and ensures that the last two cells of the X array are properly tested.

The result of executing this excerpt reveals that 19, 32, 48, 52, and 63 are retained within the X(1) to X(5) cells. Though no actual data values appear in lines 100 to 180, the sort was correctly completed. Our combined use of nested loops and their variables as subscripts permitted us to sort the contents of the X array correctly. Another sample program will help reinforce the concept of sorting and enable the reader to view the sort of data within the context of a full problem.

PROBLEM 8.5   Sorting 12 Data Items

The problem entails the sorting and processing of 12 data items held in an array. The 12-cell array is loaded 2 cells at a time in module 1. Module 2 sorts the array's contents, placing data in ascending order. The third program module outputs the contents of the sorted array, three items at a time. Use an edited format to compact the report format. The data items used are as follows:

| 42.89 | 80.68 | 106.21 | 71.19 | 55.03 | 49.57 |
| 63.07 | 42.14 | 28.77 | 95.37 | 72.85 | 101.67 |

These are the main points in the problem narrative.

1   The problem utilizes a three-module structure. Module 1 loads the array, module 2 sorts its contents in ascending order, and module 3 outputs the newly ordered array.

2   The input of data occurs two data items at a time. The array is outputted three items per line in a compact edited format. Looping sequences control modules 1 and 3. The sorting of data items occurs within a nested loop.

3   A 12-cell array is used to hold all data items undergoing processing. No other array is required.

The flowchart, program, and output of Problem 8.5 are shown in Figure 8.14.

The flowchart reveals the use of three major modules. In the initial module, data is loaded into the 12-cell array, accessing two array cells per loop. The use of nested loops is required to sort the N array in module 2. The outer I loop ranges from 1 to 11 and thus defines the interior J loop of 2 to 12. Each time N(I) is less than N(J) the loop continues and no swap is necessary. When N(J) is less than N(I), data in these cells is swapped.

Before the contents of the sorted N array are outputted, an edited format is defined. The format must accommodate the output of three data items per line within the closing looping sequence. The use of a FOR/NEXT with STEP option is coordinated with the manipulation of subscripts. This tabular output will list all 12 values in ascending order on 4 consecutive lines.

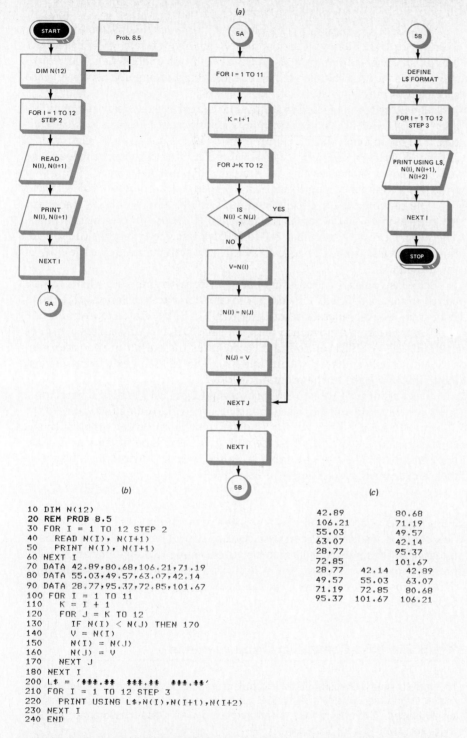

(a)

(b)

```
10 DIM N(12)
20 REM PROB 8.5
30 FOR I = 1 TO 12 STEP 2
40    READ N(I), N(I+1)
50    PRINT N(I), N(I+1)
60 NEXT I
70 DATA 42.89,80.68,106.21,71.19
80 DATA 55.03,49.57,63.07,42.14
90 DATA 28.77,95.37,72.85,101.67
100 FOR I = 1 TO 11
110    K = I + 1
120    FOR J = K TO 12
130       IF N(I) < N(J) THEN 170
140       V = N(I)
150       N(I) = N(J)
160       N(J) = V
170    NEXT J
180 NEXT I
200 L$ = '###.##  ###.##  ###.##'
210 FOR I = 1 TO 12 STEP 3
220    PRINT USING L$,N(I),N(I+1),N(I+2)
230 NEXT I
240 END
```

(c)

```
42.89       80.68
106.21       71.19
55.03       49.57
63.07       42.14
28.77       95.37
72.85      101.67
28.77   42.14    42.89
49.57   55.03    63.07
71.19   72.85    80.68
95.37  101.67   106.21
```

FIGURE 8.14 (a) Flowchart, (b) program, and (c) output for Problem 8.5.

The BASIC program opens at line 10 with a DIM statement which defines the N(12) array. The loading of this array occurs within a FOR/NEXT statement, lines 30 to 60. A STEP 2 option enables handling of two subscripted variables per loop. The 12 data items undergoing processing are specified at lines 70 to 90.

The nested loop created to sort the 12-cell array exists between lines 100 and 180. The indentation of statements helps accentuate each loop's activities. The outer loop causes I to run from 1 to 11. Line 110 acts as an index, defining K as one more than I. The K value is used as the opening value of the nested J loop and ensures that the I and J values are never equal. The J loop will always commence looping with an X(J) cell that is one above the X(I) cell.

The key comparison of cells occurs at line 130. The IF/THEN statement will branch to line 170 when N(I) is less than N(J), and processing continues. The swap of array values, lines 140 to 160, is performed when the contents of the N(J) are less than N(I). The NEXT J and I statements define the close of the nested loop.

The last phase of processing commences with line 200, where the L$ edited format is defined. This output format compactly positions three data items per line in preparation for the PRINT USING statement of line 220. This instruction is sandwiched between the FOR/NEXT sequence of lines 210 and 230. A STEP option of 3 coordinates the output of the three subscripted variables defined within line 220. The NEXT I exit from this last loop, line 230, leads to the program's close.

The output for Problem 8.5 is shown in Figure 8.14(c). It shows the dual entry of array data and four lines of output, listing the ordered sequence of the N array. These last lines list the 12 data items in ascending order, with the smallest value listed as the first item on line 1 and largest value as the last item on line 4. The use of a tabular, edited output provides an alternative means of printing a long series of data.

A Combined Student Problem

Thus far, many of our problems have been of moderate size in order to make new concepts easier to understand. Our next problem provides a means of integrating the many concepts learned in this and previous chapters into one program solution. This program will incorporate nested loops, the sorting of data, compound conditionals, the use of arrays, and a modular structure via GOSUBs.

PROBLEM 8.6   Computing Student Grades

The problem entails the computation of student grades. Student data are retained in five arrays. Within module 1, the name and the midterm and final exam grade arrays are initially loaded. Two other arrays, a final average and final class grade array, are filled with data resulting from processing.

In module 2, the program computes a final average for each student. The average is computed by multiplying the midterm grade by 0.4 and the final exam grade by 0.6. Enter each final grade into its respective array cell. In addition, this module will determine the letter grade for each student. The table of letter grades is listed below, along with the student data. Use compound conditionals to create each grade category and to assign an equivalent letter grade. Store the letter grade in its own array.

Module 3 is used to order student data in descending order. The student's final average is used to sort the name, final average, and final grade array. When one array cell is swapped, the other two cells in question must be moved. (Note: We are deliberately not using the midterm and final exam arrays.)

Module 4 outputs the student data contained in the sorted name, final average, and final grade arrays. A heading of STUDENT, FINAL AVG, and GRADE is positioned commencing with positions 1, 16, and 26. An edited format of ##.# is applied to final averages.

The required grade table and student data are as follows:

Student Name	Midterm	Final Exam		Final Avg	Grade
Arnolds	82	73		90–100	A
Bascomb	76	86		80–89	B
Conti	89	97		70–79	C
Davis	64	70		60–69	D
Enrich	44	65		0–59	F
Franklin	84	74			

These are the main points in the problem narrative.

1   The program will use five arrays, one array each for the student's name, midterm grade, final exam grade, final average, and final class grade. Each array should consist of six cells.

2   The name, midterm, and final exam arrays are loaded in module 1. The remaining two arrays, final average and class grade, are filled from the results of processing in module 2.

3   The final average is computed at 0.4 and 0.6 of the midterm and final exam grades. Compound conditionals are used to assign letter grades. The final average and letter grades are assigned to their respective arrays.

4   Module 3 is used to sort data. The three arrays involved in the sort are the name, final average, and class grade arrays. Data is sorted by final average. When data is swapped, all three arrays are handled concurrently.

5   The output of student data is reserved for module 4. Headings and an edited format are employed to prepare a compact format.

6   A modular program structure should be planned using GOSUB modules.

The flowchart for Problem 8.6 is shown in Figure 8.15.

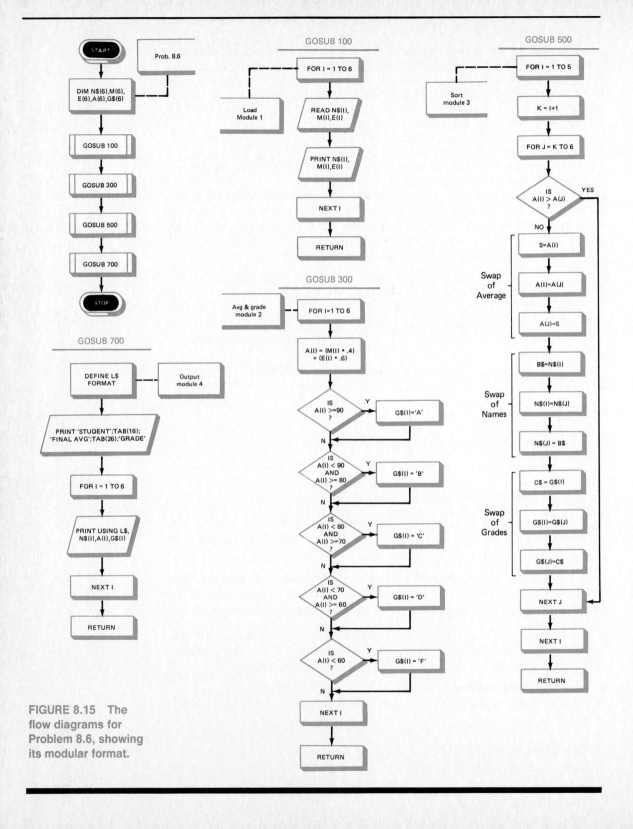

FIGURE 8.15 The flow diagrams for Problem 8.6, showing its modular format.

The main flow diagram of this solution depicts an initial definition of five arrays and four GOSUB modules. Each module is individually detailed in its own flowchart. The first module, GOSUB 100, describes the loading of the name, N$(I), midterm, M(I), and final exam, E(I), arrays within a six-loop sequence.

The second module, GOSUB 300, consists primarily of decision symbols within another six-loop FOR/NEXT sequence. Processing opens with the computation and retention of each student's final average A(I). Five decision symbols follow, each one defining a compound conditional for the indicated grading scheme. This segment of the solution assigns each student a letter grade of A, B, C, D, or F.

The sorting of data is accomplished in the third module, GOSUB 500. The short sequence focuses only on the data retained in the name, final average, and letter grade arrays. The use of three arrays requires the concurrent transfer of data, when a swap of array cells is required. Note that three sets of swapping instructions are needed to properly swap data in those three arrays. A nested loop controls the sort sequence. The principal decision is the test to determine whether the largest average values are stored in the lower arrays. Remember, we are sorting data in descending order, high to low averages.

The output of student data, sorted in module 3, is performed in GOSUB 700 — the fourth program module. After an edited line format is defined, the required headings are outputted. A six-loop FOR/NEXT sequence directs the output of data in the name, final average, and letter grade arrays. This module outputs only data that was sorted and does not concern itself with data in the midterm and final exam arrays.

The solution to Problem 8.6 results in the lengthy program listed in Figure 8.16. An opening DIM statement initializes the five arrays used to support processing. A REM statement, line 20, precedes the four GOSUB statements that define the four modules of this program. An unconditional branch, line 70, closes the program by branching to an END statement.

The GOSUB 100 module, lines 100 to 180, loads the contents of the name, N$, midterm, M, and final exam, E, arrays and defines the data used in processing. A six-loop sequence controls the loading of data into these three arrays. Data items are doubled up at line 150 to 170.

The computation of each student's final average and letter grade are assigned to module GOSUB 300. These tasks are performed within a second FOR/NEXT loop. The weighted computation of each final average, A(I), is accomplished at line 320. Five IF/THEN statements, lines 330 and 370, assign a letter grade, G$(I), to each student. Lines 340 to 360 employ compound conditional formats which parallel the grade structure.

The sort of data on a numerical basis is accomplished in the GOSUB 500 module. The main sort is performed against data held in the final average array, positioning that data in a descending order. In addition to swapping cells in the average array, companion cells in both the name and letter grade arrays are also moved. Three sets of swapping instructions, a total of nine

(a)

```
10 DIM N$(6),M(6),E(6),A(6),G$(6)
20 REM PROB 8.6
30 GOSUB 100
40 GOSUB 300
50 GOSUB 500
60 GOSUB 700
70 GO TO 800
100 REM -- LOAD MODULE 1
110 FOR I = 1 TO 6
120    READ N$(I),M(I),E(I)
130    PRINT N$(I),M(I),E(I)
140 NEXT I
150 DATA 'ARNOLDS',82,73,'BASCOMB',76,86
160 DATA 'CONTI',89,97,'DAVIS',64,70
170 DATA 'ENRICH',44,65,'FRANKLIN',84,74
180 RETURN
300 REM -- AVG & GRADE MODULE 2
310 FOR I = 1 TO 6
320    A(I) = (M(I) * .4) + (E(I) * .6)
330    IF A(I) >= 90 THEN G$(I)='A'
340    IF A(I) < 90 AND A(I) >= 80 THEN G$(I)='B'
350    IF A(I) < 80 AND A(I) >= 70 THEN G$(I)='C'
360    IF A(I) < 70 AND A(I) >= 60 THEN G$(I)='D'
370    IF A(I) < 60 THEN G$(I)='F'
380 NEXT I
390 RETURN
500 REM -- SORT MODULE 3
510 FOR I = 1 TO 5
520    K = I + 1
530    FOR J = K TO 6
540       IF A(I) > A(J) THEN 640
550       S = A(I)
560       A(I) = A(J)
570       A(J) = S
580       B$ = N$(I)
590       N$(I) = N$(J)
600       N$(J) = B$
610       C$ = G$(I)
620       G$(I) = G$(J)
630       G$(J) = C$
640    NEXT J
650 NEXT I
660 RETURN
700 REM -- OUTPUT MODULE 4
710 L$ = '\           \    ##.#        \  \'
720 PRINT 'STUDENT';TAB(16);'FINAL AVG';TAB(26);'GRADE'
730 FOR I = 1 TO 6
740    PRINT USING L$,N$(I),A(I),G$(I)
750 NEXT I
760 RETURN
800 END
```

FIGURE 8.16 *(a)* Program and *(b)* output for Problem 8.6. Four GOSUB modules define the main program of this solution.

(b)

```
ARNOLDS       82              73
BASCOMB       76              86
CONTI         89              97
DAVIS         64              70
ENRICH        44              65
FRANKLIN      84              74
STUDENT       FINAL AVG GRADE
CONTI           93.8       A
BASCOMB         82.0       B
FRANKLIN        78.0       C
ARNOLDS         76.6       C
DAVIS           67.6       D
ENRICH          56.6       F
```

statements from lines 550 to 630, control the movement of data in these three arrays. We are testing to ensure that the highest averages are retained in the first cells of the average array, as well as their related names and letter grades. A nested loop controls the sort sequence.

The output of the student name, final average, and letter grade arrays occurs within the final module, GOSUB 700. The L$ format offers an edited output, line 740. The printing of the three column headings, via TAB functions at line 720, precedes the FOR/NEXT sequence in which individual student data is outputted.

The output for Problem 8.6 appears in Figure 8.16(b). The reader may observe the sorting of data by comparing the listing of original data and the computed results of processing.

SIDE BAR 8.2   Inverting the Contents of an Array

On occasion, the need arises to output the contents of a single one-dimensional array that has just undergone a sort. The user does not want to resort that array and further complicate processing. The solution to this dilemma involves the manipulation of the array's subscripts and the output of that array in a loop.

Consider an X array of 10 cells, where the data is held in ascending numerical order. It is possible to output the contents of those 10 cells, from X(10) to X(1), using the following statements.

```
300     FOR I = 1 TO 10
310     PRINT X(11 − I)
320     NEXT I
```

The trick here is to manipulate the subscript, with the assistance of the loop variable. Though I will range from 1 to 10, the subscript will assume the values of 10 to 1 on each loop. The I value is subtracted from 11, within the subscript, thus reversing the order of output.

When I equals 1, the X subscript is 10. When I equals 2, the X subscript is computed at $9(11 − 2)$ and X(9) is outputted. The output of X(1) occurs on the tenth loop, with I equal to 10 and the subscript computed at $1(11 − 10 = 1)$. The manipulation of the array subscript permits the output of an ordered array, without resorting its contents.

An Alphabetic Sort

A natural question arises in relation to the sorting of nonnumeric data held in arrays. Is it possible to use the same sort technique used in Problem 8.6? The bubble sort handles nonnumeric data in exactly the same way as numeric data. What varies is the conditional statement used to determine the order of alphabetic characters.

The conditional statement associated with the sort of alphabetic data may be written as

```
360     IF N$(I) < N$(J) THEN 420
```

which parallels the structure of the numerical sort test. The difference lies in the computer's handling of the nonnumeric data. The computer first converts the data to an arithmetic equivalent and then sorts it. The user doesn't see the conversion of these data items, but the results are as accurate.

FIGURE 8.17 The
sort sequence applied
to nonnumeric data is
similar to the instruc-
tions used when
sorting numeric data.

```
500 REM -- ALPHABETIC SORT
510 FOR I = 1 TO 5
520    K = I + 1
530    FOR J = K TO 6
540       IF G$(I) < G$(J) THEN 610
550          C$ = G$(I)
560          G$(I) = G$(J)
570          G$(J) = C$
580          B$ = N$(I)
590          N$(I) = N$(J)
600          N$(J) = B$
610    NEXT J
620 NEXT I
```

When this logical operation is used to sort alphabetic or nonnumeric data, the user must remember to swap data held in the cells of the alphabetic arrays. Using Problem 8.6 as a model, we could have sorted letter grades and names using the set of instructions in Figure 8.17.

The nested loop is still a principal component of the sort. The test of alphabetic values occurs at line 540, where the grade array's cells are compared. If G$(I) is less than G$(J) and I equals 1 and J equals 2, the G$(1) cell contains an alphabetic character (for example, A) that should precede the value held in the G$(2) array (for example, C). If the values are reversed — that is, A is in G$(2) and C is in G$(1) — a swap is necessary. Lines 550 to 570 swap the letter grades, with the swapping of related names directed by lines 580 to 600.

Chapter Summary

8.1 Selecting One Data Item

It is possible to select particular data items by reading the contents of the entire array and testing each cell. This approach makes possible the selection of the largest or smallest value or a data item which meets a set of specific characteristics.

An integral part of the selection technique is the use of a FOR/NEXT statement and an IF/THEN statement. One array item is established as a test value to accommo-

date the comparisons of data. Each cell's data is tested, and that item retained, if it is to replace the existing value.

It is possible to load the array, inputting multiple items of data. When searching through the array, only one cell is tested per loop. Array cells tested may contain data that was originally placed there via input operations or as the result of processing.

8.2 One-Dimensional Tables

Arrays provide a means of ordering a series of data items which compose a list or table of values. Each cell holds data in a category; array cells assume the same order as the list of categories. Assuming a table of four values, a four-cell array is needed.

The key to using an array is the ability to access values from its cells. Conditional statements control access to the array. The YES branch of an IF/THEN statement defines the subscript or the specific array.

If the data held in an array remains constant, the array may be defined via READ and DATA statements. When data values vary, they can be loaded using INPUT statements.

A table of values where each category is defined by alphabetic codes may be stored in an array. A conditional statement tests these alphabetic codes to control access to individual cells.

Arrays constructed to support a range of values are similarly handled. An IF/THEN statement tests whether the value input falls into a category and assigns the array cell associated with that value. A series of conditional statements controls access to a multiple-category array.

Compound conditionals permit a logical operation to be defined using two or more conditional statements. The logical operators AND and OR may be used to link conditionals. Thus, it is possible to test whether a variable falls between a low and high value or between two codes.

8.3 Nested Loops

Nested loops position one loop within a second loop. The interior loop is repeatedly executed, while the outer loop is held constant.

In BASIC programs, nested loops are defined by means of two FOR/NEXT statements. The outer FOR/NEXT defines one loop variable, while the second is used in the inner loop. The following program excerpt illustrates a nested loop:

```
100     FOR I = 1 TO 5
110     FOR J = 1 TO 3
        .
        .
        .
200     NEXT J
210     NEXT I
```

In these statements, the outer loop executes 5 loops, while the inner loop executes 3 loops, for a total of 15 loops (5×3).

8.4 The Program Sort

Array data is ordered through sorting. The bubble sort continually searches for the lowest (or highest) value in the array. A nested looping sequence is used to construct the sort. On the first sort pass, the lowest (or highest) value is stored in cell 1. On sort pass 2, the second value is stored in cell 2, and so on.

The sorting of alphabetic data uses a similar approach to sorting data in ascending order. The program converts alphabetic data to a numeric equivalent, tests values, and places them in ascending order.

When performing sorting, the program must swap values as the contents of cells are tested. It is important to use three statements, retaining one of the shifted data items in a dummy storage area while the swap is performed. Without this, one of the array values would be lost. The IF/THEN is the vehicle for testing two array cells and determining whether their contents should be swapped. This test is repeatedly performed in a nested loop.

Key BASIC Statements

	Examples	
AND operator	30	IF A < 6 AND B > 10 THEN C = 1
	40	IF A > 90 AND B <= 80 THEN I = 2
Nested loop	100	FOR I = 1 TO 8
	110	FOR J = 1 TO 4
	.	} A total of 32 Loops
	.	
	190	NEXT J
	200	NEXT I
OR operator	50	IF X = 6 OR N$ = 'A' THEN B = 9
	60	IF X = 6 OR Y <= 10 THEN C = P(1) * R

Glossary

AND operator A component within compound conditionals which links two conditions and forces both to be met.

Bubble sort A programming technique used to sort both numeric and alphabetic data.

Compound conditional A conditional statement composed of two or more conditions.

Negative accumulator An accumulator where an amount is subtracted within a loop.

Nested loop The placement of one loop within a second loop; the outer loop is held constant while the inner loop is executed repeatedly.

OR operator A component within compound conditionals where one or the other condition is met.

Sorting The placement of data within an array in a desired order — numerically or alphabetically.

Table look-up The testing of values representing catagories, determining which cell within that array should be accessed.

Exercises

In-Class Exercises

1   The problem entails finding the smallest number in an array of 10 values. Input data to the array in module 1, two data items at a time. In module 2, search through the array and determine its smallest data item. Output that item, using the label SMALLEST VALUE. The 10 data items are as follows:

.088	.062	.082	.072	.073
.075	.093	.061	.069	.065

Write a flowchart and program for this narrative.

2   The problem entails sorting data in an array. Using the data in problem 1, load an array of 10 cells. In a second module sort this data in descending order — high to low values. Output the contents of this array two at a time and close processing. Write a flowchart and program for this narrative.

3   The problem entails estimating the money earned in a bank account. A bank account is opened at $10,000. Each month, a withdrawal of $250 is made. Interest is calculated at the end of six months at a rate of 8.62 percent on the lowest balance in the account. The interest is added to the account to start the next six-month period. How much money is in the account at the end of one year? Accumulate the interest earned and print that total out at the year's end. Use an edited format of #####.## for dollar amounts. Use a nested loop to establish the two 6-month periods. Write the flowchart and program for this problem.

Lab Exercises

1   The problem entails loading and sorting array data. Names and test scores on an achievement test are randomly entered into an array of 10 cells each in module 1. Module 2 sorts the arrays in descending order by test scores. When the score is swapped, the name cell must also be swapped. In module 3, output these reordered arrays beneath the heading APPLICANT and TEST SCORE. The data for the problem is as follows:

Name	Test Score	Name	Test Score
Karlson	76.8	Meltzger	49.3
Abbey	46.5	Zipper	82.7
Carlton	86.2	Shawnee	68.3
Leland	70.9	Harnetto	91.6
Frankel	52.4	Martin	63.1

a Write the flowchart and program to satisfy this narrative. Use nested loops to sort the data.

b Revise the solution and sort the arrays by name, not test score. Write the program and flowchart describing this alphabetic sort. Use GOSUBs to establish the three modules.

2   The problem entails computing a series of costs and loading them into an array. In module 1, data is entered into the project number array and units array, one set of values per loop. A total of six cells is involved in each array. In module 2, costs for each project are computed. The cost's formula is:

$$\text{Costs} = 275 + (.56 * \text{units})$$

The costs figure is stored in its own array in relation to its project number. The units figure is drawn from its array cell. All six cost cells are filled in module 2. In module 3, the program outputs all data. A heading of PROJECT, UNITS, and PROJ COSTS is outputted commencing at positions 1, 10, and 17, respectively. Use ##### for project and units data and ####.## for costs when printing. The data for this problem is as follows:

Proj No	Units	Proj No	Units
86113	2561	94152	7709
00614	3890	50319	4909
21009	4024	48617	5670

a Write a flowchart and program for the above narrative.

b Solve the above problem, but add a fourth module to sort the data in the costs array and all array cells related to it. Insert this module before the last output module, such that the entire report produced will be in ascending order by cost. Write the flowchart and program for this revised solution, using GOSUBs for each module.

3   The problem entails computing gold prices and involves a table look-up. A three-cell array is constructed to hold sales rates for types of gold traded by a company. The array is loaded in module 1. In module 2, the sales price for each gold sale is computed. Input on this loop are the customer's ID number, the number of ounces of gold sold, and the code for the type of gold. The sales price is computed by multiplying the number of ounces of gold by the sales rate for that type of gold. Sales rates are drawn from the list of values held in the rate array. Output on each loop the customer's ID number, the ounces sold, and the total sales price beneath appropriate headings. Use

the edited formats of #### for customer ID, ## for the ounces of gold, and #### for the sales price of the gold. The data for the problem is as follows:

Type of Gold	Sales Rate/Oz.	Customer ID	Ounces	Type	Customer ID	Ounces	Type
A	447	2006	12	B	1614	20	C
B	392	615	18	C	0933	14	A
C	365	1844	10	A	1266	16	B
		1356	15	A	1056	17	C

  a Prepare a flowchart and program to satisfy this narrative. Use GOSUBs to create program modules.

  b Revise the solutions to store all of the input data and the computed prices in arrays. Perform the computation and output in module 2. In module 3, scan through the array of sales prices and determine the largest sales price computed. Retain that price, the customer ID, type and number of ounces sold. Output these data items on four separate lines, using literals to define each.

4   The problem entails the computation of monies in a bank account. The principal in the account is $14,900. The holder of the account wishes to draw $200 per month from the account. At the end of each quarter, interest is computed at 2.64 percent on the lowest balance in that account and added to the principal. The user wishes to draw that amount monthly for 48 months or until the account falls below a balance of $6000, whichever comes first. Output the principal at the start of each quarter, the accumulated total of interest made, and principal in the account when the $6000 limit is surpassed or the 48-month limit is reached. Use the edited format of #####.## on dollar amounts.

  Write the flowchart and program to satisfy the narrative. Use nested loops to create the quarterly loop and annual loop. Note that 16 quarters constitute a 48-month period.

5   The problem entails the conversion of British currency to dollars, using rates held within a table. In module 1, an array consisting of five cells for five categories of dollar conversions is constructed. The table defines the amount in British pounds to be converted to dollars and the rate to be used when converting to dollars (for example, 50 pounds is converted at a rate of 1.562 pounds per dollar).

  In module 2, an input statement permits the user to enter the amount of currency to be converted. The processing sequence is as follows:

  a The amount in pounds is compared against the array to determine the correct rate to use.

  b The conversion is multiplied by the currency amount to produce a dollar amount.

  c A service charge of 10 percent is computed, using the dollar amount from step 2.

  d The service charge is subtracted from the dollar amount to compute the net amount actually received by the individual.

For each conversion, output on four separate lines the amount to be converted in pounds and the conversion rate to be used, the resulting dollar amount, the service charge, and the net amount received.

The data and conversion table are as follows:

Pounds to Be Converted	Conversion Rate (Pounds/$)
0–100	1.562
101–500	1.524
501–1000	1.498
1001–5000	1.476
5001 and up	1.441

Pounds Slated for Conversion*	
652	7500
243	500
1009	1800
85	800

* Conversion amounts are only handled in full pound amounts.

Write a flowchart and program to satisfy this narrative.

6 The problem entails the investment of money in a timed savings account. An investor wishes to place $7500 in an account that earns interest at an annual rate of 8.952 percent. The interest is accumulated each day, with that total being added to the principal at the end of the seventh day of the week. The updated principal amount is used to start the next seven days' investment. The seven-day cycle is used for an entire year of 52 weeks. At the end of every quarter (every 13 weeks), an amount of $500 is withdrawn from the account and reduces the principal by that amount for the next investment week. At the end of the 52-week period, output on separate lines the starting balance, the total interest earned, the total amount of withdrawals and the closing balance in the account. Use appropriate labels for each output and edit the dollar amounts as ####.##.

Write a flowchart and program for this narrative. Use a nested loop to create the 7-day and 52-week cycles. Ensure that you initialize the account and use accumulators to total interest amounts made. Compute the daily rate by dividing the annual interest rate by 365.

7 The problem entails computing and sorting student grades. In module 1, data is entered into three arrays — student name, midterm grade, and final exam grade. These inputs represent three of the six arrays which will be employed.

In module 2, each student's final average and letter grade for the course are computed. The final average is computed using a ratio of 30 percent for the midterm and 70 percent for the final exam. The final average is stored in its array. The letter grade is determined using the table that is listed below. Three letter grades of S (for superior), P (for pass), and F (for fail) are possible. The final average is compared against the grade table to assign the grade which is stored in its array.

In module 3, a student grade report is prepared. Use the headings STUDENT, FINAL AVG, and GRADE, commencing at positions 1, 18, and 30. Output each student's data beneath those headings, printing only those array's contents.

a Write the flowchart and program necessary to satisfy the above narrative. Add a fourth module in which student data is sorted by final average (in descending order) to include the student name and grade arrays. A fifth module should output the sorted data held in those three arrays. Use appropriate headings.

b Write the flowchart and program for the above narrative. Again add two modules. In module 4, sort by the student name and also swap data in the final average and grade arrays. Output those three arrays in module 5, using appropriate headings.

The data and table used in this problem are as follows:

Grade Range	Letter Grade
85 to 100	S
60 to 84.9	P
0 to 59.9	F

Name	Midterm	Final Exam
Kobb	63	87
Marshall	92	73
Abbott	43	68
Donaldson	90	83
Marche	79	92
Yancy	80	51
Scott	62	37
Randelo	93	97

Quiz Problem

The problem entails computing the cost of carpeting. Four types of carpet are marketed by a manufacturer, with the rates per square yard held in a four-cell array. This array is loaded in the initial program module.

In module 2, input on each loop the customer number, length and width of the area to be carpeted (in feet), and the type of carpet to be laid. The length and width variables are multiplied, with that product divided by 9 to compute the square yards of carpeting required. This carpeting amount is multiplied by the rate for the type of carpet desired, found from the rate array, to produce the cost. This cost is stored in an array for subsequent sorting. In loop 2, output the customer number, carpet type, square yards needed, and the related cost beneath appropriate headings. Output this data commencing with positions 1, 6, 9, and 15. Use the formats #### for customer number, ####.# for square yards, and #####.## for cost.

In module 3, sort only the cost amounts in ascending order. Output this sorted sequence in module 4. The data and rate table for this problem are listed below.

Carpet Types	Carpet Rates	Customer No	Type	Length (ft.)	Width (ft.)
A	6.95	891	B	38	18
B	8.95	2067	C	12	56
C	11.95	1458	A	35	28
D	16.95	602	D	24	15

Prepare a flowchart and program to satisfy this problem narrative.

Quiz Solution

The flowchart, program, and outputs for the quiz problem are shown in Figure 8.18. The solution uses a 1-D array, a nested FOR/NEXT loop, and single looping sequences.

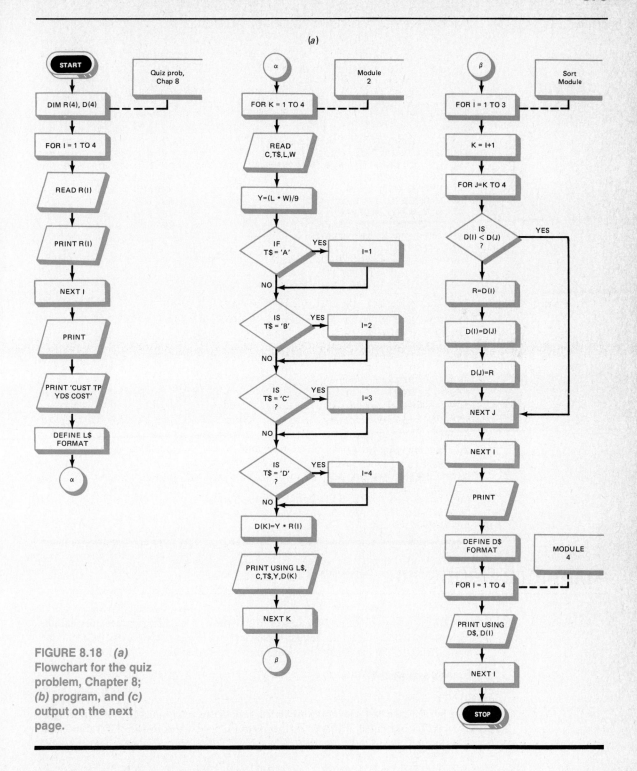

FIGURE 8.18 *(a)* Flowchart for the quiz problem, Chapter 8; *(b)* program, and *(c)* output on the next page.

FIGURE 8.18   *(Continued)*

(b)   (c)

```
10 DIM R(4), D(4)                                    6.95
20 REM -- QUIZ PROB, CHAP 8                          8.95
30 FOR I = 1 TO 4                                    11.95
40    READ R(I)                                      16.95
50    PRINT R(I)                                     4
60 NEXT I                                   CUST TP  YDS     COST
70 PRINT                                    891  B   76.0   680.20
80 DATA 6.95,8.95,11.95,16.95               2067 C   74.7   892.27
90 PRINT 'CUST TP  YDS       COST'          1458 A   108.9  756.78
100 L$ = '#### \ \###.# ####.##'            602  D   40.0   678.00
110 REM -- MODULE 2
120 FOR K = 1 TO 4                               678.00
130    READ C,T$,L,W                             680.20
140    Y = (L * W)/9                             756.78
150    IF T$ = 'A' THEN I=1                       892.27
160    IF T$ = 'B' THEN I=2
170    IF T$ = 'C' THEN I=3
180    IF T$ = 'D' THEN I=4
190    D(K) = Y * R(I)
200    PRINT USING L$,C,T$,Y,D(K)
210 NEXT K
300 REM -- SORT MODULE
310 FOR I = 1 TO 3
320    K = I + 1
330    FOR J = K TO 4
340       IF D(I) < D(J) THEN 380
350       R = D(I)
360       D(I) = D(J)
370       D(J) = R
380    NEXT J
390 NEXT I
400 PRINT
410 REM -- MODULE 4
420 D$ = '#####.##'
430 FOR I = 1 TO 4
440    PRINT USING D$, D(I)
450 NEXT I
500 DATA 891,'B',38,18,2067,'C',12,56
510 DATA 1458,'A',35,28,602,'D',24,15
600 END
```

Appendix: Debugging Hints

Working with nested loops often creates difficulties, as the programmer must handle multiple variables and track the performance of two looping sequences. Two common errors relate to the incorrect specification of loop variables.

Whose NEXT?

Through haste, programmers may improperly position the NEXT instructions associated with a nested-looping sequence, as depicted in Figure A.8.1. In this excerpt, the NEXT I statement at line 130 is incorrectly placed before the NEXT J statement. To construct the nested loop properly, the NEXT J instruction should have preceded its NEXT I counterpart.

```
 90  P = 6500
100  FOR I = 1 TO 4
110     FOR J = 1 TO 3
120        P = P - 50
130     NEXT I
140  NEXT J
150  PRINT P
200  END
```

the error message produced when
these instructions are executed

```
?NEXT without FOR at line 130
?FOR without NEXT at line 100
```

FIGURE 8.A.1 The improper specification of nested FOR/NEXT instructions will result in a program error and the inability to execute those statements.

Such an error results when the programmer follows the order of the opening FOR statements and does not recognize the positioning of the two loops involved. The inner J loop must be nested inside the outer I loop so that both loops be executed properly.

The error message printed, when an attempt was made to execute this program, identifies the misplacement of the NEXT statements. It recognizes that either NEXT statement was misplaced, not knowing the desired position of the I or J loop. The error message recognizes an error in program syntax, as well as identifying an error in the logic used to construct this solution.

A Case of Mistaken Identity

When more than one loop variable is used, programmers must exercise care that they do not conflict with other variables. The program excerpt noted in Figure A.8.2 offers a typical example of what can result if variables are carelessly specified.

The format of the solution appears correct, but a flaw exists. When specifying the interest variable I, the programmer did not recognize that it was also employed as the loop variable for the outer nested I loop, lines 110 and 200. The processing performed at lines 160 to 180 will directly interfere with the I looping sequence. The first set of loops will commence properly, but errors will result when the I variable is incorrectly employed for the computation of interest.

This error condition is recognized from the abbreviated output resulting from the program's execution. Where a total of 12 loops should ensue, only 3 loops are completed before an error occurs. The three outputs of line 140 note the performance of the three J loops and precede the latter outputs of lines 180 and 190. With I exceeding a value of 4, because of the processing at line 160, the loop is prematurely closed.

The programmer must specify another variable name for the interest computation to correct the error. This type of error is one of logic and may be caught by carefully reading your program before processing it.

FIGURE 8.A.2 The apparently correct program produces an incorrect output, revealing an error in the solution's logic.

```
100  P = 6750
110  FOR I = 1 TO 4
120     FOR J = 1 TO 3
130        P = P - 100
140        PRINT 'PRIN =',P
150     NEXT J
160     I = P * .0228
170     P = P + I
180     PRINT 'INT =',I
190     PRINT 'PRIN =',P
200  NEXT I
300  END
```

the results of processing
reveal an error in logic

```
PRIN =        6650
PRIN =        6550
PRIN =        6450
INT =          147.06
PRIN =        6597.06
```

NINE

Chapter Objectives

- Introduce two-dimensional (2-D) arrays.

- Discuss the structure of 2-D arrays and the use of row and column subscripts.

- Describe the use of FOR/NEXT nested loops when performing I/O operations on 2-D arrays.

- Discuss the conversion of categories and their relation to 2-D array subscripts.

- Introduce the MAT statement.

- Discuss the application of MAT statements to 2-D arrays and their data.

This chapter will

Introduction

An integral part of many computer applications is the access of data from tables. One-dimensional arrays are effectively employed in one type of problem, where access to a list of values requires only one means of reference. That is, only one subscript is necessary to determine which array cell to access.

Tables which require the user to specify two keys (or indexes) for a particular cell cannot be handled via one-dimensional arrays. Tables using two references require a **two-dimensional (2-D) array.** This type of array holds data within a matrix of cells, where data is fixed in specific rows and columns identified by subscripts. Tax tables, train schedules, inventory listings, and road maps are just a few examples of tables where specific data items are selected by cross-referencing columns and rows.

This chapter discusses the definition, structure, and use of two-dimensional arrays. Concepts developed in earlier chapters — nested loops, compound conditionals — provide a basis for constructing and handling two-dimensional arrays. The chapter opens with a discussion of how these arrays are configured and used as reference tables or to hold the results of processing. I/O operations relating to 2-D arrays are carefully explained. The chapter closes with a discussion of the MAT statement, which provides a means of efficiently manipulating the contents of 2-D arrays. Sample programs illustrate the application of these and other array-related statements.

9.1 The 2-D Structure

To use two-dimensional arrays properly, it is essential that users understand their structure and the way they retain data. Access to 2-D arrays requires the use of two subscripts, which when cross-referenced identify a specific cell. These subscripts define the structure of the two-dimensional array.

Rows and Columns

Many people correctly associate the structure of two-dimensional arrays with a table consisting of multiple rows and columns. Rows provide the horizontal levels of an array, where columns denote its vertical partitions. The relationship of the rows and columns composing a 2-D array is noted in Figure 9.1.

The two-dimensional array depicted consists of 4 horizontal rows and 3 vertical columns—a total of 12 cells in which data may be stored. Both the row and column numbers associated with that cell must be specified in order to reference any of these 12 cells. In Figure 9.1, the circled array cell carries the notation (2,3). This notation identifies the position of the cell in row 2, column 3. Convention has it that the first number in the parentheses denotes the row, with the second digit defining the column.

This form of notation signifies the two-way nature of the two-dimensional array. Two references, both a row and a column indicator, are needed to access any cell in a 2-D array.

Use of Two Subscripts

The need to specify both a row and a column variable essentially fixes the subscript employed with two-dimensional arrays. Paralleling the format for one-dimensional arrays, we could specify the (2,3) cell in the X array as

FIGURE 9.1   A 2-D array consisting of four rows and three columns. Each cell has its own identification code composed of a row and column number. The (2,3) cell notes its position in row 2, column 3.

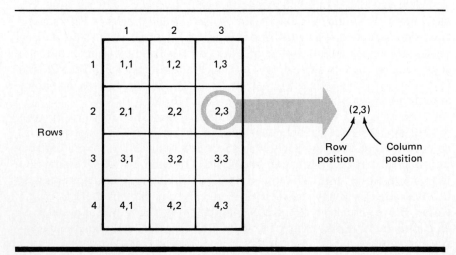

X(2,3). The variable name X indicates that this two-dimensional array holds only numeric data. A string-variable array name would define an array where nonnumeric data is retained.

To reinforce the use of double subscripts, let us consider the array cell X(4,2). This notation identifies the array cell positioned at row 4, column 2. The X(4,2) cell can hold exactly *one* item of numeric data and can be accessed by specifying that pair of row and column values.

In reexamining the cell identification of Figure 9.1, we may note qualities related to each row and column. For example, the three cells of row 1 carry the notations (1,1), (1,2), and (1,3). In each set of subscripts, the row subscript is held at 1 as each cell is in row 1. The column subscript is incremented by 1, as we pass from column 1 to column 3.

The same rationale could be applied to the cells situated in column 2. In that case, the cell subscripts are (1,2), (2,2), (3,2), and (4,2). The column subscript is held at 2 while we read down the rows 1 to 4.

The important fact gained from these observations is that we can systematically proceed along a row or down a column by indexing its subscript and holding the other subscript constant. Applying this principle, we can work with an entire row or column to perform I/O operations. This approach is used to load a two-dimensional array.

9.2 Loading 2-D Arrays

As with one-dimensional arrays, two-dimensional arrays must be loaded on a systematic basis. However, instead of using one FOR/NEXT sequence, the double subscript requires that two loops be used — one loop nested within the other.

The nested nature of these loops carries great importance, as it defines the order in which the array's cells are loaded. As we recall with nested loops, one variable remains constant while the other repeatedly loops. Since the loop variables of the nested FOR/NEXT statements act as subscripts, they define which variable is held constant and which varies. Accordingly, this sequence controls whether the two-dimensional array is loaded on a row-by-row or column-by-column basis. As the row-by-row loading sequence is most commonly used, let us examine a nested FOR/NEXT sequence in which this task is accomplished.

Nested FOR/ NEXTs

Figure 9.2(*a*) contains instructions for loading an array composed of four rows and three columns. The loading sequence is accomplished on a row-by-row basis: all three cells of one row are filled before the next row is loaded.

The DIM statement, line 10, defines a 2-D array called X, composed of four rows and three columns. The double subscript of the array name specifies

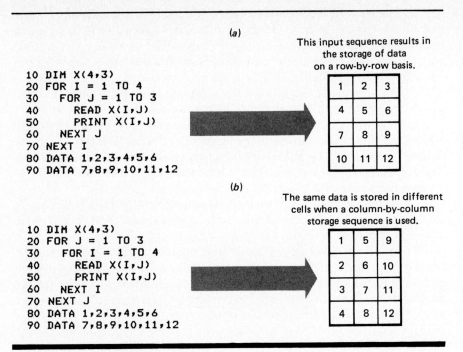

(a)

```
10 DIM X(4,3)
20 FOR I = 1 TO 4
30    FOR J = 1 TO 3
40       READ X(I,J)
50       PRINT X(I,J)
60    NEXT J
70 NEXT I
80 DATA 1,2,3,4,5,6
90 DATA 7,8,9,10,11,12
```

This input sequence results in the storage of data on a row-by-row basis.

1	2	3
4	5	6
7	8	9
10	11	12

(b)

```
10 DIM X(4,3)
20 FOR J = 1 TO 3
30    FOR I = 1 TO 4
40       READ X(I,J)
50       PRINT X(I,J)
60    NEXT I
70 NEXT J
80 DATA 1,2,3,4,5,6
90 DATA 7,8,9,10,11,12
```

The same data is stored in different cells when a column-by-column storage sequence is used.

1	5	9
2	6	10
3	7	11
4	8	12

FIGURE 9.2   The X(4,3) array can be loaded *(a)* row-by-row or *(b)* column by column. The placement of the I loop as the outermost FOR/NEXT supports the row-by-row method of loading data. Using the J loop as the outermost FOR/NEXT accesses each cell on a column-by-column basis. Note the difference in how each approach stores its data in the X array's cells.

the exact number of rows and columns. The X(4,3) designation reflects the 12 array cells constituting that array. Two indexes are necessary when accessing any cell within that array.

The nested FOR/NEXT statements, lines 20 to 70, are the key to loading two-dimensional arrays. The outer I loop is associated with the *row* position in the X(I,J) array. The J variable refers to the *column* subscript of the X(I,J) array. This nested sequence holds I constant, while J repeatedly ranges from 1 to 3.

On the first loop, when I and J equal 1, the cell X(1,1) is accessed and the number 1 stored in that cell. In the next loop, I equals 1 and J equals 2, causing 2 to be stored in the X(1,2) cell. The last array cell of that row, X(1,3), is loaded with 3 on the next loop. When J equals 3, the inner loop is closed, the I loop recycles, and the next looping sequence starts with I equal to 2 and J equal to 1.

The next looping sequence loads the three cells of row 2. The cells accessed are X(2,1), X(2,2), and X(2,3), loaded with 4, 5, and 6, respectively. With I equal to 2, the J variable runs from 1 to 3 and each cell in row 2 is assigned a single data item.

In the remaining loops, rows 3 and 4 are loaded. The subscripted variables X(3,1), X(3,2), and X(3,3) are used with row 3, and X(4,1), X(4,2), and X(4,3) cells are accessed in row 4. The X(4,3) cell is the twelfth and last cell loaded. These cells have been accessed on a row-by-row basis because of the positioning of the nested loops.

Using the same 12 data items we can create a totally different loading sequence simply by reversing the I and J loops, as shown in Figure 9.2*(b)*. The X array is loaded on a column-by-column basis; J is held constant while I varies from 1 to 4. On the first set of loops with J equal to 1, the array cells accessed include X(1,1), X(2,1), X(3,1), and X(4,1). The cells compose column 1, each cell respectively filled with the values 1, 2, 3, and 4.

With J equal to 2, a similar looping sequence occurs and the cells in column 2 are loaded. The sequence of cells involves X(1,2), X(2,2), X(3,2), and X(4,2). The third column's cells are accessed when J equals 3, again moving vertically down this column.

By comparing Figure 9.2*(a)* and 9.2*(b)* we observe the radical difference in the contents of cells loaded on a row-by-row or a column-by-column basis. With either approach, the only two cells that remain the same are the first and last cells. All other cells possess different values. Our discussion will favor the row-by-row approach, as it is the most often used. The alternate approach is presented to illustrate the loading of arrays by each column and reinforce the use of nested FOR/NEXT loops.

In both loading techniques, the X(I,J) subscripted variable was used to access each cell. The I and J subscripts were consistently used to reference the row and column positions. Only one X(I,J) array cell is handled per loop, with one data item loaded and output from that cell. Data in both program excerpts was supplied via DATA statements.

Two-dimensional arrays may be loaded on an interactive basis using INPUT statements, as shown in Figure 9.3. In the indicated loading sequence, nested FOR/NEXT statements control looping and the order in which array cells are filled. As the outer loop is controlled by the FOR I instruction, line 20, cells are loaded on a row-by-row basis. The input variable X(I,J) specifies I as the row subscript and J as the column subscript.

Interactive Loading

FIGURE 9.3   When data held within an array varies between applications, the array can be loaded on an interactive basis. A prompting INPUT statement is often helpful to the user.

```
10 DIM X(4,3)
20 FOR I = 1 TO 4
30   FOR J = 1 TO 3
40     INPUT 'ENTER DATA ITEM';X(I,J)
50     PRINT X(I,J)
60   NEXT J
70 NEXT I
```

The output of each cell, line 50, employs the same subscripted variable X(I,J). Essentially, the interactive loading sequence is the same as the READ/DATA approach, except for its online nature and its lack of DATA statements.

These differences again point to the way in which both 1-D and 2-D arrays are employed in processing. If the contents of the array remain relatively stable, then READ and DATA statements are an excellent means of loading. This is generally the manner in which arrays destined for use as tables are loaded. By contrast, arrays holding varying data are better served through INPUT statements. The flexibility offered by these interactive statements permits the user to load array data as desired. This latter approach is suited to applications in the sciences, statistics, or specialized math problems, where the data employed varies widely.

SIDE BAR 9.1   1-D Arrays versus 2-D Arrays

For many programmers, the differences between 1-D and 2-D arrays are indistinguishable. Programmers may believe — incorrectly — that the two types of array are interchangeable. Consider the following program excerpt.

```
10    DIM X(4,3), Y(12)
20    FOR I = 1 TO 4
30    FOR J = 1 TO 3      This excerpt is
40    READ X(I,J), Y(I)   wrong
50    NEXT J
60    NEXT I
```

The nested loop for the 2-D array is properly defined, as are the I and J row and column subscripts. An error occurs when an attempt is made to load the Y array in the same looping sequence. This is not possible, as I will range from 1 to 4, not 1 to 12. The first four cells of the Y array are repeatedly loaded, but the remaining eight cells remain unfilled. Where the nested loop is employed to load the 2-D array, a separate 12-loop sequence is required to handle the one-dimensional Y array.

9.3 Applications for 2-D Arrays

One of the primary uses of two-dimensional arrays is as reference tables. Two keys or indexes are needed to identify one cell in the array; the data held in that cell is then used in processing. The keys to which row and column subscript is used must be produced by the program. IF/THEN statements provide the means to test data items, assign the proper row and column subscripts, and gain access to the desired cell.

The compound conditional is vital to these tests, as it enables the program to test a range of values and determine the row and column for the array cell. In almost all problems where 2-D tables are constructed, the compound conditional is the key to determining the subscripts.

Though we cannot duplicate the entire federal tax table, we can create a hypothetical two-dimensional tax structure to illustrate how a program might use such a table. The data in Table 9.1 will be used in our first sample problem.

A Tax Table

TABLE 9.1 Proposed Tax Rates and Categories

Salary $	Dependents Declared		
	0 to 1	2 to 5	6 or more
0 to 4,999	.065	.032	.011
5,000 to 14,999	.083	.067	.021
15,000 to 39,999	.149	.093	.062
40,000 and up	.347	.258	.196

This tax table uses a two-dimensional format of four rows and three columns. Each of the 12 cells contains a distinct tax rate. To access any one cell, you must determine the salary range into which the individual falls and the number of dependents declared. With these two keys, a specific tax rate cell is accessed and that rate made available. In our hypothetical tax structure, the tax due is computed by multiplying the tax rate by the salary.

The key to accessing the proper tax cell is the use of the compound conditional. To search for the correct cell, a total of seven decisions is necessary. Four conditionals are needed to determine the row subscript, while three are used for the column subscript. By substituting these subscripts into the array's subscripted name, the user gains access to a specific cell and its tax rate when computing taxes. Let us formally define the problem and then illustrate how the array is used.

PROBLEM 9.1 A Tax Table

The problem entails the use of a tax table to compute tax rates. The tax rate detailed in Table 9.1 is loaded into a 2-D array in module 1. These rates provide the basis for computing individual tax liability.

Tax amounts are computed in module 2. Input on each loop are a name, number of dependents, and salary amount. The salary amount and dependent figure are used to access a tax rate from the table. Compound conditionals are used to test for the appropriate cell. The tax rate chosen is multiplied by the salary amount to produce the tax owed. For each person, output the name, number of dependents, salary amount, tax rate, and tax owed. Use the headings INDIVIDUAL, DEP, SALARY, RATE, and TAX OWED, commencing at print positions 1, 16, 20, 27, and 32. Apply the formats of ## to dependents, #####. to salary, .### to tax rate and #####.## to taxes owed. In addition to Table 9.1 the data for the problem is as follows:

Name	Dep	Salary	Name	Dep	Salary
Martin	0	3560	Holcroft	3	49065
Scarlatti	1	25467	Ludlam	7	13776
Ostermann	6	38554	Fontine	2	11983

These are the main points in the problem.

1 Two modules compose this solution. Module 1 loads the 2-D array, and module 2 handles the processing of taxes. Nested loops are used in module 1 for array loading.

2 On each loop of module 2, a name, number of dependents, and salary amount are inputted. The latter two inputs are used to access the correct tax rate cell.

3 Compound conditionals test each category of the tax table. Row and column subscripts are derived from these tests and used to access the proper array cell.

4 Taxes owed are computed by multiplying the selected tax rate by the salary amount.

5 Output each name, number of dependents, salary, tax rate, and taxes owed for each person. Use the indicated formats and headings, aligning each.

The flowchart for Problem 9.1 is shown in Figure 9.4. It is divided into two modules. After defining the tax array, $T(4,3)$, the initial module proceeds to a nested loop, where the array is loaded. The outer I loop represents the four rows, and the J loop defines the required three columns. The L$ format will incorporate the desired editing feature. This operation precedes the output of the desired heading and the start of module 2.

The second module requires a six-loop FOR/NEXT sequence, as we are processing one person's data per loop. The seven decisions that follow the READ symbol define the row and column subscripts for the tax array T. The first four decision symbols relate to the categorization of the rows, with the last three applied to columns.

These decisions employ both compound conditional and single-conditional statements. The initial four decisions define I, the row subscript, at a value of 1 to 4. The latter three decisions test against J, the column subscript, assigning it values of 1, 2, or 3. For example, if a salary of $3000 is inputted with three dependents, the test sequence would define I as 1 and J as 2. These subscripts are substituted into the $T(I,J)$ variable name, accessing the $T(1,2)$

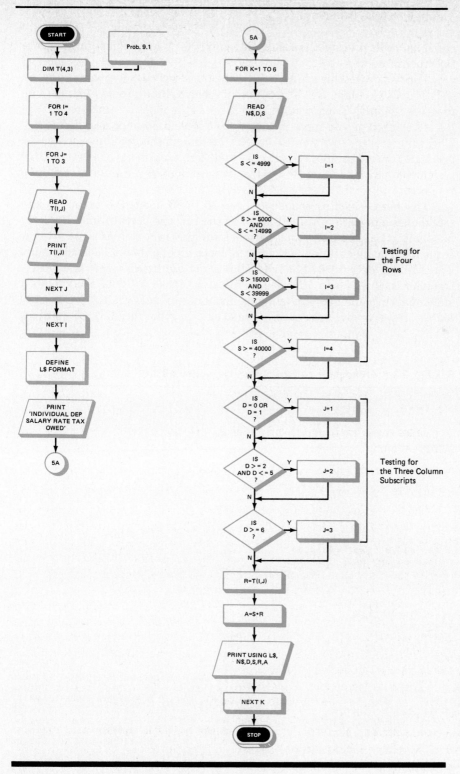

FIGURE 9.4 The flowchart solution for Problem 9.1 consists of two main processing modules. Testing to determine the proper subscripts is performed in module 2.

cell. That cell's rate, .032, is assigned to R and used in the computation of the tax amount A.

The two processing symbols following the seven decision symbols assign T(I,J) to R and compute A. The output of the five required data items per line precedes the NEXT instruction, which closes the looping sequence.

The program solution and output for Problem 9.1 appear in Figure 9.5. This solution uses two main modules, one to load the two-dimensional tax array and one to compute the taxes owed. The program opens with a DIM statement, which defines a T(4,3) tax array composed of four rows and three columns. A total of 12 cells (4×3) will hold tax rates.

The nested-looping sequence, lines 30 to 80, loads the tax array and establishes a pattern of using I and J as the row and column subscripts. By positioning I as the outer loop variable, the program defines a row-by-row sequence. The indentation of the I and J loops highlights their nested nature. The 12 rates entered within the T(I,J) array are listed within the DATA statements, lines 90 to 120. We deliberately chose to write those DATA statements in a manner paralleling their actual storage in the array. Lines 130 and 140 respectively define the L$ format and the report heading to be output.

FIGURE 9.5 *(a)* Program and *(b)* output for Problem 9.1.

(a)

```
10 DIM T(4,3)
20 REM PROB 9.1
30 FOR I = 1 TO 4
40   FOR J = 1 TO 3
50     READ T(I,J)
60     PRINT T(I,J)
70   NEXT J
80 NEXT I
90  DATA .065,.032,.011
100 DATA .083,.067,.021
110 DATA .149,.093,.062
120 DATA .347,.258,.196
130 L$ = '\            \ ## #####. .### #####.##'
140 PRINT 'INDIVIDUAL      DEP SALARY RATE TAX OWED'
200 FOR K = 1 TO 6
210   READ N$,D,S
220   IF S <= 4999 THEN I = 1
230   IF S >= 5000 AND S <= 14999 THEN I = 2
240   IF S >= 15000 AND S <= 39999 THEN I = 3
250   IF S >= 40000 THEN I = 4
260   IF D = 0 OR D = 1 THEN J = 1
270   IF D >= 2 AND D <= 5 THEN J = 2
280   IF D >= 6 THEN J = 3
290   R = T(I,J)
300   A = S * R
310   PRINT USING L$,N$,D,S,R,A
320 NEXT K
400 DATA 'MARTIN',0,3560,'HOLCROFT',3,49065
410 DATA 'SCARLATTI',1,25467,'LUDLAM',7,13776
420 DATA 'OSTERMANN',6,38554,'FONTINE',2,11983
500 END
```

(b)

```
.065
.032
.011
.083
.067
.021
.149
.093
.062
.347
.258
.196
INDIVIDUAL   DEP SALARY  RATE TAX OWED
MARTIN         0   3560. .065   231.40
HOLCROFT       3  49065. .258 12658.77
SCARLATTI      1  25467. .149  3794.58
LUDLAM         7  13776. .021   289.30
OSTERMANN      6  38554. .062  2390.35
FONTINE        2  11983. .067   802.86
```

The second phase of processing begins at line 200. A FOR/NEXT sequence of six loops is created to process one person's taxes per loop. A loop variable of K is used, as the I and J variables have already been assigned as the row and column subscripts. This is a major point, as any attempt to reuse I and J for other than those subscripts would induce errors.

The first task of the K loop is the input of each person's name (N$), number of dependents (D), and salary (S). The reading of this data, line 210, must precede the series of IF/THEN statements, lines 220 to 280. A mixture of single and compound conditionals defines the categories being tested. Lines 220 to 250 test the four salary categories, while lines 260 to 280 test the three categories of dependents.

If S is less than or equal to 4999, the tax rate must exist on the first row and therefore I equals 1. The test for the second salary category of $5000 to $14,999 is defined at line 230. If the salary input falls within that range, the tax rate exists on the second row of the tax table and I equals 2. The conditional statements at lines 240 and 250 create tests for the third and fourth salary categories and similarly define row subscripts as I equals 3 and I equals 4. Note that because of the way we have defined this series of IF/THEN statements only one row subscript (I) results. It is not possible for two I values to occur. The row subscript assigned relates directly to the dollar category in which each person's salary falls.

A similar logic is applied to the conditional tests in lines 260 to 280, where we are attempting to define the column subscript J. If the number of dependents equals 0 or 1, the tax rate falls in column 1 and J equals 1. A dependent value of 2 to 5 results in J being set equal to 2, as column 2 of the tax table holds those rates. Six or more dependents defines J at 3, the last column of rates within the array.

By systematically testing each variable, we establish a single set of I and J values for subscripts of the cell where the specific tax rate to be used is found. The actual I and J values selected are substituted in the variable $T(I,J)$ at line 290 to establish the tax rate R used in computing the taxes owed. The tax amount A is actually computed at line 300, prior to the output of tax data. A PRINT USING statement facilitates the output of five data items, each employing the L$ format.

The NEXT K statement, line 320, denotes the loop's close and precedes the data module. This second group of data relates solely to those six individuals and was specifically set apart from values composing the tax array. Lines 400 to 420 create a data module and precede the program's END statement. The output appears in Figure 9.5(b).

The key to this problem is its two processing sequences. In the first a nested loop was correctly used to load the 2-D array. In the second loop, a series of seven conditionals correctly defined the row and column subscripts necessary to access one cell in the tax array. Without these steps, a sound program solution would not have been possible.

Currency Conversion and Mixed Indexes

In Problem 9.1 we used numeric data in a two-dimensional array. A similar approach is used to define subscripts that combine nonnumeric and numeric categories. We approach the testing of these values in the same way, using conditional statements to define row and column subscripts. Here, however, an association exists between a nonnumeric value and a subscript. Our next sample problem addresses this type of 2-D table.

PROBLEM 9.2   Converting Foreign Currency

The problem entails the conversion of foreign currency into dollars. Table 9.2 defines the conversion rates for four major currencies and two amount categories. This (2,4) array consists of two rows and four columns and provides the rates for converting those currencies. The array is loaded in module 1.

TABLE 9.2   Currency Conversion Rate ($)

Amount to Be Converted	British (Pound)	German (Mark)	Swiss (Franc)	Japanese (Yen)
0 to 1000	1.58	.421	.489	.0042
1001 and up	1.54	.411	.482	.0041

A looping sequence is established for processing in module 2. Entered on each loop are an amount of currency to be converted into dollars and the type of currency (by alphabetic code). A series of conditionals establishes the appropriate row and column subscripts to enter the array. The chosen rate is multiplied by the initial amount of currency to produce a dollar amount. This dollar amount is retained in its own one-dimensional array cell, as are the two amounts originally read.

The last module serves to output the contents of the three 1-D arrays loaded during module 2. Use the headings AMOUNT, CURR, and $ AMT, commencing at positions 1, 9, and 16. Edit these outputs as #####. for the initial currency amount and #####.## for the converted dollar value. Data for this problem is as follows:

Amount	Currency	Amount	Currency
680	Pounds	6560	Francs
4476	Marks	3060	Marks
500	Francs	8260	Yen

These are the main points in the problem.

1   Three modules of processing activities exist. Module 1 loads the two-dimensional array in which currency conversion rates are held. Module 2 converts the foreign currency to dollar amounts. Module 3 serves an output function, printing a currency conversion report.

2   The conversion array consists of two rows and four columns, defined via READ and DATA statements. Three additional arrays are the initial amount of currency, the type of currency, and equivalent dollar amount arrays. Each array is one-dimensional, defined in module 2, and output in module 3.

3   The equivalent dollar amount is computed by multiplying the original amount of currency by the rate drawn from Table 9.2. A series of conditional statements defines the required array cell, testing for the amount and type of currency. The resultant dollar amount is stored in its own array, along with the original amount of currency and its type.

4   Edited formats and headings are applied to the report prepared in module 3. Each processing module is defined by a GOSUB module.

The overall structure of the program and the flowcharts for Problem 9.2 are shown in Figure 9.6, with (a) detailing the hierarchical relationship of each module. In Figure 9.6(b), the main program flowchart uses three modules to make up the total solution. The initial module defines the four arrays slated for use and the three GOSUB modules which follow it. Three 1-D arrays are employed, as is the 2-D array holding currency conversion rates.

The GOSUB 100 module loads the rate array R(2,4). The two-row and four-column structure of this array consists of eight cells, each cell individually accessed via the subscripted variable name R(I,J). One cell is loaded per loop, within a nested loop. A blank line separates this module's output from the report produced by the GOSUB 400 module.

A single FOR/NEXT sequence controls processing within the GOSUB 200 module. The K subscript continues the FOR/NEXT loop, executing exactly six loops. The currency amount and type are entered in their own arrays. Once these two items are read, a testing sequence of five decisions ensues. The comparison of the currency amount A(K) against 1000 defines either of the two row subscripts.

A series of four decisions tests for a specific currency type and assigns the column subscript J associated with that currency. Note that these tests involve nonnumeric data, each currency type defined within quotes. The C$(K) variable name denotes that the currency type was retained in a non-numeric array.

The row and column subscripts defined by these five decisions permit the correct conversion rate to be selected. The rate variable R(I,J) is multiplied by the currency amount A(K) to produce the equivalent dollar amount D(K). This amount is stored in its respective array before the looping sequence closes.

The last module relates solely to the output of data held in three arrays. After the desired edited format and report heading are defined, a six-loop FOR/NEXT sequence is initiated. Within this loop, each of the six sets of currency data are outputted on a separate line.

The program and output for Problem 9.2 are depicted in Figure 9.7. The solution follows the modular approach defined in the flow diagrams. Three modules of activity comprise the program solution.

(a)

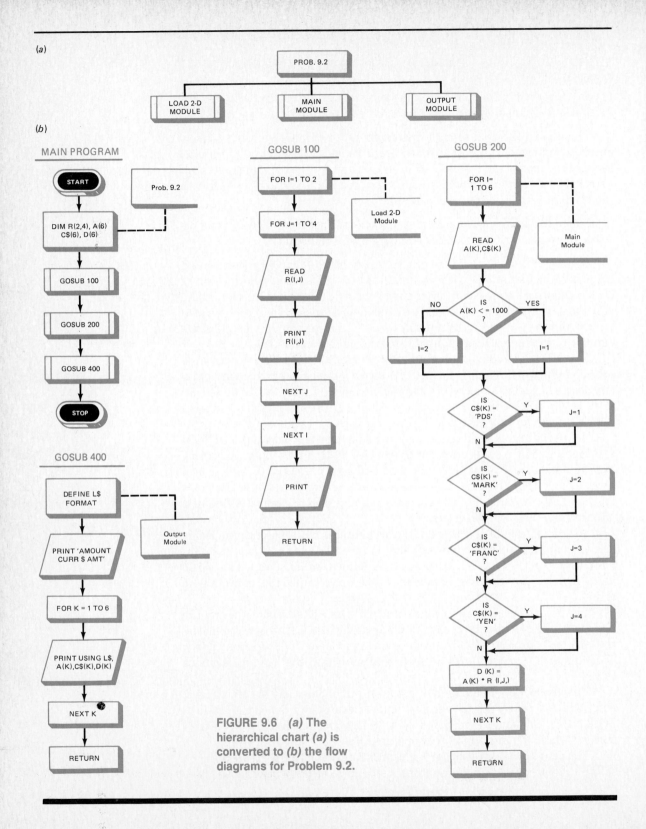

(b)

MAIN PROGRAM

START

DIM R(2,4), A(6) C$(6), D(6) --- Prob. 9.2

GOSUB 100

GOSUB 200

GOSUB 400

STOP

GOSUB 100

FOR I=1 TO 2 --- Load 2-D Module

FOR J=1 TO 4

READ R(I,J)

PRINT R(I,J)

NEXT J

NEXT I

PRINT

RETURN

GOSUB 200

FOR I= 1 TO 6 --- Main Module

READ A(K),C$(K)

IS A(K) < = 1000 ? — NO → I=2 / YES → I=1

IS C$(K) = 'PDS' ? — Y → J=1

IS C$(K) = 'MARK' ? — Y → J=2

IS C$(K) = 'FRANC' ? — Y → J=3

IS C$(K) = 'YEN' ? — Y → J=4

D (K) = A (K) * R (I,J,)

NEXT K

RETURN

GOSUB 400

DEFINE L$ FORMAT --- Output Module

PRINT 'AMOUNT CURR $ AMT'

FOR K = 1 TO 6

PRINT USING L$, A(K),C$(K),D(K)

NEXT K

RETURN

FIGURE 9.6 (a) The hierarchical chart (a) is converted to (b) the flow diagrams for Problem 9.2.

FIGURE 9.7 (a) Program and (b) output for Problem 9.2. GOSUB statements create a modular structure.

(a)

```
10 DIM R(2,4), A(6), C$(6), D(6)
20 REM PROB 9.2
30 GOSUB 100
40 GOSUB 200
50 GOSUB 400
60 GO TO 500
70 DATA 1.58,.421,.489,.0042
80 DATA 1.54,.411,.482,.0041
100 REM -- LOAD 2-D MODULE
110 FOR I = 1 TO 2
120   FOR J = 1 TO 4
130     READ R(I,J)
140     PRINT R(I,J)
150   NEXT J
160 NEXT I
170 PRINT
180 RETURN
200 REM -- MAIN MODULE
210 FOR K = 1 TO 6
220   READ A(K),C$(K)
230   IF A(K) <= 1000 THEN I=1 ELSE I=2
240   IF C$(K) = 'PDS' THEN J=1
250   IF C$(K) = 'MARK' THEN J=2
260   IF C$(K) = 'FRANC' THEN J=3
270   IF C$(K) = 'YEN' THEN J=4
280   D(K) = A(K) * R(I,J)
290 NEXT K
300 RETURN
310 DATA 680,'PDS',6560,'FRANC'
320 DATA 4476,'MARK',3060,'MARK'
330 DATA 500,'FRANC',8260,'YEN'
400 REM -- OUTPUT MODULE
410 L$ = '#####.    \     \ #####.##'
420 PRINT 'AMOUNT  CURR   $ AMT'
430 FOR K = 1 TO 6
440   PRINT USING L$,A(K),C$(K),D(K)
450 NEXT K
460 RETURN
500 END
```

(b)

```
                    1.58
                    .421
                    .489
                    .0042
                    1.54
                    .411
                    .482
                    .0041
AMOUNT    CURR    $ AMT
  680.    PDS     1074.40
 6560.    FRANC   3161.92
 4476.    MARK    1839.64
 3060.    MARK    1257.66
  500.    FRANC    244.50
 8260.    YEN       33.87
```

The program opens at line 10, defining the four arrays used in processing. All four arrays are defined by the DIM statement. The R(2,4) array holds the currency conversion rates. The A(6), C$(6), and D(6) arrays hold the currency amounts, currency types, and dollar equivalent amounts, respectively. The three GOSUB statements, lines 30 to 50, control processing.

The loading of the conversion array commences at line 100. A nested loop, lines 110 to 160, control the I and J subscripts accessing the cells of R(I,J). The eight values listed at lines 70 and 80 are loaded into the eight cells of the R array. Once loaded, the R(2,4) array is ready for use in module 2.

A single six-loop sequence is needed in the GOSUB 200 module, as only six sets of data are processed — one set per loop. The amount of currency to be converted, A(K), and currency type, C$(K), are the only two items read. After they are inputted at line 220, the testing sequence begins. The IF/THEN statement, line 230, tests the A(K) value against 1000 to define the row subscript I. As only two rows are evident in the R array, I must assume a value of either 1 or 2.

The J subscript may assume one of four values. The J subscript value relates directly to the type of currency input. Each of the four IF/THEN statements, lines 240 to 270, tests for a specific currency type and defines a value of J at 1 to 4. The definition of I and J are essential, so that the proper cell in the R(I,J) rate array is accessed. This value is used in line 280 to compute the equivalent dollar value D(K).

All output activities are assigned to the third module, GOSUB 400. The coordinated definition of the L$ format and output of the three column headings are accomplished at lines 410 and 420. The column headings were defined in one large literal. The output of the three arrays falls beneath these headings and details the results of processing, shown in Figure 9.7*(b)*.

This program illustrates that both one- and two-dimensional arrays may be integrated into a single solution. Each array type must be handled separately, as deemed necessary by processing: nested loops for 2-D arrays, and single looping sequences for 1-D arrays. Data taken from both array types may be used in computations, and those results stored in other arrays. Arrays are utilized as any other means of processing, in addition to their use as tables.

Mileage Charts

Two-dimensional arrays can retain data which is made available on an interactive basis. The key to accessing array data may be either numeric or alphabetic, depending upon the application. In our third sample program, we examine a problem where the user wants to know the mileage between cities. The user will enter the cities in question and the program will respond with a mileage figure on an interactive basis.

PROBLEM 9.3   Finding the Mileage Between Cities

The problem entails determining the mileage between two cities. A 4 × 2 array holds the mileage between cities. This eight-cell array containing the data listed in Table 9.3 is loaded in module 1.

In module 2, the user interactively inputs the two cities in question and receives the mileage between them. Use prompting literals to permit the entry of data. Use a priming read and looping sequence to control the user's request for data.

TABLE 9.3   Mileage Chart

Departing City	Arriving City	
	Chicago (CHI)	St. Louis (STL)
Boston (BOS)	963	1141
New York (NY)	802	948
Philadelphia (PA)	738	868
Wash., DC (DC)	671	793

These are the main points in the problem narrative.

1 An eight-cell, two-dimensional array holds mileage data. It is the only array used.

2 Users will interact with the computer to determine the mileage between the indicated cities. INPUT statements with prompting literals are used.

3 After searching the mileage array, output all facts with appropriate labels. A priming read and loop control are required.

The flowchart for Problem 9.3 is shown in Figure 9.8.

The solution's logic dictates a two-module approach. Module 1 loads mileage data into the $M(4,2)$ array. A nested loop, where I and J respectively serve as row and column subscripts, controls module 1.

Before opening module 2, we position two INPUT statements, which represent the priming read. We chose to make this problem interactive and thus permit users to enter their mileage requests as needed. The two INPUT statements precede the start of the looping sequence, which continues until terminated by the user. The entry of XXX for the departing city acts like a 9s decision and triggers the loop's close.

The loop uses five decisions, each designed to assign the correct row and column subscript for the $M(I,J)$ array. The test of A\$ = 'CHI' assigns either a column subscript of $J = 1$ or $J = 2$. The four decisions that follow test the D\$ variable, setting I equal to a value of 1 to 4. Both I and J are needed to select the mileage for the two cities involved.

Two outputs follow the decision sequence, advising of the mileage between the two cities selected. Within the initial output, the mileage cell $M(I,J)$ is accessed and printed. This line precedes the specification of the departing D\$ and arriving A\$ cities. The second half of the priming-read sequence, a second set of INPUT statements, is positioned prior to the loop's close. When the D\$ = 'XXX' data is input, the loop and program end.

The BASIC program and output for Problem 9.3 are shown in Figure 9.9. Program modules are defined within the program's looping sequences. A nested loop, lines 30 to 80, loads the $M(I,J)$ mileage array with the data at lines 90 and 100. The second loop extends from lines 110 to 220. The two INPUT statements represent the priming read, lines 110 and 120. As indicated, the loop continues until a D\$ value of XXX is input.

The decision sequence, lines 130 to 170, opens with a test of A\$ = 'CHI'. Abbreviations for each city's name simplify the user's input of data. The five conditional statements define the I and J subscripts and enable access to the mileage array. The contents of the $M(I,J)$ cell is acknowledged at line 180, one of the two PRINT statements in the program. The user must initially specify departing and arriving city codes to enable access to the mileage array. These codes are reprinted when the mileage associated with these cities is outputted.

The closing half of the priming read is evident at lines 200 and 210. Again, D\$ and A\$ are inputted, permitting looping to continue until D\$ = 'XXX'. No DATA statements are provided for the second looping sequence,

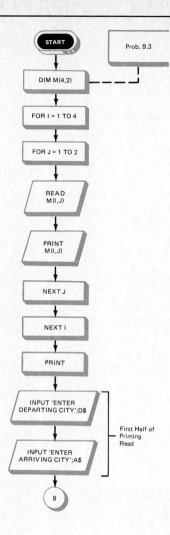

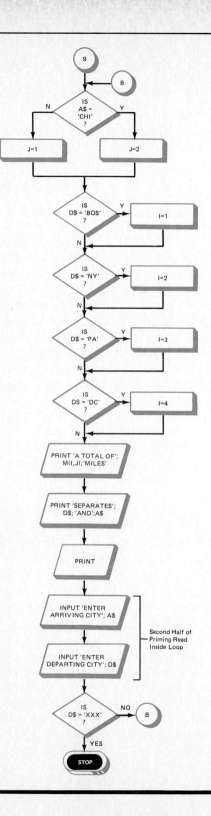

FIGURE 9.8 Flow-
charts for Problem 9.3
using an interactive
approach, thus
enabling users to
access data in a mile-
age array.

FIGURE 9.9 *(a)*
Program and *(b)* out-
put for Problem 9.3.
The use of interactive
statements is evident.

(a)

```
10 DIM M(4,2)
20 REM PROB 9.3
30 FOR I = 1 TO 4
40    FOR J = 1 TO 2
50       READ M(I,J)
60       PRINT M(I,J)
70    NEXT J
80 NEXT I
85 PRINT
90 DATA 963,1141,802,948
100 DATA 738,868,671,793
110 INPUT 'ENTER DEPARTING CITY';D$
120 INPUT 'ENTER ARRIVING CITY';A$
130    IF A$ = 'CHI' THEN J=2 ELSE J=1
140    IF D$ = 'BOS' THEN I=1
150    IF D$ = 'NY'  THEN I=2
160    IF D$ = 'PA'  THEN I=3
170    IF D$ = 'DC'  THEN I=4
180    PRINT 'A TOTAL OF';M(I,J);' MILES'
190    PRINT 'SEPARATES ';D$;' AND ';A$
195    PRINT
200    INPUT 'ENTER DEPARTING CITY';D$
210    INPUT 'ENTER ARRIVING CITY';A$
220    IF D$ = 'XXX' THEN 230 ELSE 130
230 END
```

(b)

```
963
1141
802
948
738
868
671
793

ENTER DEPARTING CITY? PA
ENTER ARRIVING CITY? CHI
A TOTAL OF 868  MILES
SEPARATES PA AND CHI

ENTER DEPARTING CITY? BOS
ENTER ARRIVING CITY? STL
A TOTAL OF 963  MILES
SEPARATES BOS AND STL

ENTER DEPARTING CITY? DC
ENTER ARRIVING CITY? CHI
A TOTAL OF 793  MILES
SEPARATES DC AND CHI

ENTER DEPARTING CITY? XXX
ENTER ARRIVING CITY? XXX
```

as INPUT statements are involved. This program's output, shown in Figure 9.9*(b)*, reflects the interactive nature of this solution.

Problem 9.3 illustrates one of the better uses of two-dimensional arrays on a small scale. These arrays are well suited to holding data to which immediate access is warranted. Once given the proper keys, the program controls access to the 2-D table, readily searching its cells and making that data available for processing. The program also shows that nonnumeric or alphabetic keys present no hinderance to accessing data from 2-dimensional arrays.

9.4 The MAT Instruction

Learning About MATs

Many users recognize the importance of two-dimensional arrays and a simpler means of working with them. To fulfill these needs, manufacturers developed a series of statements specifically designed for 2-D array manipulations. The product of these efforts is the **MAT statement.** Sample MAT statements are outlined in Figure 9.10. Users must initially acquaint themselves with a slightly different format of the two-dimensional array — the **matrix.** It consists of rows and columns, but is configured within large parentheses. Though its appearance is altered slightly, the matrix is still a 2-D array.

DIM A(3,3),B(3,3),C(3,3) defines the arrays to be used.

$$A = \begin{pmatrix} 4 & 2 & 5 \\ 6 & 3 & 9 \\ -1 & -7 & 0 \end{pmatrix} \qquad B = \begin{pmatrix} -5 & 2 & -3 \\ 1 & 7 & 9 \\ 12 & -4 & 8 \end{pmatrix} \qquad C = (\quad)$$

	Action Taken	MAT Statement	Array Configuration
1.	Setting arrays equal to each other	100 MAT C=A	$C = \begin{pmatrix} 4 & 2 & 5 \\ 6 & 3 & 9 \\ -1 & -7 & 0 \end{pmatrix}$

2. Adding arrays   100 MAT C=A + B

$$\underset{A}{\begin{pmatrix} 4 & 2 & 5 \\ 6 & 3 & 9 \\ -1 & -7 & 0 \end{pmatrix}} + \underset{B}{\begin{pmatrix} -5 & 2 & -3 \\ 1 & 7 & 9 \\ 12 & -4 & 8 \end{pmatrix}} = \underset{C}{\begin{pmatrix} -1 & 4 & 2 \\ 7 & 10 & 18 \\ 11 & -11 & 8 \end{pmatrix}}$$

3. Subtracting arrays   100 MAT C=B –A

$$\underset{B}{\begin{pmatrix} -5 & 2 & -3 \\ 1 & 7 & 9 \\ 12 & -4 & 8 \end{pmatrix}} - \underset{A}{\begin{pmatrix} 4 & 2 & 5 \\ 6 & 3 & 9 \\ -1 & -7 & 0 \end{pmatrix}} = \underset{C}{\begin{pmatrix} -9 & 0 & -8 \\ -5 & 4 & 0 \\ 13 & 3 & 8 \end{pmatrix}}$$

4. Multiplying arrays   100 MAT C=A*B

$$\underset{A}{\begin{pmatrix} 4 & 25 \\ 6 & 3 & 9 \\ -1 & -7 & 0 \end{pmatrix}} * \underset{B}{\begin{pmatrix} -5 & 2 & -3 \\ 1 & 7 & 9 \\ 12 & -4 & 8 \end{pmatrix}} = \underset{C}{\begin{pmatrix} -20 & 4 & -15 \\ 6 & 21 & 81 \\ -12 & 28 & 0 \end{pmatrix}}$$

5. Multiplication by a constant   100 MAT C=B * 2

$$\begin{pmatrix} -5 & 2 & 3 \\ 1 & 7 & 9 \\ 12 & -4 & 8 \end{pmatrix} * 2 = \begin{pmatrix} -10 & 4 & 6 \\ 2 & 14 & 18 \\ 24 & -8 & 16 \end{pmatrix}$$

6. Zeroing out all array cells   100 MAT C = ZER

$$C = \begin{pmatrix} 0 & 0 & 0 \\ 0 & 0 & 0 \\ 0 & 0 & 0 \end{pmatrix} \text{ All array cells are filled with zeros.}$$

7. Loading an array with one's   100 MAT C = CON

$$C = \begin{pmatrix} 1 & 1 & 1 \\ 1 & 1 & 1 \\ 1 & 1 & 1 \end{pmatrix} \text{ All array cells are loaded with 1s.}$$

FIGURE 9.10   MAT statements offer the user a variety of operational features which are readily accessed by means of predefined commands.

Figure 9.10 shows three 2-D arrays. The A and B arrays are depicted in the matrix form, whereas C is undefined. The matrix operations enable the user to perform many tasks. The first task involves setting two arrays equal to each other. In this case, the statement 100 MAT C = A will fill the C array with A's contents, so that both are equal on a cell-by-cell basis.

The MAT instruction eliminated the necessity to specify subscripts and design an elaborate switching procedure. The actual processing steps are shielded from the user, as the MAT statements act like predefined subprograms. They perform the desired task, once directed by the program, and relieve the user of the need to write those instructions. MAT statements are designed for very specific operations, saving users work. Specialized programming tasks must still be written by the user, however.

Reading down the remaining tasks of Figure 9.10, it is possible to observe other ways of manipulating 2-D arrays. In these cases, however, we are dealing with arrays of like size. It is not possible to use many MAT statements when arrays of different row and column sizes are involved.

One advantage associated with MAT statements is their ability to perform I/O operations. Without having to employ lengthy lists of instructions, MAT commands can read or print the contents of 2-D arrays. A comparison of MAT and conventional statements is shown in Figure 9.11.

<table>
<tr><td>(a)</td><td>(b)</td></tr>
</table>

```
10 DIM X(4,3)            100 DIM X(4,3)
20 FOR I = 1 TO 4        200 MAT READ X
30   FOR J = 1 TO 3      300 MAT PRINT X
40     READ X(I,J)       400 DATA 12,15,19
50     PRINT X(I,J)      500 DATA -6,13,17
60   NEXT J              600 DATA 0,1,5
70 NEXT I                700 DATA 8,5,-3
80 DATA 12,15,19
90 DATA -6,13,17
100 DATA 0,1,5
110 DATA 8,5,-3
```

```
the output resulting          MAT statements produce
from the nested I/O            the following output
statements

    12                            12
    15                            15
    19                            19
    -6                            -6
    13                            13
    17                            17
    0                             0
    1                             1
    5                             5
    8                             8
    5                             5
    -3                            -3
```

FIGURE 9.11 *(a)* Loading by means of a nested-loop sequence. *(b)* Loading by means of a MAT statement. The output is the same in either case.

The nested-loop sequence, Figure 9.11(a), adequately handles the loading of data into the 12 cells of the X(4,3) array on a row-by-row basis. The data items 12, 15, and 19 are placed in the three cells of row 1, with each subsequent row of cells similarly filled.

By comparison, the statements of Figure 9.12(b) accomplish the same function. The entire loading sequence, including reading and output, is invoked by statements 200 and 300. These statements read and print their data on a row-by-row basis in the same fashion as in Figure 9.11(a). By comparing the outputs from each excerpt, you can note the row-by-row handling of the MAT statement.

MAT Statements and Labor Costs

One of the best ways to comprehend a statement's function is to use it. Let us apply MAT instructions to the manipulation of 2-D arrays.

PROBLEM 9.4   Finding New Wage Rates

The problem entails estimating contract increases from labor negotiations. An existing hourly work scale is retained in a 2-D array consisting of three rows and five columns. The existing scale is listed at the narrative's end. Management wants to estimate the change in wages, if increases of 10 and 8 percent are consecutively applied in the two-year contract.

A program must be written to load the initial wage scale array and manipulate its contents. The original wage array must be outputted, as must the array holding the increases of 10 and 8 percent, respectively. These outputs will be used to evaluate the proposed wage settlement.

Wage Scales

Shift Work	I	II	III	IV	V
Morning	6.50	6.90	7.40	8.00	9.00
Afternoon	7.00	7.50	8.10	8.90	10.00
Evening	7.75	8.25	8.95	9.90	11.00

These are the main points in the problem narrative.

1   Three 2-D arrays of three rows and five columns are required. The (3,5) array will be manipulated twice to prepare wage estimates.

2   MAT statements are used to load, manipulate, and output all three arrays.

3   The original wage array is loaded. Its contents are increased by 10 percent for the first year's wage scale. The second year's estimate is an increase of 8 percent over the preceding year. Both estimates, as well as the initial wage array, are outputted.

Complete solutions for Problem 9.4 are shown in Figure 9.12.

FIGURE 9.12 *(a)*
Flowchart, *(b)* pro-
gram, and *(c)* output
for Problem 9.4. MAT
statements are
employed with arrays.

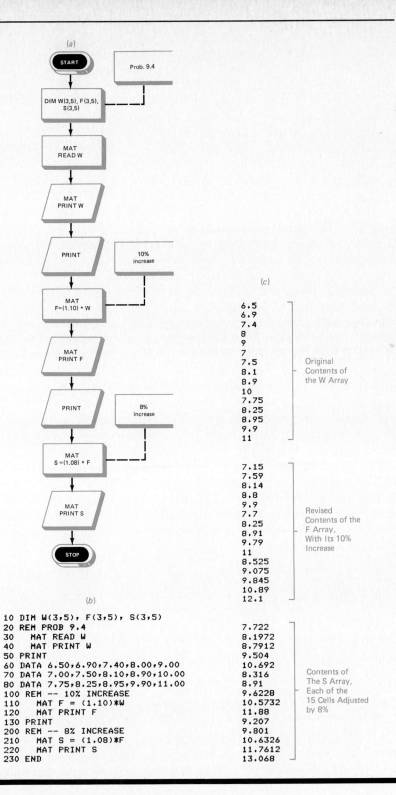

```
10 DIM W(3,5), F(3,5), S(3,5)
20 REM PROB 9.4
30   MAT READ W
40   MAT PRINT W
50 PRINT
60 DATA 6.50,6.90,7.40,8.00,9.00
70 DATA 7.00,7.50,8.10,8.90,10.00
80 DATA 7.75,8.25,8.95,9.90,11.00
100 REM -- 10% INCREASE
110   MAT F = (1.10)*W
120   MAT PRINT F
130 PRINT
200 REM -- 8% INCREASE
210   MAT S = (1.08)*F
220   MAT PRINT S
230 END
```

(c)

```
6.5
6.9
7.4
8
9
7
7.5          Original
8.1          Contents of
8.9          the W Array
10
7.75
8.25
8.95
9.9
11
```

```
7.15
7.59
8.14
8.8
9.9          Revised
7.7          Contents of the
8.25         F Array,
8.91         With Its 10%
9.79         Increase
11
8.525
9.075
9.845
10.89
12.1
```

```
7.722
8.1972
8.7912
9.504
10.692       Contents of
8.316        The S Array,
8.91         Each of the
9.6228       15 Cells Adjusted
10.5732      by 8%
11.88
9.207
9.801
10.6326
11.7612
13.068
```

The streamlined appearance of this solution results from the use of MAT statements. Each MAT statement invokes the set of instructions necessary to handle that task. Note that the nested loops normally associated with handling two-dimensional arrays are not visible. These looping sequences exist, but access to them is controlled via MAT statements.

The loading of the initial wage array W(3,5) is accomplished on line 30. Note that all three arrays are defined by the DIM statement, line 10, in preparation for their use. Initially, only the W array is handled. The output of the wage array is performed via line 40. This MAT PRINT instruction will output the W array's cells on a line-by-line basis.

The remaining processing is easily handled. The 10 percent increase in the original wage array is computed at line 110. A MAT statement results in the multiplication of the W array by 1.10, increasing the original wage array by 10 percent and storing those results in the F array. The revised contents of F are outputted via line 120 on 12 consecutive lines.

The estimated 8 percent increase in the second year of the contract is similarly calculated. At line 210, each cell of the F array is multiplied by 1.08 to produce the S array. Its output is performed at line 220, before the program is closed. Blank lines were inserted between the array outputs to improve their legibility. The finalized outputs of Problem 9.4 are shown in Figure 9.12(c).

The MAT statements offer an efficient means of performing certain standardized tasks. More specialized tasks must be handled by user-written instructions prepared uniquely for a given application. A fifth sample problem examines an application where both MAT and customized instructions are required.

Analyzing Processed Results

MAT instructions are often helpful in preparing arrays for processing. In addition to their use as tables, 2-dimensional arrays may also act as accumulators, recording processed results according to preestablished categories. Thus, for example, it would be possible to analyze processing and assign those results to specific array cells. The output of array cells would provide a summary of the processing performed.

This type of processing is often used in the social sciences, where results of the analysis are assigned to array categories. For example, the array outputs can show the number of boys versus the number of girls in a category, those achieving above- and below-average results, and so on. This 2-D array forms the framework of a table in which results categorized prior to output can be interpreted further by the user.

PROBLEM 9.5   Finding a Student Grade Profile

The problem entails analyzing student grades and providing a profile on the results. A 2-D array consisting of two rows and three columns is constructed to record grades assigned to boys and girls in a class. The grade array and grading categories are noted in Tables 9.4 and 9.5. The grade array will record the distribution of class grades and must be zeroed out before being used. Conditional statements in the main loop will assign grades and record each student's result in the proper array cell.

TABLE 9.4 Grades

Sex	S	P	F
Male			
Female			

TABLE 9.5 Grading Scheme

85–100	S	Superior
65–84.9	P	Passing
0–64.9	F	Failure

The main loop handles the processing of student grades. Input on each loop are the student's name, sex, midterm grade, and final exam grade. The final class average is computed at 40 percent for the midterm and 60 percent for the final exam. The final grade is determined by testing the final average against the grade scheme in Table 9.5. The proper array is updated according to sex and grade. Output for each student are the name, final average, and grade. Use the headings STUDENT NAME, AVER, and GRADE, each literal commencing at position 1, 16, and 23, respectively. Edit the final average with a ##.## format.

After the last student is processed, output the contents of the grade array using a MAT instruction. The data for the problem is as follows:

Student	Sex	Midterm	Final Exam	Student	Sex	Midterm	Final Exam
Martino	M	92	80	Winfield	F	80	92
Smalley	F	68	75	Griffey	F	40	68
Kiner	F	60	72	Nettles	M	72	80
Randolph	M	72	88	Baylor	M	90	81
Kemp	M	65	70	Cerone	F	86	78
Pinella	F	90	93	Gamble	F	78	70

These are the main points in the problem narrative.

1 A 2-D array is used to record the results of student grades. All cells in this array must be initialized at zero.

2 Input are the student's name, sex, midterm, and final exam grade. The final average is computed as

Final Avg = (.4 * midterm) + (.6 * final exam)

3 Final grades (in letter form) are assigned according to three defined categories. Once defined, the appropriate array cell should be updated by 1.

4 Output are the student's name, final average, and final grade. An edited output is employed, each item appearing beneath its indicated heading.

5 Output the contents of the grade array after all students are processed.

The flowchart prepared for Problem 9.5 is depicted in Figure 9.13. One main loop and three GOSUB modules are indicated. After defining the G(3,2) grades array, a MAT statement loads each of its cells with a zero. The L$ edited format is defined prior to the output of the report's heading line. A FOR/NEXT sequence of 12 loops controls the processing of student grades.

The input of student data precedes the computation of the student average A. A test of X$ determines the student's sex and assigns the proper row subscript I. Three decisions follow and determine the letter grade and column subscript J. These processing tasks are performed in separate grade modules.

The I and J subscripts are used to update the correct cell of the grade array. The output of student data follows and precedes the loop's closing NEXT statement. A blank line separates the last student's data from the output of the grade array produced by a MAT PRINT instruction.

The program and output for Problem 9.5 are shown in Figure 9.14. A single grade array, consisting of two rows and three columns, is defined at the DIM statement, line 10. A MAT statement, line 30, enters zeros into each of the six cells of the G array. During processing, data items representing each cell cause its contents to be updated by an increment of 1. Any cell retaining its zero value indicates that no students fell into that category.

Two output statements are found at lines 40 and 50. The edited L$ format for student grade data is defined before the output of the report's heading line. Three literals compose this heading line. Because of their proximity, all three were defined within a single literal of 27 characters.

The main looping sequence, in which each student's grades are processed, commences at line 60. This FOR statement loops 12 times, 1 loop for each student. A READ statement, line 70, enters the student's name (N$), sex (X$), midterm grade (M), and final exam grade (E). The midterm and final exam grades are used to compute the final average A, at line 80.

The testing sequence to determine the row and column subscripts of the grade's cell associated with that student's performance is initiated at line 90. This IF/THEN/ELSE statement tests for the student's sex, assigning a row subscript of I at 1 or 2. The testing to assign a letter grade and define the column subscript J occurs at lines 100 to 120.

Each of these conditional statements leads to one of three GOSUB modules. In each module, a grade of either S, P, or F is awarded and a J value of 1, 2, or 3 is defined. Examining the GOSUB 400, 500, and 600 modules, we can identify their respective assignments.

Whichever row I and column J subscripts are defined, both are invoked at line 130. They are substituted in the G(I,J) variable name, that grade array cell being updated by 1. A PRINT USING statement outputs student data in an edited format, preceding the loop's NEXT K statement.

The FOR/NEXT sequence executes exactly 12 loops, processing each student's data and updating the grade array's statistics on each loop. The final contents of the grade array is outputted at line 170, using another MAT statement. The MAT G statement prints the six cells of the G(2,3) array,

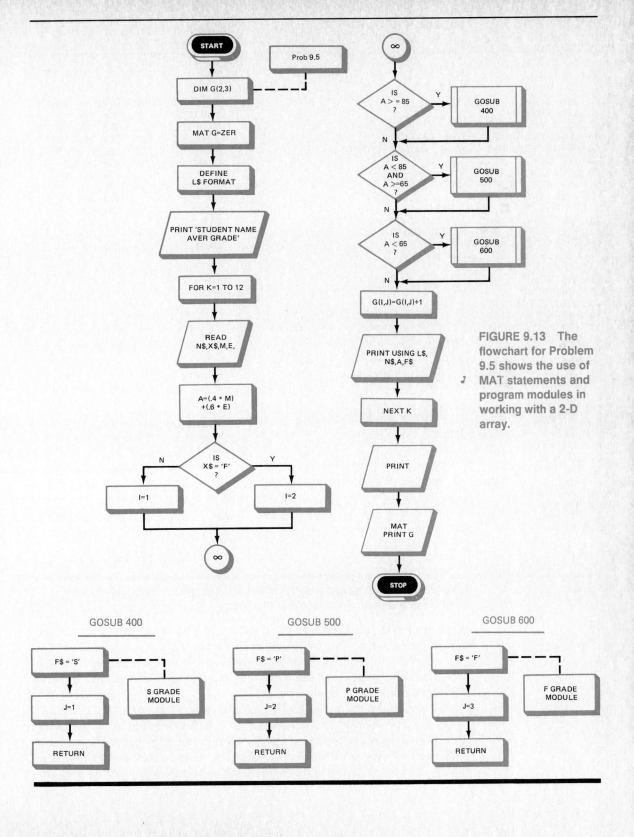

FIGURE 9.13 The flowchart for Problem 9.5 shows the use of MAT statements and program modules in working with a 2-D array.

```
10 DIM G(2,3)
20 REM PROB 9.5
30 MAT G = ZER
40 L$ = '\              \ ##.## \ \'
50 PRINT 'STUDENT   NAME AVER   GRADE'
60 FOR K = 1 TO 12
70    READ N$,X$,M,E
80    A = (.4*M) + (.6*E)
90    IF X$= 'F' THEN I=2 ELSE I=1
100   IF A >= 85 THEN GOSUB 400
110   IF A < 85 AND A >= 65 THEN GOSUB 500
120   IF A < 65 THEN GOSUB 600
130   G(I,J) = G(I,J) + 1
140   PRINT USING L$,N$,A,F$
150 NEXT K
160 PRINT
170 MAT PRINT G
180 GO TO 700
200 DATA 'MARTINO','M',92,80,'WINFIELD','F',80,92
210 DATA 'SMALLEY','F',68,75,'GRIFFEY','F',40,68
220 DATA 'KINER','F',60,72,'NETTLES','M',72,80
230 DATA 'RANDOLPH','M',72,88,'BAYLOR','M',90,81
240 DATA 'KEMP','M',65,70,'CERONE','F',86,78
250 DATA 'PINELLA','F',90,93,'GAMBLE','F',78,70
400 REM -- S GRADE MODULE
410 F$ = 'S'
420 J = 1
430 RETURN
500 REM -- P GRADE MODULE
510 F$ = 'P'
520 J = 2
530 RETURN
600 REM -- F GRADE MODULE
610 F$ = 'F'
620 J = 3
630 RETURN
700 END
```

STUDENT	NAME AVER	GRADE
MARTINO	84.80	P
WINFIELD	87.20	S
SMALLEY	72.20	P
GRIFFEY	56.80	F
KINER	67.20	P
NETTLES	76.80	P
RANDOLPH	81.60	P
BAYLOR	84.60	P
KEMP	68.00	P
CERONE	81.20	P
PINELLA	91.80	S
GAMBLE	73.20	P

```
0
5
0
2
4
1
```

(c)

The G array, the last 6 lines of output,
should be interpreted in
the tabular format below.

		Grade	
Sex	S	P	F
Male	0	5	0
Female	2	4	1

FIGURE 9.14 *(a)* Program and *(b)* output for Problem 9.5 along with *(c)* the user's interpretation of the results in the array.

outputting each cell's value on a separate line. The grade array is outputted for interpretation by the user. A blank line separates the last line of student data and the output of the grade array data. An unconditional branch at line 180 causes the program to jump over the remaining DATA statements and GOSUB modules to close processing.

The tabular output for Problem 9.5 is shown in Figure 9.14*(c)*. Note that two of the student grade cells remain at zero, indicating that no students fell into those categories. The zero entry exists in the cells equivalent to male students, receiving grades of S and F. This fact may be verified by examining the list of student grades which preceded the output of the grade array.

If MAT statements are available in your version of BASIC, you should take advantage of them. They offer a simple means of performing specific tasks without having to write those instructions. You should remember that the more specialized the processing, the greater the likelihood that a MAT statement may not be applicable.

Chapter Summary

9.1 The 2-D Structure

Two-dimensional arrays are constructed using rows and columns. Two subscripts define the row and column variables and identify the position of each cell in a 2-dimensional array. In the subscripted variable name X(I,J), I is the row subscript and J is the column subscript. An array name of X(5,3) notes the use of five rows and three columns for a total of 15 cells (5×3).

9.2 Loading 2-D Arrays

A nested loop controls the loading of a 2-dimensional array. When row subscripts are defined in the outer FOR/NEXT statement, the array is loaded on a row-by-row basis. When column subscripts are defined in the outer FOR/NEXT statement, the array is loaded on a column-by-column basis. The row-by-row loading sequence is most commonly used.

When the contents of a 2-D array are relatively stable, array data may be loaded using READ and DATA statements. INPUT statements are used where the contents of a 2-D array may vary extensively between applications. The interactive nature of INPUT statements offer the users some flexibility.

9.3 Applications for 2-D Arrays

Two-dimensional arrays are successfully used as reference tables, each array cell containing a specific fact within the table. Access to each 2-D cell requires a specific row and column cross-reference. Conditional statements test values against categories in a table and determine the proper row and column subscripts needed to access a cell.

Categories for 2-D reference tables are defined using any combination of numeric and alphabetic data. Compound and single conditionals can determine the subscripts necessary to access one cell of data. These conditionals are normally positioned within a main loop and consecutively test data for each type of subscript.

9.4 The MAT Instruction

MAT instructions are predefined sets of statements that perform specific tasks in relation to 2-dimensional arrays. Using MAT statements it is possible to perform I/O operations, load arrays with zeros or ones, or undertake arithmetic operations regarding arrays. The user need only specify a single MAT instruction to perform complex tasks involving 2-D arrays.

When loading or outputting array data via MAT statements, that data is handled on a line-by-line basis. MAT statements provide all instructions needed to perform its task.

MAT statements and conventional two-dimensional array handling sequences may be integrated into program solutions. MAT statements perform predefined tasks, while the other statements handle more specialized processing. MAT statements are employed in algebraic applications, where data is held in a 2-D format referred to as a matrix.

Key BASIC Statements

	Examples	
DIM statements for two-dimensional arrays	10	DIM X(5,4),N$(5,4)
	10	DIM X(6,2),A(9)
Nested FOR/NEXT statements with two-dimensional arrays	100	FOR I = 1 TO 6
	110	FOR J = 1 TO 3
	120	READ X(I,J)
	130	PRINT X(I,J)
	140	NEXT J
	150	NEXT I
MAT statements	30	MAT READ G
	60	MAT PRINT G
	90	MAT C = A
	100	MAT C = B * .12
	110	MAT G = ZER

Glossary

MAT statements Sets of predefined statements which can manipulate data held in 2-dimensional arrays.

Matrix The visual format adopted by 2-D arrays, often associated with algebraic problems.

Two-dimensional (2-D) array An organization of array cells where two means of reference, row and column subscripts, are required to access a specific cell of data; often used to define tables of values.

Exercises

In-Class Exercises   1   The problem entails the computation of transportation costs for three types of products. The rates for these three products are listed in Table 9.6, defined in a 2-D array. This task is performed in module 1 of the program.

TABLE 9.6 Transportation Rates (dollars per mile)

Miles to Be Shipped	Product Type		
	1	2	3
0 to 75	.62	.89	1.07
75.1 to 250	.93	1.18	1.33
250.1 and up	1.15	1.43	1.69

Module 2 controls the computation of transportation costs within a loop. Input are the account number, number of miles travelled, and product type. The latter two inputs are used to test and gain access to the 2-D array that holds rates. The actual transportation cost is computed by multiplying the respective rate by the number of miles over which it must be shipped, adding a flat fee of $125. Output on each loop the account number, the mileage to be transported, the rate used, and the computed cost. The data used for this problem is as follows:

Account No	Miles	Product
40635	156	1
11538	63	2
89384	612	1
99310	403	2
20080	29	3
33067	202	1

Write a flowchart and program to satisfy this narrative.

2 The problem entails the interactive use of a two-dimensional array. Table 9.7 provides the calories associated with different types of sweets. The user enters the number of ounces to be consumed and food type, with the table reporting the calories associated. The calorie table is noted below and should be defined in module 1 of the solution.

9.7 Calorie Chart

Ounces Consumed	Apple Pie	Ice Cream	Fudge Cake
0 to 1.9	169	300	362
2 to 3.9	338	600	598
4 to 5.9	507	900	1060
6 to 7.9	676	1200	1473

The second program module is interactive, as each request is handled on an interactive basis via an INPUT statement. Enter the ounces and food type data on each loop. A series of decisions in your program determines the row and column subscripts for the correct array cell. Output the calories, food type, and ounces to be consumed on separate lines, with appropriate labels. The data involved is as follows:

Food Type	Ounces Consumed
Fudge cake	2.5
Ice cream	5.1
Apple pie	7.0
Fudge cake	1.5

Write the flowchart and program necessary to satisfy this narrative. Use INPUT statements, defining each module within GOSUB modules.

3 A group of measurements are stored in a 2-D array. The lab technician wishes to examine these values, but reduced by 20 percent. Use MAT statements to read data into the (4,4) array, multiply its contents, and output the reduced array's data. The original array's data is as follows:

.032	.064	.070	.098
.056	.072	.088	1.09
.074	.085	1.06	1.13
.091	1.08	1.20	1.32

Write the flowchart and program to satisfy this narrative.

Lab Exercises

1 The problem entails the computation of fertilizer solutions, with rates held in a 2-dimensional array, which is loaded in module 1, using the data in Table 9.8.

TABLE 9.8 Fertilizer Solution Rates

	Type of Grass		
Sq Feet	Rye	Blue	Bermuda
0–1000	.052	.057	.063
1001–5000	.128	.136	.145
5000 or more	.143	.157	.166

Module 2 computes the number of gallons of fertilizer solution to be prepared. On each loop, the square footage to be covered and type of grass is entered via READ and DATA statements. Both variables are needed to identify the subscripts for the array cell in which the rate amount is stored. A series of decisions is needed to test for these cells. The obtained rate is multiplied by the square footage to produce the number of gallons to be prepared. A 5 percent waste figure is added to that number of gallons to produce the total gallons of fertilizer needed. Output the square footage, type of grass, and total gallons necessary beneath the headings SQ FEET, GRASS, and TOT GAL-LONS.

The data for this problem is as follows:

Sq Feet	Grass
2500	Bermuda
6800	Rye
850	Blue
4560	Rye
9200	Blue
550	Bermuda

a Write the flowchart and program to accomplish the processing described. Use nested loops to load the 2-D array and GOSUBs to create program modules.
b Write the flowchart and program using MAT statements to load the array and any looping sequence to control the loop of module 2.

2   The problem entails estimating advertising costs and the potential audience for a product. Audience response rates are held in the 2-D Table 9.9 consisting of four rows and two columns. The array is loaded in module 1.

TABLE 9.9   Costs and Rating Code

Est Costs	Rating Code	
	A	B
0 to 1000	.0012	.0016
1001 to 5000	.0015	.0026
5001 to 10000	.0024	.0032

   All processing occurs in module 2. Input on each loop each project's number, the product rating code (A or B), and the market level number. The market level number is converted into a cost figure using one of the following two formulas:

   If rating code is A, Cost = 4.13 * Level Number
   If rating code is B, Cost = 12.64 * Level number

The cost figure is combined with the rating code to enter the audience response array. A series of decisions is used to test for the row and column subscripts. The audience response rating drawn from that array is used to produce an audience response figure. The audience response figure is computed by multiplying the response rating by 10,000. Output on each loop the project number, rating code, estimated cost, and audience response amount. Use the headings PROJ ID, R/C, EST COSTS, and POT AUDIENCE, each heading commencing at position 1, 9, 13, and 23. Apply the format ##### to project number, #####. for estimated costs and ####.# for the audience's response amount.

   The data for this problem is as follows:

Project Number	Rating Code	Market Level Number
1066	B	1050
1215	A	862
1443	A	206
1732	B	663
1776	B	375
1812	B	502

Write a flowchart and program to satisfy this narrative. Use GOSUBs to create program modules.

3   The problem entails creating a mileage table for travel agents. A 2-D array is defined for the table listed below. The array is loaded in module 1.

   An interactive set of INPUT statements are used in module 2 to prompt the user. One INPUT requests the arriving city, while a second requests the departing city.

Using both cities as keys to the mileage array, the program will determine the mileage between those cities. The mileage figure obtained from the array is divided by 500 to estimate the flight time between those cities. Output on each loop are the departing city, arriving city, the mileage between them, and the estimated flight time — each output on a separate line. Use appropriate labels to identify each output.

Mileage data for various cities is as follows:

Departing Cities	Arriving Cities			
	Los Angeles (LA)	San Francisco (SFO)	Portland (POR)	Seattle (SEA)
Boston (BOS)	2779	3095	3046	2976
New York (NY)	2786	2934	2885	2815
Baltimore (BALT)	2636	2796	2751	2681
Atlanta (ATL)	2182	2496	2601	2618
Miami (MIA)	2687	3053	3256	3273

Determine the distance and time between

  a New York and Portland   **d** Miami and San Francisco
  b Atlanta and Los Angeles   **e** Baltimore and Portland
  c Boston and Seattle

Write the flowchart and program necessary to satisfy this narrative.

4 The problem entails computing the volume of cement needed for making concrete. A two-dimensional array of cement ratios is used in computing the amount of cement needed. The cement array is loaded in module 1, using the data in Table 9.10.

TABLE 9.10 Cement Ratios

Cu Yards	Concrete Type		
	Quick Set (Q)	Normal Set (N)	Slow Set (S)
0 to 9	.142	.153	.167
10 to 24	.165	.172	.188
25 or more	.179	.193	.206

In module 2, processing is performed in a looping sequence. Input on each loop the height, width, and depth of the site to be filled with concrete and the type of concrete to be used. Multiplying the first three inputs creates the cubic feet of that site. That amount is divided by 27 to determine the cubic yards of concrete to be poured. It is the cubic yards figure and type of concrete that are used to enter the array and retrieve the ratio of cement to use. Multiply the ratio by the cubic yards figure to produce the pounds of cement to use. Output on each loop the volume of concrete (cubic feet), concrete type, and the amount of cement (in pounds) to use. Use the headings VOL(CU FT), TYPE, and CEMENT(LB).

The data for this problem is as follows:

Height	Weight	Depth	Type
8	5	3	S
10	12	2	N
6	20	8	Q
3	40	4	N

Write the flowchart and program necessary to complete this narrative.

5 The problem entails identifying characteristics associated with processed results. A researcher wishes to collect data for projected management salary increases in a 2-D array consisting of two rows and three columns. A sample of the results array format is shown in Table 9.11.

The formula used by the researcher is

Income Projection $= AT^2 + BT$

where A and B are ratings related to performance from testing and past work experience, and T is the number of years in the company. The A, B, and T values are entered on each loop and substituted into that equation. Also input are the employees' project number and sex. The income projection and sex variables are used as keys to enter the results array and update specific cells. On each loop output the employee's project number, sex, and projected income estimate. After processing is complete, output the entire results array.

Use MAT instructions to insert zeros in the original results array and to output that array when all processing is over. The data for the problem is as follows:

Project No	Sex	A	B	T(Years)
10361	M	1586	40	4
11572	F	585	80	10
02389	F	508	29	6
80672	M	2500	3	1
43055	F	1260	38	5
54170	M	421	62	12
62931	M	330	56	8
09903	M	762	34	3
41183	F	160	73	7
54516	M	1480	55	5
66072	M	217	93	20
15837	F	2610	48	15

TABLE Table 9.11 Rate Array Format

Sex	Estimated Salary Range		
	0 to 10,000	10,001 to 25,000	25,000 or more
Female (F)			
Male (M)			

Quiz Problem   The problem entails using the data held in a 2-D array in processing. Mailing rates for a magazine are held in a (3,3) rate array, whose contents are listed in Table 9.12. Load the array in module 1.

TABLE 9.12   Mailing Rates

Weight (Oz.)	Mailing Zone		
	A	B	C
0–1.50	.24	.63	.89
1.51–3.00	.35	.71	.92
3.01–5.00	.46	.79	.99

Module 2 uses the mailing array. Input on each loop the subscription number, mailing zone shipped to, and the weight of the printed matter shipped. The latter two variables are used as keys to the mailing array and to derive the appropriate rate cell. The rate accessed is multiplied by the weight amount (in ounces) to compute the mailing costs. Output on each loop the subscription number, mailing rate, and cost for that material beneath the headings ID NO, MAIL RATE, and MAIL COST. The data is as follows:

Subscription Number	Mailing Zone	Weight (Oz.)
1063	A	.98
4429	B	2.17
8061	C	4.66
7553	A	3.54
4081	B	1.21
3115	C	1.88

Quiz Solution   The flowchart, program, and output for the quiz problem are shown in Figure 9.15. The solution involved a (3,3) array and the extraction of rates from it.

Appendix: Debugging Hints

A Conditional Gap

As 2-dimensional arrays retain data in a tabular form, it is essential that proper access be provided to that data. This includes the correct specification of the conditional statements defining array categories and their subscripts. Often, these conditional statements are written incorrectly.

Consider the table described in Figure A.9.1 and the categories defined. We want to establish compound-conditional statements to define each category's limits. The statements listed apparently perform this task, but a potential error exists.

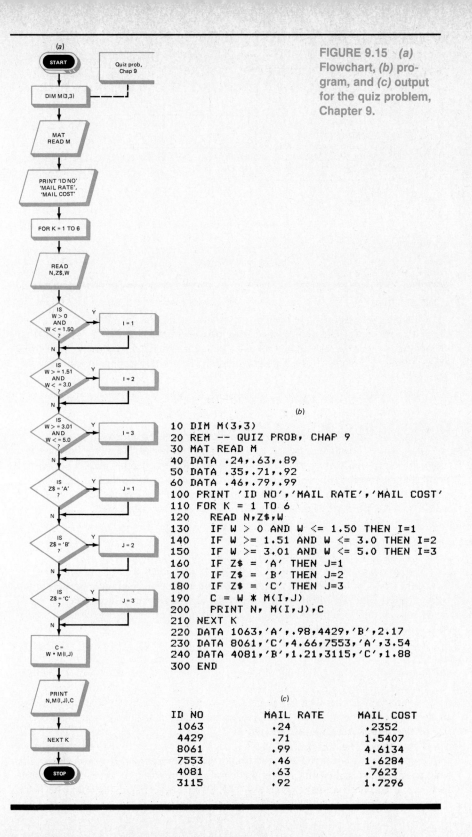

FIGURE 9.15 (a)
Flowchart, (b) pro-
gram, and (c) output
for the quiz problem,
Chapter 9.

(b)

```
10 DIM M(3,3)
20 REM -- QUIZ PROB, CHAP 9
30 MAT READ M
40 DATA .24,.63,.89
50 DATA .35,.71,.92
60 DATA .46,.79,.99
100 PRINT 'ID NO','MAIL RATE','MAIL COST'
110 FOR K = 1 TO 6
120    READ N,Z$,W
130    IF W > 0 AND W <= 1.50 THEN I=1
140    IF W >= 1.51 AND W <= 3.0 THEN I=2
150    IF W >= 3.01 AND W <= 5.0 THEN I=3
160    IF Z$ = 'A' THEN J=1
170    IF Z$ = 'B' THEN J=2
180    IF Z$ = 'C' THEN J=3
190    C = W * M(I,J)
200    PRINT N, M(I,J),C
210 NEXT K
220 DATA 1063,'A',.98,4429,'B',2.17
230 DATA 8061,'C',4.66,7553,'A',3.54
240 DATA 4081,'B',1.21,3115,'C',1.88
300 END
```

(c)

ID NO	MAIL RATE	MAIL COST
1063	.24	.2352
4429	.71	1.5407
8061	.99	4.6134
7553	.46	1.6284
4081	.63	.7623
3115	.92	1.7296

COST	A	B	C
0 - 500			
501 - 1000			

```
200 IF C > 0 AND C < 500 THEN I=1
210 IF C > 501 AND C < 1000 THEN I=2
```

(Improperly written)

Though the compound conditional statements adhere to the BASIC syntax, they are written incorrectly. Instead of specifying greater than or equal to ($>=$) or less than or equal to ($<=$) signs, the statement omits the equal sign. Thus, gaps in the categories exist at each of the opening and closing points. The correct statements should have been

200   IF C $>=$ 0 AND C $<=$ 500 THEN I $=$ 1
210   IF C $>=$ 501 AND C $<=$ 1000 THEN I $=$ 2

In this manner, gaps in defining the table's categories are avoided.

This type of error generates no computer error messages. It is not a syntax error. The error is programmer-oriented, as categories used in testing for subscripts have not been defined correctly. Data falling within those gaps would pass through without being tested or would be handled using the subscripts of the previous loop. The error would be recognized only by verifying the results of processing.

Data Entry Errors

A common mistake related to loading 2-dimensional arrays involves the attempted entry of two or more data items into one array cell. Beginning programmers believe that the two subscripts employed with 2-D arrays permit the entry of two data items, not the handling of row and column subscripts. The program excerpt in Figure A.9.2 offers a glimpse of this type of error.

The nested loops necessary to control the input sequence are properly defined in lines 20 and 30. The difficulty occurs at line 40, where the attempt to read two variables results in error. Instead of using the subscripted variables X(I,J), the user erroneously specified the X(I) and X(J) variable names. Though I and J are defined, they are employed with one array cell — not two distinct subscripted-variable names. In the indicated excerpt, only one cell should be loaded. The I and J values define the row and column subscripts for that cell.

The attempt to improperly read array data is recognized in the initial loop, and the computer is alerted to the incorrectly specified subscript. To correct the error, the programmer must replace the one-dimensional variable with the correct X(I,J) notation. Using the subscripted variable, the 10-cell array is loaded on a row-by-row basis — one cell per loop.

```
10 DIM X(5,2)
20 FOR I = 1 TO 5
30    FOR J = 1 TO 2
40       READ X(I), X(J)
50    NEXT J
60 NEXT I
70 DATA 20,63,-1,7,14
80 DATA -70,29,17,19,31
```

(Incorrect)

APPENDIX A

Extra Statements and Functions

Appendix Objectives

- Describe the use of the ON GOTO and ON GOSUB statements under controlled branching conditions.

- Introduce the trigonometric functions SIN, COS, and TAN.

- Briefly discuss user-defined functions.

- Describe the use of functions in string processing.

- Illustrate use of the LEFT, RIGHT, MID, and INSTR functions.

- Discuss the use of the RND function in generating random numbers and its impact on computer-oriented games.

Introduction

BASIC is sufficiently complex to warrant the use of many types of instructions. Though our discussions have introduced many of BASIC's principal instructions, we have not covered all the statements which the language supports. This appendix attempts to broaden the scope of the text by covering statements favored by many users. These statements range from conditional branching operations to the generation of random numbers.

A.1 Controlled Branching

In earlier solutions we employed IF/THEN statements to control the testing of codes leading to processing activities. If codes of 1, 2, and 3 defined three separate processing tasks, a sequence of three decisions was used to test those codes and branch to related processing.

The same can be done for accessing program modules defined via GOSUB statements. Conditional statements were employed to test for codes and control access to the specific modules. A sequence of IF/THEN statements enabled us to tightly control when specific processing statements were executed.

BASIC provides the programmer with an alternative to using a string of decisions to branch to program statements or modules—the ON GOTO statements.

The **ON GOTO statement** is employed when a series of codes is tested. Instead of using separate conditional statements to test for each code, the ON GOTO statement can test a group of them all at once. However, the user must ensure that the codes are in consecutive order, commencing at 1.

Figure A.1*(a)* compares the ON GOTO statement with the IF/THEN conditional instruction. Three IF/THEN statements are employed to test C for codes of 1, 2, and 3. Each instruction causes the computer to branch to a different line, when its specific code is met. Each code is an integer, possessing no decimal points. Also, no gaps exist in the code structure. The C variable is either a 1, 2, or 3. When an ON GOTO is used, however, all three tests are integrated into one statement. The words ON and GOTO are required commands, with a line number. The variable to be tested against, C, is positioned between ON and GOTO commands. The instruction is designed to automatically link the testing of coded variables and their line numbers. When C equals 1, the instruction directs the program to line 300. Similarly, when C equals 2 and 3, the program branches to lines 400 and 500, respectively. No other linkages are necessary, as the instruction coordinates the required testing and branching sequences.

The ON GOTO statement can be successfully used only when the codes are numeric and defined sequentially. Gaps within the coded sequence, alphabetic codes, negative values, and decimals render the ON GOTO ineffective. Another disadvantage of the ON GOTO is the need to use GOTO statements to return to the main processing flow. Since structured designs call for the minimal use of GO TOs, the ON GOTO statement is not popular with top-down programmers.

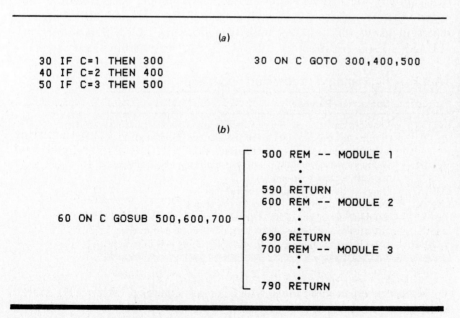

```
                        (a)

30 IF C=1 THEN 300          30 ON C GOTO 300,400,500
40 IF C=2 THEN 400
50 IF C=3 THEN 500


                        (b)

                            ┌─ 500 REM -- MODULE 1
                            │      .
                            │      .
                            │      .
                            │   590 RETURN
                            │   600 REM -- MODULE 2
                            │      .
60 ON C GOSUB 500,600,700 ──┤      .
                            │      .
                            │   690 RETURN
                            │   700 REM -- MODULE 3
                            │      .
                            │      .
                            │      .
                            └─ 790 RETURN
```

FIGURE A.1 A series of IF/THEN statements can be replaced by ON GOTO and ON GOSUB statements. *(a)* Three IF/THEN statements are replaced by an ON GOTO statement. *(b)* An ON GOSUB statement controls access to three program modules.

ON GOSUB
Statements

The **ON GOSUB statement** parallels the ON GOTO and allows the program to branch to modules of related statements.

The ON GOSUB statement is applied to situations where sequential codes are evident. Figure A.1*(b)* illustrates a program excerpt where the ON GOSUB statement is applied to codes of 1, 2, and 3.

At line 60, the variable C is tested by the ON GOSUB for the three numeric codes. If C equals 1, 2, or 3, the GOSUB modules commencing at lines 500, 600, and 700, respectively, are accessed. In all three cases, a RETURN statement is required to transfer control back to the original ON GOSUB instruction.

This last point is important and represents a major advantage over the ON GOTO statement. The RETURN statement eliminates the need for GO TO statements to return to the main flow of processing and enables the programmer to adopt a modular approach.

The ON GOSUB and ON GOTO statements may be used whenever a series of codes is evident in the processing sequence. At the programmer's discretion they can replace a series of conditional statements. Remember, for these statements to be used effectively, no gaps can exist in the numeric code sequence.

A.2 Mathematical Functions

In Chapter 7 we introduced the predefined SQR and ABS functions and applied them to processing involving arrays. The SQR and ABS functions represent just two of the user-supplied functions available with most versions of BASIC. Table A.1 provides a list of other predefined functions.

TABLE A.1   Standard Predefined Functions

Function	Operational Purpose
INT(X)	Provides the greatest integer which is less than or equal to X; truncates the decimal part of the number (for example, 7.62 becomes 7 and -5.2 becomes -6)
SGN(X)	Defines a value of $+1$, 0, or -1, depending on whether X is positive, zero, or negative
LOG(X)	Provides the natural log for the value of X
EXP(X)	Defines the equivalent of e to the power of X
SIN(X)	Establishes the sine of X, where the X angle is in radians
COS(X)	Establishes the cosine of X, where the X angle is in radians
TAN(X)	Establishes the tangent of X, where the X angle is in radians

These seven mathematical functions are specified within LET statements. For example, the instruction

60   Y = INT(X)

truncates the decimal portion of X and stores that value in Y. The variable to the left of the equal sign may be a numeric variable or a subscripted variable if an array is employed.

Of particular interest are the last three functions listed in Table A.1. These functions relate to trigonometric operations and require that the argument being used be defined in radians. This limitation means that X angle cannot be specified in degrees but must be converted to its equivalent in radians. Any attempt to enter a number of degrees for X will result in a program error.

The formula for conversion of an angle to its equivalent radian value is as follows:

One degree $= \pi/180$ radians

where pi (π) equals 3.1416. Hence, the mathematical formula for converting degrees to radians is

$$x = n \cdot (3.1416/180)$$

where n is the number of degrees in the angle specified and x is the equivalent number of radians.

It is the x value (in radians) that is substituted in the predefined function to compute the desired trig value. This instructional sequence may appear as

```
100     INPUT N
110     X = N * (3.1416/180)
120     Y = SIN (X)
130     PRINT 'THE SINE OF';N;' DEGREES'
140     PRINT 'HAS A VALUE OF ';Y
```

This excerpt commences with the input of the number of degrees, N, on line 100. At line 110, the N degrees is converted to its radian equivalent, X. The sine value of X is computed at line 120, and the result retained as Y. The outputs generated by lines 130 and 140 provide users with the result of processing.

PROBLEM A.1   Trigonometry Problems

The problem entails writing a program to solve trigonometry problems. A student must determine the side lengths of various triangles using the sine and cosine. Input on each loop is the angle (in degrees), a code for whether the sine (1) or cosine (2) is used, and the hypotenuse of the triangle. After the angle is converted into radians, that value is substituted into the SIN or COS function and multiplied against the hypotenuse producing the unknown side of the triangle. Figure A.2 illustrates relationships between the angle, sides, and hypotenuse. Output the angle, hypotenuse, and resulting side in each loop. Use headings at the top of the report and a four-loop sequence. Use an ON GOSUB to branch to the module in which each type of processing is performed. The data employed in this problem is listed below.

Angle	Code	Hypotenuse	Angle	Code	Hypotenuse
30	1	12	45	1	10
60	2	18	75	2	21

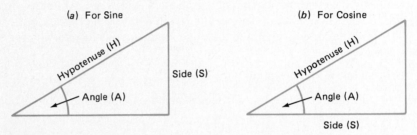

FIGURE A.2   Relationships between the angle, sides, and hypotenuse of a triangle. *(a)* For sine; *(b)* for cosine.

These are the main points in the problem narrative.

1   A four-loop sequence controls processing. Each trig function is handled within its own module, accessed via an ON GOSUB instruction.

2   The three-literal heading at the top of the report consists of ANGLE, HYPOTENUSE, and SIDE.

3   Inputted on each loop are an angle (in degrees), a function code, and the hypotenuse value. The angle is converted to radians before use in the SIN or COS function. The formula used to convert the angle to radians is

Radians = degrees ∗ (3.1416/180)

The radian's value is substituted into the trig function, where an equivalent decimal results. That value is then multiplied by the hypotenuse to produce the side value sought.

4   Processing related to either trig function is performed within its own module. This includes computations and outputs.

The flowchart for Problem A.1 is shown in Figure A.3*(a)*. Four repetitions are performed in the main flowchart. The smaller flow diagrams reflect the processing associated with sine (GOSUB 200) and cosine (GOSUB 300) values. The selection of either module is controlled via a decision which is represented as an ON GOSUB instruction in the program.

FIGURE A.3 *(a)*
Flowchart, *(b)* program,
and *(c)* output for
Problem A.1.

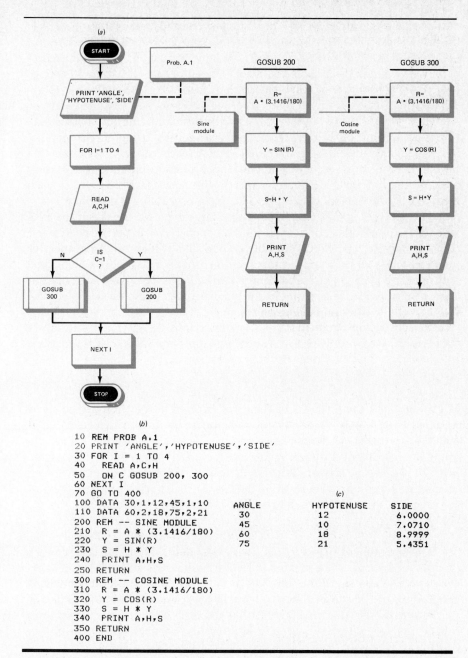

```
(b)
10  REM PROB A.1
20  PRINT 'ANGLE','HYPOTENUSE','SIDE'
30  FOR I = 1 TO 4
40     READ A,C,H
50     ON C GOSUB 200, 300
60  NEXT I
70  GO TO 400
100 DATA 30,1,12,45,1,10
110 DATA 60,2,18,75,2,21
200 REM -- SINE MODULE
210    R = A * (3.1416/180)
220    Y = SIN(R)
230    S = H * Y
240    PRINT A,H,S
250 RETURN
300 REM -- COSINE MODULE
310    R = A * (3.1416/180)
320    Y = COS(R)
330    S = H * Y
340    PRINT A,H,S
350 RETURN
400 END
```

	(c)	
ANGLE	HYPOTENUSE	SIDE
30	12	6.0000
45	10	7.0710
60	18	8.9999
75	21	5.4351

Each module is designed for one trigonometric function. The conversion of the angle A into radians precedes its use in the SIN and COS functions. The value derived by either function is multiplied by the hypotenuse to produce the side of the triangle. Output of the angle used, hypotenuse, and resultant side concludes each module's activities.

The processing defined by the three flowcharts is reflected in the actual program, shown in Figure A.3*(b)*. After the opening output of the three column headings, a FOR/NEXT loop is initiated at line 30. The data used in each of the four loops indicated is listed on lines 100 and 110. Line 40 defines the READ statement in which the angle A, code C, and hypotenuse H are inputted.

Of interest is the use of the ON GOSUB statement, line 50. This instruction tests the variable C, transferring program control to modules commencing at lines 200 and 300, when C equals 1 and 2, respectively. The statement's format incorporates the conditional test and branching operations necessary to access each GOSUB module. RETURN statements at the end of each module transfer control back to line 50, when processing is complete.

The processing in each module is similar, except for the use of the **SIN** and **COS functions.** After each module opens, the angle (in degrees) is converted to radians. The R variable is then substituted into the respective function, line 220 or 320, to compute the variable Y. The Y value is then multiplied by the hypotenuse to compute the value of the opposite or adjacent side of the triangle. The output of the angle, hypotenuse, and side is accomplished before either module is closed.

The output for Problem A.1 is shown in Figure A.3*(c)*. The results show the correct use of the ON GOSUB statement and the SIN and COS functions in calculating the side values of the four triangles.

User-Defined Functions

In Problem A.1, the formula for the conversion of degrees into radians was specified twice. In instances where a computation is used repeatedly, it is possible for the user to define that equation separately and make it generally available throughout the program. Access to a specific statement is permitted through the use of a **user-defined function.** This function is so named because it is created and defined by the user for use in that program only. In our program, we could have defined the radian computation as

```
10      DEF FNR(X) = A * (3.1416/180)
```

The line number 10 is required, as the user-defined function occupies one program instruction. The command DEF FN identifies the statement's purpose as a user-defined function. The R variable denotes the unique name assigned to the user-defined function by the programmer. This name must be specified to access this function. Either numeric or string-variable names may be used when naming user-defined functions, depending upon the type of data being processed.

The variable specified within the required set of parentheses denotes the data to be inputted to the user-defined function. The actual computation is specified after the required equal sign (=). In this notation, X acts as a dummy variable with A actually inputted prior to processing. Generally, the user-defined function is specified at the program's start and then accessed during the program's execution.

(a)

```
10 REM PROB A.1 REVISED
20 DEF FNR(X) = A * (3.1416/180)
30 PRINT 'ANGLE','HYPOTENUSE','SIDE'
40 FOR I = 1 TO 4
50    READ A,C,H
60    Z = FNR(A)
70    IF C=1 THEN Y = SIN(Z) ELSE Y = COS(Z)
80    S = H * Y
90    PRINT A,H,S
100 NEXT I
110 DATA 30,1,12,45,1,10
120 DATA 60,2,18,75,2,21
200 END
```

(b)

ANGLE	HYPOTENUSE	SIDE
30	12	6.0000
45	10	7.0710
60	18	8.9999
75	21	5.4351

FIGURE A.4 *(a)* Revised program and *(b)* output for Problem A.1. The user-defined function shortens the solution but does not affect the results.

The revised solution to Problem A.1 uses a user-defined function and reorders its processing sequence (Figure A.4). Line 20 specifies the user-defined function in which degrees are converted into radians. The three required column headings are outputted at line 30.

The FOR/NEXT statements, lines 40 and 100, define the four-loop sequence in which all processing is performed. Three variables are read at line 50. Access to the user-defined function is at line 60, where the function name is specified. The FNR command identifies the function, with the variable A providing the dataname for actual data items used. The results of converting the angles to radians is stored in Z.

The IF/THEN/ELSE statement, line 70, tests C against a code of 1 to determine whether to use the SIN or COS functions. The radian value Z is substituted into the proper trig function and produces the numeric equivalent of that angle Y. The Y value is used to compute the resulting side length, which is outputted on line 90.

No difference is apparent in the output of our revised solution, shown in Figure A.4*(b)*. Effectively, all we did was to provide a uniform means of computing radians and identify it by a unique name. Access to that function's processing required the specification of that name and the data to be used.

It should be noted that it is also possible to create user-defined functions consisting of multiple lines. This format may appear as follows:

```
100     DEF FNX(A)
.
.
.
200     FNEND
```

where 100 and 200 represent required line numbers, X the name of the multi-line function, and A the dummy argument. The commands DEF FN and FNEND identify the opening and closing lines of this function. All statements composing this multiline function appear between these two statements.

Though the multiple statement user-defined function is possible, it is not commonly used. Current programming methodology encourages the use of GOSUB modules, where a wide range of processing activities is easily undertaken.

A.3 String Processing

Until this point our discussions have focused on the handling of numeric data. It is also possible to manipulate nonnumeric or character data in a similar fashion. This type of processing is referred to as **string processing,** deriving its name from the handling of string-variable data. We intend to introduce some of the fundamental tasks which may be performed in this area to include the merging and analysis of string data.

String Configurations

In an operation similar to addition, it is possible to join two sets of string data into one. This task is generally referred to as a **concatenation.** A sample concatenation is shown in Figure A.5(a). In this program, we have defined three character strings — A$, B$, and C$ — in lines 110 to 130. The concatenation of these strings occurs at lines 140 and 150, where B$ and C$ are combined with A$. The result is two different names, outputted at lines 160 and 170.

The concatenation was accomplished by specifying a plus sign (+) between two previously defined string-variable names. In many computer-prepared documents, similar techniques are employed to create phrases and sentences which compose memos and statements.

In addition to merging string data, it is also possible to isolate specific parts of character strings. The selection of specific characters may occur at the start, middle, or end of a character string. To accomplish this selection

FIGURE A.5 A sample concatenation of string data (a) produces two different names (b).

(a)

```
100 REM -- SAMPLE CONCATENATION
110 A$ = 'EVANO'
120 B$ = 'WSKI'
130 C$ = 'VICH'
140 D$ = A$ + B$
150 E$ = A$ + C$
160 PRINT 'FIRST NAME',D$
170 PRINT 'SECOND NAME',E$
180 END
```

(b)

```
FIRST NAME     EVANOWSKI
SECOND NAME    EVANOVICH
```

process, BASIC makes available three predefined functions: LEFT, MID, and RIGHT.[1]

The **LEFT** and **RIGHT functions** are operationally similar and adopt the general format

LEFT (string, position)
RIGHT (string, position)

The term *string* notes the string-variable name to be worked on, while *position* represents the number of the character position which processing will continue to or end with. The program excerpt of Figure A.6 illustrates the use of these functions.

The 11-character variable J$ is defined at line 100. The left six characters are accessed at line 110 and assigned to K$. The LEFT function directs that the computer isolate the first six characters of J$. The word CUSTOM is so created and printed via line 120.

The RIGHT function, line 130, is similarly employed. In that statement, we direct the program to select characters commencing with position 8. The word defined by this RIGHT function is ZING.

To obtain character data within the middle of a string, the **MID function** is used. To use this function, the programmer must specify the starting character positions from which data should be drawn and the number of characters to be taken. The general format of the MID function

MID (string, position, number)

emphasizes these requirements. This format is applied at line 150 in Figure A.6*(a)*.

The MID function also accesses the J$ string. But in this case we seek string data commencing at character 4, for a total of three characters. These parameters are defined by the MID function, line 150, and assigned to M$. The three-character output for M$ defines the name TOM, which is printed via line 160.

(a)	(b)

```
100 J$ = 'CUSTOMIZING'
110 K$ = LEFT(J$,6)
120 PRINT 'LEFTMOST WORD : ';K$
130 L$ = RIGHT(J$,8)
140 PRINT 'RIGHTMOST WORD : ';L$
150 M$ = MID(J$,4,3)
160 PRINT 'MIDWORD : ';M$
170 END
```

```
LEFTMOST WORD : CUSTOM
RIGHTMOST WORD : ZING
MIDWORD : TOM
```

FIGURE A.6 Using functions, it is possible to select character data from within nonnumeric strings *(a)*. Three terms are selected from the J$ variable *(b)*.

---

[1] In other versions of BASIC, string-processing functions place a dollar sign ($) in their names. The names LEFT$, RIGHT$, MID$, and INSTR$ may be specified. Check your computer's technical manual for the correct function name.

Using the LEFT, RIGHT, and MID functions it is possible to control access to string-variable data. We can manipulate portions of character strings to allow the output of certain terms, phrases, or letters.

Searching for Characters

When working with character strings, programmers often want to scan the data for certain character groupings or codes. Many versions of BASIC assist these efforts by providing the **INSTR function.** The INSTRing function assumes the following format:

INSTR (position, string, character)

where *position* defines the character position at which the search starts, *string* the string variable to be searched, and *character* the character group being tested for. When specified, the INSTR function may appear as

90   F1 = INSTR (1,B$,'A')

In this instruction, the search starts at character 1 of a string variable called B$, and we are looking for the character A. When the character A is found within B$, the INSTR function assigns to F1 the position of the character where A was found. Note the INSTR function provides not character data but the number of the position of the desired string. If B$ does not contain an A, the number 0 is returned for F1. To further understand use of the INSTR function, examine the program in Figure A.7.

In this program, we search a character string for the letter I and the word TOM. The C$ string which will undergo testing is defined at line 110. The first INSTR function, defined at line 120, instructs that the search for an I commence with the first character of C$. Its position, when found, is recorded in W1.

The second INSTR function, line 130, performs the same search but commences at the (W1 + 1) character. This manipulation ensures that the

FIGURE A.7 The position of character data within strings is defined via the INSTR function (a). This program produces three such outputs (b).

```
(a)          100 REM -- SEARCHING FOR I'S
             110 C$ = 'CUSTOMIZING'
             120 W1 = INSTR(1,C$,'I')
             130 W2 = INSTR(W1+1,C$,'I')
             140 W3 = INSTR(1 ,C$,'TOM')
             150 PRINT 'FIRST I IS AT CHARACTER';W1
             160 PRINT 'SECOND I IS AT CHARACTER';W2
             170 PRINT 'THE WORD TOM BEGINS AT POSITION';W3
             180 END
```

```
(b)          FIRST I IS AT CHARACTER 7
             SECOND I IS AT CHARACTER 9
             THE WORD TOM BEGINS AT POSITION 4
```

second search will commence at the character position immediately following the position at which the first I was found. The (W1 + 1) computation advances the starting point of the second search by 1.

The third INSTR function, line 140, searches C$ for the word TOM. When those three characters are sensed, W3 will record the character position at which T was defined. The output of all three positions is accomplished via lines 150 to 170, each output carrying its own literal.

A.4 Random Numbers

RND Function

There are many programming applications which require data to be generated on a random or unbiased basis. This data should not possess obvious patterns or be geared to a specific answer. BASIC's vehicle for creating random data items is the *RND function,* which is used as a random number generator. The RND function is an instruction which upon command can generate numeric data that has no discernible pattern. It is ideally suited for statistical software or programs simulating gaming situations. Using RND functions, it is possible to create a variety of business conditions and test data to which users must respond.

The RND function may adopt two formats in relation to the system in which it is used. The RND function is written as

$$Y = RND$$

or as

$$Y = RND(X)$$

where the (X) argument may be omitted in some systems.

The net effect of the RND function is to generate a number between 0 and 1 in a decimal format. The resulting number may be altered by multiplication to fit into any number sequence. For example, to produce a random number between 0 and 10, we could use the following instruction:

```
40    Y = 10 * RND
```

This statement computes Y by multiplying the number randomly generated by the RND function by 10. Since that original number lies between 0 and 1, Y must fall between 0 and 10.

The resulting number possesses decimals. On occasion, users may desire to truncate those decimals and utilize only the integer portion of that data. The truncation of decimals is easily accomplished using the **INT function,** whose sole purpose is the suppression of the decimal portion of numbers. This function adopts a format of

$$N = INT(X)$$

where INT is the function name, X the numeric variable to be worked on, and N the truncated result.

PROBLEM A.2   Using Random Data

The problem entails the manipulation of an array with random data. An array consisting of 12 cells is loaded with random data, generated via a RND function. These numbers should fall between 0 to 100 and assume an integer format. In module 2, the contents of the array are sorted in descending order. The ordered array is printed in module 3, two data items per line.

These are the main points in the problem narrative.

1   An array of 12 cells is loaded with data generated by a RND function. The data should assume an integer format ranging from 0 to 100.

2   Module 2 directs the sorting of the array's data in descending order.

3   The contents of the sorted array is outputted, two data items per line, within module 3.

Figure A.8(a) shows the flowchart for Problem A.2. The initial module creates the random numbers to be loaded into the 12-cell array. Module 2 sorts its contents, and module 3 outputs the newly ordered contents of the array.

The flowchart opens with the definition of the 12-cell array, preceding the 12-loop sequence in which the array is filled. The N1 variable computes a random number between 0 and 100. The INT function converts N1 to an integer format with that value loaded into each X(I) cell per loop. The output of N1 and X(I) records the original random number and the integer counterpart loaded into the X array.

Module 2 establishes a nested-loop sequence in which data in the X array is sorted in descending order, high to low. Once the sort is completed, the contents of the array are printed, two cells at a time. A blank line separates these ordered pairs from prior outputs.

The program for Problem A.2 is shown in Figure A.8(b). A DIM statement, line 10, defines the 12-cell X array and precedes the FOR instruction that opens the required 12-loop sequence. The random number N1 is generated via the RND function, line 40. Note that we choose to specify the RND function without an argument. With equal success, we could have written line 40 as

40   N1 = (RND(1) * 100)

The argument (1) has no impact on the instruction, other than to provide a basis for generating a random number.

The decimal portion of N1 is stripped away from its integer value at line

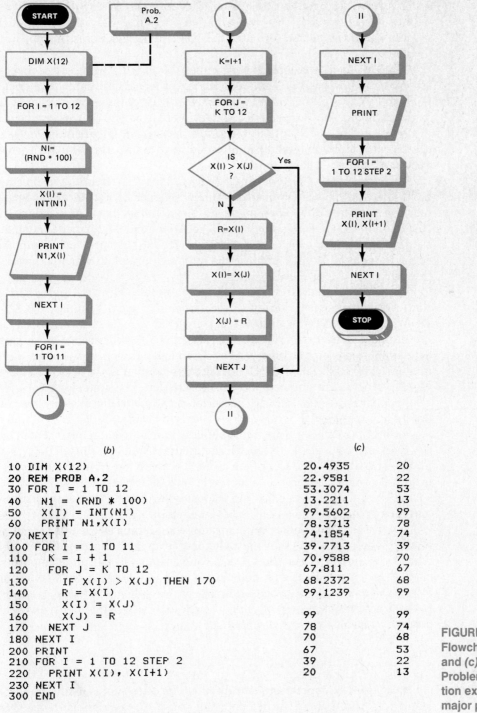

(a)

(b)

```
10 DIM X(12)
20 REM PROB A.2
30 FOR I = 1 TO 12
40    N1 = (RND * 100)
50    X(I) = INT(N1)
60    PRINT N1,X(I)
70 NEXT I
100 FOR I = 1 TO 11
110    K = I + 1
120    FOR J = K TO 12
130      IF X(I) > X(J) THEN 170
140      R = X(I)
150      X(I) = X(J)
160      X(J) = R
170    NEXT J
180 NEXT I
200 PRINT
210 FOR I = 1 TO 12 STEP 2
220    PRINT X(I), X(I+1)
230 NEXT I
300 END
```

(c)

20.4935	20
22.9581	22
53.3074	53
13.2211	13
99.5602	99
78.3713	78
74.1854	74
39.7713	39
70.9588	70
67.811	67
68.2372	68
99.1239	99
99	99
78	74
70	68
67	53
39	22
20	13

FIGURE A.8 (a) Flowchart, (b) program, and (c) output for Problem A.2. The solution exhibits three major processing sequences.

50, using the INT function. It is the integer value that is stored in X(I). The output of N1 and X(I) follows at line 60, recording the original random number and its truncated format. A NEXT I statement closes this opening module.

The sort module is constituted by lines 100 to 180. The nested sequence sorts the 12 values held in the X array, placing them in descending numerical sequence. The output of this newly ordered array is accomplished in module 3. The array's contents are printed two items per line, a FOR/NEXT sequence incorporating a STEP 2 option. The resulting output in Figure A.8(c) reveals the 12 values initially created and loaded into the X array and the sorted values in a paired format.

We must make the following advisory comment regarding use of the RND function. The user must determine whether or not an argument is required for the RND function, as its use will vary between versions of BASIC. Though the RND function will generate random numbers, the same string of random numbers is generated each time that program is run. In effect, the computer will reproduce the same set of random data in a specific program.

If the user wants a fully randomized set of data each time a program is run, a different instructional set is used. Depending on the system, the **RANDOMIZE** or **RANDOM statement** is invoked to request different sets of random data. This instruction directs the computer to commence processing data at different points within the list of random numbers and thus produce random data sets. The RANDOMIZE statement must be specified once within a program, prior to use of the RND function. This statement sequence ensures that a different set of randomized data is introduced each time the program is processed. Figure A.9 illustrates this point.

In this program, we generate 15 random numbers and retain them in an array. Of interest is the RANDOMIZE statement, line 110. The INPUT of N provides the RANDOMIZE statement with a varied key from which to commence the random generation of numeric data. Note that the RANDOMIZE statement is not positioned within the looping sequence, as it is only specified once in a program — ahead of the RND function.

The actual generation of random data occurs at line 130, where a random number is generated on each loop and stored in an array position. This array is output, three cells per line, in a second looping sequence. This output enables us to examine the randomness of each number. Two sets of output from this program are shown. Each starts with a different N value, resulting in two different sets of random data. The RANDOMIZE statement served its purpose, creating two sets of random data.

RND and Games

The RND function is often used to test strategies that have been created for simulating selected operational conditions. These tests may involve military maneuvers, corporate strategies, economic theories, or sporting events. One of the more common uses of the RND function is the generation of data for computer games.

(a)

(b)

```
10 DIM X(15)
100 INPUT 'ENTER A STARTING VALUE';N
110 RANDOMIZE
120 FOR I = 1 TO 15
130   X(I) = RND
140 NEXT I
200 FOR I = 1 TO 15 STEP 3
210    PRINT X(I),X(I+1),X(I+2)
220 NEXT I
300 END
```

Output from First Run:

```
ENTER A STARTING VALUE? 300094
 .462759       .776492       .494118
 .97628        .410621       .677205
 .367645       .111023       .357331
 .144779       .652689       .613128
 .804564       .30923        .614305
```

Output from Second Run:

```
ENTER A STARTING VALUE? 300094
 .832695       .995918       .481254
 .924262       .214284       .967346
 .875518       .546993       .402302
 .490873       .324517       .529246
 .254822       .765717       .300903
```

FIGURE A.9   *(a)* The RANDOMIZE statement causes the RND function to generate data randomly each time a program is run. *(b)* Two sets of outputs illustrate this feature.

SIDE BAR A.1   Your Game Plan

Many people are baffled as to how to design their own computer-related game. Where the program generates its data, where the decisions go, and a host of other questions confront the potential game designer.

The principal rule of any game is to clearly define the rules under which the game is played. Without these rules, it is not possible to establish the logic of a game or design the program to support the game you have in mind.

For example, if you choose to design a computerized tennis match, one of the first actions would be the serve of the ball. You could not enter a volley without having achieved the opening serve. In detailing the serve, all of the possible occurrences would have to be considered to include double faults, let serves, bad first serves, and aces. You would have to define each of these outcomes and assign each a probability and a priority of occurrence. Establishing the rules under which each outcome can occur defines the programming logic.

A good rule of thumb is to start small with one phase of a game and then add something to it. Essentially, design the module for the first serve before continuing to a second-serve module and a third module on volleys. Test ideas and new concepts before adding them to your game. This gradual development permits you to slowly evolve a solution, without having to attack a larger problem that might otherwise prove insurmountable.

For example, it is possible to simulate the flipping of a coin where two possible outcomes, heads or tails, can occur. We could establish an array to hold the simulated results of flipping the coin, analyze those results, and output them for the user. A program along these lines is presented in Figure A.10. In this initial program module, heads and tails values are randomly

FIGURE A.10 The
RND function can be
used to simulate the
tossing of a coin. (a)
This program produces
25 flips of a coin. (b)
The results of the 25
coin flips.

(a)

```
10 DIM T$(25)
20 REM -- FLIP A COIN
30 INPUT 'TYPE A STARTING VALUE';N
40 RANDOMIZE
50 FOR I = 1 TO 25
60    X = RND
70    IF X < .5 THEN T$(I)= 'H'
80    IF X >= .5 THEN T$(I)= 'T'
90 NEXT I
200 REM -- ANALYZE DATA
210 T1 = 0
220 T2 = 0
230 FOR I = 1 TO 25
240    IF T$(I) = 'H' THEN T1 = T1 + 1
250    IF T$(I) = 'T' THEN T2 = T2 + 1
260 NEXT I
300 PRINT 'NO OF HEADS =';T1
310 PRINT 'NO OF TAILS =';T2
320 END
```

(b)

```
TYPE A STARTING VALUE? 567
NO OF HEADS = 12
NO OF TAILS = 13
```

generated and stored in their array, lines 10 to 90. The analysis of the heads and tails values occurs in module 2, lines 200 to 260. The output of each total occurs in module 3, starting at line 300.

The question often asked is how each coin is "flipped." In this case, the flipping term does not reflect the actual tossing of a coin. Instead, it represents the random generation of a number which is converted to the equivalent of a tossed coin. The RND function is needed to ensure that no predictable pattern (or bias) is incorporated into the data when generated. Using the RND function, we do not have to actually flip a coin and record those results. Imagine how much work is involved in experiments where literally millions of occurrences are involved!

The program opens with the establishment of the T$(25) array, which will hold each head (H) and tail (T) value. Lines 30 and 40 invoke the RANDOMIZE function, affording us unbiased data. A 25-loop FOR/NEXT sequence is initiated at line 50 which generates the heads and tails values involved in processing.

This sequence requires some explanation, as the RND function does not directly produce H and T values. The RND function generates a decimal number between 0 and 1, line 60. The X variable represents this value and is tested to determine whether a heads or tails value was generated.

As an equal probability exists for either heads or tails, we chose 0.5 as our break-off point. If the randomly generated X value was less than 0.5, we concluded it was a head. If X is greater than or equal to 0.5, we determined that a tail resulted. Lines 70 and 80 represent these conditional statements, the definition of either value, and its storage in the T$ array. Exactly 25 values are randomly generated and converted in this fashion and made ready for analysis.

The next phase of processing, line 200, determines how many heads and tails were stored. Two accumulators are initialized, as they are needed to total the heads (T1) and tails (T2) values. A 25-loop FOR/NEXT serves to frame the processing sequence.

The individual testing occurs at lines 240 and 250, where each T$(I) value is separately compared against H and T. The appropriate accumulators are updated, as each is set within its own statement. After 25 loops, each cell has been tested and the output of T1 and T2 may occur. The output of either accumulator is preceded by its own special label, lines 300 and 310.

These outputs illustrate the successful generation of heads and tails values. Summing up the T1 and T2 values printed, we have a total of 25 which indicates each was properly defined. It should be evident that with minor modifications 100 or 1000 H and T values could be quickly generated.

The RND function can also be used on an interactive basis. That is, the user guesses at what data the RND function will generate — for example, by trying to predict the number of heads and tails that will result and comparing them to the actual output. This feature adds an element of chance and is frequently used to involve the user directly in processing. Let us examine an illustrative program which builds on this idea.

PROBLEM A.3   Rolling Dice

In this problem, the user is asked to predict the outcome of tossing dice, which can range from 2 to 12. A RND function is used to generate the value of the first die and then the second. Each die's number is added to the other to produce the dice's total. Assign this generation routine to a GOSUB module. Establish a looping sequence responsive to user-interactive inputs.

These are the main points in the problem narrative.

1   The problem requires the user to interact with the program and predict the total of the dice. This input should occur within a loop ended at the user's request.

2   Each die's amount is computed separately, within one module. Each die total is added to produce the sum of both dice. This total is compared to the user's guess. The range of dice values is 2 to 12.

3   The hierarchy of instructions should be:
   a   Note the user's prediction
   b   Generate value of die 1 via RND function
   c   Generate value of die 2 via RND function
   d   Add values and compare results
   e   Request to continue or exit loop

The program and output for Problem A.3 are shown in Figure A.11. An opening REM statement identifies Problem A.3 before defining a RANDOMIZE statement at line 30.

An INPUT statement at line 40 prompts users to enter their guess on the roll of the dice. Remember, the D value entered must be an integer value between 2 and 12. The program proceeds to GOSUB 600 to create the first die's value (line 50), assigning it to D1 (line 60). A second visit to the 600 module creates the second die's value (line 80) and defines D2. Both D1 and D2 are added at line 90 to create T, the equivalent of a rolling of the dice.

The outputs generated via lines 100 and 110 print the four variables D1, D2, T, and D, using appropriate literals. The testing of T against D is accomplished using the IF/THEN/ELSE statement, line 120. As this statement was extremely long, we chose to continue the ELSE portion of the statement on the next line. As this was the continuation of an existing statement, *not a new one,* a line number was not needed. The branches of line 120 print either a congratulatory or losing literal, dependent upon whether T was equal to D.

A blank line of output, line 130, precedes the request to continue or exit

FIGURE A.11   *(a)* Program for Problem A.3. *(b)* The program's outputs reveal the simulated rolling of dice and the user's attempt to predict their outcome.

(a)

```
10 REM PROB A.3
20 INPUT 'ENTER RANDOM VALUE';N
30 RANDOMIZE
40 INPUT 'ENTER GUESS OF DICE';D
50 GOSUB 600
60 D1 = V
70 GOSUB 600
80 D2 = V
90 T = D1 + D2
100 PRINT 'DIE 1 =';D1,'DIE 2 =';D2
110 PRINT 'DICE =';T,'YOUR GUESS =';D
120 IF T=D THEN PRINT 'CORRECT, YOU WIN!'
          ELSE PRINT 'SORRY, YOU LOSE!'
130 PRINT
140 INPUT 'WISH TO STOP - Y OR N';R$
150 IF R$ = 'Y' THEN 800 ELSE 40
600 REM -- COMPUTE DIE VALUE
610 X = RND
620    IF X < .167 THEN V=1
630    IF X >= .167 AND X < .334 THEN V=2
640    IF X >= .334 AND X < .501 THEN V=3
650    IF X >= .501 AND X < .667 THEN V=4
660    IF X >= .667 AND X < .835 THEN V=5
670    IF X >= .835  THEN V=6
680 RETURN
800 PRINT 'GAME OVER'
810 END
```

(b)

```
ENTER RANDOM VALUE? 6
ENTER GUESS OF DICE? 7
DIE 1 = 3      DIE 2 = 1
DICE = 4       YOUR GUESS = 7
SORRY, YOU LOSE!

WISH TO STOP - Y OR N? N
ENTER GUESS OF DICE? 11
DIE 1 = 2      DIE 2 = 5
DICE = 7       YOUR GUESS = 11
SORRY, YOU LOSE!

WISH TO STOP - Y OR N? N
ENTER GUESS OF DICE? 5
DIE 1 = 5      DIE 2 = 6
DICE = 11      YOUR GUESS = 5
SORRY, YOU LOSE!

WISH TO STOP - Y OR N? N
ENTER GUESS OF DICE? 6
DIE 1 = 6      DIE 2 = 5
DICE = 11      YOUR GUESS = 6
SORRY, YOU LOSE!

WISH TO STOP - Y OR N? N
ENTER GUESS OF DICE? 7
DIE 1 = 3      DIE 2 = 5
DICE = 8       YOUR GUESS = 7
SORRY, YOU LOSE!

WISH TO STOP - Y OR N? Y
GAME OVER
```

processing. The prompting literal, line 140, requests the entry of a Y or N to indicate your choice. An entry of Y leads out of the loop and ends the program with a closing GAME OVER literal. A user's desire to continue causes the program to branch to line 40, restarting the loop's activities.

The GOSUB 600 module consists of a RND function and six IF/THEN statements, where the value of each die is created. The RND function, line 610, randomly creates the number which is tested at lines 620 to 670. The net effect is to simulate the rolling of a die, without actually having dice at hand. The program branches to GOSUB 600 twice to create the D1 and D2 values independently, each value representing die 1 and 2, respectively.

Some users question whether the instructions composing the GOSUB 600 module represent the only way of computing the value of a die. The program excerpt below offers another method of computing a V value.

```
600    REM--COMPUTE DIE VALUE REVISED
610    X = RND * 100
620    Y = X/16.66
630    V = INT(Y) + 1
640    RETURN
```

In this revised module, we arrive at a die's value differently. The multiplication of the RND function by 100 creates a decimal number between 0 and 100. At line 620, that X value is divided by 16.66 to potentially create a Y value that is greater than 0 and less than 6. The die's value is finalized at line 630, where the integer portion of Y is taken and increased by 1. This ensures that an integer value of 1 to 6 is assigned.

The reader may observe the results of Problem A.3 in Figure A.11(b). The results show five attempts at guessing the value of the dice. Users might try running the same program on their own computers to test their skills.

A.5 Planning a Menu

Many software programmers prefer to provide users with a list of the processing each program can perform. This list of activities usually appears at the start of each program and is called a **menu**. The menu serves to prompt the user by describing the processing activities handled by this program by name and number. The user then specifies the desired option, and processing commences.

The use of a menu is prevalent in programs where more than one processing option exists and users must select one. As the processing of each option is completed, the menu reappears, giving the user a choice of continuing processing via a second option or closing the program's activities. Normally, interactive INPUT statements permit users to enter their choices on an online basis.

To illustrate the use of a menu, let us examine a program which offers the users four processing options.

1   Compute weekly batting averages.

2   Compute seasonal batting averages.

3   Compute slugging percentages.

4   Perform all three options.

A fifth option to close processing is also available and considered to be the last option available in most menus. It effectively provides the user with a means of closing the program.

A menu is easily integrated with structured concepts, as each option's processing is assigned to a module. The menu parallels the hierarchical structure of a program solution.

Each processing module defines an option available to the user. All options are listed at the program's start and after each module's processing is complete. An ON GOSUB instruction is often used to control access to the modules selected by the user. Figure A.12 illustrates a hierarchical relationship between the menu and the modules it supports.

The program prepared from this menu is detailed in Figure A.13. An opening REM statement identifies the program and precedes access of the GOSUB 100 menu module, line 20. The menu lists five options available to

FIGURE A.12   The relationship between each module's activities and the overall program is depicted within a hierarchical chart.

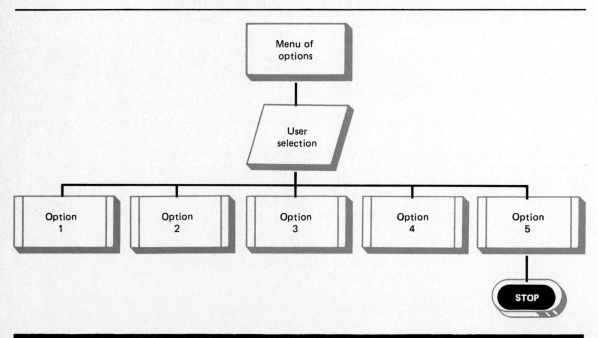

```
10 REM -- USING A MENU
20 GOSUB 100
30 INPUT 'SELECT OPTION';N
40 IF N = 5 THEN 2000
50 ON N GOSUB 200,400,600,800
60 IF N < 1 OR N > 5 THEN GOSUB 1200
70 GO TO 20
100 REM -- MENU MODULE
110    PRINT 'BASEBALL DATA -- PROGRAM OPTIONS :'
120    PRINT '   1. COMPUTE WEEKLY BATTING AVG'
130    PRINT '   2. COMPUTE SEASONAL BATTING AVG'
140    PRINT '   3. COMPUTE SLUGGING PERCENTAGE'
150    PRINT '   4. COMPUTE ALL 3 (ABOVE)'
160    PRINT '   5. CLOSE PROGRAM'
170 RETURN
200 REM -- WEEKLY AVG MODULE
210    INPUT 'PLAYER NAME, HITS, AT BATS';N$,H,B
220    W = H/B
230    PRINT N$,'HAD';H;' HITS IN';B;' AT BATS FOR AN A WEEKLY AVG OF';W
240    PRINT
250    INPUT 'CONTINUE TO NEXT BATTER - Y OR N';R$
260    IF R$ = 'Y' THEN 210
270 RETURN
400 REM -- SEASONAL AVG MODULE
410    INPUT 'PLAYER NAME, SEASON HITS & AT BATS';N$,A1,A2
420    A = A1/A2
430    PRINT N$,'HAS A SEASON AVG OF';A
440    PRINT
450    INPUT 'CONTINUE TO NEXT BATTER - Y OR N';R$
460    IF R$ = 'Y' THEN 410
470 RETURN
600 REM -- SLUGGING PCT MODULE
610    INPUT 'PLAYER NAME & TOTAL AT BATS';N$,A2
620    INPUT 'NO OF SINGLES, DOUBLES, TRIPLES, HOMERS';H1,H2,H3,H4
630    S = (1 * H1) + (2 * H2) + (3 * H3) + (4 * H4)
640    P = S/A2
650    PRINT N$,'HAS A SLUGGING PCT OF';P
660    PRINT
670    INPUT 'CONTINUE TO NEXT BATTER - Y OR N';R$
680    IF R$ = 'Y' THEN 610
690 RETURN
800 REM -- ALL 3 MODULE
810    INPUT 'PLAYER NAME, WK HITS & AT BATS';N$,H,B
820    INPUT 'SEASON HITS & AT BATS';A1,A2
830    INPUT 'SINGLES, DOUBLES, TRIPLES, HOMERS';H1,H2,H3,H4
840    W = H/B
850    A = A1/A2
860    S = (1 * H1) + (2 * H2) + (3 * H3) + (4 * H4)
870    P = S/A2
880    PRINT 'PLAYER ';N$,'SLUG PCT =';P
890    PRINT 'WK AVG =';W,'SEASON AVG =';A
900    PRINT
910    INPUT 'CONTINUE TO NEXT BATTER - Y OR N';R$
920    IF R$ = 'Y' THEN 810
930 RETURN
1200 REM -- ERROR MODULE
1210    PRINT 'YOU KEYED IN THE WRONG CODE'
1220    PRINT 'TRY AGAIN, USE MENU'
1230 RETURN
2000 PRINT 'PROG OVER'
2010 END
```

FIGURE A.13 The GOSUB 100 module within this program defines the menu of processing activities offered to the user.

the user. The input of the user's choice is accomplished via line 30 and tested in the ON GOSUB statement, line 50. Only the codes of N equal 1 to 4 are used with that instruction, branching to the appropriate module.

The code of N = 5 is specifically handled at line 40, an IF/THEN statement which branches to line 2000. A closing module was not used, as we chose to terminate the program at its logical end and not within a GOSUB module. The placement of an END statement in a GOSUB, prior to a RETURN statement, can result in an error and invalidate processing.

The conditional statement at line 60 serves to catch errors related to the user's input of the option variable N. An N value outside the range 1 to 5 can trigger an error message from within the GOSUB 1200 module. This simplified error routine helps alert the user to problems. The menu will reappear

FIGURE A.14 The output from the menu program notes the execution of options 2 and 3, with the menu displayed prior to the user's selection of the option chosen.

```
BASEBALL DATA -- PROGRAM OPTIONS :
    1. COMPUTE WEEKLY BATTING AVG
    2. COMPUTE SEASONAL BATTING AVG
    3. COMPUTE SLUGGING PERCENTAGE
    4. COMPUTE ALL 3 (ABOVE)
    5. CLOSE PROGRAM
SELECT OPTION? 2
PLAYER NAME, SEASON HITS & AT BATS? MUSIAL,120,304
MUSIAL          HAS A SEASON AVG OF .394737

CONTINUE TO NEXT BATTER - Y OR N? Y
PLAYER NAME, SEASON HITS & AT BATS? THRONEBERRY,60,270
THRONEBERRY    HAS A SEASON AVG OF .222222

CONTINUE TO NEXT BATTER - Y OR N? N
BASEBALL DATA -- PROGRAM OPTIONS :
    1. COMPUTE WEEKLY BATTING AVG
    2. COMPUTE SEASONAL BATTING AVG
    3. COMPUTE SLUGGING PERCENTAGE
    4. COMPUTE ALL 3 (ABOVE)
    5. CLOSE PROGRAM
SELECT OPTION? 3
PLAYER NAME & TOTAL AT BATS? MAYS,280
NO OF SINGLES, DOUBLES, TRIPLES, HOMERS? 57,13,8,19
MAYS            HAS A SLUGGING PCT OF .653571

CONTINUE TO NEXT BATTER - Y OR N? Y
PLAYER NAME & TOTAL AT BATS? JACKSON,256
NO OF SINGLES, DOUBLES, TRIPLES, HOMERS? 45,8,2,14
JACKSON         HAS A SLUGGING PCT OF .480469

CONTINUE TO NEXT BATTER - Y OR N? N
BASEBALL DATA -- PROGRAM OPTIONS :
    1. COMPUTE WEEKLY BATTING AVG
    2. COMPUTE SEASONAL BATTING AVG
    3. COMPUTE SLUGGING PERCENTAGE
    4. COMPUTE ALL 3 (ABOVE)
    5. CLOSE PROGRAM
SELECT OPTION? 5
PROG OVER
```

after the output of the two error messages, giving the user a chance to rekey the chosen option.

Each of the modules used in processing follows the main program, lines 10 to 70. Modules commence at lines 200, 400, 800, and 1200, in relation to the options chosen. Instructions are unique to each module, handling the processing as directed.

The output resulting from this program is shown in Figure A.14. The menu appears at the program's start and each time a module completes its course the user chooses another option. We have chosen to execute options 2 and 3. Our output reveals the processing of two persons in each module, illustrating the function of each.

The critical point to select from this program is its use of a menu. When a program has multiple options within it, a menu serves a valuable informative purpose. The menu should be written into its own module, thus providing ready access to its statements from anywhere in the program.

APPENDIX B

A Comparison of BASIC Statements

Statement	DEC — BASIC Plus	IBM PC — DOS System	Apple II BASIC
Remark	*(a)* REM (followed by note)	*(a)* REM (followed by note)	REM (followed by note)
	(b) Exclamation point (!) and note	*(b)* Single quotation mark(') and note	
LET	Optional use in statement	Optional use	Optional use
GO TO	Unconditional branch	Unconditional branch	Unconditional branch
	GO TO (followed by line number)	GO TO (followed by line number)	GO TO (followed by line number)
READ	READ $v_1, v_2, v_3, \ldots, v_n$ list of variables	READ $v_1, v_2, v_3, \ldots, v_n$ list of variables	READ $v_1, v_2, v_3, \ldots, v_n$ list of variables

Statement	DEC — BASIC Plus	IBM PC — DOS System	Apple II BASIC
DATA	DATA $d_1, d_2, \ldots d_n$ list of data items	DATA $d_1, d_2, \ldots d_n$ list of data items	DATA $d_1, d_2, \ldots d_n$ list of data items
VARIABLES	*Numeric:* 1 or 2 characters long; alphabetic character alone or followed by a digit (0 to 9) *String:* same as numeric with $ added to end of name. In EXTEND mode (optional), alphabetic character followed by 29 letters or digits	*Numeric:* variable length, must start with alphabetic character; can add a % for integer data; a ! for single precision; a # for double precision *String:* same as numeric, must end with a $	*Numeric:* variable length to 236 characters, names ending in % are integer *String:* same as numeric, add $
INPUT	*(a)* INPUT $v_1, v_2, \ldots, v_n$ list of variables *(b)* With prompting literal INPUT '_____'; $v_1, \ldots, v_n$ literal When executed a ? appears on screen or is printed on paper	*(a)* INPUT $v_1, v_2, \ldots, v_n$ list of variables Outputs a ? when executed	*(a)* INPUT $v_1, v_2, \ldots, v_n$ list of variables Outputs a ? when executed
PRINT ZONES	5 zones of 14 characters	5 zones of 14 characters	3 zones of 13 characters
PRINT	PRINT $v_1, v_2, \ldots, v_n$ list of variables separated by commas and semicolons	PRINT $v_1, v_2, \ldots, v_n$ list of variables; use of commas and semicolons	PRINT $v_1, v_2, \ldots, v_n$ list of variables commas and semicolons permitted
Printer Capacity	80 characters per line; modified to handle 132 characters	80 characters; with modification up to 132 characters wide	40 characters per line for DOS 3.3; with CPM — 80 characters per line
Screen Size	80 characters/line; upper- and lowercase	80 characters/line; upper- and lowercase	40 characters/line; uppercase only
IF/THEN	IF (condition) THEN line number *or* executable statement	IF (condition) THEN line number *or* executable statement	IF (condition) THEN line number *or* executable statement
IF/THEN/ELSE	IF (condition) THEN line number *or* statement ELSE line number *or* statement	IF (condition) THEN line number *or* statement ELSE line number *or* statement	IF (condition) THEN line number *or* statement ELSE line number *or* statement
ON GO TO	On v_1 go to $line_1, line_2, \ldots, line_n; v_1 = a$ variable of representing integer data	On v_1 go to $line_1, line_2, \ldots, line_n; v_1 = a$ variable of representing integer data	On v_1 go to $line_1, line_2, \ldots, line_n; v_1 = a$ variable of representing integer data
ON GO SUB	On v_1 GOSUB $line_1, line_2, \ldots, line_n$; $v_1 = $ variable of integer data	On v_1 GOSUB $line_1, line_2, \ldots, line_n$; $v_1 = $ variable of integer data	On v_1 GOSUB $line_1, line_2, \ldots, line_n$; $v_1 = $ variable of integer data
LPRINT	Not available	Directs output to printer attached to PC	Directs output to printer attached to PC
TAB function	Used in PRINT statement; TAB (X); $v_1, \ldots,$ where X is print position to start printing the variable (v_1) or literal following it	PRINT TAB (X); $v_1 \ldots,$ where X is position to commence printing of variable (v_1) or literal	PRINT TAB (X); $v_1 \ldots,$ where X is position to commence printing of variable (v_1) or literal
RND function	RND or RND(X), generates a decimal value between 0 and 1	RND or RND(X) generates a random number between 0 and 1	RND or RND(X), generates a random number between 0 and 1
RANDOMIZE	Randomize or random	Randomize	Not available

Statement	DEC — BASIC Plus	IBM PC — DOS System	Apple II BASIC
LIST	(a) LIST — all of program (b) LIST 100 — lists line 100 only (c) LIST 40–80 — lists lines 40 to 80	Same as DEC; may be replaced by a function key on keyboard	Same as DEC
CLIST	Not available	CLIST lists program on printer; may be replaced by function key	CLIST command available in CPM software only; prints program on printer accompanying system
LOAD	Not available	LOAD "PROGNAME" loads program onto disk; function key available	(a) LOAD PROG 10 in DOS (b) LOAD "PROG 10" in CPM loads program onto disk
SAVE	SAVE "PROG NAME" — retains program on file	SAVE "PROG NAME" — retains program on file; function key available	(a) Save PROG NAME in DOS (b) Save "PROG NAME" on CPM

C.1 File Concepts

In prior discussions, we employed READ and DATA statements and INPUT statements to define the data used in processing. These statements were employed to emphasize the relationship between variable names and the data undergoing processing.

These are not the only means of representing data or making data available for processing. BASIC affords the user the capability to retain data in files maintained within the computer. Numeric and character data may be retained in these files and accessed by programs in processing. As disk storage is most often mentioned in relation to BASIC, we will focus our discussions on use of that storage medium. Prior to those discussions, we must explain the conceptual difference between sequential and random-access files.

Sequential and Random Files

The difference between sequential and random-access files relates to the way each handles its data. In a sequential file, records are positioned immediately one after the other, forming an ordered sequence. Existing records are retained in this order, with new records added at the end of the file. To access a specific record, the computer must read through all the records ahead of it.

By contrast, random-access files offer greater flexibility. Each record in a random-access file is independently accessible because of how it is stored on the disk. Instead of being stored immediately behind the preceding one, each record is retained within a predefined storage area called a sector. Each sector provides the capacity to retain one record, which is directly accessed when its unique identification number is specified. The user's specification of that sector number will direct the computer to it and make the data stored in that sector available. Figure C.1 illustrates storage using both formats.

In this illustration, we have chosen to compose each record of exactly three fields. The name, city, and ZIP code fields for each person's record consists of 25, 15 and 5 characters each. Examining Figure C.1, we may observe how the file types differ.

FIGURE C.1 The storage formats employed with sequential and random-access files differ in their retention of data. Records in a sequential file (a) are compactly written, when compared to randomly stored records (b) which must start at specific sectors.

(a)

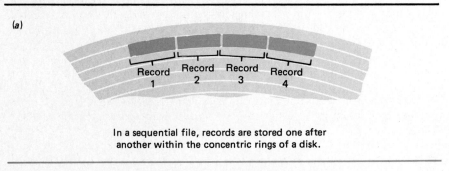

In a sequential file, records are stored one after another within the concentric rings of a disk.

(b)

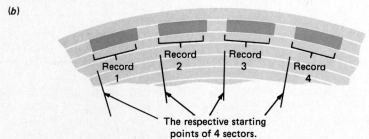

The respective starting points of 4 sectors.

in a random file, disk storage areas are divided into sectors—with each record stored in its sector, commencing at its starting point.

In Figure C.1(a), we observe a sequential file configuration where records are positioned one after the other. The semicircular format shown represents the edge of the disk on which each record is placed. Records are stored in concentric rings called tracks, each track containing as many records as their sizes allow. We show four of the records, commencing with record 1, that might appear on one track. Note that sector boundaries are not critical to the storage of data in a sequential file.

This is not the case with a random-access file. Each record must commence its storage at the start of a sector, thus permitting its independent retrieval. Each sector is identified by a number assigned to the record it retains. Each sector's start establishes the point at which that record begins.

In Figure C.1(b), 4 of the sectors on a specific track are noted, each with one record stored within it. This one-to-one relationship enables the computer to access a sector and retrieve one record. The space between a record's end and the start of the next sector is deliberately left blank.

The differences between both file types are reflected in the way each is programmed. With sequential files, the programmer directs that each record be written with the computer overseeing its storage. With random-access files, the programmer must monitor what sector is employed to retain the record. Without this knowledge, the programmer would not be able to specify the record's identifying number and access the sector at which that data is stored.

Creating and Updating Files

Two principal activities related to the use of computer files are creation and update. A file must be initially created, thus defining its structure and file type. After that, the programmer must have a means of modifying the contents of that file — updating the records stored within it. The update should accommodate the addition of new records and the modification of fields within existing records. The creation and update of files relates to both sequential and random-access files.

With sequential files, an initial number of records composes the original file. In subsequent updates, other records are added to that file's end to extend its size or to modify the contents of existing records.

Random-access files are similarly created, but update operations are often more complex. Individual records may be randomly accessed and modified, as well as added to or deleted from the file. These updates will severely affect the order of the existing file. Records must accordingly be shifted with each insertion or deletion. In random-access files, new records may be added at the file's end as well as between existing records. Naturally, the complexity of the update performed will dictate a program's size.

Compounding this problem are the differences among computer systems — especially among microcomputer (home) systems. Microcomputers, even the several models of any one manufacturer, vary in the software they use to handle files. Minor differences in hardware affect the design of file software, thus altering the syntax and statements used for a given program.

This advisory note is made to caution users and preface the discussions that follow. We will introduce sample programs, relating to different manufacturers, to create and update files. These programs are meant as representative models of file software and may have to be modified slightly, due to differences in your hardware, to have them work on your computer system. As we have no way of knowing what type of hardware you will use, we must leave the fine tuning of supporting software to you. We will, of course, explain the statements used in our file software.

Our next section deals with the creation, update and manipulation of computerized files in relation to different computer manufacturers. We will employ both sequential and random-access files in our handling of relatively simple file-processing tasks. These tasks will provide a basis for comparing manufacturers' hardware, as similar programs are written for each device.

Our attempt here is to familiarize the reader with these computer systems and introduce the user to file handling. Minor modifications in the programs described may have to be made to accommodate the uniqueness of each system, but the programs provide sufficient detail to permit comprehension and can act as stepping stones to future work. Remember, that once data is removed from a file, it is usable as any other data might be. The format of a file provides an efficient and ready means of storing data.

To standardize our discussions of files, we will utilize a record format consisting of the three fields listed below, namely:

1   A NAME field of 25 characters

2   A CITY field of 15 characters

3   A ZIP CODE field of 5 characters

All software is written to accommodate this record format. The handling of records composed of these three fields will illustrate how similar records of different lengths may be handled. Readers may utilize these programs or prototypes when writing their own file-handling software.

C.2 Working with an APPLE

The APPLE system is a microcomputer which provides for the storage of files on diskette, in either a sequential or random format. Sample programs will illustrate the handling of both file types. Our discussion will explain the specific statements used with each file type, commencing with a review of sequential files.

Sequential Files

In Figure C.2, programs relating to the creation of a sequential file and the access of records from an existing sequential file are detailed. In Figure C.2(a) we create a sequential file of records consisting of the three specified fields. In Figure C.2(b), records sequentially read from that file are output. Each program has statements requiring clarification.

The create program (a) opens with a REM statement denoting the program's purpose. Line 100 defines the Control-D character essential to outputting data records on diskette. This Control-D character, assigned the variable name D$ to simplify its use, must be used in diskette I/O operations. The definition of D$ at line 100 establishes this control code and makes it available for use throughout this program.

The Control-D character is immediately employed at line 110, where our sequential file is opened. The OPEN instruction is utilized to create a file and define its name. We have chosen to name our file, FILEA, defining that name in a pair of quotes.

	(a)		(b)
10	REM -- APPLE FILE CREATE ON DISK	10	REM -- READ DISKETTE & PRINT
100	D$ = CHR$ (4)	100	ONERR GO TO 600
110	PRINT D$: "OPEN FILEA"	110	D$ = CHR$ (4)
120	INPUT "NAME, CITY & ZIP"; N$,C$,Z	120	PRINT D$; "OPEN FILEA"
130	IF Z = − 99999 THEN 600	130	PRINT D$; "READ FILEA"
140	PRINT D$; "WRITE FILEA"	140	INPUT N$,C$,Z
150	PRINT N$	150	PRINT N$,C$,Z
160	PRINT C$	160	GO TO 130
170	PRINT Z	600	PRINT D$; "CLOSE FILEA"
180	PRINT D$	610	END
190	GO TO 120		
600	PRINT D$; "CLOSE FILEA"		
610	END		

FIGURE C.2   Two programs relating to the creation (a) and use (b) of sequential files on an Apple system.

The three data fields slated for storage on file are input at line 120. A 9s decision against the Z variable is used to terminate the looping sequence in which the file is created, prior to the close of the file and the program. The datanames used denote the data items composing the three fields.

The declaration to write the record (composed of the three fields) occurs at line 140. The Control-D character precedes the WRITE instruction, bracketed by quotes, in which the FILEA name is specified. The three PRINT statements, lines 150 to 170, are required to accomplish the writing of the three fields on diskette as a complete record. These statements must appear separately. The three variables may not be grouped into one PRINT statement. The Control-D statement, line 180, serves to transfer I/O control from the disk device to the keyboard of the CRT being used to input data, in preparation for the user's entry of the next record's fields at line 120.

The unconditional branch, line 120, closes the loop and directs the program back to the opening INPUT statement. The entry of − 99999 for Z, causes the program to branch to line 600 where FILEA is closed. The CLOSE statement parallels prior file statements, requiring the use of the D$ control variable and quotes. The file name must follow the CLOSE command, ensuring the proper closing of the correct file. An END statement is required to complete this create program.

The user can utilize the create program to enter an unspecified number of records, depending on operational needs. The (b) program of Figure C.2 draws upon the existing FILEA and outputs data held in its records.

The format of this second program reflects its purpose to read records from a sequential file and print this data in a hardcopy format. Many statements similar to those of our first program are specified in this solution. A REM statement identifies this program's opening instruction and precedes an ONERROR statement. This statement is positioned anywhere in a program and triggered by an error in the program, especially in the reading of file data. When the end of our diskette file is sensed, the ONERROR statement is activated causing the program to branch to line 600, where FILEA is closed.

The remainder of the program is fairly simple. The Control-D character required for file I/O operations is defined at line 110. At line 120, FILEA is opened for use and prepared for the reading of its records by line 130. This statement readies the file for the sequential access of data by the INPUT statement of line 140. By contrast to output operations, the three data fields are accessed together in one statement. The N$, C$ and Z variables are printed before the looping sequence is regenerated by line 160.

The net result of program *(b)* is the output of FILEA's contents. Each record is sequentially output, paralleling the file's structure. Every record's contents is printed until the file's end is reached. A program designed to add new data records at the end of FILEA is detailed in Figure C.3.

```
10      REM -- ADD TO EXISTING FILE
20      D$ = CHR$ (4)
30      PRINT D$; "APPEND FILEA"
40      REM -- ENTER NEW DATA
50      INPUT "NAME, CITY & ZIP"; N$,C$,Z
60      PRINT D$; "WRITE FILEA"
70      PRINT N$
80      PRINT C$
90      PRINT Z
100     PRINT D$
110     INPUT "ADD ANOTHER RECORD - Y OR N"; R$
120     IF R$ = "Y" THEN 50 ELSE 900
900     PRINT D$; "CLOSE FILEA"
910     END
```

FIGURE C.3   New records are appended to an existing file using this Apple program.

In a sequential file, new data records are added to the end of the existing file. Instead of merely opening the file, an APPEND statement is specified. The APPEND statement serves to open the file, as well as ready it for the addition of new data records. Line 30 of our third program illustrates this statement's format.

The remainder of the program parallels our two prior solutions. Line 50 directs that the three new data items be input, with line 60 readying FILEA for output. Lines 70 to 90 respectively write N$, C$ and Z on diskette, individual statements being required. Line 100 shifts I/O control from diskette to CRT keyboard, in preparation for the input of data at line 50.

The request to continue processing occupies lines 100 and 110. The desire to enter a new record directs the program to line 50, where a branch to line 900 causes the file to be closed. Essentially, the user is free to add as many records as necessary and close processing when those records are exhausted.

Random Files

An entirely different set of programs is employed when working with random-access files. This difference in software results from the way data is stored in a random file. Each record is individually handled and stored so that it can be retrieved separately. Two programs relating to the creation and use of random files appear in Figure C.4.

A program creating a random file is described in Figure C.4*(a)*. Its structure is

	(a)		(b)

```
10      REM -- APPLE CREATE OF RANDOM FILE        10      REM -- READ & PRINT A RECORD
20      D$ = CHR$ (4)                             20      DE = CHR$ (4)
30      PRINT D$; "OPEN FILEB, L48"               30      PRINT D$; "OPEN FILEB, L48"
110     REM -- WRITE EACH RECORD                  40      PRINT "NAME", "CITY", "ZIP"
120     INPUT "STUDENT NAME IS :"; N$             100     REM -- READ A RECORD
130     INPUT "ENTER CITY       :"; C$            110     INPUT "ENTER NUMBER OF DESIRED RECORD"; R1
140     INPUT "ZIP CODE IS       :"; Z            120     PRINT D$; "READ FILEB,R"; R1
150     INPUT "RECORD NUMBER TO USE"; R1          130     INPUT N$,C$,Z
155     IF R1 = -999 THEN 500                     140     PRINT D$
160     PRINT D$; "WRITE FILEB,R"; R1             150     PRINT N$,C$,Z
170     PRINT N$                                  160     INPUT "ANOTHER RECORD - Y OR N"; R$
180     PRINT C$                                  170     IF R$ = "Y" THEN 110 ELSE 900
190     PRINT Z                                   900     PRINT D$; "CLOSE FILEB"
200     PRINT D$                                  910     END
210     GO TO 120
500     PRINT D$; "CLOSE FILEB"
510     END
```

FIGURE C.4   Two programs for the creation (a) and reporting (b) of data in random files in an Apple system are shown.

similar to its sequential counterpart, but contains instructions uniquely suited to random files. It opens with a REM statement and the declaration of the Control-D character before using a new form of the OPEN instruction.

At line 30, a random-access file named FILEB is defined via an OPEN file instruction. The L48 component denotes the length of the record to be used; with L the code for Length and 48 the number of characters. The 48 total is derived from the sum of the length of the three fields composing the record $(25 + 15 + 5)$ and the three one-digit control characters which must be positioned after each of those fields $(45 + 3 = 48)$. The control characters are required and must be added to the other field sizes. As shown in line 30, quotes are used to frame the file-open entries.

With FILEB defined and open for use, the program's next phase deals with building the file. Lines 120 to 140 request the name, city and ZIP code data which will be written onto the disk record. Line 150 requests the number of the record in which these data will be stored. Generally, when building a file, you begin a record with number 1 and increment upward by 1. This requires that the user build an index of what data items are associated with what records, in order to retrieve desired data.

This last point tends to confuse some readers. Random files are originally written one record at a time, sequentially using record numbers. Once created, any record within the file is randomly retrievable by its record number. By keeping an index of records, the user does not have to search the file, but can specify a particular record number and retrieve that data. Line 150 accomplishes the input of the desired record identification number. A 9s decision follows that INPUT statement and permits the user to branch from the loop by entering a value of $R1 = -999$.

At line 160, the instruction to write the record at the R1 location is issued. The WRITE FILEB statement positions the diskette for output and prepares the system for the transfer of data to the diskette. The PRINT statement, lines 170 to 190, cause the data to be written on disk. The R component of the WRITE statement reminds us and the computer of the Random nature of the file.

The control D$ statement, line 200, shifts I/O control back to the keyboard in anticipation of the entry of the next record's data. The GOTO at line 210 directs the loop back to the INPUT statements which permit the entry of such data. The loop continues until the user desires to close it by keying an R1 value of −999. The branch to line 500, from line 155, precedes the closing of FILEB and the program.

A small program illustrating the use of an existing random file is shown in Figure C.4(b). Here we can selectively read through a random file and prepare a report from the records chosen. This program uses many of the statements discussed in our prior create example. Program (b) opens similarly, but adds column headings at line 40. Module 2 of the program commences at line 100.

The desired record is identified at line 110, where its number is input. That record is randomly identified via line 120, where a READ FILE statement is specified. This statement identifies FILEB, R for its random file structure and R1 as the record identification number. The actual reading of the R1 record is accomplished at line 130, where an INPUT statement accesses N$, C$ and Z from the disk. The PRINT D$ statement shifts I/O control from the diskette to the terminal, such that the three variables are output at line 150.

The request to continue processing occurs via lines 160 and 170. A user response of Y continues I/O operations, whereas an N causes an exit from the loop. At line 900, FILEB is closed and the program's processing concluded.

The update program, Figure C.5, is more complex, as it accommodates both the additions of new records and the modification of existing records. A menu at the program's start advises users of the available choices. The hierarchical chart, Figure C.5(a), notes that access to either of the two modules occurs through the menu module.

The division of responsibilities is evident in the program's structure, Figure C.5(b). The menu module is constructed within lines 100 to 160, where each of three choices is defined. A branch to line 310 leads to the ADD A RECORD module, with line 610 providing access to the CHANGE RECORD module. Prior to these activities, the file format is opened and defined at line 30.

The ADD A RECORD module is similar to the program of Figure C.4(a) where records are written onto disk. Data for the three fields is input and written onto disk. The user has the option of continuing or exiting the module. Lines 310 to 430 define the first module's actions.

The CHANGE module commences at line 610. We must initially identify the record to be modified. The record number is specified at line 620, with the record retrieved via lines 630 and 640. The current contents of the record retrieved are output at lines 660 to 680. The Control-D character, line 650, precedes this output, shifting I/O control from the disk to the terminal.

In this program, the user has the option of separately changing each field. The request to alter the NAME field occurs at lines 690 to 700. If the user desires a new name, that input is accomplished at line 710. The remaining CITY and ZIP fields are similarly handled at lines 720 to 740 and 750 to 770.

The intent to rewrite the new record at the R1 location is established at line 780. The WRITE FILEB instruction establishes the link to disk, with the three PRINT statements following it actually writing the N$, C$ and Z data on disk. The PRINT D$ returns I/O control to the CRT, prior to the request to continue processing at lines 830 to 840. The loop is executed each time a record is modified.

An important aspect to this update program is its ability to separately handle the change of each field. This enables users to change from one to three fields, at their discretion.

(a)

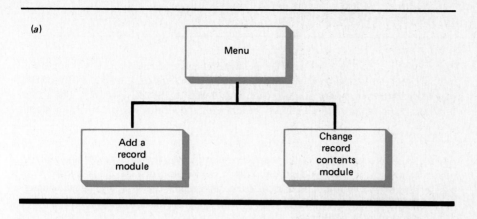

(b)

```
10     REM -- UPDATE RANDOM FILE PROGRAM        610    REM -- CHANGE RECORD CONTENTS MODULE
20     D$ = CHR$ (4)                            620    INPUT "ENTER NUMBER OF RECORD TO CHANGE"; R1
30     PRINT D$; " OPEN FILEB, L48"              630    PRINT D$; "READ FILEB,R"; R1
100    PRINT , "MENU OF ACTIVITIES"              640    INPUT N$,C$,Z
110    PRINT , "    1. ADD A RECORD"             650    PRINT D$
120    PRINT , "    2. CHANGE A RECORD"          660    PRINT "CURRENT NAME :"; N$
130    PRINT , "    3. CLOSE PROCESSING"         670    PRINT "CURRENT CITY   :"; C$
140    INPUT "ENTER CHOICE"; C                   680    PRINT "CURRENT ZIP   :"; Z
150    ON C GOSUB 310,610,900                    690    INPUT "WISH TO CHANGE NAME - Y OR N"; R$
160    GO TO 100                                 700    IF R$ = "N" THEN 720
310    REM -- ADD A RECORD MODULE                710    INPUT "ENTER NEW NAME"; N$
320    INPUT "STUDENT NAME IS"; N$               720    INPUT "WISH TO CHANGE CITY - Y OR N"; R$
330    INPUT "ENTER CITY        "; C$            730    IF R$ = "N" THEN 750
340    INPUT "ZIP CODE IS        "; Z            740    INPUT "ENTER NEW CITY"; C$
350    INPUT "RECORD NUMBER TO USE"; R1          750    INPUT "WISH TO CHANGE ZIP - Y OR N"; R$
360    PRINT D$; "WRITE FILEB,R"; R1             760    IF R$ = "N" THEN 780
370    PRINT N$                                  770    INPUT "ENTER NEW ZIP CODE"; Z
380    PRINT C$                                  780    PRINT D$; "WRITE FILEB,R"; R1
390    PRINT Z                                   790    PRINT N$
400    PRINT D$                                  800    PRINT C$
410    INPUT "ANOTHER RECORD - Y OR N"; R$       810    PRINT Z
420    IF R$ = "Y" THEN 320                      820    PRINT D$
430    RETURN                                    830    INPUT "CHANGE ANOTHER RECORD - Y OR N"; R$
                                                 840    IF R$ = "Y" THEN 620
                                                 850    RETURN
                                                 900    PRINT D$; "CLOSE FILEB"
                                                 910    END
```

FIGURE C.5   The update program for a random file uses a menu to advise users of their options. The hierarchical chart *(a)* expresses the overall logic of the program *(b)*.

C.3 Working with an IBM PC

File handling activities with an IBM PC parallel those of the APPLE system. Files must be created before they may be used in any processing. Though many of the file-related statements are similar, each is tailored to the IBM system. The three programs which follow offer a glimpse of handling sequential files in an IBM system.

Sequential Files

Sequential files are created on a record-by-record basis, the contents of the desired record being input via a keyboard and written onto disk. Once the file is created, it is possible to read its contents, manipulate data and report the results. The addition of new records to the existing file may be performed, too. The programs of Figure C.6 demonstrate two file activities.

In Figure C.6(a), a program creating a sequential file is listed. This program takes data entered from a keyboard and writes these data on diskettes. The program uses a REM statement at line 10 to identify its purpose.

An OPEN statement, line 100, prepares FILEA for use and identifies the fact that data will be output to it. The number (#1) declared at the end of the OPEN statement identifies FILEA as the first file and provides the computer a means of controlling I/O operations for that file. If more than one file is used, additional numbers (i.e., #2, #3, . . .) are specified for each, in separate OPEN statements, prior to their operational use.

The OPEN statement, specified at line 100, represents one of two formats which may be employed. This format permits the user to define a file for INPUT, OUTPUT, or APPEND operations. The second format, shown in the program of Figure C.6(b) can only define files for I/O activities. This format is subsequently explained in the (b) program.

With FILEA open for use, input operations entering the three desired fields commence at line 110. The name, city and ZIP code data are entered from the terminal. A 9s decision using the Z variable enables the user to exit the loop when desired.

FIGURE C.6   The creation (a) and use for report purposes (b) of a sequential file is illustrated for an IBM system.

```
                    (a)                                      (b)

10      REM -- SEQ FILE FOR IBM            10      REM -- READ DISKETTE & PRINT
100     OPEN "FILEA" FOR OUTPUT AS #1      20      PRINT "NAME","CITY","ZIP"
110     INPUT "NAME, CITY & ZIP"; N$,C$,Z  100     OPEN "I",1,"FILEA"
120     IF Z = −99999 THEN 200             110     IF EOF(1) THEN 200
130     PRINT #1, N$                       120     INPUT #1, N$,C$,Z
140     PRINT #1, C$                        130     PRINT N$,C$,Z
150     PRINT #1, Z                         140     GO TO 110
160     GO TO 110                           200     CLOSE #1
200     CLOSE #1                            210     END
210     END
```

Lines 130 to 150 actually perform the output of data onto disk. The PRINT #1 format dictates that the three fields be written on the file associated with #1 — which is FILEA. The use of separate PRINT #1 statements is required to output each data item onto its equivalent disk record.

An unconditional branch at line 110 completes the loop, returning control to line 110 where the input of data continues. When the 9's data is entered, the program branches to line 200 where a CLOSE statement is executed. Note that a file name is not required, as the #1 is associated with FILEA. The CLOSE #1 instruction is sufficient to close FILEA and precede the program's end. All files should be closed before a program's end.

The contents of FILEA is read and output in the program listed in Figure C.6*(b)*. In this case, FILEA is an INPUT file and is defined at line 100. In this version of the OPEN statement, "I" reflects the INPUT nature of "FILEA" and 1 its numeric designation. The pound sign (#) does not precede the file number in this format. The "O" designation is used for files serving an output function. The OPEN statement which follows could have been specified in the program of Figure C.6*(a)* with equal success.

```
100     OPEN "O", 1, "FILEA"
```

This second form of the OPEN statement does not support the APPEND file format. For APPEND file manipulations, where data is written onto the end of an existing file, the first instructional format of Figure C.6*(a)* must be used. For I/O file operations, however, both OPEN instructional formats may be interchangeably used.

An EOF conditional statement is introduced at line 110. This IF/THEN statement is tailored to test for an end-of-file condition in FILEA. The file number written into the parentheses following EOF indicates the file against which the EOF test is performed. A successful EOF check causes the program to branch to line 200, where FILEA is closed.

The actual retrieval of data from file #1 is accomplished via line 120. This INPUT statement carries with it a file number (#1) and the respective variable names of the data items being entered. All three variable names are specified in the same INPUT statement to reflect their collective input. The specification of the correct file number is a mandatory part of this statement's syntax.

The output of these three variables is performed at line 130. As this output is terminal-oriented, the PRINT statement does not specify a file number (e.g., #1). The N\$, C\$ and Z variables will occupy print zones 1 to 3 and appear beneath the headings defined by line 20's execution. Output operations will continue until the EOF condition occurs and the program is closed.

The addition of new records to an existing sequential file is employed to update a file. A sample program exhibiting these steps appears in Figure C.7, where FILEA is to be updated. This program's function is readily evident by the OPEN statement, line 100. FILEA is opened as file #1, where the APPEND command is dictated. The APPEND command only can be specified using this form of the OPEN statement.

With FILEA opened for use, update activities start at line 110. The INPUT statement shown permits the keyboard entry of N\$, C\$ and Z variable data. The writing of these data items on disk is performed via lines 120 to 140. Again, the use of separate PRINT #1 statements is mandated. The APPEND file command ensures that all records written are added to the end of FILEA.

```
10      REM -- ADD A RECORD TO EXISTING FILE
100     OPEN "FILEA" FOR APPEND AS #1
110     INPUT "NAME, CITY & ZIP"; N$,C$,Z
120     PRINT #1, N$
130     PRINT #1, C$
140     PRINT #1, Z
150     INPUT "ADD ANOTHER RECORD - Y OR N"; R$
160     IF R$ = "Y" THEN 110 ELSE 900
900     CLOSE #1
910     END
```

FIGURE C.7   The addition of new records is demonstrated for a sequential file.

A prompting input sequence, at lines 150 and 160, permits the user to continue entering new records or close processing. An entry of "Y" leads to line 110 where a new record's data is keyed. Otherwise line 900 is accessed and file #1 closed.

Random Files   Random files are conveniently handled in a fashion which parallels their usage in the APPLE system. A file must be opened, with each field defined prior to its use. Data items slated for storage must be converted to compact formats before the IBM system will accept them for storage. Different commands are employed to handle disk I/O operations. Figure C.8 provides two programs which illustrate these points.

The program in Figure C.8(a) reflects the creation of a random file where each record is stored on diskette. Figure C.8(b) denotes the reading of data from an existing file and its output. The overall logic of both programs is similar to prior solutions, but some new statements, unique to IBM systems, are introduced.

FIGURE C.8   Two programs denote the creation (a) and use for output (b) of a random file in an IBM PC.

(a)	(b)
10 REM -- CREATE RANDOM FILE	10 REM -- READ RECORD & WRITE IT
20 OPEN "R",1,"FILEB",44	20 OPEN "R",1,"FILEB",44
30 FIELD#1,25 AS BN$,15 AS BC$,4 AS BZ$	30 FIELD#1,25 AS BN$,15 AS BC$,4 AS BZ$
100 REM -- WRITE RECORD	40 PRINT "NAME","CITY","ZIP CODE"
110 INPUT "NAME, CITY & ZIP"; N$,C$,Z	100 REM -- READ/WRITE RECORD
120 INPUT "RECORD NUMBER TO USE"; R	110 INPUT "RECORD NUMBER TO USE"; R
130 LSET BN$ = N$	120 GET #1,R
140 LSET BC$ = C$	130 Z = CVS(BZ$)
150 LSET BZ$ = MKS$(Z)	140 PRINT BN$,BC$,Z
160 PUT #1,R	150 INPUT "READ ANOTHER RECORD - Y OR N"; R$
170 INPUT "ANOTHER RECORD - Y OR N"; R$	160 IF R$ = "Y" THEN 110 ELSE 900
180 IF R$ = "Y" THEN 110 ELSE 900	900 CLOSE #1
900 CLOSE #1	910 END
910 END	

In the initial file-create program *(a)*, a REM statement precedes the OPEN statement, line 20. The statement specifies that FILEB is a *R*andom file, handled via channel 1, and has a length of 44 characters. The 44-character size is computed by adding 25 positions for name, 15 for city and 4 for ZIP code. The four positions do not correspond to the normal 5-character size of ZIP codes, but to the four storage positions employed by the computer to physically retain that field in storage. The 4-position size is generally assigned to almost all numeric data items undergoing storage. IBM software possesses other storage formats for more specialized data items, where they are occasionally required in highly technical applications.

An alternate form of the OPEN statement is made available to users. This statement

20   OPEN "FILEB" AS #1 LEN = 44

specifies the same file parameters, but in a different form. FILEB is associated with channel 1, and a length of 44 storage positions. The use of this instructional format implies the existence of a random file.

The fields composing the record format of FILEB are defined in line 30. The FIELD statement specifies in sequential order each field composing the record format and its relative size. The names associated with each field define the variable name employed when each data item is to be stored. These names must be specified when preparing each variable prior to its output to and storage on disk, as shown in lines 130 to 150.

Prior to those data-handling statements, the actual data to be stored should be input. Two INPUT statements, lines 110 and 120, permit the entry of the three required fields and the number of the record where those items should be stored. The three required fields are prepared for storage via lines 130 to 150. The LSET statements, lines 130 and 140, position the N$ and C$ fields for storage and associate them with the BN$ and BC$ names. Line 150 performs a similar task for BZ$, but in addition converts the Z data to a compacted storage format. The MKS$ command directs the computer to perform this required conversion. Failure to convert data to its required format will cause a program error to occur and invalidate the storage of that data. The IBM software provides other MKS-like commands for data formats used in specialized applications. Users may separately investigate these instructions. The MKS$ format can handle almost all general applications.

With the three fields made ready by the LSET statements, the record may be written onto disk. The IBM PC uses a PUT statement to perform this output activity, *not* a PRINT statement. The PUT statement, line 160, associates its output with the FIELD #1 format of line 30 and directs that storage occur at record number R. The comma between #1 and R is mandatory. The prompting of the user, lines 170 and 180, permits the continuation of file activities or the exit from the loop. All files opened for processing must be closed, before the program's end.

Some changes appear in the read/write program, Figure C.8*(b)*. The OPEN and FIELD statements properly define FILEB and its record format. A heading consisting of three literals is defined by line 40. The number of the record to be output is requested via line 110, an INPUT statement. The actual reading of that record off disk is accomplished by using a GET statement, line 120. The GET statement is the operational opposite of the PUT statement, both dealing solely with disk storage operations.

The data record retrieved via line 120 possesses a format which must be re-converted before it can be used. If you recall, data was converted prior to its storage. The

CVS command of line 130 converts the numeric data item Z so that it may be properly output. Because of the storage format used with character (non-numeric) data, it is possible to print the BN$ and BC$ data items without converting them. Additional CVS commands are available for specialized data-handling options. Again, another set of user-prompting statements completes the loop and control processing.

The update program, Figure C.9, combines many of the features of these two programs and permits the user to add a record to FILEB or modify the contents of an existing record. This update program commences with the opening and definition of FILEB, and the presentation of a menu of activities. The three options offered include (1) the addition of a record, (2) the read and change of a record, and (3) the end of the program. The user is then free to choose and input an option.

Module 1, starting with line 300, is similar to prior program (a). It adds a record to FILEB and accomplishes the conversion and storage of that record on disk. Module 2, beginning at line 600, enables the update of each field within the existing record format. An additional change to the update program from the earlier solutions is the required conversion of data items. Lines 630, 680, 720 and 760 relate directly to this function. GET and PUT statements handle disk I/O activities. Other than these alterations, the logic employed parallels the prior update solutions. The user should read through these solutions to confirm this point and reinforce understanding.

These sample programs do not illustrate all of the various options and statements available with the IBM PC but provide a prototype with which to build other solutions. A major step in disk-handling operations is the conversion of data formats before writing data on or after reading it from the diskette. However, once each data item is correctly converted, it may be employed in any of the processing activities previously reviewed.

FIGURE C.9 The update program again uses a menu of choices to advise the user. Note the mandatory conversion of data to a compacted format and its reconversion from storage.

```
10    REM -- READ/WRITE UPDATE PROGRAM        600   REM -- READ & CHANGE MODULE
20    OPEN "R",1,"FILEB",44                   610   INPUT "NUMBER OF RECORD"; R
30    FIELD#1,25 AS BN$,15 AS BC$,4 AS BZ$    620   GET #1,R
100   REM -- MENU MODULE                      630   Z = CVS(BZ$)
110   PRINT ,"MENU OF CHOICES"                640   PRINT BN$,BC$,Z
120   PRINT ,"    1. ADD A RECORD"            650   INPUT "CHANGE NAME - Y or N"; R$
130   PRINT ,"    2. READ & CHANGE A RECORD"  660   IF R$ = "N" THEN 690
140   PRINT ,"    3. END PROGRAM"             670   INPUT "ENTER NEW NAME"; N$
150   INPUT "ENTER CHOICE"; C                 680   LSET BN$ = N$
160   IF C=3 THEN 900                         690   INPUT "CHANGE CITY - Y or N"; R$
170   ON C GOSUB 300,600                      700   IF R$ = "N" THEN 730
180   GO TO 110                               710   INPUT "ENTER NEW CITY"; C$
300   REM -- ADD A RECORD MODULE              720   LSET BC$ = C$
310   INPUT "NAME,CITY & ZIP"; N$,C$,Z        730   INPUT "CHANGE ZIP CODE - Y or N"; R$
320   INPUT "RECORD NUMBER TO USE"; R         740   IF R$ = "N" THEN 760
330   LSET BN$ = N$                           750   INPUT "ENTER NEW ZIP"; Z
340   LSET BC$ = C$                           760   LSET BZ$ = MKS$(Z)
350   LSET BZ$ = MKS$(Z)                      770   PUT #1,R
360   PUT #1, R                               780   INPUT "CHANGE ANOTHER RECORD - Y or N";R$
370   INPUT "ANOTHER RECORD - Y or N"; R$     790   IF R$ = "Y" THEN 610
380   IF R$ = "Y" THEN 310                    800   RETURN
390   RETURN                                  900   CLOSE#1
                                              910   END
```

C.4 Implications for the TRS-80

File-handling operations on the Radio Shack TRS-80 computer, with few exceptions, match those of the IBM PC. Disk records are retained sequentially or on a random format. Numeric data is stored in a compacted format to consume less space. Essentially, the program presented in Figures C.8 and C.9 are generally usable on TRS-80 systems.

Differences relate to the use of OPEN statements and their random-access format. With the TRS-80, the OPEN statement used must follow the format:

    100   OPEN "R", 1, "FILEB", 44

as the other version of the OPEN statement is not available.

The TRS-80 system also provides for the storage of integers, as well as double-precision data items. The conversionary statements used are paired as MKI$ and CVI instructions for integer data, with MKD$ and CVD instructions for double precision. The latter format is used when very small or large numbers are involved in processing and a greater degree of precision is desired. Double precision allocates double the amount of storage space for numeric data and thus permits more accurate computations.

Again, we must remind the user that minor modifications in software may be necessary, due to differences between devices — even in the same family of computers. Thus, it may be necessary to tinker with some program statements on your computer before getting a program to run satisfactorily.

C.5 Working with a DEC System

Digital Equipment hardware supports many schools and businesses, especially in the use of BASIC, in a time-sharing environment. Many students began their programming careers on DEC equipment, using RSTS/E operating system. DEC's version of BASIC, called BASIC-PLUS, is similar to other forms of the language and offers many statements to support structured programming concepts.

Its file-handling features are similar to the other versions of BASIC reviewed, but again, slight differences are evident. Sample programs paralleling the use of sequential and random files will illustrate these factors. The first two programs deal with sequential file structures.

Sequential Files

The differences between the sequential file programs employed in a DEC system and those previously discussed lie in the control statements used to define the files and the way the programs are employed.

The program specified in Figure C.10*(a)* offers the user two options. It can be used to create a sequential file where none previously existed and to append new records to an existing file. This dual capacity is designed into one program without radically expanding its size. The control commands utilized will become evident, as we review the program's syntax.

	(a)		(b)

```
10      REM -- CREATE SEQ FILE                  10      REM -- READ & WRITE FILE DATA
20      INPUT "ENTER NAME OF FILE"; F$          20      PRINT "NAME","CITY","ZIP CODE"
30      INPUT "ENTER NUMBER OF RECORDS TO       30      ON ERROR GOTO 1000
        BE HANDLED"; N                          40      OPEN "SEQ.DAT" FOR INPUT AS FILE #1
40      FILE.OUT$ = F$ + ".DAT"                 100     REM -- READ/WRITE LOOP
50      OPEN FILE.OUT$ AS FILE#1%,MODE 2%       110     INPUT #1%,N$,C$,Z
100     REM -- FILE HANDLING MODULE             120     PRINT N$,C$,Z
110     FOR I = 1 TO N                          130     GO TO 110
120     INPUT "NAME,CITY & ZIP"; N$,C$,Z        1000    IF ERR = 11% THEN CLOSE #1 ELSE PRINT "ERROR =";ERR
130     PRINT #1%,N$,C$,Z                       1010    END
140     NEXT I
200     CLOSE #1
210     END
```

FIGURE C.10   The two programs shown parallel previous solutions for sequential files. A create program (a) precedes an I/O program (b), both written for DEC systems. Single or double quotes may be used in the DEC system.

Program (a) opens with a REM statement, preceding the input of the file's name, F$. We will call our file SEQ, as it adopts a sequential format. At line 30, we enter the number of records to be processed, N, in preparation for the FOR/NEXT loop defined via lines 110 to 140.

The definition of our file is accomplished at line 40, where the output nature of this file is established via the FILE.OUT$ command. The instruction also creates the full file name of SEQ.DAT by adding the name defined with F$ to ".DAT". DEC systems require that this format be adopted.

The SEQ.DAT file is opened for use in line 50, using the expanded version of DEC's OPEN statement. FILE.OUT$ is opened as file #1%, identifying it from all other potential files. The % sign is appended to #1 to ensure that an integer number is defined. The % sign eliminates a potential decimal. The MODE 2% command is unique to DEC equipment and permits this program to support both create and update operations. Line 50 fully defines the file for output activities, via channel #1, and in relation to MODE 2% tasks.

With the SEQ.DATA file defined, the loop commences. Exactly N loops are executed, causing exactly N records to be added to a file or creating a file of exactly N records. Record data is input via line 120 and output via line 130. The PRINT #1% format ensures that the data is properly output to the correct disk. At the close of N loops, the loop is exited and file #1 is closed.

The use of the SEQ.DAT file to prepare a report is detailed in Figure C.10(b). This program is similar to prior solutions where a sequential file was read and its contents printed. A REM statement identifies Program (b)'s purpose, preceding this output of three column headings (line 20) and an ON ERROR statement. Line 30 is used to detect end-of-file (EOF) conditions and seek out data errors when working with the file. Either type of error causes the program to branch to line 1000, where the file is closed on an EOF condition or the discovered error is output. The program is then closed to further processing.

An alternate form of the OPEN statement is used at line 40. Here, SEQ.DAT is opened for input operations as file #1, as data read from the file is printed. The INPUT #1% command reads each record from disk, with the printing accomplished via line 120. Note, the #1% designation is essential for line 110 so that the disk is properly accessed. The PRINT statement does not require this, as the data is output on the user's terminal. A GOTO instruction, line 130, completes this simplified loop, continuing the reading of SEQ.DAT records until the EOF is reached or an error is detected.

We must take a moment to point out the relationship between the programs of Figure C.10. In Program *(a)*, a file named SEQ.DAT was defined, and in Program *(b)*, that file was requested at line 40. This emphasizes the coordinated nature of file manipulations. Only files that are properly named, defined, and documented can be correctly used in file manipulations. Even the best programmers can be defeated by their own sloppiness.

Random Files

In a DEC system, random-access files possess a structure unique to that system. They are created through the use of arrays to define each field within a record. Also, the manufacturer suggests that the file be defined for a finite number of records. Thus, a file is created for a specific number of records at its inception. Records are added until the file is filled; then its contents are transferred to a new, larger file. To observe the implementation of these concepts, let us examine the program of Figure C.11.

Program *(a)* describes the creation of a random file in a DEC system. The OPEN statement, line 20, creates FILEB as a data file 1%. The impact of an array is invoked at line 30, where a DIM statement defines three arrays. The N\$, C\$ and Z arrays are defined at 50 cells each, thus creating a file of 50 records. The number 50 was arbitrarily chosen, whereas a 100- or 200-record format would have been acceptable.

With FILEB defined and opened, a FOR/NEXT sequence is initiated into which the file is loaded. An INPUT statement, line 110, utilizing the required array name is sufficient to accept the three data items needed to generate a record. After the 50-record file is fully loaded, FILEB is closed.

In program *(b)* of Figure C.11, the contents of FILEB are output. The file is opened at line 20, with the array fields constituting each record dictated by the DIM statement of line 30. Three literals are output to create the report's heading.

The INPUT statement, line 100, requests the number of the record to be printed. The PRINT statement, line 110, accesses the three fields associated with the R record and outputs them. Note the entire record is accessed via its component array/field name. A prompting INPUT statement closes the loop, controlling access to the next record or the exit from the loop. When no other records are output, FILEB is closed and the program ends.

FIGURE C.11 Random files, once created via program *(a)*, may be employed for report purposes as in program *(b)*.

```
           (a)                                          (b)

10    REM -- CREATE RANDOM FILE           10    REM -- READ/WRITE PROGRAM
20    OPEN "FILEB.DAT" AS FILE 1%         20    OPEN "FILEB.DAT" AS FILE 1%
30    DIM #1,N$(50),C$(50),Z(50)          30    DIM #1, N$(50),C$(50),Z(50)
100   FOR I = 1 TO 50                     40    PRINT "NAME","CITY","ZIP CODE"
110   INPUT "NAME, CITY & ZIP"; N$(I),C$(I),Z(I)   100   INPUT "ENTER RECORD NUMBER";R
120   NEXT I                              110   PRINT N$(R),C$(R),Z(R)
130   CLOSE #1                            120   INPUT "ANOTHER RECORD - Y OR N"; R$
140   END                                 130   IF R$ = "Y" THEN 100
                                          200   CLOSE #1
                                          210   END
```

```
10      REM -- UPDATE PROGRAM              600     REM -- CHANGE MODULE
20      OPEN "FILEB.DAT" AS FILE 1%        610     INPUT "ENTER RECORD NUMBER";R
30      DIM #1, N$(50),C$(50),Z(50)        620     PRINT N$(R),C$(R),Z(R)
40      REM -- MENU OPTIONS                630     INPUT "CHANGE NAME - Y OR N";R$
100     PRINT ,"MENU CHOICES"              640     IF R$ = "N" THEN 660
110     PRINT ,"   1. ADD A RECORD"        650     INPUT "ENTER NEW NAME"; N$(R)
120     PRINT ,"   2. CHANGE A RECORD"     660     INPUT "CHANGE CITY - Y OR N"; R$
130     PRINT ,"   3. CLOSE PROCESSING"    670     IF R$ = "N" THEN 690
140     INPUT "ENTER YOUR CHOICE"; C       680     INPUT "ENTER NEW CITY";C$(R)
150     IF C = 3 THEN 900                  690     INPUT "CHANGE ZIP - Y OR N"; R$
160     On C GOSUB 300,600                 700     IF R$ = "N" THEN 720
170     GO TO 100                          710     INPUT "ENTER NEW ZIP"; Z(R)
300     REM -- ADD A RECORD MODULE         720     INPUT "ANOTHER RECORD - Y OR N"; R$
310     INPUT "ENTER RECORD NUMBER";R      730     IF R$ = "Y" THEN 610
320     INPUT "NAME, CITY & ZIP"; N$(R),C$(R),Z(R)   740     RETURN
330     INPUT N$(R),C$(R),Z(R)             900     CLOSE #1
340     INPUT "ANOTHER RECORD - Y OR N";R$ 910     END
350     IF R$ = "Y" THEN 310
360     RETURN
```

FIGURE C.12   The update program offers three choices to its users, enabling the modification of a random file.

The update program related to random FILEB, Figure C.12, is operationally similar to our prior update solutions. FILEB is opened using similar statements, which precede the menu of options available to the user. The choice made, C, leads to either of two modules or the program's close.

In module 1, commencing at line 300, a record is added to the file after its location is identified. The data composing the record is input at line 320 and subsequently output to confirm its storage. Users are free to add any number of records or close module 1.

The change module, starting with line 600, initially prints the contents of the record indicated (R), lines 610 and 620. The statements that follow individually access each of the three fields composing every record and permit the user to change them. The input of a new data field automatically updates its contents with that record. The update sequence occurs in lines 630 to 710. At lines 720 to 730, the user is prompted to continue processing or close that module.

We again remind our readers that these solutions are representative of the programs that may be used to handle computer files. Users are free to tinker with these programs to create solutions more closely tailored to their processing needs. Users should carefully acquaint themselves with the features of their system's hardware and software before commencing extensive file operations.

Answers to In-Class Exercises

1   The solution to in-class exercise 1 is shown in Answer 3.1.

2   The flowchart and checklist for in-class exercise 2 is shown in Answer 3.2.

3   The flowchart for in-class exercise 3 is shown in Answer 3.3

1   In-class exercise 1 should be keyed into the computer for the purpose of familiarizing yourself with the terminal keyboard.

2   The following sample statements are used to satisfy the two parts of in-class exercise 2.
   a   The 9s decision entered at line 30 might appear as

```
30   IF P = −99 THEN 400       or
30   IF R = −99 THEN 400       or
30   IF N$ = 'XXX' THEN 400    if nonnumeric data is used
```

   b
```
20   K = 1
60   IF K = 15 THEN 400
70   K = K + 1
```

3   Two solutions are offered for in-class exercise 3. In Answer 4.3A, a 9s decision controls looping. In Answer 4.3B, a counter is employed to complete the six loops needed for processing.

   In Answer 4.3A, we chose to use the IF/THEN/ELSE statement to compute pension amounts. This statement was replaced by two IF/THEN statements in Answer 4.3B. This change was made to illustrate how alternative computations can be performed if the IF/THEN/ELSE instruction is not available in your version of BASIC.

1   The following statements are needed to complete the program excerpts for the three parts of in-class exercise 1.
   a   The FOR/NEXT statement shown will handle 24 loops.

```
20   FOR K = 1 TO 24
60   NEXT K
```

   b   The FOR/NEXT statements, lines 20 and 50, incorporate a STEP option with an increment of .2.

```
20   FOR X = −1.8 TO 2.4 STEP .2
50   NEXT X
```

   c   A FOR/NEXT statement, with a negative increment, is inserted at lines 20 and 50, to complete this program excerpt.

```
20   FOR C = 100 TO 0 STEP −5
50   NEXT C
```

2   The solution to in-class exercise 2 is shown in Answer 5.2. A FOR/NEXT statement, using an increment of 2, is used to add the even numbers from 2 to 100.

3   The flowchart, program, output, and output format for in-class exercise 3 is shown in Answer 5.3.

Chapter 6   1   The flowchart, program, and output for in-class exercise 1 is shown in Answer 6.1.

2   The flowchart, program, and output for in-class exercise 2 is shown in Answer 6.2.

3   The flowchart, program, and output for in-class exercise 3 is shown in Answer 6.3.

Chapter 7   1   The following program excerpts satisfy the requirements in the three parts of in-class exercise 1.

   a   These statements permit data to be read into the D array, two items at a time.

```
10   DIM D(20)
20   FOR K = 1 TO 20 STEP 2
30   READ D(K), D(K + 1)
40   PRINT D(K), D(K + 1)
50   NEXT K
```

   b   These statements define a tabular output, where four items are printed per line.

```
400   FOR K = 1 TO 28 STEP 4
410   PRINT X(K), X(K + 1), X(K + 2), X(K + 3)
420   NEXT K
```

   c   An error checking sequence is built into the FOR/NEXT loop which controls the input of data into the N$ array, three items per loop.

```
100   FOR K = 1 TO 45 STEP 3
110   INPUT N$(K), N$(K + 1), N$(K + 2)
120   INPUT 'DATA OK — Y OR N'; R$
130   IF R$ = 'N' THEN 110
140   NEXT K
```

2   In-class exercise 2 illustrates the speed with which the computer can process data. It should take you a few minutes to key the data, with the processed result appearing in seconds. Use care when keying the data to avoid costly errors.

3   The flowchart, program, and output for in-class exercise 3 is shown in Answer 7.3.

Chapter 8   1   The flowchart, program and output for in-class exercise 1 are shown in Answer 8.1.

2   The flowchart, program and output for in-class exercise 2 are shown in Answer 8.2.

3   The flowchart, program and output for in-class exercise 3 are shown in Answer 8.3.

Chapter 9   1   The flowchart, program, and output for in-class exercise 1, are depicted in Answer 9.1.

2   The flowchart, program, and output for in-class exercise 2, Chapter 9, are shown in Answer 9.2.

3   The flowchart, program, and output for in-class exercise 3, Chapter 9, are shown in Answer 9.3.

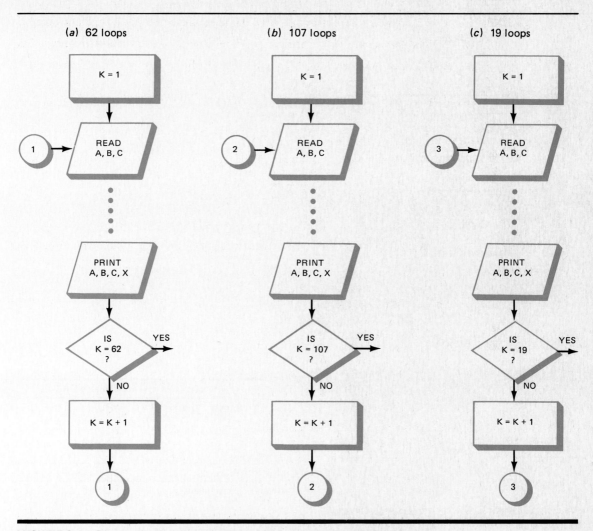

ANSWER 3.1   Completed flowchart for Figure 3.26, defining loops 62, 107, and 19.

ANSWER 3.2 Flowchart and checklist for in-class exercise 2, Chapter 3.

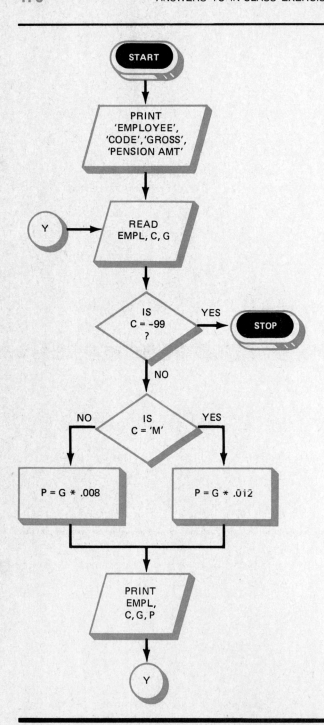

Input Data	Dataname Used
Employee name	EMPL
ID code	C
Gross pay	G

Processing	Formula Used
Pension amt	P = G * .012
	P = G * .008

Output Data	Dataname Used
Employee name	EMPL
ID code	C
Gross pay	G
Pension amt	P
Heading	EMPLOYEE, CODE
	GROSS, PENSION AMT

Decision
IS C = –99?
IS C = 'M' ?

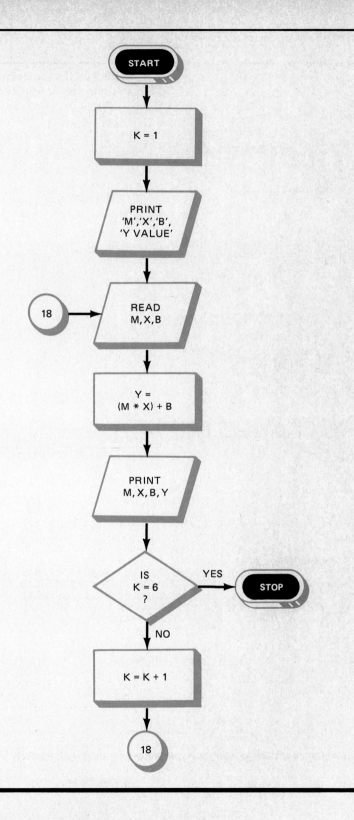

ANSWER 3.3
Flowchart for in-class
exercise 3, Chapter 3.
A counter controls the
six loops required for
processing.

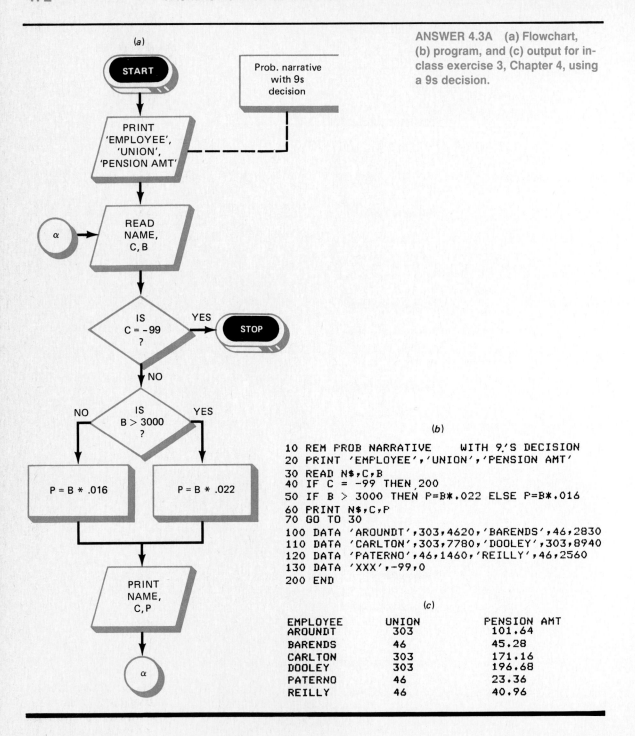

(a)

ANSWER 4.3A   (a) Flowchart, (b) program, and (c) output for in-class exercise 3, Chapter 4, using a 9s decision.

(b)

```
10 REM PROB NARRATIVE      WITH 9.'S DECISION
20 PRINT 'EMPLOYEE','UNION','PENSION AMT'
30 READ N$,C,B
40 IF C = -99 THEN 200
50 IF B > 3000 THEN P=B*.022 ELSE P=B*.016
60 PRINT N$,C,P
70 GO TO 30
100 DATA 'AROUNDT',303,4620,'BARENDS',46,2830
110 DATA 'CARLTON',303,7780,'DOOLEY',303,8940
120 DATA 'PATERNO',46,1460,'REILLY',46,2560
130 DATA 'XXX',-99,0
200 END
```

(c)

EMPLOYEE	UNION	PENSION AMT
AROUNDT	303	101.64
BARENDS	46	45.28
CARLTON	303	171.16
DOOLEY	303	196.68
PATERNO	46	23.36
REILLY	46	40.96

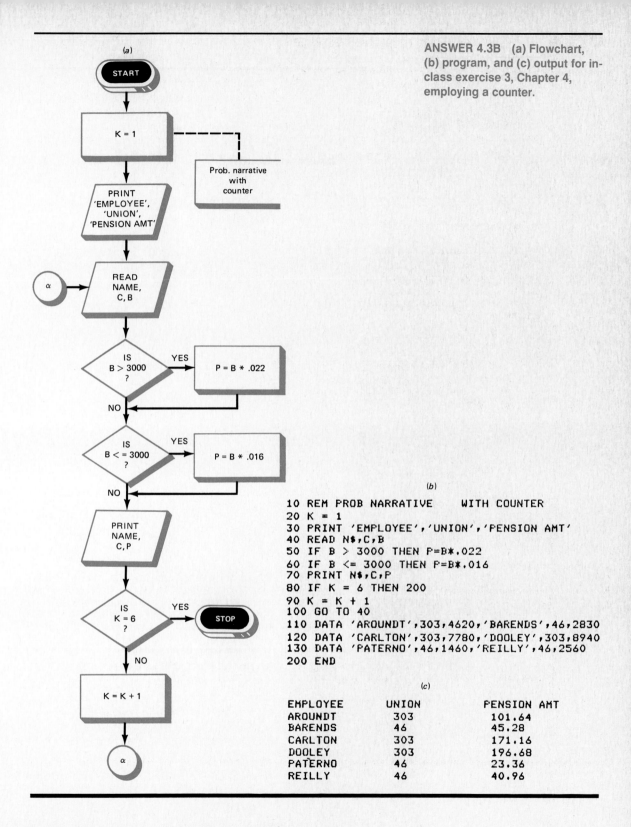

(a)

START

K = 1

Prob. narrative
with
counter

PRINT
'EMPLOYEE',
'UNION',
'PENSION AMT'

α → READ
NAME,
C, B

IS
B > 3000
? —YES→ P = B * .022

NO

IS
B < = 3000
? —YES→ P = B * .016

NO

PRINT
NAME,
C, P

IS
K = 6
? —YES→ STOP

NO

K = K + 1

α

ANSWER 4.3B (a) Flowchart,
(b) program, and (c) output for in-
class exercise 3, Chapter 4,
employing a counter.

(b)

```
10 REM PROB NARRATIVE     WITH COUNTER
20 K = 1
30 PRINT 'EMPLOYEE','UNION','PENSION AMT'
40 READ N$,C,B
50 IF B > 3000 THEN P=B*.022
60 IF B <= 3000 THEN P=B*.016
70 PRINT N$,C,P
80 IF K = 6 THEN 200
90 K = K + 1
100 GO TO 40
110 DATA 'AROUNDT',303,4620,'BARENDS',46,2830
120 DATA 'CARLTON',303,7780,'DOOLEY',303,8940
130 DATA 'PATERNO',46,1460,'REILLY',46,2560
200 END
```

(c)

EMPLOYEE	UNION	PENSION AMT
AROUNDT	303	101.64
BARENDS	46	45.28
CARLTON	303	171.16
DOOLEY	303	196.68
PATERNO	46	23.36
REILLY	46	40.96

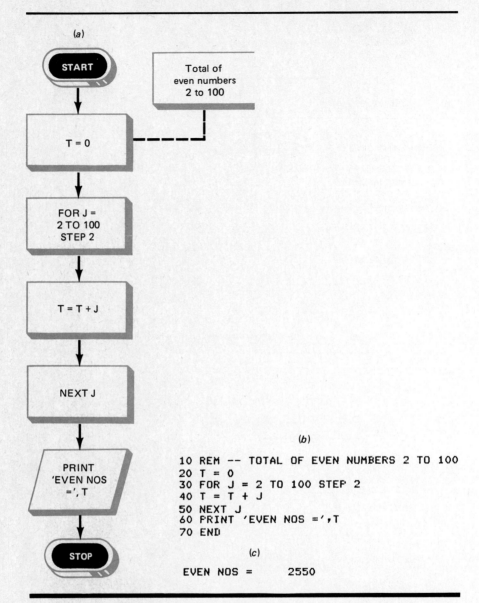

(a)

START

Total of
even numbers
2 to 100

T = 0

FOR J =
2 TO 100
STEP 2

T = T + J

NEXT J

PRINT
'EVEN NOS
=', T

STOP

(b)

```
10 REM -- TOTAL OF EVEN NUMBERS 2 TO 100
20 T = 0
30 FOR J = 2 TO 100 STEP 2
40 T = T + J
50 NEXT J
60 PRINT 'EVEN NOS =',T
70 END
```

(c)

```
EVEN NOS =     2550
```

ANSWER 5.2 (a) Flowchart, (b) program, and (c) output for in-class exercise 2, Chapter 5. This program offers only one line of output.

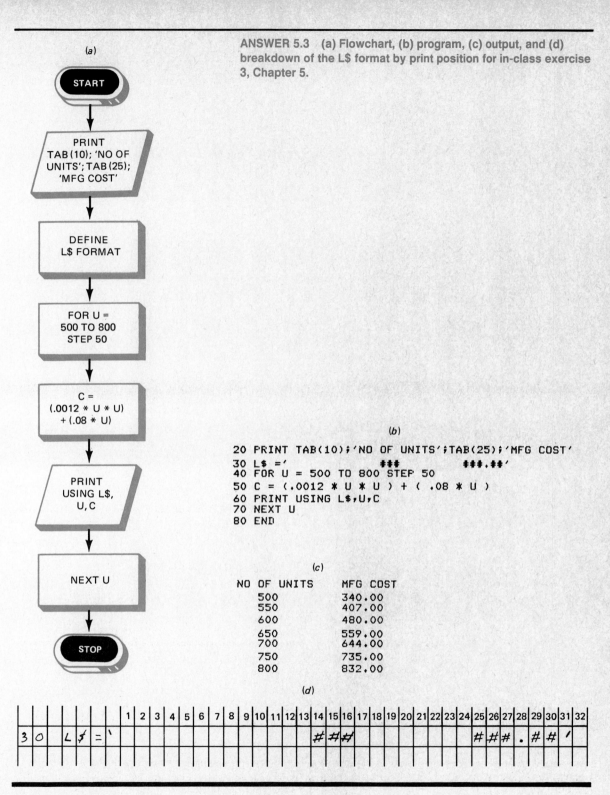

(a)

START

PRINT
TAB(10); 'NO OF
UNITS'; TAB(25);
'MFG COST'

DEFINE
L$ FORMAT

FOR U =
500 TO 800
STEP 50

C =
(.0012 * U * U)
+ (.08 * U)

PRINT
USING L$,
U, C

NEXT U

STOP

ANSWER 5.3   (a) Flowchart, (b) program, (c) output, and (d) breakdown of the L$ format by print position for in-class exercise 3, Chapter 5.

(b)

```
20 PRINT TAB(10);'NO OF UNITS';TAB(25);'MFG COST'
30 L$ ='              ###          ###.##'
40 FOR U = 500 TO 800 STEP 50
50 C = (.0012 * U * U) + ( .08 * U )
60 PRINT USING L$,U,C
70 NEXT U
80 END
```

(c)

NO OF UNITS	MFG COST
500	340.00
550	407.00
600	480.00
650	559.00
700	644.00
750	735.00
800	832.00

(d)

							1	2	3	4	5	6	7	8	9	10	11	12	13	14	15	16	17	18	19	20	21	22	23	24	25	26	27	28	29	30	31	32
3	0		L	$	=	'														#	#	#									#	#	#	.	#	#	'

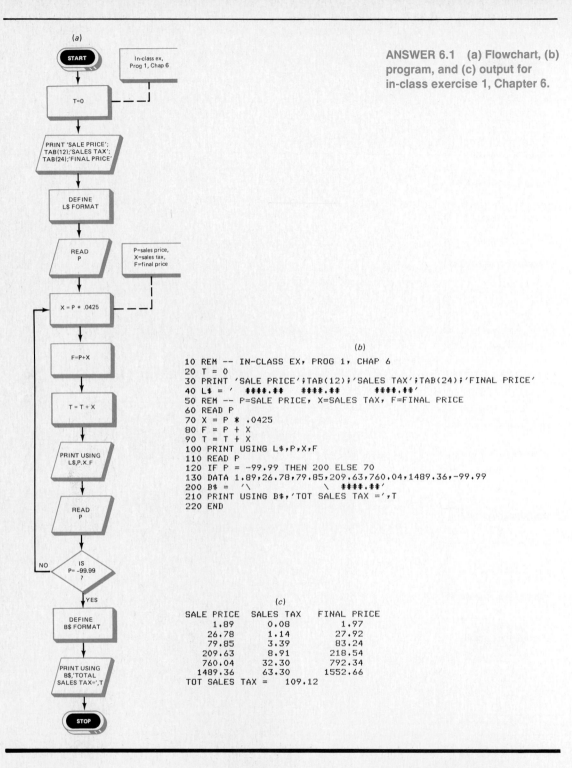

ANSWER 6.1 (a) Flowchart, (b) program, and (c) output for in-class exercise 1, Chapter 6.

(a)

START

In-class ex, Prog 1, Chap 6

T=0

PRINT 'SALE PRICE'; TAB(12);'SALES TAX'; TAB(24);'FINAL PRICE'

DEFINE L$ FORMAT

READ P

P=sales price, X=sales tax, F=final price

X = P * .0425

F=P+X

T = T + X

PRINT USING L$,P,X,F

READ P

IS P= -99.99 ? — NO

YES

DEFINE B$ FORMAT

PRINT USING B$,'TOTAL SALES TAX=',T

STOP

(b)

```
10 REM -- IN-CLASS EX, PROG 1, CHAP 6
20 T = 0
30 PRINT 'SALE PRICE';TAB(12);'SALES TAX';TAB(24);'FINAL PRICE'
40 L$ = '    ####.##    ####.##       ####.##'
50 REM -- P=SALE PRICE, X=SALES TAX, F=FINAL PRICE
60 READ P
70 X = P * .0425
80 F = P + X
90 T = T + X
100 PRINT USING L$,P,X,F
110 READ P
120 IF P = -99.99 THEN 200 ELSE 70
130 DATA 1.89,26.78,79.85,209.63,760.04,1489.36,-99.99
200 B$ = '\            \   ####.##'
210 PRINT USING B$,'TOT SALES TAX =',T
220 END
```

(c)

SALE PRICE	SALES TAX	FINAL PRICE
1.89	0.08	1.97
26.78	1.14	27.92
79.85	3.39	83.24
209.63	8.91	218.54
760.04	32.30	792.34
1489.36	63.30	1552.66

TOT SALES TAX =   109.12

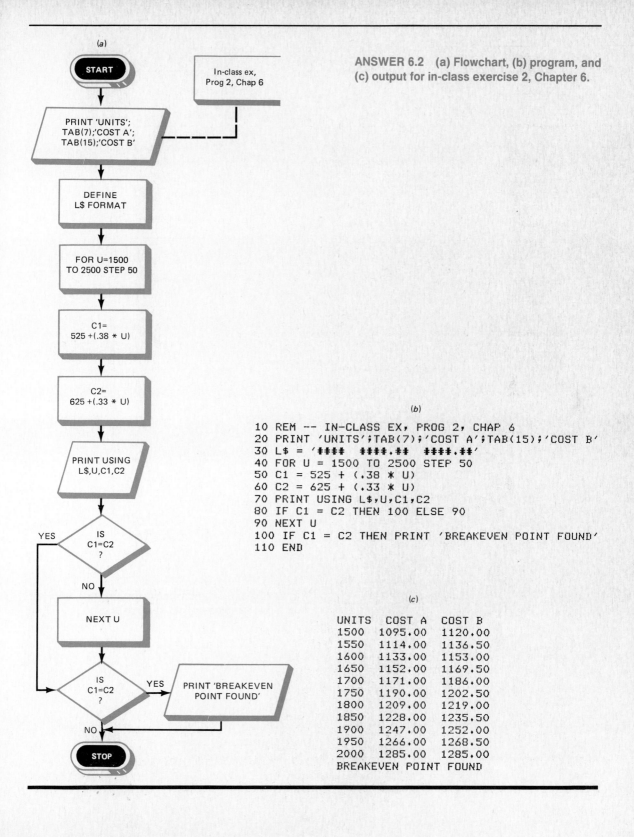

ANSWER 6.2 (a) Flowchart, (b) program, and (c) output for in-class exercise 2, Chapter 6.

(a)

START

In-class ex, Prog 2, Chap 6

PRINT 'UNITS';
TAB(7);'COST A';
TAB(15);'COST B'

DEFINE
L$ FORMAT

FOR U=1500
TO 2500 STEP 50

C1=
525 +(.38 * U)

C2=
625 +(.33 * U)

PRINT USING
L$,U,C1,C2

IS
C1=C2
?

YES

NO

NEXT U

IS
C1=C2
?

YES

PRINT 'BREAKEVEN
POINT FOUND'

NO

STOP

(b)

```
10 REM -- IN-CLASS EX, PROG 2, CHAP 6
20 PRINT 'UNITS';TAB(7);'COST A';TAB(15);'COST B'
30 L$ = '####   ####.##   ####.##'
40 FOR U = 1500 TO 2500 STEP 50
50 C1 = 525 + (.38 * U)
60 C2 = 625 + (.33 * U)
70 PRINT USING L$,U,C1,C2
80 IF C1 = C2 THEN 100 ELSE 90
90 NEXT U
100 IF C1 = C2 THEN PRINT 'BREAKEVEN POINT FOUND'
110 END
```

(c)

UNITS	COST A	COST B
1500	1095.00	1120.00
1550	1114.00	1136.50
1600	1133.00	1153.00
1650	1152.00	1169.50
1700	1171.00	1186.00
1750	1190.00	1202.50
1800	1209.00	1219.00
1850	1228.00	1235.50
1900	1247.00	1252.00
1950	1266.00	1268.50
2000	1285.00	1285.00

BREAKEVEN POINT FOUND

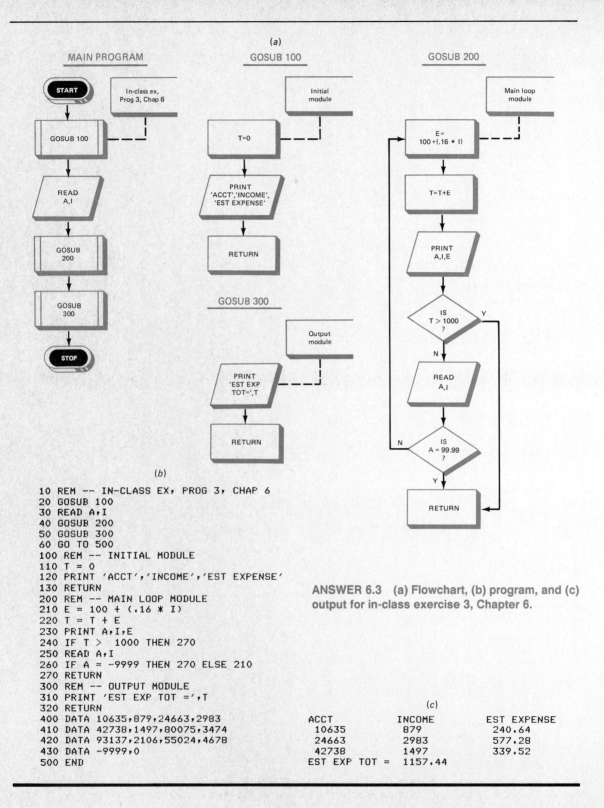

(a)

MAIN PROGRAM GOSUB 100 GOSUB 200 GOSUB 300

(b)

```
10 REM -- IN-CLASS EX, PROG 3, CHAP 6
20 GOSUB 100
30 READ A,I
40 GOSUB 200
50 GOSUB 300
60 GO TO 500
100 REM -- INITIAL MODULE
110 T = 0
120 PRINT 'ACCT','INCOME','EST EXPENSE'
130 RETURN
200 REM -- MAIN LOOP MODULE
210 E = 100 + (.16 * I)
220 T = T + E
230 PRINT A,I,E
240 IF T > 1000 THEN 270
250 READ A,I
260 IF A = -9999 THEN 270 ELSE 210
270 RETURN
300 REM -- OUTPUT MODULE
310 PRINT 'EST EXP TOT =',T
320 RETURN
400 DATA 10635,879,24663,2983
410 DATA 42738,1497,80075,3474
420 DATA 93137,2106,55024,4678
430 DATA -9999,0
500 END
```

ANSWER 6.3 (a) Flowchart, (b) program, and (c) output for in-class exercise 3, Chapter 6.

(c)

ACCT	INCOME	EST EXPENSE
10635	879	240.64
24663	2983	577.28
42738	1497	339.52

EST EXP TOT = 1157.44

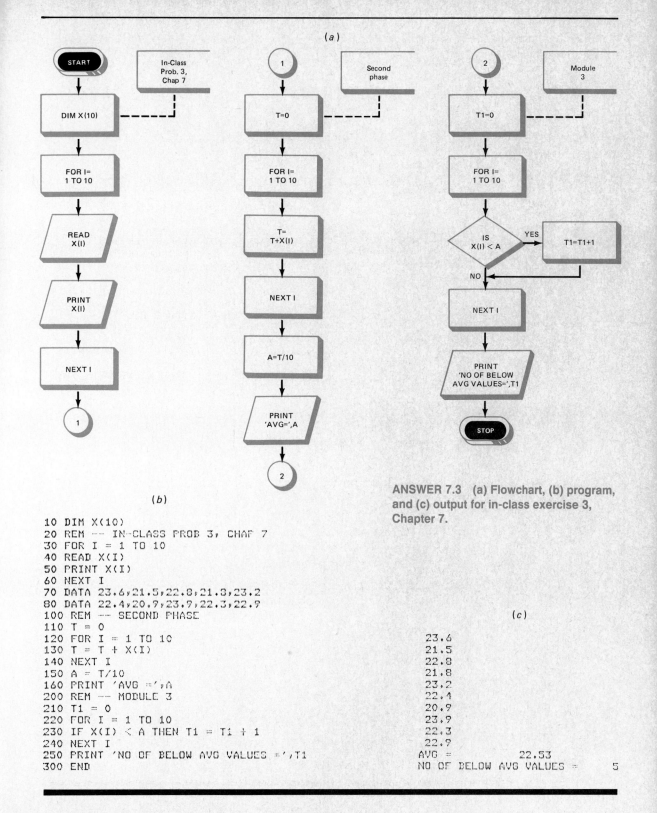

(b)

```
10 DIM X(10)
20 REM --- IN-CLASS PROB 3, CHAP 7
30 FOR I = 1 TO 10
40 READ X(I)
50 PRINT X(I)
60 NEXT I
70 DATA 23.6,21.5,22.8,21.8,23.2
80 DATA 22.4,20.9,23.7,22.3,22.9
100 REM --- SECOND PHASE
110 T = 0
120 FOR I = 1 TO 10
130 T = T + X(I)
140 NEXT I
150 A = T/10
160 PRINT 'AVG =',A
200 REM --- MODULE 3
210 T1 = 0
220 FOR I = 1 TO 10
230 IF X(I) < A THEN T1 = T1 + 1
240 NEXT I
250 PRINT 'NO OF BELOW AVG VALUES =',T1
300 END
```

ANSWER 7.3   (a) Flowchart, (b) program, and (c) output for in-class exercise 3, Chapter 7.

(c)

```
23.6
21.5
22.8
21.8
23.2
22.4
20.9
23.9
22.3
22.9
AVG =           22.53
NO OF BELOW AVG VALUES =    5
```

ANSWER 8.1 (a)
Flowchart, (b) program,
and (c) output for
in-class exercise 1,
Chapter 8.

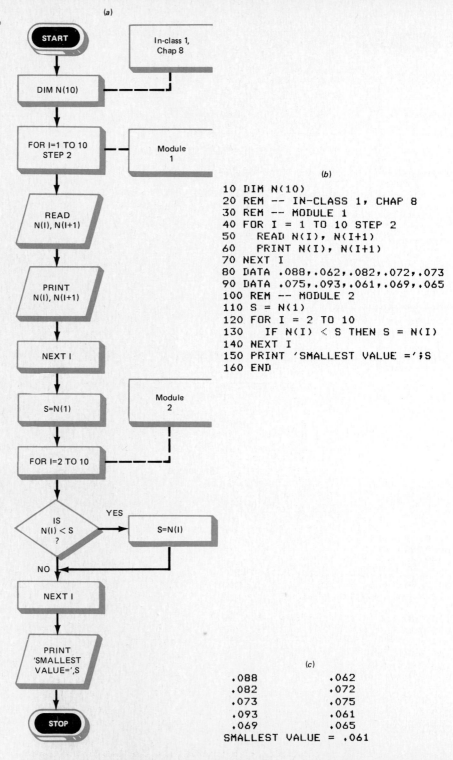

(a)

START

DIM N(10)

In-class 1,
Chap 8

FOR I=1 TO 10
STEP 2

Module
1

READ
N(I), N(I+1)

PRINT
N(I), N(I+1)

NEXT I

S=N(1)

Module
2

FOR I=2 TO 10

IS
N(I) < S
?

YES

S=N(I)

NO

NEXT I

PRINT
'SMALLEST
VALUE=',S

STOP

(b)

```
10  DIM N(10)
20  REM -- IN-CLASS 1, CHAP 8
30  REM -- MODULE 1
40  FOR I = 1 TO 10 STEP 2
50     READ N(I), N(I+1)
60     PRINT N(I), N(I+1)
70  NEXT I
80  DATA .088,.062,.082,.072,.073
90  DATA .075,.093,.061,.069,.065
100 REM -- MODULE 2
110 S = N(1)
120 FOR I = 2 TO 10
130    IF N(I) < S THEN S = N(I)
140 NEXT I
150 PRINT 'SMALLEST VALUE =';S
160 END
```

(c)

```
.088              .062
.082              .072
.073              .075
.093              .061
.069              .065
SMALLEST VALUE = .061
```

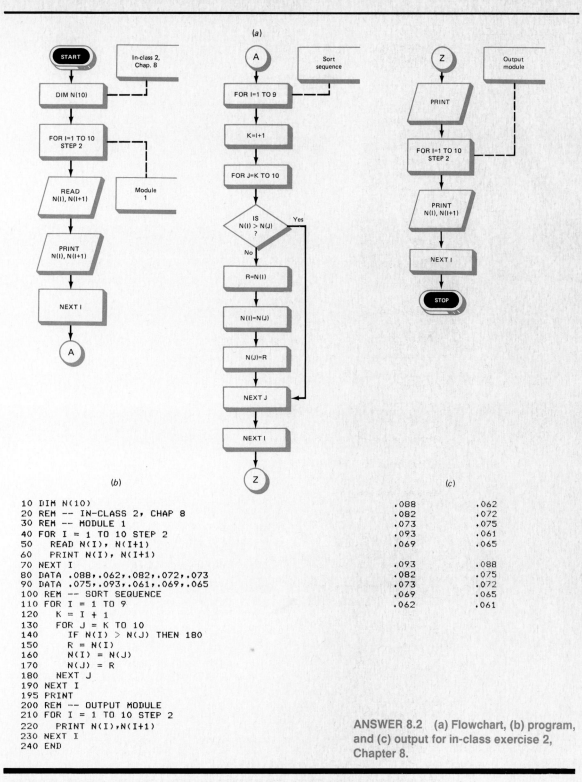

(a)

(b)

```
10 DIM N(10)
20 REM -- IN-CLASS 2, CHAP 8
30 REM -- MODULE 1
40 FOR I = 1 TO 10 STEP 2
50    READ N(I), N(I+1)
60    PRINT N(I), N(I+1)
70 NEXT I
80 DATA .088,.062,.082,.072,.073
90 DATA .075,.093,.061,.069,.065
100 REM -- SORT SEQUENCE
110 FOR I = 1 TO 9
120    K = I + 1
130    FOR J = K TO 10
140       IF N(I) > N(J) THEN 180
150       R = N(I)
160       N(I) = N(J)
170       N(J) = R
180    NEXT J
190 NEXT I
195 PRINT
200 REM -- OUTPUT MODULE
210 FOR I = 1 TO 10 STEP 2
220    PRINT N(I),N(I+1)
230 NEXT I
240 END
```

(c)

.088	.062
.082	.072
.073	.075
.093	.061
.069	.065
.093	.088
.082	.075
.073	.072
.069	.065
.062	.061

ANSWER 8.2   (a) Flowchart, (b) program, and (c) output for in-class exercise 2, Chapter 8.

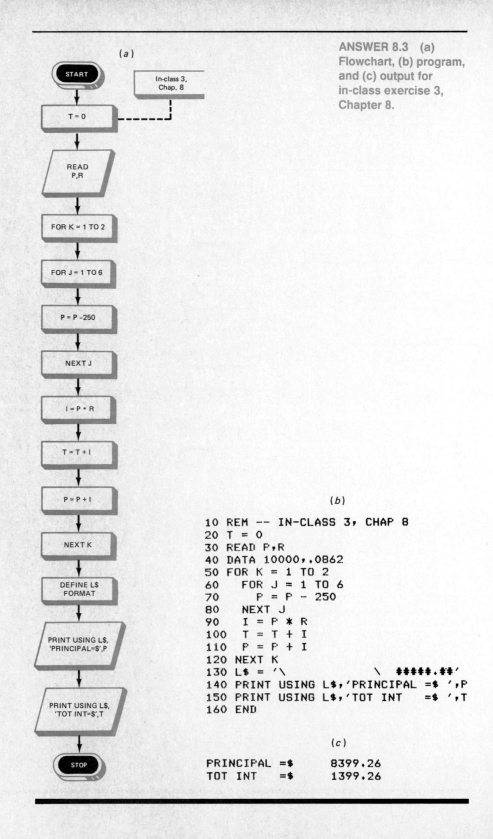

ANSWER 8.3 (a) Flowchart, (b) program, and (c) output for in-class exercise 3, Chapter 8.

(a)

In-class 3, Chap. 8

```
10 REM --- IN-CLASS 3, CHAP 8
20 T = O
30 READ P,R
40 DATA 10000,.0862
50 FOR K = 1 TO 2
60   FOR J = 1 TO 6
70     P = P - 250
80   NEXT J
90   I = P * R
100  T = T + I
110  P = P + I
120 NEXT K
130 L$ = '\                    \  #####.##'
140 PRINT USING L$,'PRINCIPAL =$ ',P
150 PRINT USING L$,'TOT INT   =$ ',T
160 END
```

(b)

(c)

```
PRINCIPAL =$      8399.26
TOT INT   =$      1399.26
```

ANSWER 9.1 (a)
Flowchart, (b) program,
and (c) output for
in-class exercise 1,
Chapter 9.

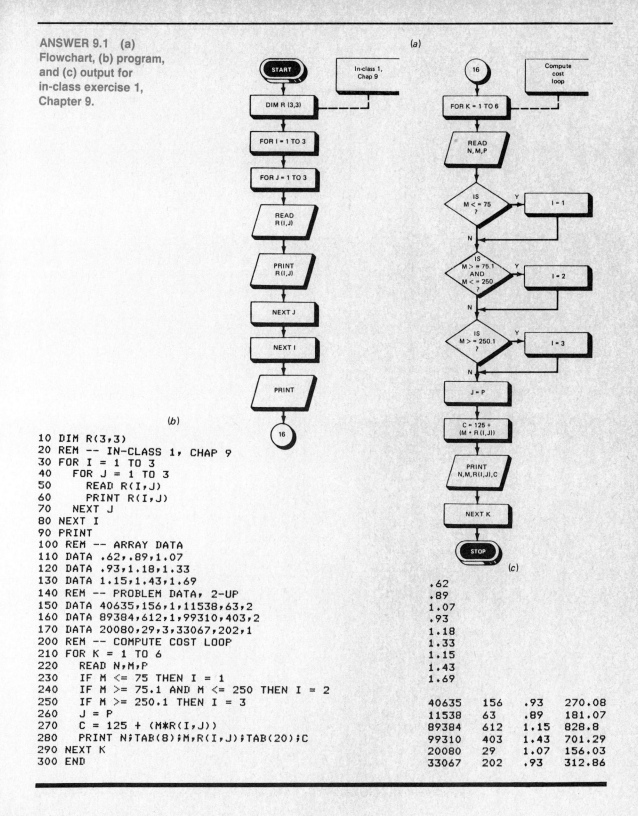

(a)

(b)

```
10 DIM R(3,3)
20 REM -- IN-CLASS 1, CHAP 9
30 FOR I = 1 TO 3
40    FOR J = 1 TO 3
50       READ R(I,J)
60       PRINT R(I,J)
70    NEXT J
80 NEXT I
90 PRINT
100 REM -- ARRAY DATA
110 DATA .62,.89,1.07
120 DATA .93,1.18,1.33
130 DATA 1.15,1.43,1.69
140 REM -- PROBLEM DATA, 2-UP
150 DATA 40635,156,1,11538,63,2
160 DATA 89384,612,1,99310,403,2
170 DATA 20080,29,3,33067,202,1
200 REM -- COMPUTE COST LOOP
210 FOR K = 1 TO 6
220    READ N,M,P
230    IF M <= 75 THEN I = 1
240    IF M >= 75.1 AND M <= 250 THEN I = 2
250    IF M >= 250.1 THEN I = 3
260    J = P
270    C = 125 + (M*R(I,J))
280    PRINT N;TAB(8);M,R(I,J);TAB(20);C
290 NEXT K
300 END
```

(c)

```
.62
.89
1.07
.93
1.18
1.33
1.15
1.43
1.69

40635    156    .93    270.08
11538    63     .89    181.07
89384    612    1.15   828.8
99310    403    1.43   701.29
20080    29     1.07   156.03
33067    202    .93    312.86
```

ANSWER 9.2 (a)
Flowchart, (b) program,
and (c) output for
in-class exercise 2,
Chapter 9.

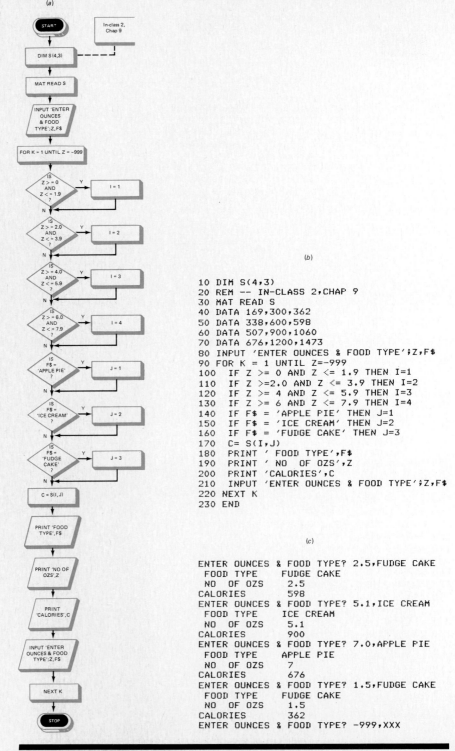

(a)

(b)

```
10  DIM S(4,3)
20  REM -- IN-CLASS 2,CHAP 9
30  MAT READ S
40  DATA 169,300,362
50  DATA 338,600,598
60  DATA 507,900,1060
70  DATA 676,1200,1473
80  INPUT 'ENTER OUNCES & FOOD TYPE';Z,F$
90  FOR K = 1 UNTIL Z=-999
100    IF Z >= 0 AND Z <= 1.9 THEN I=1
110    IF Z >=2.0 AND Z <= 3.9 THEN I=2
120    IF Z >= 4 AND Z <= 5.9 THEN I=3
130    IF Z >= 6 AND Z <= 7.9 THEN I=4
140    IF F$ = 'APPLE PIE' THEN J=1
150    IF F$ = 'ICE CREAM' THEN J=2
160    IF F$ = 'FUDGE CAKE' THEN J=3
170    C= S(I,J)
180    PRINT ' FOOD TYPE',F$
190    PRINT ' NO OF OZS',Z
200    PRINT 'CALORIES',C
210    INPUT 'ENTER OUNCES & FOOD TYPE';Z,F$
220 NEXT K
230 END
```

(c)

```
ENTER OUNCES & FOOD TYPE? 2.5,FUDGE CAKE
 FOOD TYPE    FUDGE CAKE
 NO OF OZS    2.5
CALORIES      598
ENTER OUNCES & FOOD TYPE? 5.1,ICE CREAM
 FOOD TYPE    ICE CREAM
 NO OF OZS    5.1
CALORIES      900
ENTER OUNCES & FOOD TYPE? 7.0,APPLE PIE
 FOOD TYPE    APPLE PIE
 NO OF OZS    7
CALORIES      676
ENTER OUNCES & FOOD TYPE? 1.5,FUDGE CAKE
 FOOD TYPE    FUDGE CAKE
 NO OF OZS    1.5
CALORIES      362
ENTER OUNCES & FOOD TYPE? -999,XXX
```

ANSWER 9.3 (a)
Flowchart, (b) program,
and (c) output for
in-class exercise 3,
Chapter 9.

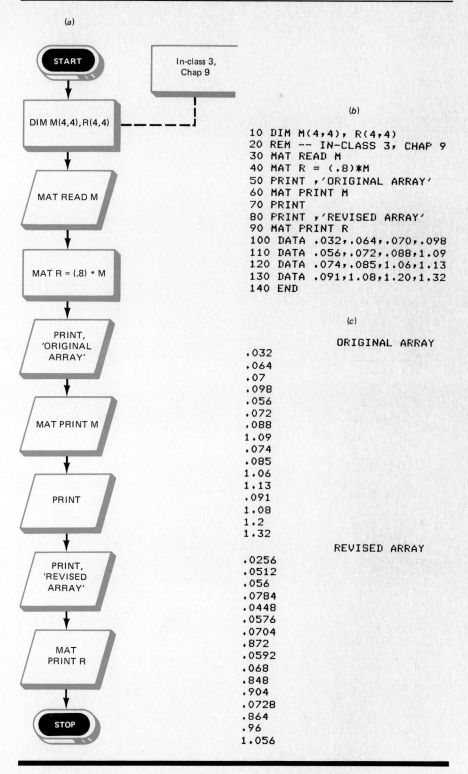

(a)

```
10 DIM M(4,4), R(4,4)
20 REM -- IN-CLASS 3, CHAP 9
30 MAT READ M
40 MAT R = (.8)*M
50 PRINT ,'ORIGINAL ARRAY'
60 MAT PRINT M
70 PRINT
80 PRINT ,'REVISED ARRAY'
90 MAT PRINT R
100 DATA .032,.064,.070,.098
110 DATA .056,.072,.088,1.09
120 DATA .074,.085,1.06,1.13
130 DATA .091,1.08,1.20,1.32
140 END
```

(b)

(c)

```
                 ORIGINAL ARRAY
.032
.064
.07
.098
.056
.072
.088
1.09
.074
.085
1.06
1.13
.091
1.08
1.2
1.32

                 REVISED ARRAY
.0256
.0512
.056
.0784
.0448
.0576
.0704
.872
.0592
.068
.848
.904
.0728
.864
.96
1.056
```

INDEX

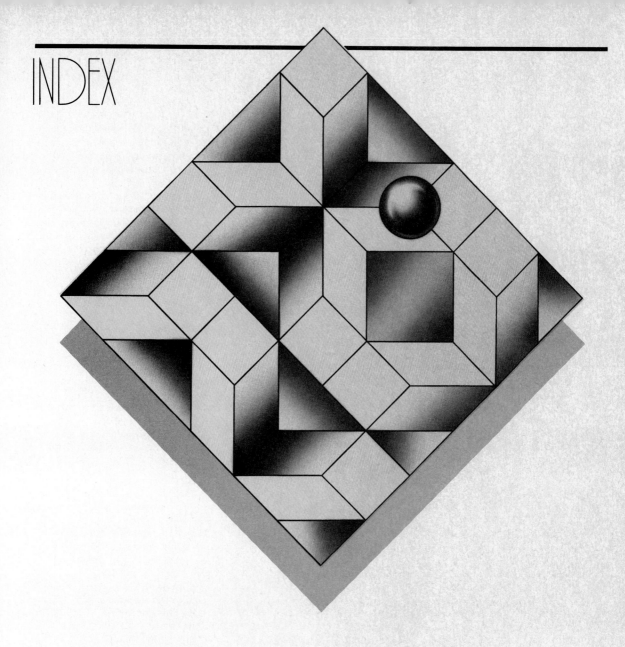

Page number in **boldface** indicates term is defined in chapter glossary.